When Israel Was Young

A History of the Jewish People
from the Beginnings to the
Roman Conquest of Jerusalem

Lester L. Grabbe

t&tclark
LONDON • NEW YORK • OXFORD • NEW DELHI • SYDNEY

T&T CLARK

Bloomsbury Publishing Plc, 50 Bedford Square, London, WC1B 3DP, UK
Bloomsbury Publishing Inc, 1359 Broadway, New York, NY 10018, USA
Bloomsbury Publishing Ireland, 29 Earlsfort Terrace, Dublin 2, D02 AY28, Ireland

BLOOMSBURY, T&T CLARK and the T&T Clark logo are trademarks of Bloomsbury Publishing Plc

First published in Great Britain 2025

Copyright © Lester L. Grabbe, 2025

Lester L. Grabbe has asserted his right under the Copyright, Designs and Patents Act, 1988, to be identified as Author of this work.

Cover design by Holly Capper
Cover image: Chronicle / Alamy Stock Photo

All rights reserved. No part of this publication may be: i) reproduced or transmitted in any form, electronic or mechanical, including photocopying, recording or by means of any information storage or retrieval system without prior permission in writing from the publishers; or ii) used or reproduced in any way for the training, development or operation of artificial intelligence (AI) technologies, including generative AI technologies. The rights holders expressly reserve this publication from the text and data mining exception as per Article 4(3) of the Digital Single Market Directive (EU) 2019/790.

Bloomsbury Publishing Plc does not have any control over, or responsibility for, any third-party websites referred to or in this book. All internet addresses given in this book were correct at the time of going to press. The author and publisher regret any inconvenience caused if addresses have changed or sites have ceased to exist, but can accept no responsibility for any such changes.

A catalogue record for this book is available from the British Library.

Library of Congress Control Number: 2025935783

ISBN: HB: 978-0-5677-1432-9
PB: 978-0-5677-1431-2
ePDF: 978-0-5677-1433-6
eBook: 978-0-5677-1434-3

Typeset by Integra Software Services Pvt. Ltd.
Printed and bound in Great Britain

For product safety related questions contact productsafety@bloomsbury.com.

To find out more about our authors and books visit www.bloomsbury.com
and sign up for our newsletters.

To

Dr. Robert Lawrence Kuhn

and

Professor Raphael Cohen-Almagor

CONTENTS

List of Tables xiv
List of Illustrations and Maps xv
List of Abbreviations xvi
Preface xviii

1 The Beginnings: History and the Bible 1
   Sources for History: How Do We Know What We Know? 1
   Why Not Just Follow the Bible? 5
   How the Historian Works 6
   How the Bible Was Written 8
   How the Bible Came to Us 9
   Conclusions 15

2 History and the Book of Genesis 17
   The Main Creation Account (Genesis 1) 18
   Another Israelite Creation Account 20
   Compare the Babylonian Creation Account 22
   Adam and Eve (Genesis 2–3) 23
   The Flood Story (Genesis 6–8) 28
   Conclusions 32

3 Israel Enters History 35
   Semitic Peoples in Egypt 35
   Palestine and the Egyptian New Kingdom 37
   "The Amarna Age" 38
   The Ramesside Pharaohs and the First Mention of Israel 39
   The Question of "the Patriarchs" 41
   Was There an Exodus? 46
   Conclusions 49

4 Israel Settles in the Land 51
   What Does the Archaeology Say? 51
   Context of the Settlement: Collapse of Empires 52
   What About the Book of Joshua and the Israelite "Conquest"? 53

Where Did Israel Come From? 56
The Times of Judges 58
The "Song of Deborah," an Early Israelite Poem 60
The Israelite Settlement: A Summary 61

5 Israel Becomes a Kingdom: Saul, David, and Solomon 65
Sea Peoples and Philistines 65
Israel Edges Toward Becoming a Kingdom 68
Samuel 69
Saul 70
Israel and Judah Separate? 72
Eshbaal 73
David 73
    Relationship of the Saul and David Traditions 75
    Origin/Early Life of David 76
    David Made King over "All Israel" 77
    David's Wars 78
    Jerusalem, David's Capital 79
    Conclusions About David 81
Solomon 82
Conclusions 85

6 The Rise of the Omrides, or How Israel Finally Became a State 87
A New Historical Source: The Court/Royal Chronicle 87
David's Kingdom Reverts to Two (1 Kgs 12–14) 90
Reigns of Rehoboam and Jeroboam (1 Kgs 12–14) 91
The Invasion of Pharaoh Shoshenq 93
Reign of Abijam of Judah (1 Kgs 15:1-8) 95
Reign of Asa of Judah (1 Kgs 15:9-24) 95
Rulers of Israel to Omri (1 Kgs 15:25–16:20) 96
Omri (1 Kgs 16:16-28) 97
Ahab (1 Kgs 16:29–22:40) 100
Jehoshaphat (1 Kgs 22) 104
Ahaziah and Jehoram of Israel and Joram and Ahaziah of Judah (1 Kgs 22:52 to 2 Kgs 9:29) 105
Elijah and Elisha and the Prophetic Narrative Cycle 106
Jehu (2 Kgs 9–10) 107
Athaliah and Joash of Judah (2 Kgs 11–12) 108
Jehoahaz and Jehoash of Israel (2 Kgs 13) 109
Amaziah and Azariah (Uzziah) of Judah (2 Kgs 14:1-22; 15:1-7) 110

Jeroboam (II) of Israel (2 Kgs 14:23-29) 111
Zechariah, Shallum, and Menahem of Israel (2 Kgs 15:8-22) 111
Jotham and Ahaz of Judah (2 Kgs 15:32–16:20) 112
Last Kings of Israel and the Fall of Samaria (2 Kgs 15:23-31; 17) 112
Conclusions 114

7 From Polytheism to Worship of One God:
Religion in Ancient Israel 115
Divine Names in the Biblical Text 115
Early Israelite Deities and Worship 116
Yahweh, a God Unique to Israel? 119
Development of Monotheism 121
Other Aspects of Israelite Religion 121
    Worship in Ancient Israel 122
    Worship Places: Temples or Sacred Space 123
    Cultic Personnel and Other Religious Specialists: Priests, Prophets, Sages, and Others 123
    Holy Days and Festivals: Sacred Time 125
    Sacred and Profane, Pure and Impure 126
    Law and Ethics 127
Temple Religion versus "Popular"/"Folk"/"Family" Religion 128
The Supposed Abominations of Canaanite Religion 129
Conclusions 130

8 Judah Rules Alone: From the Fall of Samaria to the
Fall of Jerusalem 131
Reign of Hezekiah, the Rebel Against Assyria (2 Kgs 18–20) 131
Reign of Manasseh (2 Kgs 21:1-18) 134
Reign of Amon (2 Kgs 21:19-26) 135
Reign of Josiah, the Reforming King (2 Kgs 22:1–23:30) 135
Reign of Jehoahaz (2 Kgs 23:30-34) 137
Reign of Jehoiakim (2 Kgs 23:34–24:6) 137
Reign of Jehoiachin (2 Kgs 24:6-16; 25:27-30) 138
Reign of Zedekiah (2 Kgs 24:17–25:21) 138
Conclusions 139

9 Judah and the Jews in the Babylonian and Persian Empires 141
The Jewish Communities in Babylonia 143
A Province in the Persian Empire 145
The "Repopulation" of Judah? 146
The Initial "Resettlement" of the Province of Judah 148

The Rebuilding and Completion of the Temple 150
The Appointment of Nehemiah 151
    Opposition to Nehemiah 153
    Building of the Wall 155
    The Fiscal Crisis 156
    The Remainder of Nehemiah's Governorship 158
    Nehemiah as Reformer 158
    Nehemiah's Vision for Judaea 160
    Views Different from Nehemiah's 161
Sanballat and the Samaritan Community 162
The Elephantine Jewish Community 163
The Mission of Ezra the Scribe (Ezra 7–10; Neh. 8) 166
    When Did Ezra Work? 166
Historical Problems in the Ezra Story 167
    The Episode of Marriage with "Foreign" Wives 171
    Ezra as Lawgiver 172
The Final Century of Persian Rule 174
The Book of Esther 175
The Importance of the Persian Period for Judaism 175

10 The Coming of the Greeks: Alexander's Conquests and Ptolemaic Rule 177

Near Eastern Culture and Hellenization 179
The Jews and Hellenization 181
Alexander and His Conquests (336–323 BCE) 183
Alexander and the Jews: Did He Meet the Jewish High Priest? 185
Alexander's Successors—The "Diadochi" (323–281 BCE) 186
Ptolemy I and the Jews 187
Province of Judaea under the Ptolemies 188
Judaea in the Zenon Papyri 190
The Story of the Tobiads 191
Fourth Syrian War (219–217 BCE) and Fifth Syrian War (202–199 BCE) 193
The Jews and Their Communities in Egypt 195
The Jews and Legal Practice in Egypt 197
Jewish Women in Legal Documents 199
Apocalyptic—A Hellenistic Phenomenon 200
The Beginnings of Jewish Religious "Scripture" 200
Translation of the Pentateuch into Greek 204
Conclusions 204

11 The Threat to Jewish Religion, the Maccabean Revolt, and the Hasmonaean Kingdom 207
  The First Twenty-Five Years of Seleucid Rule 207
  How the Jewish Revolt Against Seleucid Rule Began: Jason's "Hellenistic Reform" 210
  Turn About ... Jason Displaced by Menelaus 214
  Antiochus and the Sixth Syrian War 216
  Conflict and Religious Suppression in Judaea 217
  The Beginnings of the Revolt 221
  Concessions by the Seleucids to the Jews 223
  Temple Retaken and Returned to Service 225
  Final Deeds of Judas 225
  Jonathan Maccabee Becomes Leader 228
  A New Jewish Kingdom: The Hasmonaean Dynasty 231
    Simon (143–135 BCE) 231
    John Hyrcanus I (135–104 BCE) 232
    Pharisees and Sadducees 234
    Qumran and the Essenes 236
    Judah Aristobulus I (104–103 BCE) 238
    Alexander Jannaeus (103–76 BCE) 239
    Alexandra Salome (76–67 BCE) 241
  Conclusions 241

12 The Roman Takeover and the Reign of Herod the Great 243
  The Last of the Hasmonaeans: Aristobulus II and Hyrcanus II (67–63 BCE) 243
  Roman Administration in Judaea 244
  Early Career of Herod 246
  How Herod Became "King of the Jews" 248
  Antony, Cleopatra, and Herod 251
  Herod, Friend of Augustus Caesar 252
  The Rest of Herod's Reign (30–4 BCE) 254
  Family Quarrels and the Death of Herod 258
  Assessment of Herod's Reign 262

13 The First Century CE: Roman and Herodian Rule to the Fall of Jerusalem 267
  Governed by Tetrarchs 267
  Judaea a Roman Province (6–41 CE) 269
  "The Jesus Movement": Another Jewish Sect 273

Judaea Becomes Once More a Kingdom 274
Philo's Mission from the Alexandrian Jews to Caligula 278
Caligula's Attempt to Place His Statue in the Temple 279
The Rest of Agrippa I's Reign 280
The Emperor Claudius and the Jews 282
Agrippa II (44–94? CE) 284
The Emperor Nero (54–68 CE) 286
Judaea Once Again a Roman Province (44–66 CE) 287
    Cuspius Fadus (44–46? CE) 287
    Tiberius Julius Alexander (46?–48 CE) 288
    Ventidius Cumanus (48–52 CE) 288
    Antonius Felix (52–59? CE) 290
    Porcius Festus (59?–62 CE) 292
    Lucceius Albinus (62–64 CE) 292
    Gessius Florus (64–67 CE) 292
The War with Rome (66–70 CE) 294
    Beginning Stage of the War 294
    Preparations to Resist an Inevitable Roman Campaign 297
    In the Meantime ... the Situation in Rome 299
    Vespasian's Campaign Against Galilee 300
    Jerusalem Isolated and Surrounded 302
    Jewish Infighting in Jerusalem 304
    Final Siege of Jerusalem 305
    Destruction of the Temple and End of the War 308
Why Did They Hold Out? 309
Conclusions 310

14 Last Gasps: The Final Jewish Revolts under Trajan and Hadrian 313
Continued Resistance after the Fall of Jerusalem 313
The Years after the Great War with Rome 316
The Roman Emperors: Titus to Nerva 317
    Titus (79–81 CE) 318
    Domitian (81–96 CE) 318
    Nerva (96–98 CE) 319
Movements That Flourished after 70 CE 320
    The Apocalyptic Approach: The Apocalypses of Ezra, Baruch, Abraham, and John 320
    The Rabbinic Approach: Nascent Rabbinic Judaism at Yavneh (70–130 CE) 322

The Roman Emperor Trajan (98–117 CE) 326
The Revolts under Trajan 327
The Roman Emperor Hadrian (117–138 CE) 329
The Bar-Kokhva Revolt (132–136 CE) 329
Examples of "Ordinary" Lives: The Stories of Two Jewish Women 334
   Babatha 335
   Salome Komaïse 336
Conclusions 337

15 Summary: History of the Jewish People over Two Thousand Years 339

The Early Period 339
The Period of the Monarchies 341
Judaism in Transition 344
The Persian Period 350
The Coming of the Greeks 351
The Seleucids Take Over 353
The Maccabaean Revolt and the Hasmonaean Kingdom 355
The Jews under Roman Control 357
The Herodian Kingdom 358
Demotion to a Roman Province 359
Agrippa I and Agrippa II 360
Demoted to a Province a Second Time and the Path to War 361
"The Seventy Years' War" 361

References and Notes 365
Index 388
About the Author 413

TABLES

1.1 Lengths of life of the various patriarchs 14

4.1 Sites supposedly conquered and destroyed 55

6.1 Comparison of Jeroboam I and Jeroboam II stories 92

6.2 Kings of Damascus 98

6.3 Neo-Assyrian kings 98

6.4 Parallels with the Jehu dynasty 103

6.5 Omri's reign, Biblical versus extra-Biblical 104

9.1 Neo-Babylonian kings 141

9.2 Persian kings 143

10.1 Early Ptolemies and Seleucids 177

10.2 Ben Sira's references to Hebrew Bible passages 201

11.1 Seleucid kings 209

11.2 Ptolemaic kings 210

ILLUSTRATIONS AND MAPS

Illustrations

1.1 An artist's conception of the Jewish historian Josephus 2
2.1 The four-tiered universe as imagined widely in the ancient Near East 20
3.1 The Stela of Merenptah with the first mention of Israel by name 41
5.1 The Tel Dan inscription which names David and two other Israelite kings 74
7.1 The Kuntillet Ajrud Inscription that depicts Israel's God with a consort 120
8.1 Assyrian inscription showing the siege of the Jewish city Lachish 132
9.1 The Behistun inscription telling of the Persian king Darius's exploits 149
12.1 Reconstruction of Herod's temple 256
14.1 The Jewish fortress Masada 314

Maps

3.1 Ancient Near East in the third millennium BCE 36
9.1 Palestine in the Persian period 142
10.1 Alexander's conquests 178
11.1 Palestine in the Hellenistic and Roman periods 208

ABBREVIATIONS

ABD	David Noel Freedman (ed.) (1992) *Anchor Bible Dictionary*
ANET	J. B. Pritchard (ed.) *Ancient Near Eastern Texts relating to the Old Testament*
AP	A. Cowley (1923) *Aramaic Papyri of the Fifth Century BC*
BA	*Biblical Archeologist*
BASOR	*Bulletin of the American Schools of Oriental Research*
BCE	Before the Common Era (= BC)
BN	*Biblische Notizen*
CBQ	*Catholic Biblical Quarterly*
CE	Common Era (= AD)
CPJ	V. A. Tcherikover et al. (1957–1964) *Corpus Papyrorum Judaicarum*
CR:BS	*Currents in Research: Biblical Studies*
DOTT	D. Winton Thomas (ed.) *Documents from Old Testament Times*
EA	*El Amarna Letter*
GLAJJ	M. Stern, *Greek and Latin Authors on Jews and Judaism*
HSCP	*Harvard Studies in Classical Philology*
IDBSup	Supplementary volume to G. A. Buttrick (ed.) *Interpreter's Dictionary of the Bible*
IEJ	*Israel Exploration Journal*
JAOS	*Journal of the American Oriental Society*

JBL	*Journal of Biblical Literature*
JNES	*Journal of Near Eastern Studies*
KTU	Manfried Dietrich, Oswald Loretz, and Joaquín Sanmartín (eds.) (1995) *The Cuneiform Alphabetic Texts from Ugarit, Ras Ibn Hani and Other Places*
TA	*Tel Aviv*
TAD	Bezalel Porten and Ada Yardeni (1986–1999) *Textbook of Aramaic Documents from Ancient Egypt*
TSSI	J. C. L. Gibson, *Textbook of Syrian Semitic Inscriptions*
VT	*Vetus Testamentum*
WD	Wadi Daliyeh seals and seal impressions
WDSP	Wadi Daliyeh Samaria Papyri
ZAW	*Zeitschrift für die Alttestamentlichen Wissenschaft*
ZPE	*Zeitschrift für Papyrologie und Epigraphik*

PREFACE

My research career has focused on the Hebrew Bible and early Jewish history. Having written a series of academic books that covered Jewish history from the second millennium BCE to the second century CE—a period of two thousand years and more—I thought it might be helpful to cover this same ground in a single volume that was written for the non-specialist. I hope and expect that many readers will be somewhat familiar with the Bible and perhaps some elements of early Jewish history, but my wish is that even those without this knowledge can still jump in and engage with the outline of Jewish history given here. All it takes is interest in what happened to the Jews before medieval and modern times.

This book is dedicated to two individuals who have been important in engaging one way or another with my research. The first is Professor Raphael Cohen-Almagor. As a professor of politics, he founded the Middle East Study Centre at the University of Hull. This carried forward one of his main interests, which is to promote the two-state solution to the Palestinian question, but it served as a platform to a wide variety of lectures and presentations on the Middle East. It was simply amazing the number of prominent people—academics, politicians, ambassadors, and researchers—he was able bring in for public events provided by the MESC. It was a sad day when he took voluntary retirement from the University and embarked on another phase of his illustrious career.

I first met Dr. Robert Lawrence Kuhn in 1968. Our friendship began over a mutual interest in the Hebrew language but went on to encompass a variety of other topics. Our regular meetings ceased in the late 1970s when he went into business, and I subsequently emigrated for an academic career in England. Since then we have met in person only sporadically, but we still correspond over mutual interests. So now I celebrate a friendship of well over a half century with the dedication of this volume.

Lester L. Grabbe
Kingston upon Hull

1

The Beginnings: History and the Bible

The task of this book is to write a history of the ancient Israelites. In other words, we want to present a history of the Jews from the beginnings (whenever that is) to the Roman period when the Romans conquered Jerusalem and brought the province of Judaea—the Jewish homeland—formally to an end.

But when does Jewish history begin? We have information on when Jerusalem was taken over by the Romans, but where should we start with history of the Jewish people? If we go to the preeminent Jewish document, the Bible, Jewish history begins with creation. The Bible in its very first chapter—Genesis 1—describes the creation of "the heavens and the earth." The Jewish historian Josephus, writing in the first century of the Common Era, also began his *Antiquities of the Jews* with creation, but he was simply following the Bible.

If a modern historian wanted to write the up-to-date history of the Jews "from the beginning," he or she would of course have to start with the Big Bang. According to current theory, 13 or 14 billion years ago the universe expanded from a tiny point to the trillions of stars and galaxies covering billions of light years in space that we can observe today. That led to the earth about 4.5 billion years ago, to the origins of life, and finally to *Homo sapiens*—modern humans. This is all a part of a long history that came before there were any Jewish people to have concerns about their past.

Yet this immediately raises a number of central questions: *How do we know anything about the Jewish past? Indeed, how do we know anything about the past at all? And what is the place of the Bible in writing Jewish history?* We need to try to answer these questions before we can start writing our history of the people of Israel.

Sources for History: How Do We Know What We Know?

As people living in the twenty-first century, we know a lot about recent history—from school, from books, from television, and so on. But some of what we know came to most of us from their parents and grandparents who told them about things during

FIGURE 1.1 *An artist's conception of the Jewish historian Josephus.*

their lives. For example, for some readers they learned about World War II from hearing about it from their elders who had lived through it. Now, the generation that lived through the war is coming to an end, with few still alive. But for World War I, no one is still alive to tell about it. And if we go further back—to the American Civil War—or even further back—to the English Civil War—we start to get into a period beyond even memories passed down through family generations.

So how do we learn about the past that goes beyond current memory? The answer is that we know about the past because there are many sources that tell us about it. Documents of all kinds, photographs and films if we are talking about the nineteenth century or later, but for earlier periods there are formal records, such as the minutes of government meetings or war diaries. Newspapers are an important source, but also interviews about personal experiences, personal diaries, letters, and so on. This means there is a great deal of information about the recent past.

The situation is similar at first as we move further into the past: we still have many formal documents, not only of the government but of private business (records of debt, financial accounts, and the like). Although as we go back, we quickly come to a time when there was no television, then no photographs, then when newspapers also did not exist. Within a few centuries—no earlier than the medieval period—we reach a time when most ordinary people could not read or write. Yet medieval historians still have many documents available to them, produced by the clergy and the upper class who could read and write.

As we move back in time, a new discipline becomes more and more important: archaeology. It is true that archaeology has a place even in modern history. You have no doubt seen documentaries in which archaeology is used to gain access to World War I battlefields. It is even used for World War II and more recent events. But it is especially important for ancient history. Archaeology often tells us about things that are not found in written sources or only partially recorded in writing: buildings, settlements, cities, and daily life where written records are only episodic or even lacking altogether.

Archaeology will play an important role in the present book, because much of what we know about ancient Israel comes from archaeology.

We had just traced our history back to medieval times, but medievalists have an abundance of evidence compared to the ancient historian. For the historians of Greece and Rome, and especially for the ancient Near East, there are only bits and pieces—scraps of written information, some of it found only by accident—that often leaves huge gaps in our knowledge. Archaeology becomes vital here and has helped to fill in a great deal about ordinary life, yet the data in the ground are often partial, with later settlements sometimes obliterating those that came before.

This is the situation when we start to ask about the history of the early Israelites. There were no newspapers, much less TV, radio, or social media. Writing was the preserve of only a few, mainly professional scribes who jealously guarded this knowledge that was key to their livelihood. When scribes did write, it was not usually about the history of their people but concerned documents vital to their masters: business transactions, legal documents, records of debts or payments for goods, and tax receipts or bills.

Those who could write were often priests or temple personnel. Again, though, their writing was not history but frequently cultic instructions or records of divination. But the priesthood were also the ones who preserved the community or national myths, with stories about the gods and about humans of the heroic age who were often seen as the ancestors of the people. These myths and legends were in some ways the forerunners of folk or national history.

But it also became conventional for rulers to have scribes write about their accomplishments—or their alleged accomplishments, because sometimes there is reason to doubt whether they did all they claimed. When the king was regarded as (semi-)divine, his deeds—whether military conquests or building endeavors—were often described in exaggerated form to match his exalted status. These royal inscriptions were also forerunners of history writing and become sources for history in many cases, when they talk about actual rulers (as opposed to legendary figures which were also written about).

The historian of ancient times will draw on all sources possible, even those that yield only a few fragments of knowledge. This includes any written histories, which may have been preserved just in late copies, but sometimes there are early writings among papyri or manuscripts discovered where they had lain slowly decaying for many centuries. This is where archaeology becomes so important, for many important written sources (such as the Dead Sea Scrolls or papyri from Egypt or cuneiform texts from Mesopotamia) have been found by archaeologists. Other finds that tell a story are tools, weapons, coins, seals, human and animal remains, and especially pottery. More on this below.

In the ancient Near East, the Middle East of today, writing was invented in both Egypt and Mesopotamia about the same time, about 3000 BCE. The writing was not alphabetic but developed from picture writing to a system that tended to show syllables or even whole words. It was complicated, and the ability to read and write was confined mainly to professional scribes. Even kings and major officials frequently could not read or write: letters were read to them, and they dictated the reply.

Alphabetic writing was developed among the Phoenicians, though their alphabet showed only consonants. For a native speaker, the vowels were not usually difficult to supply orally, though there were occasionally ambiguities. The Hebrews adopted the Phoenician writing. So did the Greeks, but they used some of the letters (important for Semitic but not needed to write Greek) to indicate vowels. The Latins borrowed the Greek writing system, which gave us the Roman alphabet used even today in most Western countries (though a few use the Cyrillic, based on the Greek alphabet).

Knowledge of many of the ancient languages and writing systems was lost in antiquity, though Greek and Latin were known and continued to be studied through the ages. Then in the nineteenth and twentieth centuries, ancient Egyptian and cuneiform writing from Mesopotamia were deciphered and many ancient inscriptions have been rediscovered and read. Also, other lost languages have been recovered and, in many but not all cases, deciphered by scholars so that they are known, or at least partially known: Hittite, Ugaritic, Epigraphic South Arabian, Hurrian, Old Persian, and Elamite.

This means that we now have access to information from the ancient world that was not available to the Greeks and Romans or even more recent scholars until the eighteenth or nineteenth or even twentieth centuries. The written sources are only occasional, however, and often they do not tell us about history. So as helpful and useful as the inscriptions discovered in the last couple of centuries are, they still leave large gaps in our knowledge.

It was really in the nineteenth century that a new science began to be developed, though it perhaps began in the eighteenth century and the excavations at Pompeii. This was of course archaeology that we have already talked about. Although archaeology might well turn up written sources in excavation, its main contribution is to provide information on the material culture. Excavations have provided actual material objects: walls, buildings, settlement sites, camp sites, food stuffs, tools, weapons, bones, excrement, and so on. These all tell us how people lived, and some of it can even give approximate dates for aspects of the culture.

Especially important is pottery whose changing styles and manufacturing patterns often allow the dating of objects and settlement phases found in excavations. We are all familiar with china tableware that changed and adapted patterns and styles as it migrated from China to the Western world and the potteries of eighteenth-, nineteenth-, and twentieth-century England and Europe. Experts can usually place a random modern ceramic piece from its style. In the same way, pottery in the ancient world gradually evolved and developed, and careful studies cataloguing huge amounts of pottery dug up from dated contexts have enabled experts among archaeologists to give the approximate dating of excavation horizons because of the pot sherds found there.

Why Not Just Follow the Bible?

Some readers will no doubt be saying, "What is the big mystery? If you want a history of the Jews, go to the Bible. All you have to do is follow the Bible—paraphrase the biblical text—and you have your history!" *Does not the Bible give us all we would want to know about the Jews and their history? No, not at all!*

The written sources and archaeological information mean that much more is known about ancient history than in the past, even if we still do not usually know as much about it as about more recent history. But what about ancient Israel? This is a significant question, and it is important to take some time to answer it. This is what I shall do right here at the beginning of our historical quest.

My immediate answer is this: the Bible is important, but it does not tell us about a lot of things of Jewish history that we would like to know. Yet it not just a case of adding footnotes to the biblical narrative, as it were. There is much in the Bible that we cannot take at face value—there is much that we have to correct or supplement when we write the history of the Jews.

But some will immediately respond, "The Bible is central to Jewish history. Why can't we just accept it and go from there?" This response is a natural one. The Bible—meaning of course the Hebrew Bible (since the Jewish Bible is not the same as the Catholic Bible or Protestant Bible or Greek Orthodox Bible)—has been central to Jewish religion and Jewish life. Until the last couple of centuries or so, it was also the backbone for writing the history of the Jewish people: Abraham, the exodus, settlement in the land, exile from the land, and later events have been as important to Jewish people as their own more recent history in whatever community or country they lived in at the time.

Thus, every spring Jews reenacted the exodus from slavery in Egypt. They might be living thousands of years since Egyptian enslavement, but in the Passover *seder*, they relived the exodus experience and made it a part of their personal, individual history. In that sense, the Bible's history is the history of every practicing Jew.

But this is not the end of the story. For a historian to appropriate a person's religious tradition—important and understandable as it is—is not the same as writing proper history. In other words, we all participate in our own past but also the past as received in family tradition, the past as perceived by one's ethnic identity, the past as a national tradition. Each nation has its own tradition of important events that are often celebrated in national holidays. Most of us accept these even if we do not believe that things happened exactly as the tradition tells us. Most Americans celebrate the Fourth of July as Independence Day, even though most would not give any credence to the story of George Washington and the cherry tree or even that liberty and justice were experienced by all Americans in 1776.

The same could be said of the Magna Carta in Britain. At the time it was a document setting out the demands of barons and earls and other nobility in their clash with King John. It was not a defense of the rights of the peasant man behind his plough or the peasant woman grinding grain. In any case, King John quickly reneged on the promises in the document that he signed. Yet the document set out ideals that became the basis of some of the fundamentals of liberty in all Western democracies today. Thus, many would accept that liberty and justice have not been achieved for all Americans even today, but that does not negate the important symbol of the signing of the Declaration of Independence or the ideals that it set forth. Nor that the principles evinced in the Magna Carta have been realized by all citizens of Great Britain, yet its signing (even though soon royally repudiated) still has great symbolic significance as a historical event.

But isn't this the point? We can accept the symbolism and the ideals of our history without accepting that those symbols and ideals were *literally* true at the time. And as we probe further back into our more remote past, we begin to find that some events—important as they are from the point of view of present ideals—have been questioned by historians as to whether they happened literally as portrayed in ancient literature or tradition. Ancient rulers liked to be praised and flattered. Likewise, ancient writers often found it convenient to praise or flatter those wealthier or with greater power than their own. Sometimes what you wrote could mean the difference between favor and wealth or losing your head. This is why certain principles have become accepted by modern historians as the proper way to proceed. These principles make up the *historical method*.

How the Historian Works

Fake news is not a new concept. Historians have long argued that they can find more than one version of the truth—or the purported truth—in ancient historical sources. The job of the historian is to try to sort out the truth from false, or at least to distinguish between the true and the less true. This makes use of *critical analysis*, which is an important ingredient of the historical method. We need to keep in mind that "criticism" in scholarly parlance does not just mean "tearing down" or "finding fault." It comes from the original Greek word *krinō* and *kritikos*, which mean "judge." The historian has to make judgments. He or she has to examine carefully the ancient sources and decide about the accuracy and reliability of a particular writing or inscription, or the meaning of an artifact found in an archaeological dig.

The question is, how does the historian distinguish the true from the false? This is a large subject on which whole books have been written. It is not my intent to write a book on the subject at this point, but some basic principles can be outlined now.

Although we may not be aware of it, most of us exercise critical analysis of our own in our daily lives. If we hear something from a friend or neighbor or read something in a newspaper or a tweet, we usually exercise judgment about the accuracy of the information. We consider whether the information is believable from a prima facie point of view. Does it match our own experience? Considering the personalities involved, does it seem compatible with what you know of them? Does it meet with human nature or the normal human experience? Yet such reasoning might only suggest whether the information agrees with our own prejudices. The historian has to be careful not to allow his or her prejudices to determine the conclusions arrived at. Therefore, where possible the historian must go further.

The historian will want to know what all the sources say, to the extent that they are available. If you read something in one newspaper or in one social medium, you would want to compare it with what comes from other news sources or online claims. In other words, you would want to gather as much information from as many sources as possible and compare it. Of course, the fact that all the available sources may say the same thing does not necessarily confirm the story. You might think that all the sources known to you have a vested interest in presenting a particular version, or they may all be taking their information from a single prior source, in which case you are not seeing many sources but ultimately only one.

One of the first questions a historian will ask is about the viewpoint of the source of information. Is the author of the source prejudiced or biased in any way? The author will always to some extent represent the views, attitudes, and assumptions of his or her time—as modern historians will also be influenced by the worldview and perspectives of their own times—the personal background, the personal experiences, the individual education, and so on. So, we can't ignore that *all* sources have *some* bias. The question is, What is that bias and how can we get round it? To repeat, the first step is to discern the viewpoint of the source.

Then the historian will want to know whether the source was in a position to know about the incident being investigated. Perhaps the person who wrote the account was not present and is reporting only hearsay information. Or perhaps the account available was written long after the events ostensibly being described. To take an example, if there was a King Arthur of Britain, he would have lived in the sixth century, yet the detailed story of Arthur that has come down to us and influences most modern accounts was written in the twelfth century, half a millennium after the presumed historical Arthur.

This twelfth-century account (by Geoffrey of Monmouth) cannot be taken as an accurate historical source, as most historians of British history will acknowledge. Even if there was a King Arthur, the early sources tell us little about him—it is only with the much later Geoffrey of Monmouth that we get a detailed account of events. Yet he is very unlikely to have had such information at hand. It is evident that much of what he writes he simply made up. This means that if there was a historical King Arthur—which is not at all certain—we know almost nothing about him. Such is the nature of ancient history: it is not unusual to find that we know little or nothing about a particular person or event.

We always have to ask: to what extent did the writer have actual data and how much is made up? How much of the account is fact and how much just so much rhetoric and imagination? Late sources are statistically more likely to have imaginary embellishments that do not come from the original account.

Yet late sources can sometimes be very reliable. This is when they depend on an early original source. For example, our knowledge of the conquests of Alexander the Great comes from a writer of the Roman period named Arrian, five hundred years after the time of Alexander. Yet he is highly regarded by classical historians because it has been determined that he used sources that were written by individuals who served with Alexander and witnessed many of the events in which Alexander acted.

This is why the historian will go first to the *primary sources*, those close in time and space to the events being described. Yet even primary sources do not necessarily have all the information one wants, nor are they always careful about their facts. Also, as in the case of Arrian, a *secondary source* might be very reliable because it relied on good primary sources. This is one of the many judgments that the historian has to make.

The task of the historian is to evaluate sources and evidence, asking about reliability, bias, and state of preservation. History is not just the past but is what the historian can determine is knowable or believable about the past.

Yet even with sources considered reasonably reliable, the historian will always exercise critical judgment, because no source is 100 percent accurate. Something may have been omitted, or perhaps the original source did not have all the information, or perhaps the manuscript tradition has been badly preserved. One of the problems with trying to write about ancient history is that we often have only very limited source material. This means that there are gaps in our knowledge, sometimes very large gaps. The historian may try to fill these gaps by inference, creative reconstruction, or even speculation. But the reader should note carefully where historians have information and where they do not. A good historian will be honest about the state of his or her information—what actual evidence is available—but unfortunately not all are clear about where their knowledge ends and speculation begins.

How the Bible Was Written

Now we come to the Bible. How was it written? What was the intent of the writers? For example, the Bible was clearly not intended to be a history book. It is a *religious book*: it tells us about theology and religious belief, about the people of Israel, their ideas and way of life, but it also seeks to show by example and by instruction how to live. *The Bible is not a book of history; it is a book of religion with a focus on theology—the God of Israel.*

Large sections of the Bible have nothing to do with history. There are extensive passages on legal matters: correct conduct of the temple cult but also the rules by which people should live—in short, the revelation of God's law. There are the prophetic writings which contain moral guidance, religious criticism, and examples of what happens when God's law is not followed. There is the wisdom tradition that has practical advice on living or examples of how certain wise people lived. What history exists in the Bible is for the purpose of religious education and instruction and theological thought. In order to understand the Bible, we need to consider these aims of the writers.

We can begin by asking: How did we get the actual physical words of the Bible? The branch of scholarship that deals with this question is referred to as "textual criticism." It is the study of how a writer or composer gets material into written form and then how it is transmitted through the ages to appear as the readable written text in front of us that we can understand. There is no complicated theory involved, and you do not have to be a technical genius. The rules and basic process are known and used by most people in their everyday lives. They are a "common sense" understanding about how people work and think in their daily activities.

The writers of the Bible wrote in a particular context, with a particular background. They drew on current knowledge and attitudes of the people, and they wrote for those same people in their own language—not a "Holy Spirit" language but the everyday speech that people used to converse and to pass on information to each other. Of course, they sometimes used poetry, and they had different styles of writing, from formal to slang, just as is the case today. But it was the language used by the people who were receiving the written words of the Bible.

The language of what is called the Hebrew Bible (or Old Testament by many Christians) is naturally Hebrew. That was the language of the people for whom it was originally written. Some very early passages are in what has been called "Early" or "Archaic Hebrew," but this applies to only a few passages, most of which are in a form of poetry. Most of the Bible is written in "Standard Biblical Hebrew," though some books are in "Late Biblical Hebrew." Finally, some chapters in Daniel and Ezra are in Aramaic, which became the adopted language of most Jews after they came under Persian rule. Although the Persian rulers used Old Persian among themselves, most of their documents and letters were issued in Aramaic which was the common language (the *lingua franca*) of most people in the Persian Empire.

Some have assumed that divine inspiration gives the writer knowledge and understanding far beyond that of their own situation and times. But if this were the case, wouldn't the Bible appear in a modern language, such as twenty-first-century English, and wouldn't it refer to our technology of today? No, the writers of the Bible wrote in their own language and composed out of their own experience and knowledge. That is why none of the Bible is in Chinese, not even in English. No writer writes in a heavenly language, in spite of many jokes about which language God speaks. That's why there are no automobiles or airplanes or nuclear power plants or space rockets.

In the Christian Bible, the New Testament is in Greek. But the Hebrew Bible was translated into Greek, called the *Septuagint*, which was extensively used by Jews in the Greek-speaking world. The model of Greek, even in the ancient world, was the writings of Athenians in the fifth and fourth centuries BCE. This was referred to as "classical Greek." But when Greek was spread over a wide stretch of the Mediterranean and Near Eastern world after Alexander's conquest, it developed new characteristics and underwent some vocabulary and grammatical changes. This language is referred to by modern scholars as "Hellenistic Greek" or sometimes "*Koinē* (Common) Greek." The New Testament and, also, many early Jewish and Christian writings were in Hellenistic Greek. Once again, the language of the writings was that being used by those to whom they were addressed. At this time, the language of many Jews (and Christians) was Greek.

How the Bible Came to Us

So far, we have talked about the early *writers* of the Bible. But it seems evident that at least some of the text did not originate with a writer but was made up of stories and traditions told orally, perhaps by grandparents to grandchildren, or around a campfire or hearth in the evening. These stories might have been passed down through many generations without being written down, simply by *oral tradition*. Oral literature may be produced and passed on, as has been shown by studies of oral literature that exists even in some societies today. But finally, someone wrote down the stories and narratives—in the developing book we now call the Bible—because they were thought valuable and useful for religious instruction. Thus, it seems highly likely that large sections of what is now the Hebrew Bible originated and were initially preserved in an oral context and were written down only much later.

The fact was that most people could not read and write at the time of Israelite and Judahite kings. Such knowledge was not helpful to people who lived by ploughing or planting or herding cattle, sheep, and goats. Their time was occupied in making a living and providing for their families. Education was a luxury for which they did not have the means or the need. Writing was a skill for the educated scribe. But if they had been able to read, there were no books to be read! Most writing was in practical documents having to do with everyday business: receipts, bills of sale, loans, tax records.

But the scribes were mostly priests at this time, and they were also interested in religious texts. It was the task of the priests to conduct worship in the temple but also to educate. They taught the people about beliefs and how they were to live their lives. Finally, someone decided it would be helpful if there was a written book. This was the beginnings of the collection of writings that became the Bible.

It is no surprise that the priests wrote instructions and directions about worship and about conduct in everyday life. But many stories and legends that had been passed down orally over the generations also found their way into the text. They were included perhaps because they were traditional and told about the origins of the people. But many were included as cautionary tales—stories that set out right or wrong conduct, that exemplified how people should function to be good Israelites. They told how God-fearing people should live and act.

This suggests that many of the stories in the first part of the Bible were traditional material and Israelite folklore that had been passed down orally over time. But now they were finally put into written form by priests. Of course, the priests did not just take down word for word what storytellers recounted. On the contrary, they cast the stories into their own verbal form, into the wording they wanted their readers to see and hear. They shaped and edited the material that they received, and as time went on the written form was further shaped and edited and embellished by even later generations of scribal priests. New material was added to old stories, and the old stories might be updated and given new forms to suit the language and views of the new generations of readers and hearers.

As time went on, manuscripts became tattered and worn. The old scrolls were copied into new manuscripts, and the old ones discarded. Much of what we know about the Bible comes from much later copies. We have no original manuscripts of the Bible, only copies usually centuries after the text was first written down. Sometimes manuscripts were stored or hidden away and forgotten about. Unfortunately, in most cases, the material on which the text was written—usually animal skin or paper made from the papyrus plant—perished in the climate of the time. Only exceptionally was early material preserved, such as in the desert areas of Judah or Egypt where the manuscripts were not destroyed by dampness.

It is true that a few inscriptions on stone or other durable material from the ancient Israelites have been discovered. But these are not generally that helpful because the biblical text was not reproduced in inscriptions. Inscriptions were not a way of communicating with the vast majority of people, and only a very few have survived from biblical times. Yet the ones we currently know about are helpful because they show that the language and manner of writing found in the biblical text is roughly the same as that preserved in contemporary inscriptions.

Specialists continue to debate the origin and growth of the biblical writings. Part of the problem is that we do not have direct information on how the Bible was composed and have to infer this from information in the books themselves or from analogies with other known literature. It is clear that books like the Psalms developed over many generations, with later writers composing psalms that came to be added to the collection. Many of the Psalms probably originated in the temple and its liturgy. Some of the Psalms talk about events many centuries after the time of David who is credited with composing some of the Psalms. For example, Psalm 137 mentions the Babylonian captivity, which took place about 600 BC, long after David would have lived.

Apart from a few passages in "Archaic Biblical Hebrew" much of the text seems to have been written between about 800 and 500 BCE, reflecting the form of the language known as "Standard Biblical Hebrew." Other writings are composed in "Late Biblical Hebrew," which is the form of the language after about 500 or 450 BCE. For example, although the book of Qohelet/Ecclesiastes mentions Solomon as the literary persona of the writer, it is clear from the language of the book that it was written probably in the third century BCE. It uses new words or words with new meanings developed for the new situation. Daniel is probably even later (as will be discussed on p. 144).

It is not sufficient to point to early elements in a text to demonstrate an early date for it. Early elements can be found in late texts, but not vice versa. Ultimately, judging the date of a text depends on a variety of factors, but the final form of a text can be no earlier than the latest element in it. In some cases, it has been argued that an early text has "only been updated." But how is "updating" different from editing or revising or rewriting that literary critics have traditionally appealed to? It means that the text has been interfered with and does not necessarily reflect the data or message of the original text.

We know of a number of Jewish writings that were written between 800 and 100 BCE. Only some of these became a part of the Bible. How that happened is discussed in a later chapter (see pp. 201–3). But we know that the ancient procedure was to write the text in scrolls of vellum (leather) or papyrus. Who did this for the Bible is not absolutely certain but seems to have been done primarily by priests in the temple. They were the ones with the knowledge and leisure time to do this. Much of the text of the Bible was probably written by priests, but in any case, it seems to have been copied and passed down through the centuries mainly by priests.

But because manuscripts wore out and were recopied, the earliest manuscripts in our possession used to be those copies in the eighth or ninth centuries of the Common Era—our medieval times. In other words, our earliest manuscripts of a book supposed to tell us about events in early history were copied centuries— millennia—after the events they were alleged to record. Fortunately, because of the discovery of the Dead Sea Scrolls in 1947 we came to possess manuscripts of portions of the Bible from as early as 200 BCE. We also have some early translations, especially the Septuagint in Greek, that allow us to see the biblical text as it was in the century or so before the fall of Jerusalem to the Romans.

Yet in spite of some exciting and important finds in recent decades, our direct knowledge of the biblical text is still centuries later than most of the events described in it. To put it another way, *the Bible is not generally a primary source but a secondary source.* In other words, it generally does not contain a record of events by eyewitnesses but by individuals constructing a narrative to describe happenings long before their own time.

There are some exceptions to this situation. In a few cases, primary sources—real eyewitness reports—have been incorporated into the text. The book of Nehemiah seems to include portions of a report composed by Nehemiah himself. Judges 5, in an early form of Hebrew, may be a poem written by a poet who lived near the time of Deborah and Barak. The author(s) of the books of Kings seems to have had chronicles from the royal court available (see further, chapter 6, pp. 87–9). These are valuable sources. On the other hand, we have to recognize that even such firsthand accounts were added to the text by later scribes who also edited them. To what extent they might have changed the story or added details not in the original is always a question.

You might well ask, Why should we assume that scribes changed things? Couldn't scribes simply have copied the text as they found it, with no changes? The answer is that in some cases they may well have copied with few or no changes. Of course, we always have to reckon with accidental mistakes or miscopying. But we have evidence that scribes sometimes produced new or different versions of the text. We know this because *we have different versions of the same text even today.*

When we look at the biblical manuscripts among the Dead Sea Scrolls found at Qumran or elsewhere, we find not one form of the text for each book but often two or even more versions. For example, the book of Jeremiah circulated in at least two significantly different versions. We have the version in the traditional Hebrew text (known as the Masoretic text), which is also the "long version." But in the Septuagint version (the translation into Greek), the text is one-sixth shorter than the Masoretic and has certain sections in a different arrangement. This was not just a change made by the translator, however, because now at Qumran we have found a Hebrew version that coincides with the Greek. This demonstrates that the Greek was translated from a Hebrew manuscript that was shorter than the Masoretic, and had the textual arrangement known from the Septuagint.

This means that we have *two versions of the book of Jeremiah.* They are not hugely different, but there certainly are differences. Other sections of the Bible show a similar diversity. The book of Joshua in Greek is quite different in places from the Hebrew text. Which is more original? This is hard to say, since some of the differences in the Greek text could be the result of an originally different Hebrew text from which it was translated. The same applies to Job which is one-eighth shorter in Greek. Many think this was because the translator of Job into Greek shortened the text, but we do not know for sure. The books of Esther and Daniel have multiple versions, when the various Greek versions are taken into account.

We have to allow that at least some of this diversity is not due to translation technique but to a different original.

It is especially in the Pentateuch and the books of Samuel that we have proof of diversity, with manuscript evidence for at least three different versions of each. We can begin with the books of Samuel. There is the Hebrew Masoretic text used by the Jewish community today, and the Greek translation, the Septuagint. Now, among the Dead Sea Scrolls were also found some fragmentary manuscripts with passages from 1 and 2 Samuel. These had a Hebrew text that differed from the Masoretic. Especially interesting as examples are 1 Sam. 1:11 and 1:22, which differ in all three versions (a fairly literal translation is given here):

> MT: 1:11 And I shall give him to Yahweh all the days of his life and no razor will go upon his head.
> 1:22 And he will appear before the face of Yahweh and remain there forever.
> LXX (Vaticanus): 1:11 And I shall give him before you a gift until the day of his death, and wine and strong drink he shall not drink, a razor will not go upon his head.
> 1:22 And he will appear before the face of the Lord and remain there forever.
> Qumran (4QSam^a): 1:11 And I shall give him be[fore your face a Nazirite until the day of his death and wine and strong drink he shall not drink, and] no razor will go up[on his head.]
> 1:22 [And he will appear] before the face of Yahweh, and he will remain before the face of [Yahweh, and he will remain there forever, and I shall gi]ve him a Nazirite forever, all the days of [his life.]

The question is the status that Hannah's son Samuel would have. According to the traditional Masoretic text, no razor was to be used to cut his hair. A reader might think of the one situation in the Bible where a man was not to cut his hair, which was the Nazirite vow (Num. 6): the person taking that vow was not to cut his hair (Num. 6:5) but was also forbidden to drink wine or to eat grapes or eat or drink anything associated with the vine. But the Masoretic text never explicitly says that Samuel is a Nazirite. The Septuagint goes further, saying that he is not only not to cut his hair but also not to drink wine or strong drink. Yet it also refrains from saying that Samuel is a Nazirite.

But in the Qumran text, Samuel is plainly said to be a Nazirite. It is true that in 1 Sam. 1:11 a portion of the manuscript is missing (indicated by the square brackets) and has been reconstructed by textual experts. Their restoration depends on measuring how many letters might have been present in the missing portion of the text and requires considerable skill and knowledge of scribal habits. However, 1 Sam. 1:22 without question states that Samuel was a Nazirite. The chances are that both 1 Sam. 1:11 and 1:22 stated this in the original manuscript (before the bacteria, insects, and damp destroyed a portion of it).

Now, how to explain these differences between the three versions is an interesting question. All three texts *imply* that Samuel was a Nazirite, the Septuagint mentioning both letting the hair grow and not drinking wine, against the Masoretic text's single mention of not cutting the hair. But only the Qumran text makes a clear statement that he was a Nazirite. Was it a case that the Septuagint translation embellished the statement of the Masoretic text, and the Qumran writer went even further? Or was the Masoretic text at some point miscopied and the statement about Samuel's being a Nazirite was somehow left out? This is a debate for specialists, and we shall not worry about which text was likely to be more original. But what we can see without any doubt is that three different versions of the biblical text were in existence.

For the Pentateuch, we have two Hebrew versions, first, the Masoretic text in Hebrew and, second, the Hebrew text used by the Samaritan community. In addition, we have the Septuagint translation into Greek, though there is considerable support for the view that this was translated from a Hebrew text differing from

TABLE 1.1 *Lengths of life of the various patriarchs*

Biblical Text NB: the dates are all AM (*anno mundi*, the era counting from creation). SP = Samaritan Pentateuch; LXX = Septuagint Greek translation; MT = the traditional Hebrew text.	SP	LXX	MT	Jubilees
5:3: Adam begets Seth.	130	230	130	130
:6: Seth begets Enosh.	105	205	105	98
:9: Enosh begets Kenan.	90	190	90	97
:12: Kenan begets Mahalalel.	70	170	70	70
:15: Mahalalel begets Jered.	65	165	65	66
:18: Jared begets Enoch.	62	162	162	61
:21: Enoch begets Methuselah.	65	165	65	65
:25: Methuselah begets Lamech.	67	167	187	65
:28: Lamech begets Noah.	53	188	182	49–55
[5:32; 11:10: Noah begets Shem.]	[502]	[502]	[502]	[500–6]
7:11: Noah's age when flood came.	600	600	600	601–7
11:10: Shem's age at the time of the flood.	98	98	98	101
:10: Shem begets Arpachshad.	100	100	100	103
:12: Arpachshad begets Shelah [Cainan LXX, *Jubilees*].	135	[135]	35	[65]
[:13: Cainan begets Shelah LXX, *Jubilees*]		[130]		[57]
:14: Shelah begets Eber.	130	130	30	71
:16: Eber begets Peleg.	134	134	34	64
:18: Peleg begets Reu.	130	130	30	12 [*sic*]
:20: Reu begets Serug.	132	132	32	108
:22: Serug begets Nahor.	130	130	30	57
:24: Nahor begets Terah.	79	79 [variant 179]	29	62
:26: Terah begets Abram (11:32; 12:4).	70	130	130	70
17:17; 21:5: Abraham begets Isaac.	100	100	100	112
25:26: Isaac begets Jacob.	60	60	60	58

both the Masoretic text and the Samaritan Pentateuch. Although the differences are sometimes minor, there are also significant differences. Furthermore, for the book of Genesis we have the paraphrase in the early Jewish writing known as *Jubilees* (probably from the second century BCE). The book seems to have been originally in Hebrew (some Hebrew fragments were found among the Dead Sea Scrolls), though that has been mostly lost, and we know of the text from a Latin translation (only part of the text preserved) and an Ethiopic translation of the whole.

A good example to illustrate the differences between the three texts plus the version in the *Book of Jubilees* is to look at the genealogy found in Genesis 5 and elsewhere, with the lengths of life of the various patriarchs (see Table 1.1).

As is plain here, we have four different pre-Flood genealogies, with four different lengths of time for this period. Some will argue that we should simply follow the Hebrew. This sounds fine at first glance, but consider these points: (1) we have more than one Hebrew text: the traditional Masoretic text is in Hebrew, but so is the Samaritan Pentateuch; furthermore, *Jubilees* seems also originally to have been written in Hebrew; (2) Christian readers will be interested to know that the New Testament often quotes the Septuagint Greek text, even when it differs from the Hebrew; for example, the genealogy of Jesus quoted in the gospel of Luke (3:36) has an extra person in it, the person Cainan who is missing from Genesis 5:12-13 in the Jewish Hebrew text but is found in the Septuagint and also in the book of *Jubilees*.

Conclusions

This has been a very brief foray into a complex subject. But it has nevertheless put our finger on some important aspects of the biblical text. Some will say, "Just rely on the Bible and you won't go wrong." *Would that it were so!* Unfortunately, just copying out the biblical text will not give us much of a history. Which version of the Bible should we use? Should we use the traditional Jewish Masoretic text or the Samaritan Pentateuch or the Greek Septuagint version? What do we do when there are gaps—when it does not contain the information that we need to make a connected narrative?

The Bible did not fall from heaven in 1611 in a hermetically sealed package, printed by the finger of God, complete with red lettering, gold edging, leather covers, and silk marker ribbon. The most important result of our investigations is that the Bible is made up of human literature. In whatever way God was behind the producers of the Bible—which some readers will believe but others will reject or doubt—it was still made by human beings, in their language and according to conventions of their literature, with all their limitations of knowledge and expression.

Modern scholars argue that large portions of the Bible originated in an oral context and was passed down orally for a shorter or longer period of time. Oral literature had a large place in traditional communities before the modern period and was often rich and sophisticated. The conventions of creating and passing it on are now much better understood and appreciated. Also, the literature that later went on to become a part of the Bible was primarily community literature. We do not so often encounter modern literature that is genuinely a community product, but ancient literature was often a writing that had grown and been developed by many contributors and had been handed down over a number of generations.

Some single-authored works have probably made it into the Bible, such as the book of Qohelet (also called Ecclesiastes), but these are the exception. Even books that began as the work of one or two individuals were subsequently edited, shortened, expanded, added to, subtracted from, and generally reworked and rewritten over the centuries as they were passed from one generation of scribes to another. In most cases, the history of the text can only be guessed at, and its many edits are suspected but not possible to catalogue with any certainty.

The literature reflects the times of those who composed it. They were limited by their own environment and knowledge. They spoke about what they knew. They used their own contemporary language: when Hebrew was their language, they wrote in Hebrew. When Aramaic became a part of the linguistic scene, we find Aramaic (as in Ezra and Daniel). Later on, we find Jewish literature written in the common language of the Hellenistic world, which was Greek. Toward the beginning of the Hellenistic period (probably the third century BCE), the writings that were starting to be treated as authoritative and even sacred—as the Bible—were translated into Greek. This translation, referred to as the Septuagint, was produced for the benefit of those many Jews whose first language was Greek.

The actual textual evidence available to us makes plain that we have more than one version of many passages, chapters, and even whole books. Sometimes these differ only slightly, but at other times there are considerable differences. The only possible conclusion is that the original text is now unknown. We can make intelligent conjectures, but ultimately, we do not know whether we are anywhere close to the original in the surviving textual tradition. To argue that the Bible is "literally true" requires that we have a clear text and a clear means of determining its meaning. Neither is necessarily the case.

There is also the important fact that the Bible is a religious writing. Its aim was not to give us a history of the Jews. Rather, it was meant to teach us about life, about God, about worship, about theology. There may be passages that contain historical information, but their purpose is not to tell about history as such but about religious lessons, moral instruction, or theological perspectives on humans, the world, and the universe.

Our final conclusion is that the biblical text is sometimes a valuable source for the history of Israel, but at other times it cannot be relied upon. As historians we have to make critical decisions at every point. In the chapters in the rest of this present book, we shall consider the biblical accounts, yet there are many times when the history we write will differ from them to a lesser or greater extent. This will depend on the evidence, however, and will not be done arbitrarily. The reader should be able to understand why a particular position is taken on the history of the event in question.

The next chapter is an important one for determining the value of the Bible as a source for a history of the Jews. It will address specific examples of biblical stories or narratives and ask to what extent these are believable. It will ask whether we can take the Bible at face value or whether our approach should be different.

2

History and the Book of Genesis

The previous chapter explained how history—and historians—work. It also talked about the Bible, how it was written and how we got it, and its place in general in writing history. At this point, we can begin to write our history of Israel. *But important questions remain about how we use the Bible in writing this history.*

If we wanted to write a proper scientific history of Israel, as understood by present-day scientists and historians, we would probably begin with the Big Bang. About 13.8 billion years or so ago, a tiny point began to expand, creating space and time and growing into what we know as the universe. The original universe was made up of hot hydrogen gas and using the cosmic microwave background physicists have actually taken a picture of that early cosmos. As the universe expanded, the gas cooled and things became darker and darker, making up the Dark Ages of the cosmos's early history.

But about 100 million years or so after the Big Bang, gravity had condensed the gas sufficiently for the first stars to begin to form, blue giants that started the process of star and then galaxy creation. The blue giants burned fiercely and quickly burned out after a few million years. But some small stars, called red dwarfs, burned slowly and continued to exist for billions of years. One star, HD 140283, also called the "Methuseleh star" seems to have formed not long after the Big Bang and continues to exist today as one of the oldest stars in the universe.

Stars were formed, burned out in explosive supernova, and left material to condense and gradually form new stars. The mass of hydrogen gas was also a continuing source of star formation. Stars began to collect into giant clusters, then to form galaxies rotating around a center (apparently usually a giant black hole). Galaxy creation eventually led to our own Milky Way galaxy, our sun, and finally our earth about four and a half billion years ago. Life in the form of primitive bacteria arose already about three or four billion years ago, ultimately evolving into modern humans less than a million years ago.

The present chapter will examine the beginnings more specifically, looking at the first part of the book of Genesis, specifically chapters 1 to 11. It is here that Bible gives a picture of creation and the beginnings of human history that was widely accepted in the Abrahamic religions—Jews, Christians, and Muslims—until recent times. Here I summarize a good deal of material that is given in more detail in my book, *Faith and Fossils: The Bible, Creation, and Evolution* (Eerdmans 2018).

The Main Creation Account (Genesis 1)

"In the beginning God created the heavens and the earth." This is the way the first verse of the Bible is often translated, though some would argue that it should be translated, "In the beginning, when God created the heavens and the earth, the earth was …" But the first thing to notice is that the first sentence of the Bible is geocentric: it makes the earth the center of the universe. The earth is separate from "heaven" (or "the heavens"—the Hebrew word is almost always plural in form)—heaven is seen from the perspective of the earth. It is the earth that is formless and in chaos (Hebrew *tôhû* and *bôhû*), covered in darkness (Gen. 1:2). It is the earth that concerns the author: the vast universe, with its billions of galaxies and trillions of stars, was something way beyond his ken.

Playing on the "darkness" of v. 1, in Gen. 1:3 the author writes a poetically brilliant and wonderful Hebrew expression: *Yĕhî 'ôr vayhî 'ôr*, "'Let there be light', and there was light." Because of the peculiarities of ancient Hebrew grammar, the first clause seems to be a simple repetition of the second, but the sense is as given in the English translation. The simplicity, yet graphic expression of the Hebrew evokes admiration for the writer's command of vivid language. It is beautifully poetic. But is it scientific?

Notice that there is nothing that corresponds to what is known today about the beginnings of the universe or of the earth. There is no Big Bang, no expanding university, no novas or neutron stars, no solar system with planets circling a star, no black holes. Nothing here shows any knowledge or consciousness of the universe as a whole, much less a scientific understanding of it as we understand it today.

Furthermore, from a modern scientific point of view, vv. 3 to 5 are nonsense. There is "light" but no light source. Light is "separated" from darkness, even though we know that darkness is simply the absence of light. Yet the light becomes "day"; and the darkness, "night," followed by something even more bizarre: "there was evening, and there was morning—day one." There is no sun, moon, or stars: so where did "evening" come from? Where did "morning" come from? There is no sunset that marks off the evening; there is no sunrise that ushers in morning. How can it be a "day"? And where is the rest of the universe in all this?

Next, God makes a "firmament" (Gen. 1:6). What is a firmament? This is the standard English translation of the Hebrew *rāqîa'*. Just as the English word "firmament" implies something "firm," so the Hebrew word implies something of actual substance. The word *rāqîa'* in fact is used elsewhere to mean "bowl" or "basin." The Hebrew author is not simply talking about an atmosphere; he is telling us that something *solid* was created which keeps the waters "above" from joining the waters "underneath." This "firmament"—this inverted solid bowl covering over the earth—is called "heaven." Once again, there is the puzzling "evening and morning, a second day."

The story of creation continues to unfold: God now gathers all the waters into one place, to make up the "seas," letting the dry land appear, called "earth": "seas" in the plural but nothing about continents; no tectonic plates (Gen. 1:9-13). Then plants are commanded to sprout from the earth. What sort of plants? Ferns and cycads?

Horsetails? Ancient vegetation we know from the attestation of fossils? No, the author talks only of plants "seeding seeds" and "fruit trees bearing fruit with seeds." He seems ignorant of, or at least unconcerned about, other sorts of plants. He is not aware that for millions of years there were no flowering plants and no seeds as we think of them; no grass—certainly no "fruit trees bearing seeds." Also, there is the inexplicable fact that plants are in place, yet there is still no sun to provide the energy needed for plant growth. Finally, there is once again the enigmatic "evening and morning, a third day," even though the sun necessary to mark off these times of day does not exist.

This is not a scientific point of view, for it goes contrary to all basic principles of science, but it is a beautiful piece of literature, with appealing imagery, narrative simplicity, and dramatic storytelling. In vv. 14-19 God commands "lights" in the firmament. These lights are "to separate light from darkness," an astonishing statement in view of vv. 4-5 where God is already said to "separate light from darkness." The lights are never named as "sun" and "moon" here, although the terms are used frequently elsewhere in the Hebrew Bible. Why? The answer seems to be that the sun and moon were both gods among the surrounding peoples.

Finally, on the fourth day we have the heavenly bodies necessary for a proper evening and morning, night and day. But what is the location of these heavenly bodies? We know that the sun is the body around which the earth circulates and the moon a body that rotates around the earth. Yet in Gen. 1:14-18, they are both set in and thus move across the solid sky, the inverted basin holding back the waters above it. Belatedly, the "stars" are also mentioned as being created alongside the "greater light" and the "lesser light" (1:16). No modern science here. The light has been around since day one, but only on the fourth day are light sources created. The universe being described is not even Ptolemaic (the earth-centered model of the universe widely accepted in ancient and medieval times), much less Copernican. (Genesis 1 continues on, but its contents will be considered in a later section of the present chapter.)

What we have in Genesis 1 is the typical universe of the ancient Near East.

The story in Genesis 1 is brilliantly told. Perhaps the language is best described as "heightened prose," since it does not take the form found in unquestioned poetic passages. But the language, the expression, the overall message are the work of a Hebrew literary genius. On the other hand, the chapter is not the writing of a scientist in any modern sense. There is nothing in the chapter that suggests any advanced knowledge of cosmology, astronomy, geology, biology, or physical reality. All the author knows about astronomy is a basin over the earth across which the sun and moon travel each day, and it also contains the stars. But the writer clearly knows nothing of a solar system, galaxies, blue giants, red giants, white dwarfs, interstellar clouds, or supernovas.

"But," we can hear some protest, "he is not describing the universe. He is only giving things from his perspective on earth." Precisely! This is exactly the point: he is giving things from his perspective, which is one limited by the knowledge of the universe and the world as possessed by the people of the ancient Near East in his own time, whenever that was. The writer had no special knowledge of the universe or the Big Bang or the age of the earth or the development of life over billions of years. The author is very much part of his literary and thought world in the ancient Near East.

FIGURE 2.1 *The four-tiered universe as imagined widely in the ancient Near East.*

The special thing he must give us is the Hebrew encounter with God, including the belief that God somehow at some time created the world. The physical details were unknown to him, but they did not matter. He found a way to express his faith in a highly graphic, colorful, metaphorical account.

Genesis 1 is valuable, but it is valuable as religion, not science.

Another Israelite Creation Account

The connection of the biblical account of creation with the ancient Near Eastern cultures is demonstrated by the fact that *another, rather different version of creation is found in some passages of the Bible.* Notice the following passage:

> You [God] drove back "Sea" in your strength,
> You broke the heads of the large sea creatures [*Tannînîm*] upon the waters,
> You shattered the heads of Leviathan,
> You gave him as food for the inhabitants of the wilderness.
>
> (Psa. 74:13-14)

Widespread in the ancient Near East was belief in "monsters of chaos." These were the opponents of the creator god(s) and constantly threatened the ordered universe, attempting to return it to primitive chaos. Creation had been the divine imposition of order onto the primitive chaos and disorder.

In Genesis 1, God imposed order on chaos, but the object of his creation in that account were lifeless inert elements. Creation was, as one scholar put it, simply "a job of work." But in other biblical passages, creation comes about because God defeats the monsters of chaos. In Psa. 74:13-14 the Hebrew word translated "large sea creatures" (or even "whales" in some contexts) was the same word that was originally used of monsters of chaos threatening to overwhelm the world—*Tanninim*—monsters that had to be defeated by God.

Leviathan is another one of those chaos monsters. In fact, "Sea" in this context is also alive—not an inert element—threatening God and his creation, just as it does in some of the ancient Near Eastern accounts. Read this way, God is not attacking his creation—the ocean or poor whales or other large animals. This would make no sense. Rather he is doing here what Marduk or Baal or other gods do in other Near Eastern stories of creation or primordial stories in which they do battle to defeat the forces of chaos, giant monstrous creatures and the ocean personified as an opponent of the divine order. Notice some other similar passages:

The heavens praise your wonder, O Yhwh [the divine name,
    written without vowels but probably pronounced Yahweh],
Your faithfulness in the assembly of the Holy Ones.
For who in the heavens is like Yahweh,
Who can compare with Yahweh among the Sons of the Gods?
El is greatly feared in the Council of the Holy Ones …
Feared by all those around him.
Yahweh, God of Hosts, who is mighty like you, Yah?
    ["Yah" is a shortened form of Yahweh]
You rule the swelling of the Sea,
You still the surgings of its waves,
You crushed Rahab like a corpse,
With your strong arm you scattered your enemies.
                         [Psalm 89:6-10 (Hebrew 89:7-11)]

By his power he stills the Sea,
By his skill he struck down Rahab,
By his wind the heavens were calmed,
    His hand pierced the fleeing serpent.
                                  (Job 26:12-13)

Once again, the God of Israel fights against monsters of chaos that threaten the divinely created order. "Sea" here is not the watery ocean but rather an active divine opponent. The name Rahab is unique to Israel since the name is not attested in any other ancient Near Eastern literature, but he is another of the chaos monsters. The "fleeing serpent" is an expression that has parallels in Ugaritic texts in which the storm deity defeats Leviathan, who is also called the "fleeing serpent." Now we come to one of the most graphic passages:

> In that day Yahweh will punish with his sword—great, cruel, and mighty—
> Leviathan, the fleeing serpent,
> Leviathan, the twisting serpent.
> He will slay the *large sea creature* [*Tannîn*] which is in the sea.
>
> (Isaiah 27:1)

As already noted, it is obvious that Yahweh is not making war on innocent animals. Like a warrior with a sword, he is fighting the monsters of disorder that threaten to overwhelm the ordered creation. Here Leviathan is pictured as a "serpent." Interestingly, some of the same words are used here that occur in the Ugaritic texts: "Leviathan the slippery [or 'fleeing'] serpent" and "Leviathan the twisting serpent."

Ugarit was a city-state on the north coast of the eastern Mediterranean, opposite Cyprus. It flourished for several centuries in the late second millennium BCE, long before ancient Israel. Scholars acquainted with both Hebrew and the Ugaritic language and literature can easily see that the usage is too close to be accidental. The "large sea creatures" are also found in the Ugaritic text, as is Leviathan, along with the "slippery/fleeing serpent," and "twisting serpent." The Ugaritic texts from northern Syria are poetic texts that have many contact points with the language of the Hebrew Bible. The religion expressed in these ancient Ugaritic texts inhabits a conceptual world similar to the worship of Yahweh in ancient Israel. Finally, we should look at a passage which combines imagery of the age-old battle between Yahweh and the chaos monsters with the exodus and other imagery:

> Awake, awake, clothe yourself with strength,
> O arm of Yahweh,
> Awake as in days of old,
> As in generations of long ago.
> Did it not hack Rahab,
> Piercing the sea creature [*Tannîn*]?
> Did it not dry up Sea, the waters of the Great Deep?
> He established the abysses of Sea as a way for the redeemed to go over.
> And the redeemed of Yahweh will return and come to Zion with rejoicing ...
>
> (Isa. 51:9-10)

In a passage composed with great skill the poet has combined, within the space of a few lines, references to Yahweh's defeat of the chaos monsters (Rahab, the Sea Creature, the Sea itself, and the Deep). He weaves the references to these ancient foes into the story of the crossing of the sea at the exodus from Egypt and ties the whole into a hope for the future exodus in which God's people will return from their captivity in foreign lands to Jerusalem. For all this creativity, the writer was working with traditional material, and the defeat of the forces of disorder and chaos by God was a part of this tradition.

Compare the Babylonian Creation Account

These passages from the Bible can be illustrated from the Babylonian Creation Epic, called the *Enuma Elish*. The hero is Marduk, the city god of Babylon. The Babylonian epic tells of how the world of the gods was threatened by a chaos monster named Tiamat. The gods looked for a champion. Marduk volunteered on condition he be made king of the gods. The gods agreed and Marduk and his allies fought and defeated Tiamat. He then used her body, which was mostly water, to create the universe. Tiamat is split in two. Marduk uses one half to form the sky and the other half to form the earth. Even in this fantastic creation narrative, we find that there was a mass of waters above the sky and another mass below the earth.

When the *Enuma Elish* was first discovered, to scholars it looked like an astonishing parallel to the account in Genesis 1 (although the Babylonian version is far older than Genesis), but there was also an important contrast. In Genesis, creation unfolds not through a cosmic battle with the forces of chaos, but creation is simply composed of inert elements in the hands of God who shapes them into a creation but does not do battle with the forces of chaos.

Notice the important differences as well as the equally important similarities. In Genesis we find here a highly skilful and knowledgeable writer—indeed, a capable polemicist—who has written an account of creation in which God is completely sovereign. This is an obvious contrast to the Babylonian accounts. Yet a careful reading will reveal that there is influence on the text of Genesis from the Babylonian epic.

What the author of Genesis 1 has done is turn the active demonic opponents of God into inanimate material elements to be shaped by God's hands. Rather than facing in combat a powerful monstrous foe in Tiamat, the God of Genesis 1 acts on the "deep," which is lifeless stuff from which creation is begun. Indeed, for those who understand the Semitic language complex, the Babylonian language and Hebrew are related, though somewhat distantly. But the Babylonian goddess name "Tiamat" is cognate with the Hebrew word for "deep" (*tĕhôm*). This seems to be a deliberate play on words on the part of the Genesis 1 writer. In the Babylonian story, Tiamat's watery body is cut in two to form heaven and earth, while in Genesis there is a separation of the "deep" into the waters above and the waters below by the firmament (Gen. 1:6-7). In Genesis 1:21 we meet creatures: these are not monsters of chaos like Tiamat but this time are real sea animals.

The writer of Genesis 1 has turned the Babylonian version on its head. God does not fight active enemies as Marduk does but shapes and moulds natural elements to produce an ordered cosmos. Yet, as we have seen, a number of passages from the Hebrew Bible offer a rather different creation story. In Genesis 1, the story is a brilliant description of the "work" of God in forming the earth, but in some of the Psalms, in Job, in Isaiah, we find something much less polished and rather closer in tone and substance to some of the ancient Near Eastern myths. We read of the God of Israel doing battle with living creatures that represent the forces of chaos. In these passages the imagery is quite different from Genesis 1. God is a warrior who battles monsters such as Sea, Rahab, the great sea creature, and Leviathan the many headed serpent, twisting and fleeing.

Adam and Eve (Genesis 2–3)

At the end of Genesis 1, on days five and six, God creates all the animals—whether of the land, sea, or air—and finally human beings. But when we turn to Genesis 2, we suddenly find a different story. Already more than two centuries ago scholars began to notice the detailed differences between the last verses of Genesis 1 and the scenario of Genesis 2.

As the narrative of chapter 2 begins, there are no plants on the earth; this is because it has not rained and because there is no human to till the earth. God sends a water source of some sort over the earth to water it, as he creates the first man. This is completely different from Genesis 1, in which the plants were created on the third day—with no problems about rain or water—whereas humans were not created until day six. As the story unfolds, Genesis 2–3 looks like another creation story, one in some ways parallel to Gen. 1:26-28 but in other ways rather different.

As the story continues, we find the man referred to sometimes as 'ādām, which can be "man" or can be the name "Adam" (Gen. 2:20); most of the time, though, the word has the article, which translates as "the man" (Gen. 2:8, 15, 16, 18, 19, 20, 21, 22, 23, 25; 3:8, 9, 12), even though some translations still at times render it as "Adam." Whereas in Genesis 1:26 humans were created male and female on the sixth day, Genesis 2 has the man alone created. He then names all the animals (birds and land animals, though apparently not the fish). Yet within all these birds and animals, "for Adam not was found any helper suited to him" (Gen. 2:20).

This is bizarre! In Genesis 1, various animals, birds, fish, and other living things were created and told to multiply. Clearly both sexes were created together for most living creatures. Yet when God created Adam out of the dust of the earth, he was apparently rather forgetful. Instead of thinking, "I need a male and a female human," he absent-mindedly fashioned only a male. Then, he scrabbles around among the animals to find a female for Adam but—surprise, surprise!—none is found. So finally, he decides to make a female, but he does so by taking a body part from his newly created man.

What a scenario! Strangely, the man of Genesis 2 has no female counterpart, but a suitable helpmate is sought among all the birds and animals that he names before one is finally created for him. What sort of situation is this? God has no trouble creating the birds and animals male and female. Yet he creates man as a male only—and then seeks a mate among all the various birds and beasts! How peculiar! As Alice would say in *Wonderland*, it gets curiouser and curiouser.

This may sound sarcastic, as if playing for laughs. But that is not the point. If the story was meant to be taken literally, it would be comic. But the story is a very serious creation of a talented author. It is not out to tell us how humans were created but to teach us something about human society that the author wanted to get across. If we try to read the story literally, it appears odd indeed. This is further indicated as we continue to go through the story: an abundance of details cry out to the reader that the story is not meant to be taken at naïve face value. There are clear indications that this is *another* story about the creation of humans, different from Genesis 1:26-28. In this story Adam is placed in the Garden twice (Gen. 2:8, 15). In it, as just noted, Adam strangely considers taking a mate from among the various animals, even birds, but—fortunately—none suitable is found.

The story continues: after the female is created especially for him, almost as an afterthought, one of God's creatures suddenly starts talking to Eve, out of the blue. Almost like children, they are led astray, after which the man and woman are given mortality as punishment for their sin. This is true even though they were already very mortal. Then there are the curses: the serpent is told he must crawl on the ground, which he had already been doing for some time; the woman has to experience labor to produce children, which is the case with all mammals; farmers have to work the land and weed out the natural growth of plants, because crops do not sow and cultivate themselves—but what else do we expect of farming?

On the other hand, if we read the story symbolically, it makes perfect sense. It can also be reconciled with modern science. Since the middle of the nineteenth century, it has become more and more obvious to scientists that humans lie at the end of a long process of evolution which began with simple bacteria. These are not just the fulminations of a few arrogant atheists but *the view of the vast majority of believing scientists*, whether Christian, Jewish, or Muslim. Not all scientists are people of faith, but contrary to popular perception, many scientists also adhere to a religious tradition. Yet they also accept evolution as a scientific fact.

This does not mean giving up belief in divine creation. On the contrary, it is a recognition of how God actually created—not by supernatural fiat in six days but by a long process of evolution that followed the (divine!) laws of nature. Those who argue that this perspective is contrary to divine revelation ignore how the Bible originated, how it came to us, and how it is to be interpreted. Above all, they ignore nature itself, which science is unveiling with an increasing acceleration.

One example of where science has accumulated a great deal of information in recent years is the evolution of human beings. This is a huge topic and can be properly addressed only by specialists. Yet a quick overview might be helpful at this point, providing some data to better interpret the story of Adam and Eve.

Fossils of a number of different hominids have been discovered and identified in the past decades, some of them earlier than modern humans (*Homo sapiens*) and some of them living alongside them. We can mention a few here. An earlier species were the *australopithecines*, the most famous of whom was "Lucy," from about three million years ago. They walked upright but otherwise seem to have spent a lot of time in trees ("Lucy" may well have died from a fall from a branch). Their brains were no larger than those of a chimpanzee and they were not able to speak.

More similar to modern humans and later living alongside them was *Homo erectus*, originated perhaps two million years ago. At this point, we have individuals who are starting to look very much like us. They have larger brains (c. 875 cc), they walk upright in much the same way as modern humans. But there remain some questions: they may have used fire, though this is still uncertain; there are arguments that they had begun to develop speech, based on anatomy and other considerations, though this is still in the realm mainly of speculation. They were certainly toolmakers and users.

The Neanderthals were the first ancient humans discovered (in 1856). Most recently they have been put as a separate species (*Homo neanderthalis*), but despite some physical differences many Neanderthals could have passed us in the street without our thinking them different. The average brain size (c. 1530 cc) is even larger than that of modern humans (c. 1400 cc), though there is no indication that they were more intelligent. It may have had something to do with their body structure, which was much heavier, stockier, and well-muscled (though slightly shorter) than the average *Homo sapiens*. The body seems to have evolved to survive in the cold, since they lived much of the time when Europe was experiencing glacial conditions.

They do not seem to have built shelters, though they made use of caves and rock overhangs. However, they appear to have buried their dead, though whether they were the first hominin to do so is uncertain. Whether burial was accompanied by ritual and symbolism is also uncertain, although it has been proposed. The recently discovered *Denisovans* were the first humans to be reconstructed on the basis of DNA rather than fossils, but scientists are confident that this was another early human group. On the other hand, they are thought to be closely related to the Neanderthals.

These are just some of the diverse humans and near humans that existed over the past several million years. So how can we fit the story of Adam and Eve into the documented evolution of modern humans? Many theologians and biblical scholars would argue that we cannot. Adam and Eve were symbolic figures and their story teaches us certain things about human beings and the human condition. This becomes evident when we look at the "curse" that God pronounces after Adam and Eve are caught in their sin (Gen. 3:14-19).

The curse on the serpent is simply a description of its mode of life—it lives by crawling on its belly, and there seems to be a natural human antipathy toward it (though this antipathy is not confined to snakes but applies to other "creepy crawlers" such as spiders). But then the curse on the woman is very strange: "I shall make great your birth pains; in pain you shall bear children." All mammals have a form of labor in order to give birth, since the offspring has to be expelled from the womb. Humans differ from other animals in that the baby has a very large head because of development of the brain.

Ideally, the baby would be brought to full development before birth, as is the case with most mammals, but with humans this is not possible because the head would be too large for any birth canal. Human babies are born underdeveloped, which is why they are so helpless in the first year compared to many other animals. Thus, human birth is a compromise between letting the child mature as far as possible but still be small enough to pass through the mother's pelvis. The female pelvis can only grow to a certain size, which means that the baby's head must not be too large to pass through the birth canal. Tissue can stretch, but the bone of the pelvis opening limits the size of the baby's head that can be born. Therefore, human birth can be subject to greater trauma than is the case with many animals. But pain in childbirth is not a curse because of Eve's sin but the natural result of this evolutionary compromise between the maximum size of the pelvis and the maximum development of the baby at birth. Genesis 3:16 describes the human condition that has nothing to do with the sin of a first mother.

Finally, in Genesis 3:17-19 we have God's pronouncement on Adam:

Cursed is the ground for your sake. In pain you shall eat all the days of your life. Thorns and thistles shall sprout before you and you shall eat the herb of the field; in the sweat of your face you shall eat bread until you return to the earth, because from it you were taken, for dust you are and to dust you shall return.

Were thorns and thistles created at this time, or were they not part of the creation of plants from the start? Thorns and thistles are a part of nature. When farmers cultivate the soil, any seeds around will sprout, but in order to make sure that only the right crop grows, they plough or hoe or otherwise remove plants they do not want to grow there. There is nothing sinister about these other plants; they just happen to be out of place from the farmer's point of view. Growing crops requires a good deal of work; farming is a labor-intensive occupation. Anyone who has grown up on a farm knows how hard the work can be, but it is the nature of the occupation. The plight of the farmer is well described here, but there was no physical change of plants—no new plants suddenly springing up—or any change to the life as a farmer at this time.

So what we see in Genesis 3:14-19 is a description of the world that humans (and the serpent) lived in. Snakes crawl; they bite humans or are killed by humans. But this is the nature of a snake's life. No suggestion is made that snakes had legs but lost them at this point. Women experience labor to give birth to children. For most it is not a pleasant experience (until the end when they experience the joy of having a new healthy baby). Most people lived by agriculture beginning about 10,000 BCE, requiring a lot of hard work to produce enough food for themselves and their family. Adam and Eve sinned and were punished. *But nothing is said in Genesis about a fall.* Nothing is said here about nature changing. The "curses" are really just a description of life as it was lived.

As social anthropologists will tell you, these "foundation" stories—which are often fanciful—are very important for society. The details are not the important thing about them but their overall intent. Their main function is to describe society in such as way as to inculcate traditional society values in the next generation. This is why they are often handed down from one generation to the next.

Yet a few conservative theologians, while accepting that the Adam and Eve story has to be fitted into the account of human evolution, nevertheless argue that they had to be real human beings. This is said to be because Jesus believed they were actual individuals who existed. This is a problematic argument because precisely what Jesus thought is impossible to ascertain in many cases. The reason is that we do not have Jesus's own account of his thought, for he wrote nothing. What we have is the *interpretation of Jesus by the early Christians*, as found in the gospels and other parts of the New Testament.

Non-Christians will probably not be concerned about what the New Testament says about Adam. But in any case, a couple of passages in the writings of Paul should give Christians pause. The first is in Romans 5:14. In the wider passage of 5:12-21, Paul is making a point about sin. Sin and death entered into the world through one man, though all humans are subject to death *because all have sinned*. But just as death came about by one person, so life will come through one person: grace, righteousness, and life come through Jesus Christ. Paul also mentions that "Adam was a type of the one to come" (Rom. 5:14).

This reference to "type" is interesting because it refers to the exegetical technique of allegory. Allegory is found sporadically in the Hebrew Bible, early Judaism, and the New Testament. However, it was a mode of exposition widely known in the Graeco-Roman world and especially favored by certain Jewish commentators, such as Philo of Alexandria. We also find some examples in Paul. For example, in Galatians 4:21-31 he gives an allegory based on Sarah and Hagar, from the book of Genesis. Abraham had two sons, one born of a slave and one born of a free woman. These represent two covenants, but these also represent two Jerusalems, the earthly

Jerusalem and the heavenly. Hagar also represents Mount Sinai, that is, the Mosaic law, though no counterpart to Sarah is given for this aspect of the allegory. But the important thing is that the Galatians (Christians) are children of the free woman, the heavenly Jerusalem.

Now, we can ask, is Paul trying to tell us that there was a literal, historical Isaac and a literal, historical Ishmael? Is this his purpose? Of course not. He is using figures from the book of Genesis to make a point. He doesn't even mention Ishmael by name. Whether the figures mentioned in the allegory are historical or only literary is not relevant: *the important thing is what they represent.* Would it make any difference to the theological message if Abraham, Isaac, Ishmael, Sarah, and Hagar were simply figures in a fictional story? Not at all.

Let us consider another passage in which Paul uses a passage from the Hebrew Bible to make a theological point: 1 Corinthians 9:8-12. He is arguing that he has a right to be free to live his life, which includes making a living from preaching the gospel. He then quotes Deuteronomy 25:4 in v. 9, "You shall not muzzle an ox while it is threshing (grain)." What was the purpose of this law? One might think of more than one intent, but surely one purpose was concern for the welfare of the animal doing the work. Yet Paul is not interested in that, and even states, "Is it about oxen that God is concerned, or does he not speak entirely with regard to us? For he writes concerning us that the ploughman should plough in hope and the reaper should reap in hope" (1 Cor. 9:9-10). Is God concerned about the welfare of animals? Naturally! Yet Paul brushes past that to make the point that he should have his physical needs provided for as he takes the message of the gospel to others. The important issue for him is not the original context and meaning but his application of the passage to his contemporary situation.

We can now return to Romans 5:12-21. Paul's aim is clearly not to declare whether or not there was a literal Adam and Eve. He is using Adam as a counterpart to Jesus, illustrating how sin and death entered the world through Adam—though we are all subject to death because we have all sinned—but we can gain grace and life through the "second Adam" who is Jesus. Adam did not lose immortality; he was *never* immortal. He was mortal from his creation. The text makes it clear that he was prevented from gaining immortality. Paul's point is that death entered the world through the first Adam, but resurrection and life through the second Adam (= Jesus).

Paul is using a figure of speech, creating an image, illustrating a point of theology. He has no interest in discussing science, nor should Christians attempt to extract such information from these passages. The story of Adam and Eve is in the Bible because it teaches certain things, or illustrates certain things. The important conclusion is to try to learn what lesson the story imparts. Trying to deduce from the story that there must have been individuals called Adam and Eve somewhere in the history of human evolution is misplaced. It is not good science, and many of us would argue it is not good biblical exegesis.

The Flood Story (Genesis 6–8)

The interesting story of Noah and the flood is found in Genesis 6 to 8, but when we look at other ancient Near Eastern literature, we find a plethora of flood stories.

Most of these are found in cuneiform documents from Mesopotamia. When you read them, they seem to be remarkably similar to the biblical story. You could think that the Sumerians, Assyrians, and Babylonians had borrowed their versions from the account in Genesis 6–8; however, when you put the various accounts in chronological order, you will see that the early ones are earlier than the biblical version, and also the later versions are the ones most like the Noah story. *The borrowing is in the other direction: the biblical writers have borrowed from Mesopotamia, though adapting it to their own tradition.*

Documentary evidence for the development of the flood story in Mesopotamia goes back to the early Sumerian tradition. The flood is already mentioned in the *Sumerian King List*, about 2400 BCE, "The Flood swept thereover. After the Flood had swept thereover, when the kingship was lowered from heaven the kingship was in Kish" (i 39–42). There is also a Sumerian version of the flood story, the presently known tablets of which were copied about 1600 BC, but the story itself probably originated much earlier. The Sumerian flood hero's name is Ziusudra.

The next version is an Akkadian flood story, referred to by its title *Atra-hasis*, after its hero. This version is very important because it is quite complete and also is older than any parts of the Bible. The story told is similar to the Sumerian flood story but is much longer and has developed certain features that put it closer to the version in the *Epic of Gilgamesh*.

It is to tablet 11 of the *Epic of Gilgamesh* that we look for the most complete version known to us from Mesopotamia. Gilgamesh was the hero of a long epic poem that was the Mesopotamian equivalent of Homer but was much older. The version best known was in a copy that had been made in the first millennium BCE, in the Neo-Assyrian language and writing system, but it had its roots in the third millennium BCE. The hero of this epic poem was on a quest for immorality. The survivor of the flood (called here Utnapishtim) had been made immortal by the gods. Therefore, Gilgamesh sought him out because he might have the secret to eternal life. The journey was an arduous and dangerous one, but he eventually reached the abode of Utnapishtim and his wife. Utnapishtim told him the story of the flood, which took up a long section in the epic poem.

According to Utnapishtim's story, the gods are forced to swear an oath that they will not warn the humans of the flood disaster approaching. But the god Enki, the god of wisdom who had helped create mankind, used a trick. He did not tell Utnapishtim what was to happen, but instead he addressed the wall beside Utnapishtim and told the wall about the plans to send a flood and gave instructions on how to escape it. The narrative then goes on to relate in Utnapishtim's own words what he did to escape the flood:

[XI 23] Man of Shuruppak, son of Ubar-Tutu,
Tear down (this) house, build a ship!
Give up possessions, seek thou life.
Forswear (worldly) goods and keep the soul alive!
Aboard the ship take thou the seed of all living things.
The ship that thou shalt build,
Her dimensions shall be to measure.
Equal shall be her width and her length.
...

[XI 80] [Whatever I had] I laded upon her:
Whatever I had of silver I laded upon her;
Whatever I [had] of gold I laded upon her;
Whatever I had of all the living beings I [laded] upon her.
All my family and kin I made go aboard the ship.
The beasts of the field, the wild creatures of the field,
    All the craftsmen I made go aboard.
...
[XI 127] Six days and [six] nights
Blows the flood wind, as the south-storm sweeps the land.
When the seventh day arrived,
The flood(-carrying) south-storm subsided in the battle,
Which it had fought like an army.
The sea grew quiet, the tempest was still, the flood ceased.
I looked at the weather: stillness had set in,
And all of mankind had returned to clay.
...
[XI 140] On Mount Nisir the ship came to a halt.
Mount Nasir held the ship fast,
    Allowing no motion.
...
[XI 145] When the seventh day arrived,
I sent forth and set free a dove.
The dove went forth, but came back;
Since no resting-place for it was visible, she turned round.
Then I sent forth and set free a swallow.
The swallow went forth, but came back;
Since no resting-place for it was visible, she turned round.
Then I sent forth and set free a raven.
The raven went forth and, seeing the waters had diminished,
He eats, circles, caws, and turns not round.
Then I let out (all) to the four winds
    And offered a sacrifice.[1]

When the flood story in *Gilgamesh* was first discovered in 1853, its remarkable resemblance to the flood story of Genesis was obviously commented on. Which came first? Scholars agreed that the story in *Gilgamesh* was older than the one in Genesis. Yet another version of the flood story had been known for the centuries, the version of Berossus. It also had some remarkable similarities to Genesis. Berossus was a Babylonian priest who wrote an account of Babylonian myth and history in Greek about 300 BCE, shortly after the Greek conquest of Mesopotamia. His version had been known for many centuries because it was quoted by the church historian Eusebius.

The natural assumption was that Berossus's text had been influenced by the Genesis account; however, the Mesopotamian texts and subsequent study have convinced most scholars that Eusebius quoted faithfully the text that had come to him, and his version probably represents closely the text that Berossus wrote. Yet even though Berossus's text was late compared to some of the others, he evidently knew the cuneiform sources and based his account on earlier Mesopotamian texts. That is, although the translation is late, the sources were probably much earlier. Here is the main account of Berossus:

1. Cronus [Akkadian Enki or Sumerian Ea] appeared to Xisouthros [apparently the Greek form of Ziusudra, the Sumerian "Noah"] in a dream and revealed that on the fifteenth day of the month Daisios [May] mankind would be destroyed by a flood ... Then, he should build a boat and embark on it with his kin and his closest friends. Food and drink should be placed in it. He was to load into it also the winged and four-footed creatures and to make everything ready to sail ... he built a boat five stades [c. 3000 feet] in length and two stades [c. 1200 feet] in breadth ...

2. [On the third day] after the flood had come and swiftly receded, Xisouthros released some of the birds [to determine if they might see somewhere land which had arisen from the waters]. But finding neither food nor a place on which to alight, the birds returned to the ship. After a few days Xisouthros again released the birds and these again returned to the ship but with their feet covered with mud. On being released a third time, they did not again return to the ship. Xisouthros understood that land had reappeared. Tearing apart a portion of the seams and seeing that the boat had landed on a mountain, he disembarked ... It is also said that the land in which they found themselves was Armenia.[2]

When we look at all the versions of the flood story, we see differences in details but also structural similarities and even in details in all of them. The latest version in the *Epic of Gilgamesh* is the one most like the story in Genesis with regard to the birds sent out, while the earlier versions have more differences. Thus, we see versions of the Mesopotamian flood story that had a lot of differences from the Genesis story but others that were closer in some details. Of course, even Gilgamesh has differences from Genesis, but many scholars are now convinced that the flood story in Genesis originated in Mesopotamia. It was taken by Hebrew scribes and adapted to Hebrew literature conventions and to the Hebrew religion. Thus, there are differences, but there are also striking resemblances—resemblances that would be hard to explain except through literary dependence. It might seem surprising to some that a Hebrew writer would have borrowed material from Mesopotamia, but we have many examples of influence from other ancient Near Eastern and Graeco-Roman cultures on the biblical writers.

Some will ask the obvious question: "What about geology? Does it show a worldwide flood?" This is an important question because some "creationists" have asserted that there is evidence of Noah's flood in the earth itself. Unfortunately, this claim is not usually made by professional geologists—many geologists, by the way, are people of faith. Much could be written on this subject, but we shall have to be content with one example on the question.

Three evangelical Christian geologists, K. Wolgemuth, G. S. Bennett, and G. Davidson, addressed the question of the flood and geology in a lecture given at the Evangelical Theological Society.[3] They challenged the "unnecessary" dilemma often presented in the writings of many a young-earth creationist, namely that it was a choice of accepting either the standard interpretation of geology or the correctness of the biblical account. After surveying some of the major claims of what some fundamentalists refer to as a special science of "flood geology," they counter with geological data that can be studied and verified. These three evangelical geologists, along with a growing number of other Christians working in the field of geology, utterly reject this "false dilemma": "It is our conviction that this position [so-called 'flood geology'] is unreasonable from both a biblical and scientific perspective." They conclude:

> But could a tremendously violent flood account for the myriad layers of the earth's rocks and sediments, as well as most fossils? Flood Geology advocates would have us believe there is evidence on both sides of this question that must be weighed. Our observation is that honestly presented evidence leaves nothing left to debate. Deposition of all the earth's layers by a single flood is not only implausible, but utterly impossible unless God temporarily suspended His natural laws in order to establish layers and fossil beds that would subsequently communicate a story vastly different than what actually happened.

This is the overwhelming experience of geologists with a faith perspective. The so-called "flood geology" cannot be reconciled with the actual geology in the ground: the rocks simply tell another story.

Conclusions

This chapter may have seemed negative: the various biblical stories of creation, Adam and Eve, and the flood were all examined and found not to give us history. But the aim was not to be negative but to establish a positive way to work as we use the biblical text. Now that we understand better how and why the Bible was written, we can return to the question with which we began: what place does the Bible have in Jewish history? The Bible has been studied carefully from a critical perspective now for about two or three centuries. In that time, a general consensus has been developed about many points relating to the biblical account and how useful it is for ancient history of the Jews.

The first point is that much of the biblical text is much later than the events it is ostensibly describing. It begins with a story about creation that has little to do with modern science. There is no Big Bang. There is no origin of the solar system, no humble beginnings of life with bacteria, no evolution of plants and animals, no dinosaurs, no australopithecines, no *Homo erectus*, no Neanderthals. We have a worldwide flood that geologists know nothing about. Instead of languages evolving and changing over thousands of years, we have a sudden creation at the Tower of Babel—no Indo-European, no Ural-Altaic, no Proto-Semitic.

It is very important to recognize that the composers of the text were very much creatures of their own time and world. They used their contemporary language, not some ethereal celestial language or "tongues of angels." They were limited by their own environment and knowledge. They spoke about what they knew. Just as their language was the language known and used by those around them, so their knowledge of the world reflected the knowledge of the times. Here and there we see evidence of a more sophisticated, learned knowledge of the natural world, but it was knowledge attested in other literature of the time. There is no evidence that the ancient writers had insight into or knowledge of modern physics, biology, or astronomy. Just as we would not expect them to know modern English, we should not expect them to understand modern genetics or geology.

As we shall continue to see, the biblical text is sometimes useful for history and sometimes not. Yet what it does is fulfill over and over again its religious purpose, often in a remarkable literary package with admirable rhetoric and poetic imagery. These stories tell us truths about human beings, about the divine realm, and about how we should live and conduct ourselves. In some cases, if we want to know what was happening in history, we have to go to science and to other sorts of historical records. The Bible is clearly not a history book nor is it a science manual. Humans have been given the intelligence and then left to work out things for themselves. The present book is an exercise in working out for ourselves the history of Israel.

3
Israel Enters History

When Israel finally enters history, it is the Egyptians who tell us about it. As we shall see later in this chapter, the first explicit mention of the name Israel comes in an Egyptian inscription just before 1200 BCE. But we can look at possible predecessors, both from Egyptian history and from the Bible.

Throughout the second millennium BCE, Egyptians interacted with the populations of Palestine and Syria. We begin with the Egyptian Middle Kingdom (about 2050 to 1750 BCE). This was a fruitful period in Egypt's history and in many ways serves as the model for Egyptian language and culture. It was followed by a period of disunity and partial foreign domination referred to as the Second Intermediate Period (about 1750–1550 BCE). Texts and inscriptions show that many Semites came into Egypt over these centuries. This was followed by the long period of the Egyptian New Kingdom (1550–1050 BCE) when the Egyptian Empire was at its height and Palestine was under its control most of this time.

Semitic Peoples in Egypt

The Egyptians frequently referred to a group called the *Amu*. The term is often translated as "Asiatic" but seems to refer to anyone from the area of Palestine and Syria. *Amu* is the most frequent term, but they also used other terms such as "Dwellers-across-the-Sand" (*hryw-š'* and *nmɪ'w š'*). At various times the pharaoh launched military campaigns against these people in Palestine and further north. For example, a military commander named Khu Sobek was serving with the army of Pharaoh Sesostris III (c. 1837–1819 BCE), and wrote the following account:

> His majesty proceeded northward to overthrow the Asiatics. His majesty reached a foreign country of which the name was Sekmem [apparently the ancient city of Shechem, modern Nablus in Palestine]. His majesty took the right direction in proceeding to the Residence of life, prosperity, and health [he returned home]. Then Sekmem fell, together with the wretched Retenu [Canaan]. While I was acting as rear-guard then I rallied together the individuals of the army to fight with the Asiastics.[1]

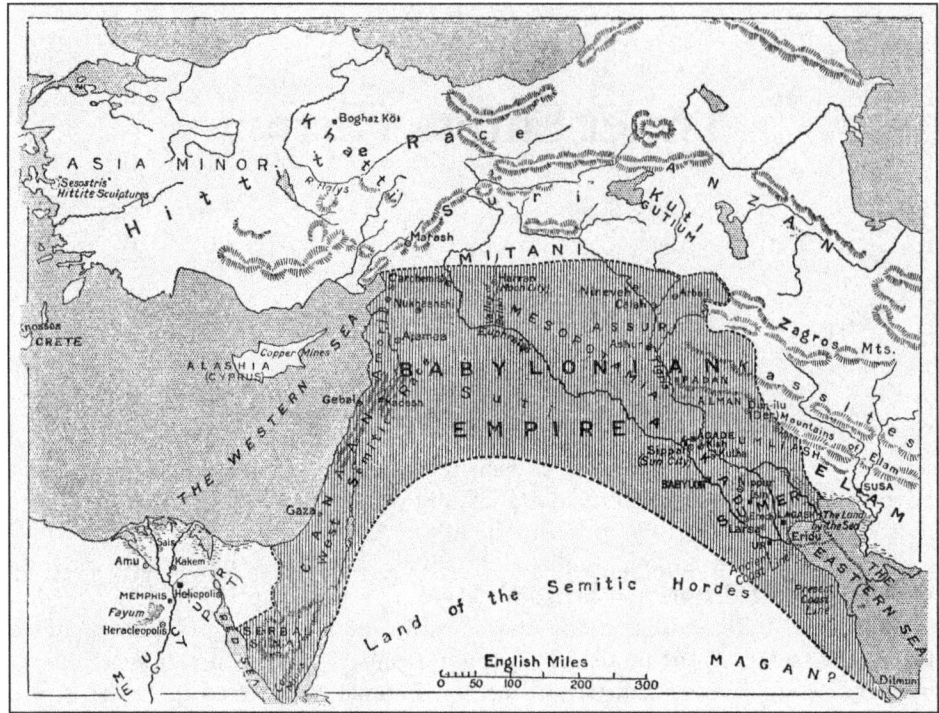

MAP 3.1 *Ancient Near East in the third millennium BCE* © Alamy.

"Asiatics" began to settle in the Delta region (northern part of Egypt, at the end of the Nile, leading to the Mediterranean) after about 2000 BCE. Many Asiatics were also serving in Egyptian households throughout Egypt, not just in the Delta, no doubt coming from a variety of backgrounds in the Levant. Many of these were probably there through enslavement, but others—free individuals—seem to have been imported to work on building projects. There were also free individuals living at various places in Egypt (some no doubt descendants of former slaves), some well-integrated into the local community, even taking Egyptian names. But others came by immigration, with Asiatics bringing their cattle and families, sometimes temporarily but at other times permanently. Quite a few of the settlers were troops, either brought there as captives of the Egyptian army or hired as mercenaries to protect and fight for the kingdom.

Beginning already with Pharaoh Amenemhet I (c. 1939–1910 BCE) subjection of the "Asiatics" (meaning mainly Canaanites), capture of their forts, and enslavement of many individuals is claimed by a number of the Twelfth Dynasty pharaohs. But inscriptions and archaeology show that these "foreigners" were also allies and trading partners. The nonroyal tombs indicate an expanding community of Egyptian-Asiatic mixed descent, sometimes over many generations. These individuals of mixed Egyptian-Asiatic heritage are often depicted uniquely in murals, different both from native Egyptians and Asiatics. Individuals labeled "Asiatic" often have completely Egyptian names and occupy a variety of posts, including officials in the administration.

But perhaps the most interesting settlers were the Hyksos. These were a group of Asiatics who settled in the Delta region. They became temporary rulers of Egypt and made up the Fifteenth Egyptian Dynasty. Before the Egyptian hieroglyphs were deciphered, we had an account of the Hyksos in the Jewish historian Josephus.[2] He claims to have been quoting from Manetho, an Egyptian priest who wrote a summary of Egyptian rulers in thirty dynasties in the Greek language, though he was drawing on native Egyptian sources. Much of Manetho's writing has been lost, and we know of it only from quotations in later writers. Normally, Manetho's account is brief, with the name of a dynasty and the names and lengths of reign of the rulers given briefly; however, Josephus's story of the Hyksos happens to be a longer narrative account.

Whether Josephus is always quoting Manetho or sometimes adding his own conclusions, he made several errors according to the latest research by Egyptologists. The Hyksos probably did not carry out a violent invasion of Egypt but originally settled peaceably over a period of time. They might not even have been a single group (though they are treated as such by the Egyptian sources). It was only after living there a long time that the settlers had become the dominant population in the region and set up their own dynasty with their own pharaoh. But this affected only the Delta: they apparently did not rule over the rest of Egypt.

The Egyptian name for them was *ḥq3w ḫ3swt*, which means "rulers of foreign lands" and was the Egyptian name for the actual Hyksos rulers, whereas the people are often referred to as *Amu*, "Asiatics." Their name had nothing to do with "shepherds" (Josephus explains their name as "shepherd kings"). This "Hyksos rule" seems to have lasted only about a century. They (or at least some of them) left (or were driven out) and moved into southern Palestine (but contrary to Josephus there is no evidence that they settled at or founded Jerusalem).

Finally, Josephus claims they were "our ancestors," that is, the ancestors of the Israelites. It is true that they may have been distantly related to the ancestors of the Israelites, though we cannot be certain about this. What we can say is that the Hyksos, as well as the other Semitic groups and individuals, who came into Egypt in the early second millennium BCE may have been distantly related to the later Israelites. However, none (so far as we can tell) were the direct ancestors of the Israelites we know from the Bible.

Palestine and the Egyptian New Kingdom

The Hyksos were finally driven from Egypt by Pharaohs Kamose and Ahmose who founded the Eighteenth Dynasty, which began the Egyptian New Kingdom. The New Kingdom (c. 1550–1050 BCE) was made up of the Eighteenth, Nineteenth, and Twentieth Dynasties, at a time when Egypt was at its height. The Egyptian texts are abundant during this time and tell us a good deal about the area of Palestine or Canaan. It is because of these texts, especially the Amarna Letters (see below), that we can begin to write a history of the land of Canaan. These texts also enable us to compare the history gleaned from contemporary writings with that which seems to be given in the Pentateuch of the Bible.

But the first point to note about Canaan (Palestine) is that it was ruled over by Egypt almost the entire period of the New Kingdom. When we survey the military activities of the Egyptian kings for the Eighteenth and Nineteenth Dynasties—a period of more than three hundred years—we find that there was seldom any length of time when Canaan was not under the Egyptian thumb. The pharaohs were either mounting military campaigns into Palestine and southern Syria or they were administering the territories as possessions and colonies.

The process began with the first king of the Eighteenth Dynasty, Ahmose (c. 1539–1515 BCE) who besieged and captured the city of Sharuhen where some of the Hyksos rulers and upper class had taken refuge (archaeology indicates the bulk of the Hyksos population remained settled in the Delta). Sharuhen seems to have been in southern Palestine. Over the next century, most or all of the rulers—Amenhotep I, Thutmoses I to III, Hatshepsut, and Amenhotep II—made excursions into Canaan. Perhaps most famous is Thutmoses III (c. 1479–1420 BCE) who conducted nearly twenty campaigns into Palestine and Syria, including the remarkable capture of Megiddo about 1450 BCE.

"The Amarna Age"

The rest of the fourteenth century BCE—from about 1350 to 1300—is covered by the "Amarna Age." King Amenophis IV (c. 1353–1336 BCE) was the famous Akhenaten who decided to worship a single deity, the Aton or sun disk, and moved his court to a newly built capital at Amarna. This new royal residence and worship was not popular with the influential civil administrators and certainly not the clergy of the traditional gods. The result was that when Akhenaten died, Amarna was abandoned, and his son Tutankhamun and other successors reverted to traditional worship.

But in the nineteenth century copies of letters were found in the site of Amarna that had been left when the administration moved back to Thebes. These letters, written on clay tablets using the contemporary diplomatic language of Akkadian, provide a two-decades-wide window that lets us see what was happening in Syria and Palestine. There were nearly four hundred of these "Amarna letters," of which more than three hundred were correspondence with rulers—kinglets—of city-states in Canaan and Syria that were the vassals of Egypt. We know of the main city-states of Hazor, Megiddo, Shechem, Jerusalem, Gezer, Gath, Ashkelon, and Lachish. The Amarna letters describe a situation in which the various city-states were jockeying for position, whether to gain power and territory or to defend themselves against takeover by neighboring city-states or perhaps even a combination of both.

The situation in Palestine can be well illustrated by looking in particular at two Canaan city-states that were under Egyptian rule, Jerusalem and Shechem. Among those who wrote letters to the pharaoh from the southern part of Canaan was the king of Jerusalem (Urusalim), Abdi-Heba. The name Abdi-Heba means "servant of the (Hurrian) goddess Heba"; however, as far as we can tell, he was a native Canaanite, one of the many kinglets of the Canaanite city-states. We have six letters from Abdi-Heba, plus a couple of other letters that refer to him. As will be clear, we need to keep in mind that only Abdi-Heba's side of the story is given in his letters. He claims to be a victim of treacherous neighbors and asks for Egyptian help against them. But we need to consider his allegations alongside other letters, letters from those very same neighbors who accuse him of treachery, aggression, and disloyalty toward the pharaoh!

But it is true that Abdi-Heba was struggling against rivals, especially the ruler of Shechem, one of the more powerful kingdoms in Canaan at this time. When Shechem's ruler Lab'ayu died, Abdi-Heba of Jerusalem evidently took the opportunity to try to expand his territory to the west. This was at the expense of the kingdom whose ruler was Shuwardata, probably Gath. This was why the latter complained to the Egyptian king that Abdi-Heba had become another Lab'ayu throwing his weight around (as EA 280 indicates). However, in the political maneuverings and shifting alliances that one expects of the region at this time, Shuwardata and Abdi-Heba were able to make common cause when they were both threatened by *Apiru* (as indicated in EA 366, a letter from Shuwardata).

What we find in Canaan in the Amarna Letters is a situation that we shall see later with the rise of early Israel. The two kingdoms of Jerusalem and Shechem are similar to the territories of Samaria and Judah when the Israelite monarchy began. Although Judah/Jerusalem was evidently the weaker and less prosperous region, it could still command resources and power to assert itself and attempt to expand its control over neighboring territories. (See further on p. 72 in chapter 5.)

To summarize this discussion of the Amarna letters, what we can find from the various letters is that there were a number of competing city-states: they squabble among themselves and complain to the pharaoh, each maneuvering for position and seeking advantage for itself in competition with its neighbors, constantly playing off one another in relation to the Egyptian king. What we do not have is any indication of an Israel settled in the land, or even of Israelites migrating from captivity in Egypt to the Promised Land. Jerusalem was controlled by a Canaanite ruler, not the tribe of Judah or Benjamin. Nothing in the Amarna Letters matches up with the account of Israel as found in the Bible.

The Ramesside Pharaohs and the First Mention of Israel

It is the period of the thirteenth century—about 1300 to 1200 BCE—that we first find reference to Israel by name. This was in a context different from anything we find in the Bible, however. The question of the sojourn in Egypt and the exodus will be looked at later in the chapter (pp. 46–9), but the context of Late Bronze Palestine and the later Egyptian New Kingdom are important.

In the new Nineteenth Dynasty, Ramesses II (1279–1213 BCE) is often seen as the pinnacle of pharaonic rule. He had a long reign of sixty-six years and was a great military leader, at least in his younger years. Of his many campaigns into Palestine, Phoenicia, and Syria, the most famous was probably the battle of Qadesh in Syria against the Hittites. Strangely, Ramesses II has often been proposed as the pharaoh during whose reign the exodus from Egypt by the Israelites supposedly took place, as for instance in the Cecil B. DeMille movie, *The Ten Commandments*. How this could have happened under one of the strongest of the pharaohs who had a firm hold of the whole region well into Syria and reigned for so much of the thirteenth century seems not to be considered. Furthermore, Ramesses II did not drown in the Red Sea! One cannot imagine an Egypt devastated by plagues, with a huge population leaving the country, and an army destroyed in the wilderness near the Red Sea as compatible with anything we know about this ruler, not to mention other problems with the idea of an Israelite exodus (see below pp. 46–9).

Ramesses II was succeeded by his younger son, Merenptah (1213–1203 BCE), who was already middle aged. Egypt suffered a Libyan invasion allied with a number of the Sea Peoples in the fifth year of his reign. They were met in the western Delta region and defeated. Merenptah set up an inscription which was mainly devoted to the Libyan victory. However, toward the end of the inscription some Palestinian cities plus Israel are mentioned:

> The princes are prostrate, saying: "Mercy!"
> Not one raises his head among the Nine Bows [traditional enemies of Egypt].
> Desolation is for Tehenu [Libya]; Hatti [the Hittites] is pacified;
> Plundered is Canaan with every evil;
> Carried off is Ashkelon; seized upon is Gezer;
> Yanoam [city in northern Palestine] is made as that which does not exist;
> Israel is laid waste, his seed is not;
> Hurru [Canaan] is become a widow for Egypt!
> All lands together, they are pacified;
> Everyone who was restless, he has been bound by the King of Upper and Lower Egypt.[3]

As noted, this reference to Israel is tacked onto the main inscription at the very end. How the statement here relates to the Libyan invasion—if at all—is unclear. Some have argued we have no evidence Merenptah conducted a campaign into Palestine by his fifth year. In answer to this, others have pointed out that the Amada Egyptian inscription refers to Merenptah as "conqueror of Gezer," and it is now widely agreed that the water source referred to in Josh. 15:9 and 18:15 should be translated "the spring of Merenptah"—which indicates the pharaoh must have come into that area himself.

A great deal has been written about this mention of Israel since the stela was discovered a century or so ago, but there is room for only a few issues to be discussed here. First, it should be noted that "Israel" is one of four entities, along with Ashkelon, Gezer, and Yanoam. In Egyptian writing many nouns were accompanied by a determinative, a sign that indicated the category of noun it was. In this case, the names of three of the places are designated by determinatives as indicating "foreign country," or foreign city-state. But Israel is accompanied by a determinative that indicates it is a "foreign *people*," not a geographical site. Although there has been debate, most Egyptologists now see the use of this determinative with Israel as significant: they were a people and might not even have had a fixed abode at this time.

A second point is that all four are listed between two mentions of "Canaan" ("Hurru" seems another name for Canaan here). The three cities are all thought to be in Canaan; therefore, it is likely that "Israel" was also in Canaan, but beyond this general region we have no hint. The statement sometimes made that Israel was in the central hill country of Palestine at this time has no support from the Merenptah inscription. Finally, this Israel was destroyed—or at least, badly defeated—by Merenptah. There is no relation between this inscription and the biblical description of the exodus from Egypt or the Israelite settlement in the land.

The Question of "the Patriarchs"

The Merenptah Stela is the first mention of Israel by name in an external source. Yet we have a lengthy account of Israel's ancestors in Genesis in the so-called "patriarchal narratives." According to them, it was with Abraham and his descendants that Israel's history first began, and some think this is correct. I beg to

FIGURE 3.1 *The Stela of Merenptah with the first mention of Israel by name.*

differ! Recent study has given biblical historians a quite different perspective on the patriarchal narratives.

Most biblical scholars have long tended to view the early chapters of Genesis—the stories of creation, Adam and Eve, the flood, the Tower of Babel—as Hebrew legend. Yet in the 1950s and 1960s, a school of thought called the Biblical Theology Movement came to dominate much work being done by academic biblical researchers. One of the central pillars of the Biblical Theology Movement was the "revelation of God in history," with the mantra that adherents would "take the Bible seriously" as history. They wanted to focus on the text, like many lay Christians, but without viewing it from a fundamentalist viewpoint.

The Biblical Theology Movement was embraced by scholars from a variety of religious traditions. There was of course a debate, with North American scholars tending to give more credence to the narratives while the Europeans were more skeptical, but a variety of views was advanced on both sides of the Atlantic. Some of the prominent representatives were students or followers of William F. Albright. Albright was not a fundamentalist, nor were most of his followers, but their language at times seemed to espouse a literal interpretation of the Bible. Many conservative evangelical Christians welcomed the teachings of the Albright school, assuming (wrongly!) that its members believed in the Bible in the same way they did.

As it turned out, despite their language Albright's followers did not believe that "the acts of God in history" really involved literal miracles, such as the Red Sea parting before the Israelites for them to walk through dry shod. Yet a version of the "patriarchal period," which saw some sort of history beginning with Genesis 11:26, was accepted by many biblical scholars in the 1950s, 1960s, and into the 1970s.

If you work from the genealogies and other chronological information in the Bible, the patriarchal period began about 2000 BCE, but some have dated it differently. For example, the patriarchs have been put in the fifteenth century BCE by some. One well-known but somewhat eccentric scholar made Abraham a "merchant prince" in the Amarna period (fourteenth century BCE). Albright wanted him to be a donkey caravaneer; in any case, the Albright school was particularly effective in promoting the idea that the patriarchal traditions contained "substantial historicity" from around 2000 BCE. Yet this consensus began to come unravelled in the 1970s.

In 1974, Thomas L. Thompson published his study, *The Historicity of the Patriarchal Narratives: The Quest for the Historical Abraham*. A study by another scholar was published in 1975, completely independent of Thompson but coming to similar conclusions. They both argued that the content of the biblical patriarchal narratives was filled with anachronistic data and could hardly represent genuine history of the early second millennium BCE. Albright had died in 1971 and was no longer around to dominate the discussion, and these two studies had a significant impact.

Yet shortly after Thompson's book appeared, a new discovery seemed to give considerable support to the more conservative view. Beginning in 1975 was the discovery and initial decipherment of the archives of the ancient city of Ebla. Ebla was especially important because it was near Palestine and might tell us something about it. The archaeological site is at modern Tell Mardikh, about 35 miles southwest of Aleppo in Syria. Seventeen thousand tablets were discovered in the archaeological dig. These tablets show that Ebla's power waxed and waned, though it sometimes controlled the Euphrates Valley and the Taurus foothills. Eventually, Ebla seems to have been destroyed about 2300 BCE.

One of the scholars working on Ebla was the epigrapher, Giovanni Pettinato, a specialist in ancient writings of Syria and Mesopotamia. Soon after the textual discovery, Pettinato began to give interviews—sometimes to fellow scholars but also to the popular press—in which he presented astonishing Eblaite parallels to texts from the patriarchal chapters of Genesis. On the basis of what he was (allegedly) told by Pettinato, one biblical scholar (a student of Albright) wrote a rather polemical article in which he attacked Thompson and others for not accepting the historicity of the patriarchs.

In the article he referred to the "recent archaeological discoveries" that he asserted had supported the basic factuality of the patriarchal narratives "while effectively under- cutting the prevailing skepticism and sophistry of the larger contingent representative of continental and American scholars." While he admitted that the narratives contain an "admixture of the legendary and the mythical," he still asserted that they give us information allowing scholars to say something about the dates (at least, of some of them), the places from which they came and to which they went, their work, and even about their legacy of faith and practice.

He went on to refer to a tablet with the names of the five cities of the plain (those cities allegedly existing alongside Sodom and Gomorrah [Gen. 14:8] which were destroyed in Genesis 19)—in the same order as in the Bible—though he admitted he had not seen the tablet and was relying on a conversation with Pettinato. But on that basis, he concluded that Thompson and others (who dated the Genesis narratives to the first millennium BCE) had jumped in the wrong direction: instead of dating the book of Genesis later, he wanted to date it even earlier!

But just as the article was going to press, some disturbing news arrived: Pettinato had apparently retracted some of his identifications. The article was printed as written, but an introductory text did bring the readers' attention to Pettinato's alleged retraction. The result was that the article's defense of historicity, based on the biblical text, was essentially negated. It took a while to settle down, but within a few years the use of Ebla as a defense of the patriarchal narratives had been silenced. When Pettinato's book (1991) appeared in English, there was no mention of Sodom and Gomorrah or the cities of the plain! Today there continues to be lively interest in and discussion about Ebla among scholars, but they seldom relate to the biblical text. Ebla has ceased to appear in standard scholarly discussions about Genesis.

The basic problem with finding history in the "patriarchal age" is that the only information preserved has been what could be found in the text of Genesis—there was no direct external confirmation, either epigraphic or literary. None of the patriarchs has been found attested in extant sources. This means that the arguments in favor of historicity have generally attempted to present a circumstantial case for regarding the Genesis narratives as containing historical data.

Yet those who advocated a historical status for the patriarchs were not stupid. Most of us now think they were wrong, but their concerns should not be dismissed lightly. It is the nature of scholarship that there are "fashionable" trends, when everyone seems to think in a certain direction, but then the next generation rejects this trend and goes in a different direction. Those who took the patriarch narratives as historical were biased in part by religious beliefs sincerely held and in part by the trends of their own times. It would be useful now to look at some of the issues that concern the historicity of the patriarchs, the arguments used to defend historicity, and the reasons why they are now widely rejected. For reasons of space, however, these can only be briefly summarized.

The first thing we should note is the number of *anachronisms* in these chapters in Genesis. The patriarchal narratives in their present form reflect a later time, with many details possible only for a historical period much later than the early second millennium BCE: the Philistines in the land (they only came after about 1200 BCE, as part of the migration of the Sea Peoples); Arameans (Gen. 22:21; 24:10) who are first attested about 1100 BCE in an inscription of Tiglath-pileser I; Arabs who first occur about the ninth century (Gen. 26:12-18); and the Chaldeans (Gen. 11:28) who are attested after 1000 BCE but are mainly important in the Neo-Babylonian period.

Most specialists think the mention of *camels* in Genesis is an anachronism. There has been something of a debate over the matter: Albright had already argued that this was anachronistic and made Abraham a donkey caravaneer, but some conservatives had claimed evidence for the domestication of camels at an earlier time. The evidence for the domesticated camel in Palestine, however, seems to be no earlier than the Iron Age, with the concentration of bones at Tell Jemmeh, apparently a caravan center, focusing on the seventh century BCE. The most recent research concludes that the introduction of domestic camels to the southern Levant occurred not earlier than the last third of the tenth century BCE, in other words only about 950 BCE or later—long after any alleged patriarchal age.[4]

Archaeology has sometimes been drawn on in support of the view that the stories of Abraham and his offspring were "substantially historical," but the most up-to-date studies are mainly negative. The primary centers of Transjordan and the Negev that are associated with the patriarchs in Genesis lack remains for the early second millennium BCE. At the important site of Beersheba (Gen. 21-22) there are no remains for that time, while investigation of the "cities of the plain" (Gen. 14:8; 19:24-29) have also found nothing. On the one hand, many of the main cities known to have existed at the time are absent from the text; on the other hand, no period in the early or middle second millennium BCE is known when all sites in the patriarchal narratives were settled: it was not until the end of the second millennium that this complete settlement of those sites took place.

It was once assumed that the patriarchs were nomadic and that this was uniquely in line with the early second millennium BCE context. One of the critiques of the biblical picture of the patriarchs is that a *nomadic lifestyle* is not the key to understanding early Israel. Unfortunately, some of the models developed by biblical scholars were ignorant of the wide range of nomadic pastoralist modes of living, which have turned up in investigations by contemporary anthropologists studying the question. "Pastoral nomad" covers a wide spectrum of living modes, from those who grow crops alongside their animal husbandry and have close contacts with the settled community to those who live away from the settled areas and have a very mobile way of life. Pastoralists and farmers generally have a mutually beneficial relationship and usually live together in harmony.

Many parallels can be found to the *names* in the patriarchal narratives. Names cannot be proof, of course, because the patriarchal names can all be found in the telephone book of almost any large Western city today. As Thompson points out, most of the names have typical Northwest Semitic structure. It is striking that some of the names for Abraham's ancestors in Genesis 11:20-32 are actually *topographical names in the region of Haran*, as known from Mesopotamian texts: *Peleg, Serug, Nahor, Terah*, and *Haran are the names of places*, not persons. It is as if someone wrote a biography of George Washington and said his ancestors were Boston, New York, and Philadelphia.

Traditional *social customs* have been one of the main pieces of evidence. For example, the Genesis commentary of the *Anchor Bible* drew many parallels from the Nuzi texts to illustrate passages in the patriarchal narratives. There are several problems with these examples. The first is that the Nuzi texts come from the fifteenth century BCE, long after the time of the patriarchs as many date them. Nuzi was a major city in the Mitanni Empire which arose in the mid-second millennium BCE and covered the eastern part of Asia Minor. The cuneiform tablets from Nuzi often relate to business and family matters.

A second problem with the Nuzi parallels alleged for patriarch customs was the argument that the custom was not understood by the biblical writer—a rather strange way of arguing for authenticity and reliability! In fact, many of the alleged Nuzi customs are not parallel to the biblical passage, or either the Nuzi text or the biblical text have been misunderstood or misrepresented. For example, Gen. 15:2-4 states that Abraham's servant Eliezer was his heir; however, God promised that Abraham would have his own son who would be his heir. The argument was made that according to Nuzi custom an adopted son ceased to be the heir if an actual son was born. Yet it turned out that disinheriting the adopted son when a natural-born son appeared was actually *contrary to the Nuzi custom!* This alleged parallel was not parallel to Genesis at all. Abraham's and Isaac's passing their wives off as sisters (Gen. 12:10-20; 20:1-2; 26:1-11) was said to reflect a Nuzi custom of adopting the wife as a sister. In fact, the biblical text does not actually suggest such an adoption but, in any case, the Nuzi practice was actually misapprehended by some modern scholars.

Genesis 23 gives the story of how Abraham purchased a cave at Hebron to bury Sarah his deceased wife. It was argued that this reflected intimate knowledge of Nuzi custom and practice, but specialists in the Nuzi archives have not found the arguments convincing: "the customs in real estate transactions and feudal dues [alleged for Genesis] are unlike anything known" in Asia Minor. The best parallel to Genesis 23 seems to come from the Neo-Babylonian period, more or less a millennium after the supposed Nuzi parallels. In the end, none of the customs allegedly demonstrating an early second millennium background for the patriarchal stories seems to have stood up to careful scrutiny.

A good example of late material seems to be the *Joseph story*. The main study remains that of the Egyptologist Donald B. Redford, *A Study of the Biblical Story of Joseph (Genesis 37–50)*. He investigated the Egyptian parallels and references in the account. What he found was that some of the parallels indeed occur as early as the Middle Kingdom (c. 2000–1750 BCE), but we must keep in mind that some elements found early also occur in later Egyptian history. Furthermore, a number can be found only in later periods, in the Saite period or afterward (after about 650 BCE). The overall evidence found by Redford in the story suggested that the narrative was written between about 700 and 400 BCE; some would date it even later. Some examples of late or anachronistic elements include the following:

- Gen. 41:43: *Abrek* (אברך) is thought to be from a Akkadian word *abarakku*, one of whose meanings is "chief steward of a private or royal household." There is also the Phoenician word *hbrk*, which some interpret as "vizier" or similar, and may also be a borrowing from Akkadian. Although Egyptian words have been proposed, connection with the Akkadian language looks the most likely solution. But Egyptian officials are unlikely to be using an Akkadian word in the Middle Kingdom.
- The name Potiphar (פוטיפר) is clearly of Egyptian origin; it means, "he whom Re gives" (*P3-di̓-p3-R'*) and is attested only from later times, from the Saite to the Ptolemaic period.
- Gen. 40:15: "land of the Hebrews [העברים]" as a designation for Palestine would not have been used in the early second millennium BCE. No such usage occurs in Egyptian texts of the Middle and New Kingdoms. It occurs in late texts, however, from the Saite, Persian, and Ptolemaic periods.
- 41:42: a "gold chain around his neck" is a gift to Joseph. The Egyptian phrase "gold of honour" (*nbw n[.y] hsw.t*) is attested from the New Kingdom. What is significant about the Joseph example, however, is that a foreigner is invested with honor and given an administrative position. This is not so far known in New Kingdom or earlier, though there is an example from the time of Psammetichus I (seventh century BCE) in which a foreigner (a Greek) is granted a "golden collar" for his neck and given command of a city.

To conclude about the patriarchal narratives in Genesis, the anachronisms and late elements in the text show that these chapters were written down much later than the second millennium BCE. The narratives reflect a historical period a thousand years or more after the supposed activities of the patriarchs. They are generally thought to have been written down no earlier than about 900 BCE, with some of the material much later. The Joseph story seems to have a context in the Saite period or later (after 650 BCE). Many of the best-fitting parallels to customs in Genesis arguably stem from the Neo-Babylonian period (c. 610 to 540 BCE). The inventive ability of the writer(s) is shown by Abraham's alleged ancestors, which are simply the names of Mesopotamian cities.

In the opinion of most scholars today, the stories of the patriarchs do not contain "substantial history."

Was There an Exodus?

At the end of Genesis, the family of Jacob is settled in Egypt. The first few chapters of the next book, Exodus, continue the story of the family, now represented as a community or even nation. Known as the "descendants/children of Israel" they are oppressed and made slaves, with an attempt even made to kill all male babies. But a leader is raised up in the person of Moses, an Israelite reared in the court of pharaoh. A major concept in the biblical text is that, after ten plagues sent by God, the ancestors of Israel went out of Egypt "with a high hand" (Exod. 14:8), and that they entered the Promised Land after a period in the wilderness. That the Egyptians allow the Israelites to leave but then pursued them with the idea of killing many and returning the rest to slavery adds dramatic tension to the narrative.

This story of the sojourn in Egypt, the ten plagues, the first Passover, and the exodus from Egypt is an inspiring one. It has helped to sustain the Jewish people through the persecutions of many centuries and has been seized on by other downtrodden peoples—such as black slaves in the pre–Civil War American South—for hope of future freedom and salvation. No historical study can take away this prototype of hope and inspiration that the exodus story puts forward. But stories can be inspiring and provide stirring models without being literally true. Look at some of Jesus's parables, for example, or some of the Hasidic tales recorded by Martin Buber. In this final section in this chapter, we shall briefly investigate the historicity of the sojourn in Egypt and the exodus:[5]

- *The most important point to note is that there is nothing in Egyptian texts that could be related to the story in the book of Exodus.* No Egyptian document, inscription, or piece of iconography depicts, recounts, or refers to an exodus as described in the Bible. According to the plain statement of the text, six hundred thousand men of military age came out; when we count in the elderly, women, and children, the number would have been at least three or four million. Yet there is no period in the second half of the second millennium BCE when Egypt was subject to a series of plagues, deaths of children, physical disruptions of the country, or the loss of huge numbers of its inhabitants.
- Some have argued that Egyptological elements within the text fit the period of Ramesses II, but this is not sufficient. One must show that they do not fit any other period in history. As it happens, a number of the Egyptian elements in the exodus story are anachronistic.
- The term "land of Goshen" occurs only in late texts (Gen. 45:20; 46:28, 29, 34; 47:1, 4, 6, 27; Exod. 8:22; 9:26). A number of recent scholars have agreed that the name derives at a late period from the name of the Qedarite leader whose area of control evidently related to the northern Egyptian and Delta area (cf. the name "Geshem" in Neh. 2:19; 6:1-2, 6).
- The cities Raameses (Pi-Ramesse) and Pithom (Exod. 1:11) are crucial. Pi-Ramesse is widely identified with Qantir, though one scholar asked where the "Pi" (Egyptian *pr* "house") of Pi-Ramasse had gone. Contrary to some views, the name Ramesses and Pi-Ramesse are attested long after the city of Ramesses had disappeared about the mid-eleventh century BCE. No agreement about the identity of Pithom had been reached for a long time. Many have now argued that Tell el-Maskhuta is Pithom (Egyptian *pr-'Itm* "the house of Atum"), but this site was not settled between the sixteenth and the seventh centuries. The nearby site of Tell el-Ratabah is another possibility, but it was reoccupied only about 1200 BCE.

- A further consideration concerns the orthography of "Ramesses" (רעמסס in Hebrew) in Exod. 1:11. The name as found in the Bible (Gen. 47:11; Exod. 12:37; Num. 33:3, 5) is spelled with the Hebrew letter *samek*, a late transliteration, whereas an early form would have had the letter *shin* (שׁ). The transcription of Egyptian *s* (*ś*) with Hebrew *samek* occurs only at a later time. This shows that the Egyptian name Ramesses entered the Hebrew text no earlier than the eighth century BCE: "the name Ramesses in Ex 1:11 points to the first millennium BCE," was the conclusion of a biblical scholar who works in Egyptian.[6]

- In dating the time to which the textual data point, one must consider not only the sites named but also any important ones that are omitted. Particularly notable for its absence is the site with the classical name of Sile. This was a strongly fortified frontier site and armory built in the New Kingdom. The Egyptian name of Sile was *Ṯrw*, known already in the Middle Kingdom and as a fortress in the reign of Thutmose III (c. 1479–1425 BCE). Yet *Ṯrw*/Sile seems to find no place in the biblical account. This indicates that the narrative of Exodus is no earlier than the Saite period or later (eighth to fifth century BCE).

- The supposed route of the exodus from Egypt. The text does not reflect the fifteenth or thirteenth BCE but the seventh or eighth. The largest portion of the Edomite Iron Age sites mentioned in the "forty years of Israelite wandering in the wilderness" that have been excavated originated only in the seventh or eighth century. Overall, the Negev and Transjordanian sites and settlements are mainly later than the Late Bronze Age (that is, later than 1200 BCE). Only at the end of Iron II (that is, later than 900 BCE) were most of the sites that can be identified actually occupied. Most scholars argue that the itineraries in Exodus and in Numbers 33 are the result of late editing of several different traditions that do not presuppose the same route.

- Lack of archaeological evidence for an exodus. No event of the size and extent of the exodus could have failed to leave significant archaeological remains. According to the book of Numbers (10:11; 12:16; 13:26; 20:1, 22; 33:36) much of the "forty years of wandering" was spent near Qadesh-barnea. This and related sites in Sinai and southern Palestine should yield ample evidence of a large population in this region. Even if they lived in tents, they might have built temporary shelters or stock pens of brush. They would have had regular fires for cooking or warmth. They would have made toilet facilities. Some objects, such as the jewelry "borrowed" (looted) from the Egyptians, would have been lost and become buried. People and animals would have died and been buried or left their bones. Hundreds of thousands of people living on one site over many decades would have left a mark, yet we find nothing. Qadesh (Tell el-Qudeirat) itself has been extensively excavated but shows no habitation between the Middle Bronze and the tenth century BCE or even later.

The evidence shows that a large population of Israelites, living in their own section of the country, did not march out of an Egypt devastated by various plagues and despoiled of its wealth and spend forty years in the wilderness before conquering the Canaanites. On the other hand, this does not rule out the possibility that the text contains a distant—and distorted—memory of an actual event, as many scholars have long argued. Some feel that the tradition is so strong in the Bible that some actual event must lie behind it, though it might well be only a small group of (slave?) escapees fleeing Egypt (a view long and widely held).

The exodus story as we have it is not a monolith but is made up of elements from a variety of periods and milieus. Although there may well be early elements within the exodus narrative, some perhaps even going back to Ramesside times, the form of the story as we presently have it in Exodus and Numbers contains data that are most closely associated with the Saite and Persian periods, or about the seventh to fifth centuries BCE.

Conclusions

The earliest known reference to Israel is found in an inscription of Pharaoh Merenptah about 1200 BCE. This chapter has looked at that reference and then tried to find out if there was other possible material on the early history of Israel. What we found was that Semitic groups were migrating temporarily or even settling permanently in Egypt from about 2000 BCE on. Several inscriptions from the Middle Kingdom mention such Semitic groups, some perhaps related to what became Israel later on. Then there was the Hyksos Dynasty in the Second Intermediate Period, which ruled for about a century (c. 1630–1530 BCE). The Hyksos may have been distantly related to the later Israelites.

In the Amarna letters we find detailed accounts of events in Canaan and Syria, covering the period about 1350 to 1325 BCE. Israel is not mentioned in these important letters and nothing in them seems to relate to the Israel known to us. They indicate that no Israel was in the land of Canaan before about 1325 BCE. The Merenptah stela does suggest that an entity called Israel was in Canaan, but where and in what mode is uncertain. The hieroglyphic determinative with the name Israel is that for a people, but whether these people were settled down or were rather moving through the land as a mobile community cannot be known from the information in the inscription.

This brings us to the stories in the Pentateuch, especially Genesis and Exodus. We have looked at the first few chapters of Genesis in previous chapters of this book. We saw that the biblical story of creation, of Adam and Eve, of the flood, and the Tower of Babel did not coincide with scientific information now available to us. These are legendary accounts that teach certain basic truths but cannot be taken literally as chronicles of history. When we come to Genesis 12 and the story of Abraham, it was once widely asserted in scholarship that we were now dealing with serious history. After important studies and debates, however, it seems clear that we are still encountering legendary material in Genesis 12–50. The actions of the patriarchs are models of virtue but are also sometimes cautionary tales of how not to live or act. The stories are filled with anachronisms and historical improbabilities and were probably written down a millennium or more after the alleged events and individuals in the stories. We can glean little or nothing of the early history of Israel from the patriarchal narratives.

As we read farther into the text, we reach the book of Exodus. The most important conclusion about it arises from the earlier survey of Egyptian history: there were very few periods during the Late Bronze Age or the Egyptian New Kingdom when Palestine was not firmly under Egyptian control. It is in that context that Israel is first mentioned about 1208 BCE by Merenptah, showing that Israel already existed by the end of the Late Bronze Age. But what exactly that entity of Israel consisted of is uncertain, and there is the important question of where it resided.

No Egyptian king is named in the biblical text, and no reference to the exodus or associated events is found in Egyptian texts. There are no Egyptian references of any kind that relate to Joseph, the descendants of Jacob, Moses, the ten plagues, or the exodus. It does seem strange that there is not even a hint in Egyptian literature, iconography, or legend that any of this happened. It is even stranger that there is no early archaeology relating to the Israelites in the major areas of the exodus, especially around Qadesh-barnea or further north in the Transjordanian region.

Thus, when the some scholars relate the exodus story to the sixth century BCE or the Saite period or the Persian period, they are not necessarily being less true to the text than some conservative evangelicals—who incidentally also happily overlook or ignore aspects of the text when they try to find a place for it in the thirteenth or fifteenth centuries BCE. One of the first things they usually try to do is explain away the textual statements about six hundred thousand armed men, plus women, children, and animals, coming out of Egypt on the first Passover night. Reading the biblical text as literally and/or historically true is not necessarily a better way of reading it than is reading Shakespeare as literally and/or historically true.

4
Israel Settles in the Land

As discussed in the previous chapter, the first mention of Israel (in the Merenptah stela) associates it with the land of Canaan. We have a story in the books of Joshua and Judges in which the people of Israel march out of the desert, conquer Transjordan, cross the Jordan River, and subdue Canaan—all in the space of a few years.

No one questions that Israel settled in the land of Canaan! Yet already a century ago there was a dispute about how the Israelite settlement came about. Was it a unitary conquest as depicted in Numbers and Joshua, as those of the Albright school claimed? Or did "nomads" gradually filter in from the surrounding wilderness and desert areas and settle down—mostly peaceably, though with perhaps the occasional violent clash—over several generations, as many German biblical scholars believed? The followers of Albright claimed to have archaeology on their side, but did they? Beginning in the 1970s the debate heated up to encompass scholars from around the world.

What Does the Archaeology Say?

It is a bit naughty to ask the question, "What does the archaeology say?" because archaeology does not speak!—in spite of sweeping statements by some archaeologists and biblical scholars. Archaeology is simply the inert stuff in the ground: the artifacts, the remains of buildings, the bones of humans and animals, plant debris, pots and pans, excrement, and all the rest of material deposited in the earth over the centuries. It is *archaeologists* who spout words—it is they who tell us what this residue lying in the ground means for history. In other words, archaeology is an interpretative science, just like historians who get their history from written sources. Whatever the source, the writing of history relies on human interpretation.

Yet this does not negate the value of archaeology—on the contrary! A written text—whether ancient or modern—is the product of the human mind. The reader is at the mercy of the writer who may be telling the truth, a partial truth, or lying like a dog. But an object in the ground has its own existence. It can be touched, collected, and catalogued. It is not (usually) invented. Sometimes there is doubt, but the practice among professional archaeologists to catalogue carefully what they find before interpreting it makes this less likely than perhaps in the past when recording of finds was sometimes careless. And, of course, we should be very leery of treasure hunters whose only concern is to find valuable objects and do not follow the code of conduct for digging as professional archaeologists do. Or the hobbyists who have a theory and want to excavate solely "to prove" it, ignoring any counterevidence and the wealth of overall data that the archaeological dig can provide.

The historian has access to the finds of archaeology and also to the debates, disagreements, and differences of interpretation between archaeologists. Most historians are not themselves archaeologists, but they can make use of archaeological finds as they can any other historical source. The non-archaeologist may not always be able to decide between competing archaeological theories, but often the careful historian can judge who is most likely to be right or at least reckon when it is wisest not to choose a side in the debate.

When it comes to the Israelite settlement, there is general agreement about what is found in the ground and the overall picture produced by these finds. There are disagreements about how to interpret some of the finds, but there is now a much greater consensus than there was back in the early and mid-twentieth century when several schools of thought divided historians of early Israel and how it became a state. We can now investigate the archaeological work of the past few decades that provides an insight into the Israelite settlement. (For the technical terms used for the various archaeological periods, an approximate date is usually provided.)

Context of the Settlement: Collapse of Empires

In order to set the scene for the settlement of Israel in the land of Canaan, we need to consider the larger context in the eastern Mediterranean and the ancient Near East. The decades before and after 1200 BCE were momentous ones, not just for Israel: the whole of the region underwent a large upheaval. Few of the peoples and societies were left without major changes. Canaan was only one of the areas that was transformed at this time.[1]

The Late Bronze Age ended with a major collapse that seems to have affected the whole of the eastern Mediterranean. The exact cause of this collapse about 1200 BCE is uncertain, though a momentous climate catastrophe in the form of a long-term drought in much of the ancient Near East has been proposed. In any case, the general prosperity of the LB age in Palestine came to an end sometime about 1200 BCE. However, it is *important not to think of a sudden collapse; on the contrary, it was gradual, over decades, perhaps even as long as a century*. There was the destruction of the main Palestinian centres: Akko, Hazor, Megiddo, Beth-Shean, Lachish, and Ashdod. But this was over time, and the sites in the lowland areas were mainly destroyed in the twelfth century rather than the thirteenth.

Yet the *"conventional wisdom" that the Palestinian city-state system came to an end at this time oversimplifies what happened. But a significant event was the decline and disappearance of the Egyptian presence, by about 1130 BCE if not earlier.* Some city-states probably did decline or disappear with the destruction of their urban centers, but the rural sector generally experienced continuity, both demographically and culturally. We have now set the stage for the Israelite settlement, but as we shall see, the archaeology and other sources of evidence do not generally support the biblical picture. Let us look carefully at what actual data we have on the settlement.

- The foremost point is the greater development in northern Palestine as contrasted with southern Palestine. This was largely due to geographical factors: topography, geology, soil, rainfall, climate in general. The region of Judah was less fertile, had a lower density of population, and developed economically more slowly than Samaria. The sudden growth in the hill country. The central hill country between the Jezreel Valley and Jerusalem was only sparsely settled during most of the Late Bronze Age (about 1500 to 1200 BCE). This changed drastically in the Iron I period, which produced a "settlement wave of unprecedented intensity," with about 250 established sites by the late Iron I, most of them small. This increase was largely in the north, especially in the areas of Ephraim and Manasseh, and almost entirely north of Jerusalem.
- This growth was slower in Judah. The "Benjaminite or Gibeon-Bethel plateau" (between Bethel and Jerusalem) was a region of rapid growth of small settlements. The Judaean Hills further south eventually also underwent settlement as well but approximately a century later than the Central Highlands.
- The Shephelah (Lowlands) was a fertile region, but it was dominated by the Philistines until later during the Judaean monarchy. It is often assumed that Judah controlled the Shephelah from an early time, but this seems incorrect. It was only after the destruction of Gath by Hazael about 835 BCE that Judah was able to expand into the Shephelah.

What About the Book of Joshua and the Israelite "Conquest"?

When we read the Bible, we have a picture of "Israel" as a group of settlers and settlements that arose after a conquest of Canaanite cities. This has conventionally been dated to the Iron I period. But now many reject this depiction of an Israelite conquest and settlement. Why is this? What about the book of Joshua?

As we discussed in the preceding chapter, there is no historical or archaeological evidence of a large body of Israelites—several million according to the biblical text—leaving Egypt, marching through the desert, and massing on the Transjordanian side of the Jordan River. "But," one might ask, "many cities were destroyed by the Israelites, according to the book of Joshua. What does archaeology say about them?" This is a good question and the key to evaluating the account according to Joshua.

Were there many Canaanite cities destroyed at this time, as the Bible pictures it?

We can actually start a bit earlier, with the book of Numbers. According to Numbers 21:1-3, Israel, on its way to the Promised Land, attacked and destroyed the city of Arad in the Negev. Likewise, the city of Heshbon in Transjordan was also taken (Num. 21:25-26). *Arad* was abandoned at the end of the Early Bronze Age (c. 2650 BCE) and was not rebuilt until the eleventh century BCE. *Heshbon* was only excavated beginning in 1968. No Bronze Age remains were found, only a possible unwalled village from sometime after 1200 BCE. *From the information currently available, neither Arad nor Heshbon were inhabited at the time of the alleged attacks from conquering Israelites.*

When the city of *Hazor*, in the northern part of Galilee, was excavated in the 1950s, it seemed to fit the description in Joshua 11:1-11. Hazor had been a great city in the Late Bronze Age, but sometime in the thirteenth century it was destroyed. It lay abandoned for a time but then was settled by a group whose material culture was different from the Bronze Age inhabitants. This was interpreted as destruction by Joshua, abandonment for a time, then resettlement by Israelites. However, in the 1980s and 1990s further excavation work was undertaken, which provided data that went against the Joshua 11 account.

There was evidence of a major conflagration in the thirteenth century that affected the monumental buildings, but none of the smaller-scale domestic and cultic buildings in the lower city were burnt or violently destroyed. Especially important was the fact that no archaeological evidence of warfare—no evidence of human victims—no evidence of weapons—was found anywhere on the site. This strongly indicates that the *destruction of Hazor was not the result of a military conquest but of an internal revolt*. During that revolt the symbols of a hated elite (such as statues) were destroyed by an uprising of the formerly subservient part of the population.

More widely in the *Galilean area*, a number of small settlements existed, the majority established in the twelfth and eleventh centuries. Their material culture suggests continuity from the Late Bronze into Iron I and indicates that the population was indigenous rather than immigrants as pictured by the biblical text (contrast Josh. 19:24-48). The suggestion that a new population took control appears to have no archaeological support.

Jericho was a major engagement according to Joshua 6. When the site was excavated in the 1930s, the archaeologist thought he had found evidence of Joshua's destruction of the city at the end of the Middle Bronze Age; however, when further excavation work was done by Dame Kathleen Kenyon in the 1950s, it was found that the main destruction of the city happened in the sixteenth century BCE, long before any possible time for Joshua. There was no Late Bronze Age walled city to be destroyed by any supposed Israelite campaign. At most there was a minor unwalled settlement, hardly the stuff for mighty walls to come tumbling down at the sound of Levitical trumpets. Finally, recent carbon-14 dating has indicated that the destruction of the Middle Bronze city was about 1550 BCE. There seems no way to salvage a destruction of Jericho by Joshua from the archaeological data.

Lachish seems to have been destroyed about 1135 BCE. Some have wanted to associate the destruction with an Israelite invasion (Josh. 10:31-3). The problem is that the site remained abandoned and uninhabited for about two centuries, which seems strange if the biblical text is correct, since it would have been part of the heritage of the tribe of Judah (Josh. 15:39). Now, the destruction has frequently been associated with the coming of the Sea Peoples (on these, see pp. 65–8). Specifically, the city could have been destroyed by the invading Philistines.

Other sites said to have been destroyed by the Israelites (according to Joshua) do not match the archaeology: *Ai* (Josh. 7–8) had been destroyed about 2400 BCE and lay unoccupied until rebuilt about 1200 BCE; no evidence exists for a city at *Gibeon* (Josh. 9) during the Late Bronze Age (only a few tombs); also no evidence of a settlement at *Hebron* (Tell er-Rumeida) during the Late Bronze Age (Josh. 10:36-7) except for a few tombs; *Debir* (Khirbet Rabud) was not destroyed at this time (as alleged by Josh. 10:38-9); neither was *Tirzah* (Tell el-Farah North), despite Josh. 12:24, while *Taanach*'s signs of destruction date to the twelfth century, after the time of Joshua's alleged activities (Josh. 12:21).

Thus, when we examine the Canaanite cities allegedly conquered and destroyed by the Israelites, we often find the archaeology of those cities telling us a different story. Notice a summary of what the archaeology says about the main sites we have been discussing:

When we look at the cities actually destroyed at the end of the Late Bronze Age, these were once simplistically associated with an Israelite conquest under Joshua. But more careful observation shows two important considerations:

- The various destructions of Canaanite centers were not more or less simultaneous as Joshua depicts it but rather took place over a long period of time, at least a century.

- Of the dozen cities or so associated with the Israelite invasion in the book of Joshua, only a couple (primarily Hazor and Dan) show a resettlement pattern that would match the new Israelite population settling down.

We would expect that after the conquest Israelites would have settled in the most fertile and hospitable parts of the country, yet we find hardly any new settlements in Iron I in those areas, whether the coastal plain, the Shephelah, or the northern

TABLE 4.1 *Sites supposedly conquered and destroyed.*

Biblical Site	Biblical Passage	Results of Archaeology
Arad	Num. 21:1-3	Not occupied at that time
Heshbon	Num. 21:25-26	Not occupied at that time
Jericho	Josh. 6	Only small settlement? (see discussion on p. 54)
Ai	Josh. 7-8	Not occupied at that time
Gibeon	Josh. 9	Little occupation at that time
Jerusalem	Josh. 10:1-27	No destruction at that time
Jarmuth	Josh. 10:3-27	Not occupied at that time
Makkedah	Josh. 10:28	Not occupied at that time
Libnah	Josh. 10:29-30	Unidentified
Lachish	Josh. 10:31-2	No destruction at that time
Eglon	Josh. 10:34-5	Unclear
Hebron	Josh. 10:36-7	Little or no settlement
Debir	Josh. 10:38-9	No destruction at that time
Hazor	Josh. 11:1-11	Destruction (see discussion on p. 54)
Taanach	Josh. 12:21	No destruction at that time
Tirzah	Josh. 12:24	No destruction at that time

valleys. On the other hand, archaeology shows a burgeoning of new settlements in the central hill country, a region that hardly features in the book of Joshua or its account of the Israelite settlement.

Where Did Israel Come From?

Recognizing that the picture in the book of Joshua is very misleading, we still know that there was an Israelite settlement. Once we understand that various people indeed settled in the Canaanite highlands in the Late Bronze or Early Iron I period, the next question is: Who were these people? Were they all one ethnic group or were they from a variety of groups? In order to answer this, we need to consider some of the possible groups associated with Palestine at that time.

Canaanites. In some biblical passages the Canaanites seem to be a tribe or ethnic group. But in most of our sources, including many biblical passages, "Canaanite" is simply a reference to anyone who dwells in the country or territory of Canaan. *It is a geographical term, not an ethnic term.* All the people who lived in the region of Canaan could be called "Canaanite," including any Israelites who lived there. According to many biblical passages (such as Gen. 17:8; Exod. 6:4; Lev. 25:38; Deut. 32:49; Josh. 14:1), Israel considered the "land of Canaan" their heritage; therefore, they were Canaanites. It is likely that the settlers included farmers migrating from other parts of Canaan, people of the Canaanite lowlands who left their villages and farms and even the Canaanite cities and made these remote regions their home. Basically, it included any number of Canaanite people seeking a better life by cultivating land in the sparsely settled country of the highlands.

Shasu. This is a group referred to in a number of Egyptian texts. In many passages they appear as an ethnic group. Yet they are also associated with certain geographical areas. They are often connected with the area of southern Transjordan, particularly Edom, Seir, and Transjordan east of the Arabah. It is frequently assumed that the Shasu were pastoralists (often referred to as "nomads"), but nomadic pastoralism covers a wide-ranging spectrum and can include those who raise crops, engage in trade, or even go raiding or robbing caravans—alongside their livestock husbandry. The Shasu were not the only pastoralists. One of the results of recent study is that society in Palestine tended to oscillate between pastoralism and settled farming over a climate cycle of several centuries. When the climate got drier, many of the population turned to pastoralism and lived in tents or other temporary accommodation. When rainfall increased on a permanent basis, they would settle down and depend on settled farming for a living.

Apiru. When the name *Apiru* was first found in the Amarna letters, some transcribed the name as *Haberu*. This was due to the peculiarities of the cuneiform writing system. In any case, it is cognate with the Hebrew word "Hebrew." However, this word was originally *not an ethnic term but referred to a particular social class of people who were outside the social system.* They could be "migrants" or "refugees," but they were often seen as "outlaws" or "brigands." This included escaped slaves and other refugees of all sorts. Those who fled to the highlands were often designated as *'apiru* in Egyptian sources, but that tells us little other than that they were seen as displaced persons and potential troublemakers. We have evidence that sometimes these outsiders banded together and lived by raiding or stealing; at other times, they seem to have sold their services as mercenaries. But just as the medieval Vikings were also farmers and settlers, as well as warriors and raiders, so too did those referred to as *'apiru* pursue more than one way of making a living.

Philistines. We first hear of them in Egyptian texts where they are one group of the Sea Peoples (on the Sea Peoples, see chapter 5, pp. 65–8). These were tribes, mainly from the Aegean, who made raids on Egyptian territory. There were several tribes, but it is the Peleset—the Philistines—that concern us here. Although Genesis (mistakenly) has Philistines in the Canaan in the second millennium BCE, we know they did not reach Palestine until after 1200 BCE. But sources show that they settled in the southeast of Palestine, including the coastal plain and were later to have conflicts with the nascent Israel.

Various ethnic groups immigrating to the region. The collapse of urban culture in the entire Aegean-Anatolian-Syro-Palestinian region and the migration of large groups came in the thirteenth to eleventh centuries. The Aramaeans gradually took over large tracts in Mesopotamia and Syria. Migration in Iron I because of destruction in Asia Minor means that various groups reached Canaan and played an important part in settlement. Some migrants also came from the Transjordanian area across the Jordan River into Canaan. It was once argued that major groups from Asia Minor and Syria picked up sticks and moved south. But there is little or no evidence for such large movements of people into Palestine. On the other hand, here and there are references to small groups of people whose ancestors seem to have originated a long way away but chose to settle and live in Canaan. We therefore have some evidence of migration of at least small groups: Hittites in Hebron; Hivites in western Benjamin and perhaps around Shechem; Jebusites from the Hittite Empire; and Girgashites from Anatolia. Only two of the alleged seven pre-Israelite nations were autochthonous, that is, native to the region.

Perhaps the most widespread thesis is the concept of beginning Israel as a "mixed multitude," an idea that goes back at least to the mid-1980s. According to this theory, the population that became Israel was made up of a diverse group of people. The different groups or populations who contributed to the highland settlers seem to have included the following (some of whom came from groups listed above):

- The pastoralist population who had derived from an originally settled population that in past centuries had turned to pastoralism because of adverse conditions. This included the Shasu centered on the Dead Sea region who also engaged in copper mining and smelting among their community endeavors. Pastoralists are often more or less invisible in the archaeology, but the indication is that many existed. The majority of this "new" population seem to be those pastoralists who lived in the hill country and went on to form the bulk of the new settlers. These pastoralists and the settled population generally had a symbiotic relationship, in which livestock and animal products were traded for grain and other agricultural products, to mutual benefit.
- In the early stages of the Iron I, the new settlements had a strong tendency to arise in the vicinity of Late Bronze urban centers. This indicates that the settlers were not primarily rebels against the city rulers and administrators.

- Farmers and others of the rural Canaanite population who left a sedentary lifestyle and withdrew into the highlands because of the systems collapse of the Canaanite lowlands.
- *Apiru*, individuals on the margins of society who had sought refuge in the highlands for a variety of reasons (as refuges, escaped slaves, etc.) and lived by raiding, mercenary activity, and perhaps subsistence agro-pastoralism.
- Egyptian administrators who had married local women and settled locally on retirement.
- Other ethnic groups who had recently migrated to Canaan from outside and were still not integrated into the lowland or urban populations. Some of these may have been associated with the caravan trade. Some may have been migrants from Transjordan.

Some researchers have argued that the early Israelites were primarily from one particular group. At the moment, the consensus seems to be that the early Israelites were mainly "Canaanite," that is, they arose in Canaan among the indigenous inhabitants of the land. Yet some have argued that they arose primarily from the Shasu; indeed, some make "Shasu" and "Israelite" practically synonymous. Some argue that the "Israel" mentioned in Merenptah's famous inscription is actually pictured fighting the Egyptians in the scene labeled by the name "Shasu." This goes far beyond the evidence, and many experts contradict this equation.

Some have wanted to find Israelite characteristics that would show up in archaeological finds. Thus, it was once suggested that a number of innovations in technology took place in the central highlands: terracing, plastered cisterns, the "Israelite house," collared-rim jars, and use of iron. Unfortunately, it seems there is no list of technologies that is exclusive to this region and time or that can serve as "Israelite ethnic markers." A favorite supposed sign of being Israelite relates to pork consumption—or the absence of it. The subject is a complicated one: there is indeed a considerable drop in evidence for swine in the highlands during Iron I and Iron II, in contrast to the Late Bronze Age and also the Iron I and II coastal plain where pigs remained a part of the diet. But important studies have concluded that "no human behavioral evidence exists to indicate that pig avoidance was unique to any particular group in the ancient Near East ... Lots of people, for lots of reasons, were not eating pork."[2]

The Times of Judges

The book of Judges is a curious book. The first thing that strikes the reader is that it contradicts the book of Joshua in many ways! Having finished Joshua, in which the Israelites conquered and settled Canaan after only about five years, the interested student will be astonished to read in Judges 1 that much of the land remained to be subdued. According to Judges 1, there had been no quick conquest of the land by a unified Israel under Joshua; rather, the taking of territory came mainly after Joshua's death, and in many cases the Israelites lived alongside Canaanites.

A second impression on perusing the book is that it seems to be filled with legendary figures and stories of activities by an individual tribe or two. For example, one can hardly credit the story of Samson (Judg. 13–16) with the label of "authentic history"; on the contrary, Samson seems to be in much the same category as Jack the Giant-killer in the fairy tales of the Brothers Grimm or Paul Bunyan of American folklore. To take another example, the account in Judges 3:12-30 ostensibly concerns the figures of Ehud and Eglon, but these are geographical terms: Ehud a Benjaminite clan, and Eglon, a town in the Judaean foothills.

The book of Judges comes across quite differently from Joshua: Judges 1 begins by stating that at the time Joshua died there still had been no major conquest of the land or defeat of the Canaanites. Far from being conquered and under Israelite rule, the lowlands and many of the main cities were still controlled by the native inhabitants who fought with chariots of iron. As noted above, if one had read Joshua for the first time and then moved to Judges without knowing anything about its contents, it would have produced considerable consternation, because a number of the things supposedly accomplished by Joshua had to be done again (e.g., the tribal military campaigns in Judg. 1:19–36 versus Josh. 16–19).

Yet on the face of it, the book of Judges seems to reflect in a general way the state of Canaan in the Early Iron Age, especially the presence of several small, semi-independent polities fighting for status and even survival among themselves. The picture of disunity, with a variety of often uncooperative peoples and tribes in the land—each out for personal gain and advantage—seems to fit the general situation during the Iron Age I (about 1200 to 1000 BCE). The developing settlements no doubt sometimes cooperated for mutual benefit but also sometimes quarreled over resources and territorial control. There is a certain resemblance between some of the "judges" in the book and the Canaanite kinglets known from the Amarna period (see pp. 38–9 above). To take the example of Shamgar ben Anath. Only a brief sentence or two are given about him (Judg. 3:31; 5:6), and he seems to have been an embarrassment for the narrator, perhaps because of being apparently a worshiper of the goddess Anat. Yet he was included rather than omitted from the record as would have been easy, so he seems to have been someone who could not be overlooked. He reminds one of Abdi-Heba of Amarna Jerusalem who was a local leader and had a goddess as part of his name.

But apart from this general picture, the stories in Judges are largely illusory if one looks to them for genuine historical memory of detailed events. This is because *the book reflects an overall theological design rather than a historical one*. It is mainly made up of a series of episodes that follow a *common theological pattern*:

- Israel sins,
- Israel is punished by being made subjects of a foreign people,
- Israel cries to Yahweh,
- Yahweh sends a deliverer who leads them in throwing off the foreign yoke.

Astonishingly, this all follows a schematic forty/eighty-year cycle. This artificial structure is clear through much of the book, yet this is not the way history works. These stories, in addition to their entertainment value, had an important content relating to morality, which is probably the main reason they were told. But our concern is with their historicity. Yet despite our lack of confidence in the details of the narratives, actual persons and/or events might lie behind some of the stories in Judges.

The narrative of Judges is divided between heroic deliverance figures ("major judges") and civic leaders ("minor judges"). The "minor judges" get little actual space but are presented in two brief lists (Judg. 10:1-5; 12:7-15). For example, Shamgar ben Anath was discussed above. Some have suggested that he was a Canaanite tribal leader rather than an Israelite. However, we must keep in mind that Israelites were polytheistic at this time. Some families might have had personal attachment to a particular god or goddess even though they probably also worshiped the tribal God Yahweh (on this, see further in chapter 7).

The judge named Jerubbaal has a name that means something like "Let Baal be great"; Judges 6–8, 6:32 give a nonsensical etymology of his name. He is only later identified with Gideon, which suggests that we are dealing with two separate individuals. Whether the person of Gideon was a person or just an invention of the storyteller, the story may be about military action against the Midianites west of Shechem in the tenth century. As for the Abimelech, the supposed son of Gideon (Judges 9), the presumed oldest tradition seems to concern a struggle between two 'apiru groups or outlaw gangs over control of Shechem that ended in the destruction of the city (late eleventh or early tenth century BCE). In any case, Abimelech looks more like the king of a Canaanite city-state rather than an Israelite tribal leader.

Jephthah occurs in the list of "minor judges" but also appears as a heroic or deliverer figure. It has been suggested that an old savior tale lies at the heart of this story. Perhaps it was about a border dispute with the Ammonites, conducted by an 'apiru group led by Jephthah, between the town of Gilead (south of the Jabbok River) and the town of Mizpah (north of the Jabbok) no later than the tenth century BCE.

To summarize, one cannot rule out that some actual historical core can be found in some of the "deliverer" stories, but when we turn the statement around, demonstrating such a core of history is very difficult. Despite references to "all Israel" only one or two tribes are normally involved in the action in an episode; the Song of Deborah (Judges 5) is the only passage with more than two tribes. The geographical distribution of the stories shows a deliberate attempt by the author to fill in the territory of the Northern Kingdom to cover the Israelite hill country, Gilead, Jezreel, and the northern border areas (remarkably similar to the description in 2 Sam. 2:9). The amount of confirmed historical data in Judges seems small.

The "Song of Deborah," an Early Israelite Poem

When it comes to searching for historical accounts, the "Song of Deborah" (Judges 5) seems to be an exception. The reason is that the language is an example of early poetry—perhaps written in the tenth century BCE—which would put it close to the events described. The list of Israelite tribes differs in several ways from all other lists (Machir instead of Manasseh [Judg. 5:14]; Gilead instead of Gad [Judges 5:17]). Judah, Simeon, and Levi are all absent. The reason for the differences might well be that this is an independent tradition, one rather earlier than some of the other traditions in the book of Judges. Therefore, the account in Judges 5 will be accepted as representing in essence a particular situation and battle in the Jezreel Valley in the tenth century.

The list of tribes is given below (Judg. 5:14-18). This looks like a list of the contents of Israel after it had become a state under Ishbaal's (Ish-bosheth's) rule (2 Sam. 2:9):

Judges 5	2 Samuel 2:9
Ephraim	Ephraim
Benjamin	Benjamin
Machir	
Zebulun	
Issachar	
Reuben	
Gilead	Gilead
Dan	
Asher	Ashurites?
Naphtali	
	Jezreel

Benjamin, Ephraim, and Machir represent approximately the segment of the Israelite kingdom in Canaan before the time of Omri (the place of Issachar, Zebulon, and Naphtali is uncertain). From the geographical point of view, Judges 5 represents Israel before Omri's rule (after which it expanded greatly; see further in chapter 6).

Making use of chapter 5 does not give credence to the rest of Judges as a historical source. In one area, however, Judges as a book may reflect an older linguistic usage: the title "judge" (Hebrew *šôfēṭ*). Although the word means "judge" in a judicial sense in most Hebrew usage, the reference to persons by this title in Judges means something like "political/military leader," which seems to be an older usage. Thus, here and there may be reliable early traditions, but demonstrating them is difficult; the book is generally too problematic to use as a historical source.

The Israelite Settlement: A Summary

The context for this chapter has been the eastern Mediterranean and ancient Near East during the Early Iron Age. The Late Bronze Age had seen the Mediterranean world expand into an interconnected cosmopolitan realm, but the end of the Late Bronze Age presided over a general collapse of trade and communication, with many cities destroyed along the Mediterranean coast and sometimes further inland. We cannot get away from the fact that Egypt controlled Palestine until the end of the Late Bronze Age (c. 1200 BCE). Our focus has been on the Iron I period, beginning about 1200 BCE and ending with the invasion of Pharaoh Shoshenq I (about 950–925 BCE).

Toward the beginning of Iron I (before 1100 BCE), Egypt withdrew from Palestine. Some of the Sea Peoples—mainly the Philistines—had settled in southern Palestine, beginning about 1200 BCE. Once Egypt withdrew, the various small kingdoms and city-states were left on their own to try to survive or to expand and take over territory at the expense of others. This was the story of Canaan in the Iron I period (c. 1200–1000 BCE). This was the context in which Israel made its start.

The singular most significant point arising from the archaeology is the rapid expansion of settlement in the central hill country in Iron I, mainly small sites. Continuity of pottery styles in the Jezreel and Beth-Shean Valleys indicates that it was the indigenous inhabitants whose population began to increase, rather than new settlers from outside. In the Ephraimite and Manassite regions population increase was unprecedented. The "Benjamin Plateau" (between Bethel and Jerusalem) was another area of sustained growth in the Early Iron Age. The increase was much slower in the Judaean Hills and south than in the north but nevertheless developed a momentum later in Iron I, while its main growth came in Iron IIA (after 1000 BCE).

A very important question is, who were those who settled in the central highlands at the end of the Late Bronze and beginning of the Iron I? Several observations need to be made that are relevant to the highland settlements:

- "Israel" did not begin with the settlement of the hill country in the Iron I. An entity called Israel was already in existence in the Late Bronze Age, even if we know little about it.

- Many of those settling the highlands would have come from other areas of Canaan: peasants and farmers from the rural areas but also villages and farmsteads surrounding the Canaanite cities. Also inhabitants of Canaanite cities, who had lived within the city walls, but who went out each day to engage in agriculture work.

- Nomadic pastoralists who decided that they wanted a more settled life. This would have included some of the Shasu. But recent scholarly study has shown that the highland population often altered between being pastoralists (when agricultural conditions were not good) and being farmers (when conditions were favorable). So apparently some of the settlers were former pastoralists who chose to farm instead of (or in addition to) pastoralism.

- There were also likely some foreigners brought in as administrators and garrison troops for Egyptian centers in Canaan, who settled there after their service was complete. And we must also reckon with a few migrants from abroad who saw opportunities in the Canaanite highlands.

We can conclude that the Israel that settled in the highlands probably had a variety of origins. Yet this disparate group of settlers gradually coalesced into tribes. That is, they came to see themselves as people related by supposed ancestral descent (whether actual or fictional does not matter, since tribal genealogies are often cleverly created rather than an actual record of descent). But tribal identity is a later development, when the settlers of diverse origins came to see themselves as having a good deal in common and that coalescing into a community would have distinct advantages.

Like the story of the exodus and the wandering of millions of Israelites in the desert for forty years, the book of Joshua describes a *fictional* conquest of Canaan.

Although this picture was once widely accepted, the past half century or so of archaeological excavations has convinced most scholars that no Israelite conquest took place. Instead, it is thought that however Israel originated, it became mainly associated with the greatly expanded settlements of Iron I in the central highlands. This is confirmed in certain ways by the book of Judges, which gives a quite different picture of Israel's settlement, with Israelite communities existing alongside the Canaanites. In fact, the Israelites were originally Canaanites—inhabitants of the territory of Canaan—before taking on the Israelite identity.

The book of Judges describes a Canaan made up of a variety of independent tribes and peoples, often squabbling among themselves. Judges 5 seems to describe an Israel in which independent tribes sometimes worked together for a common good but for the most part pursued their own ends. Some of the tribal and other groups known to us from biblical genealogies might have originated in this period, though we know that others are probably creations by much later story tellers and scribes. Local leaders might have given rise to some of the stories in the book of Judges, but it is doubtful if much historical memory about specific individuals remains here. Yet the general picture of a disunited series of autonomous (or partially autonomous) peoples is quite believable. The book also confirms what we know from other sources: Judah was originally separate from Northern Israel and had its own history and identity.

It is plausible that a line stretched from the "Israel" mentioned by Merenptah to the kingdom of Israel several centuries later. With these two centuries after the first mention of an "Israel," the highland settlers had reached a point that they were willing to unite behind a common identity and a common leader. Thus began monarchic Israel whose story we take up in the next chapter.

5
Israel Becomes a Kingdom: Saul, David, and Solomon

In the two previous chapters (chapters 3 and 4) we saw how Israel was first mentioned in an Egyptian inscription of Pharaoh Merenptah and how archaeology shows a rapid and vast increase in small settlement sites in Canaan, particularly in the central hill country in what is called the Iron Age I (c. 1200–1000 BCE). The results of recent archaeology contradict the picture of a unified Israelite conquest of Canaan as depicted in the book of Joshua.

In the present chapter we shall consider how the hill country settlement that we associate with early Israel developed into a kingdom and a more-or-less unified people. First, we must consider the people that seem to be Israel's primary opponent at this time, the Philistines. Then, we shall look at the early Israelite kings and how the kingdom that they ruled took its place in the Palestinian region of the time. Finally, we shall examine each of the early kings in succession—Saul, David, and Solomon—and consider the rise of the Israelite monarchies, the two separate kingdoms of Israel and Judah. It is the period of the monarchy before the split into two separate kingdoms which this chapter will look at.

A major problem is that, except for one significant mention, we have no reference to Israel in inscriptions or other sources from the surrounding nations at this time. All we have in the way of written accounts are the biblical narratives of 1 and 2 Samuel and 1 Kings. But these were written much later than the events they describe, while the books of Chronicles are even later and almost entirely made up of material taken from Samuel and Kings. There is also archaeology, and it will be an important source of information, but exactly how to interpret it is sometimes disputed. Therefore, throughout this chapter we shall continue to exercise critical judgment as to how much of the biblical text to accept at face value.

Sea Peoples and Philistines

We know about the Sea Peoples mainly from the references to them in Egyptian inscriptions. The Pharaoh Ramesses III states that in his eighth year (c. 1175 BCE) he fought them. He gives a picture of a massive invasion from both land and sea by a coalition of five tribes of the Sea Peoples. But we must take account of the rhetoric of the pharaoh's account. Egyptologists now recognize that Ramesses's claims were part of conventional propaganda to show that he fulfilled his duties as the son of the sun god to protect the Egyptian people. We now know that he exaggerated or even completely invented victories over the Nubians and Asiatics, and his account of the Sea Peoples may also be exaggerated. Yet the Sea Peoples were nevertheless very real. We can summarize the current views on the Sea Peoples as follows:

- It was not necessarily a unified movement but was made up of different groups at different times. Five (sometimes more) tribes are listed: Lukka, Sherden, Weshesh/Ekwesh, Shekelesh, Tjeker/Sekel, Teresh, Denyen, but the most famous—and the one that concerns us here—the Peleset (*prst*) or Philistines. They came from "islands in the midst of the sea," which is how the Egyptians referred to Crete and the Aegean archipelago (cf. the biblical "Caphtor" [Amos 9:7; Jer. 47:4]). But other considerations suggest a variety of Mediterranean and Anatolian origins.

- Although only warriors are pictured in the sea battle, we have other reliefs that show families and livestock, with household goods in ox carts. This suggests the migration of peoples rather than just an army of conquest. These migrants (women, children, and elders are depicted) may have come overland from the north into southern Palestine.

- A sea battle seems to have taken place in the region of the Nile Delta (as the reference to "river mouths" implies), but the land battle is more of a problem. It may have been further north, perhaps on the Phoenician coast or northern Palestine. In any case, Ramesses III's "victory" might have been an attack on a few contingents of migrating peoples but hardly the bulk of them.

- After the battle with the Egyptians, there is evidence that the Philistines settled in the coastal region of southern Palestine. Whether they were settled in the coastal plain by Egyptian coercion or whether they took the area by force in spite of what the Egyptians could do is debated. But this is where we find them in the biblical text.

- The immigration into the Philistine coastal plain may have been a prolonged one, perhaps even over a time frame of fifty or a hundred years. It has been suggested that the Sea Peoples assisted in bringing an end to the Hittite Empire, the kingdom of Ugarit, and the city state of Amurru. More recent study has been more skeptical, even though these states and empires did end in violence about this time. In any case, by 1150 BCE or a little later, Egypt no longer had the strength to prevent the Sea Peoples' migration.

The Philistines were one of the named tribes of the Sea Peoples. We have to keep in mind that the picture of the Philistines given by the biblical text is manifestly wrong in certain parts; for example, the Philistines have been anachronistically projected back as settled in the land in the early second millennium BCE at the time of the so-called patriarchs (Gen. 21:22-34; 26:1-18). Yet we know that there were no Sea Peoples settled in the land until after 1200 BCE. The settlement of some of the Sea

Peoples in south Palestine and along the coast created a new element within Canaan that was to have profound significance for the developing state of Israel. As one archaeologist who has excavated extensively in the old Philistine area explained it, the Philistine settlement was most probably a complex process that took place over an extended period of time and included both violent interactions and peaceful integration.[1]

Much work has been done on the Philistines in recent years, especially in archaeological excavations of Philistine city remains. Judging from what we presently know, the story of the Ark of the Covenant and its capture by the Philistines (1 Sam. 4–6) is not intrinsically unbelievable overall. Unfortunately, many of the welcome recent archaeological finds do not impinge directly on the Bible. For example, the pebbled hearth that has been noted as characteristic of the Philistine area for many centuries seems not to be reflected in the biblical text. There are several examples where text and archaeology interact which we can survey briefly.

- *Lists of Philistine cities* (Josh. 11:22; 19:43; Judg. 1:18; 1 Sam. 6:17; Jer. 25:20; 2 Chron. 26:6). Five cities have become known as the Philistine Pentapolis: Ashdod, Gaza, Ashkelon, Gath, and Ekron. Gath was destroyed by the Aramaean king Hazael about 830 BCE and ceased to be a major Philistine site (2 Kgs 2:18). Yet the biblical text seems to remember the original importance of Gath, which suggests an early memory. But the biblical picture of this Pentapolis, with a council of *seranim* (rulers) making decisions for it as pictured in the text (e.g., 1 Sam. 5:8, 11), seems to be incorrect.
- *That the cities of Gath to Ekron were returned to Israel after the Ark incident* (1 Sam. 7:14) is clearly unhistorical in the light of archaeology: we have no evidence of Israelite occupation of this region in the material culture of this time. Indeed, 1 Sam. 17:52 evidently has Ekron in Philistine hands when David was young, not too many years afterward.
- *The architecture of Philistine temples.* This is known from excavations: the placement of the pillars supporting the roof in the Philistine temple (Judg. 16:25-30) looks like a match to those found in archaeological excavations. Yet we must qualify this positive statement with two more negative ones. First, the statement that there were people on the roof who could observe events on the ground floor of the temple (as if overlooking an unroofed courtyard) is not confirmed by anything so far found. Second, this description of a Philistine temple could date from a much later period, since temples existed in Philistine towns until very late (for example, 1 Macc. 10:84; 11:4).
- *Achish, king of Gath* (1 Sam. 21:11, 13; 27:2-4, 11; 1 Kgs 2:39). This is the only evidence for such a person; however, we have an inscription from the seventh century BCE in the name of "Achish, ruler of Ekron." The fact that the writer remembered the city of Gath as being important might mean that the name of an early king of Gath named Achish was also preserved in the tradition.

- *That the Philistines controlled the working of metal in the region (1 Sam. 13:19-21) is very unlikely.* It seems an absurd notion that Israelites had to go to Philistia just to sharpen their farm implements, not only paying a very high price but also taking the time and trouble to travel there and back. To renew a ploughshare that had been blunted or even damaged by stones would probably cost two-thirds of a sheqel (the value of a *pîm* in the Hebrew text, a weight which has been found in archaeological digs), but this charge would seem extremely expensive simply to sharpen a sickle. Moreover, the Israelite farmer could easily have found appropriate whet stones in the environment to use to sharpen a sickle or mattock. What we find in 1 Sam. 13:19-22 is a statement of theology, not contemporary metal technology.

We can conclude that the picture of the Philistines in the biblical text is a mixed one, speaking from a historical perspective. There is a remarkable memory of the importance of Gath, even though this city fell into decline at an early time. But some other references to the Philistines have been contradicted by archaeology or other information available to us. We can now turn to Israel itself and start to examine how it grew from a people and collection of villages into a kingdom and state.

Israel Edges Toward Becoming a Kingdom

The initial growth in the Central Highlands (that we described in chapter 4) was mainly in small sites, individual homesteads, and the like, though there were also villages. But these seemed to have developed and thrived without any central authority or control by a major urban site. This brings up the question of why the Israelite kingship originated or Israel became a state. In the Bible, we have a strong argument *against* having a king in 1 Samuel 8. This suggests that becoming a monarchy was debated by Israelites, though whether this was before they had a king or only later when they experienced some negative aspects of monarchy is not clear.

One reason for becoming a kingdom that has often been put forward is the "Philistine threat," that is, that the Philistines were trying to expand their territory to include the highlands. Yet there are problems with this proposal. First, there was little reason for the Philistines to want to expand their territory into the highlands. They already had control of the coastal plain and probably also the Shephelah (lowlands, between the highlands and the coastal plain) during this period. The Philistines had little need to make incursions into the Palestinian hill country except as a defense mechanism. *If there was a clash between the people of the hill country and the Philistines, it is likely that Israel initiated it.*

Would the highlanders have had the strength or resources for a wholesale invasion of Philistine territory? It seems unlikely. Instead, they would have made the occasional raid to carry off livestock, stored grain, and other spoils, until finally the Philistines demanded retaliation by their leaders. At this point, the Philistines might have organized an extensive campaign against the Israelites—to punish them and to discourage further raids. This might have included outposts to secure some sort of border with the highlanders (cf. 1 Sam. 14:1-14). But the highland tribes might well have reacted—as we know from other Near Eastern tribes—by countering with further aggression and even an aim to expand their settlements in the lowlands at the expense of the Philistine cities who controlled the region.

The reasons for the development of a state in the highlands are no doubt complex, but the settlement of the Philistines and other Sea Peoples in the south of Palestine and along the coast had added a new element to the population of Canaan. Gradual removal of Egyptian control before 1100 BCE, whether in manned fortresses or the threat of raids against Canaan's inhabitants, allowed a number of groups to thrive. In short, the highland tribes were in competition with other groups in the region (including the Philistines).

Perhaps one important factor was a growth in population: a critical mass of settlers was reached without which certain things could not happen, but this was more significant in the north and decreased as one went south, with the area south of Jerusalem still being mainly pastoral. But this rapid settlement of the hill country was followed by collapse toward the end of Iron I (in the eleventh century BCE), which put pressure on the loose collection of highland peoples. It seems that at some point a dominant ethnic consciousness came about in this region. Part of the reason might be by force: an "Israelite" group—a tribe or coalition of tribes—might have conquered or otherwise taken over some other smaller groups and assimilated them (as suggested in the book of Judges). But this move toward unity would have been enhanced by the successful cooperation of several tribes in a common cause (e.g., against a common enemy as against Sisera in Judges 4–5).

Regardless of why, Israel did choose a king and become a small kingdom. The process is outlined in the biblical text with the description of Saul's reign. Although we shall not be able to confirm many of the details, the story of Saul as the first king seems to be historical and to show some coincidence between the archaeology and the biblical text.

Samuel

We begin not with Saul as such but with the story of Samuel, which takes up the first part of the book of 1 Samuel. Samuel was in many ways a continuation of the line of judges described in the book of Judges: he is said to have "judged" Israel (1 Sam. 7:15). He was both priest and prophet, but he was also a political leader, at least during the first part of his life. We do not normally expect either priest or prophet to be the king (or a similar figure). Yet we know that after the fall of the monarchy when Israel no longer had a king, the high priest of Judah was also a political leader of the Jewish community and sometimes had prophetic functions. So Samuel is not an unlikely figure.

One could easily argue that Samuel was an invented character. But a little reflection would indicate that a religious figure—priest or prophet—might well have been associated with the rise of the monarchy in Israel. You might think of the Archbishop of Canterbury in English history. Although the archbishop was a religious figure, he had considerable power, including the power to crown the monarch. We also know that some archbishops were very political, even holding civic office along with their ecclesiastical duties. Just as the history of the English monarchy includes the activities of many of the Canterbury archbishops, Samuel who had both priestly and prophetic functions, as well as a community leadership role, could have been a necessary figure. He could well have been an important shamanistic figure and king maker in the period at the beginnings of an Israelite state.

Saul

Perhaps the best reason for believing that Saul was a historical personage is that he was plainly a problem for the narrator of 1 and 2 Samuel. It seems clear that the narrator wanted to tell the story of David but had to deal with Saul as well, even though he would rather have ignored or forgotten about him. According to narrative logic, the rulership and dynasty should have begun with David. The whole story of the monarchy is of the legitimacy of the Davidic dynasty and the illegitimacy of the northern kingship. The Northern Kingdom should not have existed, and the northern kings were presented as usurpers. But how is this is to be explained, if David was also a usurper—not part of the dynasty originally chosen by God?

The narrator of 1 Samuel has to present it that Saul's dynasty was not just wiped out, but that his descendants were declared null and void as far as kingship was concerned—a rather strange concept, if it was the king and dynasty originally chosen and anointed by Yahweh. If Saul's rulership and dynasty could be overturned, why not that of David? Why should not his throne have been overthrown with Solomon who also went astray? Yet the narrative insists on treating David's line quite differently from that of Saul.

Thus, it seems that the narrator was stuck with Saul and his family. The existence of Saul as the first king of Israel does not strike the critical reader as a likely fictional scenario, even if some aspects of the relationship and interaction between Saul and David could easily find their place in a work of fiction. The tradition was too firmly settled and known to the people to have been given major changes, such as dropping Saul altogether. Even though there is absolutely no evidence for Saul apart from the biblical text, there is good reason to believe there was a historical Saul.

What else can we say with more or less confidence about this figure? As has long been observed, 2 Sam. 2:9 describes Eshbaal (or Ishbosheth), Saul's son and successor, as ruling over "Gilead, the Ashurites, Jezrel, Ephraim, and Benjamin." This is reasonably much of the territory ascribed to Saul, though his control probably did not extend as far north as Galilee. Saul's final battle is set in the Jezreel Valley by the biblical text, but it seems strange that the Philistines would have been active so far north. There is no indication that either Saul or the Philistines controlled this territory.

Except for one foray into Gilead, the early Saul traditions are confined to the Benjamin Plateau and the southern Ephraim hill country. The hill country north of Bethel is almost entirely absent from the Saul narrative. But this restricted area for Saul is especially important because it does not include Judah, for reasons that will be noted later in the chapter (see p. 72). Apart from some territory on the other side of the Jordan, the core of Saul's fiefdom is the central hill country, which archaeology suggests is the center of the Iron I settlement area in Palestine.

Saul is probably to be dated to the Late Iron I period—likely sometime shortly before 1000 BCE. He is associated with Gibeon, an important town of Benjamin that lies on one of the main trade routes between the Jordan Valley and the coast. Many of Saul's activities could have been accomplished in two years, though he probably ruled longer than that (cf. 1 Sam. 13:1 whose text is often thought to be corrupt). Much of the Saul tradition involves fighting against the Philistines. If Saul arose to defend Israel against them, it may be because they were seeking to put a stop to highland raids once and for all by a major campaign against Israel, perhaps even establishing border fortresses to counter raiding parties. 1 Sam. 14:1-14 suggests that Saul's son Jonathan attacked one of the garrisons that the Philistines had established to protect against Israelite raids.

In sum, we should not think of an Israelite David being threatened by a Philistine Goliath; rather, the Philistine cities and Israel were simply rivals in the same narrow region of Palestine. This interpretation seems to be supported by the archaeology. The Galilee region and northern valleys prospered during the Iron I for the most part, but some of the main sites were destroyed in the later Iron I. Radiocarbon dating now suggests that these destructions were not a unitary event but happened over a period of some decades. The subsequent material culture implies that invaders from the central highlands were the cause of the destructions.

Here are some salient points about the Saul tradition. First, Saul looks like a chieftain, with a court that meets under a tree (1 Sam. 22:6). We have two versions of how he became king: one is that he was anointed by Samuel (1 Sam. 9:1–10:16), which looks like a self-serving account from a prophetic source that wants to make Saul subordinate to the prophet Samuel; the other—more likely to be reliable—is that he arose as a deliverer (1 Sam. 11:1-15). That he and his son Jonathan led an Israelite military band against the Philistines is one of the main foci of the tradition and is plausible.

The other focus is Saul's attempt to counter his rival David for leadership. Again, this is plausible, partly because it was to some extent embarrassing for the author to have to catalogue David's failures and weakness in having to flee from Saul. But this means that the Saul tradition has been filtered through the distorting lenses of the Davidic tradition, with contrasting views: David mostly positive and Saul often negative. Although contemporary scholars have differing views of Saul, there seems to be a common core to many of them.

Saul was the petty king of Gibeon with Benjaminite roots but a successful leader who had the support of the people and was the first to develop a standing army. He was not only able to unite the Israelite tribes but also to incorporate Canaanites and other minority groups into the emerging state. He expanded into surrounding territory to create a state called "Israel." Attempts to control local trade routes and find markets brought him in conflict with the Philistines and other independent states. Possibly he died trying to expand further north (into the Jezreel/Beth-Shean area of Canaan?). Loyalty to Saul continued after his death, creating rebellions and other problems for David; indeed, David almost wrecked the monarchy by his sabotage of Saul's rule to gain the throne for himself.

Saul's kingdom seems to have been an example of a chiefdom, but also of a tribal state with a simple governing structure. Saul appears as a charismatic leader, but also the leading families (i.e., the tribes) chose him as their king: power was apparently invested for the most part in various clan leaders. Further discussion of Saul will occur in the account of David.

Israel and Judah Separate?

As we discussed Saul and how he established a kingdom in Benjamin and further north, we pointedly left Judah out of the picture. Why was this? The answer is that the northern tribes and Judah seem to have been separate from the beginning. Although they may have been related in some way, there is evidence that Judah saw itself as separate for the most part. Here is why.

One of the factors of historical development often forgotten is the difference between Israel in the north and Judah in the south. There was a considerable disparity of natural resources and economy between the two, with Judah continually the poorer. In Judah the agriculture was largely subsistence and disadvantaged by lack of good soil for grain-growing and rainfall of 300 to 500 millimeters per annum. The better soils around Hebron had their value reduced by low rainfall. This meant that pastoralism was an important pursuit. In competition with Israel, Judah definitely came off second best. When Palestine entities are finally named in the inscriptions of other nations, such as the Assyrians in the first millennium BCE, there is already a division between Israel and Judah.

This long-term division is also hinted at in biblical passages, in spite of a supposed 12-tribe nation. The most important of these is Judges 5 (also discussed in the previous chapter, pp. 60–1). As one of the earliest passages in the Hebrew Bible, it seems to have been written not long after the events it describes. It lists several tribes of Israel that cooperated in opposing the predations of Sisera. The important point is that Judah was absent, even though from other biblical passages we would have expected it to be here.

Another passage is 2 Sam. 2:3-4, which states that David and his family settled in Hebron, along with the men of his band and their families. Then, "the men of Judah" came and made him king "over the house of Judah." Clearly, the "house of Judah" was separate from Saul's kingdom of Israel, as is further made clear when Abner schemed to transfer the kingdom of Israel ("the house of Saul") to David's rule (in 2 Sam. 3–4). This finally happened when "all the elders of Israel" came and made David king over Israel (2 Sam. 5:1-3). That this was a temporary uniting of what had been a division between the two peoples is acknowledged in 2 Sam. 5:5: "he [David] reigned over all Israel and Judah."

This division is confirmed by archaeology. As already discussed (p. 53 in the previous chapter), the area south of Jerusalem only began to grow gradually through Iron I, with the main growth later (after about 1100 BCE). Although Jerusalem and Hebron were major sites, there were only a few urban areas between them and also little settlement south of Hebron. This was in contrast to the region between Jerusalem and Bethel, which made up the Benjaminite Plateau and grew quickly in the Iron I. Judah's growth came mainly in the Iron IIA (c. 1000–900 BCE), with penetration into the desert fringe and an increase in the population of the southern regions of the Judean Hills.

Eshbaal

Eshbaal, the son of Saul, became king of Israel after the death of Saul. He also seems to have been a problem for the narrator. He is not necessary for the story: David could have become king of Israel on the death of Saul, a simpler and more straightforward scenario. Yet the writer seems to have been stuck with an Eshbaal tradition too strong to be ignored; in the books of Samuel, he called him Ish-Bosheth ("man of shame") instead of his proper name, "man of Baal." The writer of Chronicles gives his correct name (cf. 1 Chron. 8:33). When one asks whether the account of Eshbaal's reign is historical, the answer seems to be that he must have been a historical character who succeeded Saul as king. Furthermore, Eshbaal's own relative Abner conspired to deliver Saul's—Eshbaal's—kingdom to David, a scenario that looks plausible.

The territory ruled by Eshbaal was evidently also that ruled by Saul (2 Sam. 2:9), with Benjamin at its heart. The brief rivalry between David's and Eshbaal's kingdoms does not take up much narrative space, until Abner brings Israel over to David. The reality may have been different: Eshbaal may have ruled for a couple of decades or more. He is given only two years by 2 Sam. 2:10, but this is at the same time as David is said to have ruled seven years in Hebron, while there was a "long war" between the two kingdoms. But let's face it: the narrator was not particularly interested in the kingship of Eshbaal!

David

The David traditions are in part bound up with the Saul traditions, and they need to be evaluated together. One of the concerns in the early part of the story is to legitimate David—strongly suggesting that David was a usurper. My position here is that David seems to have ruled over a united Kingdom of Israel that included Judah. This is a notable historical point where I differ from some recent researchers who want to keep David separate from the Northern Kingdom. But in my view the tradition combining Saul, Eshbaal, and David together is too strong to dismiss. Many of the details are unlikely to be credible, and the question of whether David ruled over a large kingdom is almost certainly to be answered in the negative. David's "United Monarchy" is quite different from the one portrayed in the biblical text and seems not to have been much of an advance on Saul's chiefdom or tribal kingdom, as we shall see. David's "United Monarchy" was very small indeed.

It is finally with David that we have some evidence outside the Bible. This is from the Tel Dan inscription which came to scholarly attention only in the 1990s (discussed further in chapter 6, pp. 105–6). The reading of interest here is the phrase *bytdwd*, which is widely accepted as meaning "House of David." The inscription seems to be a description of the defeat (and execution?) of two Israelite kings, but these kings apparently belonged to the "dynasty ('house') of David," showing that the line of Judahite kings was thought to originate with David. Just to be clear, the

FIGURE 5.1 *The Tel Dan inscription which names David and two other Israelite kings.*

Tell Dan inscription is not a contemporary reference to King David but rather an account by a later Aramaean Hazael king who defeated Israel and Judah about 830 BCE. The existence of a "house of David" leads to the strong presumption that David existed, since a number of local dynasties in the region were named after founders who are also attested in historical records.

David is inextricably associated with the south of Palestine. This is basically the region of Judah (Judah as a tribe may be a late development). As has been discussed (p. 53), the Judahite territory—meaning primarily the territory between Jerusalem and Hebron but also some settlements further south—began to grow only in the Late Iron I, probably not long before the birth of David. The Judaean Hills had been only sparsely settled by that time. Yet Hebron was an urban center and the expansion in the Judaean region, although delayed compared to the Central Highlands, should not be overlooked. There was a settled agrarian population and no doubt many pastoralists as well. This included clan leaders or elders, and apparently the concept of a "tribe of Judah" had eventually developed. This was to become the core of a "Judahite kingdom." But David was also strongly identified with Benjamin, which was the core of Saul's kingdom.

Relationship of the Saul and David Traditions

In this chapter we are arguing that there is a historical core to both the Saulide and Davidide traditions. There are several reasons. There is first of all the saying, "Saul has slain his thousands, but David his tens of thousands" (1 Sam. 18:7; 21:12; 29:5). Not a major piece of information but nevertheless one worth noting, and one likely to be early according to some commentators. It shows the intimate connection between the David and Saul traditions.

Second, one of the major characteristics of the David tradition is the extent to which his reign is legitimated by various means, which strongly suggests that David was in some sense a usurper:

- Comes as an apprentice to Saul's court (1 Sam. 16:14-23).
- Performs personal duties for Saul's health (1 Sam. 16:14-23).
- Fights as a champion against Israel's enemies (1 Sam. 17).
- Marries the king's daughter (1 Sam. 18:17-27).
- Wins her hand by warrior-worthy deeds (1 Sam. 18:25-27).
- Anointed by a prophet-priest (1 Sam. 16:1-13).
- Even the king's son and heir (Jonathan) recognizes David's right to rule (1 Sam. 18:1; 20:12-17; 23:16-18).

Why go to all this trouble to make David's rule legitimate if he had been accepted as the first king of Judah by the tradition? This suggests that the present picture of the text—that he was not the first king but effected a change of dynasty—was not a secondary creation but one already there in the tradition when the text was redacted.

Third, one could take the example of Michal. She could have been added to the tradition simply to give a further negative picture of Saul, since her story is ultimately a negative one in which she is rejected and childless though remaining David's wife. But her story is more complicated and interesting than this. For example, she helps David escape from her father by a clever deception (1 Sam. 19:11-17). After she was married to another man, David expended some effort to get her back (2 Sam. 3:12-16).

Fourth, there is also the story of Jonathan. Again, he could serve just as another reason to bolster David's legitimacy: even the heir to the throne supports David's right instead of his own. But why make him such an integral part of the story, if that were his only purpose? Not least is the question of why Jonathan did not succeed his father. The many hazards to an heir not only growing up but acquiring the necessary military prowess and confidence of the troops meant that prime heirs did not always gain the throne. But we might have expected a different sort of story, if it was simply a literary invention to enhance David's right to the throne.

Finally, we have to ask: if the Saul tradition was simply about the first king of Israel, separate from Judah, what happened to his dynasty? We know that, at a later time, kings well attested in historical sources ruled over Israel. But if the Saul tradition was completely independent of the David one, what happened to the Israelite monarchy that had begun with Saul? Did it simply peter out? If so, what filled the vacuum, and how did it get started up again? It is such questions that make us turn to the David tradition and ask whether it is not historically correct that David in some way was the successor on the throne of the inchoate state of Israel begun by Saul.

It is as if the Davidic and Solomonic traditions are *necessary* to fill the gap between Saul and the history of the two kingdoms or monarchies of Israel and Judah. If so, then the concept of the "United Monarchy" could be correct, after all—but only in a particular sense. That is, the first king Saul ruled over a portion of the central highlands, mainly Benjamin, though apparently not Judah. The Judahite David— possibly a tribal leader of Judah but perhaps being appointed as a sort of king of Judah, as the text suggests—took over from Saul (or Saul's son), establishing some sort of rule over both the southern Central Highlands (up to Bethel), especially Benjamin, and the Judaean highlands.

Origin/Early Life of David

Saul may have had connections with the tribal and clan leaders of Judah, even though he does not appear to rule over Judahite territory. Two stories are given about David's rise to power and to being the son-in-law of Saul. According to one (1 Sam. 16:14-23) he was a musician who came to Saul's court and helped him to appease his demons by playing on the lyre. The other story is that David secured his place in Saul's court by his military exploits. The idea that Saul was able to draft in soldiers from Judah, including David's brothers, is an unlikely one. On the other hand, Saul's army might have attracted young men from Judah as volunteers who wanted the mercenary pay and the excitement.

Yet there may be another explanation for the association of David's family with the court of Saul. Surprisingly, although David grew up in Bethlehem, an area of Judah, he is not referred to as a "Judahite" but is said to be from "Israel" (1 Sam. 18:18; 27:12; 2 Sam. 5:1). David's father Jesse is named as an "Ephrathite" in 1 Sam. 17:12. But Ephrathite usually refers to people from Ephraim (for example, Elkanah in 1 Sam. 1:1). Does this indicate that David's family was part of an Ephraimite clan which had settled in Bethlehem? If he was related to an Ephraimite clan, Saul might have had the responsibility and privilege of giving orders to his family even though they were in Judahite territory. It would also explain why later on the elders of Israel were favorable toward him.

To return to the rise of David, the first story claims that Saul was troubled by an "evil spirit from Yahweh" (1 Sam. 16:14-23). A search is made, and David is engaged to play the lyre to provide relief for Saul when the evil spirit came upon him. He enters Saul's service; Saul likes him and makes him one of his arms-bearers. He is a valued member of Saul's court and has a personal relationship with Saul. It is important to keep this in mind because of what comes later in the story.

We now come to the crucial episode ascribed to David: the contest with Goliath (1 Sam. 17). The story is filled with contradictions and dubious data. First, the story of David's coming forward to fight Goliath has Saul asking, "Whose son is the lad, Abner?" Abner does not know, either. After he slays Goliath, David is brought to Saul who puts the same question directly to him: "Whose son are you?" and David answers that he is the son of Jesse (1 Sam. 17:53-8).

This scenario is incredible! According to the biblical text, David was brought into Saul's court long before and has been there for months, playing the lyre to Saul personally to soothe his "evil spirit." Furthermore, Saul likes him so much that he makes him a personal arms-bearer. Yet we are now told that Saul does not know who he is. This is not to mention how incredible it would be for Saul to have taken a dangerous gamble to risk defeat of his army and the war through single combat, by letting an unknown shepherd boy tackle the mighty and feared hero of the enemy that none of his seasoned warriors would dare fight!

Goliath's armor has been much discussed. Half a century ago it was remarked that "the narrator ... has put together the wholly singular weaponry of Goliath from diverse elements of military equipment known to him" at a rather later time.[2] It has been argued that Goliath's armory represents a Greek hoplite soldier of the seventh century, though some parts of the description rather fit Assyrian equipage. We can rightly ask: is an actual soldier with his weaponry being described, or is the image of Goliath simply made up eclectically for a particular effect on the reader? In any case, a later time than the Iron I or Early Iron II is being represented.

But the *coup de grâce* to the credibility of the story is found in 2 Sam. 21:19. In this account of one of "David's mighty men," *it is clearly stated that the otherwise unknown Elhanan son of Jaareoregim slew Goliath*! It seems that Elhanan's deed has somehow come to be credited to David, just as various anecdotes get attached to famous people even though they originated with someone more obscure. Could David's surprising victory become transferred to Elhanan? Very unlikely—the path of transfer is invariably from the less known to the more famous. It makes a much better story to attribute the slaying of Goliath to the youthful David rather than recognize it was one of David's warriors who did the deed.

While the David-and-Goliath story is not believable, the idea that David impressed with his military prowess fits the image of David throughout much of his adult life, when he was a military commander. Although Saul did not rule over the Judaean territory, he seems to have had quite a bit of influence—or possibly it was just a matter of intimidation. When David was supposedly on the run from him, he was able to chase him through the southern area without hindrance (1 Sam. 22–26), and some of the local people reported on him to Saul (1 Sam. 23:7-13; 24:2; 26:1). It may be that the Judahites did not wish to bring Saul's wrath down on themselves and did not support David so that Saul would leave them alone.

But it may well be that David—acting as an *apiru* or bandit leader, like the El Cid of medieval Spain[3]—was regarded with suspicion by the local people. According to the biblical text, he only raided Philistine territory but left the Judahites alone (1 Sam. 26). Yet this could simply be the bias of the surviving text, whereas David may have actually taken what his band needed from all sides, including from the people and villages of the Judahite peoples. If so, he would have had his supporters but also those who feared him and would not help him unless they were forced to.

David Made King over "All Israel"

The biblical text makes it clear that David was the successor of Saul. The reign of Eshbaal intervened, but already when Saul was alive, he saw David as his rival and successor, which is why he pursued him. After Saul's death, David was able to bring together the population from Jerusalem south under his control. According to 2 Sam. 2:1-4, David settled in Hebron with his followers and their families. What negotiations he carried out are not described, but we must expect that he had communications and discussions with the leaders of the various clans in the region. The result was that "the men of Judah" came to David and anointed him king over the "House of Judah."

David ruled over Judah from Hebron allegedly for seven and a half years (2 Sam. 5:4). This number is probably more believable than the thirty-three following years of rule, because they add up neatly to forty years as king—a gross unlikelihood! During his seven years in Hebron, David had conflicts with Eshbaal's men, but then Abner got in touch with David and proposed to make him king over Israel as well (2 Sam. 3:12-21). Although Abner was subsequently killed by David's army commander Joab, Eshbaal was also assassinated. After that "all the elders of Israel" came to David in Hebron, made a pact with him, and anointed him king over "all Israel and Judah" (2 Sam. 5:1-5).

David now ruled over a "United Monarchy"; however, this was hardly the glorious empire later described in the biblical text—especially the mighty empire described for Solomon's reign. It is clear that, in addition to the small territory of Judah, David had only taken over the small kingdom of Saul/Eshbaal. This latter amounted mainly to the region of Benjamin and southern Ephraim. There is no indication that David ever ruled the core of what became the Northern Kingdom of Israel after the death of Solomon—that is, the region of Samaria.

The division of David's kingdom between Judah and Israel is indicated by the narrative about Absalom's rebellion later in David's reign (2 Sam. 15–20). The supporters of Absalom seem to have been mainly Israelites (2 Sam. 18:6-7). One of the main opponents of David at this time was Shimei, a Benjaminite (2 Sam. 16:5-8; 19:17-18); another was Sheba, also a Benjaminite, whom "all the men of Israel" are claimed to have followed (2 Sam. 20:1-22). But when David's troops win the battle it is the elders of Judah who invite him to return, and Judahites escort him back to Jerusalem (2 Sam. 19:12-16). Yet men of Israel are miffed at this exclusive Judahite escort and argue that they should have been included. Even if most of the details given here depend on the narrator's imagination, the basic division between Israel and Judah even in David's kingdom appears to be attested in the passage overall.

David's Wars

According to the text of 2 Samuel, David continued Saul's fight with the Philistines, especially in 5:17-25 and 8:1. Yet contrary to the account regarding Saul, there is very little description of wars with the Philistines. What appears to have happened is that *David arranged a truce with the Philistines that allowed a peaceful coexistence throughout his reign.* The two Philistine cities Gath and Ekron were rivals at this time. David's dealings were primarily with Gath (e.g., 1 Sam. 27:3; 2 Sam. 15:18-22). If he had conflict with Philistines, it was probably with those from Ekron. There are a number of arguments in support of this.

First, David's wars with the Philistines in 2 Sam. 5:17-25 seem only a passing episode, with little consequence. The motive for the Philistines to attack him also looks rather trumped up. Indeed, these campaigns (and the statement in 2 Sam. 5:25) fit Saul better and might have been borrowed from the Saulide tradition. In any case, any conflicts between David and the Philistines appear brief and early in his reign and, as noted, would probably have been with Ekron. Second, David does not defeat the Philistines (only the tacked-on summary statement in 2 Sam. 5:25 claims this), yet the threat simply disappears from the text. Third, we also have the reference to the six hundred warriors from Gath, under the command of Itai, who assist David at the time of Absalom's rebellion (2 Sam. 15:18-22). Fourthly, Achish king of Gath is clearly at peace with Solomon after the time of David (1 Kgs 2:39-40). Finally, Judah seems to have expanded into the Shephelah in the first half of the ninth century, yet there is no evidence of conflict with Gath which would have dominated the area as a large city at this time. This further suggests that an earlier agreement (presumably the one made in the time of David) was still in effect.

Yet if David did not fight with the Philistines (or did so only initially), was he seeking an essential expansion of his territory? According to 2 Samuel, David fought a variety of the surrounding peoples, including the region of Aramaean rule (2 Sam. 8; 10:1–11:1; 12:26-31). The proposed extension of control into Edom and Transjordan (see below) is possible, but defeat of the Aramaeans—even placing a garrison in Damascus (2 Sam. 8:6)—looks contrived. The area of Aram was a long way to the north of David's core territory. A compelling case has been made by an Israeli scholar that this fight against and defeat of Hadadezer of Zobah is a only a literary creation by a later scribe earnestly desiring to big David up.[4]

Although David worked to expand the size of his kingdom, there is no indication that he captured the northern hill country or the Jezreel Valley and Galilee. Essentially, he is said to have expanded his territory into Moab and Ammon, that is, northern Transjordan (2 Sam. 8:2; 10:1-14; 12:26-31) and into Edom (2 Sam. 8:13-14). To what extent he expanded west into the Shephelah is discussed in the next section.

Jerusalem, David's Capital

The stories in Judges (1:21) seem to remember a Jerusalem that came into Israelite hands only relatively late and continued to have the earlier people as a part of the population for some time afterward. What the various traditions suggest, therefore, is that there was a collective folk memory of a time when Jerusalem was not Israelite. This memory also recalled that the city came into Israelite hands much later than some of the surrounding territory. This is a remarkable memory, especially if we keep in mind that it would have been more convenient to believe that Jerusalem was conquered with the rest of the territory and divided up by the Israelites without any complications.

Yet the text acknowledges complications: Jerusalem is sometimes the property of Judah (Josh. 15:63; cf. Judg. 1:8) and sometimes within the territory of Benjamin (Josh. 18:28; Judg. 1:21). In both cases, it recognizes that some of the original inhabitants, the Jebusites, continued to live in the city, alongside the Judahites (Josh. 15:63) or Benjaminites (Judg. 1:21). Despite this tradition, 2 Sam. 5:6-9 asserted that the city was not in the hands of Judahites/Benjaminites but required David to conquer the city from the Jebusites again. David took the city and renamed it "the city of David."

The story in 2 Sam. 24:16-25, when attention is carefully paid to the original Hebrew text, confirms that Jerusalem had a mixed population and an unusual history. This is part of an incident in which a plague was devastating Israel because of David's sin. To stay the plague, David was told to set up an altar on the threshing floor of "Araunah the Jebusite," which he purchased. The name "Araunah" is curious. It does not look like a typical Hebrew name, and in 2 Sam. 24:16, the word occurs with the Hebrew definite article ("the Araunah"), which is not normal with names. It has been explained as a Hittite word meaning "aristocrat" or a Hurrian word meaning "lord." Either explanation suggests that the owner of the threshing floor was the (former?) king or lord of the city, which is also one way of reading the Hebrew text of 2 Sam. 24:23: "Araunah the king gives all to the king (David)."

The text indicates that it was this threshing floor that later became the site of the temple built by Solomon, but the episode suggests the size of the Jebusite city was not large. *Current archaeological study suggests that Jerusalem was unwalled and unfortified between the Late Bronze Age and Iron IIB (sixteenth to mid-eighth centuries BCE), and thus Jerusalem was "at best modest."*[5] Based on the work of the famous British archaeologist Dame Kathleen Kenyon, it is apparent that Jerusalem of the tenth and ninth centuries was a small town occupied mainly by public buildings, not exceeding 12 hectares (about 30 acres) and approximately two thousand inhabitants or even fewer.[6] For the Jerusalem settlement to be little more than a town at the time of David is not a problem. This was probably all that was needed for David's state, considering its small size and complexity. It was certainly an advance on Saul's open-air court under a large tree (1 Sam. 22:6)!

Jerusalem was small, with a minimal population by later standards, but it was not negligible, especially for its time. Especially important is a major "monumental" building project, the "stepped stone structure" (built into the slope from the City of David down to the Kedron Valley). The dating of the stepped stone structure is confirmed by the pottery in the structure and the fill, which puts it to the tenth or early ninth century.[7] To construct it would have taken considerable resources in material and manpower. These were evidently provided by the areas around Jerusalem, including the Benjaminite Plateau to the north with its towns and villages. This confirms that these regions were under Jerusalem control and a part of the kingdom of Judah.

Considerable excitement was caused when one archaeologist recently argued that a building at the top of the stepped stone structure dates to David's time and could be his palace.[8] This appears to be an important site and—if confirmed—would be another example of monumental architecture from the time of David. Acceptance of this interpretation is by no means universal, however. The main problem is its dating. In response to the original claims about the "David's palace" building, a study by four archaeologists gave quite a different interpretation of the site, concluding that the building is most likely late Hellenistic—nearly a millennium after the time of David![9]

The recently excavated Khirbet Qeiyafa (c. 25 kilometers/15 miles southwest of Jerusalem) has been the occasion of much discussion, in large part because of the claims of the excavators that the site was Judahite and disproved those who doubted the biblical account of David.[10] Qeiyafa was a short-lived site that was in existence only for some decades before being destroyed or abandoned (and not revived until the Hellenistic period). It was probably built on a previously uninhabited site in the period about 1025 to 950 BCE. However, none of the material objects found there were exclusive to Judah, whereas some finds (such as hearths) were uniquely associated with Philistines. When Judah later built towns in the Shephelah, the ruined site of Qeiyafa was left untouched, further suggesting it had not been a Judahite town.

Conclusions About David

What we find in 1 and 2 Samuel is the story of a young Judahite warrior made good. He seems to have grown up in a society that was not heavily stratified; nevertheless, there was no doubt tribal leadership, with Judahite elders and perhaps even a tribal chieftain or chieftains. Was David the heir of one of these tribal leaders? There are also some hints that his family was not so humble. After all, he was brought into Saul's court, unlikely to happen to a complete nobody. In any case, David became some sort of *'apiru* leader such as we find in Amarna Palestine (cf. chapter 3, pp. 38–9): surprisingly, this image appears to be agreed on by archaeologists who otherwise take somewhat different views on the "United Monarchy."

In the biblical story, David fits the image of the hero figure; there are many folkloristic elements and a variety of traditions; yet there are also traditions with some interesting twists, such as the willingness to acknowledge some of David's weaknesses, the need to legitimate David from a variety of angles—suggesting that he was not seen as legitimate by everyone—and the admission that David did not do certain things that we might have expected. One of the interesting points about the Davidic tradition is how "lumpy" it is. That is, it often disagrees with what we would expect from the biblical text as a whole. To summarize, we can note some of the points that emerge from a look at the Saul and David traditions:

- The tradition recognizes that David was not the first king.
- Saul came to the throne probably as a military leader by popular acclaim (1 Sam. 11:1-15), whereas the prophetic tradition that the king was subject to Samuel's choice and censure is unrealistic (1 Sam. 9:1–10.16; 10:23; 13:2–14:52).
- The apparent boundaries of Saul's kingdom (2 Sam. 2:9) is reasonably in line with the natural and demographic resources in Cis-Jordan, though it probably did not extend north of Bethel.
- A strong link is made between David's rise and Saul's court, but much of this looks like a deliberate attempt to legitimate David as king from a variety of angles: anointing by Samuel (1 Sam. 16:1-13); armor-bearer in Saul's court who plays the lyre for him personally (1 Sam. 16:14-23); slaying of Goliath (1 Sam. 17); and marriage to Saul's daughter (1 Sam. 18:17-27).
- Contrary to expectations David does not build a temple (though a strenuous effort is made for him to do everything short of the actual building).

- Both Saul and David were mainly military leaders.
- The text itself does not suggest an extensive administrative apparatus in the case of either Saul or David.

Two further points put David at odds with the general trend of teaching and piety in the Hebrew Bible. First, David's sons acted as priests at this time, possibly even before he took Jerusalem (2 Sam. 8:17). Being from the tribe of Judah or possibly Ephraim (see p. 76), David and his family should not have been able to be priests. But the tradition that all priests were supposed to be Levites from the family of Aaron is probably a later one. Second, David made the Jebusite priest Zadok one of his two chief priests. It has long been recognized that Zadok was formerly a priest from the Jerusalem cult that was functioning prior to the takeover by David.

What these facts show us is that many of the religious sensibilities that we associate with Israelite worship and Judaism developed at a later time. The Bible gives us only the later religious regulations, but we still find hints that things were not always as they are pictured later. For further on the development of Israelite religion, see chapter 7.

Solomon

According to the Bible, Solomon's kingdom could not be more different from Saul and David's! The narrative about Solomon's reign (1 Kgs 2–11) strikes the reader as quite unlike those about the kings before him. Almost from start to finish Solomon fits the image of the great "Oriental despot/emperor." It is essentially a folktale about an Eastern potentate—a royal legend. Solomon controls a vast territory and possesses great wealth, with absolute sovereignty over his subjects. Of course, he marries the daughter of a country of similar power—suggesting equality with Egypt in this case—and harnesses the best craftsmen and materials from legendary Tyre to build his city. His capital city consists of great palaces and a magnificent temple, with gold like dust and silver so abundant it is of little account.

His household overflows with luxuries, his table groans under the weight of exotic fruits, meats from rare animals, and every sort of desirable food for consumption. He boasts a harem of a thousand women, all of whom he apparently services. His wisdom is legendary, and he exceeds all others in intellectual skills. His reputation reaches far and wide, and rulers from distant lands travel to see such a supreme example of power, wealth, and wisdom—only to find that the reports were understated. His ships travel to the ends of the earth for rare and astonishing goods. Unlike David's "lumpy" story, one is immediately struck by how uniform the tale about Solomon is. It looks like the product of a master creator of sagas about great men.

Much of Solomon's rule looks and feels like a fairy tale. Thus, it looks difficult to discover much in the Solomon story that strikes the critical reader as likely to be historical. Although the story of David has him expanding his territory via conquests, there is nothing to suggest that he rules all of Palestine, much less the land beyond. Yet according to the text Solomon controls all the land between Egypt and the Euphrates (1 Kgs 5:1, 4)—even though he fought no battles! There is not a hint that David could monopolize the trade in horses between Egypt and Mesopotamia, as Solomon does (1 Kgs 10:28-29).

As for the wealth invested in the House of Yahweh, this is commensurate with the quantity of gold that Solomon receives each year: 666 talents plus the revenue from trade and commerce (1 Kgs 10:14-15). Only a great empire, such as that of the later Persians, could collect so much wealth: according to Herodotus (3:91) the vast Persian Empire, stretching from northern India to the Aegean, collected 14,560 talents of silver in tribute annually—the equivalent of 1,120 talents of gold. *The idea that Solomon could raise 666 talents of gold plus much additional wealth each year is a gross flight of fancy on the part of the writer.*

As for Solomon's marriage to pharaoh's daughter, many Egyptologists are of the opinion that it is very unlikely since it was clearly the custom for the reigning king to marry his daughters only to those within Egypt itself, not foreigners.[11] Although some have claimed that this was done during the Egyptian Third Intermediate Period—which began just before the time of Solomon—no examples of the marriage of a reigning Egyptian king's daughter to a foreign ruler have in fact been found.[12] It is possible that someone from the Egyptian court, perhaps distantly related to the pharaoh, was in fact the one whom he married. But as one scholar concluded, "it is best at this time to avoid placing any weight on the reports of Solomon's marriage to an Egyptian princess."[13]

In this story, though, the height of marvels is Solomon's great wisdom (1 Kgs 10:3, 6-8, 23-24), even if there is precious little in the way of examples of how this is demonstrated. The one example of the two prostitutes claiming the same child is a facile one, in no way comparable to examples found in other wisdom stories. For example, in another Oriental tale (the story of Ahiqar) the wise man skillfully addresses the challenge to the king to build a city in the sky, much more impressive than Solomon's supposed manifestation of wisdom.

Of course, this is only part of the story, since there are also passages in which a negative picture of Solomon is painted. 1 Kings 11 has many such statements or examples. The account of Solomon has been edited from different perspectives over the centuries. The existence of a King Solomon is not to be discounted, however. His name echoing the old god of Jerusalem (Shalim/Shalem) is suggestive of reality rather than simply the piety of the David story. Also, he began his reign with the bloody elimination of rivals, though the idea that he took his throne in the midst of adversity, which he overcame, could be a part of the stereotype. The writer probably saw nothing bad in this.

Overall, there is little in the Solomon story that looks on the face of it to be historically reliable. Yet one cannot help being intrigued by the story that he built the Jerusalem temple. This sort of story is what we might expect, and the description of the wealth and rare construction of the temple fits the legend well. Yet David—the expected temple-builder—did not construct it, and we find nothing in the stories of the later kings that might hide such a building (with the possible exception of Jehoash who is said to collect money to repair the temple: 2 Kings 12). This suggests that a temple to Yahweh was built in Jerusalem at a fairly early time.

Note, however, an oblique reference to a temple in the time of David in 2 Sam. 22:7; also, it seems unlikely that Jerusalem had no Jebusite temple when it was captured by David. If so, Solomon might have only enhanced a preexisting temple, though he could also have constructed a new one to replace the one already there. We might think of "Herod's temple" (see chapter 12, p. 255) which was not a new temple but was so rebuilt and remodelled by Herod as to take on his name. Possibly here we have a genuine remembrance that has been expanded into a great legend.

We further have the ascription of materials supplied by Hiram of Tyre. How credible is this? Early annals of Tyre have been alleged to exist. For example, Josephus refers to them, though it is clear that he cites them from more recent Greek historians, such as Menander (of Pergamum?) and an unknown writer named Dius.[14] Although there is some genuine cultural memory in Menander's account, the original Phoenician writer from whom Menander took the details would have been writing long after the Hiram of the tenth century BCE. This Hiram's reign is blown up into a Golden Age of Tyrian history, parallel to Solomon's in Israel. This is why the eighth-century biblical writer was able to draw on the Hiram story, which he got from somewhere, as contemporary with Solomon. But most of the details are the invention of the writer. From several considerations, therefore, the Phoenician contribution to the temple story has been blown into a legendary extravaganza.

The episode relating to the Queen of Sheba illustrates the historical problem (1 Kgs 10:1-13). The Sheba story has all the marks of a folktale (though it has been incorporated into the text by a literary writer). The main figure has no name: she is simply "the Queen of Sheba." She herself is a representative of wealth, wisdom, and power. Yet her function in the story is to marvel at all that Solomon and Jerusalem have to show her: despite all her own wealth and wisdom, Solomon's are much greater. He leaves her speechless.

This story has been defended as historical by explaining it as a journey to establish trade relations between southern Arabia and Israel, by appealing to developments in southern Arabia by the tenth century BCE. The appeal to a trading network is a strange defense of historicity, considering that the biblical text says not a word about such a purpose! On the contrary, according to 1 Kgs 10:1, the queen of Sheba came to Solomon "to test him with riddles," not to establish trade relations. The well-known scholar of the ancient Near East, Professor Mario Liverani, encapsulates the problem in a nutshell: "the story of the Queen of Sheba's visit is too much like a fairy-tale in style and in use of narrative themes to be regarded as anything other than a romance from the Persian era."[15]

We can summarize our discussion of Solomon's reign by accepting that Solomon was historical but that he differed considerably from the biblical picture. To evaluate the story of Solomon, we can note that the king's name suggests that he was non-Judaean in origin. The Bathsheba story, which clearly discredited David's reputation, was not suppressed because there was a worse story: Solomon was not David's son! He became king through a *coup d'état* by getting rid of the Jerusalem elite. He was no monotheist, because the Judaean tribal deity Yahweh had only a subordinate position in the Jerusalem pantheon. Solomon's alleged building program of cities and monumental buildings cannot be confirmed archaeologically.

In conclusion, we can say that it looks as if some of the achievements of later Israelite kings—such as Omri and Jeroboam II—are here ascribed to Solomon. There are also numerous parallels with achievements by Assyrian kings in the latter part of the Neo-Assyrian Empire. But Solomon's accomplishments go far beyond even these, demonstrating how the imagination of the writer soared astronomically!

Conclusions

In this chapter we discussed the rise of Israel to become united into an early kingdom. Why then did the disparate peoples—perhaps constituting tribes by this time—decide to unite into one people or unit? The answer is not simple and would probably involve a number of considerations. The "Philistine threat" has often been invoked, though the Israelites may well have brought this "threat" down upon themselves because of becoming a thorn in the side to the Philistines with raids into the coastal plain for booty and supplies. In any case, if they were to fight a common enemy, it would have made sense to unite under a military leader that all had confidence in. The idea that the first king was a military leader is very believable.

There seems to be sufficient evidence to assert that Saul, Eshbaal, David, and Solomon existed as historical individuals. The archaeologist Amihai Mazar summarizes the situation as he sees it, based on the available archaeology:

> It is certain that much of the biblical narrative concerning David and Solomon is mere fiction and embellishment written by later authors ... David can be envisioned as a ruler similar to Labayu [from the Amarna letters] ... In such an environment, a talented and charismatic leader, politically astute, and in control of a small yet effective military power, may have taken hold of large part of a small country like the Land of Israel and controlled diverse population groups under his regime from his stronghold in Jerusalem, which can be identified archaeologically. Such a regime does not necessitate a particularly large and populated capital city.[16]

Saul was evidently the first king, primarily a military leader, and was overthrown by David who was declared king of the small southern area of Judah. But the circumstances described in which Saul's kingdom, centered on Benjamin, voluntarily joined with David's tribe to form a united monarchy are plausible. Much in the David tradition would be compatible with that. But the "United Monarchy" under David is basically a Jerusalem city-state or a Davidic chiefdom or a David tribal state—it is not the same as the great "United Monarchy" of the Bible. It seems unlikely that David controlled anything beyond a limited territory centered on the southern hill country and Jerusalem, which overlapped with territory earlier controlled by Saul.

What is surprising is that without any description of new conquests or major changes to David's state, Solomon suddenly presides over a huge empire, stretching from Asia Minor to Egypt, over which he establishes economic and commercial control and brings in unheard-of wealth. There is nothing in the text to prepare us for the sudden change with Solomon's kingdom. It soon becomes obvious that we are dealing with a typical tale of an Oriental potentate of great wisdom, enormous wealth, and many women. There are reasons to think Solomon existed (including his name, from a local deity of Jerusalem), but much of the description of his kingdom and his reign are incredible. Even the demonstration of his wisdom depends on a banal tale of two prostitutes.

6

The Rise of the Omrides, or How Israel Finally Became a State

In the previous chapter we saw how Saul began to unite the various Israelite groups into some sort of kingdom—some would call it a "tribal kingdom." David brought in the region of Judah and ruled a sort of "united kingdom," but this was still an inchoate political entity that covered only a small territory in the central hill country of Judah (evidently with the region of Samaria, the Jezreel Valley, and Galilee still outside this Israelite kingdom). David's son—if he was his son—Solomon is not said to have engaged in warfare, much less to have conquered new territory. Despite this, the text ascribes unimaginable riches and a great portion of the Levant and southern Syrian to his rule. Although this "fairy tale" cannot be taken at face value, there was still probably a historical Solomon who ruled over a small kingdom with Jerusalem as its capital.

In this present chapter, we finally leave behind the silence of the surrounding peoples about Israel and begin to find some references to Israel in the writings of Israel's neighbors. We were not completely bereft of contemporary information in the earlier period, because we have always had archaeology. Archaeology was very important and remains very important, but from this chapter on we also have valuable written sources. We of course have the biblical text, but as already explained in chapter 1, the extant text is not usually contemporary with the events described but was composed much later for the most part. However, as we shall see, we may here and there have some early information in it—in excerpts from a court or royal chronicle. The present chapter takes us to the fall of Samaria at the hands of the Assyrians and the end of the Northern Kingdom.

A New Historical Source: The Court/Royal Chronicle

It was long ago suggested that an important source for the author of 1 and 2 Kings was an official court or royal chronicle. It was somewhat like a ship's log, except that it was maintained by a court scribe. Any activities of the king would have been considered important and recorded in some form or other. Please note that we are speaking of *extra-biblical chronicles*, not the biblical books of Chronicles (which are always capitalized). A brief survey of commentaries shows that this *Chronicle of the Kings of Israel* and the *Chronicle of the Kings of Judah* or something similar are often assumed to be important sources.

Court chronicles are well known from other peoples in the ancient Near East. The ones available are not generally "day books" but set out year by year. The events of each year are recorded briefly, and an entire year often needs only a few lines. Sometimes the entire reign of a king is summarized in a few lines of script and not year by year. A number of these chronicles from Mesopotamia are known and have been published in accessible editions and translations. The court chronicles from ancient Israel and Judah also seem to have been set out with a few lines devoted to each king. We appear to have a reference to Israelite and Judahite chronicles in the books of Kings themselves (e.g., 1 Kgs 14:19-20, 29-31; 15:7-8, 23-24, 27-31; 16:5-6, 10-14, 18-20, 27-28).

It has usually been assumed that the author used two sources, which he synchronized himself: a royal chronicle from the Northern Kingdom and one from the Southern Kingdom. But the author of kings was probably from Judah and writing either at the end of the kingdom of Judah or, more likely, after the fall of Jerusalem. It is quite plausible that he had access to a copy of the Judahite royal chronicle, but would he have had sight of a royal chronicle for the Northern Kingdom which had fallen a century or even two earlier, with many nobles taken captive? It seems unlikely.

Yet when we look at Mesopotamian chronicles, we find examples of those that recorded happenings in more than one kingdom. They provide excellent comparative evidence of how a single chronicle might well include accession data from neighboring countries. For example, *Chronicle 16, From Nabonassar to Šamaš-Šuma-Ukīn*, sets down the parallel histories of Babylonia, Assyria, and Elam, even though the author was probably a Babylonian.[1] Here is a brief excerpt from *Chronicle 16*:

[The third year of Nabonassur,] king of Babylon,
Tiglath-pileser III ascended the throne of Assyria.
The same year [the king of Assyria] went down to Akkad,
plundered Rabbilu and Hamranu, and deported the gods of Shapazza.
In the time of Nabonassur Borsippa
revolted against Babylon; (however,) the battle that Nabonassur
conducted against Borsippa has not been written.
The fifth year of Nabonassur, Humbannikash I
ascended the throne of Elam.
The fourteenth year, Nabonassur became ill and
died in his palace.
For fourteen years Nabonassur ruled Babylon.
(Nabu-)nadin-(zeri) ascended the throne of Babylon.

When we compare *Chronicle 16* with what we find in the books of Kings, we see a remarkable parallel in that the reigns of the kings of more than one kingdom are recorded and synchronized. Therefore, it is not necessary to assume the author of Kings had two chronicles before him (although this is of course not impossible) since all the chronicle data in 1 and 2 Kings could have come from a single chronicle, the *Chronicle of the Kings of Judah*. This chronicle would have given brief but factual information on each king of Judah but also recorded the accession and deaths of the neighboring kings in Israel. This chronicle had several characteristics:

- It would be fairly concise, devoting only a paragraph to each king. Even if individual years were sometimes recorded, these would have been very short.
- The basic data included for each king would be the time of taking his throne, his father, and the length of his reign. The Judahite chronicle seems to have been unique, however, in also including the name of the king's mother—this is not found in any other Near Eastern chronicle. In addition, some of the main events of his reign would be included (if there were any): battles, invasions, revolts, building projects, other significant events, personal matters relating to the king (e.g., major illnesses), and the cult.
- Data on its main (and dominant) neighbor and rival, the Kingdom of Israel, including synchronism of the reigns of the Israelite and Judahite kings (for the period up to 720 BCE when Northern Israel was conquered by the Assyrians).
- *Moral or religious judgment about the king would not be contained in the chronicle*. Statements about whether a king was good or bad, and moralizing comments on his reign, were the contribution of the editor/compiler of the books of Kings. No royal chronicle would criticize the king or his actions!

Other (often legendary or semi-legendary) material was used by the author of Kings to fill out the narrative but not taken from any chronicle; however, much of the reliable data—the data confirmed by other ancient Near Eastern sources—was taken from the *Chronicle of the Kings of Judah*.

Here is an example from the reign of Abijam of Judah (1 Kgs 15:1-8). This gives us a flavor of how the writer used the chronicle information, but also alongside other information from other sources (or perhaps coming only from his own imagination), to compile his account. The information that is likely to have come from a chronicle is given in italics:

> ¹*Now in the 18th year of King Jeroboam, son of Nebat, Abijam became king over Judah.* ²*He ruled three years in Jerusalem, and the name of his mother was Maacah daughter of Abishalom.* ³And he walked in all the sins which his father had committed before him; his heart was not whole with Yahweh his God like the heart of David his father. ⁴But for David's sake Yahweh his God gave him a lamp in Jerusalem to raise up his son after him and to establish Jerusalem. ⁵For David did what was right in the eyes of Yahweh and did not turn aside from all that he commanded him all the days of his life, except concerning the matter of Uriah the Hittite. ⁶*And there was war between Rehoboam* [read Abijam?] *and Jeroboam all the days of his life.* ⁷And the rest of the deeds of Abijam, and all that he did—are they not written in the Book of the Chronicles of the Kings of Judah? There was war between Abijam and Jeroboam. ⁸*Abijam slept with his fathers, and they buried him in the city of David. Then Asa his son became king in his place.*

This shows two formulae (stereotyped statements), one about the accession of the king and the other about the death of the king. The information in these two formulae was probably borrowed from the *Chronicle of the Kings of Judah* (written in italics in the quotation). When we examine these two formulae, it becomes clear that the opening formula is similar to chronicle entries in other ancient Near Eastern chronicles. This opening formula seems to contain certain sorts of information that is conventionally found in official chronicles.

The text in regular Roman type (vv. 3-5) is the contribution of the Judahite author of Kings, either his own statement or theological judgment or material from other sources. It is unlikely that both the italicized statement in v. 6 and that at the end of v. 7 are exact quotations from the court chronicle, but the chronicle must have had a statement on the war. It illustrates that *the author adapted material from the chronicle and did not always just quote it verbatim*. Verse 8 is unlikely to have come verbatim from any chronicle, but it is conceivable that a chronicle might regularly have a statement that a king "slept with his fathers and his son reigned after him."

An important conclusion immediately manifests itself: *all of the factual information in this passage could have come from a chronicle*. In addition to the information in vv. 1-2, a chronicle entry might well have mentioned that Abijam waged war against Jeroboam all his reign (vv. 6-7). The statements in vv. 3-5 are mainly theological pronouncements but do not constitute "information," in the sense of telling us something about the king's reign. Thus, the summary of Abijam's reign is made up of reliable chronicle material but also other material (probably less reliable) based on other sources or just the author's imagination.

David's Kingdom Reverts to Two (1 Kgs 12–14)

As noted in chapter 5, the events during the reign of Solomon are difficult to assess because so much is legendary. But what becomes clear is that either during his reign or after it, the simmering divisions within Israel came to the surface. According to the surface picture of the biblical story, a single nation of Israel split into two rival nations because of petty issues under Solomon's son Rehoboam and his nonroyal opponent Jeroboam. The text presents it as the privileged heir of Solomon arrogantly refusing to listen to the demands of the people to ease some of the burdens created by the ruling family.

Solomon seems to have made use of forced labor for some of his projects. This was not unusual in the ancient Near East—in addition to paying taxes, people also often had to donate a certain number of days of work to the state. But like taxes, this donated labor—"corvée labor"—was not welcomed by the people who had to do it. One of Solomon's officials—a man by the name of Jeroboam who had fled to Egypt but had now returned—is said to have led the delegation to Rehoboam. To what extent the story and its details are accurate can be debated, but what is clear is that the groups that had been united by David had reverted to the natural division between north and south. Saul had brought together Benjamin and other Israelite groups, while David had joined together the region that we now call Judah with Saul's tribal coalition.

But careful consideration of the geopolitical facts, as well as a number of biblical passages that are easily overlooked, shows that the union of two ethnic groups under David was an artificial one. It is obvious historically that both Judah and Israel each had its own national identity and was separate from and a rival of the other from an early period. This was already discussed in chapter 5 (p. 72). Although we cannot be confident of the details, the split of the kingdom back into Judah and Israel after Solomon's death seems to be correctly remembered by the text.

Reigns of Rehoboam and Jeroboam (1 Kgs 12–14)

It has been argued that Jeroboam I's reign has been modelled on that of Jeroboam II, to create details for a reign of the earlier Jeroboam that in fact never took place. It is true that we have strong evidence of the existence of Jeroboam II, primarily 2 Kgs 14:23–15:1 (see below, p. 111). The activities of Jeroboam I are interwoven with events during Solomon's reign and Rehoboam's reign, primarily 1 Kgs 11:26-40; 12:2-3, 12, 15, 20; 12:25-13:10; 13:33–14:20; 14:30–15:1. But let's compare the reigns of the two Jeroboams as recounted in the texts of 1 and 2 Kings (see Table 6.1).

When we compare the reigns of the two kings as recounted in the biblical text, we find almost no correspondence. About the only thing they have in common in the literary accounts is that they were both kings of Israel. Whether or not the account of Jeroboam I is fictional, it is not modelled on the reign of Jeroboam II. There may have been a small amount of borrowing from Jeroboam II's reign, but Jeroboam I seems to have had a place in the *Chronicle of the Kings of Judah*.

It so happened that this *Chronicle of the Kings of Judah* is first quoted during the reign of Jeroboam I. Thus, we have in 1 Kgs 14:19-20 a passage with the standard formula linking the information to a chronicle:

> The rest of the actions of Jeroboam, how he fought and how he ruled—are they not written in the Book of the Chronicles on the Kings of Israel? The time that Jeroboam ruled was 22 years, then he slept with his fathers, and his son Nadab ruled after him.

1 Kgs 14:29-30 also looks like a quotation from a chronicle:

> The rest of the actions of Rehoboam and all which he did—are not they written in the Book of the Chronicles on the Kings of Judah? A state of war existed all the days between Rehoboam and Jeroboam.

It is important to note that, judging by these standard literary formulas, the writer of 1 and 2 Kings has begun to draw on a chronicle during the reigns of Rehoboam and Jeroboam. He apparently did not have this chronicle available for the reigns of David and Solomon.

Egypt plays an important role in the story of Jeroboam I. According to 1 Kgs 11:40, he was allowed to settle in Egypt by Shishak (probably Pharaoh Shoshenq I). One Egyptologist has argued that the core of the statement is likely to be historical.[2] He notes that we have several instances in Egyptian and Mesopotamian sources in which a foreign prince or official sought exile in the Egyptian New Kingdom.

Jeroboam was supposed to have resided in three cities at different times: Shechem, Penuel, and Tirzah. Shechem was in existence once again during the Early Iron Age IIA, the time of Jeroboam I. Archaeology shows an early destruction, which has been associated with Shoshenq I. The next stratum has been dated to the late tenth and the ninth centuries BCE and has been described as "the tangible evidence of Jeroboam I's rebuilding (1 Kgs 12:25) and a return to city status."[3] Tirzah is discussed below

TABLE 6.1 *Comparison of Jeroboam I and Jeroboam II stories.*

1 Kings	Jeroboam I	2 Kings	Jeroboam II
11:26	Son of Nebat	14:23	Son of Joash.
14:20	Reigned 22 years		Reigned 41 years.
11:28	Over Solomon's corvée		
11:29–39	Promised 10 tribes by prophet Ahijan of Shiloh		
11:40	Flees to Egypt to escape Solomon's wrath		
12:20	Israel summons Jeroboam and makes him king		
12:25	Fortifies Shechem, lives there; fortifies Penuel		
12:26–33	Sets up calves for worship in Dan and Bethel		
12:33–13:9	Sacrifice at Bethel interrupted by man of God		
14:1–18	Wife consults prophet Ahijah but ill child dies		
		14:25	Restored territory of Israel from Lebo-Hamath to the Sea of the Arbah [Gulf of Aqabah]. Done according to the prophecy of Jonah.
		14:26	Yahweh took mercy on the bitter situation of Israel.
		14:27	He chose not to blot out the name of Israel but delivered them through Jeroboam.
		14:28	Jeroboam recovered Damascus and Hamath [to Judah in Israel?? (textual corruption?)].
14:20	Succeeded by his son Nadab.	14:29	Succeeded by his son Zechariah.
15:1	Abijam becomes king of Judah in Jeroboam's 18th year.	15:1	Azariah becomes king of Judah in Jeroboam's 27th year.

(p. 97). Unfortunately, there seems to be little information on the archaeology of Penuel.

Jeroboam is also associated with cult sites in Dan and Bethel, but the archaeology of the sites presents something of a problem. So far, no cult site has been found in Bethel, though it is so strongly attested textually that it seems difficult to dismiss it. Similarly, it was argued that Dan was not inhabited in the time of Jeroboam, the Early Iron Age IIA. But recent studies assert that some have been misled by assuming that no pottery was found in Stratum III of Dan (from the time of Jeroboam I) because no such pottery has been published. Yet, a good deal of such pottery has in fact been found, and the existence of this stratum—which some thought was nonexistent—is in fact well supported by the material culture.[4] Thus, there is presently an indication that evidence for the existence of the cult site at Dan during the time of Jeroboam I is available, though the final conclusion must await the full publication of the pottery.

Yet, this is not the whole story. Even if the cult site at Dan was in full operation in the late tenth and early ninth centuries, did the Kingdom of Israel extend that far north at that time? According to the reconstruction of several scholars, it did not reach that far north, even under Omride rule.[5] Thus, on the basis of one set of criteria we are left with the possibility that no cult site existed at Bethel, while the cult site at Dan was not in Israelite hands.

But the final word has not been spoken. Perhaps there is something about the site at Dan that we do not know, which would put it in Israelite possession at this time, as some have indeed argued.[6] Likewise, the textual attestation of a cult site at Bethel is strong, which makes one wonder if perhaps such a site will eventually be turned up by archaeologists. It may well be that the bull cults of Dan and Bethel belong to a different time and a different king from Jeroboam I but perhaps not. In my view, the question remains open, but we have to accept the verdict "not yet proved" for the present.

The Invasion of Pharaoh Shoshenq

According to 1 Kgs 14:25-28 a king Shishak of Egypt came up against Jerusalem in Rehoboam's fifth year and took all the treasures of the temple. This supposed raid of Shishak has been seen as a major event in Israel's history and a means of determining its early chronology, as well as allegedly providing evidence within the archaeology (because of the assumed destruction of various Palestinian sites). When an inscription of Shoshenq I (c. 943–923 BCE), founder of the Twenty-Second Dynasty, was discovered at Karnak listing many topographical sites in Palestine, a connection was made with the passage in the Bible and has been the standard view ever since.

All seem to agree that Shoshenq's expedition was a signal event in Israel's history, but precisely what happened on the ground and even when the invasion took place is considerably disputed. The conventional view is heavily informed by the Bible. According to it, Shoshenq's army made a number of destructive raids on various parts of Palestine, destroying many sites in the Negev and even as far north as Megiddo; however, Jerusalem did not fall because the pharaoh was bought off by Rehoboam. There have always been some problems (not always acknowledged), nevertheless, especially the fact that Israel and Judah are not mentioned specifically, that no site in Judah occurs in the inscription (except perhaps for Arad in the Negev), that the toponyms cannot be worked into any sort of itinerary sequence, and that the biblical text says nothing about an invasion of the Northern Kingdom. A recent study[7] that investigated Shoshenq's inscription in the context of other Egyptian triumphal inscriptions notes the following points:

- Triumphal inscriptions were designed to extol the pharaoh's exploits, not provide historical data.

- The reliefs glorify all the exploits of the king rather than a particular campaign.
- The topographical lists are not laid out according to any system that allows a reconstruction of the military route.
- The sites listed may in some cases be those attacked, but others not attacked—indeed, friendly towns and allies—might be listed as well.
- The lists were apparently drawn in part from military records and onomastical lists, which means that some data of value for certain purposes may be included.

The implications of these conclusions are considerable. Rather than recording a particular campaign into Palestine, Shoshenq's inscription may include more than one. This would help to explain the vague nature of the inscriptions that accompany the topographical lists, without clarifying the reasons for or objectives of the "invasion." More puzzling is the lack of any reference to Judah or Jerusalem as such. The argument has been made that this was in a section of the inscription that is no longer readable. But this argument is not compelling since the section that would have contained mention of Judah and Jerusalem is quite clear and intact.

What is becoming more likely in the light of recent study is that at least part of Shoshenq's aim was the production and trade in copper. Copper from Cyprus had ceased at this time, and Palestine was the main source for Egypt. Yet we know that Shoshenq pushed on north as far as the Megiddo and the Jezreel Valley, which might have given him access to the copper trade routes. A stela naming this pharaoh was found in Megiddo: Shoshenq would hardly set up his stela in a ruined city, which suggests that Megiddo was occupied (not destroyed!) to become a regional headquarters and administrative center.

It may be that Judah or, more probably, both Judah and Israel were regarded as vassal states by Shoshenq. They would not only have paid tribute but would also, no doubt, have been required to assist Egypt in acquiring copper. Regardless of any uncertainty in the reading of the inscription, the general direction of march seems clear.[8] Not only the Gibeon region but also the region of Samaria (Tirzah, Zemaraim) and the Transjordan territory (Mahanaim, Penuel) that seemed to be a part of Jeroboam I's kingdom also appear to be included. How we are to interpret this? One could conclude that Judah/Rehoboam was spared but that the northern region/Jeroboam was attacked. This would argue that Shoshenq was more or less happy with Judah/Rehoboam, which is why no sites in Judah are recorded in his list of toponyms. But he was unhappy with Jeroboam, for whatever reason. Possibly he was even supporting Rehoboam against the "rebellion" of the northern tribes. In any case, the line of march suggests that he was going up against Jeroboam. The biblical text places it under Rehoboam; however, some have wanted to put it earlier, in Solomon's time.[9]

An examination of the toponyms named on Shoshenq's inscription does indeed suggest that Judah was spared since none of the toponyms named are located there. (One site is "Greater Arad," generally agreed to be Tel Arad in the Negev, but the Negev was probably not part of Judah at this time.) But what about the tribute taken from Rehoboam according to 1 Kgs 14:25-28? Nothing supports the biblical statement. If Jerusalem paid tribute, it seems paramount that Shoshenq would have mentioned it, yet the place in the list where Jerusalem would have been mentioned has no obliterated or questionable names. Also, the argument that the tribute was paid to the Pharaoh at Gibeon goes nowhere—he still would have listed Jerusalem.

One suggestion is that this story was simply a creation of the biblical writer, as a way of explaining what happened to Solomon's alleged enormous wealth that was clearly no longer there in subsequent centuries. On the other hand, if Judah was already submissive to Egypt and paying annual tribute, it might not have been listed.

Reign of Abijam of Judah (1 Kgs 15:1-8)

The rule of Abijam, son of Rehoboam, in Jerusalem is essentially a blank (the text was quoted above, p. 89). We learn only that his mother was Maacah and that he reigned three years. The war with Jeroboam, begun under his father, continued. Otherwise, all we have are the standard statements made about every king of the Northern Kingdom and most kings of Judah—that he was wicked! We do not even know whether his successor Asa was his son or his brother: 1 Kgs 15:8 says Asa was Abijam's son, but his mother was the same as Abijam's (1 Kgs 15:10; the word for "father" ['āv] and "brother" ['āḥ] are similar in Hebrew, so this could be a scribal error).

Reign of Asa of Judah (1 Kgs 15:9-24)

The short description of Asa's reign focuses on his righteousness, but the question is how much of the data might have come from an official chronicle, as opposed to the contribution of the Kings' author who was interpreting any information from a source and also making theological statements and judgments. The following *could* have come from an official annal, because they are the sort of things that a court chronicle might well record:

- Deposed the queen mother (Maacah who was his mother or possibly his grandmother).
- Deposited his father's and his own votive objects in the temple.
- Bribed the Aramaean Bar-Hadad son of Tabrimmon son of Hezion to attack Israel (so Baasha would cease to build Ramah that blocked movement from Judah to the north).
- Built Geba and Mizpah of Benjamin.
- Had an ailment in his feet.

The removal of the queen mother is a unique event in biblical history, partly because it is the only passage that talks about a queen mother. If the queen mother had an official function in the Judahite monarchy, we have no information on it. According to the text's theological interpretation, she was removed from office because she made a cult object for Asherah. This appears prima facie unlikely, since it has recently become acknowledged that according to Israelite belief Yahweh had a female consort Asherah (see further the discussion in chapter 7, p. 120–1). This female "partner" was eventually dropped from the divine story, but that apparently did not happen until the seventh century, several centuries after Asa. Thus, the statement that the queen mother was removed because of making an Asherah cult object is likely to be an interpretation rather than information from a chronicle. The same judgment applies to Asa's removing the $q^e\underline{d}ēšîm$ from the land. This term has often been translated as "male cult prostitute," but this is now generally rejected: there is little or no evidence of cult prostitution (whether male or female) in Canaanite religion, as was once assumed. (On these points relating to religion, see further in chapter 7, p. 129.)

The information on bribing Bar-Hadad looks more authentic. The question is whether Israelite territory extended this far north at that time. Thus, the biblical author might have had useful information, but it is also possible that he is creating a scenario from knowledge of Israelite territory at a later time? Some think that it was Jeroboam II who had dealings with Bar-Hadad, and the biblical writer has confused the two. Our problem is that our knowledge of the Aramaean kingdoms that dominated Syrian history in the first millennium BCE is defective, which often makes it difficult to judge biblical statements on the question. But it looks as if the narrator of Asa's reign has mistakenly drawn on knowledge of a later Aramaean king named Ben/Bar-Hadad and the list of later conquered territory (as known, for example, in 2 Kgs 15:29—compare with 1 Kgs 15:20) to fill out his narrative.

Yet it does look as if the narrator has recognized the conflict between Judah and Israel over the territory of southern Benjamin. As was noted in the previous chapter (p. 72), Jerusalem probably came to dominate the Benjaminite Plateau in the time of David. Archaeology also appears to confirm this conflict, since sometime after 900 BCE the settlements on the Benjaminite ridge disappeared, while about the same time the Judahite site of Mizpeh was fortified. What this indicates is that Israel succeeded in gaining control of the northern part of Benjamin, but Judah established its northern border by turning Mizpah into a fortified site to keep control of the Benjaminite Plateau.[10]

There is also the matter of Asa's defeating Zerah the Cushite ("Ethiopian"), though this episode is found only in 2 Chron. 14:8-14 and is absent from 1 Kings. Some have tried to defend this as authentic even though the writer of Kings knows nothing about it. It was once suggested that "Zerah" was a reflex of the name of Pharaoh Ororkon I who lived about this time, but Egyptian philologists now refute any connection between the names. The name is neither Nubian nor Egyptian but biblical (Gen. 36:17; Josh. 7:1; 1 Chron. 1:37; Neh. 11:24). The Egyptologist B. U. Schipper examined the story in the light of biblical and Egyptian considerations and concluded that 2 Chron. 14:8-14 is "in no way a historical document from the ninth century but an example of Old Testament theology from the post-exilic period."[11]

Rulers of Israel to Omri (1 Kgs 15:25–16:20)

Several short-lived rulers of the Northern Kingdom filled in the time between Jeroboam and Omri; the only one who ruled for any length of time was Baasha.

First, Nadab the son of Jeroboam ruled for two years (1 Kgs 15:25-31). All we know of him is that while laying siege to Gibbethon in Philistia, he was struck down by Baasha. Baasha then proceeded to kill all members of Jeroboam's house (1 Kgs 15:29-30). Baasha ruled for twenty-four years, and there is a fair amount of text on his rule (1 Kgs 15:27-30, 32-34; 16:1-6), yet we know little about him other than that he began to build Ramah and that his "house" (relatives) was destroyed, like that of Jeroboam. Baasha was succeeded by his son Elah (1 Kgs 16:8-14) who ruled two years. His chariot commander Zimri killed him while he was drinking in the capital Tirzah and then proceeded to kill all males of the house of Baasha. But Zimri lasted only seven days, because the army chose their commander Omri who then besieged Zimri in Tirzah, and the latter committed suicide (1 Kgs 16:15-20). Omri consolidated his rule by defeating a rival Tibni who also had a following among the people (1 Kgs 16:21-22).

Omri (1 Kgs 16:16-28)

Omri became king only fifty years after the death of Solomon, if the figures of the MT can be trusted. From the biblical text you would be led to believe that Omri was not very important: he has only twelve verses devoted to him. The essence of his life is that he was the army commander declared king by the army when Zimri assassinated Baasha. Omri established his kingdom by going against Zimri, who committed suicide, and defeating and killing the other rival for the throne, Tibni. Omri then purchased the hill of Shemer and founded a new capital for the Northern Kingdom, Samaria. Otherwise, he is simply dismissed as wicked.[12]

Yet we know from Assyrian texts that Omri was a significant individual who gave his name to his kingdom: the Assyrians long called the Northern Kingdom *Bit-Ḥumri* ("House of Omri"). The Assyrian records thus confirm the existence and importance of Omri, though they say nothing further about him. Yet we also find a reference to Omri in the stela left by Mesha, the king of Moab, about 800 BCE. This "Moabite stone" (also called "The Mesha Stela") states that Omri "oppressed" Moab for his lifetime and half the lifetime of his son, forty years, before Mesha threw off the Israelite yoke (see further about the Moabite stone and this figure under "Ahab," p. 102–3).

Several of the previous Israelite kings had their capital at Tirzah. Tirzah is widely identified these days with Tell el-Farʿah (North). The stratum associated with the reign of Jeroboam I ended in destruction, which has been connected with the taking of the city from Zimri by Omri. In the next stratum of the city there is an "unfinished construction" phase, which has been interpreted as Omri's rebuilding efforts, which were abandoned when he decided to move his capital to the new site of Samaria. Thus, the archaeology of Tirzah seems to fit with the data in the Jeroboam I account, while the archaeology of Tirzah and Samaria matches the biblical statements on Omri.

Although the biblical account of Omri is quite short, a good portion of the concrete data probably come from a royal chronicle. Here is my suggestion of the material taken from a chronicle, as found in the biblical description:

¹⁵*During the 27th year of Asa king of Judah Zimri ruled seven days in Tirzah, and the people camped at Gibbethon which belonged to the Philistines.* ¹⁶*And the people camped there said, "Zimri has plotted and struck down the king." And in the camp they made Omri, the commander of the Israelite army, king of all Israel at that time.* ¹⁷*And Omri—and with him all Israel—went up from Gibbethon and besieged Tirzah.* ¹⁸*It was when Zimri saw the city was taken, he went into the citadel of the king's palace, set the palace on fire over him, and died in the fire.* ²¹*Then the people of Israel were divided, half the people following Tibni son of Ginah, to make him king, and half following Omri.* ²²*The people who followed Omri were stronger than those who followed Tibni son of Ginah. Tibni was killed, and Omri reigned.* ²³*In the 31st year of Asa, king of Judah, Omri became king over Israel for 12 years, reigning six years in Tirzah. He purchased the hill of Samaria from Shemer for two talents of silver. He built on the hill and called the name of the city that he built Samaria, after the name of the (previous) owner Shemer.*

Although this material might not be a literal quotation from the royal chronicle, the content is likely to have come from it. This illustrates how the writer of Kings has used the royal chronicle to fill out the factual side of his account. What becomes clear

TABLE 6.2 *Kings of Damascus*

References to these kings in Assyrian inscriptions is also included:
Hadadezer
Hazael
    Eighteenth year of Shalmanezer III (*ANET*: 280)
    Twenty-first year of Shalmanezer (*ANET*: 280)
    Fifth year of Adad-nirari III (*ANET*: 281–82)
        —Arslan Tash ivory: reference to "Mari" (though possibly Bir-Hadad):
Bir-Hadad ben Hazael
    Zakkur inscription (*ANET*: 219–20)
    "Mari" (though possibly Hazael)
Rezon (Raqianu)
    Tiglath-pileser III (c. 737) tribute list

TABLE 6.3 *Neo-Assyrian kings*

The dates given for the reigns of kings are not necessarily definite. In some cases, there is disagreement even among specialists. For the first century of the Neo-Assyrian Empire (to c. 934 BCE), we have little information except that they were harassed by the Aramaeans.
Ashur-Dan II (934–912).
Adad-narari II (911–891).
Tukulti-ninurta II (890–884).
Ashur-nasir-pal II (883–859).
Shalmaneser III (858–824).   Sixth year: met by coalition of twelve kings led by Hadadezer of Damascus, including "Ahab of Israel" (*A-ḫa-ab-bu* ᵐᵃᵗ*Sir-'a-la-a~-a*) who had "2000 chariots" (2 LIM GIŠ.GIGIR.MEŠ) and ten thousand troops.

Tenth: opposed by Hadadezer of Damascus.
Eleventh: opposed by Hadadezer of Damascus, together with twelve kings.
Fourteenth: has army of 120,000; opposed by Hadadezer and twelve kings.
Eighteenth: opposed by Hazael (*Ḫa-za-'e*-DINGIR) of Damascus whom he imprisons in his city and burns his gardens. Received tribute from "Jehu son of Omri" (*Ia-a-ú* [var. *Ia-ú-a*] DUMU ᵐ*Ḫu-um-ri-i*).
Undated inscription: Hadadezer passed away and "Hazael, son of a nobody" (*Ḫa-za-a'*-DINGIR DUMU *la ma-ma-na*) took the throne.

Shamshi-adad V (823–811).

Adad-narari III (810–783). Returned to Syria and Mediterranean (c. 805–796), though number of campaigns uncertain. Received tribute from "Mari" (*Ma-ri-i'*) of Damascus and "*Iu-'a-su* of Samaria (*Sa-me-ri-na-a-a*) [var. land of Omri (*Ḫu-um-ri-i*)]." Mari equals Hazael according to one reading of the Arslan Tash ivory, but not all agree.

Shalmaneser IV (782–773). A campaign led by the *tartanu* (field marshall) marched to Damascus and took tribute from Ḫadiiāni of Damascus.

Ashur-dan III (772–755 BCE).

Ashur-narari V (754–745 BCE).

Tiglath-pileser III (744–727 BCE). Number of campaigns to the west:
743: defeated coalition led by Mati'el of Arpad (Arpad fell in 740).
738: defeated coalition led by Azriyau (of Iaudi?); tribute paid by number of northern Syrian states and by Rezin (*Ra-ḫi-a-nu/Ra-qi-a-nu*) of Damascus, Byblos, Tyre, and Menahem of Samaria (*Me-ni-ḫi-im-me* ᵘʳᵘ*Sa-me-ri-na-a* + *a*).
734: annexed Aram (*Bīt-*ᵐ*Ḫa-za-'i-i-li*), captured Gaza (ruler Hanunu), and established Assyrian rule to the Egyptian border.
733–732: Syro-Palestinian rebellion led by Rezin of Damascus. Damascus survived a siege in 733 but apparently fell in 732 (gap in the annals) and made into an Assyrian province. Pekah (*Pa-qa-ha*) of Samaria (*Bīt-Ḫu-um-ri-a*) defeated and killed; Hosea (*A-ú-si-'i*) took the throne.

Shalmaneser V (726–722 BCE). Little known of him except his siege of Samaria.

Sargon II (721–705 BCE). Babylonia rebelled at his accession, under Marduk-baladan II who maintained his position with the help of Elam. A major offensive in 710 forced Marduk-baladan to flee to Elam. Sargon was welcomed into Babylon and recognized as king of Babylon. Rebellions in Syria and Palestine at his accession. Claims to have conquered Samaria in his first year, but unlikely; however, he probably did carry out the deportation of some of the Samarian population.

Sennacherib (704–681 BCE). Marduk-baladan II seized Babylonian throne at beginning of his reign.
Marduk-baladan forced to flee, and Bel-ibni put on throne (703 BCE). Campaign into marshes of the south (700 BCE). Marduk-baladan fled across Persian Gulf; later died in Elam in exile.
701: campaign against Judah, though ultimate goal probably conquest of Egypt.

Esarhaddon (680–669 BCE). Conquest of Egypt in 671. Egyptian king Taharqa fled but family captured. Most areas of Syro-Palestine submissive, but troubles with Phoenicia. Sidon rebelled (c. 680); recaptured (677 BCE). But Tyre then rebelled and allied with Taharqa of Egypt. City was besieged but apparently not forced to submit. New expedition in 669, but Esarhaddon died on the way.

Ashurbanipal (668–627 BCE). His reign in many ways the height of the Assyrian Empire but had come to edge of a precipice. Collected a famous library of much Mesopotamian literature. Had trouble holding Egypt. Taharqa rebelled and made secret alliance with other princes such as Necho I who were supposedly Assyrian allies. Plot discovered and most punished except for Necho. Syro-Palestine generally acquiescent. Besieged Tyre about 662. Tyre not taken but submitted. Rebelled again about 644, and Assyrians plundered mainland city. His brother Shamash-shuma-ukin rebelled in Babylon, encouraged by Elam. Revolt put down and Elam invaded with great ferocity, with Susa destroyed.

---

when putting all our information together is that Omri was a very important king who gave a major impetus to the development of Israel into a state.

Ahab (1 Kgs 16:29–22:40)

Ahab evidently continued the work of his father in the evolution of Israel into a significant political entity in the Levant. As we shall see, Israel's military was substantial and a leading contribution to a military coalition of the region. The biblical text focuses on the religious question, highlighting Ahab's impiety and especially that of his foreign wife Jezebel, but this is the judgment of a devout writer from a later age with different standards of godliness and appropriate worship. What has become clear in recent scholarship is the extent to which Ahab, along with his father Omri, made Israel into a kingdom with international connections, a formidable military, and a leading power in the eastern Mediterranean.

With Ahab's reign we suddenly find ourselves with an embarrassment of riches, relatively speaking, for we have far more potential sources than for most of the Israelite and Judahite kings.[13] Far from removing problems and difficulties, however, they seem only to raise new ones, especially when it comes to reconciling the biblical text with the primary sources. First, much of the text is actually taken up with the story of Elijah the prophet, and prophetic legends cannot be taken as necessarily reliable for historical purposes, since one of their aims is to enhance the power and reputation of the prophet. Thus, Elijah is presented as opposing Jezebel single-handedly, even though the text itself admits that there were many who had not worshiped Baal (1 Kgs 19:14 versus 19:18). Indeed, many think that the text has misrepresented the situation with Jezebel (see pp. 107–8 under "Jehu").

The essential information on Ahab is summarized in a biblical passage that appears to come from a court chronicle of some sort. The material that seems based on the chronicle record is given in italics, while the comments of the writer of Kings is put in square brackets:

> *Ahab son of Omri ruled over Israel in the 38th year of Asa king of Judah. Ahab son of Omri ruled over Israel in Samaria 22 years.* [Ahab son of Omri did evil in the eyes of Yahweh more than all who preceded him. He made light of walking in the sin of Jeroboam son of Nebat.] *And he took to wife Jezebel daughter of*

Ethbaal, king of the Sidonians. [He went and served Baal and worshiped him.] *He set up an altar to Baal in the House of Baal which he built in Samaria.* [Ahab made an Ashera, and did additional things to annoy Yahweh, the God of Israel, more than all the kings of Israel who preceded him ...]. *The rest of the deeds of Ahab and all that he accomplished and the house of ivory and all the cities that he built—are they not written in the Book of the Annals of the Kings of Israel? And Ahab slept with his ancestors, and Ahaziah his son ruled in his place.* (1 Kgs 16:29-33; 22:39-40)

It is clear that we do not have the chronicle itself but an extract that has been excerpted and inserted into the biblical text, along with edits and editorial comments. The bracketed material is clearly editorial material that was not a part of the original chronicle. But some of the material in italics is unlikely to be a verbatim quote from a chronicle. For example, it is not certain that the chronicle mentioned building a temple and altar for Baal, but this is a factual statement and might be taken from the chronicle.

On the question of Baal, however, we must keep in mind that the writer/editor is a later Judahite writer with a particular view of worship. At the time of Ahab both Israel and Judah were polytheistic societies, who worshiped Baal and Asherah as well as Yahweh. Also, the House of Baal was apparently built for Jezebel as a private royal chapel, since she herself was a Phoenician and considered Baal as her chief deity. Finally, Ahab was himself a worshiper of Yahweh. We know this because his chief palace overseer Obadiah was a devoted Yahweh worshiper, and Ahab could hardly have been ignorant of that (1 Kgs 17:3). Furthermore, his two sons had theophoric names that contained a form of the divine name Yahweh (the element *-yahu*, found in Ahaziah [1 Kgs 22:40: Hebrew *'ăḥaziyāhû*] and Jehoram [2 Kgs 1:17; Hebrew *yəhôrām*]), which would hardly have been the case if he had been a Baal worshiper. For further information on Israelite religion, see chapter 7.

According to the biblical text, Ahab spent his reign fighting Aramaeans, specifically a king called Ben-Hadad. Israel was generally the underdog who came off the worse in these conflicts (see especially 1 Kgs 20 and 22). The Assyrian inscriptions give a quite different story, and it is important to understand why this is important. Of course, the Assyrian inscriptions have their own biases and interests, but modern scholars are aware of this and read them critically. The Assyrian inscriptions are so significant, however, because they are contemporary or nearly contemporary with the events they record, unlike the biblical text that was finalized long after the events. Here is the main Assyrian account from the military campaign of year six of the Assyrian emperor Shalmaneser III for the year 853 BCE (the statement on Ahab is in italics):

I departed from Argana and approached Karkara. I destroyed, tore down and burned down Karkara, his ... royal residence. He brought along to help him 1,200 chariots, 1,200 cavalrymen, 20,000 foot soldiers of Adad-'idri (i.e. Hadadezer) of Damascus

... , 700 chariots, 700 cavalrymen, 10,000 foot soldiers of Irhuleni from Hamath, *2,000 chariots, 10,000 foot soldiers of Ahab, the Israelite (A-ḫa-ab-bu ᵐᵃᵗSir-'i-la-a-a)*, 500 soldiers from Que, 1,000 soldiers from Musri, 10 chariots, 10,000 soldiers from Irqanata, 200 soldiers of Matinu-ba'lu from Arvad, 200 soldiers from Usanata, 30 chariots, 1[0?],000 soldiers of Adunu-ba'lu from Shian, 1,000 camel-(rider) s of Gindibu', from Arabia, ... ,000 soldiers of Ba'sa, son of Ruhubi, from Ammon—(all together) these were twelve kings.

According to these early extra-biblical sources it was the Assyrians that Ahab fought, and *he was part of an anti-Assyrian coalition in which the Aramaeans were his allies.* This is an essential contradiction that cannot be lightly dismissed or trivially harmonized. There is no question that Assyria dominated the history of the Levant at this time. Assyria was attempting to expand its tentacles toward the Mediterranean, and the small kingdoms of Syria and Palestine were in its sights. The biblical text's ignoring of the Assyrian problem is a major historical blunder that cannot be overlooked. *Either the writer was grossly ignorant, or he wilfully changed the true situation, by making the Aramaeans rather than the Assyrians the enemy, for theological reasons.*

In the sixth year of his reign, beginning about 853 BCE, the Assyrian King Shalmaneser III (858–824) marched west to make conquests in the Syrian area. Shalmaneser's inscriptions (one of them quoted above) show that Ahab was allied with Hadadezer of Damascus and ten other rulers in a coalition opposing the invading Assyrians at Qarqar in 853 BCE. This coalition of a dozen local kings was able to fight the Assyrians to a standoff at this time and for perhaps another decade or so. Note also that Ahab had the largest number of chariots—two thousand—which shows that he was one of the strongest members in this alliance.

It should be noted that Assyria was in a continual struggle with Hadadezer's coalition from his sixth year until at least the fourteenth year. Ahab is unlikely to have left the coalition during this time; it is only in the eighteenth year that a new king of Israel is mentioned, and the coalition under Hadadezer is defeated. Ahab would not have fought the Aramaeans in his last few years when he was part of the coalition organized by Hadadezer. It was only when Ahab was out of the way that the coalition was defeated.

Yet an explanation of the biblical picture that has become widely accepted in scholarship suggests the following: 1 Kings 20–22 is made up of material from the later Jehu dynasty (e.g., 2 Kgs 13), which has been mistakenly assigned to the reign of Ahab. In other words, the stories making Ahab fight the Aramaeans might have been transferred from the later Jehu dynasty (long after Ahab's death) when Israel was indeed weak in relation to the Aramaeans.[14] See Table 6.4.

Another issue concerns the relationship of Omri's kingdom with Moab. According to 2 Kings (1:1; 3:4-5) Moab was under the dominion of Israel but managed to break free after Ahab's death. No suggestion is made in the biblical text as to who subjugated Moab in the first place. The Mesha Stela states that Omri "oppressed" Moab for his lifetime and half the lifetime of his son, forty years, before Mesha threw off the Israelite yoke. There is a remarkable coincidence between the biblical and the extra-biblical data.

One particular problem is the dating of Moab's vassalage to Israel. A period of forty years is mentioned in the Mesha Stella inscription, obviously a round number. Omri is associated with the conquest of Moab; however, it is rather curious that Ahab is not mentioned at all, though the expression "his son" might have been taken as a derogatory reference by not actually naming Ahab. But we can go further: it is interesting that the length of reigns of Omri and Ahab together total thirty-four

TABLE 6.4 *Parallels with the Jehu dynasty.*

1 Kings	*2 Kings*
19:15: Hazael to be anointed over Aram	8:7-15: to be anointed by Elisha
20: king called Ben-Hadad throughout chapter	
20:26-27: only tiny army in Israel	13:7: only tiny army left to Israel by Aram
20:26: defeat at Aphek	13:17: Aram to be defeated at Aphek
20:34: Ben-Hadad restores cities	13:24-25: cities from Ben-Hadad, son of Hazael
22:4: fight for Ramoth-Gilead	10:32-33; 9:14; 8:28: Gilead lost in Jehu's time

years according to the biblical text (1 Kgs 16:23, 29), not far from forty years. Then, "half the reign of his son" could be a reference to Jehoram (Ahab's son and Omri's grandson) rather than Ahab ("son" being used generically for a more remote descendent, "grandson" in this case). After all, the Moabite scribe was making a general point, not giving a blow-by-blow historical narrative. Moab rebelled in the reign of Jehoram according to 1 Kings 1:1. This gives us

Omri's reign—12 years

Ahab's reign—22 years

Jehoram's reign 12 years: "half" = 6 years

Total—40 years

This fits both the biblical data and the information from the Mesha stela. Only a coincidence—or was Mesha giving us a reasonably accurate dating?

One of the areas of difficulty often discussed is the number of chariots possessed by Ahab, according to the Assyrian texts. Some have said this was impossible: chariots at that time were like tanks in a modern army. Israel could not be that strong, some allege. Yet the text clearly reads "2,000 chariots" (2 *lim* GIŠ.GIGIR.MEŠ in the Akkadian inscription): this figure is clearly written; we are not dealing with a damaged text. Yet the text is often emended. But this emendation is erroneous, for two reasons.

First, the resources needed to maintain a large force of horses is not the precise equivalent of the economic support needed for manufacturing and supplying a modern tank regiment. Two thousand chariots would need a large herd of horses, but these would not necessarily have been kept permanently in stalls. Grassland unsuitable for crops could still provide good grazing for horses kept in reserve until a national emergency arose. A second point is that this force may not have been supplied by the kingdom of Israel alone. 1 Kgs 22:4 suggests that Judah was subordinate to Israel, perhaps being a vassal, as was Moab. Also, Tyre and Sidon (marriage to Jezebel made them allies) are not mentioned in Shalmaneser's inscription, either as opposing his advance or as paying tribute. The resources of these kingdoms could have supplemented those of Ahab, helping to fill out the numbers of his chariots.

Another famous incident is that of Naboth's vineyard, but there are good reasons for thinking this story actually originated in the Persian period and is only a subsequent insertion into the Ahab story.[15] Further information on Jezebel is given

TABLE 6.5 *Omri's reign, biblical versus extra-biblical*

Biblical	Extra-biblical
Omris' reign short/insignificant	Omri remembered by Assyrians, who used the names Bit-Ḫumri and ^{mar}Ḫumri for Israel
Ahab fights Aramaeans	Ahab allied with the Aramaeans
Aramaean king is Ben-Hadad	Aramaean king is Hadadezer
	Ahab fights the Assyrians
Ahab weak	Ahab has 2,000 chariots
Mesha tributary of Ahab but frees himself	Mesha king of Moab but throws off Israel's yoke
1 Kgs 22:40: Ahab died natural death (contrast 1 Kgs 21:27-29 with 22:38).	

below (pp. 107–8). Regarding the Elijah and Elisha stories that form a part of the Ahab and sons' story, see pp. 106–7 below. We can summarize by saying the "facts" of Ahab's rule seem to be the following, if we discount the theological editorializing and the various legendary accounts:

- Began his reign in the thirty-eighth year of Asa of Judah.
- Reigned twenty-two years.
- Married Jezebel, daughter of the king of the Sidonians, illustrating international connections and perspective. He appears to have dominated Judah and possibly also Tyre and Sidon who had become his allies with his marriage to a Sidonian queen.
- Caused the nation to prosper economically, allowing him to build an ivory house (i.e., one housing carved ivory objects) and a number of cities.
- Built a temple to Baal, evidently for his queen Jezebel, but he himself was primarily a worshiper of Yahweh.
- Fought the Assyrians as a member of a coalition that included the Aramaeans as an ally.
- Some think he died fighting the Assyrians, but the statement that he "slept with his fathers" implies a peaceful death.

Jehoshaphat (1 Kgs 22)

The reign of Asa's son Jehoshaphat is summarized in 1 Kgs 22:41-7. He is labeled as righteous by the biblical writer, though it is admitted that the high places continued to function. Of course they did! because the concept of centralized worship apparently arose only much later (see chapter 7, p. 123). The other point made is that he was a great warrior (1 Kgs 22:46). Earlier in 1 Kgs 22, he is supposed to have supported Ahab in one of his battles (exactly what this battle was is problematic because the enemy is said to be the Aramaeans, which evidently were not the enemy during Ahab's reign), which supports his reputation as a military leader, but we have no references to him outside the biblical text.

Jehoshaphat's treatment in 1 Kings is surprisingly brief. It is in the book of 2 Chronicles that we have an extensive discussion of his reign. The long additional section in 2 Chronicles 17, 19, and 20:1-30 has Jehoshaphat ruling a magnificent kingdom in which the Torah is taught, the nations round about send gifts, a formidable military force is organized, and a great coalition of Moab, Ammon, and Seir is defeated. In light of our downgrading of Solomon's grandiose kingdom (chapter 5) to something less impressive than that given by the biblical text, the description of Jehoshaphat's Judah according to 2 Chronicles seems rather unlikely. It exemplifies the way in which the Chronicler has enhanced the theological picture, compared to Kings, and is generally less trustworthy as a historical source.

Ahaziah and Jehoram of Israel and Joram and Ahaziah of Judah (1 Kgs 22:52 to 2 Kgs 9:29)

We actually have little information on the kings themselves (confined to 1 Kgs 22:52-4; 2 Kgs 3:1-3; 8:16-29; 9:15-29). The text gives priority to the story of Elisha the prophet, which complicates the narrative. Whereas a historian's interest is primarily on the political and related developments, the biblical writer was most impressed by the theological aspect of Elisha and his supposed activities. Basically, all the text says about the Israelite king, Ahaziah son of Ahab (who ruled only two years), is that he was wicked. The twelve years of his brother Jehoram are also dismissed as wicked, except that he removed the "pillars of Baal" set up by Ahab (2 Kgs 3:2). The circumstances and significance of this are not presented to the reader, but as mentioned earlier, Jezebel's cult was a private one confined to herself and her servants. It may be that Jehoram found the cult symbol of the "pillars of Baal" too provocative for the Israelite population and removed them for this reason.

The next king of Judah was Joram son of Jehoshaphat. Joram was said to be wicked and to have married Athaliah, sister of Ahab (2 Kgs 8:26, though 8:18 seems—mistakenly—to identify her as a daughter of Ahab). Also, under him Edom rebelled and broke away from Judahite rule (2 Kgs 8:20-22), according to the text. His son Ahaziah (whose uncle was Ahab of Israel) was king of Judah after Joram. He allied with Jehoram of Israel, and both fought against Hazael, king of the Aramaeans. Jehoram was wounded and went to Jezreel to recover. While Amaziah was visiting him there, Jehu rebelled and killed both Jehoram, king of Israel, and Amaziah, king of Judah, at the same time (2 Kgs 9:16-28).

An extra-biblical source that may tell us something about these events is the Tel Dan inscription. The following is my reading of the first fragment found in 1993 with a minimum of reconstruction:[16]

```
     ] my father went up [              ]
my father lay down (died?). He went to [Is-]
rael earlier in the land. My father [(or "in the land of my father")]
I—Hadad went before me [           ]
x my king. And I killed of [them char-]
ot and thousands (or 2,000) of riders [       ]
```

           king of Israel. And I kill[ed   ]
      xx "house of David" (*bytdwd*). And I set [   ]
           xx the land. They x[   ]
      another, and xxxx [ki-]
      ng over Is[rael   ]
      siege over [   ]

The second fragment (actually two fragments that fit together) does not clearly join onto the first. Some have tried to join the two or three fragments to reconstruct one long inscription. This may seem more satisfactory to some, but it strikes me as pure speculation. I read the second fragment as follows, with little hypothetical reconstruction:

           ] and cut [   ]
           ] battle/fought against xx [   ]
      ]x and went up the king x [   ]
      ] and Hadad made king [   ]
           ] I went up from Sheva'/seven [   ]
      seven]ty tied/harnessed x[   ]
      Jeho]ram son [   ]
      Ahaz]yahu son [   ]

This inscription has been subject to a number of interpretations, some of which are quite compelling, but they rely generally on the reconstruction of the original editors. However, it does seem to me that in the last two lines the restoration of "J(eh)oram" is virtually certain, and of "Ahaziah" quite reasonable. If so, this favors assigning the inscription to Hazael and the interpretations that follow from it.

We know of Hazael from the biblical text but especially from the Assyrian inscriptions. He was king of Damascus about 842 to 800 BCE. According to the biblical text, he was anointed king by the prophet Elisha (2 Kgs 8:7-15). He fought against Jehoram of Israel and Ahaziah of Judah at Ramoth-Gilead. According to the Assyrian texts, he was attacked and besieged in Damascus but managed to survive. He took Israelite territory in Gilead east of Jordan (2 Kgs 10:32-3). He also conquered the Philistine city of Gath and threatened Jerusalem (about 830 BCE) but was bought off (by Joash who was king of Judah at that time: 2 Kgs 12:18-19).

Basing themselves on the Tell Dan inscription a number of scholars have recently argued that Jehoram and Ahaziah were slain by Hazael, not Jehu. Can this interpretation be reconciled with the biblical text which has the two kings slain by Jehu? This is not difficult, since Hazael would have considered the actions of Jehu, who was his vassal, as his own actions. It was not an uncommon practice in royal inscriptions for the ruler to claim for himself the actions of his subordinates.

Elijah and Elisha and the Prophetic Narrative Cycle

As discussed in chapter 7 (p. 125), the prophetic narrative is an important feature in the books of Kings. In some cases (for example, the story of Ahab), for the reign of a particular king the biblical text devotes most of the space to stories about prophets. Elijah is a central figure in the Ahab story, and his successor Elisha is a major character in the stories of some of the successors to Ahab. The Elijah and Elisha stories take up a good deal of the reigns of the Omride kings. Some of these prophetic stories may be part of the earliest layer in the narrative of 1 and 2 Kings. Yet many of the prophetic stories are late. For example, as we have it the story in 1 Kgs 13 (about a prophecy against Jeroboam) comes from a time three hundred years later than Jeroboam, because of the reference to Josiah (1 Kgs 13:2). This is followed directly by another prophetic story, which has to do with the illness and subsequent death of Jeroboam's son and the prophecy of Ahijah that Jeroboam's family will be wiped out (1 Kgs 14:1-18).

The Elijah story makes him primarily an opponent of Baal. This might well be a correct memory, since there is likely to have been a "Yahweh-alone party," alongside the normally polytheistic society of Israel at the time.[17] If Elijah opposed Baal worship and even had Baal cult functionaries slaughtered, it is hardly any wonder that he attracted the wrath of Jezebel, since he was attacking her national god (on Jezebel and religion, see p. 101). The miracle stories, including his being taken up to heaven, are what we expect to find in such prophetic legends and are not of interest from a historical point of view (though they may tell something about the phenomenon of prophecy in Israel).

As with Elijah, the Elisha story may contain genuine remembrances of a prophet who was leader of a prophetic community but who occasionally interacted even with the royal court. Yet many of the details are nothing less than miraculous. Certain religious figures gather stories around themselves that include the performance of miracles and other supernatural acts. This process of embellishing the stories of "holy men" with wondrous deeds is known throughout history. In some cases, these stories simply confirm the importance of the prophetic figure to the community who remembered him and preserved his memory and story. These tell us about prophetic tradition but not much about history. Yet since kings at the time did consult prophetic and mantic figures, the details of the Elijah and Elisha stories that relate to kings like Ahab may have a foundation in the history of the king in question.

Jehu (2 Kgs 9–10)

With Jehu we once again have an Israelite ruler who is mentioned by the Assyrians. Jehu was the grandson of Nimshi (2 Kgs 9:2); for this reason, his dynasty is often referred to as the "Nimshides." According to the text of 2 Kings, Jehu began his reign with a blood bath: he first slaughtered the kings of both Israel and Judah, next he had Jezebel the queen mother killed by being thrown from her window; he then had seventy sons of Ahab executed by their guardians, relatives of Ahaziah slaughtered, and the other members of the house of Ahab killed. Immediately afterward, he had all the Baal worshipers assembled at the temple of Baal in Samaria and proceeded to butcher them. Despite this zeal, which Yahweh supposedly commended, Jehu still followed in the ways of Jeroboam. Hazael of Damascus began to take away territory, including the areas of Gilead and Bashan, northeast of the Sea of Galilee (2 Kgs 10:32-3).

Jehu's slaying of Jezebel is a curious incident. Since the Ahab story had painted her as completely wicked, it is hardly surprising that Jehu had her put to death.

But as already noted, her story is that of a foreign princess brought to Samaria as Ahab's wife and queen. She naturally brought her own cult, and her husband had a temple to Baal constructed for her. The biblical text claims that she persecuted the prophets of Yahweh (e.g., 1 Kgs 18:4), but religious persecution was not normally the actions of a polytheist. Furthermore, as noted above (p. 101), Ahab was himself a worshiper of Yahweh and is said to have consulted prophets of Yahweh about the future (1 Kgs 22:6). The children that he and Jezebel produced incorporated "Yahweh" in their names, indicating worship of Yahweh (1 Kgs 22:40; 2 Kgs 1:17; 3:1). It seems that Jezebel's persecutions took place only in reaction to Elijah's attack on the Baal cult personnel.

One will notice that the concern of the text is, once again, the Aramaeans. Nothing is said about the Assyrians, yet it was the Assyrians who made Jehu pay tribute to them. Shalmaneser III (who had fought Ahab) took tribute from Jehu, and he appears to be bowing to the Assyrian king on the Black Obelisk, which has the inscription: "At that time I received the tribute of the inhabitants of Tyre, Sidon, and of Jehu, son of Omri (*Ia-ú-a mâr Ḫu-um-ri-i*)."[18]

Much has been made by some writers about the designation of Jehu as "son of Omri." One explanation is that the writer of the inscription did not know that Jehu was not a son of Omri but a usurper to the throne. However, the other inscriptions of Shalmaneser show that the Sumerian ideogram rendered DUMU "son of" (read as *mār* in Akkadian) is used in a number of cases simply to designate a citizen of a particular country, though the person so designated usually happens to be the king. See the designation of Adramu, king of Hamath, as DUMU *A-gu-ú-si*; Aḫunu, king of Adini, as DUMU *A-di-ni*; and Ḫaiiānu, king of Gabbari, as DUMU *Gab-ba-ri* in the Kurkh Monolith.[19] Thus, I would argue that "son of Omri" simply means "king of Bit-Humri (Israel)."

Once the coalition assembled by the Aramaean ruler Hadadezer had broken up, Hazael alone stood against the Assyrians. Jehu, along with other small kingdoms of the region, submitted to the Assyrians and paid tribute. Campaigns against Hazael are mentioned for Shalmaneser III's eighteenth (841 BCE) and twenty-first years (838 BCE). After that the Assyrians ceased to march into the western part of their empire for several decades, leaving Damascus to dominate the region. The picture of Hazael and his son Bar-Hadad (called Ben-Hadad in the biblical text) as causing trouble for Israel is a realistic one (2 Kgs 10:32-33; 12:18-19; 13:3-6; see further pp. 109–10).

Athaliah and Joash of Judah (2 Kgs 11–12)

The account of Athaliah's attempted coup and the temple repair under Joash might not have come from a chronicle. Both involve priests and the temple, but whether they were based on oral tradition or a written source is unknown. As the daughter of Omri (or possibly Ahab), Athaliah had been married to Jehoram son of Jehoshaphat king of Judah (2 Kgs 8:18, 26). She was the mother to Jehoram's son Ahaziah (who was assassinated by Jehu), and she seized the throne of Judah after Ahaziah's death (2 Kgs 11:1-3). Jehoram's young son Joash was hidden away, however, to prevent his being killed by Athaliah, according to the text. After the passage of several years, the high priest Jehoiada arranged to have Joash crowned king, at which point Athaliah was herself taken out and executed. Whether things happened exactly as the text suggests is a question, but the basic scenario looks credible: such attempted coups and rivalry over the throne are widely attested in history. It is also likely that something was recorded in the royal chronicle, though whether any of the present biblical text is taken from this chronicle is uncertain.

The main action described for Joash is that he ordered money to be collected and used to repair the temple (2 Kgs 12). Religion also features in another event ascribed to his reign: after his coronation, the high priest supposedly had a temple to Baal torn down and its priest slain (2 Kgs 11:18). Although this might be possible, one must ask, When was this temple to Baal built and who by? One suspects a literary creation in which Jehu's destruction of the temple for Baal in Samaria has been duplicated here. Joash is said to be a righteous king: is he righteous because of the deeds recounted, or are the deeds created because he had a reputation of being righteous? Two episodes could have come from a court chronicle: the first is the attack of the Aramaean King Hazael (2 Kgs 12:18-19): this fits the archaeology of Gath; the other is that Joash was assassinated in a conspiracy (2 Kgs 12:21-22). This latter point is very intriguing: Why would his courtiers—their names are even given in the text—assassinate him? There was presumably a reason, but the text is silent on why this rather drastic deed took place.

Jehoahaz and Jehoash of Israel (2 Kgs 13)

The next two kings of Israel were Nimshides, part of the Jehu dynasty. First was Jehu's son Jehoahaz under whom Israel was harassed and its territory diminished by Hazael the Aramaean and his son Ben-hadad (Bar-Hadad in Aramaic: 2 Kgs 13:1-9). It is the small size of his army and other details that make some scholars think that some material in the Ahab cycle actually belongs to Jehoahaz but was taken over (by accident or design?) into the Ahab account (as discussed on pp. 102–3). He was followed by his son Jehoash about whom we know little. We have only the Elisha prophetic legend that says Jehoash could have destroyed the Aramaean oppression if he had only read Elisha's mind and extended his symbolic act!

The one item that could have come from a chronicle is that once Hazael died, Jehoash began to recover some towns (under his successor Ben-hadad/Bar-Hadad) that had been taken from Israel by Hazael (2 Kgs 13:25). The reason for this recovery is not given by the biblical text (which only relates it to the actions of Elisha), but the Assyrian records help us out. After many decades during which the Assyrians did not campaign to the Mediterranean, they once again intervened in the west under Adad-nirari III (c. 806–796).

We know that a coalition of small states, including Bar-Hadad, son of Hazael, attacked Zakkur of Hamath (according to the Zakkur Inscription) and apparently went on to challenge the Assyrians. Not only does the biblical text have the sequence Hazael, followed by Bar-Hadad (Hebrew Ben-Hadad), but the "savior" of 2 Kings 13:5 is probably a reference to the Assyrian help. The Zakkur inscription probably alludes to this same anti-Assyrian coalition, whereas Zakkur is pro-Assyrian and seems to have been delivered by Assyrian intervention. The Joash of Israel who is being relieved of the oppression from Bar-Hadad is mentioned in the el-Rimah Assyrian inscription as paying tribute to the Assyrians.

Finally, the fall of Damascus about 802 BCE, as described in the el-Rimah and other inscriptions, would have taken the pressure off Israel and others who were under the yoke of Damascus. About 780 to 775 BCE Shamshi-ilu the Assyrian commander for the region collected tribute from Ḥadiiāni of Damascus. This would suggest that Damascus was not able to do just anything it wished. Thus, although the biblical text cannot be confirmed in detail, the general picture given fits the situation in the last part of the ninth century and beginning of the eighth, as we know it from extra-biblical sources.

Amaziah and Azariah (Uzziah) of Judah (2 Kgs 14:1-22; 15:1-7)

Amaziah is supposed to have been righteous like his father Joash (though the high places were admittedly not removed, but we would not have expected them to be objected to at this time). Unsurprisingly, he executed those who had assassinated his father. He supposedly defeated the Edomites and captured Sela. But when he challenged Jehoash of Israel to battle, Amaziah was soundly defeated, captured, had to pay tribute and send hostages, and have part of the wall of Jerusalem destroyed. Like his father, he was slain in a conspiracy (though he fled to Lachish, trying to escape). All of this is plausible, but none of it can be confirmed because there are no extra-biblical sources. Unfortunately, there are still some major disputes about interpreting the archaeology of Edom that might otherwise help us here.

Amaziah was succeeded by Azariah (called Uzziah in 2 Chronicles 26). Once again, he is supposed to have been righteous, even though he did not remove the high places. In other words, he followed the normal religious expectations of his own time rather than the later judgment of the biblical writers (see chapter 7, p. 123). His reward was to be stricken with leprosy, and his son Jotham became co-ruler (2 Kgs 15:5). (Although co-rulership is often postulated in order to overcome chronological problems, this is one of the few actually attested in the text.)

2 Chronicles 26:5-20 is a curious text that gives all sorts of information not in the text of Kings: Uzziah is supposed to have made various conquests against the Philistines, Arabs, and Ammonites, to have built major fortifications and expanded the military, and to have extended cultivation and prosperity. But then in a state of hubris, he tried to offer incense in the temple, against the protests of the priests, and was struck with leprosy. Again, this shows the bias of the biblical writer, who was probably a priest or Levite.

In fact, the king was the chief religious figure in the kingdom and had every right to offer in the temple (see chapter 7, p. 124). David and Solomon had offered sacrifices, as was normal for Judahite kings at this time. The Chronicler's version seems to be the product of a vivid imagination, based on later priestly prejudice. Yes, Uzziah evidently contracted leprosy (this information probably came from a royal chronicle), but it was hardly because he offered incense in the temple.

Jeroboam (II) of Israel (2 Kgs 14:23-29)

Once again, the biblical text makes light of an Israelite king that other sources indicate was a significant ruler. The main judgment of the text is that he was wicked, yet it knows that he restored the northern part of Israel at the expense of the Aramaeans: 2 Kgs 14:26-27 is almost apologetic that this recovery was allowed to happen! The exact territory recovered is unclear since the portion of the text that might have come from a chronicle (2 Kgs 14:28) seems to be in disorder; the suggestion is that much of Syria was taken, but this is unlikely. The important historical point, though, is that Jeroboam II reversed the ascendancy of Damascus over Israel; however, it should be noted that the reason is primarily that Assyria had returned to the west and was putting unstoppable pressure on the Aramaeans.[20] Jeroboam took advantage of the Assyrian attack to open another front against Bar-Hadad, ruler of Damascus.

In addition to the references in the Assyrian inscriptions and the biblical material, we have the so-called Samarian ostraca, which appear now to be dated to the reigns of Joash and Jeroboam II. These are receipts for the delivery of various products (usually wine and other food stuffs) to the palace in Samaria. Scholars have interpreted these as showing that Omri set up a military regime in which the court moved around the country, but the leading families were linked to it by a requirement to contribute products from their own estates to the court. The Samarian ostraca consist of more than a hundred receipts written on pot sherds, which was customary at the time when paper had not been invented and writing on papyrus or vellum was expensive. An example of one of them is the following (Samarian Ostracon 58): "In year 15, to Bedeiah, [wine of] the vineyard of the Tell." One of their contributions to history is the many names of individuals and families in Israel. As will be discussed in chapter 7 (p. 118), they show that Baal was worshiped alongside Yahweh in Israel at that time.

Zechariah, Shallum, and Menahem of Israel (2 Kgs 15:8-22)

Jeroboam's son Zechariah lasted only six months before being assassinated in a conspiracy by Shallum, but the latter was then killed only a month later by Menahem. The text says that Zechariah was wicked, though exactly how he accomplished this wickedness in a reign of half a year is not stated. Strangely, no such condemnation is made of Shallum, though this was probably an oversight on the part of the writer.

Menahem began his rule not only with executing Shallum but then attacking Tiphsah and committing an atrocity against the inhabitants for not submitting (which was to massacre the people and rip open all the pregnant women). But the main event was that Tiglath-pileser III (here called Pul) of Assyria came against Israel and required a tribute of a thousand silver talents. Menahem raised the funds by requiring 50 shekels from all the "men of substance" (if this is what the Hebrew phrase means) in the kingdom. Since there are usually 3,000 shekels in a talent, this suggests sixty thousand "men of substance." This sounds exaggerated, but did all the tribute come from their contribution? Are these figures even accurate, or might there be scribal errors? The problem is that Tiglath-pileser's tribute list in the Calah Annals includes Menahem of Samaria as one who paid tribute to him, but the amount is not given.[21]

Jotham and Ahaz of Judah (2 Kgs 15:32–16:20)

Uzziah's son Jotham is said to have been righteous, even though the high places remained in place; once again the reason for this judgment that Jotham was righteous is unclear. Apart from some renovations to the temple, the main claim to fame of his reign, as mentioned by the text, is that Rezin of Damascus and Pekah of Israel began an assault on Judah. Also, Rezin took back the Red Sea port city Elath from Judah (2 Kgs 16:6), though the text seems confused to whether it was "Aramaeans" or "Edomites" who settled there ("Aramaean" and "Edomite" are very similar in Hebrew).

The main attack on Judah came under Jotham's son Ahaz, however, according to both 2 Kgs 16:5-9 and Isaiah 7. They failed to overcome Israel because Ahaz sent a bribe to Tiglath-pileser III; that is, he made himself a vassal of Assyria, which meant that he was required to pay an annual tribute. But Assyria now attacked Damascus and killed Rezin.[22] The Assyrian king also removed Pekah from being king over Samaria and replaced him with Hoshea (for more details, see next section). The main part of the account is once again about a religious matter. Ahaz is supposed to have engaged in a religious apostasy by building another altar in the temple, alongside the original. This altar was possibly a copy of an Assyrian altar, which probably made the matter seem even worse to the author of Kings. In order to pay tribute to the Assyrians, he stripped metal from the temple.

Last Kings of Israel and the Fall of Samaria (2 Kgs 15:23-31; 17)

Menahem's son had been Pekahiah; the only datum in the text is that his two-year reign was another example of wickedness. He was assassinated by his aide, Pekah, who seized the throne. At some point, Pekah apparently allied with Rezin the Aramaean (discussed in the previous section). Although the "Syro-Ephraimite war" (2 Kgs 15:29; 16:5-9; Isa. 7) is not described as such in the Assyrian annals, it is compatible with everything so far known. In the end, though, both Rezin and his alleged ally Pekah lost out. Tiglath-pileser III took Damascus about 732 BCE and exiled many of the Aramaeans.[23]

The Assyrian king had Pekah removed for disloyalty and replaced by Hoshea.[24] The Assyrian account is remarkably close to 2 Kgs 15:30. Perhaps the one discrepancy is whether Tiglath-pileser or Hoshea deposed Pekah, but this is probably a matter of wording. The removal of Pekah is not likely to have happened without Tiglath-pileser's ultimate say-so, and one suspects that Hoshea acted only when he knew that he had Assyrian backing. Hoshea, the last king of Israel, was apparently put on the throne by the Assyrian King Tiglath-pileser III (745–727 BCE).

This at least is the Assyrian's version, even though the biblical account sounds a bit different (2 Kgs 15:30, but compare 17:1-3). At any rate, the passage claims that Hoshea plotted to break free from the Assyrian yoke by appealing to So of Egypt (2 Kgs 17:4).

The passage is straightforward and, although it is not mentioned in the extant Assyrian annals, it fits with their statements on Hoshea and the fall of Samaria.[25] But who is this So, king of Egypt? The name (Egyptian *Wsrkn*), as well as the historical circumstances of the time, correspond to Osorkon IV.[26] Osorkon evidently felt that he had nothing to gain by attempting to support Hoshea and refused, which made it easy for Shalmaneser V (726–722 BCE) to punish Hoshea. However, a few years later Osorkon did send a military force to help out Hanunu of Gaza who rebelled against Assyrian rule. In this case, the Assyrian king Sargon II (721–705 BCE) defeated the combined forces of Gaza and Egypt, and Osorkon sent a gift (or tribute) of twelve fine horses to Sargon. Osorkon had provided aid to Hanunu for the simple reason that Gaza served as a buffer state between Assyria and his territory in Egypt (which was the eastern part of the Delta).[27]

The Mesopotamian sources also fill in a great deal about the siege and capture of Samaria and deportation of many Israelites, but they also raise a number of questions. The biblical text refers to Shalmaneser (2 Kgs 17:3; 18:9) who was the Assyrian King Shalmaneser V (727–722 BCE); however, the Assyrian inscriptions mention the two Assyrian Emperors Shalmaneser V and Sargon II (722–705 BCE), who were probably brothers. The question is, which king captured Samaria and deported its inhabitants? Although the biblical text says that Shalmaneser captured Samaria, Sargon in his inscriptions claims to have conquered the city.

In the past some have accepted the claims of one king, and some have accepted the claims of the other. Yet the argument that the various sources can be reconciled is probably correct, though more than one solution is possible. The account in 2 Kgs 17:3-6 that this siege and capture of Samaria took place in the time of Shalmaneser V is supported by the *Babylonian Chronicle* (i 27–31), but since he died about that time, Sargon may have been the one to finish the task, at least the removal of the population (if the city had already fallen under Shalmaneser). One recent persuasive thesis has been presented that there were two conquests of Samaria, one by Shalmaneser V in 723 BCE and another by Sargon II in 720 BCE in response to a rebellion of Ilu-bi'di of Hamath.[28]

It seems likely that both Shalmaneser V and Sargon II were in some way involved in the end of Samaria. Yet there is no evidence in the archaeology that the city was destroyed. Perhaps the biblical text does not clearly envisage a destruction of the city, but the archaeological evidence also seems to be against a wholesale deportation of the population, contra 2 Kings 17. Archaeology suggests that a small portion of the Israelite population was removed and replaced by outside settlers, but not the wholesale removal of Israelites as the biblical text claims.[29] As to the question of whether the Israelites were really taken to the places alleged in 2 Kgs 17:6 and of whether peoples from the places listed in 2 Kgs 17:24 were actually brought in, there is now some evidence that some movement of populations between the two regions actually took place.[30] But the great deportation as described in the biblical text is definitely to be queried. The evidence is that most of the Israelite population continued to live where it had always been.

Conclusions

This chapter has looked at the material stretching from the death of Solomon to the fall of Samaria. We have no extra-biblical information on the splitting of the kingdom under Rehoboam and Jeroboam, and it is difficult to verify the details. Yet there are two factors that suggest the biblical account embodies actual events, at least in outline. First, we have clear evidence in extra-biblical sources of two kingdoms in Palestine, the Kingdom of Israel and the Kingdom of Judah. We also have evidence that this division between Judah and Israel was a long-standing situation: what was unusual was that they were temporarily united under a single ruler in the time of David and Solomon. The second factor confirming the situation is that the biblical narrative leads up to Omri and Ahab who are known from inscriptions of surrounding nations.

Thus, most likely after Solomon's death, the polity over which he ruled reverted to its natural division into two communities. It is in the period of history covered by 1 Kings 16 to 2 Kings 17 that we start to have considerable extra-biblical parallels. There are many statements that are supported by these extra-biblical sources or that at least have a prima facie probability, even if there is no external support. Yet if we look carefully at the material of this text, we see few passages of any length that seem to be straightforward historical narratives. For example, the reign of Omri is described succinctly and with the surface appearance of factuality, but the reign of Ahab is dominated by stories about the prophets Elijah and Elisha.

In some instances, we evidently have material from a court chronicle or the like (though it may be a paraphrase of such a chronicle rather than directly excerpted from the chronicle itself). But the quality of the material is made clearer in many cases when it is contrasted with the parallel account in 2 Chronicles. Where the latter has a more extensive account, it is obvious most of the time that it did not have additional sources or—if so—that they were not of the same quality as those in the books of Kings. So we can conclude that in spite of all the necessary qualifications the narrative in the books of Kings has useful data for reconstructing the history of Israel and Judah, if it is used carefully and critically.

7

From Polytheism to Worship of One God: Religion in Ancient Israel

This chapter will be eye-opening to many, but some may find it disconcerting or even downright sacrilegious. This is because it may go contrary to preconceived views about Christian or Jewish religion. Indeed, it will present a picture that—at least in part—differs from the picture of the biblical text. But those who are willing to come with me through the text and the evidence of history will find an exciting odyssey that is religious affirming rather than destructive. For the biblical text itself gives surprising data that is often overlooked even by those very familiar with the text itself.[1]

The Bible pictures the Israelite religion as pure, monotheistic, and different from the false worship of all other nations and peoples, especially the Canaanites. This is the surface image, at least, and causes us little surprise. On the other hand, if one takes a broader view, religion in early Israel was typical Northwest Semitic belief and worship. This is shown by several lines of evidence:

- The variety of names for the Israelite deity.
- The picture shown by certain early biblical texts that have escaped pious editing.
- The theophoric names of Israelites, that is, the personal names that have a divine name incorporated within them.
- The evidence found in some inscriptions and iconographic images.
- Certain finds of archaeology.

This is not to deny that Israelite worship developed unique characteristics and came to establish strong boundaries against other religions, but this took a long time to develop.

Divine Names in the Biblical Text

The name most frequently associated with the God of Israel in the biblical text is *Yhwh*. The vowels have not been preserved, only the consonants, though it is often reconstructed as *Yahweh* based on its appearance as *Iaō* in later Greek and Latin texts[2] and on the form of the name as it occurs in theophorous names in vocalization in the biblical text (-*yāh* and -*yāhû*).

We shall discuss the many occurrences of the name Yahweh presently but first let us notice some of the other names and titles used for the deity. For many other names and titles occur in the biblical text, though not easily recognized in English versions because they are often rendered in Bible translations as epithets or descriptions rather than as names.

One important name is that of *El*, which is used for the Israelite God but can also mean just "god" in a generic sense. This is in line with much Northwest Semitic usage in which *El* (or the earlier form *Ilu*) could stand both for the head of the pantheon (the god El) and for the word "god, divinity" in general. Another term that can be both a divine name and also a generic word for "god" is *Eloah*. This is found in several biblical passages (e.g., Isa. 44:8; Psa. 18:32; 2 Chron. 32:15; Dan. 11:37-8), but most often it appears as a plural, *Elohim*. The plural form has an unusual usage in the Bible that seems to be unique to Israel. When used with a plural verb, it simply means "gods" and refers to non-Israelite gods. But it occurs frequently with a singular verb (equivalent to saying in English, "the Gods is") where it refers exclusively to the Israelite God.

Another divine name is *Shaddai*, used, for example, in a number of passages in Genesis (17:1; 28:3; 35:11; 48:3; 49:25), sometimes combined with the name El. It is also the divine name found through most of the poem of Job and seems to be the prime divinity for the original composer of the book's core (the name Yahweh occurs in Job only in the introduction and conclusion). Genesis 14:18 attests the deity *El Elyon*, not known anywhere else. However, the name *Elyon* by itself also occurs in Num. 24:16, Deut. 32:8, and Isa. 14:14, while the Ugaritic equivalent (`ly`) is applied to Baal.[3] The point is that these other names may once have applied to other members of the pantheon (just as El did) but have become assimilated to the one God Yahweh.

A number of these divine names have been used to make up names of Israelites as known in the Bible. That is, the personal name incorporates one or more of the divine names. These are known as "theophorous names." The names with El included Israel, Elijah, Elisha, Samuel, and many more. There are also names with Shaddai (e.g., Num. 1:5-6: Shedeur, Zurishaddai; Num. 1:12: Ammishaddai). But perhaps most interesting are the many Israelite personal names that include the divine name Baal. Considering the biblical polemic against Baal, one might have expected not to see such names, but they are found in surprising contexts. One of Saul's sons has a name compounded with Baal: Eshbaal ("man of Baal") and Jonathan's son was Meribbaal. These names are often overlooked because the Samuel texts substitute surrogate names compounded with the word "shame" (Ishbosheth [2 Sam. 2:8]; Mephibosheth [2 Sam. 21:7]), but they are correctly preserved in 1 Chronicles (8:33-34; 9:39-40).

Early Israelite Deities and Worship

There is evidence that the general worship of Yahweh was widespread in Israel (which we shall look at in more detail in the next section), but the Israelite people were not originally monotheistic. This is shown by a number of passages. Some biblical texts suggest a time when Yahweh was only one deity alongside others; indeed, some passages make him a subordinate to El. Scholars had long wondered whether the reading of the Hebrew text of Deut. 32:8 was not due to a later editing because of the Septuagint text, which seemed to presuppose a different Hebrew original. The suggestion of another more original Hebrew reading seems now to have been confirmed by a Hebrew manuscript from Qumran (4QDeut[j] = 4Q37) which reads "[according to the number of] the sons of God" (*bny 'lhym*). The passage goes on to say that Jacob is Yahweh's portion (Deut. 32:9). Putting all this information together indicates that Deut. 32:8-9 originally read something along the lines of the following:

> When Elyon gave the inheritance of the nations,
> When he divided the sons of Adam (or man),
> He established the boundaries of the peoples
> According to the number of the sons of El.
> For Yahweh's lot is his people
> And Jacob his inherited portion.

This suggests that Yahweh (as one of these sons of El) received Israel as his particular inheritance, whereas the other sons of El received other peoples as their inheritance.

One image found extensively among the ancient Near Eastern peoples is that of the divine assembly or divine council in which the chief deity presides over a variety of gods. Perhaps one of the clearest examples of Yahweh himself having a divine council is 1 Kgs 22:19-22 in which he presides over the "host of heaven." The heavenly council in Israel originally seems to have consisted of El as the "chairman," with other subordinate deities—including Yahweh—sitting around the table. Such a situation in which Yahweh is merely one among the sons of El in the divine assembly is found in Psa. 89:7-8, which reads (literally):

> For who in heaven compares to Yahweh?
> Who is like Yahweh among the sons of the Elim (gods)?
> El creates awe in the council of the Holy Ones.
> He is great and strikes fear in all about him.

Here Yahweh is a son of El, among other sons, even if he is said to be incomparable to his fellow sons of El. Similarly, Psa. 82:1 says, "God stands in the divine council, he judges in the midst of the gods."

A number of other passages also give a mythical picture of Yahweh not found in most biblical texts (see chapter 2). Just to give a quick reminder: the Ugaritic myths speak of a battle in which Baal defeats Yamm, while some passages speak of other monsters of chaos defeated by Baal. Similarly, the Babylonian creation epic *Enuma Elish* speaks of the god Marduk's defeat of Tiamat from whose body he created the heavens and the earth. Unlike Genesis 1, these passages suggest that God created by defeating various monsters of chaos who appear as supernatural beings. The Hebrew and Ugaritic texts are not only similar in theme but even share some of the same basic vocabulary, since the Hebrew and Ugaritic languages are closely related.

These various passages are isolated survivals of older beliefs that had been obliterated or reinterpreted by the dominant monotheistic view of Yahweh that controlled the final shaping of the biblical text. A few verses escaped editing, however, confirming what we now know from inscriptions: Yahweh was originally conceived as one god among many, perhaps even subordinate to and a son of El. He created by fighting and defeating various monsters of chaos, such as Leviathan, Tannin, and Rahab, much as Baal did in the Ugaritic texts. When monotheism became the dominant view, these older views were simply expunged or, in some cases, they were reinterpreted so as not to be an embarrassment to monotheistic views.

That Israel and Judah were not originally monotheistic is indicated by the Samaria Ostraca (chapter 6, p. 111). A variety of theophorous names are found in the texts known so far; of these, eleven are compounded with Yahweh while six have Baal. There is no way to see any social distinction in the names: one has the impression that these were common, ordinary names about which people would not have thought very much except perhaps in a cultic context. It would appear that Baal and Yahweh were worshiped happily side by side.

This original polytheistic worship is partly disguised by the later biblical editors who charge the Israelites with a penchant for "falling away" from true worship into paganism, idolatry and worship of other gods. Actually, they were not "falling away"; rather, monotheistic worship had not yet been established among the people. To balance this, one might well point to the opposition to Baal worship in the time of Elijah. However, it is not entirely clear that this is as simple as it looks, for the "Baal" of Jezebel was most likely a Phoenician god—and thus a foreign cult—introduced into Israel. It was symbolic of a foreign queen and would have been opposed by certain traditionalists. The fact that all the Baal worshipers could supposedly fit into the small Baal temple (2 Kgs 10:18-28) is evidence that this particular form of Baal worship was not a widespread alternative to Yahweh worship.

When we look more carefully, we find that worship of Yahweh was also well established, as clearly shown by the names found in Ahab's family and associates. Ahab's chief minister was named Obadiah ("servant of Yahweh": 1 Kgs 18:3) and his two sons had theophorous names that included Yahweh in them (Ahaziah and Jehoram), showing that Ahab was a Yahweh worshiper. Finally, the prophets Ahab consulted were prophets of Yahweh (1 Kgs 22:5-28). Although the text accuses him of Baal worship (1 Kgs 16:31-32), we see no actual evidence that he promoted Baal worship beyond the royal cult specifically established for his wife. The opposition of Elijah and others was probably political opposition to Jezebel, even if disguised as religious piety.

It is true that the text as found in the final form of the Bible presents this alternative worship in Israel and Judah as an act of apostasy, but this was a much later perspective: at the time, there was no hint that such worship was criticized or opposed. If there was criticism, it was likely to have been a minority movement. One theory is that there was a "Yahweh-alone" movement.[4] This is the view that certain groups and individuals favored the sole worship of Yahweh, with other gods ignored. This was not necessarily monotheism, since such worship could focus on one god without denying the existence of other gods—what we call *henotheism*.

Evidence for worship of multiple deities in ancient Israel is found in an Assyrian inscription of Sargon II relating to the plunder of Samaria about 720 BCE. The Nimrud Prism states as follow (4.29–33, minor restorations not indicated):

29) With the power of the great gods, my lords,
30) against them I fought.
31) 27,280 persons with their chariots
32) and the gods in whom they trusted, as spoil
33) I counted.

He was evidently referring to Israelite statues of gods that he took away as spoil. That is, the temple(s) of Samaria contained images of more than one god, and the Assyrians took these away as spoil as was their custom.

Finally, the Jewish military colony at Elephantine (see chapter 9, pp. 163–6 for further information) was almost certainly pre-Persian, probably being established during the Neo-Babylonian or possibly even in the Assyrian period before the fall of Jerusalem in 587/586 BCE. The community had its own temple to *Yhw*, a name probably pronounced Yahu or Yaho, a form of Yahweh. A list of contributors to the cult indicates that other divinities also had a place. Specifically listed are Eshem-Bethel and Anat-Bethel and Anat-Yahu.[5] It has been suggested that these were actually only hypostases of Yahweh. This might well have been the case by the Persian period, though there is no doubt that they originated as goddess figures in the earlier Israelite religion. Perhaps we are witnessing an evolution toward monotheism in this late period.

Archaeology has also given a good deal of information that confirms this textual picture.[6] Just to give a couple of examples, one of the most striking objects is the Taanach altar, usually dated to the tenth century and found at what seems to be a *bamah*, or open air, cult site. The Goddess Asherah seems to have a prominent place on it. Another striking object is the bronze bull of the "Bull Site." Again, it was found as the focal point of a cult site. It is not always possible to tell who used a particular cult site or the god represented (is the bull Yahweh or Baal?), but the archaeology amply demonstrates the variety of worship that texts have also delineated.

Yahweh, a God Unique to Israel?

The deity most frequently and strongly associated with ancient Israel is Yahweh. Apart from the biblical text, the name Yahweh is clearly attested first in the Moabite stone or Mesha Stela from the ninth century BCE (on this, see chapter 6, pp. 102–3). The Moabite King Mesha took the city of Nebo from Israel and dedicated the "vessels of Yahweh" to his god Chemosh. Among the Khirbet Beit Lei inscriptions (about 600 BCE) is a reference to a Yahweh who is apparently the god of Jerusalem.[7] The name is also found in a seal from the early eighth century, allegedly found in Jerusalem, which reads "Miqneyaw servant of Yahweh" (*Mqnyw 'bd Yhwh*). The ostraca from Arad dated to about 600 BC contain a number of blessings and invocations in the name of Yahweh.[8] There is also a reference to the "house of Yahweh" (*byt Yhwh*), which is probably the local temple (Arad Ostracon 18.9). The Lachish ostraca, evidently from the last days of the kingdom of Judah, contain a number of invocations using the name of Yahweh ("may Yahweh give health/good news"; "as Yahweh lives").[9]

The linguistic data attesting worship of Yahweh come from what were both the Northern Kingdom and the Southern Kingdom. Yahweh appears to have been a national or ethnic god, much as Chemosh was the god of the Moabites, Qaus the god of the Edomites, and so on (cf. 1 Kgs 11:33). This does not mean that Yahweh was the only god worshiped in Israel and Judah, as we have already seen, but he seems to have been the main object of devotion for most Israelites. His is the name most widely attested. Where did Yahweh originate? An indication of where the name originated may be found in some Egyptian inscriptions of the Late Bronze Age (about 1550–1200 BCE): "the land of the Shasu, Yahu." Although the name seems to be geographical, it is possible that there is a connection with the divinity Yahweh. Thus, to the best of our current knowledge Yahweh originated in Palestine and his worship was confined to the peoples of Palestine.

However, evidence has more recently been found for Yahweh worship in the area of Syria in a text from Hamath.[10] But there is no supporting evidence that Yahweh was part of general worship over the region. Rather, it looks more likely that Yahweh worship had been transplanted from Palestine in some way. In all the inscriptions and linguistic data from the surrounding region, there is nothing to indicate that Yahweh was worshiped generally over the entire region.

Recent finds have been even more revealing. An inscription found in 1975/1976 at Kuntillet Ajrud in the Negev (dated about the eighth century BCE) is conventionally read, "I blessed you by Yahweh of Samaria and by his Asherah."[11] Similarly, in Khirbet el-Qom near Hebron, another inscription was been found and dated to the seventh century.[12] It is very difficult to read, but the consensus is that it contains a similar statement. *These inscriptions indicate that Asherah is Yahweh's consort.*

FIGURE 7.1 *The Kuntillet Ajrud inscription that depicts Israel's God with a consort.*

The biblical text itself suggests goddess worship in several passages: it refers to "Asherah," though at times this seems to designate a cult object, especially when appearing in the masculine plural ("Asherim"). Yet a number of passages seem definitely to refer to a goddess. 1 Kings 15:13 mentions the cult object made for Asherah. This was presumably in the temple; indeed, 2 Kings 23 vv. 4 and 7 mentions vessels of Asherah (among others) and cult personnel dedicated to Asherah in the Jerusalem temple, and 2 Kgs 21:7 also speaks of an image of Asherah in the temple. 1 Kgs 18:19 designates "the prophets of Asherah," alongside the prophets of Baal, which can only be a reference to a goddess. Jer. 44:17–19 and 25 mention worship of the "Queen of Heaven" who is likely to have been Asherah.

Development of Monotheism

The discussion so far has shown how worship in Israel and Judah was polytheistic through the monarchy, even though worship of Yahweh as unique to Israel received special attention. The criticism of worship of gods other than Yahweh comes mainly from the editors of the text who worked at a later time, when monotheism was the general view. The question, then, is how early monotheism developed. In the biblical text Yahweh is clearly equated with El and with other divine names. It would not be surprising for El and Yahweh to be assimilated over time even if they were once separate deities. The various other male deities are also equated with Yahweh (except for Baal). In my view, we find monotheism already in Isaiah 40–55 (often called Second Isaiah) with the author's denial of the existence of other gods: Yahweh alone is without beginning or end, and there is nothing like him (Isa. 46:9; 48:12-13). This looks to me like monotheism, and many other scholars would agree with this conclusion.[13]

Astral imagery of the late eighth and seventh centuries had disappeared from seals and seal impressions of the Jerusalem elite by the early sixth. Also, we find that the blessing and salvation functions of Yahweh's "Asherah," found earlier in several inscriptions, had ceased by the sixth century, apparently absorbed by Yahweh by the time of the Lachish and Arad ostraca (somewhere around 600 BCE). This has been interpreted as indirect evidence of Josiah's reform and a move in the direction of monotheism.

Apart from the biblical text, one of the first and best indications of monotheistic, aniconic worship is found in Hecataeus of Abdera, a Greek writing about 300 BC: "But he [Moses] had no images whatsoever of the gods made for them, being of the opinion that God is not in human form; rather the Heaven that surrounds the earth is alone divine, and rules the universe."[14]

Other Aspects of Israelite Religion

Apart from the question of Israel's deity, other aspects of Israelite worship and belief can be briefly outlined here.

Worship in Ancient Israel

Any description of Israelite religion must take stock of its complexities: it involved prayer, ritual activity (which apparently included singing), and sacred days and religious festivals that included feasting and social events. Yet one cannot get away from the fact that the sacrificial cult, especially blood sacrifice of certain animals, lay at the heart of worship in Israel. The idea of real sacrifice seems to be ubiquitous among human societies the world over. Even those which have abandoned animal sacrifice in their contemporary form, especially in the developed countries, have sacrifice as a part of their past. Christianity of course has the sacrifice of Christ at its center, but sacrifice is an important metaphor in most religions even if literal sacrifice no longer exists.

A number of theories have been advanced as to the meaning of sacrifice. One is the idea of a gift that might serve to appease the wrath of a god or to evoke his good will toward the offeror or both. The idea of a gift to the deity is found behind a number of sacrifices, but it is not a universal explanation since there is much about sacrifice that it does not explain. Another idea is communion with the deity, since in many sacrifices most of the animal was consumed at the sanctuary by the family of the sacrificer. Yet many sacrifices cannot easily be seen as a meal with God. For example, burnt offerings could hardly be a communal meal since they are entirely burned on the altar. A popular idea is that of substitution: the idea that the victim takes the place of or in some way represents the offeror.

Regardless of what metaphor the sacrifice might function as, central to most sacrifices are the notions of expiation, cleansing, and reestablishment of cosmic—or at least microcosmic—harmony. If evil cannot be removed, sin wiped away, pollution purified, and harmony restored, there would be little point in sacrifice. Therefore, regardless of the precise terms in which sacrifices are conceived (substitution, ritual detergent, scapegoat), the desired outcome is clear. In the scapegoat sort of ceremony, the negative deeds are heaped onto the head of the victim (the scapegoat) who is then separated from the community. In other cases, the victim is in some way identified with the offeror even if precise identification is not required. The laying of the hands on the victim by the offeror in Israelite sacrifice may have a function along these lines. But regardless of the rite, the desire is to cause the sins, pollutions, illness, or troubles to vanish.

We also have to recognize what is often overlooked by modern readers of the Bible: the Israelite cult, like all religious ritual, was extremely meaningful to the participants even if we do not always understand it from our time and culture millennia later. A number of recent studies have focused on the symbolism of the cult and attempted to decipher the priestly worldview which lay behind it. For example, some have argued that a complex creation theology is presupposed and represented by the cult. The priestly view had a cosmological and sociological dimension, as well as a cultic one. To express this, it made distinctions between holy and profane, clean and unclean, life and death, order and chaos. As for the various sacrifices carried out in Israel, there is a detailed description in Leviticus 1–7.[15] These are the

Burnt Offering ('ōlāh) Lev. 1:2-9; 6:1-6.
Cereal Offering (minḥāh) Lev. 2:1-16; 6:7-11.

Sacrifice of Well-being (šĕlamîm) Lev. 3:1-16; 7:11-18; 7:28-34, sometimes translated as "Peace Offering." Three sorts of sacrifice seem to be included: (1) the *freewill offering (nĕdāvāh)*, (2) the *votive offering (neder)*, and (3) the *thanksgiving offering (tōdāh)*, though some passages suggest that this last is a separate offering (cf. Lev. 22:21, 29; Jer. 17:26; 2 Chron. 29:31-33; 33:16).

Sin Offering (ḥaṭṭā't) Lev. 4:1-35; 6:17-22.

Guilt Offering ('āšām) Lev. 5:1-26; 7:1-10, though the distinction between the "sin offering" and the "guilt offering" is not clear.

The *Daily Offering (tāmîd)* Lev. 6:12-16 was a special sacrifice, offered twice a day, once in the morning and once in the evening.

The daily offering was extremely important in antiquity because it was the chief sign that the temple was functioning, with God accessible to the people. The times when the daily sacrifice was stopped were times of dire consequences, as when the temple was destroyed by Nebuchadnezzer or the Romans, or when the sacrifice was stopped by force in the time of the Maccabees.

Worship Places: Temples or Sacred Space

In ancient Israel, various worship activities naturally took place in the home, especially prayer. But the main regular worship places for the community were high places and temples, until the end of the monarchy. Synagogues evidently arose only in the third century BCE in Egypt and did not spread to Palestine itself until the first century CE (or possibly the first century BCE). The main function of the synagogue seems to have been a substitute for the temple which was inaccessible most of the time to Jews outside Palestine. But certain cultic activities could take place only in the temple, especially that of animal sacrifice, which was central to Israelite worship as we have just discussed.

Although the Hebrew Bible rails against high places in many passages, it is clear that high places were important places of worship in the pre-monarchic and monarchic periods.[16] The high place was a type of temple, but other more conventional temples seem to have existed as well: the Jerusalem temple, apparently one at Bethel, another at Tel Dan and, at least in the postexilic period, one on Mt Gerizim. The Idumaean ostraca of the fourth century BCE refer to a "house of Yahu" which is probably a local temple.[17] One of the best-attested temples outside Jerusalem is the one built by the Judahite community at Elephantine in Egypt and functioned mainly during the Persian period. Also, at the time of the Maccabean revolt (discussed in chapter 11), the displaced high priest Onias built a temple in Leontopolis in Egypt. Thus, the idea that the Jerusalem temple was the only legitimate one was only late in development and was also not always observed, even by religious Jews.

Cultic Personnel and Other Religious Specialists: Priests, Prophets, Sages, and Others

Anthropologists sometimes refer to various religious figures in society as "religious specialists." We find a number of these in ancient Israel, as described in my study,

Priests, Prophets, Diviners, Sages: Religious Specialists in Ancient Israel. We can briefly outline these figures and their functions here.

First, there is the *king*. This may seem surprising to many, but multiple biblical passages make clear that the king is the primary cultic figure, in charge of the temple, all personnel who served there, and the practice of religion generally (1 Kgs 4:2-5, 6-8; 1 Chron. 22:1–23:6). Of course, it is not surprising that attempts were made (by priestly editors!) to configure the text in such a way that the king was subject to the priests (e.g., Deut. 17:14-20; 2 Chron. 26:16-21). The temple was the king's chapel, and at various times he led the religious ceremonies (1 Kgs 3:4-15). For example, Solomon built (or renovated) the Jerusalem temple and was the first to sacrifice there (1 Kgs 3:4; 5:15–6:38; 7:13-51; 8:1-64). The Israelite and Judahite kings acted much as other kings in the ancient Near East, which included important cultic functions. The king was considered the son of God and had a special religious place in the national order (cf. Psalm 2).[18]

Almost all religions, especially those with temples, appear to have cult personnel of some sort. Ancient Israel may not originally have had a hereditary *priesthood*, since we have accounts of a variety of figures who took on cultic duties (the young Levite Jonathan [Judges 17–18]; Samuel [1 Sam. 1–3]; David's sons [2 Sam. 8:18]). We also have the curious figure of Zadok the priest under David. Zadok is first mentioned in 2 Sam. 8:17, but the text is problematic. It seems to say that Zadok is son of Ahitub and Ahimelech is son of Abiathar; however, elsewhere Ahitub is the father of Ahimelech who is father of Abiathar (1 Sam. 22:20). This suggests that the text is corrupt here and that the original had a genealogy of Abiathar, like that in 1 Sam. 22:20, but not of Zadok.

Thus, Zadok first appears, without father or mother or genealogy, in 2 Sam. 15:24-36. It has long been noted that Zadok's sudden and mysterious appearance is probably due to his being a priest of the old Jerusalem Jebusite cult whom David took over to consolidate Jebusite and Jerusalemite inhabitants. David is pictured as having two chief priests, Abiathar and Zadok; at the end of his life, however, Abiathar was disqualified and banished (1 Kgs 2:26-27), leaving only Zadok. The possibility that Zadok was "imported" into the Israelite cult from the old Jebusite religion might seem strange at first, but to repeat what was said earlier, Israel originally did not have a hereditary priesthood, and we have accounts of a variety of early figures who took on cultic duties.

But at some point, a hereditary priesthood was appointed, with various ranks that exercised a variety of specialized duties. Although the biblical text gives an overall impression of a priestly structure that goes back to Moses, many discrepancies between texts leave us with no doubt that the temple priesthood reached a fairly stable configuration early in the Second Temple period only after a long period of struggle between rival factions.[19] But that struggle finally subsided to leave a priestly structure that seems then to have continued without major changes until the fall of the temple in 70 CE. It eventually included not only Aaronites (altar priests) and Levites (assistants to the priests), but also a number of other classes of temple servant with (sometimes more menial) duties in the temple (Ezra 2:41-58; Neh. 7:44-60). The following are the various temple personnel as found in Ezra and Nehemiah:

Priests (Ezra 2:36-39//Neh. 7:39-42; Ezra 7:7, 24)
Levites (Ezra 2:40//Neh. 7:43; Ezra 7:7, 24)
Singers (Ezra 2:41//Neh. 7:44; Ezra 7:7, 24)
Gatekeepers (Ezra 2:42//Neh. 7:45; Ezra 7:7, 24)
Netinim servants (Ezra 2:43-54//Neh. 7:46-55; Ezra 7:7, 24)
Solomon's servants (Ezra 2:55-57//Neh. 7:57-59)

Another set of religious figures, figuring prominently in the Bible, are the *prophets*. We have not only stories about prophets (especially in Samuel, Kings, and Chronicles) but a number of books that are alleged to be by prophetic figures: Isaiah, Jeremiah, Ezekiel, and the Twelve Minor Prophets. Prophets did not form a coherent body but tended to be individuals who claimed to have a divine call, though some had disciples who may have been a sort of "apprentice" prophet (e.g., Elisha who followed Elijah). Even where more than one prophet existed contemporaneously, we seldom see them acting together or even interacting with each other. The whole subject of prophecy is a complex one; see my full study, *"The Spirit of the Lord Came upon Me": Prophets in Ancient Israel from a Cross-Cultural Perspective*.[20]

A further notable group in the Bible are the *sages or "wise men."* A few individuals are labeled "wise man" or "wise woman" in the biblical text (e.g., 2 Sam. 14:2; 1 Kgs 2:9; Jer. 18:18), but we have a collection of "wisdom books" that were presumably the written products of sages: Proverbs, Job, and Qohelet (Ecclesiastes). Wise men are often named as advisors in foreign courts such as Egypt (Gen. 41), Babylon (Dan. 2, 4–5), or Edom (Obad. 1:8). Many of those so labeled were no doubt engaged in the scribal profession. Ben Sira associates wisdom specifically with the *scribe* (Sir. 38:24–39:11). They were the ones who had the training and leisure to concern themselves with wisdom and learning. The term "secular wisdom" has been used of the biblical wisdom tradition, but this is clearly inappropriate. Although the wise may not always have been religious figures as such, the wisdom of the wisdom books clearly represents a religious perspective. Also, many scribes were priests or Levites.

Holy Days and Festivals: Sacred Time

The concept of sacred time is taken for granted in most forms of liturgical worship. The weekly Sabbath and the annual festivals are described in Leviticus 23, as well as being referred to in other passages (e.g., Deut. 16:1-17). They correspond with the holy days known from later in Second Temple Judaism and historical Judaism even to today. There are hints at other festivals or observances, however. The most obvious one is Purim, which is described in the book of Esther, though it was never designated a holy day. We also have some references to "fasts" in Zechariah (7:5; 8:19), which might be observances that pertained for a time but were dropped.

Although the new moon in its calendrical function is mentioned in Leviticus, it is not labeled a holy day in any passage, but some scholars have thought that it was one of the original holy days, perhaps even a forerunner of the Sabbath. Other celebrations are known, though do not seem to have been holy days as such and are not treated in the same way as the annual Sabbaths. Hanukkah comes from the time of the Maccabees. We know from the Qumran Temple Scroll that there were Feasts of the Firstfruits of Oil, of the Firstfruits of Wine, and of the Wood Offering (11QT 19-25) in its cultic calendar. Josephus mentions a Festival of Woodgathering in passing (*War* 2.17.6 §425), and Nehemiah 10:35 makes a point about bringing the wood offering for the altar in the temple.

Leviticus 25 describes the sabbatical year and the jubilee year. These were not holy as such but designated certain required observances. We know from later indications that the sabbatical year was observed.[21] Farmers would have to let their cultivated land lie fallow. However, there is no evidence that the jubilee was ever kept; it seems to have been only theoretical.

Sacred and Profane, Pure and Impure

The two related pairs of sacred/profane and pure/impure are important for Israelite religion, as indeed they are for most religions. The two pairs of concepts are parallel but not the same, and they must not be confused. "Sacred/profane" come from Latin terms: "sacred" means that associated with the divine or its power or its sphere; a synonym is "holy." "Profane" is the broader ordinary sphere that we all live in. "Profane" is not a negative term; it simply means that which is not sacred. For a general discussion, one can consult the famous book by R. Otto, *The Idea of the Holy* (German original 1917), which still has value. The importance of "the sacred"—whether space, time, or objects—is its function as a "focusing lens" that concentrates attention on the activities of a particular time and place and invests them with a particular significance in relationship to the divine.

In Israel and Judah, the sacred or holy mainly had to do with the temple. The temple had sacred space: the "holy place" and the "holy of holies" or "most holy place." It also had sacred objects, including the altar for sacrifice, the incense altar, the table of showbread, the lampstand (*menora*), and various altar vessels. Certain things could be set aside for worship, thus becoming sacred, including certain animals designated for sacrifice (Lev. 27:9-13) or property donated to the temple (Lev. 27:14-29). Tithes allotted to the priests and Levites were sacred and were to be eaten according to specific regulations (Lev. 27:30-3).

Another of the basic concepts of Israelite society, as it relates to religion and the cult, is that of ritual purity and pollution. "Clean" (*tāhōr*) and "unclean" (*tāmē'*) were very important images. Ritual purity is perhaps one of the most misunderstood concepts in the religion of ancient Israel. Contrary to what we moderns might suppose, it has little or nothing to do with hygiene or with clean/dirty in a physical sense. For example, in the Israelite system, excrement was not usually included in the category of unclean, even though ancient Israelites had much the same view toward it that we do today. At the most basic level, to be clean allowed one to enter the sacred sphere, the temple—to participate in the cult—whereas those unclean were prohibited.

It was no sin to become unclean. Many activities caused impurity, including many of the normal aspects of daily life: menstruation, nocturnal emission, contact with the dead, touching or eating unclean (non-kosher) animals, and childbirth. When one contacted uncleanness, it seems to have been important to remove it and become ritually pure as soon as possible, even when access to the cult was not likely in the near future. Also, being pure is not the same as being sacred. Impurity can cause the sacred to become profane in some cases, but one can be ritually pure in a profane context.

Purity and impurity are not to be equated with "evil" and "good." To be impure does not mean that one is "bad," nor are you "good" just because you are ritually pure. Perhaps the best way to understand these regulations about purity and impurity is to see them as a language, in the broad sense of the term, communicating to those within the society the "correct" attitudes toward relations between the sexes, marriage, kinship, and intercourse with outsiders. Ritual cleanliness tells the people how to classify the entities—human and animal—who inhabit the world around them and communicates to the society how to fit in new forms that enter its world.

Law and Ethics

The term "law" (*tôrāh*) is used many times in the Hebrew Bible, usually in reference to God's law. This includes statements about the "book of the law," which also relates to divine instructions. Law is a concept widespread in the ancient Near East, even if the vocabulary in reference to it is not necessarily standardized in the way it is in the Hebrew Bible. We should also keep in mind that much we find regarding ethics is found in legal sections of the Hebrew Bible, though ethical instruction is also found in the prophetic and wisdom literature, as well as exemplified in narrative sections. In addition, Mary Douglas (1999), in her analysis of Leviticus, has emphasized the implications of both the teachings and the structure of the book for matters of ethics and morality.

A number of law codes from Mesopotamia have surfaced in the past century, the most famous as well as the most extensive and developed of these being the Codex Hammurabi. The relationship between the law codes and the legal documents from actual life is an interesting one that may throw light on the relationship of law in the Bible to practice in Israel.[22] It is by no means straightforward. The law codes were not, as one might expect, analogous to a statute book that judges would consult for information and guidance. On the contrary, actual legal decisions never refer to the law codes as precedent or authoritative legislation. Yet the codes were largely based on standard legal process as it functioned in society at the time. There is a certain utopian quality about the codes, but they are more than just theory. The situation in Israel seems to be similar.

As with the ancient Near Eastern law codes, the laws in the Pentateuch did probably bear some relation to actual practices within society. They were not completely divorced from how the society really worked, but they were not law codes in a modern sense. Within the biblical tradition itself, there are indications that actual society did not necessarily work according to the principles laid down in the biblical text. A prime example of this is adultery. According to Leviticus 20:10, adultery was to be punished with death. Elsewhere, though, the dangers of adultery (if caught) are not said to be a public stoning but the wrath of an irate husband who will not be appeased until he has done some rather unpleasant things to the adulterer

(Prov. 6:24-35). We have little indication that adultery was ever an occasion for a public trial and execution as the law envisages.

To conclude, there is a broad similarity in law over much of the ancient Near East from Israel to Mesopotamia. Each people selected, modified, refined, and developed the tradition in its own way, but a significant overlap is still easy to spot in the extant literature. Israel evidently drew on the common legal and ethical tradition of its world so that differences are generally those of detail and emphasis rather than conceptualization. However, there is one major difference from the "law codes" known elsewhere in the ancient Near East: the biblical text mixes civic, religious, cultic, and ritual law in the same texts. Since much of Leviticus is cultic material, this is not generally paralleled in the legal texts of Mesopotamia and elsewhere (though there may be parallels in ritual texts). It is mainly regarding Leviticus 19–20 that legal comparisons can be made.

Temple Religion versus "Popular"/"Folk"/"Family" Religion

There are some problems with using the terms "popular," "folk," or "family" religion. First, this might imply that such religion is less important or even less religion. Such is not the case: popular/folk/family religion is as legitimate and as much religion as any other. A second problem is a tendency to see this type of religion in a different category from other types of religion. This is erroneous: while perhaps having its own social and practical characteristics, it does not differ from any other type of religion. In the ancient Near East, we can perhaps talk about three spheres of religion: the cult of the ruler, the national cult or cult of the national god (which might be the same as the ruler cult, but not necessarily), and local or family or "popular" cults.

In Israel and Judah, the distance between the temple cults and family cults might not have been that great. Yahweh worship seems to have been widespread (though other deities were worshiped alongside Yahweh, if apparently less popular), and with a multitude of altars it was common for ordinary people to attend worship in a temple or holy place (cf. 1 Sam. 1). What tends to characterize popular religion is the devotion to a particular deity for personal concerns and favors and the practice of the "esoteric arts" for personal benefit: cults (including underworld cults) relating to the dead, healing, curses/blessings, magic, and divination.[23] For example, toward the close of the Judahite monarchy, a goddess seems to have been popular alongside Yahweh, perhaps even his consort (Jer. 7:18).

Temple religion came to be perhaps the main manifestation of Israelite religion before it became a book religion, but both these were probably post-exilic developments. That is, temples existed in preexilic times, including in Jerusalem, but it was probably only in the Persian period that the Jerusalem temple became the only one in many people's eyes (though there still existed temples on Gerizim, at Elephantine, in Leontopolis and possibly at Iraq al-Amir in Transjordan).

As for Judaism as a "religion of the book," I have argued that it was a development only toward the end of the Second Temple period.[24] As already noted above, the center of temple religion was the sacrificial cult. Although the book of Leviticus is a late writing, it is likely that the cult described there had continued in broad outline for many centuries. The book of Leviticus is not a handbook for priests as some have suggested.[25] The priestly knowledge was most likely passed down by word of mouth and apprenticeship training without being committed formally to writing; however, in the late Persian period the Torah was finally formalized and propagated.

Other manifestations of popular religion are known, though some became proscribed (despite their evident popularity): the cult of the dead, Molek worship, and the teraphim. The teraphim is mentioned in a number of passages (1 Sam. 15:22-23; 2 Kgs 23:24; Ezek. 21:26-27; Hos. 3:4; Zech. 10:2). A recent study of the teraphim argues that they were a common shrine to the ancestors kept in the home.[26] Even the future King David had one, which his wife placed in his bed to deceive Saul's men so that he could escape (1 Sam. 19).

The Supposed Abominations of Canaanite Religion

Many scholars once followed the text and assumed that Israelite worship was to be contrasted with that of the Canaanites. Especially they accepted the judgment that Canaanite worship was an abomination or, at least, had abominable aspects to it. By taking this point of view, they could accept the command in some passages that Canaanites were to be wiped from the face of the earth. This position is no longer that of most scholars who recognize that Israelite worship was originally much like that of the other Canaanites, before it developed into monotheism. Let us considerable briefly some of these alleged "abominations" that have been associated with the religion of the Canaanites.

One that can be quickly dismissed is the idea that there was ritual bestiality in the worship. This was based on a passage in the Ugaritic texts in which Baal copulates with a heifer.[27] It must be recognized, however, that Baal is here and elsewhere pictured as a bull. This is a mythical passage in which Baal takes an animal form, just as we find some of the gods doing in Greek myths. There is no evidence that bestiality was a religious act or even accepted generally in Canaanite society.

A subject of considerable controversy is that of cultic prostitution. According to some of the Greek writers, worship in Babylonian temples required all women to prostitute themselves at one time in their lives (Herodotus 1.199). We also have some evidence of "sacred marriage" rites in Mesopotamia, which might have involved the king and queen or the king and a priestess in ritual sex, though this is now disputed.[28] Among the cult personnel at Ugarit was a figure called *qdšm*, which some originally defined as "male prostitute." But now most regard it as just an ordinary cult functionary. Most of the biblical references using sexual phraseology for "pagan" religion can be interpreted as symbolic language for religious straying, and there is really little support for the oft-repeated assertion that cultic prostitution formed a part of the non-Yahwistic cults.[29]

Finally, there is the question of child sacrifice. We know that child sacrifice was a regular or occasional occurrence in some ancient societies. It is often alleged (by ancient sources and modern) that the Carthaginians regularly sacrificed firstborn male infants. However, this has also been disputed, based on examination of infant remains found in the burial place referred to as a "Tophet." The Tophet is also referred to in biblical texts (2 Kgs 23:10; Jer. 7:31-2; 19:6, 11-14), and some have seen the phrase, "passing sons and daughters through the fire" (e.g., Deut. 18:10; 2 Kgs 3:10), as a reference to child sacrifice. All we can say at the moment is that the practice of infant sacrifice in Carthage and Phoenicia is controversial.[30] The same applies to the biblical statements, which are potentially ambiguous.

Conclusions

Early Israelite religion was typical of that known from other Northwest Semitic texts. It had a pantheon similar to that attested in the Ugaritic and Phoenician texts, with the god El at its head, though worship of Yahweh seems to be unique to Israel. This chapter has traced Israelite religion from its polytheistic period to one in which monotheism prevailed, at least in the written text. Popular religion, however, was slower in leaving some honoring of other gods, even though Yahweh worship seems always to have been the dominant form of religious practice. Worship even of Yahweh originally took place in a variety of sites. Even when the cults of the high places were discontinued in favor of the Jerusalem temple, we have indications of temples to Yahweh elsewhere: Mt Gerizim, Elephantine, Leontopolis, and apparently even others.

A variety of religious specialists existed in Israelite society, including not only priests, prophets, and sages but also the king as the chief priest and head of the Jerusalem cult. Indications within the text suggest the priesthood had a complicated development before it came to consist primarily of Aaronites (altar priests) and Levites (assistants to the priests) in the later Second Temple period. The contrast with Canaanite religion made by the text is not justified by what we know of Canaanite worship. The call in some passages to exterminate the Canaanites because of their religion should excite the same revulsion as any of the demands for genocide known from modern times.

8
Judah Rules Alone: From the Fall of Samaria to the Fall of Jerusalem

The Assyrian capture of Samaria brought the Kingdom of Israel to an end. But the Kingdom of Judah continued for another century and more, though it was a vassal state under Assyrian domination, then Egyptian domination, and finally the Babylonian thumb.[1]

Reign of Hezekiah, the Rebel Against Assyria (2 Kgs 18–20)

The reign of Hezekiah is an event about which we have a considerable amount of information, especially in the biblical text but also in the Assyrian records. These accounts focus particularly on the invasion in 701 BCE of the Assyrian King Sennacherib (705–681 BCE). Only an outline of the information and historical problems can be given here.[2]

The account of Hezekiah's reign begins with a religious and cultic reform (2 Kgs 18:3-6). This reform was once widely accepted in scholarship, but now many question whether it is valid.[3] The problem is that Hezekiah's reforms look very much like the reforms later ascribed to Josiah. Did Josiah try to revive what failed under Hezekiah, or did the biblical writer borrow from Josiah's story to improve Hezekiah's piety by literary invention? A possible answer might come from temples at Arad and Beersheba. The excavation of them found that the cult objects had been buried and the temples dismantled, events that were originally dated to the time of Hezekiah. The argument was that the temples were cancelled because of Hezekiah's reform. Now, however, this event has been redated to the time of Manasseh or even later, not Hezekiah.[4] Also, it not certain that burying the cult objects was to cancel them—it might have been to preserve them! A study of the *bāmôt* or high places also does not support a cult reform in the time of Hezekiah, for we have archaeological evidence that they continued.[5]

Archaeology has found some interesting information about Hezekiah's reign. It provides evidence from the stamps on storage jar handles that foodstuffs were collected from various areas of the kingdom and stockpiled in central areas, especially Jerusalem, to withstand an attack and siege by a foreign army. We also have the Siloam tunnel that was dug to bring water from the Gihon Spring to within the city walls. This has been traditionally assigned to the reign of Hezekiah, though the inscription found in the Siloam tunnel has now been redated to the time of Manasseh or another ruler by some recent studies. In any case, it is clear that Hezekiah prepared his kingdom for a rebellion against Assyrian rule, which he initiated by ceasing to pay tribute to the Assyrian king (2 Kgs 18:7-8). This action brought down the wrath of Sennacherib on Judah.

The analysis of the biblical narrative has been an important part of the discussion relating to the historicity of Sennacherib's campaign against Hezekiah. First, 2 Kgs 18:14-16 had already been recognized as taken from a good early source. But 2 Kgs 18:17–19:37 was made up of two parallel accounts (more or less duplicated in Isaiah 36–37) but were less trustworthy even though containing some historical data.[6] The sources created a basic problem: according to the biblical text, the Assyrians were destroyed (by an angel, no less!), and Judah was saved, but according to the Assyrian records, Jerusalem was besieged, and Hezekiah submitted and paid a large tribute.

Attempts to rationalize the various narratives in the biblical text already began in the infancy of Assyriology, with the suggestion that Sennacherib invaded Judah twice. According to this thesis, Hezekiah submitted and paid tribute as a result of the first invasion in 701 BCE, but during a second invasion (after 689 BCE) Judah was "delivered" (whether divinely or by circumstances) by destruction of the invading Assyrian army.[7] However, this argument was refuted point by point by further study—there was only one attack on Hezekiah by Sennacherib, that in 701 BCE.[8] Although Sennacherib's reign is not well documented after 689 BCE, there does not seem to be any room for another campaign to Palestine.

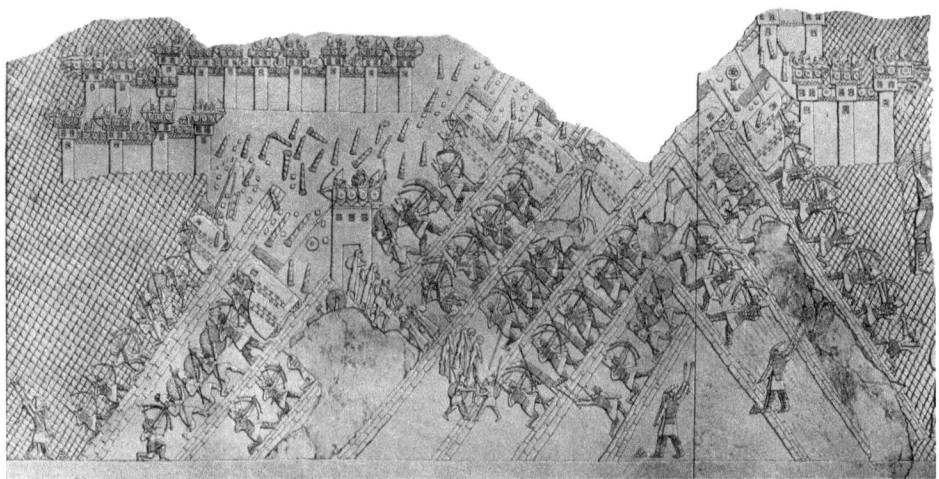

FIGURE 8.1 *Assyrian inscription showing the siege of the Jewish city Lachish.*

Here is the historical situation according to the latest information and studies.[9] The firmest datum we have is that at the end of the eighth century there was an invasion by the Assyrian King Sennacherib, because Hezekiah ceased delivering his tribute to Nineveh (both the Assyrian records and the biblical account tell us this). This invasion can be precisely calculated to 701 BCE. We have detailed descriptions in the Assyrian annals, including mention of local Palestinian rulers by name (e.g., Hezekiah), and the widespread destruction of many towns and villages in Judah has left a distinct mark in the archaeological record. There is substantial agreement that reliable memory of this is found in 2 Kgs 18:13-16, and rather less reliable memory in various other parts of 2 Kings 18–20//Isaiah 36–37.

Sennacherib invaded, destroyed much of the countryside of Judah, and besieged Jerusalem. Some catastrophe affected the Assyrian army, however, and it returned home, abandoning the siege of Jerusalem without taking the city. The Greek historian Herodotus gives an account of this incident and may provide a clue to what happened to the Assyrian forces.[10] There are also Egyptian data crucial to the question: the Nubians controlled Egypt at this time, and the Egyptian pharaoh Taharqa may have threatened the Assyrians with his own army (2 Kgs 19:9). It has also been argued that Sennacherib faced a revolt in the heartland of Assyria. All these factors were enough to make him break off his campaign in Judah without taking Jerusalem or capturing Hezekiah. King Hezekiah was thus able to stay on the Judahite throne, despite being a "rebel" in Assyrian eyes. Nevertheless, Sennacherib imposed heavy tribute on him, and he paid it. The figures given in 2 Kgs 18:14 and the Assyrian records for the tribute are very similar. Sennacherib had amply demonstrated to Hezekiah that the Judahite king could not break away from Assyrian rule.

One puzzle has been Hezekiah's dates of rule. According to 2 Kgs 18:1 Hezekiah became king in Hoshea's third year, while Samaria fell in Hezekiah's fourth year. If so, the events of 701 would have taken place about Hezekiah's twenty-seventh year. Yet 2 Kgs 18:13 makes this his "14th year." The question has been much debated, but a recent study of seal impressions with dates from the reign of Hezekiah seems to solve the problem.[11] These were used to seal gifts to the king of goods from various estates: they thus give an impression of the economy. They come to an end in the twenty-sixth year, on the eve of Sennacherib's invasion. After that, many of the cities and villages named in the bullae had been destroyed and the economic situation Judah was now very bad, thus confirming that Hezekiah's twenty-sixth year was about 702 BCE, just before Sennacherib's army destroyed much of the countryside in Judah. It seems that the reference to the "14th" year was some sort of scribal error.

We know from Sennacherib's inscriptions that the Assyrian king was assassinated, just as 2 Kgs 19:37 says; however, it was not immediately after the Judahite invasion, as the biblical text suggests but much later, in 681 BCE. An important study has shown that the name of Sennacherib's assassin had been wrongly interpreted for many years.[12] It should be read as Arda-Mulišši of which the biblical Adrammelech (2 Kgs 19:37) is a garbled but recognizable form.

A further question is how to take the visit of Merodach-baladan (called "Berodachbaladan" in 2 Kgs 20:12) to Jerusalem. Because a king of Babylon, Marduk-apla-dan actually existed, some have wanted to suggest that this is a plausible story: the

Babylonian king, who was rebelling against the Assyrians, was seeking support and allies. This might seem to be a valid argument until one considers the distance that Judah lay from Babylon and the lack of any possibility of giving help. The story looks more like an explanation of why Jerusalem fell to the Babylonians rather than a reliable historical datum.

Reign of Manasseh (2 Kgs 21:1-18)

The name of Manasseh is one of the most infamous in the biblical text. He is perhaps equaled—but not surpassed—only by Ahab and Jezebel. This suggests that the long reign ascribed to him is likely to be factual, because a long life was often thought to show that the person was right with God. What emerges from recent study, however, is the importance of the reign of Manasseh. Far from being a time of depravity and fear, many think it represents a remarkable recovery from the devastations of Sennacherib. It must have given many Judaeans a return to some sort of prosperity and hope for the future.

What the archaeology suggests is that Judah made a significant recovery from the disaster of 701.[13] The important agricultural region of the Shephelah remained sparsely populated, probably the larger part of it having been removed from Judahite control. Elsewhere, though, settlements were reestablished in destroyed southern areas, possibly with even a population increase. Settlements were also pushed into the marginal desert areas to make use of all possible land for agricultural purposes. Manasseh seems to have been responsible for building a city wall (2 Chron. 33:15), which could be the one dating from the seventh century discovered on the eastern slope of Jerusalem's southeastern hill.[14] It has also been proposed that Manasseh built some prestige projects, including the Siloam tunnel and a palace at Ramat Raḥel.[15]

Manasseh's existence is well attested in the Assyrian inscriptions. He is named as an apparently loyal subject paying the required tribute to both the Assyrian rulers Esarhaddon (681–669 BCE) and Ashurbanipal (669–631 BCE), though it has been pointed out that Manasseh's tribute is smaller than that of his neighbors. He also supplied military assistance for Ashurbanipal's attack on Egypt. In addition, there is some evidence of the part played by Judah in the economy of the Assyrian Empire, a role that would have benefited the inhabitants of Judah. The territory of Judah formed a significant link in the caravan trade from Arabia, which the Assyrians would have controlled. The Idumaean plateau gained a significant population at this time, with the trade route leading through the valley of Beersheba and the southern coastal plain to Gaza. There are indications of contact with South Arabia, and the seventh-century forts at Qadesh-Barnea and Haseva might have been built with the protection of this trade in mind. A major olive oil production center existed at Tel Miqne (usually identified with ancient Ekron); however, the olives were not grown locally but would most likely have been imported from the Samarian and Judaean highlands.

As far as Manasseh's "apostasy" is concerned, this probably only refers to the popular religion honored by the people of the countryside. That is, nothing innovative from a religious point of view happened under him; rather, he was just blamed for what had been the traditional religion among the people for many centuries. This does not, though, rule out foreign influence, such as from Assyro-Aramaic astral cults (see further in chapter 7, p. 121).

One of the most curious episodes related in the Bible is about Manasseh's deportation to and imprisonment in Babylon, followed by a return to Jerusalem and his throne and by repentance from his wicked deeds. This story is found in only one passage, significantly in Chronicles (2 Chron. 33:10-17), but not a hint is found in 2 Kgs 21:1-18. Furthermore, other biblical passages know nothing of Manasseh's repentance (Jer. 15:4; 2 Kgs 23:12; 2 Chron. 33:22). If Manasseh actually did all this, why would the writer of Kings omit it? He was either ignorant of the information or he deliberately suppressed it.

It is difficult to believe that if such an incident took place, he had no information, so we must assume that he knew of Manasseh's repentance but purposefully ignored it. Is this likely? Yes, perhaps if the idea of an act of repentance on Manasseh's part created problems with his underlying pattern of presentation, but this would be a serious reflection on the claim made by some that the biblical writer wanted to write history. In sum, though, the story of Manasseh's having been arrested and taken "with hooks and bound in bronze fetters" to Babylon is unlikely (if not impossible), an important reason being his evident loyalty to the Assyrian rulers. His father Hezekiah's difficulties with the Assyrians would have taught him this!

Reign of Amon (2 Kgs 21:19-26)

We have no data on Amon other than what is in the Bible. It was unusual for a king to be assassinated, and there is nothing about Amon to give this a literary significance. Thus, it is likely to have happened. However, the figures given for his age look suspect: although it is theoretically possible that he had a child at age sixteen, this seems highly improbable, especially for an heir to the throne. Possibly the problem is with the age of Josiah (see next section), though in cases of the sudden death of a king a minor child might well take the throne.

Reign of Josiah, the Reforming King (2 Kgs 22:1–23:30)

Despite the importance given to Josiah in the biblical tradition, neither the surviving Babylonian nor Egyptian records contain any reference to him. We are left with archaeology and the biblical text with which to make sense of his reign, though the Egyptian material and the Babylonian chronicles provide useful background and contextual information. Many past reconstructions have depended on the picture in 2 Chronicles, even in those aspects which differ at significant points from those in 2 Kings. I have considerable difficulties with this approach and give preference to the data in 2 Kings 22–23.

The first point to note is the finding of a religious book in the temple. This of course contradicts the many passages in the Bible up to this point that the "law book of Moses" had been widely known and promulgated. On the contrary, it quickly becomes clear in these chapters on Josiah that no such law book had been around. Indeed, it is not even clear that the book found in the temple was meant to be the whole Pentateuch. It was long ago recognized that most of the alleged reforms of Josiah could have come from the book of Deuteronomy alone. Thus, the biblical text itself makes it clear that neither the "law of Moses" nor other biblical books were known up to this time. Whatever book was found and proclaimed at this time was new to most of the Jewish people, including apparently the ruling elite and the priesthood.

One theory that has held considerable sway for a number of decades is that Josiah was attempting to create a "greater Israel," perhaps on the model of the Davidic kingdom. There are many obvious parallels between Josiah and David, though one could put these down to literary creation rather than actual activity of the ruler. The "righteousness" of both kings is the most obvious contact, but the conquest of territory is another that many scholars have managed to glean from the biblical material: the attempt to return to an expanded kingdom of Judah and a recovery of former glory. It has been plausibly argued that, although Josiah's reform was indeed religious, the basis of it was economic.[16]

A recent study however, has found that there was no political vacuum that gave Josiah room to try to found a new Davidic "empire."[17] Rather, the declining Assyrian power in the west was matched by the growing power of Egypt; indeed, there may have been an orderly transfer of territorial control by mutual agreement. It seems evident that Judah was a vassal state during the entirety of Josiah's reign, first under the Assyrians and then under the Egyptians. This gave only very limited scope for expansion of territory. There is some evidence of shifting the border as far north as Bethel. However, the expansion further north into the Galilee or west into the area of Philistia are unjustified from either archaeology or the text.

It was once conventional to accept Josiah's reform at face value, but the question is currently much debated.[18] We have no direct evidence outside the biblical text, which makes us at least ask whether it is an invention of a "Deuteronomist school" that some think was operating at this time and controlling the written message. The alleged absence of any reference to this reform in the book of Jeremiah has always been a major puzzle, since Jeremiah would have lived through this period. Some have found allusions here and there, but one has to admit that they are surprisingly obscure. Considering Jeremiah's overall message and position, he should have embraced such a reform and made copious comments about it. Some have seen evidence in the material remains, but others have argued against it.[19]

The central passage is 2 Kings 22–23, however. It is widely agreed that this passage has been the subject of editing by editors. But several scholars have argued cogently that at the heart of 2 Kings 22–23 is a simple list of reform measures affecting mainly Jerusalem and perhaps Bethel.[20] Although later editors have added an expansive superstructure that makes the reform much more extensive in scope and geography, a short original list of reform measures appears to be supported by the archaeology and iconography. 2 Kgs 22:3-7 has the reform follow the discovery of the law book in the temple, in Josiah's eighteenth year; this is more likely than the "12th year" in 2 Chron. 34:3-7. There is also another substantial consideration: the dating of the reform seems about 622 BCE, which puts it at the height of the crisis in Assyria during the revolt of Babylon in 626 to 623 BCE. It may be that the problems of Sin-shar-ishkun, the Assyrian ruler, were sufficient to give Josiah confidence to initiate his reforms without being in danger of attracting Assyrian disapproval.

Many have followed the narrative of 2 Chron. 35:20-27, which has Josiah die in a pitched battle. This seems unlikely, however, since Judah (which had now become an Egyptian vassal state) is not likely to have been in a military position to challenge the Egyptian army. On the other hand, a vassal king would have been expected to appear before the new ruler to pay him homage and swear allegiance. The new ruler in this case was the Pharaoh Necho II (610–595 BCE). Doubts have been expressed about the fate of Josiah for some considerable period of time.[21] 2 Kings is clearly reticent to tell what happened, but the historical circumstances strongly suggest that when Josiah met him at Megiddo, Necho had him executed for suspected disloyalty of some sort. This is also the message one gains from a close reading of the Hebrew text of 2 Kgs 23:29.

Reign of Jehoahaz (2 Kgs 23:30-34)

Nothing is known of Jehoahaz, though he has only a brief reign of three months. What does fit is that he would have been removed from the throne by the Egyptians who were probably in control of the region at this time, having replaced the Assyrians. The Judaeans had chosen Jehoahaz as Josiah's successor, but Egypt did not approve and removed him after only three months, replacing him with Jehoiakim (2 Kgs 23:30-34).

Reign of Jehoiakim (2 Kgs 23:34–24:6)

Jehoiakim is known only from the biblical text, yet his reign illustrates the external politics of the ancient Near East at this time and fits in well with them. Judah was clearly an Egyptian vassal, since it was the Egyptians who put Jehoiakim on the throne. But in Jehoiakim's fourth year, Nebuchadnezzar gained control of the region after the battle of Carchemish, and Judah became the vassal of the Babylonians. He then rebelled after three years. Why? The answer is that in 601 BCE Nebuchadnezzar fought a costly battle with Necho II: *Babylonian Chronicle 5* says "they inflicted a major defeat on one another"—that is, both sides suffered severe losses. It took Nebuchadnezzar's army several years to recover. It was after this battle that Jehoiakim rebelled. It was not until two years later that Nebuchadnezzar retaliated by fostering raids against Judah, and it was not until late in 598 BCE that he sent an army against Jerusalem. Apparently, Jehoiakim died in the meantime, and his son Jehoiachin surrendered to the Babylonians after a reign of only three months (2 Kgs 24:1-17).

Several other biblical passages seem to have misunderstood this event or simply got it wrong. 2 Chron. 36:6 states that Nebuchadnezzar besieged Jerusalem and took Jehoiakim captive to Babylon, while Jeremiah 22:18-19 predicts that he would have the "burial of an ass" (i.e., his carcass would be dragged outside Jerusalem and left exposed and unburied). Neither appears to be what happened: from 2 Kings 24 it looks as if Jehoiakim died a natural death only a couple of months or so before Nebuchadnezzar set siege to Jerusalem. When Nebuchadnezzar arrived, Jehoiachin was now ruling, but he quickly surrendered to the Babylonian king and paid the price for his father's rebellion. But then there is Daniel 1:1-2, which gives a completely confused account, saying that Nebuchadnezzar took Jerusalem in Jehoiakim's "3rd year." The siege was actually in his seventh year. The statement in Daniel is likely based on a misreading of the narrative in 2 Kings and 2 Chronicles.[22]

Reign of Jehoiachin (2 Kgs 24:6-16; 25:27-30)

Although he reigned only very briefly, Jehoiachin is well attested. In the biblical writings his name is mentioned not only in 2 Kings and 2 Chronicles but also in Jeremiah (22:24, 28; 27:20; 28:4; 29:2; 37:1; 52:31), Ezekiel (1:2), and Esther (2:6). Jehoiachin is known (though not by name) from the *Babylonian Chronicles*, which tell of Nebuchadnezzar's taking of Jerusalem and his carrying of the Judaean king into captivity. Jehoiachin's name has also been preserved in the Jehoiachin tablets from Babylon, which list rations allotted to Jehoiachin and members of his family.[23] Thus, this young ephemeral ruler is better known from extra-biblical sources than the famous Josiah.

Reign of Zedekiah (2 Kgs 24:17–25:21)

The last king of Judah is known from the *Babylonian Chronicles* as the king placed on the throne by Nebuchadnezzar after his conquest of Jerusalem in early 597 BCE, though his name is not given. We have no Mesopotamian historical sources after 594 when the *Babylonian Chronicles* come to an end. Yet the inscription of Pharaoh Psammetichus II (595–589 BCE) describing a tour of Palestine fits a situation in which the king of Judah was constantly looking for ways to free himself from the overlordship of Nebuchadnezzar.[24] The rebellion and final siege and capture of Jerusalem are, unfortunately, not known from any Mesopotamian source. The Egyptians were supposed to have assisted Zedekiah temporarily by sending an army, which caused the Babylonians to lift their siege, but the Egyptians withdrew, and the Babylonian siege was resumed (Jer. 37:4-11).

The pharaoh at the time of the Jerusalem siege was Apries (589–570 BCE, called Hofrah in the biblical text [Jer. 44:30]).[25] According to these sources, Apries brought Phoenicia into submission. Jeremiah 27:3 indicates that Tyre and Sidon supported Zedekiah's rebellion. Apries's actions seem to fit into this context. In view of the detailed information confirmed for 2 Kings in the period before this, the reasonableness (for the most part) of the picture in 2 Kings, and the general background situation in the ancient Near East, the overall picture and the approximate date for the destruction of Jerusalem are acceptable from a historical point of view.

It was finally in 587 or 586 BCE that Jerusalem fell to the Babylonians. This began what is sometimes called the "exilic period" in the history of Judah. Only some thousands of Jews—mainly from the ruling and artisan classes—were taken captive. It is clear from archaeology that the bulk of the population remained in the land. But this was the foundation of a new Jewish center that continued until modern times—the Jewish community in Babylonia.

As a sort of appendix to the story, the last few verses of 2 Kings (25:22-26) describe the brief governorship of Gedaliah who was assassinated by Ishmael. This Ishmael then took some Jews to Egypt. This story is given in greater detail in Jeremiah chapters 40 through 44 (which is told from Jeremiah's perspective), with Jeremiah one of those taken to Egypt. Some seals with the name "Gedaliah" have been found, but there are problems with associating them with this Gedaliah. Another seal with the inscription, "Ishmael son of the king" has a better chance of being an authentic reference to the figure of 2 Kgs 25:25-26 and Jeremiah 40–44.[26]

Conclusions

In this chapter the Kingdom of Judah alone remained, in the aftermath of the Kingdom of Israel's cessation. It was dominated by foreign empires all the century and a half of its sole existence. From a historian's point of view, two comments can be made: first, the narrative in Kings is generally more trustworthy than that in the books of Chronicles; second, we have found generally that the narrative became more trustworthy the later the events were recorded (we are referring to the broad outline, not necessarily the details). I hasten to add that we are talking about *history* only, not the theological value of the text. After all, stories, anecdotes, parables, and the like can have tremendous religious worth without having to be historically true.

With the reign of Hezekiah, we have a considerable amount of extra-biblical data, especially from Assyrian sources with regard to the invasion of Sennacherib in 701 BCE. Hezekiah's religious reform has been questioned, however, with many convinced it was simply a literary duplication of Josiah's reform. The reign of Manasseh was an interesting investigation, since it seems to have been much more successful than given credit for in the biblical text. The text focuses on the religious situation, but it seems that the general religious practice among the populace continued much as it had in the past with little innovation. It's just that the textual editors, working at a later time, had rejected the earlier mode of worship in Judah.

When it comes to Josiah, we have the surprising fact that no mention of him is found outside the biblical text. On the other hand, the Assyrian Empire was rapidly withdrawing from the west and being replaced by Egyptian rule. The Egyptian texts were not generally as helpful with historical data. Yet there are good reasons to accept that there was a core to Josiah's religious reforms, though they were much less extensive than the present text suggests. The story about finding the law book in the temple illustrates what has long been suspected: the supposed "law of Moses" was composed probably in the eighth or seventh century BCE or later. The Josiah account makes it clear that this law was not known earlier, even by the ruling class and the priesthood. Later editors have tried to insert it into the narrative, but it took a long time to develop, both orally and in written form. As for Josiah's death, a careful reading of the text in Kings suggests that Josiah was executed by Pharaoh Necho. This fits the situation much better than the account in 2 Chron 35:20-27 that has Josiah meeting Necho in battle.

The coincidence of history and the biblical text is made even clearer in the Judahite rulers after Josiah, where for several years we have detailed historical information. Indeed, there are times that we can write the history of Judah almost year by year in the decade between 605 and 594 BCE (at which point the *Babylonian Chronicles* cease). Nebuchadnezzar's first taking of Jerusalem is found in both the *Babylonian Chronicles* and the biblical text, but the events between 601 BCE and 597 BCE fit very well what we know about the history of the time. There are no extra-biblical references to the final fall of Jerusalem 587/586 BCE, but the extent of knowledge that the biblical writer seems to have at this point gives us some confidence that things happened much as recounted, at least in broad terms.

9
Judah and the Jews in the Babylonian and Persian Empires

This history of the Jews did not come to an end, of course, with the fall of Jerusalem to the Babylonians. Judah was now under Babylonian rule, and the ruling class—the royal family, the intellectuals, the officials—had largely been deported to Babylonia. Yet contrary to the impression of the biblical text, a sizable population remained in Judah. Most of the inhabitants of Judah still lived there, that is, those that had survived the war with the Babylonians and its aftermath.

Less than half a century later, the Neo-Babylonian Empire fell to the Persian army, led by the Persian King Cyrus. Judah was now a province in the Persian Empire. The primary language of the Persian bureaucracy was Aramaic, and Judah was known by its Aramaic name of Yehud. The Persian-period Yehud and its history that emerges in this book differs from the prima facie picture in the biblical text. It also often looks quite different from the history of Yehud found in many standard handbooks, monographs, and commentaries. There are a number of reasons for this, as we shall see as we make our way through the biblical books and the other historical sources for this period.

We begin by looking at what we know of the Jews under the rule of the Neo-Babylonian Empire. But this rule was short lived—less than fifty years. Much of our story will be taken up by what we know of the Jews under Persian rule, which lasted for two centuries and was often seen as positive in the Jewish literature that has come down to us.

TABLE 9.1 *Neo-Babylonian kings*

Nabopolassar	626–605 BCE
Nebuchadnezzar II	605–562 BCE
Amel-Marduk	562–560 BCE
Neriglissar	560–556 BCE
Labashi-Marduk	556 BCE
Nabonidus	556–539 BCE

TABLE 9.2 *Persian kings*

Cyrus the Great	539(559)–530 BCE
Cambyses	530–522 BCE
Darius I	522–486 BCE
Xerxes I	486–465 BCE
Artaxerxes I	465–424 BCE
Darius II Ochus	424–404 BCE
Artaxerxes II Memnon	404–359 BCE
Artaxerxes III Ochus	359–338 BCE
Arses	338–336 BCE
Darius III Codommanus	336–331 BCE

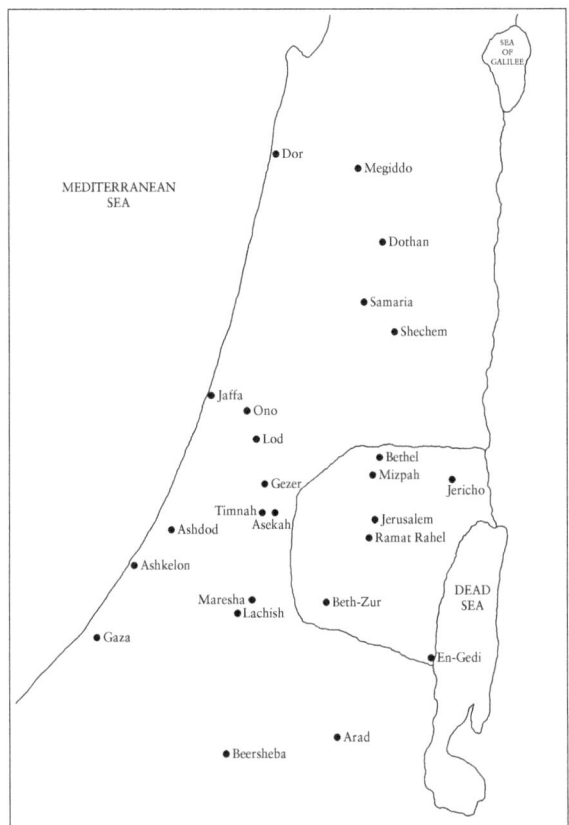

MAP 9.1 *Palestine in the Persian period. Originally created for* History of the Jews and Judaism, Part I: Yehud, *2004.*

The Jewish Communities in Babylonia

When Jerusalem fell in 587/586, many thousands of the population were taken captive to Babylonia, but recent studies indicate that the bulk of the population (though considerably reduced because of fighting and other events) remained in

Palestine. Those taken to Babylonia settled down, built up their communities, and became integrated into the society. The result was a community with two centers, one in Palestine and one in Mesopotamia (plus an additional small community in Egypt). The exact size of the community in Babylon is difficult to determine, though judging from the situation in later centuries under the Parthians, it became a relatively large and thriving one. If so, it seems that those who returned to Palestine in the reign of Cyrus and in the intervening decades down to the time of Nehemiah were very much in the minority when compared with either the indigenous Palestinian population or those who remained in the Babylonian region.

The Neo-Babylonian Empire (c. 626–539 BCE), despite the leadership of such dynamic individuals as Nebuchnezzar II, was short-lived. In about half a century it was taken over by the Persians, which had been a vassal of its erstwhile ally who were the Medes. In histories of the Jews, the period from the fall of Jerusalem to the Persian conquest of Babylon is often referred as the "exilic period." Beginning in the Neo-Babylonian period and continuing into the Persian period, we have some limited information on a number of displaced communities of Jews and other groups in the ancient Near East, most of them due to forced deportation rather than voluntary relocation. Yet we can consider ourselves fortunate in having a window also into some of the Jewish communities in what became known as the "diaspora."

The book of Jeremiah (particularly ch. 29) and some passages of Ezekiel (such as chs 8, 14, 20, and 33) touch upon the situation in some of the communities of Judaean exiles that happened under the Babylonians. We also have the book of Tobit. Although claiming to be about an exile from Northern Israel, the book was actually about Judaeans. The setting of the story is Mesopotamia, which suggests that it most likely originated in the eastern Jewish diaspora probably in the third century BCE. It fits in well with the conditions of the exiled communities, whether under the Assyrians, the Babylonians, or the Persians.

Tobit gives us the story of a pious Jew who was blinded during an act of charity. He then sends his son to a distant city to retrieve a deposit of money that he had left there. His son Tobias makes the journey but meets up with his cousin Sarah who has had successive husbands slain by a jealous demon. Tobias overcomes the demon with the help of the archangel Gabriel and marries Sarah. They return to Tobit with the money and live happily into old age. The work appears to be one of the earliest Jewish writings to deal with Jews in the diaspora.

There is very much an emphasis on the family in Tobit. The family functions both as a refuge from the outside world and an entity to which one owes various duties, such as help to relatives in times of trouble. Above all is the need to marry those related. Although the family is a social matter, it cannot be separated from the practice of religion. The importance of proper burial is depicted. There is quite a bit of what many would call moral teaching, such as almsgiving and the "negative golden rule" (do not do to others what you would not want done to you [Tobit 4:15]). Also exemplified are the proper observance of the festivals (Tobit 2:1-5), temple worship (Tobit 1:4-6), the necessity for observing the food laws (Tobit 1:11), and tithing (Tobit 1:6-8). The authority of the "scriptures" (the "book of Moses" and the prophets are specifically mentioned [Tobit 1:8; 2:6; 6:13; 7:11-13; 14:3]) is alluded to.

The situation of the Jews under the Babylonians and Persians does not seem to have been particularly different from that of the Northern Israelites under the Assyrians. Babylonian tablets confirm the presence of Jehoiachin in Babylon, along with his sons and other Judahites, listing rations that were distributed. The royal family consists of "Ya'u kīnu (Jehoiachin), king of the land of Ya[hu-du] (Judah)" and "the five sons of the king of Yakundu by the hand of Kanama."[1]

Some recently published cuneiform tablets show Jewish communities in Babylon, which seem to have originated in the captivity by Nebuchadnezzar.[2] The tablets range in date from Nebuchadrezzar, year 33 (c. 572 BCE) to Xerxes, year 13 (c. 473 BCE). Apparently, of some six hundred different names, approximately 120 contain a form of Yahweh. The Jewish settlers were engaged primarily in agricultural activities. These texts refer to a "city of Judah" or "city of the Jews/Judahites" in Mesopotamia.[3] This is not unusual because other cities named after ethnic groups are known, such as "city of the Arabians" and "city of Tyrians." One document has twelve Hebrew names and claims to have been written in the "city of Judah" about 498 BCE in the region of Borsippa and Babylon. The texts are typical of what one might expect to find in an archive of this nature: receipts for sales of various sorts, promissory notes and notes of indebtedness, and leases of property or labor.

Some may be asking, what about Daniel? As we shall see (in chapter 11) this book was not written during the Neo-Babylonian or Persian period but probably about 165 BCE during the Maccabean revolt. But the book does refer to some of the Neo-Babylonian and Persian kings. Does it tell us anything about the Jews in Babylon during those kings' reign? We have no Babylonian information on a dream by Nebuchadnezzar as described in Daniel 2. The Babylonian kings did not attempt to compel worship, which means that Daniel 3 about Daniel's friends in the fiery furnace is unlikely. The story in Daniel 4 about Nebuchadnezzar's madness is probably a story about Nabonidus who went against the powerful Marduk priesthood and spent a decade away from Babylon in the desert city of Tema.[4]

When it comes to Belshazzar in Daniel 5, we happen to know a lot about Belshazzar and his father Nabonidus who was the last king of the Neo-Babylonian Empire.[5] Although Belshazzar acted for his father while the latter was in Tema, Belshazzar was nevertheless never declared king. In any case, Nabonidus had returned to the city by the time of the Persian siege of the city of Babylon. He is referred to as the king whom the Persians defeated, where Belshazzar is not mentioned and may not even have been alive at that point. Finally, there was no "Darius the Mede."[6] Babylon fell to Cyrus's army, and he arrived to rule in the city not long after it surrendered. All in all, the book of Daniel tells us little or nothing about the Neo-Babylonian or Persian periods, but it does tell us a lot about the time of the Maccabees, as we shall see in chapter 11.

When we come to the Jews in Mesopotamia during Persian rule, we have an important witness in the Murashu texts. This group of documents come from the personal archive of a family business firm in Nippur circa 455 to 403 BCE.[7] The Murashu archive has been of special interest to scholars of the Hebrew Bible because several individuals prominent in the firm were evidently Jews, judging by their names. The Murashu house was a business and financial establishment that made loans and managed estates for absentee landlords (through a complicated system of leases and contracts). It employed a number of servants and agents, some of whom seem to have been Jewish. Genealogical relations indicate, however, that Jews did not necessarily take "Jewish" names, and there may be many more named individuals who were Jews than it is possible to recognize now.

As far as we can tell, Jews seem to have been well integrated into society. They do not appear to have lived in a "Jewish quarter" but in various villages in the Nippur area. As far as occupations are concerned, they were smallholders and lower-rank officials. Nothing in fact clearly distinguishes them from other members of the Babylonian society in which they seem to have functioned comfortably. This is no doubt why few felt the need to return to the homeland of their ancestors when Persian rule replaced Babylonian. There may have been some opportunity of advancement under Persian rule. This is indicated by the Jewish court apologies such as Esther and Daniel 1–6. One does not have to assume the historicity of the specific stories to appreciate that it was possible for a Jew to rise not only in society but even in the Persian court.

A Province in the Persian Empire

The Neo-Babylonian Empire came to an end with Cyrus's conquest of Babylon in 539 BCE. The Persians divided their territory into a few large satrapies, but these were further divided into provinces. The province of Judah (Yehud) was part of the large satrapy of Babylon and Ebir-nari (the western part of the Persian Empire). It was rather isolated, physically and economically. A benefit was that Yehud was not likely to be the object of attack because it had little strategic value. Although a Persian garrison may have been established there (at least some of the time), it was not a major line of defense for the Persian Empire. On the negative side, there was little opportunity for the inhabitants to improve their lot. The subsistence economy perpetuated itself without the means for radical change.

Most of our knowledge of Judah is based on archaeology. Those who remained in Judah or chose to return there could gain some comfort from being in the Promised Land, but the realities of life were not particularly paradisial. The country was small with a backward economy and surrounded by neighbors who at times could be hostile and who were sometimes treated with suspicion even when they appeared to be friendly. The economy was mainly agrarian, with any skilled handicrafts and manufacturing at a minimum, at least in the early part of the postexilic period. The best of the farmland was no longer within the borders of the province. Most of the Shephelah had long been taken away, and even the southern area of Judah was now in the hands of Idumaeans and/or Arabs. Much of the country was made up of the Judaean hill country. A diversity of soils and climates allowed a variety of crops and livestock. Good years gave a sufficient harvest and even a surplus, but there were on average three or four bad years in every ten. Several bad years in a row—which was not so infrequent—could be disastrous.

Because of the Babylonian conquest, there had been a sharp decline in urban life but continuity in rural settlements in the highlands, particularly between Hebron and Benjamin. As we might expect from the text, Jerusalem and the cities of the west were destroyed, following which we have a collapse in the east (the Judaean desert, the Jordan valley, the Dead Sea region) and south (the south Shephelah and the Negev). Benjamin and the Judaean highland, which apparently escaped the Babylonian destruction, contained most of the population. As for Jerusalem itself, signs of the Babylonian destruction are found throughout the city. Surprisingly, there is no evidence of settlement then until the middle of the Persian period: Jerusalem seems to have been uninhabited during the four decades or so of the "exilic period" (i.e., to about 540–530 BCE). The capital had apparently been moved to Tell en-Nasbeh (Mizpah), and Benjamin was where most people in the province now lived.

We have no credible evidence that there was any particular Persian interest in Yehud or that it received special favors from the emperor or other high Persian officials. Yet it can be shown that Judah had its own governors for part of the time, the present indication being that this arrangement dated from the beginning of the Persian period. The main task was to collect the taxes that were set by high administrators, even by the king himself. Even with its own governor, however, the priests in general and the high priest in particular played a major role in the leadership of the community. The succession of high priests is especially important for this reason. Judah had some of the characteristics of a temple state in that the temple and priesthood were prominent (whether formally or informally) in the administrative apparatus. Thus, the structure of administration initiated in the early Persian period was to continue for much of the history of the country during the Second Temple period.

The "Repopulation" of Judah?

The book of Ezra tells of the reconstruction that followed the destruction of Jerusalem and the half century of Babylonian rule. Unfortunately, while some parts of the book seem to be valuable history, this is mixed with fictional fantasy and discerning between one and the other is not always an easy task. The book begins with a decree of Cyrus I, known as "the Great" ruler of the newly established Persian Empire, for Jews to return to Palestine from Babylonia and rebuild the temple (Ezra 1:1-6).

It appears to be true that Cyrus allowed displaced peoples to return to their homelands. This is indicated by the decree recorded on the *Cyrus Cylinder*, but it must be noted that Cyrus's decree seems to have been a general policy, not one on behalf of a specific people, like the Jews. The propagandistic nature of Cyrus's decrees has long been clear, and we should be careful about taking such pronouncements at face value. The religious policy of the Persians was not that different from the basic practice of the Assyrians and Babylonians before them: they tolerated—but did not promote—the local cults (except for the traditional temples in the Persian heartland). It seems very unlikely that Cyrus would have taken the trouble to issue a decree specifically on behalf of a minority ethnic group in the first year of his reign nor do the parallels cited above suggest otherwise. Also, the Ezra "decree" is in Hebrew, whereas the expected scribal language would have been Aramaic.

Furthermore, this alleged decree in Ezra, despite its short length, is full of biblical theology. The reference to a prophecy of Jeremiah in 1:1 may not be a part of the decree, though this is not certain, but the decree refers to "Yahweh the God of Israel" (Ezra 1:3). The province was always referred to as "Judah" and the people as "Judahites" by non-Jews, never as "Israel." What is the likelihood that an official Persian decree would have such statements of Jewish theology? On the other hand, they are precisely what we would expect from a Jewish writer inventing a decree to support his perspective.

One of the curious features found in the book of Ezra especially, but also in Nehemiah, is that the people returning from Babylon were coming back to resettle a land that supposedly had remained uninhabited since the Babylonian captivity. Ezra-Nehemiah (especially Ezra 2//Neh. 7) presents a picture of thousands of exiled Jews returning to an empty land under Zerubbabel and Joshua. The literary tradition about the Babylonian captivity is ambivalent. 2 Kings 25 suggests a major removal of population at various points, but it admits that the "poorest of the land" remained in Judah (2 Kgs 25:12). The expression "poorest of the land" should be taken with a grain of salt since they were also the only ones supposed to have been left after the deportation in the time of Jehoiachin a decade earlier (2 Kgs 24:14).

Yet according to 2 Kings 25 and Jeremiah, there were plenty of nobles, soldiers, priests, and even the odd prophet around after this—and they were strong enough to withstand a siege by the Babylonians for several years (2 Kgs 25:1-3). After the fall of Jerusalem, both 2 Kings 25:22-26 and Jeremiah 40–43 show not only a large group of Jews, with a governor in the person of Gedaliah, but also a good deal of general activity. This is hardly the description of an empty land. A group (including Jeremiah) is said to have fled to Egypt, but it seems difficult to see this number as being large.

According to the biblical texts, the actual numbers of deportees was quite small, relatively speaking: ten thousand at the time of the captivity of Jehoiachin (according to 2 Kgs 24:14); Jer. 52:28-30 reduces this to three thousand, though that might be Jerusalem alone, with the entire total under Nebuchadnezzar being fewer than five thousand. Thus it is difficult to speak of actual numbers, but the impression given by the numbers alone in 2 Kings and also at the end of Jeremiah is that only a minority of the population was removed from the land. On the other hand, 2 Chronicles gives a different story. It claims not only that all those who survived the siege were taken to Babylon but also that the land observed its neglected sabbatical years (2 Chron. 36:20-21). That is, the land was not being worked; hence, one could only conclude from the text that it was empty.

This fiction of an empty land after Nebuchadnezzar's campaign is also the picture in Ezra-Nehemiah. When the original settlers come from Babylonia at the beginning of the Persian period, they return to their old habitations (Ezra 2:1//Neh. 7:6: "each to his own city"). Nothing is said about any Jews already living in Palestine or about any contest over ownership of the property. The people already in the land are labeled "foreigners." Later on, the text implies that they are basically Canaanites (Ezra 9:1). *All this is contradicted by the full evidence: the concept of an "empty land," as well as a "mass return" at the beginning of the Persian period, is only a myth created by the author.*

This is precisely what the archaeology indicates: there is no evidence of large increases in the population at any time in the Persian period.[8] The population was only about thirty thousand at its greatest—in spite of the alleged forty thousand plus pictured as returning by Ezra 2//Neh. 7. Jerusalem was only a small settlement early in the Persian period.[9] Furthermore, the end of the sixth and beginning of the fifth centuries saw a significant reduction in population, especially in the Benjamin area. The returnees were likely to have been a few thousand at most, probably over a period of time—over decades or even a century or more.

The conclusion seems straightforward: some biblical texts (but not all!) simply refuse to admit that there were Jewish inhabitants of the land after the deportations under Nebuchadnezzar. Unlike under the Assyrians, there is no suggestion that the Babylonians brought in any foreign peoples to replace those deported. One can only conclude that many, if not all, these "peoples of the land" were the Jewish descendants of those who were not deported. In the eyes of the author of Ezra-Nehemiah, these peoples were no longer kin; the only "people of Israel" were those who had gone into captivity. The writer ignores the significant community formed by the descendants of those who were not exiled by the Babylonians but remained in the land and continued to live there.

The Initial "Resettlement" of the Province of Judah

Despite the alleged Cyrus decree, we have no indication that the Persians were interested in the rebuilding of the temple and the reestablishment of the sacrificial cult. It was the Jews themselves who wanted the temple and set out to restore it. But in Ezra the laying of the foundations of the temple is ascribed—confusingly—to two different individuals at two different times, Sheshbazzar in the first year or two of Cyrus, and Zerubbabel at the beginning of Darius I's reign (Ezra 1:7-11; 3). This contradiction, however, allows us to make judgments about what the sources tell us and perhaps to reconstruct a more complicated beginnings of the Persian Judah.

It is clear that the biblical emphasis is on Zerubbabel and Joshua, a situation that we find not only in Ezra but also in the prophetic books of Haggai and Zechariah. These latter also cover the beginning of Darius's reign. What they show is that the person of Sheshbazzar has been largely overlooked. In Ezra 1 he seems almost superfluous; however, Ezra 5:13-16 gives us an entirely different perspective: Sheshbazzar is not just an inessential functionary with the redundant task of schlepping a few pots and pans to the temple. On the contrary, his mission was to journey to Jerusalem to be the first governor of the Persian province and to begin the momentous task of rebuilding the temple. Yet, for reasons that we are not told, Sheshbazzar's mission seems to have failed. This is why a decade or more later Zerubbabel and Joshua came to resume the serious work of building that had somehow been interrupted.

Ezra 2:1-2 states that Zerubbabel brought a group of Jews along with Joshua as high priest. Although the placing of the passage suggests it was shortly after Cyrus's decree in 537 (which ignores Sheshbazzar's alleged activities), the books of Zechariah 1–8 and Haggai make it clear that his activity was in the reign of Darius, a good decade or more after Cyrus. Whether he came with a group is unknown, but the numbers were likely to have been small when the demographic situation known from archaeology is considered. It is clear that the list in Ezra 2, with its parallel in Nehemiah 7, does not relate to the time of Darius but much later, perhaps even a

FIGURE 9.1 *The Behistun Inscription Telling of the Persian King Darius's Exploits.*

century or more later. Also, it is not a list of returnees but a sort of census of those living in the land.

Zerubbabel certainly seems to have been appointed as governor (Hag. 1:1; 2:2, 21) but this would probably have been by the regional satrap rather than the central Persian court. More problematic is the question of his work on the temple. According to Ezra 3 and 4, Zerubbabel and Joshua began to work immediately after arriving—while the previous work done by Sheshbazzar is completely ignored. Yet the building activity is said to have been stopped by directives from the Persians, caused by accusations of "enemies." According to Ezra 5:1-2, the two prophets Haggai and Zechariah served to goad the Jewish leadership into resuming work on the temple. As a result of Haggai's and Zechariah's prophecies, the work is resumed, without official permission, about 520 (the second year of Darius). We know from references in cuneiform texts that Tattenai was the governor responsible for the subsatrapy of Ebir-nari, of which Judah was a province.[10] Fortunately, according to the text, the Persian bureaucracy was able to produce the necessary documentation to allow them to continue, and according to Ezra 5:1–6:15 they brought the work to a conclusion about 516 BCE.

Reading the book of Ezra, it all looks straightforward. But when we then read the prophecies of Haggai and Zechariah 1–8, we have a *much different story*. The prophets complain that the temple lies in ruins and call on the people to build it

(Hag. 1; Zech. 4:1-8). There is no mention of (a) any previous activities by anyone (whether Sheshbazzar or Zerubbabel) and (b) absolutely nothing is said about any opposition or a Persian decree against the project. *In Haggai the problem is not the opposition of "enemies" or the prohibition of the Persian administration. The problem is, rather, the people who are more concerned about living in "luxurious" houses than building the temple (Hag. 1:2-4, 9).* They are called on to go to the local hills for timber for building (not to faraway Lebanon for cedar wood, as in Ezra 3:7). The problems suffered by the people come not from adversaries or government officials but drought and poor crops (Hag. 1:5-6, 9-11).

Thus, we have three separate accounts of how the rebuilding of the temple began: (a) by Sheshbazzar (Ezra 1), in the reign of Cyrus (c. 536 BCE), (b) by Zerubbabel (in the reign of Darius), with the work interrupted (Ezra 4–6), (c) by Zerubbabel without interruptions (Haggai, Zechariah).

While one could try to harmonize these accounts by force, such heavy-handed literalism would ignore the nature of the sources. We are not dealing with historical narratives but three theological accounts that, incidentally, contain some historical information. As historians, we have to try to reconstruct what actually happened from such contradictory data.

The Rebuilding and Completion of the Temple

Much of the narrative of Zerubbabel and Joshua relates to the rebuilding of the temple. Yet neither Joshua nor Zerubbabel are mentioned in connection with the ceremony over the temple's completion. This has led to speculation that Zerubbabel and possibly also Joshua were removed by the Persian authorities because of messianic pretensions, either on their own part or on the part of others, perhaps without their consent. Some scholars have suggested that the leading circles of the returnees from Babylonian attempted a restoration of the monarchy in the early Persian period.

Certainly, Haggai and to a lesser extent Zechariah seemed to have seen Zerubbabel as a potential Davidic king over a new Jewish state, but this proves nothing about Zerubbabel's own aspirations or those of the other community leaders. Considering the confidence placed in him by the Persians in choosing him as governor, Zerubbabel was probably more of a realist than the prophets. Whatever the views of Haggai and Zechariah, we have no indication that Zerubbabel himself aspired to royal status or accepted their acclaim at face value. While he may have suffered as a result of messianic stirrings in certain quarters, more likely is that he fulfilled his term of office in the normal way and retired; likewise, Joshua the high priest.

The key to the lack of mention of Zerubbabel and Joshua is probably the date of the temple's completion. Based on Ezra 6:15, this date is normally given as 516 BCE. But as already discussed, the date of building and completion of the temple depends on contradictory *literary* accounts. The first point to note is that this information relating to the completion of the temple has no basis in any known historical source. None of the sources likely to have been available to the writer mention this date. A second point relates to the resources available for temple building, which were unlikely to have been sufficient to allow completion so soon—whether material or manpower. As already noted, the total population at the beginning of the Persian period was likely to have been no more than thirty thousand, including both returnees and native inhabitants. The workers available for the temple would have been very limited. The reality was that the community was also having difficulty with producing sufficient food (Hag. 1:5-6), which was not unusual because of the geography and ecology of the region.

Thus, the claim of the text that the temple was completed in five years almost certainly goes beyond socioeconomic reality. Even accepting that Sheshbazzar had done some work in getting it started, the community is not likely to have had either the resources of material or manpower to complete the work in so short a period of time. An analogy might be the medieval cathedrals that usually took decades—sometimes even centuries—to build. *The one solid datum we can be confident of was that the temple was built.* But the lack of archaeological study of the site means that much else is very uncertain. Yet to assume that the temple was built over a period of time in the last part of the sixth century and was finished by perhaps 500 BCE or not long afterward does not seem unreasonable.

The Appointment of Nehemiah

Ezra 1–6 gives a narrative that purports to tell us about the community in Yehud, ending with the completion of the temple, after which there is a historical blank in the literary sources until the narratives of Ezra 7–10 and Nehemiah: the narrative leaps ahead from about 500 BCE to the middle of the fifth century—to about 445 BCE. My view is that of many scholars: the mission of Nehemiah preceded that of Ezra, in spite of the order of events in the Ezra-Nehemiah narrative. The reasons for dating Ezra to about 398 BCE—later than Nehemiah—will be discussed when we talk about Ezra (p. 166).

In the case of Nehemiah, we are very fortunate in having a writing of Nehemiah himself in the "Nehemiah Memoir" or "Nehemiah Memorial" (NM). This means that we probably know more about Nehemiah than practically any other Judahite of the Persian period. There are two problems with using the NM, however: the first one is that the original writing has been edited into the broader literary context of the book of Nehemiah.[11] The second problem is extremely important because it is too frequently ignored: Nehemiah gives *a* perspective on events but not *the* perspective. That is, the NM represents Nehemiah's own rather individual viewpoint on events, which was clearly not the outlook held by other individuals and groups.

According to Neh. 1, Nehemiah was cupbearer to Artaxerxes the king. Is this credible? We must keep in mind that there were two sorts of cupbearer. There was the royal office of "cupbearer to the king" given as an honorary title to high Persian nobles, usually members of the royal family, who would have been intimate with the king and served in his very presence. We need to be careful, however, for the term "cupbearer" could also refer to someone of lesser rank: to the person who served the king at the table without suggesting a high Persian noble. He carried out his duties in the king's presence and might well come to the king's attention or be known to him for this reason, but his role was basically that of a glorified waiter. Nehemiah was evidently one of this latter sort.

The position is also supported by the description of Nehemiah's journey. Although accompanied by a personal bodyguard, he undertook his journey to Jerusalem with some letters of support that he presented to the appropriate Persian officials. But he was not given authority over the established officials in the region of Ebir-nari. The only special authority he had was to obtain timber from the king's park for some of his building work. This is consistent with the view that Nehemiah received a favor from the king but was not a particularly high official in the Persian administration.

In the text, Nehemiah's commission seems straightforward enough: he simply requested, "Send me to Judah, to the city of my ancestor's graves, and I will rebuild it" (Neh. 2:5). That he would have felt the need to do this seems self-evident and self-explanatory. Yet we soon learn that there is more to it than that. For example, his building project evidently includes building not only the wall but also the building or repair of the "temple fortress" and even his own house (Neh. 2:8). Then, after a delay of several chapters, it is suddenly revealed that he occupies the office of governor of Judah (Neh. 5:14-18; cf. 8:9; 10:2).

Thus, even though the narrative presents Nehemiah's activities as a personal mission and says nothing about a commission from the king, there are hints there was more to it. This has led a number of scholars to suggest other reasons for Nehemiah's mission or at least to have seen resonances elsewhere in the ancient world. A favorite argument has been that Nehemiah was sent by Artaxerxes to secure the western borders of the Persian Empire, for example, against an invasion from Egypt.

It is true that Persia was conscious of possible rebellion in Egypt; indeed, in the latter history of the Persian Empire Egypt was a problem because of unrest and rebellion. But there is no indication that the Persian administration saw Egypt as a threat to the rest of their empire. Even if the Egyptians might have seemed to present a threat, the Persian concern would have been with the area of Phoenicia and the coast. There seems little reason to worry about an inland area like Judah, and if the roads were to be guarded, why did Jerusalem—which was rather out of the way— need fortifying? This suggestion makes Judah much more important in the Persian thinking than it was likely to have been.

In conclusion, we cannot rule out some sort of Persian imperial project, but we also cannot rule out that Nehemiah was primarily carrying out his own personal mission, compelled by his own vision of how things should be in Judah and Jerusalem. Nor can we rule out a combination of the two, but the text gives little support to such an idea. Judging from the text, the activities of Nehemiah related to inner-Judaean measures. There is not the slightest hint that he was implementing specific imperial policies or directives (beyond his general commission as governor to support the Persian system).

Opposition to Nehemiah

What immediately strikes one on reading the book of Nehemiah is the amount of opposition to his activities. A persistent theme through the book is the resistance to his measures that Nehemiah encountered, which seem to have arisen from the start

(Neh. 2:10). We can divide this opposition into two main camps. First, there were Nehemiah's potential rivals at governor level: Sanballat, Tobiah, and Geshem the Arabian. These were local members of the Persian administration who apparently worked together to mutual advantage. We know from primary sources that Sanballat was governor of the province of Samaria, that Geshem was probably an Arab ruler over a considerable territory in Idumea and/or Transjordan, and that Tobiah was probably a member of an old Jewish upper-class family with an estate in Transjordan and perhaps governor over that region.

In this case, the opposition between these individuals and Nehemiah would be quite understandable. It is the perennial political rivalry between officials of a governmental regime, especially one in which local governors of far-flung areas had a certain amount of autonomy. This type of rivalry was mild compared to what we read of between satraps in the Persian administration who, in many cases, became almost independent kings with their own armies and absolute power in their own satrapies. Achaemenid history is filled with examples of unruly satraps who gave pain not only to their fellow satraps but to the king himself. That Persian officials governing contiguous areas might have had little love lost between them needs no explanation. From that point of view the conflict between Nehemiah and the others is what we should expect.

A second reason for opposition was clearly the personality of Nehemiah himself. Time and again his actions are confrontational or, at best, insensitive toward those around him in the province of Judah. He evidently had the knack of antagonizing those who were part of the local administration. This is shown from the very start. No sooner had he arrived in Jerusalem than he made a night inspection of the wall, yet he did this without the knowledge of the local officials (Neh. 2:11-16). Why this secretive reconnaissance? He does not explain, and it makes little sense. All he had to do was tell the local officials that he had come with authority to build the wall and then go out in broad daylight for a proper inspection with those who would be doing much of the supervisory work. We have no evidence that the local people or officials were suspicious of him; on the contrary, the work of building was apparently undertaken with considerable enthusiasm (cf. Neh. 2:17-18). Yet his actions declared from the start that he did not trust the other Jewish officials.

A major question is, how much of the opposition was genuine and how much was an invention of Nehemiah's? As just noted, some rivalry would have been par for the course, but some of the language used by Nehemiah looks suspiciously like hyperbole, as well illustrated by Nehemiah 4. One has the impression that a set of murdering bandits is about to fall upon the poor builders of the wall, that they were opposed by a set of vicious and wily foes who are described in practically demonic terms. Yet at no point does anyone so much as utter "boo" to them. We should not need to be reminded that we have only Nehemiah's version of the situation. The text in Neh. 4:6-7 is difficult and probably corrupt, but his claim to be able to read Sanballat's mind is simply incredible. If Sanballat was planning a raid on Jerusalem, he is hardly likely to tell the local Jews about it (as is implied in Neh. 4:6). If he wanted to stop the building of the wall, why would that have endangered "your sons and daughters, your wives and homes," as suggested in Neh. 4:8? One cannot help wondering if the danger from Sanballat was purely a figment of Nehemiah's overheated imagination.

Nehemiah 6 is one long harangue about those who were less than enthusiastic about the governor of Judah. According to Nehemiah's version of events, his main antagonist Sanballat allied with Geshem the Arabian to "do evil" to him (Neh. 6:2). They sent a message suggesting a meeting. Nehemiah "knows" that this is a mere ruse to get him away by himself to do some unspecified nastiness to him, so he refuses repeated requests to have a meeting (Neh. 6:2-4). How does he know it is a trap? Nothing in the text suggests that he does know; in other words, he is only guessing.

But in all this verbal argy-bargy is the factor that would have been uppermost to Persian provincial governors: the satrap. The satrap was the ultimate boss of both Nehemiah and Sanballat—and he would have taken a dim view of physical or military conflict between provincial governors on his watch. Yet there is resounding silence regarding the satrap.

Perhaps the Sanballat contingent was out to rid themselves of an opponent. But would the Persian satrap, who was ultimately responsible for law and order in his satrapy, allow one governor to murder another? We have to accept the possibility that Sanballat and his supporters may have had a genuine desire to reach an agreement, no doubt to mutual advantage but nevertheless an offer to shake hands and make up. In any case, to attempt to murder Nehemiah would have been a risky undertaking for Sanballat and likely to bring the wrath of the satrap down on him. Yet nowhere in Nehemiah's account does he mention the satrap or how he expected to account for his actions to him.

The accusation that Nehemiah was seeking to set himself up as king seems to have struck a chord (Neh. 6:6-9). Nehemiah rejects this as preposterous, but his own actions belie his suggestion that it was all made up. Nehemiah was too astute to try to rebel against the Persian Empire, as charged by Sanballat; however, the accusation that there were prophets making such claims is quite believable (Neh. 6:7). This would have been a difficult charge to make if no such prophecies were known. As a politician of some knowledge and ability, Nehemiah probably had no plans to proclaim himself the Judaean king; nevertheless, you do not have to have the title of "king" to act like one. No wonder some scholars have suggested that he took the role of petty tyrant in Judah.

Nehemiah's relationships with prophets were interesting (and, incidentally, give us some insight into the prophetic scene at the time). He seems to have had opponents as well as supporters among the prophets. But how he "knows" that Shemaiah had been hired by his opponents to intimidate him is not discussed. The same seems to apply to the prophetess Noadiah. She prophesied something that Nehemiah did not like but that she was actually an opponent of Nehemiah is uncertain. They may simply have been acting by the divine spirit within them like any other prophet.

Of all Nehemiah's opponents, the most interesting is Tobiah "the Ammonite slave" (Neh. 2:10, 19). This designation by Nehemiah was no doubt intended to be a derogatory epithet. The term "slave/servant" (*'eved* in Hebrew) is ambiguous and can designate anyone from the humblest slave to the high government officials who were "humble servants" of the king. Nehemiah's sobriquet is likely to be sarcastic because it fails to recognize Tobiah's Jewishness. Tobiah was not ethnically an Ammonite. He only lived in the old Ammonite region, as we know from information on his descendants (see chapter 10, pp. 191–3). Nehemiah sees Tobiah as one of the conspirators again him, yet Tobiah was from an influential Jewish family and had relations and connections in Jerusalem (Neh. 6:17-19). At a later date, the high priest even allowed him to set up an office in one of the storerooms in the temple area (Neh. 13:4-9). Tobiah was clearly a man of stature in Jerusalem, as well as his home area.

This example of Tobiah begins to help us see part of the cause of the problems. Nehemiah presents the situation in black-and-white terms. As he saw it, people were either for him or against him, and if you supported Tobiah, you were against him. But others among the Jewish leadership did not see it that way. They did not seem to oppose Nehemiah as such, and most of them worked on the wall without hesitation, yet they also saw no reason to treat Tobiah as an enemy. So they tried to maintain good relations with both Tobiah and Nehemiah; moreover, they even attempted to reconcile the two by speaking well of Tobiah to Nehemiah (Neh. 6:18-19). It did not work because Nehemiah was determined to have nothing to do with Tobiah.

Building of the Wall

Nehemiah 3–4 is devoted to the building of the city wall. This task also seems to have been accepted by the Jerusalem authorities without any quibbling. The fact that many of them seem to have worked on the section of the wall nearest to their own homes would have been an additional inducement (Neh. 3). There are some indications of friction, such as the statement that although the Tekoaites repaired, "their nobles" refused to help (Neh. 3:5); however, the reason is not explained.

The work in Nehemiah 4 is given in the context of opposition from Sanballat, but as already noted, it is not at clear that Sanballat was so bothered. According to Neh. 7:1-5, as soon as the gates were set on their hinges, Nehemiah established a guard routine. His lack of trust in those about him is once again indicated by his appointing his brother Hanani to oversee this procedure. Hanani (also apparently mentioned in Neh. 1:2) is indicated by the context to be a literal brother of Nehemiah. It is possible that the first part of 7:2 should be translated, "Hanani my brother, even Hananiah the captain of the acra"; in other words, only one person—not two—is put in charge. All the officials were required to live in Jerusalem (Neh. 11:1). The rest of the people drew lots. The aim was to make a full tenth of the population of the province live in Jerusalem. If one-tenth of the inhabitants of Yehud lived in Jerusalem, this would give more power to Nehemiah himself. Archaeology suggests that at this time Jerusalem did contain about 10 percent of Yehud's population, perhaps three thousand out of a population of about thirty thousand. The effect of building the wall, setting up gates, and increasing the population greatly was to increase the importance and prominence of Jerusalem. *It also made it possible to control the activities of the city's population.*

The dedication of the wall is described in Neh. 12:27-43. The emphasis in this ceremony is naturally on the priests and Levites who make up the bulk of the procession around the city walls. This is the only account in the biblical text of a city wall's being dedicated in this manner. The ceremonies described seem more appropriate to the dedication of the temple; however, it would be thoroughly within Nehemiah's character to give the completion of his building work a divine dimension.

The Fiscal Crisis

With Nehemiah 5, we find a situation that is not clearly dated. To what extent it relates to the building of the wall is an important question, but it seems impossible to answer it from the available data. Some of "the people and their wives" cried out because they had had to sell property or, in some cases, even sell their own children into slavery to buy food or pay taxes. This was an all-too-familiar situation that arises among the peasant population. They would normally be farming at subsistence level, which would give enough to eat, and one hoped a small surplus to buy goods that could not be produced on the farm, to pay taxes, and to meet other expenses. But most farmland was in areas that were marginal enough to have a fair number of bad years. In such years, it was normal to take out a loan to tide the family over until a good year let them pay it back. The problem is that several bad years could come in a row. We also do not know how the tax was calculated. Tax on produce would usually be a percentage of the crop, but a poll tax would probably remain the same even in bad years.

There was clearly a major problem. Unfortunately, Nehemiah could not handle the matter quietly and effectively to resolve the problem, as a good administrator would. Inevitably, he makes a major issue of it, which is the way of the demagogic politician. Nehemiah censures the nobles and leaders publicly for pressing for the repayment of loans, citing his own example of buying back some Jews who had been sold into slavery. He says they have nothing to say for themselves, but this is hardly surprising since Nehemiah himself had gathered a crowd against them (Neh. 5:7-8), again, the action of a demagogue.

He states that he and his servants also have claims against debtors but promises to give them up, thus setting himself up as a righteous example. He then calls the priests and makes "them" swear to keep the promise to return confiscated property (Neh. 5:12). What part do the priests have in this episode? Some have taken it that the priests are seen as accomplices along with the nobles and officials, but they have not been mentioned up to this point. Why should they have been omitted if Nehemiah saw them as guilty along with the rest? It looks more like the priests being called on to witness the oaths, as representatives of the deity in whose name the oaths are being sworn.

One of the problems of interpreting this chapter is what Nehemiah actually did. Did he require the creditors to write off the debts entirely? This looks to be the case on the most obvious reading of the passage. What about the much-criticized nobles? It is important to remind ourselves that we do not have their side of the story. No doubt some had exploited the poor and deserved the censure, but did all? How many of them were not in a financial position to write off large unpaid debts? If those to whom they loaned money could not pay them, could the creditors still pay their own taxes? Had they themselves borrowed money that they expected to pay back when they in turn received payment for money loaned out? The assumption seems to be that the nobles had inexhaustible wealth, and that cancelling debts was of no consequence to them, but why should we assume this? We also find that Nehemiah was no different from those he criticized: he himself was evidently a noble and he, too, had made loans. But if he could support his gubernatorial expenses out of his own pocket (if he did), he might have been in a better position to write off loans than his fellow nobles.

The most important question, though, is this: What did Nehemiah do for the long-term good of the poor? It was a nice gesture to tell the nobles to cancel their debts. What is often overlooked is the result of this, which was that they would cease to make loans to the poor. Then when the tax demands came that could not be paid or when there was a bad year requiring a loan to get the farmers through, who was going to loan them money to pay it? Nehemiah's intervention had ensured that no one would lend money in the future because they had no way of getting it back! The essential principle of loaning against collateral had been outlawed, so there was no incentive to make a loan.

Nehemiah completes his account by enumerating the amount consumed daily at the governor's table and then boasting that he had not availed himself of the governor's food allowance to pay for these expenses (Neh. 5:14-18). Most commentators have viewed his measures with favor, but they usually have not probed beyond the rhetoric to consider the practical implications. Nehemiah has presented himself as a champion of the poor and oppressed, but a close reading of Nehemiah 5 shows elements not entirely consistent with this glowing self-evaluation. Nehemiah mentions that, among other things, an ox a day was served at his table. Over the twelve years of his governorship, this represented more than four thousand cattle—a herd large enough to stock a medium-sized Texas ranch!

Who paid for these, not to mention a flock of sheep six times this size and countless thousands of fowl? Nehemiah pats himself on the back by claiming that he did not collect the governor's tax, in contrast to previous governors, but he is coy about who did pay. One assumes he either collected funds from some other source or he had a private income. But previous governors may not have had such advantages. On the one hand, one has to ask why Nehemiah needed a retinue of 150 locals who ate at his table daily (not to mention visitors from abroad). When we think of the size of Yehud at this time, with a population of probably no more than thirty thousand people, why did a governor need such a large group of administrators, friends, and hangers-on? Was Nehemiah simply indulging in the conspicuous consumption that was characteristic of the Persian government?

The Remainder of Nehemiah's Governorship

A number of Nehemiah's other activities are not clearly dated. One of the main sections with a good deal of miscellaneous material is 12:44–13:31. Four points are emphasized about Nehemiah's achievements in 12:44–13:31: First are the organization and maintenance of the temple cult and its personnel, of which several examples are given. Second would be the repair of the wall, whose completion begins the section (and already described above). Third, the issue of interaction with foreigners is mentioned several times. Finally, the enforcement of Jewish law generally is a topic of some importance.

The importance of paying the temples' dues is emphasized in Neh. 13:10-14. Nehemiah returns from an appointment with the king in Babylon to find that the tithes and other offerings were not being paid, so that the Levites and singers were working in the fields to make a living. Two other examples relate to the general opposition to things foreign. In Neh. 13:4-9 Tobiah insinuates himself into the temple precinct (though it is clear that he has the permission of the high priest). Nehemiah is naturally furious; however, one suspects his reaction is as much because of the success of his (supposed) enemy as of a religious objection to "foreigners." As already noted, Tobiah was undoubtedly Jewish and therefore hardly "foreign." Similarly, when a son of Joiada the son of the high priest had married Sanballat's daughter, Nehemiah drove him out of Jerusalem (Neh. 13:28). Thus, zeal against intermarriage and intercourse with outsiders is difficult to distinguish from straightforward animosity toward an opponent. On the question of Neh. 13:15-22, see the next section.

Nehemiah as Reformer

As has been emphasized above, what we have in the book of Nehemiah is by and large Nehemiah's own assessment of himself plus what an admiring editor passed on to later generations in the present book. Nehemiah portrayed himself as a courageous reformer who championed the poor and oppressed and who was zealous in enforcing the law of God in the province. Where he presents himself in particular as a reformer (or at least is seen by moderns as a reformer) is especially in the two areas of his economic measures (Neh. 5, discussed above) and his religious reforms relating to the intermarriage with "foreigners" and to keeping the Sabbath (Neh. 13).

This has led a number of scholars to make comparisons with classical Greek reformers, such as Pericles and Solon.[12] Solon's reforms parallel Nehemiah's mainly in the area of cancelling debts and releasing those enslaved because of debt (Aristotle, *Athen. Polit.*, 5-9). It is alleged that the complaint of the Athenians was similar to that of those who came to Nehemiah. They wanted redemption from slavery, the abolition of debts, and the redistribution of land. Both Solon and Nehemiah enacted measures to secure the first two but the third was resisted. We know about the reforms of Solon and Nehemiah because both individuals wrote justifications of their actions for posterity. The comparisons between the Greek and the Hebrew are interesting; however, this appears to be not because of any organic connection but probably because in each case the individual is a politician rather than a hereditary ruler and thus needed to gain a certain amount of popular support.

The problem with such comparisons is that they often represent an idealized view of Nehemiah on the part of the modern scholar. We can only summarize a much longer discussion of the question.[13] First, a brief overview of Solon's reforms: there are many historical problems with determining precisely what the crisis was and exactly how Solon addressed it.[14] The issue seems to have been partly a class-based one, with conflict between the old aristocracy and the mass of the people, but in reality it was apparently much more complex than that.

Two groups of poor seem to have been in difficulties, the *peletai* (apparently those who earned their living by working for others) and the *hectomoroi* ("one-sixthers," who were bound to pay a sixth of their crops and produce to the aristocracy). Many of them had borrowed on credit, with their bodies as security. If they defaulted on the loan, they could be sold into slavery, even abroad. In addition, party-political concerns were apparently a major issue, since much of the political power had previously been in the hands of a few wealthy aristocrats.

Possibly the most important of Solon's reforms had to do with long-term economic development. Simply cancelling debt would not necessarily help the poor; indeed, it would have made it even harder for them initially, since creditors would have been reluctant to make loans in the aftermath of the reforms—a point I have already made above. Solon's reforms included not just social reform but political, legal, and economic reform. As will be obvious, there is an interesting parallel to Nehemiah in the cancelling of debts, but otherwise Nehemiah did not carry out full-blown economic or political reform. Solon therefore does not serve as much of a model for Nehemiah, since most of his reforms went far beyond anything that Nehemiah is suggested by the text to have done.

Another comparison is that of Pericles.[15] Here the parallel is quite different: Pericles's reforms have little in common with Solon's. Pericles did not carry out the wide-ranging legal, social, economic, and political reforms that his predecessor had done. Pericles's main action comparable to Nehemiah's was in the area of intermarriage with aliens (Aelian, *Varia Historia* 6.10). He has been credited with introducing pay for jury service and service in some of the other institutions that had previously been done without remuneration. However, this brought financial costs, and Pericles felt the need to reduce the number of citizens who might benefit.[16] It was this that led to his Citizenship Law of 451 BCE, decreeing that only ones whose mother and father were both citizens could be a citizen. Nehemiah's breaking up of marriages in which a Jew had a non-Jewish wife might seem to provide a parallel, but it would be a minor one at most. Since Pericles did not forbid marriage or attempt to break up unions, there is little resemblance to Nehemiah.

To summarize, only one aspect of Solon's reforms is reflected in Nehemiah's actions, that of relieving certain individuals from the threat or actual condition of servitude because of debt. Nehemiah thus helped some individuals, but he did little or nothing for the long-term well-being of the people. Solon was hardly a model for Nehemiah; on the contrary, Nehemiah's rulings possibly only made things worse in the long run, whereas Solon's reforms set Greece on a path to future development and recovery, whatever temporary hardships they might have caused. The comparison with the reforms of Pericles—which seem to have little in common with Solon's—look rather ill fitting. Pericles enacted a law that limited Athenian citizenship to the offspring of both a citizen father and a citizen mother. He did not forbid marriage or attempt to break up unions; in this his actions were very different from Nehemiah's.

The second area where Nehemiah presents himself as a reformer is religious observance (Neh. 13:4-31). A special point is made about enforcement of the sabbath (Neh. 13:15-22). He took a number of steps, which included putting a stop to Jews' working and trading on the day, but especially he forced traders to cease their activities in Jerusalem on the Sabbath. His actions in this case look almost as much an issue of exclusion or control of "foreigners" as of observance of the Sabbath itself. To what extent the Sabbath was simply being brought forcibly to people's attention and to what extent new modes of observing it were being introduced is difficult to say. This is one of the few biblical passages in which Sabbath observance is the main issue. Sabbath observance of some sort probably has a long history in Israel, but the complete cessation of work and trading may not have been envisaged until a rather later time.

Nehemiah was especially zealous in preventing the mixing of Jews with outsiders. This seems to have been part of the motive behind shutting the city against traders on the Sabbath: it would have reduced the influence of Phoenicians and other outsiders on the native inhabitants of the city. Another passage is in Neh. 13:23-28 in which some Jews had allegedly married "Ashdodite, Ammonite, and Moabite women." Finally, he expelled the grandson of the high priest from the community for marrying the daughter of Sanballat.

There are some other references to mixed marriages: Neh. 13:1-4 (in which Nehemiah is not mentioned) and Neh. 9–10 (in which Nehemiah's name occurs but only as one of the signatories while the action is taken by the community as a whole).

Nehemiah's Vision for Judaea

We now come to the crux of the matter: Nehemiah was indeed a reformer with a program that explains a number of his actions. Some of how he related to the people of Yehud seems to have been down to Nehemiah's personality, but what eventually emerges is a man obsessed with a particular vision of the province of Yehud and of Judaism in its widest sense. The various measures instigated by Nehemiah—whether the repair of the wall, the opposition to Sanballat and other "foreigners," the ban on mixed marriages, or even the regulations about the Sabbath—were not just miscellaneous *ad hoc* decisions. Rather, they look distinctly like part of a complete program.

His goal seems no less than to make Judah into an isolated puritanical theocratic state. This program is nowhere explicitly laid out in the book, but the whole thrust of the book is toward this goal. Even the wall building could be seen as a part of this program. There is no indication in the book that Jerusalem needed a wall for physical protection. Most of the people of Judah lived in unwalled villages or in otherwise vulnerable circumstances. A wall can also be a means of controlling those enclosed by it; it can close people off into a ghetto. This seems to have been an important purpose of Nehemiah's wall.

The concept of "foreignness" was another major weapon. All those not a part of the community of returnees are labeled "foreign" in Ezra-Nehemiah, which also seems to be Nehemiah's strategy. The bulk of the inhabitants of the region were the descendants of those Jews not deported to Babylon. It was among this group that religious and ideological ideas at variance with those of Nehemiah and his supporters were most likely to be found. Tobiah was a leading representative of the native Jews who had remained in the land and thus of particular danger to Nehemiah's plans. No wonder Nehemiah was outraged with him!

Views Different from Nehemiah's

When we look at Nehemiah's approach, we might think that this is the biblical perspective—the only perspective. But we need to keep in mind that the Bible is not monolithic. On the contrary, there are different views within it. In this case, we have two other biblical books that are customarily dated to the Persian period. These are the books of Ruth and Jonah, and the book referred to as "Third Isaiah" (Isa.

56–66). But these seem to take a different view of "foreigners" than that found in Ezra-Nehemiah.

According to the book of Ruth, a Moabite woman had married a man of Judah. After his death, she still considered herself a part of her husband's people with close attachment to her mother-in-law, Naomi. She eventually married Boaz, another Judahite, and had a child by him who became an ancestor of King David. Anyone reading the book of Ruth alongside Ezra-Nehemiah could not escape the contrary message: foreigners can become good Jews, foreign wives can be exemplary followers of divine law, and there is no reason to think that their offspring should be excluded from the community as polluted or illegitimate.

Additionally, Jonah gives a message that is compatible with the thought-world of Ruth. It takes the fearsome Assyrians who had devastated the Kingdoms of Israel and Judah—an enemy of the Jews if there ever was one—and makes them objects of pity, compassion, and forgiveness in the eyes of Yahweh. The foreigner is not to be despised but treated sympathetically; it may be that they will eventually come to worship the God of the Jews. As long as they are willing to heed Yahweh, they can take their place alongside the Jews as recipients of divine blessings. Again, this is not a conclusion likely to endear itself to the followers of Nehemiah.

Finally, we have another passage that is likely to date from the Persian period. This is a passage from Third Isaiah (Isa. 56–66): the passage Isaiah 56:3 and 6-8 is quite radical in comparison with other texts of the time. It says essentially that foreigners can have an equal share in the temple and the altar, if they keep the sabbath and other aspects of Yahweh's covenant. Foreigners could not only join the community but could even share in its worship in the temple. What could be further from the sentiments of Ezra-Nehemiah? So, as important as Nehemiah is in Jewish history, his way of thinking was not that of all Jews—not by any means.

Sanballat and the Samaritan Community

Samaria was another Persian province within the larger satrapy of Ebir-nari. As we know from later inscriptions, the people living there claimed to be Israelites.[17] This claim appears to be correct because (as already noted in chapter 6, p. 113) only a small portion of the population in the Northern Kingdom was taken captive to Mesopotamia. The Samaritans were not "Jews" but were related to them, while the Jews are nowhere called "Israelites" at this time by outsiders, according to presently available sources. The majority of Samaritan names are Yahwistic, indicating that Yahweh was their main deity, just as he was of the Jews.

Although the precise administrative structure is nowhere described, we have the names of some governors and other officials. The book of Nehemiah talks about Sanballat without explicitly mentioning that he is governor of Samaria. We have the names of a number of Samarian governors named in contemporary sources. Governors are named as witnesses in some of the documents among the Samarian papyri found at Wadi Daliyeh (chapter 10, p. 186): "[H]ananiah governor of Samaria"; the name, however, may be "['A]naniah."[18] Another apparent reference to the governor is possibly to someone named "Joshua," though only one or two letters of the name are preserved in the photograph: "[before Josh]ua son of Sanballat and Hanan the prefect."[19]

As we shall see in the next section, Delaiah and Shelamaiah are identified as "sons of Sanballat governor of Samaria" in the Elephantine papyri.[20] Neither is certainly named as governor, though Delaiah acts alongside the governor of Judah in another document, raising the possibility that he was governor of Samaria at that time.[21] On Samarian coins *dl* may be an abbreviation of "Delaiah," and *šl* an abbreviation for "Shelamaiah," though the term "governor" is not used. A further governor may be named on a seal impression: "[to Is]aiah son of [San]ballat, governor of Samaria."[22] This gives us the following list of *possible* Samarian governors:

Sanballat "the Horonite" (Nehemiah)

Delaiah (Elephantine; coins?)

Shelemaiah (Elephantine; coins?)

Sanballat, different from the above (seals, coins)

Isaiah(?) (seal)

Joshua(?) (Samarian papyri; seal)

Hananiah or ʿAnaniah (Samarian papyri)

There are a lot of uncertainties even with so short a list. Not all are certainly governors and some of the names are no more than intelligent guesses. In addition to governors, we also have some names of the high officials known as "prefects." Apart from Hanan (noted above), another is "Isiyaton the prefect," and possibly a third: "Aqabiah [the prefect]."[23]

Despite the difficulties, some have wanted to add even further names to the list, including a "Sanballat III." But the existence of this individual depends entirely on Josephus, with all the problems that this entails. Josephus clearly knew little about the Persian period. In this case, he writes that at the end of the Persian period the high priest Jaddua had a brother named Manasseh who married Nikaso the daughter of Sanballat.[24] The Jerusalem elders gave him an ultimatum, to either divorce his wife or give up his priestly duties, but his father-in-law Sanballat offered to build a temple on Gerizim and make him its high priest. Manasseh accepted this offer, and many Jews who had married foreign wives deserted to him and settled in Samaria.

Shortly after this, Alexander invaded. The Jerusalem high priest Jaddua remained loyal to Darius, but Sanballat took soldiers and joined Alexander in his siege of Tyre. Sanballat obtained Alexander's permission and proceeded to build the temple he had promised to Manasseh; however, he died shortly afterward. When Alexander had finished taking Gaza, he marched in anger to Jerusalem to punish the Jews for remaining loyal to Darius. On the way, though, he had a dream and, when he reached Jerusalem, instead of punishing the high priest he dismounted and prostrated himself and honored the high priest and the Jewish god. Such is the story in Josephus.

But what seems perfectly obvious is that Josephus's story of Manasseh and Nikaso is a version of the story found in Neh. 13:28, except that it has been moved a century later. Since Josephus's story of Manasseh and Nikaso looks like a development of this verse, Neh. 13:28 is more likely to represent or at least be closer to the original than would be Josephus's version. Jaddua, the high priest in Josephus's story, has a name in Greek that appears to be a reflex of the Joiada of Neh. 13:28. It looks very much like Josephus has taken the Sanballat of Nehemiah and placed him in the Alexander context, to make his own literary creation. The episode of Alexander's encounter with the Jerusalem high priest is patently a legend with little foundation in reality, as we shall see (chapter 10, pp. 185–6). The figure that some interpret as "Sanballat III" is a phantom—a mistaken displacement of Sanballat I to the end of the Persian period by Josephus.

Among the Samarian coins are several with the letters *sn*, which seems to be an abbreviation of the name *Sanballat*, especially since one coin has the name written out almost in full.[25] These coins fit best with the "Sanballat II" who is attested in the primary sources.[26] As for the governor Hananiah or the individual on the seal impression who may be Joshua and who may have been governor, we have no evidence that they were members of the Sanballat family, as some have assumed. The assertion that the government of Samaria was kept in the Sanballat family throughout the Persian period is simply conjecture and nothing more. Finally, there seems to be archaeological evidence of a Persian-period Samaritan temple on Mount Gerizim, but contrary to some claims this seems to be dated to the late fifth or early fourth century—probably the time of Nehemiah and Sanballat I.

The Elephantine Jewish Community

In addition to the Jews in Yehud, we have already noticed that we have some information on the communities that were forcibly settled in Babylonia. Another community that we know about was settled in Elephantine, an island in the Nile near Aswan in Egypt. Documents and other data from the community became known to us, relating to the period after Nehemiah's governorship, from the latter part of the fifth century BCE. Relevant papyri and ostraca appeared on the antiquities market through much of the 1800s. Eventually, the site was located and excavated archaeologically beginning in 1904. The finds from Elephantine allow us to get much closer to the daily lives of the community than is the case for most Jewish communities in the Second Temple period. Sadly, only a brief sketch can be given here.[27]

The site in original documents is called "Jeb." According to one letter, the colony was flourishing with its own temple when Cambyses conquered Egypt about 525 BCE. The most exciting—and distressing—event came about 410 BCE when the temple was apparently destroyed by the priests carrying out the cult of the ram goat Khnum who had a temple nearby. According to the Jewish version (which is the only one we have—nothing from the Egyptian side of this event has survived), the priests of Khnum instigated an attack on the temple of Yahu and effected its destruction (after it had apparently stood for more than a century).

One cannot help wondering about the cause—or one of the causes—of the destruction. A recent study suggests it escalated from the incident of a stolen jewel that was possessed by the Egyptian community but ended up in the hands of Jewish traders.[28] On the other hand, the Khnum priests were already not completely happy about the official recognition of the neighboring Jewish community. As worshipers of the ram god, it is possible they objected to the sacrifice of lambs at the Yahu temple. The Passover Papyrus, which is one of the documents in the archive, may have been the response to a request from the Elephantine Jewish community for permission to carry on the traditional pascal celebrations in the face of opposition (a missing part of the papyrus makes interpretation difficult). If so, the stolen jewel might have been the last straw.

The community wrote to various officials for permission to rebuild this temple: Bagohi, the governor of Judah; the Jerusalem high priest Johanan; Ostanes, an important figure among the Jerusalem nobles; and Delaiah and Shelemiah, the sons of the Samarian Governor Sanballat. For some strange reason, they did not write to the Egyptian Governor Arsames, or at least no such communication has been preserved (though a copy of the memorandum from Bagohi and Delaiah may have been sent to Arsames). These requests were made over a period of several years (from 410 until after 407 BCE).

Much has been made of the lack of a reply to their letter to the Jerusalem high priest, often with the conclusion that the priest did not reply because Jerusalem disapproved of the Elephantine temple. That is of course possible, but there are many other possibilities. There are an awful lot of swamps, bars, and brothels between Jerusalem and Elephantine: perhaps the letter never reached its destination in Jerusalem. Or perhaps the high priest received the letter, consulted his advisors, and then replied, but his reply failed to reach the Elephantine community. These are all possibilities; we simply do not know.

Finally, the community sent a proposal with two new aspects: first, holocausts (animal sacrifice) would not be offered, only incense and meal offerings; also, the community would pay silver (the amount is now lost in a damaged part of the papyrus) and a thousand measures of barley (perhaps about 55,000 litres). Whether these were the necessary concessions to secure agreement is a matter of speculation, but it was after this offer was made that approval came in the form of a memorandum from Bagohi (governor of Judah) and Delaiah (governor of Samaria).

A number of the documents fall into the category of an archive of a particular family, including the individuals Jedaniah, Mibtahiah, and Anani. Especially important is the "communal archive" of Jedaniah who was an important figure in the community. This archive contains documents important for the temple of Yahu, including letters about Passover observance, the destruction of the temple, and requests for rebuilding. Indeed, much of what we know about the community relates to the temple of Yahu. Quite a few documents mention it in passing. We are fortunate in having several writings that discuss ownership of real estate property, from which the actual location of different domiciles in Elephantine can be reconstructed, even if with some uncertainty. A sale of property dated to 402 BCE mentions the apparently rebuilt temple of Yahu as forming part of the property's boundary. There is also a list of payments or gifts of money on behalf of the Jewish garrison to "Yahu the god," dated to 400 BCE. The documentation ceases in 399 BCE, and the ultimate fate of the community is unknown.

One of the values of the Elephantine documents is the insight they give us into the practice of religion by the Jewish community of Jeb. The priests of the temple of Yahu are referred to by the term *khn*—compare the normal Hebrew term for priest, which is *kōhēn* (as opposed to *kmr*, which is used of pagan priests, such as the priests of Nabu, Baal, and Khnum). We also have the names of some of these priests at Elephantine. The most important is Jedaniah, son of (Gemariah?; the name is partially destroyed), who was clearly a community leader, as indicated by many of the ten documents in the "Jedaniah archive." He is the main figure writing to Bagohi, the governor of Judah, about the destruction of the Jeb temple and the desire of the community to have it rebuilt. Other named priests are Johanan and Shelem[iah?].

In addition to priests, there are references to the office of *lḥn*, which seems to be some sort of "temple servant" in the temple of Yahu, perhaps the general manager of the temple, including responsibility for general upkeep and maintenance. If so, it would be analogous to the Levites in the Jerusalem temple, though, interestingly, the term used is not "Levite" or any other term used in the biblical text. Most of the twenty or so occurrences of this term are to Ananiah (or Anani) son of Azariah, the man who married the slave Tamet. The office *lḥn* is mentioned as a way of defining Anani(ah), but no elaboration of the term or its meaning can be found in the extant texts at Elephantine. One has the impression that while there were a number of priests, there was only one *lḥn* in the temple of Yahu. His wife Tamet (or Tapamet) is also a "female temple servant" (*lḥnh*) of the temple of Yahu.

The weekly Sabbath is mentioned several times in the Elephantine papyri, though the broken context makes it difficult to interpret some of the references. One ostracon from the early fifth century tells of sending some legumes by boat, and the boat is to be met by the recipient on the Sabbath to take charge of the cargo. Another ostracon of about the same time asks for goods (including salt) to be dispatched, apparently before the Sabbath. Finally, an ostracon of a similar date seems to ask for something to be sent, apparently on the Sabbath, though the word in question is damaged. The impression is that the Sabbath was known and given a particular designation but was not observed in any strict sense. This might fit a transition period in which the place of the Sabbath in society was being very much debated.

Likewise, we hear of the Passover. The Passover is mentioned in passing in a number of ostraca, indicating that it was a normal celebration. The most famous text is the so-called Passover Papyrus, yet this is a very curious text.[29] It does not in fact contain the word "Passover," since the text is fragmentary. In any case, the content of the sections preserved is about unleavened bread, removal of leavening, and other aspects of Passover observance, though nothing about the Passover lamb. Only the left-hand side is preserved, making reconstruction of the original text problematic. The purpose of the text is unclear. The letter comes from a man named Hananiah, a Jew, but he claims some sort of communication from King Darius (II) to Arsames the satrap of Egypt.

In summary, the traditional festivals and holy days known from the Elephantine papyri are the weekly Sabbath, Passover, and possibly the Feast of Weeks. Most surprising is that the Day of Atonement does not appear, but it is also absent from Ezra-Nehemiah. What to make of this is difficult to say. *But although many legal and quasi-legal texts are known from Elephantine, they do not seem to have known of the "Book of the Law"—the "Books of Moses" or the Pentateuch.*

The name "Moses" does not appear anywhere in these texts. Considering that a number of traditional Jewish practices are attested and that worship of Yahu is regularly carried out in the local temple, it seems unlikely that lack of Moses's name is accidental, especially when you consider that "Aaron," "Levites," and many of the common sacrifices of Leviticus, and even the Hebrew word *torah* (or its presumed Aramaic equivalent *dat*) are also absent from the extant texts. The Elephantine community clearly did not have or know of the *law book* that Ezra is claimed to have brought (Ezra 7). Yet you do not need a law book for traditional religious observances. Many of these celebrations had been in the community for many generations.

As noted above, although we have no evidence of a response to the letter from Elephantine to the Jerusalem high priest, there was very evidently communication between the two communities. This looks to be obvious if the Jews of Elephantine were aware of who the current high priest was. It therefore seems likely that Jerusalem would have communicated any urgent religious matters to the Elephantine community, such as the promulgation of a new law book like the Pentateuch. The silence about such a book cannot be judged as purely accidental. If Ezra promulgated the Pentateuch, as seems the case, this was after the extant Elephantine documents were written (see further on pp. 200–3).

The Mission of Ezra the Scribe (Ezra 7–10; Neh. 8)

When Did Ezra Work?

Our first task is to find out when Ezra came to Jerusalem and did his work. Nehemiah is said to have come to Palestine in the twentieth year of Artaxerxes (445 BCE), returned to Babylon in the thirty-second year (433 BCE), and come back again to Palestine sometime after this (Neh. 2:1; 13:6-7). According to the order of events in the book of Ezra-Nehemiah, the priest and scribe Ezra came some years before Nehemiah, in the seventh year of Artaxerxes, or 458 BCE. This traditional dating came under attack with the rise of critical scholarship and was generally rejected by most scholars.

The critical view that seems most cogent to me is that Ezra came in the seventh year of Artaxerxes II, or 398 BCE. The reasons for arguing this are as follows:[30]

- The careers of Ezra and Nehemiah are actually recounted separately, apart from a few verses which are probably editorial: the inclusion of Nehemiah in Neh. 8:9 is not found in 1 Esdras 9:49, while Ezra's name seems secondary in Neh. 12:36. Furthermore, the same problems of mixed marriages and keeping God's law are addressed by both Ezra and Nehemiah. While it seems strange that Nehemiah would have had to address the same problems only a decade or so after Ezra—indeed, while he was still in Jerusalem—it would not be strange if a general relapse had taken place in the three and a half decades from about 432 to 398 BCE.

- The wall of Jerusalem was not built until Nehemiah's governorship, yet Ezra 9:9 indicates a wall was there when Ezra arrived. A wall for "Judah and

Jerusalem" would certainly imply a literal wall around Jerusalem. Also, the Hebrew word for "wall" (*gādēr*) is used in Mic. 7:11 to mean a city wall.

- The high priest in the time of Nehemiah was Eliashib, but in the time of Ezra it was Johanan *son of* Eliashib (Ezra 10:6, though according to Neh. 12:11, the term "son" should probably be interpreted in the sense of "grandson").

- The lack of any knowledge of the "book of the law" at Elephantine or in Yehud before about 400 BCE goes very much against Ezra's coming to promote the Torah before 450 BCE. Hence, if the "seventh year of Artaxerxes" is a reliable date, then taking it as a reference to Artaxerxes II makes the most sense.

Historical Problems in the Ezra Story

Our knowledge of Ezra comes entirely from the Ezra tradition, which means Ezra 7–10 and Nehemiah 8 in the Hebrew (and Aramaic) Ezra-Nehemiah. There is also the Greek 1 Esdras, which has none of the Nehemiah material and in my opinion represents an earlier version of the Ezra tradition. Ezra then disappears from Jewish literature until the book of 4 Ezra (or 2 Esdras) about 100 CE. Other references to this period refer only to Nehemiah or to Zerubbabel and Joshua (Ben Sira 49:11-13; 2 Macc. 2:13), whereas Ezra is completely ignored. Thus, for any knowledge or understanding of Ezra we have nothing to go on other than our critical analysis of this Ezra tradition.

Unfortunately, a careful reading of the Ezra story in Ezra 7–10 reveals many contradictions, incongruities, anachronisms, and absurdities. The story of Ezra seems straightforward enough at first glance. He is introduced by his genealogy, tracing his ancestry back to Aaron the priest (Ezra 7:1-5). He is also identified as a scribe and one devoted to study of the law (Ezra 7:6, 10). He received a document from King Artaxerxes permitting him to return, to bring with him various people and gold and silver for the temple, and to teach the law (Ezra 7:12-26). When he arrives, he finds a problem in that certain people have intermarried with "foreigners." He sets about resolving this problem, which is how Ezra 7–10 ends, though an additional section on the reading of the law (Neh. 8) should be included here.

Once one goes beyond the surface, though, problems immediately manifest themselves. The first problem is the letter of Artaxerxes in Ezra 7. This is sometimes referred to as the "Artaxerxes rescript," but it (along with the other "documents" in Ezra 4–6) is not a straightforward Persian document. A careful study of the alleged Persian letters in Ezra 4–7 shows that they cannot belong to the time of the Persian Empire.[31] To summarize a long and technical discussion, the letters in their present form belong to the period after the conquests of Alexander:

- The form and orthography of the Aramaic language used is post-Achaemenid.
- The epistolary form of the letters is best paralleled in the Greek tradition.
- Some of the content of the letters shows lack of knowledge of the Persian Empire.

Yet the letters are probably not complete fabrications: in some cases the letters may indeed be complete inventions by the editor of the book, but in other cases our information suggests that they may well be based on genuine Persian correspondence which was then worked over by Jewish editors at a later time. The letter in Ezra 5:7-17 looks the most authentic.

The Artaxerxes letter of Ezra 7:12-26 has some features that suggest a genuine Persian document, but other aspects of it are problematic in language and background, suggesting an original document that has been heavily edited at a much later time by Jewish scribes. The first statement is that anyone of the "people of Israel and its priests and Levites" who wants to go to Jerusalem has permission to go with Ezra (7:13); a couple of verses later "the God of Israel whose dwelling is in Jerusalem" is mentioned (Ezra 7:15). *Yet foreigners never refer to Judah or its people as "Israel"; these are phrases that would be used only by a Jew writing with a theological purpose, not by a scribe (whatever his ethnic affinity) drawing up a document in the Persian chancellery.*

The king and "his seven counsellors" also allow Ezra to "regulate" or "act as overseer over" Judah and Jerusalem by the "law (Aramaic *dāt*) of your God in your hand" (Ezra 7:14). These "seven counsellors" appear in no other document relating to the king in the Persian period. That the king had counsellors is par for the course; *that he would have shared his authority by issuing decrees or orders in the names of counsellors as well as his own is unthinkable.* Next, Ezra is given permission to convey the silver and gold which the king and his counsellors have generously offered to the "God of Israel [*sic*!] whose dwelling is in Jerusalem" (Ezra 7:15). *Even the king and his counsellors tacitly place themselves under the sovereignty of Yahweh in this letter, which is hardly credible.*

Furthermore, "all the silver and gold found in all the satrapy of Babylon" is to be given over to the house of their God in Jerusalem; this is in addition to all the gold and silver freely donated by the people and priests (Ezra 7:16). This money is to be used for purchasing animals, grain, and drink to be offered on the Jerusalem altar (Ezra 7:17). Whatever money is left over can be used for whatever the priests want, according to God's will (Ezra 7:18). Any other needs, such as of temple vessels, are to be paid from the royal treasury, up to 100 talents of silver (Ezra 7:19-22).

This generosity of the Persian government goes far beyond the realms of reality— they can be nothing more than flights of fantasy. The king and his counsellors give donations, the people and priests given donations, Ezra is allowed to take all the silver and gold found in the satrapy of Babylon. As if that is not enough, Ezra can take up to another 100 talents of silver from the treasury as "petty cash." God has indeed given Ezra favor in the eyes of the king! But there is more to come: it was forbidden to tax the priests, Levites, temple singers, and other temple servants (Ezra 7:24). No wonder that Ezra offers such profuse praise to God at the end of the chapter (Ezra 7:27-28)! *This is not the decree of a Persian king but the wishful thinking of a Jewish apologist.*

After riches comes political power: Ezra is told that he is "to appoint officials and judges to be judging all the people in the region of Ebir-nari, both those who know the law and those who do not," according to the wisdom of the law in his hand (Ezra 7:25-26). He is to teach those who do not know the law. It is often suggested that this "obviously" refers only to Jews, but such interpretations prefer to apologize for the text rather than read it for what it says. There is no basis in the decree itself for the interpretation that Ezra's authority is limited to Jews. The overt referent is all the people in the satrapy west of the Euphrates, and the mention of the "law of your God and the law of the king" suggests that not just Jews are being talked about. The intent of the phrase seems to be that "the law of your God" is treated the same as "the law of the king." Any who do not obey are to be punished as appropriate.

Ezra has clearly been given some very sweeping powers. The extent of these powers is hinted at in Ezra 8:36 where the orders of the king are handed over to the "satraps and governors of the province Beyond-the-River." The element blatantly missing in all this handing out of power is the satrap of Ebir-nari. It is unlikely that Ezra would be allowed to impose his own choice of judges and magistrates and also the laws of his god on all of Ebir-nari, much less without reference to the powerful satrap of this region, yet the satrap is completely ignored. Although the power and office of the satrap varied from place to place, time to time, and even individual to individual, they were usually members of the royal family with a great deal of independence and power, including military command and troops. It is unthinkable that Ezra would be allowed to interfere in the legal and judicial system of the satrapy without some reference to the satrap.

The preparation for the journey to Jerusalem and the activities once Ezra arrived there are described in Ezra 8 (the journey itself, as so often in the biblical text, is passed over in silence). He collects a group of those who wish to return, including priests. Finding that there are no Levites among them, he sends to Casiphia and manages to convince a handful of Levites and a couple of hundred temple servants to accompany him. Why he needs Levites is not discussed other than their designation as "ministers for the house of our God" (Ezra 8:17)—but *Levites had already been ministering in the temple for many decades, perhaps even a century or more*, if Ezra 1–6 is to be believed.

Next Ezra proclaims a fast (8:21-23). Why? Because Ezra is "ashamed to ask the king" for a bodyguard of soldiers and horsemen to protect them on the journey. This might sound like a simple case of putting his faith in God rather than men. However, the narrative goes on to state that the gold and silver gathered to take to Jerusalem was committed to the care of twelve priests for the journey. Here the story becomes completely incredible: the gold and silver said to have been donated for the Jerusalem temple amounted to 650 talents of silver, 100 talents of gold, and various expensive vessels for the temple. A talent was usually about 3,000 shekels, the preserved shekel weights being about 10 grams each (a convenient figure, though it might be a bit heavier, even up to 14 grams). A talent was thus approximately 30 kilograms (roughly 65 pounds); 100 talents of gold was about 3 metric tonnes of gold. In this case, the silver amounted to about 19,500 kilograms or 19.5 tonnes of silver. To this were to be added the hundred silver vessels of a talent each, twenty of gold, and two of an exceptionally fine quantity of bronze. Leaving out the two bronze vessels, *it all adds up to more than 25 metric tonnes of silver and gold—truly a king's ransom!*

It is difficult to grasp how much wealth Ezra's small band was allegedly transporting from Babylon to Judah. According to Herodotus 3.91, the entire satrapy of Ebir-nari produced tribute of only about 350 talents of silver per year. This would make the 120 talents of gold (including the gold vessels) equivalent in silver to 1,560 talents.

Adding up the gold's silver equivalent with the actual silver, we find that Ezra's treasure comes to a total equivalent of more than 2,300 talents of silver.[32] According to the text, the entire income of the satrapy of Ebir-nari for six and a half years has been assigned to Ezra. Considering that the entire Persian Empire under Darius is said to have yielded 14,560 talents of silver a year, *we are expected to believe that a tiny province on the edge of the empire has had 15 percent of the annual Persian income assigned to it.*

This, in itself, is incredible, but it raises a further serious question: Is it likely that the Persian king, having himself donated a large quantity of precious gifts, would have allowed Ezra to risk transporting this all without military protection? *Far from Ezra's being embarrassed to ask for a guard, the king would have insisted on it!* The textual statement that the precious metal was assigned to just twelve priests to be "guarded diligently" (how?) over hundreds of miles looks just silly (Ezra 8:24-31). Keep in mind that Nehemiah made no objection to the armed escort provided by the king (Neh. 2:9)—and he was not transporting vast quantities of wealth!

Finally, when Ezra arrives in Jerusalem, he hands over the "orders to the royal satraps and governors of the satrapy Ebir-nari" (Ezra 8:36). How he was able to do this is not stated. It seems to be implied that all twenty-three or so satraps—plus dozens or hundreds of governors—assembled in Jerusalem expressly to receive their orders. Can you imagine twenty-three high nobles—some Persian princes—leaving their domains to travel hundreds of miles to Jerusalem, just to receive orders from this Jewish priest? Once again, the text of Ezra presents us with a very unrealistic scenario.

The Episode of Marriage with "Foreign" Wives

The next part of Ezra's story is an episode relating to marriage with "foreign wives" (Ezra 9–10). Officials (of Jerusalem? of the province?) approach Ezra to tell him of the problem that some have intermarried with the "peoples of the land" (Ezra 9:1-2). What does Ezra do? He has been given the power and authority to teach and enforce the law over the entire satrapy, and to appoint judges to fulfill this task. Yet when confronted with an actual situation, there is only stupification instead of decisive action. Ezra tears his garments and hair and sits on the ground in the square (Nehemiah, on the contrary, tears the hair of his opponents [Neh. 13:25]). After sitting in the dust until evening, he then prays (Ezra 9:3-15). Perhaps mourning and prayer might be what we expect of a pious priest, but we should also expect action from this powerful individual.

Action does come about in Ezra 10, but who initiates it? Surprisingly, not Ezra. A great crowd of people gather round him, weeping. It is one of these, Shecaniah son of Jehiel, who recommends a course of action to be followed, primarily the swearing of an oath. Finally, Ezra does something decisive: he accepts this advice and acts on it. Then he goes off to fast. In the meantime, "they" (not Ezra, interestingly, but perhaps some of the officers [Ezra 10:7]) send out a decree for all Jews to assemble in Jerusalem. The rest of the chapter describes the measures taken, in which Ezra seems finally to play a full part in causing some Jewish men—some important officials—to cast off their wives and children.

So far, the narrative has established Ezra's character—or lack of it. But the question is this: How credible is this scenario? From a modern point of view, most of us would express disgust and even horror that men cast out their wives and children like this. Furthermore, there is the fact that these "foreign wives" could only have been *Jewish women*—women from Jewish families that had not been taken captive at the time of Nebuchadnezzar. The author of Ezra-Nehemiah simply refuses to accept that the bulk of the Jewish community included Jews who were descendants of those left in the land after the Babylonian captivity.

But when we analyze it carefully, we find numerous reasons to doubt that this story represents historical reality. The following considerations give grounds for thinking the author of the book has created an imaginary scenario that feeds his view of piety: (1) the situation in Ezra 9–10 looks remarkably parallel to Nehemiah 9–10 and might be modeled on that passage; (2) a number of the names in the list in Ezra 10:18-43 seem to be borrowed from the list in Ezra 2//Nehemiah 7; (3) the men named, including a number of priests, were not likely to submit quietly to being forced to give up their wives and families; (4) as just mentioned, the wives in question seem more likely to be the descendants of Jews who were not deported rather than actual foreigners; (5) and such a situation would almost certainly come to the attention of the Persian administration who would not be pleased with the potential instability being created.

We can compare Ezra 9–10 with Neh. 13:23-28. In the latter passage, Nehemiah talks about Jews who had married inhabitants of Ashdod, Ammon, and Moab. He intervened, though it is not clear that he broke the marriages up, but he did drive out the son of the high priest who had married a daughter of Sanballat (Neh. 13:28). This looks much more realistic. The marriages described are with individuals outside the Judahite community, and it fits Nehemiah's personality to intervene vigorously. Thus, there was probably some intermarriage with outsiders on the margins of society, but it was unlikely to have been a major issue. Thus, the passage in Neh. 13:23-28 looks realistic, but the actions in Ezra 9–10 look like a scene from a novel.

Ezra as Lawgiver

There is no doubt that many problems exist with the Ezra tradition, from a historical point of view. We have just outlined some of these: the story was written with a theological aim and has the primary goal of teaching theological lessons. Yet it is very likely that there was a historical Ezra. The focus of the Ezra tradition is on law, the Book of the Law (*tôrāh* in Hebrew; *dāt* in Aramaic). Take away the law, and the Ezra tradition evaporates. If there is anything historical about the Ezra tradition, it is the law. It seems likely that any historical figure in the Ezra tradition had something to do with Jewish law.[33] Much of the content of the Pentateuch was already in existence—whether in oral or written form—but it had not been written down into the final text that it now has.

Did Ezra edit the Pentateuch, or direct a team in editing it, or assist in editing it? Was his job only to go to Yehud and promulgate the new Book of the Law? Or was he possibly both the foregoing: an editor and a teacher? If we follow the Ezra tradition, we might tend to say, "All of the above." Even though Ezra is ignored or omitted in several traditions, no one else after the time of Moses is given credit for writing/editing the law. In spite of statements about Nehemiah in the book of Nehemiah[34] and elsewhere (e.g., 2 Macc. 2:13-15), he is not made a writer or promulgator of the *Torah*.

It is clear from the Elephantine papyri, as well as indications in Ezra-Nehemiah itself, that the Pentateuch was not in existence until the late Persian period, probably after 400 BCE. What seems clear is that the community at Elephantine did not know any "Book of the Law of Moses" before the year 400 BCE. The Pentateuch as we know it seems to be later than this time. The Jewish community at Elephantine was in contact with the various Palestinian provinces, including Judah and Jerusalem, and was well aware of who the current high priest was. It therefore seems likely that Jerusalem would have communicated any urgent religious matters to the Elephantine community, such as the promulgation of a new law book like the Pentateuch. The silence about such a book in the Elephantine letters cannot be judged as purely accidental.

Whatever written traditions existed among the Jews by the beginning of the Persian period, it was in the Persian period that the need for written records of the Jewish religious traditions would have been first strongly felt. The reason is the changed status of the government of Judah. Judah was no longer a nation—not even a vassal state—but functioned as a small distant province within the Babylonian and then the Persian Empire. There was no native king and clearly no prospect of one in the foreseeable future. A major break in religious continuity had occurred with the loss of the monarchy (the king had previously acted as the main religious figure and religious official). The temple personnel—the high priest in particular—would have been seen by the community as filling this vacuum in leadership. It is at such times that a people are conscious of a break in its history. It is at such times that attempts are often made to collect, organize, and record the traditions that up to then had been the repository of the national folk memory.

It is in the early Greek period that the Pentateuch is first clearly attested. It might be referred to by Hecataeus of Abdera in Diodorus 40.3.6 when he mentions a "written" book of law among the Jews about 300 BCE.[35] Clearer is Ben Sira writing about 200 BCE, in the section 44:1–49:16, known as the "Praise of the Ancestors." His statements suggest a version of the Pentateuch at least in outline similar to our present one. We know, of course, that the text of the Pentateuch continued to circulate in several forms even to the present, but a recognizable version is likely to have been available—and considered authoritative—by 200 BCE.[36] Part of the consideration is that the Pentateuch was translated into Greek in Alexandria about the mid-third century (discussed in the next section). We also need to consider the time it would take after completion to become widely accepted as sacred literature. Putting all the information together, there seems to be good evidence that the *torah* in much the form as we know it—the "five books of Moses"—is a product of the Persian period.[37] This does not, of course, rule out further textual and even literary developments in these books in subsequent periods.

A number of passages in Ezra-Nehemiah assume that the law was long known. But what is surprising is that when one reads carefully, there are also passages that suggest the Pentateuch was not known to the community, or at least not in the form that the Pentateuch now takes. When we read Ezra 7 and Nehemiah 8, it seems clear that the law is being pictured as a new one. The immediate consequence of reading this book is to find that they should be keeping the Feast of Tabernacles, including spending the eight days of the festival in booths, "which the Israelites had not done from the days of Joshua" (Neh. 8:17). This is despite such passages as Ezra 3:2-6 that state that long before Nehemiah and Ezra the Jews of Jerusalem were celebrating the festival according to the law of Moses! Both situations cannot be right.

The only logical conclusion is that the Ezra's law as such was new, and much of its content came as a surprise to the Jews of Yehud. Thus, the literary picture of Ezra-Nehemiah is a contradictory one. On the one hand, it wants us to believe that the law of Moses was known and practiced from the beginning of the return. On the other hand, it also gives the distinct impression that the book of the law read by Ezra was new to the people. The dichotomy can be explained by assuming that the *first is the ideology of the author* (Moses wrote the Pentateuch long ago and Israel has been following it) while *the second is much closer to reality: the "book of Moses" was probably something that took shape in the Persian period—after 400 BCE.*

Thus, Ezra as the lawgiver is a strong one in early Judaism. What is perhaps more important is that no other figure (apart from Moses) is accorded the position of lawgiver in any of the traditions. Wherever there is a legislator other than Moses in the Bible, it is Ezra. The Ezra tradition is, consequently, believable when it has him associated in some way with the Book of the Law. A request by Ezra or a Jewish group or even the Jews of Judah to promulgate a newly created "Book of the *Torah* of Moses" would probably have met with a favorable response from the Persian government.[38]

The Final Century of Persian Rule

A curtain comes down over events in Yehud toward the end of Nehemiah's governorship, and we are left in the dark of how things developed. We have to make room for the Ezra tradition, but it is too unreliable to allow its narrative of specific events. All we can say is that apparently the existence and contents of the Pentateuch were disseminated in some fashion. The last century of Persian rule is frustrating because the narrative sources come to an end. We have the curious episode of the high priest's alleged killing of his brother in the temple (Josephus, (*Ant.* 11.7.1 §§297–301). But if the incident did occur (some strongly doubt it), it was only a blip in Jewish history.[39]

Two events that might have affected Yehud are the "Revolt of the Satraps" and the "Tennes Rebellion." Both have been seen by some as major events for the region of Phoenicia and Palestine, with potentially serious effects on the history of Judah. The Tennes rebellion, especially, is routinely referred to in the scholarly literature discussing this period of time, but both are often appealed to in support of theories about the history of Yehud. Yet there are major questions about both these events, especially with the reconstructions sometimes made by historians.

First, the "Revolt of the Satraps": according to Diodorus Siculus (15.90), a great revolt of Ionic cities, along with an uprising of some of the Asia Minor satraps, took place against Artaxerxes III (359–338 BCE). Tachos, the king of Egypt, took advantage of this by gathering ships and mercenaries to fight against the Persians. There are problems with Diodorus's account, however, one of the main ones being the lack of any other continuous narrative of the revolt. Some occasional references (e.g., Pompeius Trogus, the Greek orators, monuments) give a rather different (and more complicated) picture. There was revolt—or revolts—but probably less serious than Diodorus states: "We are not dealing with a general, coordinated conflagration on the western front in 361 but rather with a series of limited local revolts over the course of a decade."[40]

As for the Tennes Rebellion, our main source is also Diodorus Siculus. A number of points about his account are problematic and other issues are still opaque to the modern historian.[41] The precise dates of the revolt are uncertain, but it appears to have been rather more short lived than the dates 351 to 345 often given. The reasons for the revolt are unclear. The sources seeming to associate the Jews with the rebellion are "suspect and contradictory," especially on the chronological level.[42] Most of the archaeological sites allegedly destroyed lie outside Judah proper, with the exception of Jericho. The archaeology of Jericho does not appear to be precise enough to demonstrate a destruction at this time. In sum, although the rebellion of Tennes was potentially serious, it seems to have collapsed suddenly without any major fighting. The only city destroyed was Sidon, and this is alleged to have been burnt by the Sidonians themselves. There is little evidence that other areas of Phoenicia suffered from fighting, much less Samaria or Judah or other areas of the Palestinian interior.

The Book of Esther

The book of Esther is ostensibly set in the Persian court and—on the surface—might be able to give us information about the Jews of the Persian period. The question is whether it really knows anything about the events, or the context envisaged in the book. First, the text presents textual problems in that the story itself exists in more than one version and has a long history of development, which raises the question of which version we should use to ask questions about historicity. There are also some indications that it was written, or at least completed, in the Hellenistic period. Finally, the term "novel" (or perhaps more generously, "historical novel") has often been applied to it. Even if the story is a fiction, it is still possible that the book contains genuine historical remembrances and knowledge of certain customs and practices; for example, the author appears to know the city of Susa, which features heavily in the story.

On the other hand, the story it purports to tell about a Jewish adviser to the king and his niece who became queen consort is clearly unhistorical. A study of Persian history fails to find a Queen Vashti or a Queen Esther for King Xerxes I—or any other Persian king, for that matter. Persian kings practiced endogamy, with spouses chosen from a limited number of noble families.[43] Xerxes would not have married outside this narrow circle even among the Persian nobility, much less a woman plucked from the streets, as it were. We also find no Mordecai, or anyone like him.

The book represents a genre sometimes known as the *Diasporanovelle*, a "novel of the diaspora."

On the positive side, it shows that it was possible for Jews to rise within court circles, though how high any of them went is a matter of speculation. It also has the function of describing the origins of the festival of Purim, not one of the original Hebrew festivals nor considered a holy day but one that became an important traditional celebration, nonetheless. A final point is that the book gives another example of a Jewish heroine, alongside women such as Ruth, Jael (in Judg. 4–5), and Judith. It is perhaps this feminist aspect that has spawned the great interest in the book recently, along with its textual complexity.

The Importance of the Persian Period for Judaism

Despite the many gaps in our knowledge, we have more than enough data to recognize that the Persian period was one of the most crucial in the history of the Jewish people and the Jewish religion. It is not because Cyrus personally issued a decree authorizing a rebuilding of the temple and permitting a return of Jewish exiles. Neither is it because of the allegations that Zerubbabel and Joshua led a mass return from the exile to an empty land, nor that Darius paid for the temple cult and warned Judah's enemies not to interfere. It is not because Ezra and Nehemiah came as reformers to purify the community and cult from sin and evil practices. It is not because Mordechai and Queen Esther saved the Jewish community from extinction. It is not because Jews were in high office or Persian kings lavished the Jews with wealth and favorable decrees over and above all other peoples of the empire. These were all clearly fictional events, as we have seen.

No, the Persian period is important for the Jews because at that time there were important developments for the Jews and Judaism. Yehud was a small, backward province with a rural subsistence economy. Jerusalem, perhaps the only urban area, was still no more than a few thousand people at best. Judah did not hold a strategic position from a geographical point of view and contributed only a small amount to the imperial coffers. It could have disappeared from Persian history, and no one would have noticed. But the Persian period was important because it was a day of small things (Zech. 4:10). Its accomplishments were not of might nor power but of the spirit (Zech. 4:6). Intellectual and religious developments began in the Persian period that were to become dominant in later Second Temple Judaism, some of which would carry over into Judaism to this day. Monotheism may already have existed in some circles before the postexilic period, but it came to be widely disseminated in the Jewish communities in the Persian period. Yahweh became the sole Jewish God, with other gods considered nonexistent. Holy day celebrations became fixed in the Persian period, such as the Sabbath and many of the annual festivals.

Yet it was first and foremost in the area of scripture that the seeds of later Judaism were sown. It is true that Judaism remained a temple-centered religion for many centuries. But alongside temple worship was developing a "religion of the book." First in the diaspora and then in Judah itself the written word came to be more and more the focus of religious practice until, with the temple destroyed, the book was the tangible possession still left with the Jews. Yet that book came about because some unknown individuals, probably a handful of temple personnel, took existing oral traditions, some written documents, stories, and teachings, and began to put these together into a coherent theological narrative to tell their story—not "just as it happened" but in a form that expressed what these traditions meant to them and their support group.

By the end of the Persian period, this "law book" of the Pentateuch had gained a certain authority and began the long process of becoming a religious canon. Some other writings were probably also coming to have "special" religious significance (see chapter 10, pp. 200–3). None of the other peoples of the Persian Empire probably noticed, including the Persian overlords. This was just one of the "small things," so vital for later Judaism, to which the Persian period gave birth.

10
The Coming of the Greeks: Alexander's Conquests and Ptolemaic Rule

In the past, the Greek conquest of the ancient Near East was seen as world changing. Greek culture was viewed as different, even foreign, and Hellenization was a Greek swamping of Oriental culture. Allegedly, most of the Eastern peoples welcomed—at least, accepted—this cultural change, except for the Jews. The Jews were adamantly opposed to Hellenistic culture and firmly resisted it. Allegedly. As will become abundantly clear in the first section of this chapter, this scenario is a gross caricature in almost all its aspects.

What we shall do is discuss the implications of the Greek conquest for the Jews not only of Palestine but those in the Jewish diaspora that had become widespread in the early years of the Greek kingdoms. We begin with Alexander, but much of this chapter will involve Jewish history during the Ptolemaic rule of Palestine, which lasted until the reign of Antiochus III (223–187 BCE), known as "Antiochus the Great." But first we must understand the cultural phenomenon of Hellenization.

TABLE 10.1 *Early Ptolemies and Seleucids*

Alexander the Great (336–323 BCE) Period of the Diadochi (323–281 BCE)	
Ptolemaic Rulers	**Seleucid Rulers**
Ptolemy I Soter (323–282 BCE)	Seleucus I Nicator ([321]312–281 BCE)
Ptolemy II Philadelphus (282–246 BCE)	Antiochus I Soter (281–261 BCE)
Ptolemy III Euergetes I (246–221 BCE)	Antiochus II Theos (261–246 BCE)
Ptolemy IV Philopter (221–204 BCE)	Seleucus II Callinicus (246–225 BCE)
Ptolemy V Theos Epiphanes (204–180 BCE)	Seleucus III Ceraunus (225–223 BCE)
	Antiochus III the Great (223–187 BCE)

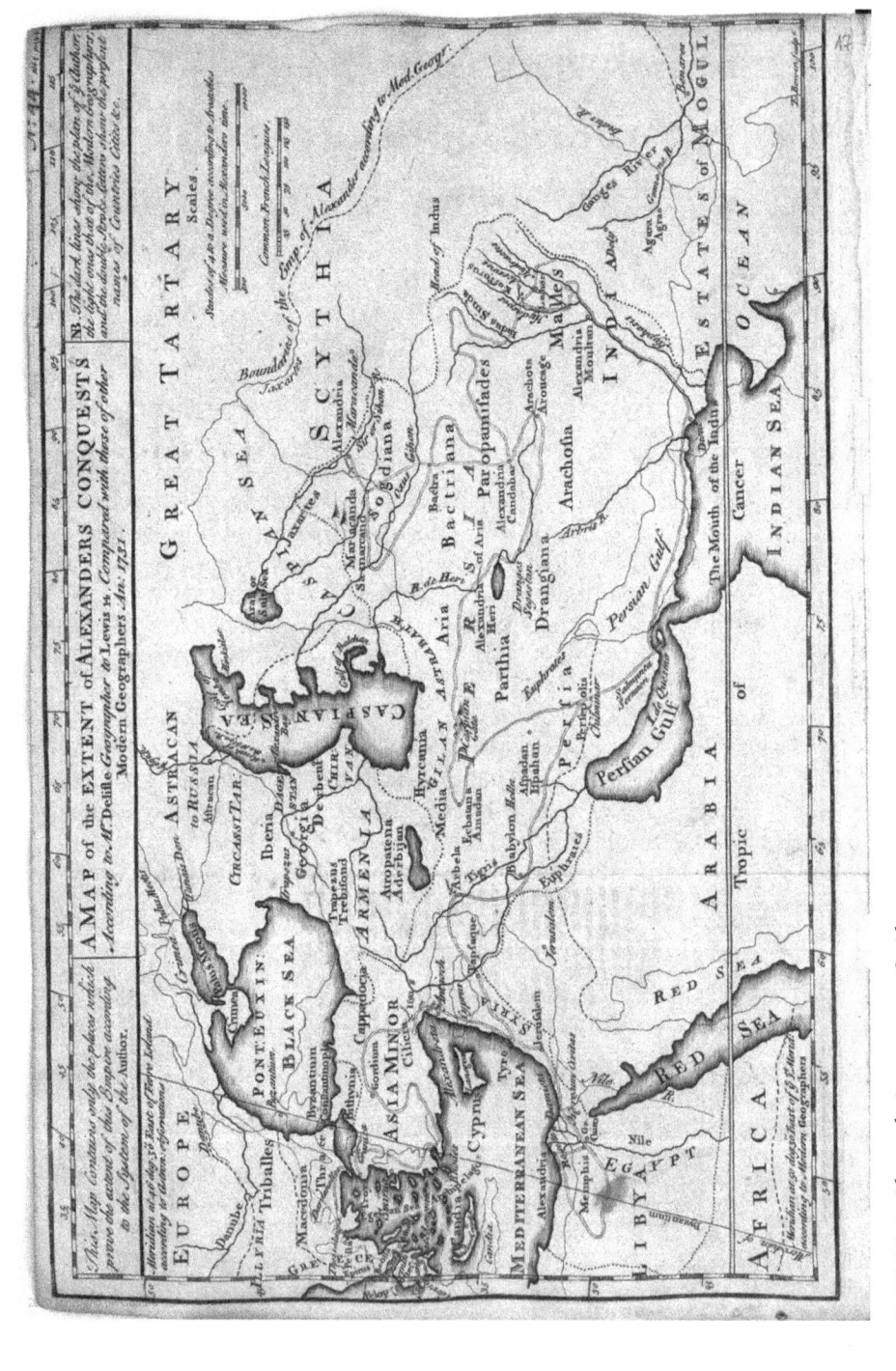

MAP 10.1 Alexander's conquests © Alamy.

Near Eastern Culture and Hellenization

The Jews were only one of a number of peoples in the ancient Near East, and none of them particularly welcomed the Greeks. The Greeks came as conquerors, but then so had the Assyrians, Babylonians, and Persians. The peoples of the various Near Eastern regions had had to accommodate overlords and adapt to their requirements for many centuries. The question is, were the Greeks any different? First, let us consider how the Hellenistic world differed from the culture of "classical" Greece:[1]

- Landholding of the Hellenistic period was primarily the large estate (usually of the king or his officials) rather than the small holding.
- Government was primarily the monarchy governing a large territory or empire rather than the small city-states. The foundations of new cities in Greek mode preserved the myth but not the substance of independent rule.
- Written laws rather than unwritten custom played a greater part during the Hellenistic period.
- The cult of the city god(s) of the classical period gave way to the imperial cult plus a variety of local (but nonpolitical) or individual cults.
- Private citizens were much more important to the classical city-state, tying individual endeavors in commerce, art, and philosophy closely to politics. In the Hellenistic world, the individual (even the wealthy) was more concerned with private affairs than with politics.
- Both the army and the administration tended to be the occupation of professionals in the Hellenistic world, rather than in the hands of amateurs as in classical Greece.
- The arts and sciences of the Hellenistic period were also much more characterized by professional preoccupation and systemization. Hence, the large production of handbooks, collections, and imitations of classical models.

A variety of institutions served as conduits for the passage of Greek elements into the Near East. Certain customs, practices, and features were seen as specifically Greek and adoption of them an accommodation to the conqueror's world. Beginning with Alexander himself and continuing with his successors, hundreds of Greek foundations on the model of the Greek *polis* (city) were established in the conquered areas. In some cases, native cities were refounded as Greek cities, but in many cases the city was new. The basic function of such cities was practical. Most were settled by veterans of the Greek campaigns, rewarding them for their service and providing a means of making a living for themselves and their families.

While the new cities did serve as a vehicle for bringing Hellenism to the Orient, the Greek was a new element in the mix and did not displace the millennia-old cultures that already existed there. From the Greek point of view, the "barbarians" could be said to be Hellenized by this spread of Greek settlements among them. As a result, Greek culture and civic life made its way to the most remote parts of Asia. *But the native culture was not eliminated and did not disappear, and the Greek was limited to certain spheres.*

Although it is often asserted that Greek became the official language of the conquered territories, this seems an oversimplification: the Seleucid Empire was multilingual, with local languages continuing to be used in official documents (with perhaps a few exceptions). A similar situation pertained in Egypt. Although Egypt is famous for its finds of papyri in Greek, the accumulating evidence suggests that at least as much written material was produced in the Demotic form of the Egyptian language during the same period of time.

Greek certainly did function as a *lingua franca* in many parts of the Hellenistic East, as Aramaic had done under the Assyrian, Neo-Babylonian, and Achaemenid Empires. Royal inscriptions and many other sorts of documents were issued in Greek, yet there was no attempt to impose it as the sole language of administration. Traders no doubt found some acquaintance with Greek useful not only in dealing with officialdom but also for getting around in areas with a multitude of local languages. If the buyer or seller whom one was dealing with knew a second language, however, in many parts of the Seleucid Empire it was more likely to be Aramaic than Greek. Most of the Jews of Palestine also used Aramaic as their first language, even those who knew some Greek.

The spread of Greek institutions and culture to the remotest parts of the Greek Empire can be seen in the Greek remains in such unlikely places as Ai Khanum, and the island of Failaka (ancient Icarus) in the Persian Gulf. The presence of Greek communities, as indicated by inscriptions, architecture, and literary remains shows that no region could escape some influence. The question is to what extent the Greek presence produced merging, adoption, or change in the indigenous cultures. An older view emphasized the Greek influence on the original civilizations of the ancient Near East and the dominance of Greek institutions. It also presented the concept of a blending or "melting together" as if the Greek and the Oriental had blended together into one giant cultural amalgam (often referred to by the German term *Verschmelzung*). The most recent scholarly study has recognized not only the Graeco-centric view of so much older scholarship but has found evidence in new discoveries as well as old that the earlier cultures were far from obliterated under Greek rule.[2]

Hellenization was a long and complex phenomenon. It cannot be summarized in a word or a sentence. It was not just the adoption of Greek ways by the inhabitants of the ancient Near East or of Oriental ways by Greeks who settled in the East. Hellenistic civilization was *sui generis*—it was its own thing—and must be considered from a variety of points of view, for it concerned many different areas of life: language, custom, religion, commerce, architecture, dress, government, and literary and philosophical ideals. Hellenization represented a process as well as a description of a type of culture.

Whatever Alexander's ideals may have been, his successors were highly Graeco-chauvinist. Pride of place in society was to go to Greeks alone, with the natives usually at the bottom of the pyramid. Greek ideals were preserved in the Greek city foundations, with citizenship and membership of the gymnasium (the education and social center of most Greek cities) jealously guarded for the exclusive privilege of the Greek settlers. Orientals might live in the Greek cities but they were not citizens and were mostly barred from becoming so. There was no interest in cultural imperialism as such by the Greek rulers.

Over a period of a century or so after Alexander's death, however, things gradually began to change. Local nobles and chieftains were often of use in the Ptolemaic and Seleucid administrations, and they employed Greek secretaries. A good example of this is the Jewish noble Tobias for whom we have a number of letters in Greek (see p. 190). These individuals were also likely to see the need to have their sons given a Greek education. Thus, already early in the Greek period, we find educated Orientals who have some knowledge of Greek.

There was also the phenomenon of Orientalization of the Greeks. This was equally a complicated process that affected different parts of the Hellenistic world differently. For example, in Egypt the Ptolemaic kingship was quickly assimilated to the Pharaonic tradition. Each new ruler was considered a son of the sun god Re and given a variety of traditional Egyptian names and titles. In the hieroglyphic inscriptions no distinction is made between the Ptolemies and the native Egyptian pharaohs of previous generations. Yet the dealings of the Ptolemies with other states and with Greek cities was done in the normal Greek way, and the court was typically Hellenistic. Only the last Ptolemy (the famous Queen Cleopatra) learned to speak the Egyptian language.

The life of the average Near Eastern person was not strikingly affected by the coming of the Greeks. The poor peasant continued to work the land, only noting that he had a new landlord or had to pay taxes to a new regime. Yet in stating this, one must not forget that the day-to-day life of the bulk of the population in the Near East probably changed little in the five millennia between 3000 BCE and 1900 CE. The coming of the Greeks did not radically change their lives—but neither did the coming of the Assyrians, the Persians, the Romans, the Arabs, the Turks, or the British. On the other hand, there were constant reminders of the new culture, most obviously in the language of administration and commerce.

As an analogy, one might consider the Anglicization of India in the nineteenth century or the Westernization of Japan in the post–World War II era. Anglo-India was very much a complex synthesis of the two cultures, with administration and communication dominated by the English culture and language, but the life of the ordinary Indian continuing much as it had been. Also, the influence worked both ways. Englishmen who lived in India soon adopted a way of life and cultural tradition that was often quite different from that in Great Britain, and they came to occupy a sphere that was neither that of the average Indian nor of that of the home country. Similarly, Japan has become very Westernized, but one could hardly conclude that the native customs and culture have been ousted or submerged. This would be abundantly clear to anyone who read Jake Adelstein's book *Tokyo Vice* or watched the TV series based on it.

The Jews and Hellenization

The question of Hellenization and the Jews has long been a major debate in scholarly study. As should now be clear, the question of the Jews and Hellenization is not different from that of Hellenization and the ancient Near East in general. It still seems to be received wisdom that Jews were not comfortable under Greek rule. This is somewhat surprising, not only in light of discussion in recent years but also the recognition of Mesopotamian and Persian influence on Judaism.[3] A variety of religious cults flourished under the Persians, but no one seems to assume that this posed a threat to Judaism. Yet for some reason, Judaism is seen as uniquely incompatible with Hellenization. The question is, how did the Jews see themselves in this new Hellenistic environment?

To begin, for the first century and a half of Greek rule there is no evidence that the Jews saw anything different or more threatening than they had under previous empires. The Greeks were just another conquering power, and until well into the second century BCE the Jews had no more problem with them than with the Persians, Babylonians, or Assyrians. We know that this changed under Antiochus IV who attempted to suppress the Jewish religion. But the point is that this religious persecution of Antiochus was a unique event in the ancient world—and it led to the violent Maccabean revolt. Antiochus's actions traumatized the Jews, and later writers often used minor elements of Greek culture as symbolic of this threat to Judaism. But in the pre-Maccabean period, no such views appear to be found among the surviving sources.

Recent study has shown that one can no longer talk of Judaism versus Hellenism nor of Palestinian versus Hellenistic Judaism. To do so is to create an artificial binary opposition and to reduce an enormously complex picture to stark, unshaded black and white. It also treats a lengthy process as if it were a single undifferentiated event—as if conception, pregnancy, birth, childhood, and adulthood could be simultaneous. We can summarize the situation of Jews and the Hellenistic world by the following points:

- *Hellenism and Hellenization was a culture whereas Judaism was a religion.* Many aspects of Hellenistic culture were irrelevant to Jewish religious views. Other aspects were viewed as irrelevant by some Jews but highly subversive by others. It is as if—to take a modern analogy—the only form of Judaism allowed to be "Jewish" was Orthodox Judaism. This may indeed be the view of some Orthodox Jews, but it is hardly the perspective of Conservative, Reform, Karaite, Falasha, and other forms of Judaism. It is not the job of the historian to take sides or adopt the denominational prejudice of the sources.

- *Those called "Judaizers" (or, misleadingly, "orthodox" in some modern works) were not totally opposed to all aspects of Hellenistic culture.* What they opposed were certain things affecting their religion, though this opposition sometimes used—or reacted to—cultural symbols as a means of expressing their loyalty to a particular form of Judaism.

- *The attitudes of those called "Judaizers" seem to have covered a wide spectrum, including the Hasidim, the Maccabees, those who refused to defend themselves against their enemies on the sabbath, the partisans of Onias, and those who wrote Daniel 7–12. The same is true of the so-called Hellenizers.* To be a "Hellenized Jew" did not mean to cease to be a Jew. Take, for example, Philo of Alexandria (discussed in more detail in chapter 13, **pp. 278–9**). Here was a man with a good Greek education, who wrote and thought in the Greek language (probably knowing little or no Hebrew), and lived a life that in many daily habits did not differ from the Greek citizens of Alexandria, yet who considered himself nothing less than a loyal and pious Jew.

- *The native cultures continued to thrive to a greater or lesser extent all over the Near East, not just in Judaea.* Greek remained a minority language and did not displace the many local languages nor the old *lingua franca* of Aramaic. Hellenization as a process—not just a static culture—continued with the coming of the Romans and the growth of their empire.
- *It is indeed true that Jews were unique and did not lose their identity—a fact with which some writers on the subject seem obsessed—but one could also make the same statement about many of the native peoples.*
- *In accommodating to Hellenistic culture, the Jews always maintained one area that could not be compromised without affecting their Judaism, that of religion.* The Jews were unique in the Graeco-Roman world in refusing to honor gods, shrines, and cults other than their own. Thus, even those Jews who were most at home in the Hellenistic world, such as Philo, still found themselves marked out—and marked off—by this fact. For the vast majority, this was the final barrier that could not be crossed; we know of only a handful of examples from antiquity in which Jews abandoned their Judaism as such. Thus, however Hellenized they might be, observant Jews could never be fully at home in the Greek world.

To conclude this discussion, we can consider an anecdote ascribed to Clearchus of Soli (said to be a pupil of Aristotle) in which Aristotle describes an encounter with a Jew in Asia Minor:

> "Well," he [Aristotle] replied, "the man was a Jew of Coele-Syria [Syria Palestine]. These people are descended from the Indian philosophers. The philosophers, they say, are in India called Calani, in Syria by the territorial name of Jews; for the district which they inhabit is known as Judaea. Their city has a remarkably odd name; they call it Hierusaleme. Now this man, who was entertained by a large circle of friends and was on his way down from the interior to the coast, not only spoke Greek, but had the soul of a Greek." (Quoted in Josephus, *C. Apion.* 1.22 §§179–80)

I draw your attention to two points that this anecdote illustrates: one was that a "Greek" was one who spoke the language and had the "Greek soul"; the other is that the protagonist of the anecdote is Jewish. Jews were as much a part of the Hellenization process as any other native peoples.

Alexander and His Conquests (336–323 BCE)

Much has been written about the life of Alexander, and no attempt is made here to survey it in detail. Alexander was only twenty years old when his father Philip II was assassinated in 336 BCE but was quickly acclaimed by Philip's trusted generals and by the army. His immediate concern was to secure Greece under Macedonian control since the treaties imposed by Philip would not necessarily be accepted as continuing after his death. If there was any question about Alexander's leadership ability, it was soon silenced by his brilliant maneuvers in swiftly squelching the anti-Macedonian developments in Thessaly and cowing the rest of Greece. Before 336 was out, he had been formally elected head of the Corinthian League, which included all the important states of Greece except Sparta. By early 335, Alexander was already facing a variety of threats to his rule. But he dealt with these, and by the end of 335 he was able to return to Macedonia and prepare for the invasion of Persia.

Alexander crossed the Dardanelles in the spring of 334 BCE with a force of about thirty thousand plus a five-thousand-man cavalry. The Greek invasion had in fact caught the Persians by surprise. Many of the cities of Asia Minor were Greek, though with Persian-appointed tyrants or oligarchies. He advanced south through Ionia and reached the Cilician Gates (the pass through the Taurus mountains) before the Persians had properly secured this pass. So far, Alexander had met little effective opposition from the Persians. One of their strengths should have been their fleet; however, Alexander concentrated on a policy of land conquest.

The crucial battle with Darius III was at Issus in the autumn of 333 BCE. The result was disastrous for Darius. He personally escaped, but his family—wife, mother, and daughters—was captured. The Persian had hired mercenaries who were by and large Greek; these left the battlefield, and most made their way to Egypt. The Phoenician cities welcomed Alexander, with the exception of Tyre, which required a siege of seven months to conquer. It fell in mid-summer of 332, and the various peoples of the southern Levant then submitted to the Greeks. As Arrian tells us, directly after the siege and conquest of Tyre "Alexander now determined to make his expedition to Egypt. Palestinian Syria (as it is called) had already come over to him, except for a eunuch named Batis, who was master of the city of Gaza" (*Anab.* 2.25.4). *This shows that the various provinces and groups in this region—including the Jews of Judaea—had submitted to Alexander's rule*, a point that will be important when we discuss Alexander and the Jews. Of the cities and peoples in the region, only Gaza refused entry to Alexander and, like Tyre, had to be besieged.

Egypt submitted without resistance late in 332 BCE. Alexander spent the winter there, founding the city of Alexandria. He also visited the famous oracle of Ammon in the oasis Siwan. This is significant because it shows that the historian Arrian was quite happy to record religious activity on the part of Alexander. In the spring of 331 he was back in Syria. A revolt in Samaria was put down (discussed further on p. 186), though this was apparently after Alexander had already marched east with the main part of his army. Darius met him a second time, on this occasion at Gaugamela on October 1, 331 BCE. Just as at Issus, Darius was defeated, and the fate of the Persian Empire was now sealed. Alexander went on to Babylon, which welcomed him without a fight in 330 BCE. Some months later, the Persian king was assassinated by one of his own satraps.

With Darius dead, Alexander proceeded formally to succeed him. This was an important step because Alexander was not just king of Macedonia but now also ruled over the Persians. He took up many of the customs of the Persian monarchy, which became a source of friction with his own men who were used to the Macedonian customs of kingship. The main custom objected to was that of obeisance (*proskunēsis* in Greek), which the Greeks interpreted as prostration, an act reserved for the gods. Alexander's actions not only went contrary to the rather egalitarian tradition of the Macedonians but, in the opinion of many, was crossing the border into impiety. Several individuals were later to pay with their lives for not showing sufficient enthusiasm for the new custom.

In 329 BCE, Alexander moved on further into the eastern realms of the Persian Empire and reached northern India (modern Pakistan) by 326. But at this point, his soldiers mutinied and refused to go any further (though Alexander may have orchestrated this as an excuse for his own decision to end his campaign without losing face). He returned to Babylon and set about consolidating his rule. Already in the brief remaining year or two of his life, there were mutinies and executions because of unhappiness among many Greeks who did not approve of his "Orientalizing" policy or his manner of rule. It all ended abruptly in 323 BCE when Alexander died at Babylon at the age of only thirty-two.

Alexander and the Jews: Did He Meet the Jewish High Priest?

In addition to the proper historical narratives about Alexander, there grew up a legendary account (or actually several related but differing accounts) that often has little to do with the real historical Alexander. A prominent episode in this legendary account is that of Alexander and the high priest of the Jerusalem temple. This incident has long been doubted in modern scholarship. Little is said about Judaea in the historical accounts of Alexander.

The story in Josephus (*Ant.* 11.8.1-6 §§304–45), the earliest extant source, says that Alexander came to Jerusalem to punish the Jews for refusing assistance in the siege of Tyre, but on the way, he had a dream featuring the Jewish high priest. When Alexander was met by the high priest as he came to Jerusalem, instead of punishment he gave honor to him. But no such incident is recorded in Arrian, Quintus Curtius, or the other genuine historians. Yet it is very unlikely that they would have omitted a visit of Alexander to Jerusalem. For Alexander to visit the holy places of other peoples was not unusual: his ostensible reason for besieging Tyre was that the city refused his request to worship at the temple of "Hercules" (the Greek name for the Phoenician city god Melqart), while later he made a special effort to cross a stretch of desert to visit the Egyptian shrine in the oasis at Ammon. If the Alexandrian historians mentioned these events, they would have mentioned a visit to Jerusalem.

Furthermore, there is simply no place in Alexander's advance down the Mediterranean coast to fit in such an event: immediately after the fall of Tyre, he received messengers with an offer of terms from Darius. These he refused but went directly down the Phoenician coast to Gaza, which he besieged because it refused entry to him. When Gaza fell after a two-months siege, he went straight on to Egypt. In any event, why would the Alexander historians have omitted a trip to Jerusalem? We have no indication that Alexander required the peoples of the interior of Syria-Palestine to help him besiege Tyre, much less a small community up in the remote hill country.

But as already noted (p. 184), directly after the siege and conquest of Tyre, the various peoples of Palestinian Syria submitted to him (all except Gaza). We do not know when or where or how the Jews formally accepted Greek rule, but Arrian's silence suggests that there was nothing exceptional about their submission. Alexander no doubt received the fealty of the Judaean nation at this time, as he did that of other peoples, but representatives would have come to him (perhaps at Jamnia), not he to them in Jerusalem. Only Gaza held out; if the Jewish high priest had also done so, we would have heard about it.

One other event involving the Palestinian region is recorded by the historian Quintus Curtius (4.8.9-11): after Alexander had left the region and marched east into Persia, the inhabitants of Samaria revolted and assassinated the governor appointed by Alexander. Not only did Alexander have the rebels and their leaders punished, he also apparently had the city resettled by Macedonians.[4] Evidence of this has now been found by archaeologists in caves at Wadi Daliyeh near the Jordan River (about 14 kilometers or 9 miles north of Jericho). The finds of human remains and papyri show that several hundred people from Samaria died in these caves about this time. The Wadi Daliyeh papyri were seen as the archives of individuals fleeing from the destruction of Samaria, who took refuge in caves near the Jordan but were nevertheless tracked down by the Greek soldiers and slaughtered there. The few citizens who escaped the destruction of Samaria were assumed to have moved to the area of ancient Shechem and settled there.

Alexander's Successors—The "Diadochi" (323–281 BCE)

Alexander died so young and so suddenly that he had not appointed a successor to his newly conquered empire. But he left a pregnant Persian wife, Roxane, and a younger (half-)brother, Arrhidaeus (allegedly mentally deficient but whom the army proclaimed as Philip III). When Roxane gave birth, the boy, Alexander IV, was to rule jointly with Arrhidaeus. But alongside them were powerful generals who were companions of Alexander and had fought with him. Although initially acting as regents, it was only a matter of time before the main generals sought to take over the empire that they had helped to subdue. This led to the forty-year period of "the Successors" (referred to as *Diodochi*, the Latinate version of the Greek term). There is little point in rehearsing the many maneuvers and battles but a few points are worth noting:

- During the wars of the Diadochi, Palestine was fought in and over many times. We have no details for the most part, but the fighting may at times have had a devastating effect on the population and economy of the country. The book of *1 Enoch* talks of fallen angels coupling with human women who have "giants" as offspring. Some have seen these "giants," who devastate the earth, as symbols of the Diadochi whose military activities seemed to threaten the inhabitants of the country.
- One of the key players was Ptolemy son of Lagos. He was early assigned Egypt as his satrapy and managed to hold onto it, in spite of various threats and invasions from his fellow generals.

- When Seleucus was ousted from rule of Babylonia in 316 BCE, he fled to Ptolemy for protection. Ptolemy helped him regain his throne over Babylonia.
- It was the battle of Ipsus that formed the final carve-up of Alexander's realm: Ptolemy over Egypt; Seleucus over Babylonia, Asia Minor, and the eastern regions of the empire; and a general by the name of Lysimachus over Greece and the Aegean.
- Ptolemy was not at the battle of Ipsus. As a result, Syro-Palestine was assigned to Seleucus in the settlement that followed (301 BCE). This was a fact that was to have major consequences for the future history of the region.
- This basic three-fold division of Alexander's Empire remained for two centuries until it was finally ended by the Romans: Greece and Macedonia under the Antigonids (who had displaced Lysimachus), Syria and Mesopotamia under the Seleucids, and Egypt under the Ptolemies.

Ptolemy I and the Jews

With Syria-Palestine now under Ptolemy's control, along with Egypt, the question is how the Jews fared. The only possible direct evidence about Judaea at this time is given in a single reference by Josephus who states that Ptolemy I took Jerusalem on the Sabbath by pretending to enter to sacrifice at the temple (*Ant.* 12.1.1 §§3–10; *Ag. Ap.* 1.22 §§209–12). Josephus goes on to say that Ptolemy took many captives, not only from Judaea but also from Samaria, and settled them in Egypt. Also later, many other Jews were attracted by Egypt and immigrated there voluntarily.

One further incident has been ascribed to Ptolemy, but it presents historical problems. Josephus (*C. Apionem* 1.22 §§187–91) refers to the "chief priest" Hezekiah (Ezekias in Greek), "a man of about sixty-six years of age, highly esteemed by his countrymen, intellectual, and moreover an able speaker and unsurpassed as a man of business." Hezekiah asked Ptolemy I for permission to lead a group of Jews to settle in Egypt after the battle of Gaza in 312 BCE. It may be that this refers not to the high priest of the temple but another senior priest who led some of his fellow Jews and even priests to settle in Egypt.

One valuable source on the Jews is Hecataeus of Abdera, a Greek who seems to have had contact with Jews or at least access to a Jewish written document. One passage shows knowledge of the name of the Jewish God: "among the Jews Moyses [Moses] referred his laws to the god who is invoked as Iao" (Diodorus 1.94.1-2). The most important passage is his long description of the Jews, as quoted by Diodorus of Sicily (40.3.1-7). Only a portion of it needs to be quoted here:

(4) But he [Moses] had no images whatsoever of the gods made for them, being of the opinion that God is not in human form; rather the Heaven that surrounds the earth is alone divine, and rules the universe. The sacrifices that he established

differ from those of other nations, as does their way of living, for as a result of their own expulsion from Egypt he introduced an unsocial and intolerant mode of life. He picked out the men of most refinement and with the greatest ability to head the entire nation, and appointed them priests; and he ordained that they should occupy themselves with the temple and the honours and sacrifices offered to their god. (5) These same men he appointed to be judges in all major disputes, and entrusted to them the guardianship of the laws and customs. For this reason the Jews never have a king, and authority over the people is regularly vested in whichever priest is regarded as superior to his colleagues in wisdom and virtue. They call this man the high priest, and believe that he acts as a messenger to them of God's commandments. (6) It is he, we are told, who in their assemblies and other gatherings announces what is ordained, and the Jews are so docile in such matters that straightway they fall to the ground and do reverence to the high priest when he expounds the commandments to them. And at the end of their laws there is even appended the statement: "These are the words that Moses heard from God and declares unto the Jews."

Hecataeus's story claims that Moses and his followers were expelled from Egypt as lepers, but otherwise much of what he says is positive and shows some knowledge (if imperfect) of Judaea and the Jews. He is clearly ignorant of the monarchy period of Jewish history (when there were Jewish kings) but knows only the situation in the Greek period when the high priest acted as the representative of the Jewish community to the administrative powers. But this quote is valuable because it gives us a picture of Judaea in the Second Temple period.

Province of Judaea under the Ptolemies

The forty years of fighting after Alexander's death finally came to an end with the death of the main protagonists by the year 280 BCE. Much of the third century BCE was dominated by the Syrian wars. These constituted an ongoing conflict between the Ptolemaic and Seleucid Empires over Syro-Palestine. The council of victors after the battle of Ipsus (301 BCE) had awarded Syria to Seleucus because Ptolemy had not participated in the battle; however, Ptolemy occupied the area and refused to concede the territory. Seleucus did not press the point because Ptolemy had aided him when he was driven from Babylon. Yet the subsequent Seleucid rulers spent the next three-quarters of a century trying to regain what they viewed as rightfully theirs.

How the Jews of Palestine were governed by the Ptolemies is still not clear. No direct evidence for a single governor over Syro-Palestine has yet appeared in our sources. We know that the possessions of the Egyptian Empire outside Egypt were divided into hyparchies, with the hyparchy being the primary administrative unit. It is possible that the entirety of Coele-Syria (Syria-Palestine) was regarded as a hyparchy, but probably it was divided into several hyparchies, of which Judaea would have been one. The chances are that the hyparchy or province of Judah maintained somewhat the same borders as it had under the Persians. The only officer mentioned in this connection is the financial official. In any case, a considerable amount of central administration was done from Alexandria, which suggests that—at least for certain things—Palestine was viewed merely as a part of Egypt and administered more or less as if it were another nome (Egypt itself was subdivided into provinces called "nomes").

The basic administrative unit was the village (*komē*), however, and the Ptolemaic administration carefully supervised this level as well as the higher ones. Each village had a civil mayor who was probably a local man, but there were also royal officials. There were government officials in every city and village, so that the Egyptian government did not lack the means of control and supervision down to the lowest level. Thus, although it is not clear that there was a regional governor between Alexandria and the individual towns and villages, a financial minister was responsible for overseeing the collection of revenues for the region.

The place of the temples in the administration of Egypt is potentially of great importance when we ask about administration in Judah. The Jerusalem temple was very similar to Egyptian temples, with many obvious features in common. It is likely that the Egyptian government would have been inclined to deal with Judah as they dealt with temples inside Egypt. The Ptolemies were cognizant of the power of the priesthood in Egypt and worked hard to keep it on their side. This means that in Judah, where the temple was at the center of the administration, this was permitted as long as it delivered the required tribute.

A number of sources mention "temple states" about this time, especially in Asia Minor. The province of Judah could be called a "temple state" in the sense simply that the priests were in charge of civil as well as cultic affairs. Like Greek cities, these temples were under the authority of the king, whatever fictional facade of independence might have been maintained. The temple states referred to here and there seem to have had a similar structure: the high priest as dynast, a village or villages that served as economic centers, territory with agricultural land worked by temple servants who were under the orders of the high priest. Whether the Jerusalem temple owned large amounts of land is a moot point, though it is clear that the high priest and other individual priests possessed land. But the temple had a regular and substantial income from donations and tithes of the people within the state of Judah.

As well as the high priest, our sources also agree that a council of elders or senate was important in the leadership of Judah, called a *gerousia* in Greek. This *gerousia*, otherwise often referred to as the Sanhedrin, was an important institution in Judah over many centuries. The *gerousia* or Sanhedrin was at the disposal of the high priest, to give advice and counsel. The exact balance of power between the high priest and Sanhedrin is nowhere discussed but probably varied over the centuries; however, the high priest was apparently always the final authority.

It is also about the middle of the third century BCE that we first find references to synagogues in Egypt. Several inscriptions show that "prayer houses" were dedicated to the reigning monarch and, incidentally, indicate for the first time that a special Jewish place of worship existed apart from the Jerusalem temple. Unfortunately, we have no further information about the services conducted or the organization of the synagogue. The synagogue originated in the Jewish diaspora where Jews did not have access to the temple. It seems clear that synagogues were not needed in Palestine where Jews were within journeying distance of the temple. It was only a couple of centuries later that synagogues finally appear in Palestine itself.

Judaea in the Zenon Papyri

We have little explicit mention of Jews before the second half of the third century BCE. But two sources of information are of particular importance because of what they tell us about the Jews living in the area of Judaea. The first is the tour of the region by Zeno, or Zenon, the agent of the Egyptian finance minister, and the archive of his documents discovered by modern archaeologists. The other is the semi-legendary account of the Tobiad family given by the Jewish historian Josephus, discussed in the next section.

The Zenon archive is a collection of papyri from among those discovered at ancient Philadelphia in Egypt during World War I. They constitute the document deposit of an individual who was the agent of Apollonius the finance minister of Ptolemy II. In the year 259 BCE Apollonius sent Zenon on a lengthy tour of Palestine and southern Syria to take care of various sorts of business. After his return, Zenon continued to correspond with certain individuals whom he had met on his travels. Thus, the archive contains documents not only from Egypt and Palestine for the year 259 but also for several years afterward. It constitutes what we might call official "public" correspondence but also letters relating to Zenon's (and Apollonius's) private affairs. The result is a wealth of material throwing light on the trade, administration, culture, and historical events in Palestine and Egypt for this period.

We can begin with an important document from the archive, a slave sale (*CPJ* 1.1). It refers to an individual who will become important in our history of the period. The person is Tobias, a Jewish nobleman who occupies a prominent place in Palestinian society, being the head of a cleruchy of cavalry in the Transjordanian area. The cleruchy was a military settlement of people given land by the king in exchange for military service when they were needed. This Tobias later writes to the finance minister Apollonius with gifts and even sends presents to King Ptolemy II himself, along with a letter (*CPJ* 1.4; 1.6). Among the papyri is an interesting letter to Zenon concerning a man who seems to be a local Jewish individual named Jeddous:

> [Alexan]dros to Oryas, greeting. I have received your letter, to which you added a copy of the letter written by Zenon to Jeddous saying that unless he gave the money to Straton, Zenon's man, we were to hand over his pledge to him (Straton). I happened to be unwell as a result of taking some medicine, so I sent a lad, a servant of mine, with Straton, and wrote a letter to Jeddous. When they returned they said that he had taken no notice of my letter, but had attacked them and thrown them out of the village. So I am writing to you (for your information). (1.6)

This interesting episode—and one not without its humorous side—seems clear in its basic outline: an official attempted to collect a debt from Jeddous that he owed to Zenon. The official does not go himself, giving the excuse of being ill, but sends a poor servant. Jeddous takes no notice of the legal letter, but instead expels them from the village by violence! This shows that local people could assert themselves even against officialdom. Some of the other points arising from the Zenon papyri can be summarized as follows:

- Local figures such as Tobias (and Jeddous) seem to have exercised considerable power and autonomy, whether in relation to the Ptolemaic government or to whatever provincial administration was exercised from Jerusalem.
- Information on Tobias can be fit with other sources to reconstruct some of the history of what seems to be an important Jewish family dynasty in the Transjordanian region, as we shall see in the next section.
- The importance of Greek language and the need for those in power to work in the Greek medium is indicated by these letters. Tobias clearly had a Greek secretary, and if he did not already possess a Hellenistic education himself, the pressure to give such to his sons would have been very strong.
- There is no indication that Tobias was anything but a loyal Jew, yet the letters suggest a person who was not, for example, bothered by a standard polytheistic greeting to the king in the letter.
- The many references to Jews show them as one of the varieties of ethnic groups in Egypt carrying on daily life much as the others. There is no indication that the Jews were singled out for special treatment (either positive or negative) or that they were less integrated into society than the other groups. Vis-à-vis the native Egyptians, however, the Jews were generally treated as Greeks.

The Story of the Tobiads

We now come to the account of the Tobiads, which continues the family history of the Tobias of the Zenon papyri just discussed. A significant section of Josephus's treatment of the Ptolemaic period is taken up with the story of Joseph Tobiad and his sons (*Ant.* 12.4.1-11 §§154–236). Much of what we know about the Jews of Palestine at this time is found in this story. The story has often been called a "romance" because it clearly contains novelistic elements. Although the story is based on actual people and events, a number of the important elements in Josephus's account are fiction. Nevertheless, the story is supported in its essential features by information from other sources.

The Tobiad family was already an established noble institution of some wealth and power well before the third century. It is evident that the Tobias of the Zenon papyri held a position of control and influence in the Palestinian area (see previous section). But it also seems likely that this family is already mentioned two centuries or more earlier in the person of Tobiah at the time of Nehemiah (Neh. 4:1; 6; 13:4-9; see **p. 153** in chapter 9). According to the Tobiad romance, Joseph (probably the son of the Tobias of the Zenon papyri) gained the tax-farming rights of the entire region of Syro-Palestine.

Tax farming was a process by which the rulers parceled out the collection of certain taxes in the region to private individuals. The tax farmer would put in a bid to collect a certain amount of tax and guaranteed that money to the government. If he then failed to collect that amount of tax, he had to make up the difference from his own resources. On the other hand, if he was able to collect more than the amount he had bid for, he could keep the difference as his own profit. The secret was to know how much could be collected and to put in a bid that allowed you to collect more than your bid so that you made a profit. On the other hand, "you cannot get blood from a stone": those bidding had to be realistic about the amount of tax that the province was actually capable of paying. Exacting too much would impoverish the region.

Part of the story consists of an important episode relating to Joseph and the Jerusalem high priest Onias II. According to Josephus's account, the high priest refused to pay a tribute of 20 talents to the Ptolemaic government. His nephew Joseph Tobiad enlisted support among the people, borrowed money from friends in Samaria, and, by political skill and greasing palms, managed to obtain the tax-farming rights for Coele-Syria. This alleged rivalry between the high priest Onias II and Joseph Tobiad looks real. We have two powerful families, one of which owes its power base to the temple and the hereditary office of priesthood, while the other took it from its noble inheritance of societal position and land.

Rivalry and jockeying for position must have been endemic to Jewish society over the centuries. Yet the two families also had much in common and evidently intermarried (Onias was Joseph's maternal uncle, after all). One has the impression that the next high priest (Onias III) was on good terms with Joseph's son Hyrcanus Tobiad, showing that bitter rivalry was not the only option. These two influential families seem to have dominated the society of Judah, but they may not be the only ones. The situation in Palestine during the Ptolemaic period appears to have lent itself to mafia-style activity on the part of such families.

According to the story, Joseph became wealthy and retired after a career of some two decades, to be replaced by his youngest son Hyrcanus; however, Hyrcanus angered both his father and his brothers by using his father's money to obtain the tax authority over the heads of his brothers. This episode in the story probably represents a romantic interpretation of a situation very much governed by political circumstances. Since Joseph ended his career and Hyrcanus began his just before the Fifth Syrian War (c. 202–199 BCE), it has been concluded that the family was split between pro-Ptolemaic advocates (Hyrcanus) and pro-Seleucid advocates (Joseph and his other sons). This is possible but uncertain. After all, Hyrcanus kept money in the temple under Seleucid rule (2 Macc. 3:11), and we have no indication that there was any secret to this.

Of particular interest is the ancestral home of the Tobiads. The Zenon papyri quoted above (p. 190) indicates that the home of Tobias was across the Jordan. It has usually been associated with 'Iraq al-Amir. There is evidence that 'Iraq al-Amir was already the (or at least *a*) Tobiad residence at an early time. Archaeology suggests a Persian settlement, as well as an early Hellenistic one. The name "Tobiah" is carved twice in the cliff facade and dated palaeographically earlier than the second century by most.

To summarize, the situation in third-century Palestine gave an impetus to enterprising individuals to establish or strengthen a local power base, especially if they were willing to take some risks. The Oniads were a family from which the Jerusalem high priest traditionally arose. It appears that the Oniads (with the approval of the

Jewish community) stepped in to represent the province of Judah to the Ptolemaic government. This logically meant that the high priest was responsible for seeing that tribute/taxes were collected and sent to Alexandria. Yet the environment also encouraged others to find a niche within the power network. The Tobiad family was long established on the other side of the Jordan and seems to have had power and wealth already for several centuries. The Zenon papyri indicate that the Tobiads were at home in the Greek world, with perhaps even a Greek education already by the mid-third century.

The apparent rebellion of Onias II against Ptolemaic rule (for rebellion is what his refusal to pay tribute meant at its most basic level) afforded Joseph Tobiad the chance to take a leadership position with the approval of many of those in Judaea, and his diplomatic skills in dealing with the king gave success to his grab for power. Disaster was averted for the Jewish community, now that Joseph had paid the amount owed, and he obtained a Ptolemaic office or at least a source of potential revenue. He made sure that it paid and put his family in a position of influence head and shoulders above all other Jews in the region and perhaps most of the other native families of power. But although some of Joseph's position came at the expense of the Onias, it must not be forgotten that the high priest retained an important office. Why did Onias refuse to pay? He may have thought the Seleucids were about to take over the region, as they eventually did.

Fourth Syrian War (219–217 BCE) and Fifth Syrian War (202–199 BCE)

The sources are by and large silent about events relating to Judah for some decades after the Zenon papyri come to an end about 250 BCE. The Tobiad romance fills us in to some extent, as we have just seen. The Fourth Syrian War, culminating in the battle of Raphia (217 BCE), was an important test for both the Seleucid and the Ptolemaic kings. For the new Seleucid king, Antiochus III (223–187 BCE), it could have been a chance to take the contested region of Syro-Palestine back once and for all and bring to an end the dispute that had divided the two empires since the year 300. As soon as Antiochus III came to the throne, he seems to have had recovery of these domains at the forefront of his strategy. For Ptolemy IV (221–204 BCE) it was a test of his leadership and whether he would continue to hold this important Egyptian province of Syria and Palestine. For the inhabitants of the region, including the Jews of Judah, it would determine whether they were Ptolemaic or Seleucid subjects.

The main account is found in a long section in Polybius (5.30.8–87.8). It began shortly after Antiochus III came to the throne, with plans to invade Syro-Palestine. Ptolemy's ministers conducted a delaying tactic by sending a mission to negotiate with Antiochus, while in the meantime gathering and training an army. Surprisingly, this included native Egyptians, whereas previous Ptolemaic rulers had mainly relied on Greek soldiers. Antiochus agreed to a winter armistice with Ptolemy and returned to Seleucia, with negotiations continuing. With the return of spring in 218, negotiations were getting nowhere, and Antiochus resumed his attempted subjugation of Syro-Palestine.

He took a series of towns in Palestine and Transjordan. In the spring of 217 BCE, both sides decided that the time for a final reckoning had come, and their actions culminated in the battle of Raphia. A lot is known of the battle of Raphia, but the details are not important for our purposes. Suffice it to say that Antiochus was beaten and sustained heavy losses and sent ambassadors to negotiate peace. Ptolemy was apparently happy to come to terms, since he had succeeded beyond all expectations; in the end Ptolemy seems not to have struck the best deal he could have.

According to the historian Polybius (5.87.5-7), Ptolemy toured around various towns in Syro-Palestine for several months after the battle. The Demotic text of the *Raphia Decree* gives further information: "He went in to the temples which were there. He offered burnt offerings and libations, and all the inhabitants who were in the cities received him with joyful hearts and celebrated feasts."[5] Thus, Polybius and the *Raphia Decree* together leave an image of Ptolemy's touring around Syro-Palestine, visiting various towns and offering sacrifices at the different temples in thanks to the gods for his victory. The question is, how was Judah affected by the events surrounding the battle of Raphia? It is entirely possible that Antiochus's army included some Jews, though we have no direct evidence one way or the other.

The Jewish book of 3 Maccabees (1:6-13), however, makes the following statement with regard to Ptolemy IV's actions after he had defeated the Seleucids:

> Since the Jews had sent some of their council and elders to greet him, to bring him gifts of welcome, and to congratulate him on what had happened, he was all the more eager to visit them as soon as possible. After he had arrived in Jerusalem, he offered sacrifice to the supreme God and made thank-offerings and did what was fitting for the holy place.

The passage goes on to say, however, that Ptolemy tried to enter the temple. This statement sounds rather suspect, because it fits later Jewish propaganda about religious persecution so well.

It would occasion no surprise if the people of Judah invited the king to visit their temple and city of Jerusalem, nor if the king had accepted the invitation. What looks like novelistic and theological invention, on the other hand, is the idea that he tried to force his way into the temple. The Ptolemies were very careful to respect the native temples, and this seems to have been the case with regard to temples outside Egypt as well as those within. It is highly unlikely that Ptolemy would have done anything to cause religious offense. But Ptolemy IV may well have visited and offered sacrifice at the Jerusalem temple in 217 BCE, most likely at the invitation of the priests and the people of Jerusalem.

When Ptolemy IV died and the new ruler, Ptolemy V (204–180 BCE), came to the throne in 204, Antiochus III took the opportunity to try again. We do not have a detailed description of the Fifth Syrian War, but it is the one in which Antiochus III finally succeeded in taking back Coele-Syria for the Seleucids. The city of Jerusalem had been fortified by the Ptolemies, but the Jews opened its gates to Antiochus's army in 200 BCE. They provided for the soldiers and the elephants. Antiochus later wrote a letter (discussed in detail in chapter 11) thanking them and undertaking to pay for the expense of repairs to the city that had been damaged in the fighting, as well as providing certain other privileges. The Jews were now under Seleucid rule.

The Jews and Their Communities in Egypt

We have already described how a large number of Jews settled in Egypt in the early Greek period (p. 187). Many Jews had made Egypt their home, probably from the reign of Ptolemy I. At the same time, Josephus (*Ant.* 12.1.1 §§7, 10) suggests that many Samaritans had settled in Egypt as well. At this point, we shall look at this important branch of the Jewish diaspora. As it happens we have a number of statements about Jewish communities and also individual Jews living in Egypt, mainly from papyri and other sources from the Ptolemaic period and later that were discovered in the nineteenth and early twentieth centuries.

The lower social and economic classes are generally less well represented, and women are less visible than men. It is often in the legal context that women and lower-status persons in general are part of the papyrological record. In addition to scattered references, we have Jewish communities linked to specific places, such as Edfu and Thebes, in Upper Egypt; and Trikomia, Samareia, Heracleopolis, and Boubastos, in Lower Egypt.[6] From literary sources (such as the *Letter of Aristeas* 308) we also know of a community in Alexandria—just as one would expect. There were no doubt other communities, and there may well have been Jewish individuals living in non-Jewish communities. There is no way to quantify the number of Jews living in Egypt, but the impression from the extant references is that the size of the population was not insignificant.

One of the most significant papyrological archives for Jewish studies from Ptolemaic Egypt was published only recently and relates to the Egyptian city of Heracleopolis.[7] The data from these papyri clarify a number of moot points about the Jewish communities in Egypt, including organization and the place of the Jewish and Greek legal and juridical traditions in Jewish life. Although these texts relate to the mid-second century BCE, the information contained in them speaks to the entire period of Ptolemaic rule.

Heracleopolis was organized as a *politeuma*. In this context the Greek term *politeuma* relates to a political or cultic association in a Greek city. It can also refer to an ethnic association, and this meaning has been emphasized in discussions about the Jews. In recent decades, the conventional interpretation has been to view the various Jewish communities in the diaspora as constituting *politeumata* (the Greek plural of *politeuma*). All *politeumata* from the early Ptolemaic period appear to have originated in a military context: they were associations of soldiers. As we shall see, many Jews in Egypt were members of military colonies.

The *politeuma* had a governor and a body of governing officials called "archons." The archons were elected for a year; the governor is best explained as the leading archon, though how he was chosen and his exact duties are not indicated in the extant papyri.[8] The archons had the same powers of jurisdiction as other Ptolemaic officials and also similar responsibilities, parallel to the powers of the commander over the local fortresses. A member of the *politeuma* was called a "citizen." Some of the published documents refer to village elders as implementing decisions of the archons.

The Jewish *politeuma* was evidently not a vehicle for religious independence or self-governance; on the contrary, it tied the community strongly into Ptolemaic society, although there is no evidence that royal approval was needed to establish such an association. Religious and cultic freedom was there without forming a *politeuma*; on the other hand, the officials of the *politeuma* had a certain juridical authority, even over non-Jews, and could be useful to Jews who were not members of the *politeuma*.

Another Egyptian village that has recently come to our attention is Samareia. It is of interest for two reasons: one is its name, which appears to be derived from the Palestinian site Samaria, and the other is the presence of a large proportion of Jewish settlers. The texts of the archive have apparently all been published (cf. *CPJ* 1.22; 1.28). They span a period of more than five hundred years, from 254 BCE to 289 CE, but the core collection is from the century between the middle of the third and the middle of the second century BCE. Of the eighty-five persons named in this core group of texts, more than half are Jewish and possibly as many as 75 percent (up to sixty-five persons). This makes the village of Samareia a significant Jewish settlement for study of Jews in Egypt.

When we ask about the daily lives of Jews, the answer is not necessarily easy to give. The reason is that most documents are legal documents or relate to taxation. The result is a somewhat distorted picture, in which women are seldom mentioned (though they are not infrequent in legal documents), and the only aspect of daily life is that relating to the judicial or administrative system. But we see a number of occupations, and they give us some idea of the variegated types of lives that Jews lived in a multicultural society. These include business contractors (*CPJ* 1.24), brick makers (1.10), potters (1.46), guards (1.12), scribes (1.137), policemen (1.25), and even Jewish tax farmers (1.90; 1.107).

It seems likely that the largest proportion of the Jewish immigrants made a living through agrarian activity or the military. We have clear evidence that some Jews were a part of the military—indeed, this may have been the dominant profession among Jewish immigrants in the early days of Ptolemaic rule. Surprisingly, some modern scholars have denied that Jews could be soldiers, yet the data to the contrary are abundant. There is a good deal of information on Jews who occupied a piece of land given to support military settlers. We have lists of military settlers that include many individuals identified as "Jew," sometimes with plots of land listed and even the taxes on them (*CPJ* 1.29-32). This refers to the general Hellenistic practice of, first, rewarding or paying off veterans but, second, of maintaining a military reserve by providing allotments of land to soldiers.

These were usually in the form of a military colony in the Seleucid realm but might be individual plots in Egypt, though we have evidence of military settlements under the Ptolemies as well. They served not only as a reserve to be drawn on in time of war but also as a local police force; hence, they were often settled in troubled areas as a way of bringing them under control. The soldier did not usually farm the plot himself but leased it to a native peasant who worked the land and provided the military family's income through rents. A good portion of the Jews in Egypt in the early Ptolemaic period seem to have been members of military colonies, living in settlements with land provided by the government but being expected to mobilize and fight in the Ptolemaic army in times of war.

In some cases, the size of the land indicates that the individual would be an officer. One Jewish settler has a house with courts and attached buildings, suggesting some wealth (*CPJ* 1.23). In the papyri are numerous references to two groups, members of active military units and members of the "reserves." In addition to lists of military settlers that include many individuals identified as "Jew," we find other references to individuals who are said to be "a Jew in the reserves," usually a party or sometimes just a witness in a document. One of the drollest incidents concerned three Jewish thieves: they got into a vineyard and stripped the grapes from a number of vines; however, it was apparently only a case of drunken vandalism, though they also assaulted the guard when he tried to stop them. They were members of the reserves, though we do not know what happened to them (1.21).

As so often, we have no way of knowing how many Jews served in the military, but it is certainly a part of the social picture. It is also part of the economic picture because the professions as a whole are part of this picture. Just as for any other young Hellenistic man who found he would receive no family property or was tired of following the plough, the military might be a convenient alternative. And, if he served as a veteran and survived, he might receive land as part of a cleruchy settlement and be better off than if he stayed at home and continued the family tradition. This was perhaps one of the small but new opportunities available under Greek rule.

The Tobias of the Zenon papyri was in charge of a cleruchy or military colony of soldiers which included cavalry (*CPJ* 1), though the actual settlers seem to have been a mixed group and not just Jews. Several examples from the Zenon papyri include men on active service. In a deed of renunciation (1.18) each of the parties is designated as a "Jew," but one of them is a *dekanikos* in a military unit—probably a sort of cavalry officer (1.18). Others refer to Jews who are *taktomisthos*, a military rank of some sort, perhaps with paymaster duties (1.24; perhaps 1.22). One of the witnesses for the payment on a house is an individual named Iasibis, probably a Jewish name, who holds the rank of commander in a detachment of cavalry (1.27).

On the one hand, some Jews seem to have been fairly low in the class system. Three farmers (Jews, judging from their names) rented some farmland, only to complain that a portion of it could not be sown (*CPJ* 1.37). A farmer specifically labeled a Jew presented a petition protesting against a sharp rise in the amount of rent he was paying (1.43). Two individuals (one a Jew by his name and possibly the other as well) complain to Zenon that he failed to provide the promised assistance to water the land they had rented from him (1.13). Judging from the small size of the plots cultivated, they were poverty stricken. Some Jews worked as field hands (1.36), shepherds (1.38), or vinedressers (1.14-15). On the other hand, some were evidently well-off. To be a tax farmer required a minimum of means to back up the bid. Others owned vineyards (1.41), livestock (1.28), and other property (1.36; 1.47).

The Jews and Legal Practice in Egypt

Jews feature in many legal documents from Ptolemaic Egypt. The Ptolemies operated two legal systems. One was for the native Egyptians and was conducted in the Demotic language. The other was for the population descended from the Greeks and used the Greek language. The Jews usually had their cases heard in the Greek system. The documents preserved include many complaints made against individuals identified as Jews. For example, a Jew promised to allow a party to a contract to shear some sheep, but he is alleged to have sheared them himself and made off with the wool (*CPJ* 1.38). A mare and carriage were supposed to be delivered by a Jew to a certain individual, but the latter claims in a letter that they have not shown up (1.135). One person claims his cloak was stolen by a Jew of the same village who then fled to the synagogue with it (1.129). Finally, one of the most unusual documents (from the third century) mentions a joint owner of a ship who is Jewish, judging by his name: Dositheos. He might be the Dositheos son of Drimylos, known from 3 Maccabees 1:3.

The question arises as to whether the Jews might have had their own laws and/or court system. The answer is that we hear nothing in the papyri of special Jewish courts. When Jews are mentioned in a legal or juridical context, it is the Greek courts (or officials of the Greek administration) who are involved. As for the question of whether Jewish law had a special place in regular court decisions—whether legal decisions might be based on Jewish law—this has been suggested, but the issue is a complicated one. It seems that only two examples can be found in which Jewish law might have been applied by the courts. As it happens, both relate to marriage.

The first is with regard to a woman who writes to the king, complaining that her husband has cast her out of his house and has refused to return her dowry (*CPJ* 1.128). The woman claims that she was the man's wife "according to the civic law of the Jews." It has been argued that Jewish law, based on Deut. 24:1, is being invoked here by the husband, at least by implication.[9] The first problem is that when it comes to the husband's actions no Jewish law is explicitly referred to. Although Jewish law allowed divorce (as did Greek and Egyptian law), there was no right for the husband to retain his wife's dowry; on the contrary, the dowry was the wife's possession and would be passed to her children, not to her husband. Further, we do not know the ethnicity of the wife: her name is Greek, but many Jews had Greek names. Her husband is labeled a Jew but not the wife; however, the petition is in the first person, and she is unlikely to give herself ethnic labels. Thus, there is no appeal to Jewish law in the petition to King Ptolemy. As far as I can see, this example tells us nothing about Jewish law one way or the other.

The only possible example of a specific Jewish legal practice is found in a case of Jewish family law.[10] It has to do with the breaking of a betrothal: a Jewish father had promised his daughter to the petitioner but then gave her to another man without first providing a "divorce certificate" to the original betrothed man. We know from later Jewish practice that not only a marriage but also a betrothal required a bill of divorce before it could be broken off officially. It was not certain that such a practice could be projected back into Hellenistic times, but this document suggests that it may already have been a Jewish custom. Yet no specific reference is made in the case to the fact that either the father or the daughter is Jewish, which is rather surprising. In such a case, the petitioner is not appealing on the basis of Jewish law but rather on general principles of fairness and broken promises. This makes this case rather uncertain as an example of Jewish law being applied in the Ptolemaic legal sphere.

When it comes to practicing their religion, we have a number of indications, though detailed descriptions are not usually available. The impression is that Jews generally avoided the pagan deities of the Greek and Egyptian communities around them. A few Jews seem to have borne names that had pagan theophoric elements (names that included the names of pagan gods), but for the most part they elected to use "neutral" Greek names or Greek names that translated Hebrew names. A list relating to deliveries of bricks implies that nothing was delivered on the Sabbath, suggesting that the day was observed by the brickyard owners (*CPJ* 1.10). There is also clear evidence of synagogues operating as a normal part of the community (1).

Jewish Women in Legal Documents

Legal documents seem to provide us some of the most detailed information on women, since they are frequently omitted from other sorts of papyrus documents. Many of these relate to marriage or property, both areas where most women would have been involved in one way or another. It was Egyptian custom that women as well as men inherit property. Thus, contrary to common assumption, Jewish women could and did inherit property. It was Egyptian practice to divide the property among all heirs, female as well as male. This sometimes caused resentment because it often led to fragmentation of family property. But one calculation suggests that in sales of land in Demotic contracts in Upper Egypt, 22 percent of vendors and 27 percent of buyers were women.[11] We do not seem to have any examples involving Jewish women, but quite a few naming Egyptian women have been published. One example is a document among the Hawara papyri, in Demotic with a Greek docket, which records the sale of one-third of a house to an Egyptian woman.[12]

Yet we do have Jewish women named in other documents. Two Jews, a man and a woman, filed countersuits against each other in a Greek court, the man accusing the woman of causing him to lose 200 drachmas and she claiming that he insulted her:

> Dositheos son of ... Jew of the Epigone, to Herakleia daughter of Disdotos, Jewess ... abused me saying that I had told certain persons that (you are a ...) woman, and on my abusing you in return you not only spat on me but seizing the loop of my mantle ... you ceased your insults ... to which I have born witness. Wherefore I bring an action of assault against you for 200 drachmai, the assessment of damages. (*CPJ* 1.19)

The case was decided in her favor because the man failed to appear to defend his accusation.

A document contains the petition to the king by a wife (probably but not certainly Jewish) against a Jewish husband. He divorced her but apparently shut her out of the house and refused to return her dowry (*CPJ* 1.128):

> To King Ptolemy greeting from Helladote, daughter of Philonides. I am being wronged by Jonathas, the Jew ... He has agreed in accordance with the law

of the Jews to hold me as wife ... Now he wants to withhold, ... hundred drachmai, and also the house ... does not give me my due, and shuts me out of my house ... and absolutely wrongs me in every respect. I beg you therefore, my king, to order Diophanes, the strategos, to write to ... the epistates of Samareia not to let ... to send Jonathas to Diophanes in order ... (*CPJ* 1.128, ellipses part of the original)

The papyri contain a few other examples mentioning Jewish women. We have a divorce certificate involving a Jewish man and wife. A Jew complains to the village scribe that his pregnant wife was assaulted by another Jewish woman and fears a miscarriage (*CPJ* 1.133).

Apocalyptic—A Hellenistic Phenomenon

One particular development was not confined to the Jews: apocalyptic. Jewish apocalyptic texts are already attested at least as early as the Ptolemaic period (e.g., 1 Enoch 1–36) and perhaps earlier, depending on one's definition. Some elements within 1 Enoch (such as the fallen angels myth) appear to go back to the Persian period. Thus, it probably emerged in identifiable form among the Jews in the Persian period (see the so-called Isaiah Apocalypse—Isa. 24–27) but was to be found all over the Near East and also the Graeco-Roman world over the next several centuries. Among the Jews the classic apocalyptic texts are Daniel 7–12, 2 Baruch, 4 Ezra, and 1 Enoch (cf. also the New Testament book of Revelation, which has many Jewish elements). Outside the Jewish community we find apocalypses in Egypt (e.g., the *Potter's Oracle*, the *Lamb of Boccharis*, and the *Demotic Chronicle*) and in Persia (e.g., the *Zand i Vohuman Yasn*, also known as the *Bahman Yasht*; the *Ardā Wirāz Namag*; and Kartir's *Vision* or *Heavenly Journey*).

The origin of apocalyptic among the Jews has been long debated. There are definite affinities with prophetic texts but also with wisdom literature, in particular with what is referred to as "mantic wisdom." A good argument can be made that some apocalyptic texts could be products of the priestly establishment. Some have seen the origin of apocalyptic in the decline of prophecy; however, it is not clear that prophecy "declined" as such during this period. A number of individuals are said to have prophesied during the Persian period (e.g., Haggai, Zechariah), and prophetic-type figures are attested over the next several centuries in Judaism. I have argued that apocalyptic is a form of prophecy, but it obviously has its individual characteristics that tend to distinguish it from classical prophecy as found in the prophetic section of the Bible.[13]

The Beginnings of Jewish Religious "Scripture"

As we saw in the previous chapter (pp. 171–3), the Pentateuch was probably edited into much its present form toward the end of the Persian period; however, it is in the early Greek period that the Pentateuch is first clearly attested. It seems to be referred to by Hecataeus of Abdera in Diodorus 40.3.6 when he mentions a "written" book of the law.[14] This and other indications suggest that the Pentateuch was available and widely circulated in the Jewish community by the coming of Alexander. Putting all the information together, there seems to be good evidence that the Torah as we know it—the "five books of Moses"—is a product of the Persian period.[15]

It is at the end of Ptolemaic rule—about 200 BCE—that we get a remarkable indication of those religious writings that had become widely known and authoritative among the Jews. This is in the writings of Joshua ben Sira, often simply called Ben Sira. He was a sage and teacher at the end of Ptolemaic rule and the beginning of Seleucid rule over Judah. Although not a priest himself, he was closely associated with the temple and priesthood. He wrote a wisdom book in Hebrew sometime around 200 BCE. Some fifty to seventy-five years later his grandson translated and adapted it for Greek readers.

Ben Sira's book is very important for trying to get a handle on the development of scripture. The most important section for our purposes is the "Praise of the Fathers" (Sir. 44–50), which goes through the heroes (no heroines are listed) of Israel, extending from Adam to Ben Sira's own time. The accompanying table shows the extent to which Ben Sira's account follows the text of our Hebrew Bible, often in some interesting details. He apparently knew the Pentateuch, the Prophets, and some of the Writings. He does not know Ezra and of course not Daniel (which had not been written by his lifetime). He ends with a non-biblical character, his hero, Simon

TABLE 10.2 *Ben Sira's references to Hebrew Bible passages*

Ben Sira	Hebrew Bible
(49:16 Adam)	Gen. 2–3
44:16 Enoch (walked with Yahweh and was taken)	Gen. 5:24
(49:14 Enoch taken away)	Gen. 4:25
(49:16 Seth)	Gen. 4:26
(49:16 Enosh)	Gen. 6:9
44:17-18 Noah (was found righteous, perfect)	Gen. 6:10, etc.
(49:16 Shem)	
44:19-21 Abraham (father of many nations)	Gen. 17:5
Covenant in the flesh	Gen. 17
Promise to bless the nations through his descendants	Gen. 12:2-3; 22:15-18
Inheritance from Euphrates to ends of the earth	Gen. 13:14-17; 15:18
44:22 Isaac	Gen. 21–22; 24–28; 35
44:23-24 Israel/Jacob	Gen. 25; 27–35; 42–50
(49:15 Joseph)	Gen. 37; 39–50
(Dead body provided for)	Gen. 50:25
45:1-5 Moses	
Performed miracles	Exod. 7–14
In king's presences	Exod. 7–14
His meekness	Num. 12:3, 7
Given commandments for his people	Exod. 19–24

TABLE 10.2 *Continued*

45:6-22 Aaron	
Description of priestly garments	Exod. 39:1-31
Dathan, Abiram, Korah	Num. 16
Priests have no inheritance	Num. 18
45:23-26 Phinehas, son of Eleazar	Num. 25
Covenant of priesthood forever	Num. 25:13
46:1-6 Joshua, son of Nun	
Sun stood still	Josh. 10:12-14
Hail sent down on the enemy	Josh. 10:11
46:7-8 Joshua and Caleb opposed rebels and allowed to go into inheritance	Num. 14:6-38
46:9-10 Caleb	Judg. 1:10-15
46:11-12 Judges	Judges (entire book)
46:13-20: Samuel	
Prophet	1 Sam. 9:9
Pledged from mother's womb	1:11
Established the kingship/anointed princes	8–10, 16
Visited the settlements of Jacob	7:16-17
When pressed by enemies, offered sucking lamb	7:9-11
God thundered from heaven against Philistines	7:10
Had taken no bribe	12:3-5
Pronounced king's fate from the grave	28
47:1: Nathan successor to Samuel	2 Sam. 7
47:2-11: David	
Killed lions and bears	1 Sam. 17:34-37
Slew the giant with a slingstone	17:49-50
Women ascribed ten thousands defeated by him	18:7
Defeated the Philistines and other enemies	2 Sam. 5–12
Added string music to altar celebration of festivals	1 Chron. 16; 23:5; 2 Chron. 7:6
47:12-22: Solomon	
Built house in God's name	1 Kgs 6
Wise when he was young	5:9-14
Fame reached wide	5:14; 10:1, 23-24
Astonished by wisdom and proverbs	5:9-14
Heaped up gold like iron, silver like lead	10:21, 27
But gave himself over to women	11:1-5
Division of kingdom but something left to David	12:20
47:23-24: Rehoboam and Jeroboam	
Rehoboam lacked sense and caused the people to rebel	12:1-19
Sinner (Jeroboam) who caused Israel to sin and, eventually, to go into captivity	12:25–13:5; 2 Kgs 17:21-23
48:1-11: Elijah	
Shattered their staff of bread and shut the heavens	1 Kgs 17–18
Brought down fire three times	18:38; 2 Kgs 1:10, 12
Brought dead child to life	17:17-24
Heard threats/punishment at Sinai/Horeb	19:5-18

Anointed prophet in his place	19:19-21
Taken up in whirlwind	2 Kgs 2:11-12
Destined to come before day of Lord, to turn hearts of parents to children	Mal. 3:23-24
48:12-16: Elisha	
Did twice as many miracles	2 Kgs 2:9
Performed miracles after death	13:20-21
48:17-25: Hezekiah	
Cut through rocks to bring water	20:20; 2 Chron. 32:30; Isa. 22:9-11,
Sennacherib's invasion	18-19; Isa. 36–37
Saved by prayer through Isaiah	19:5-7, 14-34; Isa. 37:5-7, 14-34
Angel struck down Assyrian army	19:35-36; Isa. 37:35-36
Isaiah turned back the sun and saved life of king	20:1-11; Isa. 38:1-8
(Isaiah) foretold what would happen in future	Isaiah (entire book)
49:1-3: Josiah	
Destroyed the idols and practiced virtue	2 Kgs 22–23
49:7: Jeremiah	
Made prophet in the womb	Jer. 1:5
Sent to root out, pull down, destroy, and to build and plant	1:10
49:8: Ezekiel	
Vision of creatures with chariot throne	Ezek. 1, 10
49:9: Job	Job (entire book)
49:10: Book of Twelve	Twelve Minor Prophets
49:11: Zerubbabel	
Like signet ring on God's hand	Hag. 2:23
49:12: Jeshua b. Jozadak	
Rebuilt the altar and erected the temple	Hag. 1–2; Ezra 3–6
49:13: Nehemiah	
Rebuilt Jerusalem's walls and defences	Neh. 3–4

the high priest (50:1-29), but it is clear that he gives more than just a collection of oral traditions or material derived from several sources; for the most part he looks to be following a text much like the one we possess today.

In evaluating these close parallels and allusions in Ben Sira, one must keep in mind that slightly different versions of some parts of the Bible circulated in Hebrew until at least the first century CE, and translations of variant Hebrew texts remain in use even today. In some cases, the differences between the various forms of the text are not very significant (e.g., the MT, LXX, and Samaritan Pentateuch of the Torah), but in other cases there are rather more substantial differences (e.g., the book of Jeremiah). Just as important, however, is the fact that the many "parabiblical" traditions known to us from Second Temple Jewish literature are not found in Ben Sira's account. The most reasonable conclusion from these considerations is that Ben Sira had essentially the present biblical text of the Pentateuch, Joshua to 2 Kings, 1 and 2 Chronicles, the Prophets, and the book of Job in front of him.

Translation of the Pentateuch into Greek

We end this chapter with what might seem a slight example that needs little attention. In fact, this incident—the translation of the Hebrew five books of Moses into Greek—was one of the most important events happening in Jewish history during the Ptolemaic period. It is easy to overlook it, but it was one of the most significant events at this time. The matter is complex because the Bible evidently did not yet assume a central place in Judaic religion.

The translation of the Pentateuch into Greek illustrates several things about Judaism during the first part of the Greek period. First, it shows that the primary language of the diaspora community was now Greek. Second, this community felt a need to have the five "Books of Moses" available to them in their own language. Third, the very fact that having their own version of the "scriptures" easily accessible was important to them shows the large place that "scripture" had assumed in their religion. The center of worship remained the Jerusalem temple for most Jews at this time. This had clearly been the case in the Persian period, when the rebuilding of the temple assumed such a central urgent necessity for the Jewish community in Palestine, and we have no reason to think it had changed in the third century. Yet the Egyptian Jews lived in a diaspora community to whom the temple was not easily available. It would hardly be surprising if the significant size of the diaspora community under the Greeks had not started to create changes in perception about how to practice their religion when the temple was not easily available.

The translation demonstrates the way in which the written word was starting to become the central religious focus in diaspora communities. The text had not yet replaced the temple, nor did it really do so until the temple was destroyed in 70 CE. But from this time on, we find an increasing concentration on the text until Judaism could be called a "religion of the book," with the "Law of Moses" as the heart of the faith. In hindsight, we can say that this translation of the Pentateuch into Greek was one of the most significant events for Judaism as a religion.

Conclusions

When Alexander's army marched into Syria, nothing much probably seemed to have changed—they had just exchanged Persian rule for Greek rule. Yet in some ways Jewish life was to change forever. More military conflicts followed: the forty years of the Diadochi had seen armies march across Palestine many times. But in 301 BCE Ptolemy took Palestine and retained it for the next century, no doubt a welcome event for most Jews, at least initially, because it inaugurated a period of peace and stability. The Ptolemaic possessions in Palestine and Syria seem to have been governed as if they were only another province of Egypt, administered from Alexandria but with Egyptian agents in the various cities and villages to see that the appropriate taxes were paid and the Ptolemaic interests served. Whether there was one governor over the entirety of Coele-Syria is not clear, but the region was divided into "hyparchies," perhaps equivalent to the old Persian provinces. Each village had its officials and tax agents, bringing Ptolemaic supervision down to the lowest level of society and making it difficult to avoid the multitude of taxes that weighed on the individual.

Yet taxes were a part of every regime and tell only a partial story. In fact, there seems to have been a general rise in prosperity of the region through the third century, and Judah benefited significantly. It may well be that Jerusalem became more involved in trade activity than has been previously recognized, though this is difficult to determine. As the Tobiad family increased their own wealth—as they seem to have done, probably as tax farmers—the region would have profited, with supplies to purchase, staff to hire, wages to spend, and benefactions undoubtedly made to the temple and perhaps other institutions in Jerusalem. There are indications that over half a century Jerusalem became much more affluent.

Josephus states that Ptolemy I found the Jews useful as soldiers and used them in his garrisons (*Ant.* 12.1.1 §8). Contemporary sources seem to confirm that many Jews served in the military. The basic means of providing defense of the country was by military colonies, known as "cleruchies." They served not only as a reserve to be drawn on in times of war but also as a local police force; hence, they were often settled in troubled areas as a way of bringing them under control. The Tobias of the Zenon papyri was head of such a military cleruchy, though the actual settlers seem to have been a mixed group and not just Jews. Yet Jews in Egypt engaged in a wide variety of occupations, some evidently being low in income and social status, but others became prosperous and had considerable wealth. We have less direct information on the Jews of Palestine, but it seems likely from archaeology and past practice that the vast majority of Jews in Judah were engaged in agrarian activities.

Several "Syrian Wars" took place in the third century BCE, culminating in the Fourth Syrian War, the battle of Raphia in 217 BCE. This context is important for understanding the history of Palestine, even if detail about the Jews is lacking. For the Jews, the semi-legendary story of the Tobiads is about the only source of narrative history for this period. According to it, the high priest Onias II refused to pay a tribute of 20 talents. The reason for this act of rebellion—for that is what it amounted to—is uncertain, though the suggestion that he was expecting or hoping for a transfer of rule to the Seleucids is a plausible one. In any event, his nephew Joseph Tobiad enlisted support among the people, borrowed money from friends in Samaria and, by political skill and greasing palms, managed to pay the tribute and avoid a confrontation. In the process, he gained a considerable increase in the traditional Tobiad power base (already established centuries before).

It seems likely that he obtained some sort of office or source of income, such as local tax-farming rights (though unlikely for the whole of Coele-Syria, which looks like typical storytelling hyperbole). Modern scholarship would date this to the reign of Ptolemy III or IV. Whether there was a breach between Joseph and his son Hyrcanus is debatable; in any case, the view that Hyrcanus was pro-Ptolemy is belied by the later situation in which he seems to have operated openly in Seleucid Jerusalem. This incident also shows that there was no permanent gulf between the Tobiads and Oniads: both were powerful families, each with their own power base but also intermarried. The conditions in Ptolemaic Palestine seem to have lent themselves to mafia-style tactics on the part of enterprising individuals willing to take some risks.

How much Jewish literature was produced during this time is unknown, but some writings can be dated to the early Hellenistic period with relative certainty. Religious literature, including writings that eventually became a part of the Bible, was naturally important. A collection of "scripture" had accumulated by the end of the Persian period and continued to develop in importance, though it by no means constituted a fixed canon or a fixed text. The translation of the Pentateuch into Greek was a milestone. It was not only a unique event in history up to that time but it also demonstrated the way in which authoritative writings were beginning to be a central part of the Jewish religion, at least in the diaspora. The written word did not replace the temple until its destruction several centuries later, but the process had already begun for Judaism to be a "religion of the book."

11
The Threat to Jewish Religion, the Maccabean Revolt, and the Hasmonaean Kingdom

From about 200 BCE, Judah was now under Seleucid rule. At first nothing seems to have changed. But after only a quarter of a century, a series of events began that were to have major consequences for the history of Jews and the religion of Judaism. This chapter covers these events: the initial phase of Seleucid rule, the Hellenistic reform of Jerusalem by Jason, the attempted suppression of Judaism by Antiochus IV, the Maccabaean revolt, and the rule by the Hasmonaean dynasty. This was a dynamic period of 150 years that included an independent Jewish kingdom for the first time in four centuries. It is also during this period that the major Jewish sects seem to have arisen, and the data on these will also be sketched out.

The First Twenty-Five Years of Seleucid Rule

Seleucid rule began well. Antiochus III had ended a century of Ptolemaic rule by taking back Coele-Syria (Syria Palestine) in the Fifth Syrian War (202–199 BCE). The province of Judaea and many of the Jews outside it in Syria were now under Seleucid rule. Yet the Jews had acted wisely not only by opening the gates of Jerusalem to Antiochus's troops but also providing much-needed supplies to him. Antiochus reciprocated with a decree that recognized traditional Jewish rights and religious requirements and, especially, the temple in Jerusalem (*Ant.* 12.3.3-4 §§129–46). The majority of the Jews appeared to approve of Antiochus III's rule, no doubt in part because of his decree. Antiochus's decree is very interesting: unlike the fantastical offerings of the invented Persian decrees in Ezra, the privileges granted by Antiochus are generous but limited, practical, and appropriate to the situation; they can be summarized as follows:

- Restoration and repeopling of Jerusalem, which had been damaged in the fighting.
- An allowance of animals and supplies for altar sacrifices.

MAP 11.1 *Palestine in the Hellenistic and Roman periods.* © Lester Grabbe.

- Timber and other materials for repair allowed to be brought in toll free.
- The traditional form of governance according to Jewish law allowed.
- The Sanhedrin, priests, and other temple personnel relieved of the poll tax, crown tax, and salt tax.
- The tribute from the province reduced by a third.
- Those enslaved in the war set free and their property restored.

Nevertheless, there were some ominous clouds on the horizon. For one thing, Seleucid expansion brought the Seleucid Empire into conflict with the Romans who were also extending their influence eastward. The Romans had conducted a war with Philip V of Macedonia, the so-called Second Macedonian War (200–196 BCE). Now Antiochus foolishly toppled into a war with the Romans, which was both unnecessary and also disastrous for him. After a defeat at Magnesia in 191 BCE, the treaty of Apamea in 188 placed heavy restrictions on Antiochus, including a war indemnity and the requirement for a son to be sent to Rome as a hostage. Thus, the future Antiochus IV was sent to Rome about 188 BCE and remained there until about 176. Antiochus III himself died in 187 BCE and was succeeded by his son Seleucus IV (187–175 BCE). Seleucus reigned quietly for the most part and did not engage in military ventures. He paid off much of the war indemnity but fell behind in payments toward the end of his reign, which left his successor to finish the final instalments. Seleucus IV apparently had a financial quarrel with Judah, as reflected in the tale of Heliodorus and the temple treasure (2 Macc. 3), even if the precise situation is not clear. Seleucus's life ended prematurely when he was assassinated, allegedly by this same Heliodorus, which left a power vacuum.

Normally, the son of the ruler would take over on the death of the father, but Seleucus's older son, Demetrius, had just settled in Rome as a hostage for the Seleucids'

TABLE 11.1 *Seleucid kings.*

	Seleucus I Nicator ([321]312–281 BCE)
	Antiochus I Soter (281–261 BCE)
	Antiochus II Theos (261–246 BCE)
	Seleucus II Callinicus (246–226 BCE)
	Seleucus III (226–223 BCE)
	Antiochus III the Great (223–187 BCE)
	Seleucus IV Philopator (187–175 BCE)
	Antiochus IV Epiphanes (175–164 BCE)
	Antiochus V Eupator (164–162 BCE)
Antiochus VI Epiphanes Dionysus (c. 145–138 BCE)	Demetrius I Soter (162–150 BCE)
	Alexander Balas (150–145 BCE)
Antiochus VII Euergetes Sedetes (138–129 BCE)	Demetrius II (first reign: 145–140 BCE)
	Diodotus Tryphon (c. 142–138 BCE)
	Demetrius II (second reign: 129–126 BCE)
Antiochus VIII Gryphus Epiphanes Philometor Kallinikos (126–96 BCE)	Alexander II Zabinas Theos Epiphane Nikephoros (c. 128–123 BCE)
Antiochus IX Cyzicenus Philopator (116–96 BCE)	Demetrius III Eucaerus Theos Philopator (96–87 BCE?), one of several claimants to the Seleucid throne
Seleucus VI Epiphanes Nicator (96–94 BCE)	
Antiochus X Eusebes Philopator (95–92 or 95–88 BCE?)	Philip I Epiphanes Philadelphus (94–83 or 94–75 BCE?)
Antiochus XI Epiphanes Philadelphus (94–93 BCE?)	
Antiochus XII Dionysus Epiphanes Philopator Callinicus (87–82 BCE?)	
Antiochus XIII Philadelphus Asiaticus (69–64 BCE, often seen as last Seleucid king)	

TABLE 11.2 *Ptolemaic kings.*

Ptolemy V Theos Epiphanes (204–180 BCE)
Ptolemy VI Philometor (180–145 BCE)
[Ptolemy VII Neos Philopator]
[Cleopatra II]
Ptolemy VIII Euergetes II Physcon (145–116 BCE)
[Cleopatra III]
Ptolemy IX Soter II Lathyrus (116–107, 88–80 BCE)
Ptolemy X Alexander I (107–88)
Berenice IV (58–55 BCE)
[Ptolemy XI Alexander II]
Ptolemy XII Neo Dionysus Auletes (80–58, 55–51 BCE)
Cleopatra VII (51–30 BCE)
Ptolemy XIII (51–47 BCE)
Ptolemy XIV (47–44 BCE)
Ptolemy XV Caesarion (36–30 BCE)

keeping the peace (in place of his uncle, Antiochus IV). Seleucus's other son, Antiochus, was only about four or five years old. But Seleucus's brother, Antiochus, was in Athens, apparently on his way back home from being a hostage in Rome. Antiochus took advantage of the power vacuum by quickly sailing from Athens to Antioch and taking the Seleucid throne as Antiochus IV Epiphanes. He further legitimated his rule by marrying Seleucus's widow and adopting the young Antiochus as his son.

We know of Antiochus IV from Jewish sources but also the Greek historians.[1] Recent study has found Antiochus IV a much more positive and able character than emerges from some ancient authors and, especially, many modern treatments. He had little difficulty in taking the throne from his nephew (who may have already been proclaimed king), though they apparently ruled as supposed joint rulers for a few years (before the younger Antiochus was evidently executed by his uncle). Thus began the reign of one of the most promising and possibly one of the most able of the Seleucid rulers; however, like his father he had history against him.

How the Jewish Revolt Against Seleucid Rule Began: Jason's "Hellenistic Reform"

One of the most remarkable events in ancient history is the Maccabean revolt against the Seleucid Empire. History is filled with revolts of conquered people who attempted to regain their freedom, but the interesting thing about what happened in Judah is that it eventually succeeded. Nevertheless, exactly how the revolt began is complicated, especially because our sources give more than one account of events leading up to the actual revolt. In the narrative that I give here, I follow mainly the account in 2 Maccabees 4:7-34, which is the only detailed one, but I have attempted to insert information from the other accounts where this seems appropriate. Twenty-five years of Seleucid rule went by fairly smoothly, but not without some upsetting events. The main one affecting Judah was the Heliodorus episode (2 Macc. 3) in which Seleucus sent his official Heliodorus to confiscate the temple treasury. The confiscation apparently did not take place (allegedly because of supernatural intervention by an angel)—but the actual details are obscure. In any case, Seleucid rule was ostensibly not more oppressive than that of the previous imperial rule that Jews had endured for centuries under the Neo-Babylonians, Persians, and Ptolemies. Yet things changed almost immediately when Antiochus IV came to the throne in 175 BCE, though the reasons are complex.

Antiochus IV began his reign in September 175 BCE. What actions did he take with regard to the Jews? If we follow 1 and 2 Maccabees, the answer is surprising: *he took no action with regard to the Jews!* From the main Jewish sources of 1 and 2 Maccabees, we have no indication that Antiochus had any particular interest in the Jews. True, the first encounter with the Jews does seem to have come about fairly soon after he began his reign, but it was not inaugurated by him. On the contrary, it was Jason from the Jewish side who took the initiative and approached Antiochus with a very attractive proposition.

Jason was the brother of the Jerusalem high priest Onias III, but he had ambitions to become high priest himself. So he went to Antiochus IV and offered to pay 360 talents of silver, plus another 80 from another source, a total of 440 talents of silver to be given the high priesthood in place of his brother (2 Macc. 4:8). He also offered another 150 talents to be able to build a gymnasium in Jerusalem, making 590 talents in all. Although not stated explicitly, the request to build a gymnasium and draw up an ephebate list seems clearly part of an initiative to have Jerusalem made into a *polis*—that is, a city organized in the Greek manner.

There were many important urban areas of the ancient Near East that were organized as Greek cities (*poleis*), not only cities that had been newly founded by Alexander and his successors but also some of the ancient traditional sites. In such a system, some of the population (though by no means all) would be citizens, with particular privileges. Their children would become "ephebates" or candidates for citizenship, which they would gain formally at a certain age. Preparation for citizenship included attendance at an educational institute called the "gymnasium." This was not just a place for exercise, though physical training was an important part of the education. In its origins, the gymnasium prepared young men for war. With time, however, the military training became less accentuated, and a good deal of emphasis was placed on the intellectual requirements of citizenship, especially use of the (Greek) language in both writing and speech; rhetoric, since citizens might be required to speak in public; and Greek literature (with an emphasis on Homer).

Any proposal to Antiochus that seemed likely to bring revenue into his coffers would probably meet with his approval. This does not mean that he was short of funds, but any extra income would still be welcome. In this case, there were many positive features to Jason's offer: it made no difference to Antiochus who was high priest in Jerusalem; in any event, the office was still in the family; Jason had at least showed some sign of having a bit of gumption and might turn out to be useful in other ways; above all, he seems to have paid cash on the barrel head. Finally, Antiochus appears to have encouraged a number of the native cities in his empire to become *poleis*, so Jerusalem was not an exception.

Jason was obviously interested in a *cultural transformation* of Jerusalem. But this brings up an important question: did Jason and his supporters also have a vision of a different future for the *Jewish religion* from the one suggested by its past? This has often been assumed, but there are a number of issues to consider. Judging from the names in the books of Maccabees, many of the leading figures in Judaea at this time were thoroughly Hellenized, with Greek names (alongside their native ones). Such individuals would have supported Jason's move and may even have encouraged him in his enterprise. As educated and status-bearing individuals, the priests would have been at the forefront of this acculturation process.

Of course, the books of Maccabees opposed Jason's enterprise. They claim that Jason "set aside the customs valid for the Jews by royal philanthropy, negotiated through John the father of Eupolemus" at the time of Antiochus III's initial conquest of Syria Palestine (2 Macc. 4:11). They go on to say this about Jason:

> [13]It was thus a peak of Hellenism and an explosion in the adoption of foreign customs through the excessive wickedness of the impious Jason—who was no high priest. [14]The priests were no longer devoted to the service of the altar, but treating the temple with contempt and neglecting the sacrifices, they hastened to participate in the lawless public spectacles in the arena after the summons to the event. [15]They set at nothing the ancestral honours but regarded the Hellenic status symbols as the best ... (2 Macc. 4:10-15)

It is clear that 2 Maccabees thinks Jason was acting contrary to the law. The question is whether this was correct: What exactly did Jason do that was wrong? What *specific act* of breaking the law does the text of 2 Macc. 4:10-15 name? The author of this passage throws lots of adjectives and adverbs around: "wicked," "unlawful," "ungodly"—*yet a close look shows that this account does not at any point tell us anything concrete about any unlawful acts. He has simply thrown a lot of metaphorical dust in the air.*

It would probably be agreed, at least by most readers, that Jason should not have taken the high priesthood from his brother Onias. If there is a sin or crime or wrongful act, this would have been it. But beyond that, 2 Maccabees gives *no specific examples of anything unlawful*. The most he can say is that the priests were not as intent on their service at the altar as they should have been, but even this may be a matter of interpretation. We know the daily *tamid* offering did not cease because when it was stopped a few years later, it was an extremely traumatic experience (see further on p. 219). Were the people who brought their various sacrifices not being attended to? Were there long queues of tired people dragging along to the temple thirsty sheep and goats bleating away, because the priests were not doing their job? No indication of any such thing occurs in the sources.

As far as we can tell, the cult continued as normal. What is alleged is that priests left the altar at a certain time of day to attend the sports in the wrestling arena. But priests were not required to be on duty twenty-four hours a day. There were more priests than were needed to take care of the sacrificial system, and eventually a system developed in which they were divided into twenty-four courses. They were on duty for a week twice a year and, in addition, all were on duty for the festivals. So who were the priests who went to the wrestling arena? Were they priests on duty? Or were they priests who were not on duty and were looking for things to occupy their time? Or has the writer simply created a caricature? In any case, no specific law was broken or the writer would have told us. Considering the author's earnest desire to attack Jason, his descent into mere rhetoric, without specific examples, speaks loudly that Jason upheld the law and the correct temple procedure.

In this whole chapter, only one possible example of a breach of the law is alleged by 2 Maccabees, which states that when quinquennial athletic games were held, Jason sent Antiochian envoys from Jerusalem carrying 300 silver drachmas for the sacrifice of Hercules. But the messengers thought it improper for the money to be used for pagan sacrifice and instead spent it on the equipment of warships (2 Macc. 4:18-20). However, one should look at this account carefully. First, if Jason planned to send 300 silver drachmas to Tyre, he would pick his couriers very carefully—men he could trust. There was a plethora of distractions between Jerusalem and Tyre: taverns, brothels, markets, traders, and so on, and 300 drachmas was a lot of money.

But if he chose trustworthy men, they would also be people who would not take the money for one purpose and then use it for something else when they got there. Second, it is easy to allege that it was intended for another purpose, but where is the evidence? The money was not in fact used for a pagan sacrifice but for warships. This all suggests that Jason originally sent the 300 drachmas as a gift with the intent that the silver be used to buy warships. Someone, however—perhaps even the author of 2 Maccabees—simply put the worst possible interpretation on the act.

One other allegation is—surprisingly—not found in 2 Maccabees. Rather, one source states that those who built the gymnasium "removed the marks of circumcision." It is not easy to evaluate whether this is anything more than a wild allegation because it is mentioned by no independent sources (such as 2 Maccabees). However, even if we take it at face value and put the worst interpretation on it, there are still two points to be kept in mind. The first point concerns the operation itself. There is a description of "uncircumcision" in an ancient medical text.[2] Without going into gruesome detail, it would have been very painful and would have required considerable motivation to undergo it! We can be confident they were not queuing up at the surgeon's door.

If some did go through with this, it would most likely have been to compete in athletic contests in other cities. Second, it must be pointed out—contrary to common assumption—that there is no evidence that exercises were done in the nude in the Jerusalem gymnasium, even if this was common in a Greek context. 2 Maccabees does not suggest that they were, and Thucydides (1.6.5-6) shows that it was not necessarily always the custom. They could, therefore, have done their exercises in loincloths. It is further sometimes pointed out that it was also normal for the Greek gymnasia to be dedicated to Hermes. But we have no hint that this was the case in Jerusalem. We have to keep in mind that the author of 2 Maccabees is looking for *any possible* indication of scandal, and he is able to give none. His silence about both concerns is a strong indication that there was neither nude exercise nor any pagan ceremonies connected with Jason's gymnasium.

We now come to the all-important question: What was the reaction of the people to all this activity in association with Jerusalem's becoming a *polis*? In handbooks one often reads statements along the lines that "the orthodox Jews in Jerusalem were incensed at these things."[3] There are two problems with such statements. First, the question of who is "orthodox" is begged. Who determines who is orthodox; who are we to say who was considered pious at the time and who was not—and by whom?

The second problem is closely related: it concerns the reaction of the people. And what was their reaction? The answer is, *there was no negative reaction from the people of Jerusalem.*

Some of those living in the country may have been displeased with what was happening, or at least skeptical about it, though we do not know for sure. But what we *do* know is that many people embraced this new Hellenistic city, because they became a part of it. It is clear from both books of Maccabees that there were no riots and demonstrations against Jason's plan. Indeed, the people of Jerusalem even welcomed Antiochus in magnificent fashion when he visited Jerusalem a couple or so years later, before his first invasion of Egypt (2 Macc. 4:21-22). Apart from Jason's act of taking the high priesthood itself, there is little evidence of a breach of the Torah. As it was, Jason's power base continued to be one traditional to the high priest: the temple and cult.

There seems little reason to suggest that Jason did not think of himself as anything but a loyal and law-abiding Jew and a credit to the office he held. However, there was an important consequence: Jason's brother Onias, who was displaced as high priest, had a son also named Onias. This Onias would have been the high priest Onias IV if his father had not been forced out of office. Rather than remain in Jerusalem, he fled to Egypt and founded his own temple in a place called Leontopolis (now Tell el-Yehudieh). That continued as a very minor rival to the Jerusalem temple for two hundred years—until it was closed by the Romans after the fall of Jerusalem.

Turn About ... Jason Displaced by Menelaus

Jason's Hellenistic office lasted only about three years before he was displaced by another individual named Menelaus (2 Macc. 4:23-26). Menelaus was one of three brothers. Simon was an officer of the temple, mentioned in 2 Macc. 3:4-6 who had had a disagreement with Onias over the running of the city market. A third brother was Lysimachus, who features in the account below. In spite of some claims that these brothers were simply lay Jews, this conclusion is scarcely credible. Textual scholars are generally agreed that the reading "tribe of Benjamin" in 2 Macc. 3:4 should read "tribe of Balgea," a priestly family, as other manuscripts show. Simon was captain of the temple, a priestly office. When Menelaus became high priest, there is no evidence of opposition from the people, which surely would have happened if he had not been of priestly descent.

Since Jason had in essence double-crossed his brother, there is no reason why others could not play that game. This Menelaus did precisely what Jason had done: he went to Antiochus and offered him even more money to hold the office of high priest. Menelaus is said to have added a further 300 talents to the amount being paid by Jason. This was a large sum by any standards, and if it was meant to be an annual contribution as seems likely, it made the annual payment from Judah an impossible sum. We know it was impossible because Menelaus did not pay it! But if Menelaus *offered* this amount of tribute, Antiochus would have accepted it, whatever reservations he might have had about the province's being able to bear it. Therefore, what we see is another example of the struggle over the priesthood which seems to have a long history.

Menelaus soon got into trouble because he was not paying the money he had promised to Antiochus (2 Macc. 4:27-34). He was summoned to appear before the king, but when he arrived, the king was away dealing with a revolt. Menelaus had to appear before another high minister named Andronicus who was temporarily in charge of the running of the kingdom. Here was a chance to gain time, so Menelaus is alleged to have stolen some of the golden temple vessels, giving some to Andronicus and selling others in the area of Tyre. If 2 Maccabees is to be believed, he in this way not only gained a breathing space with regard to his debt but also bribed Andronicus into murdering Onias III (the original high priest displaced by Jason).

Back in Jerusalem rumors had begun to spread about the stolen temple vessels, which gives us a crucial piece of historical data (2 Macc. 4:39-42). *What was the people's reaction to the (supposed) theft of the temple vessels? They rioted in the streets.* This account puts a number of the previous events in perspective. The people of Jerusalem—many of them citizens of the "Hellenistic *polis*"—were not indifferent to matters of religion. They had the same regard for the temple and its cult as their ancestors had. It was a most sacred place and not to be treated lightly. As already argued, Jason had not compromised the temple or priesthood. But selling off temple vessels was a breach of its holiness and a serious affront to the religious susceptibilities of the people, who proceeded to take action.

Lysimachus, Menelaus's brother who was governing while the latter was away, came out with a large band of armed soldiers to attack the rioting crowd. But this was no ordinary mob. They were out in such numbers and so agitated by the rumors of the temple desecration that they drove off the soldiers and even killed Lysimachus. As soon as the fighting had ceased, the *gerousia* or governing council of elders (known in other texts as the Sanhedrin) sent a delegation to complain to the king. Unfortunately, for whatever reason (bribery?), the king sided with Menelaus and his faction and executed the delegates from the council.

But it is important to recognize that the "rioters" and the members of the council of elders were all citizens of Jerusalem, evidently the very people who had welcomed the Hellenistic reforms of Jason. Their motivation in resisting Menelaus was purely religious. There is no question that the so-called Hellenizers of the Jason faction took the temple, the cult, and the Jewish religion very seriously, and they were willing to put their lives on the line to defend it. This distinction in approach and attitude between Menelaus and Jason has often been overlooked. The interpretation of the data suggests that Jason was an ideologue, perhaps to some extent a dreamer, who admired Greek culture and who saw the adoption of some aspects of it as beneficial to his people. But Menelaus looks more like an opportunist, whose actions are those of a man out to gain whatever he can for himself without regard for the consequences to the Jewish people.

Putting together the information from the various accounts, we seem to have a picture of basically three groups of people among the Jews of Judah at this time. There was a segment of the population, probably many of them living in the country and making their living from agriculture whose contact with Greek culture and the Greek world was minimal, who took a quite conservative approach. Yet it would be very unhistorical—anti-historical, even—to take sides religiously and use such terms as "pious" and "orthodox" for such people.

Another group, which evidently included the high priest Jason, was open to Hellenistic culture but religiously conservative and upheld the continuation of the temple and its cult as previously. This included members of the council of elders of the Hellenistic city of Jerusalem who opposed Menelaus and his brother Lysimachus. It included the inhabitants and citizens of Jerusalem who attacked Lysimachus's troops and ended up killing Lysimachus himself for allegedly selling off temple vessels. Surprisingly, from all we can determine, it included the Hasmonaean family, when it comes on the scene. As we shall see, the Hasmonaeans were broadly sympathetic to Hellenistic culture of this sort.

A third group were those who supported the Seleucid government and continued to do so even during the Maccabaean revolt. This evidently included the high priest Menelaus. Although often labeled an "extreme Hellenist," his precise views on Hellenistic cultures are actually not very clear, but his support of the Seleucid government—even at times against his own people—is blatantly evident. This group also includes those Jews who manned the Seleucid fortresses, including the Jerusalem Akra, alongside the troops of the Seleucid government. At various points in the books of Maccabees disparaging references are made about such individuals (e.g., 1 Macc. 3:15; 6:21; 7:5; 9:23, 25, 58, 69, 73; 10:61; 11:25). We must keep in mind, though, that the Maccabaean authors were happy to label even the "moderate Hellenizers" in this way. In any case, the precise proportion of the population who fell into this grouping is very difficult to determine; however, the bulk of the population does not seem to be in the category that supported Menelaus.

Antiochus and the Sixth Syrian War

Holding on to the ambitions of a proper Seleucid Empire, Antiochus spent the first five years of his reign accumulating the necessary resources to bring this about, which was to invade Egypt. It was during this time (c. 174 BCE) that he was quite happy to receive the large sum of money from Jason, and a few years later (c. 171 BCE) an even larger promise of funds from Menelaus. It is alleged that Antiochus intended to gain control of Egypt: by becoming king according to some, or as the power behind the throne, according to others. The trouble was that the Ptolemies were also plotting to take back Coele-Syria and Phoenicia that they had lost to Antiochus III.

Although he probably did not attack first, Antiochus was clearly prepared for war. This may be why he visited Jerusalem about 172 BCE (2 Macc. 4:21-22), where he was enthusiastically welcomed by Jason and the citizens of Jerusalem (though it did not prevent Jason being displaced by Menelaus shortly afterward). Jerusalem was close enough to the Egyptian border to be part of an inspection tour and also a stage for a show of Seleucid force from the army accompanying Antiochus.

Thus, with this plotting on both sides the Sixth Syrian War (170–168 BCE) seems inevitable. Who started the war is to some extent a fruitless debate, since they were both preparing for war. But it appears that Ptolemy VI took the initiative by advancing into Syrian territory in late 170 or early 169 BCE. Antiochus responded with a counterattack that soon turned into an invasion of Egypt itself. Antiochus was successful, taking a great deal of booty and arranging the Ptolemaic government in a way that would favor him and the Seleucid administration in general. He returned in triumph about September 169 with his army and much wealth for his coffers.

On his way back, at this time he apparently visited Jerusalem. There is some debate as to whether this visit took place after his first or his second invasion of Egypt. But it makes most sense that this visit to Jerusalem took place after the first invasion because Antiochus came to Jerusalem peacefully, which was not the case after the second invasion. Antiochus was taken on a tour of the temple by Menelaus (2 Macc. 5:15-16)—a clear breach of the law—and then appropriated much of the temple treasury before going on his way back to Antioch. It was probably the case that Antiochus justified this seizure of temple treasure as payment for the back tribute still owed by Menelaus.

Antiochus' arrangements in Egypt did not last: almost immediately Ptolemy VI associated his brother (Ptolemy VIII) and sister (Cleopatra II) on the throne with himself, clearly contrary to Antiochus's own interests. Antiochus felt he had no choice but to invade Egypt again, which he did only a year later in the spring of 168. This seems to have been successful initially (it has even been argued that Antiochus was declared king of Egypt at one point in the campaign), but then the Romans intervened. A Roman mission that was already in the region confronted Antiochus and gave him the ultimatum of withdrawing from Egypt or being an enemy of Rome. The story is an interesting one.

The Senate had passed a motion requiring Antiochus to withdraw, but it was to be delivered only if the Romans won the battle of Pydna (fighting against the Macedonians). When they did win, the Roman commander Popilius Laenas then approached Antiochus at Eleusis (a suburb of Alexandria)—they both knew each other—and greeted him from a distance but refused to shake hands. Instead, he handed him the senatorial decree. After reading it, Antiochus said he would need to consult with his Friends. Popilius took the staff he was carrying and drew a circle around Antiochus. He then said the Seleucid king had to make his decision before stepping outside the circle. Antiochus, after a few minutes' hesitation, agreed to the Senate's demands, at which point Popilius shook his hand warmly.

Conflict and Religious Suppression in Judaea

As his army withdrew from Egypt, Antiochus heard about the fighting in Jerusalem, which he interpreted as a rebellion in Judaea—indeed, there may have been an actual revolt. The reason according to 2 Maccabees 5:5 is that a false rumor had reached Jason in Transjordan (where he had taken refuge) that Antiochus had been killed. Evidently, Jason interpreted this as a heaven-sent opportunity to try to take back the high priesthood that he thought was rightfully his—since he had stolen it fair and square from his brother. His calculation was partially right in that Jason's troops quickly retook Jerusalem, but Menelaus holed up in the city's strong point, called the Akra, and could not be dislodged.

Antiochus immediately sent an army to put down the assumed rebellion (it is not clear whether he led it himself). What happened next remains obscure in both 1 and

2 Maccabees. In the six months between when Antiochus withdrew from Egypt in July 168 and the cessation of the temple cult in December 168, our sources relate a number of puzzling events that allegedly led up to the suppression of Judaism. Trying to sort out the precise sequence of events that preceded the prohibition of Judaism and the Maccabaean revolt is a difficult one. This is due not only to differences between the sources but also to complications within them pointing to intrigues and intricate maneuverings on the part of various interests and factions.

We left Jason besieging Menelaus who was holed up in the Akra. But eventually, for whatever reason, Jason himself was forced to flee. The sources now relate a series of actions that do not make complete sense:

- Antiochus had heard that Jerusalem was in revolt and brought his army against the city, killing forty thousand inhabitants and enslaving another forty thousand.
- Antiochus left a viceroy named Philip to keep the people in line (also, a similar officer in charge of Samaria).
- Later he sent Apollonius, commander of the Mysians, who took Jerusalem with violence, killing and enslaving a large number of people: his orders were to kill all the adult men and sell all the women and children into slavery. But already most of the population had been killed or enslaved when Antiochus's troops first arrived!
- Finally, sometime after this, Geron the Athenian was sent to compel the Jews to leave their ancestral laws.

When we analyze carefully this alleged chain of events, we find multiple unanswered questions: if Antiochus's army took the city and put down the revolt, why was there need to send Apollonius the Mysiarch to take the city by subterfuge sometime later? Moreover, Apollonius is ordered to kill all the men and to enslave the women and children, a strange move after Antiochus's army had already slain or enslaved practically all of them! And why did Antiochus feel it necessary even after that to send Geron the Athenian to set up pagan worship in the temple when the supposed revolt of the Jews had long since been dealt with? We are simply not given sufficient data and can only make informed guesses at best.

The best we can work out is the following: first, there is no clear evidence that Antiochus himself took part in capturing the city. Rather, the actions ascribed to him are probably those of Apollonius; that is, Apollonius was sent to put down a rebellion. The fight between Jason and Menelaus had given the impression of a revolt or perhaps had shown the continuation of one. When Apollonius got there, the city was already peaceful (apparently because Jason had already left the scene), but he took it by a ruse and carried out Antiochus's orders. After this, Philip the viceroy was sent. It looks as if he led a Syrian military detachment to be installed in Jerusalem. Philip remained there, with Menelaus continuing as high priest, until the actual Maccabaean revolt began.

The real puzzle is why, a little later, Antiochus sent Geron to crush the Jewish religion. This religious suppression would have been unique in antiquity. Religious intolerance has historically been a practice of monotheistic religions, primarily Christianity, Judaism, and Islam. While Judaism itself was often seen by the Greeks and Romans as intolerant, polytheism was usually tolerant by its nature. Antiochus was no religious zealot. He had no occasion to suppress Judaism for ideological reasons, while Jews outside Palestine itself and even in the very capital of Antioch evidently carried on with their worship without hindrance.

We further have the strange statement in 1 Macc. 1:43 that Antiochus issued a decree that all his subjects were to abandon their native laws and become one people. It goes on to state that the "Gentiles" and "even many from Israel" obeyed this decree. This is blatantly false. The various ethnic groups under Seleucid rule were as attached to their local customs as much as the Jews were. Furthermore, there is absolutely no evidence in any of the Seleucid sources that Antiochus issued such a decree. But we do know that an "abomination of desolation" was established in the Jerusalem temple. What this consisted of is not completely clear, but notice the facts:

- The temple was dedicated to Zeus Olympius (2 Macc. 6:2).
- The primary cause of pollution and sacrilege was something erected on the altar of burnt offering (1 Macc. 1:54; 4:43-47). This included a pagan altar (*bōmos*) on top of the original altar in the temple courtyard (1 Macc. 1:59). According to other sources (e.g., Diodorus 34–35.1.3-4), swine were offered on this altar, though why 1 and 2 Maccabees would have omitted this fact is a major question.
- There was a monthly celebration of the king's birthday (2 Macc. 6:7).
- Worship of Dionysus took place on the king's feast day, with processions in his honor (2 Macc. 6:7).

There is no indication that an idol of any sort was placed in the temple, as would be expected with a Greek cult. It is almost inconceivable that the presence of such would have been ignored by Daniel or 1 and 2 Maccabees. The cessation of the *tamid* offering was seen as shaking the cosmos to its foundations: how much more the statue of a pagan god set up in the Holy of Holies! The silence of Daniel and 1 and 2 Maccabees seems a strong argument against any such statue, even though some late sources assert the erection of an image.

To return to the important question of why Jewish worship was suppressed and the worshipers persecuted, some have tried to resolve the problem by arguing there was no religious suppression. But there are too many counterarguments to accept this thesis. Note the following points:

- Although the harrowing story of the martyrdom of the mother and her seven sons in 2 Maccabees 7 is a literary fiction, it shows that the author of the book thought there was real religious persecution.
- Daniel not only speaks of pollution of the temple but in Dan. 11:33 appears to talk of individuals killed for their religious beliefs or deeds.
- There is the death of Eleazer for religious reasons (2 Macc. 6:18-31). Likewise, the accounts of the women executed for having their sons circumcised (2 Macc. 6:10; cf. a similar account in 1 Macc. 1:60-61) and those killed while keeping the Sabbath in caves outside the city (2 Macc. 6:11).

- The *Testament of Moses* 8 speaks of a persecution. Circumcision is specifically singled out as a factor (*T. Moses* 8:1, 3). This looks like a reference to the Maccabaean crisis.
- Diodorus 34–35.1.3-4 states that Antiochus wanted to counter Jewish hatred against the rest of mankind. As a result, he sacrificed a great sow on the altar and then sprinkled their holy books with the meat juices; further, he compelled the high priest and the other Jews to eat of the meat.
- Tacitus, *Hist.* 5.8.2 speaks of Antiochus trying to get rid of Jewish superstition.
- The letter of Antiochus IV making concessions to the Judaeans (2 Macc. 11:27-38) mentions that the Jews wanted to use their own foods and follow their own laws. This indicates that these practices had been officially suppressed for a time. See also the letter of Antiochus V (2 Macc. 11:23-26).

These sources show how complicated the matter is. The pollution of the temple and altar (from the Jewish point of view) is confirmed. Granted, some of the accounts of persecution—and certainly many of the details—are fictional. Yet too many statements from independent sources about religious persecution cannot be dismissed. Especially decisive seem the statements in the Seleucid letters: there were decrees affecting Jewish foods and other religious laws. Thus, along with pollution of the temple and pagan sacrifices, which all accept, there were also attempts to suppress the Jewish religion, though some could be measures taken only by local officials.

To summarize, there seems no doubt that Antiochus's measures to establish his authority are correct. Judaea had rebelled in his eyes, and he needed to make an example of it. Yet also suppression of Jewish worship would no doubt have been a watershed, not only in Jewish history but in the history of antiquity, because it was not the custom to forbid local religious expression. *Make no mistake: there was religious persecution.* From the Jewish point of view, no greater attack on their religion could be made than expunging the *tamid* offering or polluting the altar with pagan sacrifices.

Another thesis to explain the persecution is the argument that Antiochus promoted the cult of Zeus Olympus and deified himself in the image of Zeus. But there is a major objection to this concept: Where in our sources is any statement connecting Antiochus's alleged religious devotion to Zeus in his political actions as king, whether against the Jews or otherwise? No such statement is found. Whatever Antiochus's personal religious devotions, there is no evidence that he attempted to impose Zeus worship or anything like it on his subjects, especially the Jews.

This conclusion is reinforced by the description of the temple site when Judas retook it from the Seleucids: "weeds growing up in the courts as in a forest" (1 Macc. 4:38). This indicates no activity had been going on there for some time. If the Seleucid military garrison in the Akra had instituted their own (pagan) worship in the temple, there is no reason why they should have then abandoned it. The description in 1 Maccabees makes it appear as if the desecration was a deliberate attempt to pollute the temple as punishment for the Jewish revolt, but once this was done, the site was then left deserted. There was no introduction of another continuing cult, whether Greek or Oriental.

From various statements and hints within the sources, it appears that Menelaus was in some way a direct or indirect cause of the persecution. 2 Macc. 13:3-8 seems to blame Menelaus for the situation. Josephus, who does not appear to know 2 Maccabees, nevertheless states that Menelaus "had compelled the Jews to violate their ancestral religion" (*Ant.* 12.9.7 §385). Menelaus was apparently purely a power seeker. He did, for example, conduct Antiochus into the temple, perhaps even the Holy of Holies, according to 2 Maccabees 5:15, though Jason on a similar visit of Antiochus did not carry out such a sacrilegious act (2 Macc. 4:21-2). Some have even argued that the imposed cult was the product of Menelaus himself as part of a power play.

Antiochus was no ideologue: any measures he took would almost certainly have been (in his eyes) for pragmatic reasons. Was this where Menelaus came in, perhaps advising the king that their religion was what caused the Jews to act in certain ways? This seems certainly a possibility. In any case, the order was an unusual—unprecedented—one and had consequences that Antiochus probably could not have begun to predict. If he had had any inkling of what the results would be, it is very doubtful that he would have given the order. Nor should we forget that some of the problem may have been the excesses of overzealous local officials.

The pollution of the temple and the cessation of the daily (*tamid*) offering took place on Kislev 25, 145 of the Seleucid era (1 Macc. 1:54). This appears to be the date November/December 168 BCE. It was once popular to give the date as 167 BCE; however, in recent years, a number of researchers have proposed 168 BCE, which is the date I also argue for.[4] Note that the cleansing of the temple took place *before* Antiochus's death; we know he died in November/December 164 BCE.

The Beginnings of the Revolt

According to 1 Maccabees 2, the fightback against Seleucid religious suppression began with Mattathias, the father of the Maccabaean brothers. There are a number of reasons to doubt this. Mattathias is completely ignored by 2 Maccabees, which focuses on Judas. A number of issues that are associated with Mattathias actually seem to have come up later in Hasmonaean history, such as the question of fighting on the Sabbath, which perhaps came up about 161 BCE (cf. 1 Macc. 9:43-49). Mattathias and his deeds are nowhere else referred to in 1 Maccabees after ch. 2, especially in the summary of Maccabaean deeds in 1 Macc. 14:27-45. Although Mattathias is mentioned as the father of Simon (1 Macc. 14:29-30), nothing is said about his part in initiating the revolt, this despite mention of Simon's brothers fighting.

A further complication is that resistance seems to have got underway before the Maccabees came on the scene. For example, we later read of the Hasidim who are clearly a resistance group not initially affiliated with the Maccabaean circle (1 Macc. 2:42). 2 Macc. 5:27 states that Judas and ten associates fled into the countryside when the persecution started in Jerusalem. There they lived like animals for a period. This suggests little support or organization for the initial resistance of the Hasmonaean family. Rather than others joining them (as 1 Macc. 2:42-43 alleges), it may be that it was they who joined others.

The Hasmonaean family eventually established leadership over the movement but, regardless of its precise origins, the Jewish resistance under Judas and his brothers took some time to get under way. The first actions seem to have been against "apostate" Jews rather than the Seleucid soldiers (1 Macc. 2:44-48; 3:8). As so often in such situations, the community was divided, and former neighbors and even kin were at each other's throats. Fellow Jews also made an easier target. The village of Modein, the home of the Hasmonaean family, served as the natural center of operations. Although itself close to the Seleucid garrisons at Jerusalem and Gezer and easily approachable by a hostile force, it was right next to the Gophna Hills to which the Jewish fighters could easily retire if threatened. Judas also raised his army from among his kin and fellow countrymen (2 Macc. 8:1). The resistance was conducted by guerrilla tactics initially and probably did not worry the Seleucid central government at first; however, the local administration saw the need of doing something about the harassment.

According to 1 Macc. 3:10-12, the first attempt to crush the revolt came from Apollonius, who led a force from Samaria. Apollonius was probably a garrison commander, possibly the same individual as the commander of the Mysians mentioned earlier (1 Macc. 1:29; 2 Macc. 5:24). No real details are given except that Apollonius was himself killed (with Judas taking his sword and fighting with it the rest of his life). Next was Seron who advanced via Beth Horon (1 Macc. 3:13-26). Unfortunately, this battle is also described in rather vague, often biblical, language, again suggesting that the author had little actual knowledge of the engagement. This was evidently a defeat for the Seleucid forces, but despite the rather pious language this was no miraculous win for the Jews. Seron's troops were defeated at the ascent of Beth Horon, a favorite spot for ambush (as the Romans found almost 250 years later [Josephus, *War* 2.19.8 §§546–50]).

1 Macc. 3:27-37 now suggests that Antiochus's entire attention was focused on Judah and the rebellion under Judas, and he paid his army a year's wages and planned to send his entire force against Judah. This is wishful thinking on the part of the author: contrary to this picture, Antiochus had far more important things demanding his attention. The effect of the Maccabaean revolt on the Seleucid Empire at this early stage were like the bites of a gnat on an elephant.

It is doubtful that news of the Jewish defeat of Apollonius and Seron had even come to Antiochus's ears, but if it had, it was not likely to have seemed very significant to him. He had organized an enormous celebration and military display of his power at Daphne in 166 BCE. He then embarked on a campaign to the Upper Satrapies—that is, the eastern part of his empire whose response to Seleucid rule was often lukewarm. The greater part of his army went with him across the Euphrates.

However, Judas's gang was causing problems at the local level and was brought to the administration's attention by Philip, the local governor in Jerusalem (cf. 2 Macc. 5:22), who realized he needed help to gain the initiative against the resistance (2 Macc. 8:8-9). A force under Gorgias was sent. One can see an example of Judas's tactical skill in this case. He evidently had good intelligence (cf. 1 Macc. 4:3) and was aware that Gorgias planned to attack the Jewish camp near Mizpah. Judas took a mobile force by night to Emmaus and attacked the Seleucid camp at daybreak. The Syrian soldiers were quickly defeated and fled. Judas had the camp set on fire, no doubt to intimidate the troops returning from Gorgias's thwarted raid. The returning Syrians were sufficiently demoralized that they too were quickly put to flight by Judas's men.

It is important to assess the military situation, since the narratives in 1 Macc. 4:1-24 and 2 Macc. 8:8-36 emphasize a miraculous victory through divine aid. In the second encounter, even though Judas had only about six thousand men (2 Macc. 8:16, 22), his force was probably about the same strength as the Syrian unit that he first attacked. This resulted not only in an enormous boost to Jewish morale and reputation but also in the capture of considerable funds, weapons, and other goods important to keep the resistance going. Included in this was a large sum of money left by slave dealers, who had accompanied the Seleucid army in hopes of great profits from selling captured Jews as slaves. The Syrian commander Nicanor, however, managed to escape the battlefield and make his way to Antioch (2 Macc. 8:34-36). Thus, in one of those unusual happenings that history occasionally throws up, a spectacular victory was won contrary to normal expectations. But Judas's admirable tactics hardly achieved a miracle.

Next, Judas defeated Timothy and Bacchides, killing twenty thousand and capturing high fortresses (2 Macc. 8:30-6). Judas's revolt now seems to have been perceived seriously enough to engage the attention of the Seleucid Vice-Regent Lysias, left in charge of Antioch when Antiochus took his army to the east. The battle with Lysias was probably the prelude to the retaking of the temple. It was evidently the summer of 165 BCE when Lysias himself led an invasion force. The number given for the Syrian force is the usual exaggeration, but interestingly the Jews are credited with ten thousand men.

Although 1 and 2 Maccabees make this another Jewish victory, this seems doubtful. Lysias had superior numbers, and a major defeat as described would have led to a panic-stricken rout, yet Lysias is described as conducting an orderly retreat. But if he was not defeated, why did Lysias withdraw to Antioch? Both 1 and 2 Maccabees ascribe it simply to divine favor and Jewish bravery. The actual reason is probably more prosaic and realistic.

Concessions by the Seleucids to the Jews

At this point we find a series of four letters in 2 Maccabees that seem to give us important information about diplomatic moves on the part of both the Jews and the Seleucids at this time. These maneuvers would have affected Lysias's fight with Judas. The important thing is that these seem to be original documents that give us valuable information about events. The earliest letter appears to be that of Antiochus IV to the Jews, which reads as follows (2 Macc. 11:27-33):

> King Antiochus to the council of elders of the Jews and to the other Jews, greetings. [28]If you are well, this is as it ought to be, which is what we wish; we are also in health. [29]Menelaus has informed us that you want to return home to take care of your own affairs. [30]To those returning by the 30th of Xanthikos [February/March,

probably in 164 BCE] the right hand is given without fear, ³¹allowing the Jews to use their own foods and laws just as formerly, and to let no one bother them in any manner concerning things done in ignorance. ³²I have also sent Menelaus to comfort you. ³³Be in health.

This letter from Antiochus IV himself seems to withdraw the primary causes for Jewish agitation. The letter was evidently not addressed to Judas and his group but, rather, to the governing council of Jerusalem and to "other" Jews. What seems to be the case, though, is that Judas and his followers ignored this amnesty.

However, we have another letter, this time from Vice-Regent Lysias, which appears to be a response to a Jewish delegation. This delegation does not appear to be from Judas but other Jews. Again, it is not the Maccabaean movement but other Jewish factions who are seeking to reconcile with the Seleucids. Nevertheless, it fits with Lysias's evident desire for negotiations with Judas (2 Macc. 11:17-21):

> ¹⁷Lysias to the Jewish community, greetings. John and Absalom, who were sent from you, furnished me with the administrative document copied below [this document is now lost] and made a request concerning its contents. ¹⁸Whatever then it was necessary to present orally to the king [Antiochus IV], I stated plainly; and whatever was feasible, he has granted. ¹⁹If then you will preserve good will toward the government, in the future I shall attempt to be responsible jointly for good things. ²⁰But concerning the details I commend them for discussion with you by your representatives and mine. ²¹Farewell.

This letter seems to show that Lysias withdrew his army from Judah back to Antioch at this time because of attempts at negotiations. Antiochus apparently supported representatives from some of the Jews when they approached Lysias to ask for terms. Why would the Jews have asked for a truce if Lysias had been trounced in battle as 1 and 2 Maccabees claim? This provides good grounds for judging that the battle between Lysias and Judas was at least a standoff and more likely a defeat for the Jews. (See below for another letter, to Lysias from Antiochus V at a slightly later time.)

Lysias's letter may have been copied to a Roman delegation, for a Roman delegation in the region sent the following letter (2 Macc. 11:34-38):

> Quintus Memmius, Titus Manius, ambassadors of the Romans, to the people of the Jews, greetings. ³⁵Lysias the relative of the king has conceded rights to you, and we consent. ³⁶But whatever he determined to bring to the attention of the king, you give it thought and then send someone immediately concerning your views, in order that we might make suggestions to you, as is appropriate. For we are approaching Antioch. ³⁷Therefore, hurry and send someone, that we might also know of your decision. ³⁸Be in health.

The Roman letter was evidently a response to Lysias's (and perhaps also Antiochus's) concessions. Roman involvement is interesting, showing that they were still closely monitoring Antiochus's activities. But they also show an interest in Jewish affairs. *From this time on, the Romans are solidly a part of Jewish history.*

The fourth letter is quoted in the next section.

Temple Retaken and Returned to Service

We now come to the climax of the Hasmonaean revolt: the retaking and restoration of the temple. Because of Lysias's withdrawal and the general military situation, Judas felt sufficiently encouraged to march on Jerusalem and retake the temple area. There was apparently no resistance, but Judas appointed a guard to keep the Syrians holed up in the Akra while the temple was cleansed and rededicated. Although Judas and his brothers were members of a priestly family, the cleansing of the temple was delegated to other priests who evidently maintained a certain independence *vis-à-vis* him (1 Macc. 4:42-58).

According to 1 Macc. 4:52-59 and 2 Macc. 10:5, this rededication was accomplished on 25 Kislev. 1 Maccabees states this was an exact three years after it was first polluted, which would bring it to November/December 165 BCE. One suspects that since they were near the third anniversary of the pollution, Judas specifically planned the rededication to fall on that exact day of the month. Or they simply put it about that it was rededicated exactly three years after the Abomination of Desolation was set up, regardless of the exact real date. On the other hand, there would have been too many witnesses to displace it very much. It was a memorable event of Jewish history, still commemorated in Judaism today by Hanukkah or the Festival of Lights.

This cleansing of the temple took place before the death of Antiochus IV on November/December 164 BCE. We also have the fourth letter. This one is clearly from Antiochus V (because he refers to the death of his father) that would have come about the spring or summer of 163 BCE (2 Macc. 11:23-26):

> [23]King Antiochus to his brother Lysias, greetings. After our father joined the gods [i.e., died], the ones who desired to be calm went to the king about their own business, [24]We heard, however, that the Jews had not consented to the conversion to Hellenistic ways by our father, but chose their own way of life and pleaded to be permitted to have their own law. [25]Since this nation has chosen to be free from disquiet, we have decided to restore to them their temple and to let them conduct their life according to the customs of their forefathers. [26]It is well, then, that you send a message and give your right hand, so that seeing our policy, they might be reassured and live cheerfully, achieving their own goals.

This letter is the culmination of a series of proclamations and negotiations. What they show in their totality is that the situation had reverted to the *status quo ante* with regard to the temple and the practice of Judaism (although the earlier letter of Antiochus IV seems to have already conceded this). Of course, the "restoration" of the Jerusalem temple to the Jews (in Antiochus V's letter) was in some sense a matter of indifference, since the Jews had already retaken it and reinstated the cult there. But now what they were doing was official and could not be interfered with by the Seleucid garrison in the Akra of the city.

Final Deeds of Judas

Just as there were perhaps four important initial military campaigns of Judas against the Seleucids, before the retaking of the temple, so there were four further battles after the retaking of the temple and the death of Antiochus IV. For the next year,

Judas seems to have been able to operate free from bother by the Syrians; instead he turned his attention to the local neighbors in Idumaea, Galilee, and Transjordan. Part of the campaign during these months was rescue operations to help Jews being attacked in areas outside Judaea itself.

Many Jews were brought back as refugees from Galilee, Golan, and Transjordan. This includes a rescue mission north into Galilee by Simon, pursuit of the Seleucid commander Timothy into the Transjordanian area by Judas and Jonathan, a rescue mission into the Golan by Judas and Jonathan, an abortive attack by the Jewish commanders Joseph son of Zecharias and Azariah against Gorgias, and a campaign by Judas and his brothers against Idumaea (though Gorgias is said to have escaped). In any event, there seems to have been no official state persecution of Jews.

As indicated by 1 Macc. 6:18-27, Judas was also busy in Jerusalem itself. He had not only retaken the temple area but was now besieging the Seleucid garrison in the Akra; it had to be dealt with. Thus, shortly after Antiochus IV's death, Lysias found it necessary to embark on a second expedition (summer 163). Judas left off the siege of the Akra to come to meet the Syrians and was defeated in a battle near Beth-Zechariah (2 Macc. 13:19-23 makes it victory for Judas!). Lysias then took Beth-Zur, with the defenders agreeing to surrender the fortress in return for a promise of safe conduct. He now laid siege to the temple, though Judas himself slipped off to his old base in the hills.

Lysias did not press his siege of the temple, however, but came to terms with the defenders so that he could return to the capital. Evidently, the reason Lysias had to return to Antioch was that Philip, Antiochus's vice-regent, had returned from the east with Antiochus IV's body but was now set on taking over rulership of the kingdom (1 Macc. 6:55-63; 2 Macc. 13:23-24). In the end, he was not successful: Lysias and the king returned and quickly defeated and killed Philip.

Lysias's basic concession was to confirm the freedom of the Jews to practice their traditional religion. Although this had already been done earlier, it was important to provide further guarantees. Also, the Jews had it in writing from the Seleucids that the temple was lawfully in their hands and not just being occupied by them against Seleucid will. The letter from Antiochus V makes this clear (2 Macc. 11:22-26, quoted above p. 225). At this time, probably on his way back from Judaea, Lysias had Menelaus executed. The exact reason is not made clear, but it was likely due to the realization that no peace with the Jews would be possible as long as Menelaus continued to hold the office of high priest.

After the execution, another priest named Alcimus was appointed to take Menelaus's place (cf. 1 Macc. 7:5; 2 Macc. 14:3-13). The next skirmish was with Nicanor who had been made governor of Judaea (2 Macc. 14:12). Apparently, a truce was negotiated for a time, but it eventually broke down. Nicanor's forces were defeated and fled to Jerusalem. They joined battle again on Adar 13, 161 BCE, and Nicanor was defeated and killed. Judas declared Adar 13 a public holiday known as Nicanor's Day. This is a day before Purim and did not become a traditional Jewish holiday, perhaps becoming assimilated to Purim.

It seems to have been about this time that Judas sent an embassy to Rome to make a treaty. 1 Macc. 7:50–8:1 places the embassy directly after the defeat of Nicanor, when "the land of Judah had rest for a few days." This recent Jewish victory over Nicanor could be taken as evidence of their freedom. It is doubtful that the Romans would have made an alliance with a people ostensibly still a part of the Seleucid

Empire. But the relations of Rome with the Seleucids was a bit tense at this time, since Demetrius I had left Rome without Senate approval and become a contender for the Seleucid throne. Thus, from both the Maccabaean and the Roman perspective, this was probably a good time to be sending an embassy to Rome.

If Judas had expected military assistance, however, he was in for a heavy dose of reality: the Romans were not in the business of giving military support unless it directly affected their own needs. The Senate was happy to make treaties and even to make promises, but the conditions of the treaty recorded in 1 Macc. 8:23-30 show no promises of military muscle. Instead, the clauses of alliance (1 Macc. 8:26, 28) say that each will not aid the enemy of the other—nothing more. The Romans were not going to send troops to fight on Judas's side. This was their standard policy.

In the wake of Nicanor's defeat, Bacchides (along with the high priest Alcimus) was sent to invade Judaea. The two armies met at Elasa, perhaps about 15 kilometers (10 miles) north of Jerusalem. Judas was killed in this encounter. His death marks the beginning of a hiatus of several years when we hear little or nothing further about his followers. The Maccabees were still a long way from gaining control of Judaea and even further from independence of Syrian rule. Judas's body was buried in Modein (1 Macc. 9:19). There was, of course, no assistance from the Romans. Judas's luck had now run out and so had apparently the fortunes of the Maccabees. They would now be on the run for many years.

We can now briefly assess the achievements of Judas Maccabbaeus. The Maccabaean evident desire to take on the Seleucid Empire was in many ways ill conceived. But by appropriate tactics, adequate resources, and sheer good luck Judas and his band—now an army—had done well, but there had been no miracles: most of its success is fully explicable by normal military factors:

- Many of Judas's actions were against fellow Jews.
- The actual numbers of Seleucid troops are usually grossly exaggerated by the Jewish sources while the Jewish numbers are often far too low.
- Judas's force was regarded by the Seleucids only as a nuisance at the beginning.
- Luck seems to have played an important part, as it has in many famous victories and defeats.
- Jewish sources sometimes ignore defeats or even make defeats appear as victories for the Jews.

Judas's contribution lay not in miraculous victories against overwhelming odds but in a much more practical sphere: developing a regular trained army.

Judas of course accomplished more than just the military side of endeavors. One of his main achievements was retaking the temple and putting it back into operation. Ultimately, this is what the revolt was about, and it was probably Judas's initial goal. But having accomplished that, he seems to have set his sights higher: to the independence of Judaea as Jewish state once more. This was not the aim of most of his fellow countrymen, however, and support for him seems to have fallen off drastically once peace and their religious rights were restored. As we shall see, this independence did come about, but it was because of circumstances beyond the fighting abilities and resources of the Jews of Judaea.

Jonathan Maccabee Becomes Leader

With the death of Judas Maccabee there is a good deal of uncertainty about the immediate events in the Maccabaean camp. Nevertheless, the "friends" of Judas chose his brother Jonathan to succeed him. The Jews as a whole, however, now seem to have acquiesced to the continuance of Seleucid rule. They evidently found the new high priest, Alcimus, acceptable, and they had freedom to practice traditional Judaism. To what extent they continued to follow Judas is a question. Judas still had a (small) army and still engaged in fighting the Seleucids, but his support among the populace appears to have declined considerably. Once Judas was removed from the scene, the followers of the Maccabees were few, while the Seleucids were able to take back any administrative control they had lost and to place Jews loyal to themselves in positions of leadership.

There was now a new pretender to the Seleucid throne. About 162 BCE Demetrius the son of Seleucus IV escaped from Rome where he had been sent as a hostage to replace his uncle Antiochus IV in 176. In late 162 or early 161, Lysias and the young Antiochus V were defeated and executed by Demetrius. Alcimus went to Demetrius for confirmation of his high priestly office and, at the same time, asked for help against the Maccabaean group who was opposing him (1 Macc. 7:5-7; 2 Macc. 14:3-13).

Jonathan's military force now appears to have been quite small, too small to tackle the Syrian army, and he and his band were very much being chased. For the Syrians were not content to let things stand as they were, and a general called Bacchides pursued Jonathan. He probably recognized that this group would continue to be a thorn in the side unless destroyed once and for all. Unsuccessful in taking Jonathan's group, Bacchides had to content himself with fortifying various sites with garrisons and taking hostages from the leading Jews (1 Macc. 9:50-53). It was apparently early in 160 BCE that the high priest Alcimus suddenly died. His death was the occasion for Bacchides to return to Antioch, which allowed a period of calm for Jonathan.

Bacchides renewed the fight after two years (1 Macc. 9:57-73). But Jonathan acquitted himself well enough that he was able to negotiate with the Syrian general, which led to a truce and the release of hostages, and Bacchides left the land. Jonathan was no longer being harassed by Syrian troops. This opportunity for a period to rest and recuperate would have been greatly welcomed by Jonathan's followers who had been fighting for nearly a decade. The agreement with Bacchides no doubt included nominal submission to the Seleucid administration of Judah.

Although there is no indication that the bulk of the population wished to pursue the Maccabaean goals, especially those that involved continuing to fight the Seleucid army, there was evidently a great deal of good will toward the Hasmonaean family. After all, they had been the ones to lead the nation in the return to religious freedom. This would have been especially true in the rural areas away from Jerusalem and perhaps a few of the major towns. Many would have looked up to Jonathan as their natural leader, as long as they could get on with their lives. This suggests that he was viewed as the leader for many in Judah (cf. 1 Macc. 9:73).

The real opportunity for the Maccabees came some years later in 153–152 BCE. This was because a new situation developed, when Alexander I Balas became the rival of Demetrius I for the Seleucid throne.[5] Alexander claimed to be the son of

Antiochus IV and thus rightful heir to the throne. Unlike Demetrius I who left Rome without permission, Alexander first sought formal permission from the Senate, then set out to try to take the Seleucid crown. Demetrius, knowing that he needed all the allies he could get, sent an offer of peace to Jonathan.

The letter gives Jonathan the authority to assemble an army and to be given the Jewish hostages in the Akra (1 Macc. 10:25-45). Jonathan had had his headquarters at Michmash (1 Macc. 9:73), but now he moved to Jerusalem and began fortifying it. Once he had established his headquarters in the provincial capital with Seleucid authority, those who opposed him (whether Jews or others) were left with little support. The Seleucid garrisons in the various strongholds began to evacuate them: only in the Akra in Jerusalem and in Beth-Zur did opposition continue (1 Macc. 10:7, 14).

Having heard of the concessions made by Demetrius, Alexander Balas now made his own promises to Jonathan, which included making him high priest. The impression left by our sources is that no new high priest had yet been appointed in Alcimus's place, and it had been vacant for seven years. Jonathan had also been given the title of "Friend," which was a significant honor for a Seleucid king to bestow on anyone: the king's Friends were the inner circle of counsellors and associates. These new titles allowed Jonathan to wear both a purple robe and a golden crown. Jonathan therefore donned these at the Feast of Tabernacles (apparently in 153 BCE), thus formally beginning the tradition of the Hasmonaean high priesthood.

To counter Alexander Balas, Demetrius I offered a long list of privileges in a letter "to the Jewish nation." Jonathan and his advisers evidently did not believe Demetrius's promises and continued to favor Alexander. The wisdom of such a choice was demonstrated soon afterward when Alexander defeated and killed Demetrius in battle about 150 BCE and commenced his rule (150–145 BCE).[6] While Jonathan was able to gain by playing off the two Seleucid rival claimants to the throne, much depended on his own skill in negotiating and defending his corner in Judaea.

Alexander made Jonathan general and governor of the province of Judaea (1 Macc. 10:65-66). Despite the honors and concessions, Judaea was still a province overseen from Antioch and the Jerusalem Akra was still in the hands of a Syrian garrison. Judaea was by no means united behind Jonathan even yet, and a delegation from the Jewish opposition to Jonathan's rule attempted to see Alexander. But he refused them a hearing. It should also be noted that Jonathan was apparently assisted—and constrained—by a council of elders (1 Macc. 1:6, 35).

In 147 BCE the son of Demetrius I, later to become Demetrius II (145–140, 129–126 BCE), sailed from Crete to attempt to take back his father's kingdom from Alexander Balas.[7] He appointed a certain Apollonius governor of Coele-Syria (1 Macc. 10:69). Apollonius sent a letter, challenging Jonathan to fight him. Since Alexander was busy making secure his position in Antioch, Jonathan could not count on his help. Jonathan joined forces with Simon his brother and pursued Apollonius's forces to Azotus (Ashdod). Jonathan won a major victory and burned the temple of Dagon in Ashdod where many of Apollonius's soldiers had taken refuge. Ashkelon submitted without a fight, and in gratitude Alexander also gave Akkaron (Ekron) and its territories to Jonathan. He had now gained control over much of the old area of Philistia.

At this time, the king of Egypt, Ptolemy VI Philometor, was hoping to bring Coele-Syria back under Ptolemaic rule (cf. 1 Macc. 11:13). This led to another "Syrian War" (the Seventh Syrian War—147–145 BCE) between Egypt and the Seleucid Empire. Ptolemy provided forces that helped Demetrius to defeat Alexander and establish his rulership in the year 145 BCE.[8] Ptolemy VI himself died shortly after Alexander's defeat and death, leaving the field clear for Demetrius II.

Taking advantage of the struggle over the Seleucid throne, Jonathan laid siege to the Akra, which was still in Syrian hands now two decades after the rededication of the temple. Demetrius demanded an accounting from Jonathan, but the latter came away with major concessions from the king. Demetrius II was soon glad of Jonathan as an ally, for troubles developed between him and his army and also with the citizens of Antioch.[9] Jonathan requested that Demetrius turn the still unconquered Akra over to him and remove the troops in the other citadels in Judah. The Syrian ruler was glad to make any promises necessary to gain loyal troops. A force of three thousand Jewish soldiers was dispatched to Antioch and arrived in time to help Demetrius put down a revolt of his own citizens in the city.

Following this victory, Demetrius evidently reneged on any implied concessions, but the situation was quickly overtaken by events, for there was suddenly another pretender to the Seleucid throne. Diodotus Tryphon, who had been a general of both Demetrius I and Alexander Balas, took advantage of the unrest against Demetrius II. Tryphon proclaimed Antiochus, the young son of Alexander Balas, king as a rival to Demetrius II, leading a revolt against him.[10] In the resulting engagement (probably in the summer of 145 or 144 BCE), Demetrius II was defeated but fled, and the new king, with the name of Antiochus VI Epiphanes Dionysus, wrote to Jonathan to confirm him in his offices, including that of high priest. Simon Maccabee was appointed general over the Seleucid armies from the region of Tyre to the borders of Egypt.[11] Jonathan was probably commander over the whole of Coele-Syria (cf. 1 Macc. 11:60).

Despite his initial defeat, Demetrius II was still alive. A long civil war continued between him and Tryphon/Antiochus VI. Therefore, it fell to Jonathan to make his area secure for Antiochus VI.[12] This he did with the help of his brother Simon. Jonathan then set in motion a program that looked very much like a movement to secure independence. He made Judah more secure by building additional strongholds, including the defenses of Jerusalem. It was also about this time (perhaps 145/144 BCE) that Jonathan was alleged to have renewed the treaty with Rome (1 Macc. 12:1-23).

But Jonathan's plans were cut short by Tryphon (1 Macc. 12:39-53). The latter first marched to Beth-Shean in Judaea where he was met by Jonathan. He honored Jonathan and gave him gifts, with a display of entirely peaceful intentions. Once in the city, though, the Jewish bodyguard was slaughtered and Jonathan taken captive. Tryphon set out to put pressure on Judah (1 Macc. 13:1-30). It now fell to Simon Maccabee to oppose Tryphon's attack, which quickly followed. Tryphon attempted to negotiate by claiming that Jonathan was only a hostage for money owed to the Seleucid government. Simon paid the ransom (100 silver talents) and sent Jonathan's sons as hostages, as Tryphon had demanded. But it was all to no avail, for Tryphon only pressed the attack without releasing Jonathan. He finally executed Jonathan at a place called Baskama. Simon buried Jonathan in Modein and also erected monuments to him, their parents, and the dead brothers.

Only Simon remained alive of the four Maccabee brothers. Jonathan's period of rule had been an important and successful one in the long term. He had gone from a period of little power and a handful of followers to high priest and formal leader of the nation. He had had to fight many battles to do this and was evidently not inferior to Judas as a military leader. Yet he had made the real gains by political moves, primarily exploiting the rivalry over the Seleucid throne. Except for misjudging Tryphon, which cost him his life, he might have continued to lead the emerging nation. Judah was not yet independent of Seleucid control, but large steps had been taken in this direction. For this, Jonathan deserves much credit.

A New Jewish Kingdom: The Hasmonaean Dynasty

Simon (143–135 BCE)

Simon was now the last of the Maccabaean brothers and the third to become leader of the Hasmonaean movement. From an overall point of view, he continued on the same basic road as Judas and Jonathan, evidently aiming at an independent Jewish state. The majority of the Palestinian Jews seem by this point to have accepted the Hasmonaeans as leaders. With this popular backing and a temporary calm, Simon was in a position to continue the efforts of his brothers to bring about the independence of the state (1 Macc. 13:33). Tryphon had shown his true colors as far as the Jews were concerned, and Simon took the logical step of negotiating with his rival Demetrius II who had not disappeared from the scene.

Demetrius II once again made a variety of far-reaching concessions in a letter to Simon, even including permission to mint his own coinage. This time Demetrius was not in a position to withdraw his offer, and the writer of 1 Maccabees could write that in the first year of Simon—the 170th year of the Seleucid era (143–142 BCE)—"the yoke of the Gentiles was lifted from Israel" (1 Macc. 13:41-42). *There is no doubt that this was a significant date and event since Judah had been a vassal state of one sort or another for about six hundred years.* Subsequent events were to show that this state of "liberation" was short-lived—the Seleucids still claimed the territory and at times still imposed their rule—and Simon himself died violently as had all his brothers. Judaea was now an independent state in name, as proclaimed internally, but the reality was somewhat different. *Nevertheless, as a psychological high point the formal proclamation of liberty should be given its due: it formally marked a new phase in Judaean history.*

In Simon's third year, a stela was erected that recounted his and his brothers' deeds and confirmed him in the office of high priest (1 Macc. 14:27-47). Despite the adulatory language of the decree, it was plain that Simon's powers—as high priest, leader, and military commander— were being granted by a coalition of "priests and people and rulers of the nation and the elders of the country" in a public assembly (1 Macc. 14:28). Finally, the decree was ratified by "all the people" (1 Macc. 14:46). The fact that Simon's powers had to be officially granted, including his high priestly authority, indicates many still needed convincing to accept these. They were apparently negotiated with various power groups, which is why they were declared only in his third year.

Simon is also said to have renewed the treaty with Rome (1 Macc. 14:16, 24). There are a number of problems with the account as it stands, but it still appears genuine at its core: Simon thought renewing the treaty was worth a half-tonne golden shield as a gift to the Senate. One important accomplishment of Simon was at last taking the Akra and expelling the Syrian garrison from it in about May 142 BCE, since this removed the last formal symbol of Seleucid rule over the country (1 Macc. 13:49-52).

After Demetrius II had made concessions to Simon to enlist his friendship, he was too busy to be concerned with Judaea. Early in 139, he marched east against the Parthians. The Parthians had become a major threat to the Seleucid Empire by this time. After some initial successes in the Upper Satrapies, Demetrius was taken captive by the Parthian leader. Demetrius's wife sent for his brother Antiochus to marry her and take the throne as Antiochus VII Sidetes (138–129 BCE). The child-king Antiochus VI had died about 142–141 BCE, leaving Tryphon as the Seleucid pretender and rival. Antiochus VII attacked Tryphon about 138 BCE and besieged him in Dor. He applied to Simon for aid and no doubt received it (1 Macc. 15:10-14, 25-26). Tryphon managed to escape from Dor but was tracked to Apamea and met his death there in 137 BCE.[13]

With Tryphon out of the way, however, Antiochus VII turned on Simon with demands which showed that he considered Judaea still a Seleucid vassal (1 Macc. 15:27-36), demanding back tribute and damages to the tune of 1,000 silver talents. Simon's counteroffer of 100 talents was considered only an insult and an excuse to declare war on him. The reason is not hard to guess: Antiochus sorely needed funds for his fight against Tryphon. Antiochus sent an army against Judah (1 Macc. 15:38–16:10). Simon was now too aged to take to the field (1 Macc. 16:2-3), but his sons John and Judah assumed command and were able to defeat the Seleucid force.

After a rule of about seven years, Simon was invited to a banquet near Jericho by his son-in-law, Ptolemy son of Abubus, the Jewish governor over the plain of Jericho (1 Macc. 16:11-17). Ptolemy used the occasion to assassinate Simon and imprison Simon's wife and two other sons, but the third son, John Hyrcanus, was forewarned and managed to escape. Thus, the last of the Maccabaean brothers met his end by violence, demonstrating that the promised peace of Simon's rule was more apparent than real. Nevertheless, Simon's achievement was considerable and his reign an important watershed in Jewish history. Perhaps the symbolism was more important than the reality—the Seleucids had by no means abandoned their claim to Judaea as one of their provinces—but the image of Israel being free from the "yoke of the Gentiles" in the 170th Seleucid year (= 143–142 BCE) was a powerful one.

John Hyrcanus I (135–104 BCE)

After his escape from Ptolemy's murderous plot, Hyrcanus fled to Jerusalem, where the people refused entry to Ptolemy. It seems likely that in this time of crisis Hyrcanus was able to rally support and take charge by means of his military resources. With his forces mobilized, he immediately turned the attack on Ptolemy who washed up in a fortress above Jericho called Dagon but besieged him without success. Ptolemy held out until the sabbatical year (when farmers allowed the land to remain uncultivated—Tishri 135–Tishri 134 BCE), when Hyrcanus terminated the siege.

Ptolemy then murdered Hyrcanus's mother and two brothers before escaping to Philadelphia.

Soon afterward, Hyrcanus himself was besieged in Jerusalem by Antiochus VII, the cause apparently being the cities that Simon had taken from the Syrians. Antiochus showed his generosity—at least in religious matters—by allowing a truce during the Feast of Tabernacles. Agreement was finally reached between Antiochus and Hyrcanus that tribute would be paid. In addition to receiving payment, Antiochus also tore down the defensive walls of Jerusalem. The agreement between Hyrcanus and Antiochus VII put them on good terms. Thus, when Antiochus marched east against the Parthians about 130 BCE, Hyrcanus accompanied him with a contingent of Jewish troops, though allowance was made for Jewish religious observances. Antiochus VII engaged the Parthians and was killed in the fighting (c. 129 BCE). Antiochus was succeeded by his brother Demetrius II, whom the Parthians released from his captivity and allowed to become king again. Hyrcanus apparently got off lightly in the Parthian campaign with his troops mainly intact, judging by the military expeditions he undertook after Antiochus VII's death.

For most of the rest of his reign, Hyrcanus was free to conduct his own affairs with little interference from the Syrians, the reason being the rivalry between the two lines of contenders for the throne. He gave no further tribute or help to them after the death of Antiochus VII; instead, he took the opportunity to expand his territory, which he did with considerable success. One of his most significant acts was the siege and capture of Shechem and Mount Gerizim, at which time he allegedly destroyed the Samaritan temple, which the archaeology seems to confirm. Coins found at the site suggest it was probably about 112/111 BCE.

He next took some of the major cities of Idumaea, extended his rule over the entire country, and is said to have forcibly converted the inhabitants to Judaism. Forced conversion is generally not very successful, yet Josephus (*Ant.* 13.9.1 §258) states that the Idumaeans continued to be Jews. The next area to fall was the city of Samaria itself. Hyrcanus may have begun the attack, but at some point, he turned it over to his sons, Aristobulus and Antigonus. When it fell, Hyrcanus could take control of the whole region. They then moved on to Scythopolis (Beth-Shean) and took the territory between it and Mount Carmel.

Hyrcanus sent at least two embassies to Rome. The Senate was happy to renew the treaty of friendship and alliance but stated that the matters imposed by Antiochus VII would have to be considered at a later time when the Senate had more "leisure." This demonstrates once again that the Romans were hesitant to get involved in affairs not their own.

The Jews in Palestine were apparently thriving at this time. Nevertheless, opposition developed and Hyrcanus had to spend some time putting down rebels. Josephus makes the Pharisees his opponents, relating an anecdote about Hyrcanus and the Pharisees. According to Josephus (*Ant.* 13.10.5-7 §§288–99), Hyrcanus had himself been a Pharisee but, after falling out with them, he became a Sadducee. In any event, he soon reduced the opposition and spent the rest of his reign peacefully, dying a natural death after a rule of thirty-one years.

In order to fill out the history of Hasmonaean rule, we now need to consider briefly the main sects that appear in the sources about this time but then continue to surface in later Jewish history. The Pharisees and Sadducees are first mentioned in sources for the reign of John Hyrcanus, but archaeology indicates that the site at Qumran was also inhabited about this time. A group called the Essenes have been connected with the Qumran community, a theory that we also need to examine.

Pharisees and Sadducees

It is appropriate at this point to go back a bit to the beginnings of the Maccabaean revolt. This is when a group known as the *Hasidim* first appeared (the name is the supposed Hebrew original of what are called the *Asiaidoi* in the Greek texts). They are mentioned only in a few passages in 1 and 2 Maccabees. About all we are told is that they were a group of "mighty warriors" who joined the Maccabees (1 Macc. 2:39-42), that they were the first to seek peace after Alcimus was made priest (1 Macc. 7:12-16), and that they were a group led by Judas Maccabaeus (2 Macc. 14:6). These statements leave many questions; in any case, these few data already contradict some assumptions, but they tell us next to nothing about the group.

Unfortunately, the Hasidim are the major component of a number of theories that have been widely espoused. One is that they were the ancestors of both the Pharisees and the Essenes. They have also been described as the "orthodox" who opposed the "Hellenizers" under the Hellenistic reform of Jason and Menelaus—terminology that we have already seen as wholly inappropriate. The list of their characteristics goes on and on in popular literature, little if any of it based on the actual original data. We do not know for certain that the Hasidim were a definite organized group; but even if only one particular group is in mind, we know little about it other than that it was not the author of Daniel 7-12 (as some propose) and that its relationship—if any—to the Essenes and Pharisees is unknown.

The main problem with the *Sadducees* is that we have not a line of their own writings or thoughts—as far as we know—and the sources we do possess are generally hostile. Evaluation of the data we have is very difficult. The earliest references to the Sadducees indicate that they are a political party with the Pharisees as their primary rivals, but no particular religious beliefs are indicated. Otherwise, in later literature they tend to be characterized by particular religious positions, but these do not form a coherent set of beliefs. The following is only a reconstruction whose tentative nature has always to be acknowledged:

- The most certain conclusion is that the group first appeared as a political entity (whatever its origin and other characteristics) and continued to exist in some form until after the fall of Jerusalem, possibly even into the second century CE.
- Several bits of information suggest some sort of connection with the priestly establishment: (a) The name Sadducees is often thought to be derived from "Zadok," the name associated with the altar priests. A group known as the "Boethusians" are thought to be associated with the Sadducees or even another name for them. The name may be derived from the family of Boethus, who provided a number of high priests. (b) They are said to differ from the Pharisees in rejecting tradition and accepting only the authority of the written word, which seems also a priestly characteristic. (c) Their method of reckoning Pentecost (which differs from that of the Pharisees) seems the

most natural one from the biblical text, again pointing to a priestly practice. (d) The Acts of the Apostles (4:1; 5:17) associates them with the high priest: "But the high priest rose up and all who were with him, that is, the party of the Sadducees."

- Josephus states that they were to be identified with the upper socioeconomic class, which is compatible with a close connection to the priestly establishment and membership on the Sanhedrin (cf. Acts 23:6-9). However, this is not to suggest that the two were coextensive: not all Sadducees were inevitably priests or perhaps even wealthy, nor were all priests or upper-class individuals necessarily Sadducees.

As for the *Pharisees*, so much has been written about them without good evidence, or even without any evidence, that it is difficult to discuss them. Unlike the Hasidim and the Sadducees, the Pharisees will come up at various points in our subsequent history. My conclusions about the Pharisees (including their relationship to the Sadducees), based on a careful analysis of the available sources, are the following:[14]

- The Greek sources (and possibly rabbinic literature) make both the Pharisees and the Sadducees important at least some of the time, beginning about the reign of John Hyrcanus (135–104 BCE). They also make the Sadducees and Pharisees rivals, both seeking political power at the expense of the other.

- There may have been certain socioeconomic differences between the groups in that the Sadducees are said to have the support of the wealthy and prominent persons, whereas the Pharisees have the support of the masses (Josephus); on the other hand, popular leaders do not necessarily come from the lower social strata, and some priests are said to be Pharisees.

- The Sadducees and Pharisees are also alleged to differ on a number of religious beliefs. The Pharisees are especially characterized by the traditions of the fathers, whereas the Sadducees do not accept as authoritative anything not in the written Scripture. The Pharisees believe in the survival of the soul and rewards and punishments in the afterlife; the Sadducees reject this. (If the Boethusians are to be associated with the Sadducees, the two groups also differ on the counting of the wave sheaf day and the celebration of the Feast of Weeks.) According to Josephus, the Pharisees (like the Essenes) have a reputation for knowing the future.

- Two of our sources seem to make the Pharisees especially concerned about halakic matters (matters relating to religious law). The gospels have them particularly exercised about tithing, ritual purity (washings), Sabbath observance, and the like. According to rabbinic literature, the *Pĕrûšîm* and *Ṣaddûqîm* (usually identified with the "Pharisees" and "Sadducees") also have certain halakic differences. The Pharisaic agenda according to the gospels—as far as one can determine it from the few brief references— accords well with the contents of the earliest rabbinic writings, the Mishnah/ Tosephta (with the exception of the gospels debates about the messiah and the question of the government of Judaea, subjects that do not come up in early rabbinic writings).

- Those sources that give the Pharisees a general dominance of religious belief and practice are those that come later in relation to parallel sources. Thus, it is only two later passages in the *Antiquities* that state that public worship is carried out according to Pharisaic regulations and that the Sadducees are required to follow them even when they hold office. This is not stated in the *War* and is not borne out in Josephus's other passages on the Pharisees. The one exception is the reign of Alexandra, the Hasmonaean queen; indeed, the statement of Josephus about the Pharisees controlling the king and high priest fits well with her reign. Similarly, although the gospels give considerable prominence to the Pharisees as opponents of Jesus, it is only the late Fourth Gospel that suggests they can cast people out of the synagogues. It is also the later passages in the book of Acts that suggest the Pharisees make up a significant part of the Sanhedrin (though they are still not dominant).

Qumran and the Essenes

Most of what we know about the Essenes comes from the statements made by such contemporary or near-contemporary authors as Pliny, Philo, and Josephus. Both Josephus and Philo (one or more accounts) agree on a number of points about the Essene community:

- Number about four thousand males (*Ant.* 18.1.5 §20; *Probus* 75).
- Live in many towns and villages (*War* 2.8.4 §124; *Probus* 76; *Hyp.* 11.1).
- No wives, women, or marriage (*War* 2.8.2 §§120–1; *Ant.* 18.1.5 §21; *Hyp.* 11.14-17).
- Community of goods and communal meals (*War* 2.8.3 §122; *Ant.* 18.1.5 §20; *Probus* 85-86; *Hyp.* 11.4-5).
- Work at agriculture and crafts (*Ant.* 18.1.5 §19; *Probus* 76; *Hyp.* 11.6, 8-9).
- No swearing of oaths (*War* 2.8.6 §135; *Probus* 84).
- No changing of clothes (*War* 2.8.4 §126; *Hyp.* 11.12).
- No slaves (*Ant.* 18.1.5 §21; *Probus* 79).

Josephus's *War* makes a number of points that do not occur in Philo:

- Oil defiling (*War* 2.8.3 §123).
- Prayers to the sun (*War* 2.8.5 §128).
- Daily schedule of work (*War* 2.8.5 §§128–32).
- Bathing before eating (*War* 2.8.5 §129) and if touched by an outsider (*War* 2.8.10 §150).
- Speaking in turn (*War* 2.8.5 §132).
- Study of the writings of the ancients and medicines (*War* 2.8.6 §136).
- Regulations for admission to (*War* 2.8.7 §§137–42) and expulsion from the order (*War* 2.8.8 §§143–4).

- Preservation of angels' names (*War* 2.8.7 §142).
- No spitting in company or to the right (*War* 2.8.8 §147).
- Strictness in observing the Sabbath (*War* 2.8.8 §147).
- Foretelling the future (*War* 2.8.12 §159).
- Also a group who marries (*War* 2.8.13 §160).

When the Dead Sea Scrolls were discovered, the question was asked about the relationship of the Qumran group (the ones who had preserved and hidden the scrolls) to the known Jewish sects. It was quickly suggested that the Qumran people were Essenes. Some even now assert this without proof or qualification. We can say with some confidence that the Qumran group was in some way related to the Essenes, but the relationship may have been more complicated than some have recognized. It should be noted that many of the Dead Seas Scrolls relate to the Bible or show no connection with any sect; however, there is a group of "sectarian" scrolls that have much in common and seem to be the product of a particular religious group.

To discuss this question of the Qumran identity, two of the seminal "sectarian" writings will be drawn on: the *Damascus Document* (CD) and the *Community Rule* (1QS). The reason is that both of these contain regulations about the organization of a community and are generally agreed to be related to each other. They will be compared with the classic statements on the Essenes by Philo and Josephus.

- *Settlements of the Essenes*. Philo (*Probus* 76; *Hyp.* 11.1) and Josephus (*War* 2.8.4 §124) indicate communities in a variety of towns and villages; this also seems to be the view of the *Damascus Document* about its own communities (CD 7.6; 12.19-14.16; 19.2). The statement of Pliny the Elder (5.73), on the other hand, indicates only one settlement: on the northwest shore of the Dead Sea. Although the exact spot is not indicated, it looks to be in the same general location as Qumran.
- *Community of goods*. Philo (*Probus* 85-86; *Hyp.* 11.4), Josephus (*War* 2.8.3 §122; *Ant.* 18.1.5 §20), and 1QS (1.11-12; 5.1-22; 6.16-23) agree that property was held in common. All new entrants turned over their property to the community on attaining full membership.
- *Regulations for assemblies*. The members were to sit according to a particular order (*Probus* 81; 1QS 6.8-10), to speak in turn (*War* 2.8.5 §132; 1QS 6.10-13), and not to spit (*War* 2.8.8 §147; 1QS 7.13).
- *Procedures for entry*. The sources agree that a period of probation was required. Josephus (*War* 2.8.7 §137–42) describes it in three stages, each lasting a year. 1QS 6.13-23 mentions two stages, each of a year, though a further, less formal stage preceding these is not incompatible with Josephus's data.
- *Rigor in keeping the Sabbath*. Josephus (*War* 2.8.9 §147) states that they were more particular in their Sabbath observances than any other group. This seems to be confirmed by such regulations as those found in CD 10.14–11.18.

- *Women and marriage.* The ancient sources agree that the Essenes were celibate, except that Josephus asserts there was one group who married for purposes of procreation. The scrolls present a diverse picture: the *Community Rule* is silent on the subject. However, the *Damascus Document* (CD 7.6-7; 12.1-2; 15.5; 16.10-12; 7.6-7//19.2-3), the *War Scroll* (1QM 7.3) and 1QSa 1.4, 9-11, all indicate the presence of women; the *Damascus Document* also seems to have in mind the intention of procreation (CD 4.10–5.2). Skeletons of women and children were found in the Qumran cemetery; on the other hand, these were few and on the outskirts of the cemetery rather than in the main part of it, which might suggest women were not generally present. Thus, some Essene communities (including Qumran?) seem to have been composed of celibate men, but others were made up of married families.

Most scholars find it difficult to believe that the agreements between Pliny, Philo, Josephus, the archaeology, and a certain group of the scrolls can be mere coincidence. The view is that either we must postulate another unattested group at Qumran that had certain unique characteristics in common with the Essenes or we must assume that Qumran is somehow related to the Essenes. The latter explanation seems the most logical, but being related is not necessarily the same as being identical.

Whatever the group at Qumran was, it was very small and certainly not the four thousand Essenes given by Philo and Josephus. It was evidently founded by an individual called the "Teacher of Righteousness" (despite many suggestions, no consensus about his identity has emerged). The group was opposed by the "wicked priest," usually seen as a pun on the Hebrew term for "high priest" in the Jerusalem temple. Most have identified this "wicked priest" with one of the Hasmonaean priest-kings, but the range of suggestions has been wide: Jonathan, Simon, John Hyrcanus, Alexander Jannaeus, or even a succession of Hasmonaean figures.

The most likely explanation is that the Qumran group began within the Essene movement but broke away. Several references to the "Man of Lies" looks like an internal reference to the leader of the parent group, but we must keep in mind that a sect's bitterest attacks may be against those closest to it ideologically. No history of the larger movement can be traced, but the Qumran group survived the (real or imagined) attacks of the "Wicked Priest" and the death of the "Teacher of Righteousness," and continued to flourish, perhaps with only one short break in settlement—or perhaps none at all—until the destruction by the Romans who overran the area of Qumran about 68 CE. The group is not likely to have survived these events.

Judah Aristobulus I (104–103 BCE)

To return to the history of the Hasmonaean kingdom, we have the peculiar statement that John Hyrcanus had left his wife in charge of the kingdom. Her eldest son Aristobulus disputed the matter with her and soon gathered the reins of government into his own hands, imprisoning his own mother and even starving her to death. He also imprisoned his brothers, apart from Antigonus. Even though Aristobulus reigned for only one year, most of the description of his reign is taken up with how he was tricked by the queen and her advisers into having his brother Antigonus killed.

The little that we learn about Aristobulus's reign can be summarized in a few brief points: he was supposedly the first to actually take the title of king, previous Hasmonaean high priests having acted as rulers but not having used the actual title. He minted coins. He had the title *Philhellene* ("lover of Greek things"), which suggests that he contributed to certain building projects in Greek cities. He took the area of Ituraea (in southern Lebanon) and required the inhabitants to adopt circumcision and live according to Jewish law. This suggests that he continued with Hyrcanus's policy of expanding the borders of Judah but also of forcible circumcision for those living in the boundaries of Judaea. Unlike the Idumaeans, however, the Ituraeans do not appear to have continued to follow Jewish law when they broke free from Jewish control.

Alexander Jannaeus (103–76 BCE)

Our main source (the Jewish historian Josephus) gives more detail about Alexander Jannaeus than any other Hasmonaean ruler. Most of what we learn about Alexander's reign is devoted to two issues: further expansion of territory and the internal Jewish opposition to his rule. At Aristobulus's death, his widow, Alexandra Salina or Salome, released the brothers from prison but appointed Alexander Jannaeus ruler. Jannaeus put to death one remaining brother, but another one was allowed to live a private life. The evidence tips the balance toward Aristobulus's widow becoming Jannaeus's wife and, later, a Hasmonaean ruler in her own right.

At the beginning of his rule, Alexander Jannaeus continued the territorial expansion initiated by his father Hyrcanus I. This entangled him in what has been called the "War of the Scepters," which involved the rivals over the Seleucid throne (now Antiochus VIII and Antiochus IX), a local ruler named Zoilus, Ptolemy IX Soter II (Lathyrus) (116–96 BCE) who controlled Cyprus, and his mother Cleopatra III Berenice who controlled Egypt. Cleopatra had the Jewish Generals Chelkias and Ananias. Jannaeus approached Cleopatra with gifts, and her Jewish general Ananias also spoke on his behalf, so that she made an alliance with Jannaeus.

Jannaeus lost no time in continuing with his territorial conquests. But then a revolt developed. It began at the Feast of Tabernacles when he was pelted with citrons while sacrificing in his capacity as high priest. The exact reasons for this opposition are not clear; however, it was not a sectarian dispute (contra a later anecdote) but a serious rebellion. Jannaeus evidently contained the revolt, killing six thousand of his opponents, showing that a major revolt against Jannaeus's rule had developed.

Having quelled the revolt, at least temporarily, Jannaeus continued with his wars of conquest. This time he moved east, taking Moab and Galaaditis (Gilead). He also attacked the Arab king Obodas I but was decisively beaten and almost killed. The defeat by the Arabs seems to have encouraged his opponents since he now had a civil war on his hands which took up the next six years. He is alleged to have killed fifty thousand of his own countrymen during this time. The climax came when his Jewish opponents called in Demetrius III (one of the new rivals for the Seleucid throne) from Damascus about 90/88 BCE. Demetrius and Jannaeus met near Shechem, with large numbers of Jews fighting on both sides, though Jannaeus's mercenaries also took part.

Demetrius seems to have got the better of the contest, and Jannaeus fled. However, those Judaeans who had asked for Demetrius's aid now abandoned him and many Jews rallied to Alexander Jannaeus. The new balance of military manpower meant that Demetrius had little choice but to retire from the country. After Demetrius III had left Judaea, the revolt against Jannaeus continued, but he brought it to a close by driving many of his opponents into a city and taking it. He then had eight hundred of the captured men crucified and their families slaughtered before their eyes, while he and his concubines feasted and watched the spectacle. The unprecedented action made a great impact on his opponents, and eight thousand of them fled the country as long as Jannaeus was alive. The incident also seems to be referred to in a Qumran writing, the commentary on Nahum 2:12 (4QpNah 1.6-7): "Interpreted, this concerns the furious young lion [who executes revenge] on those who seek smooth things and hangs men alive, [a thing never done] formerly in Israel."

It is important to note at this point that many writers state wrongly that Jannaeus's opponents were Pharisees. Josephus, who relates the story, is not afraid to refer to the Pharisees, but in neither of his accounts does he suggest that Jannaeus's opponents were Pharisees or that those crucified were Pharisees. The expression "seekers after smooth things" in the Qumran texts is often said to refer to Pharisees. This may indeed *sometimes* be the case, but there is no clear evidence that the term always has Pharisees in mind—it could just refer to opponents in general. No doubt Pharisees were among Jannaeus's opponents and probably also made up some of those crucified, but there is simply no evidence that all those revolting against Jannaeus were Pharisees; on the contrary, the numbers alleged would suggest they encompassed a great many groups in Judaean society.

With his enemies now out of the way, Jannaeus was left to get on with his external military activities for the rest of his reign. He soon developed quartan fever but nevertheless kept to the field until his death. At the end of Jannaeus's reign Judah's territory included the cities of Syria, Idumaea, and Phoenicia. If this is correct, Jannaeus's territory was the largest extent of Israel since the time of the monarchy. While besieging a fortress in Transjordan, Alexander Jannaeus died at the age of forty-nine, after reigning twenty-seven years.

One account in Josephus claims that before his death, Jannaeus advised his wife Alexandra Salome to make peace with the Pharisees, grant them a certain amount of power, and pretend to have disapproved of her husband's activities. The result was that they gave the king a magnificent funeral with many eulogies. This is another incident that has led some scholars to infer that most of the opponents of Alexander were Pharisees. Against this are several considerations, including the fact that Josephus mentions the Pharisees only at this point in the narrative of Jannaeus. On the contrary, he at no point suggests that those who opposed, fought, and were killed by Alexander were specifically Pharisees. Therefore, one can only conclude that Pharisaic opponents—which most probably existed—were only a part of the opposition against him.

Alexandra Salome (76–67 BCE)

The one feature that stands out in Josephus's accounts is the extent to which the Pharisees dominated the reign of Alexandra. Under Alexandra, the Pharisees clearly possessed considerable political clout, including the ability to get rid of a number of their enemies. It finally reached the stage that some eminent citizens appealed directly to Alexandra (with the aid of her son Aristobulus) for a guarantee of safety. This Pharisaic attempt to get rid of some of Jannaeus's ministers seems real enough, showing that at this time they were not just a religious sect but a firm political movement wanting to take power. To appease those who had been loyal to Jannaeus and now to herself, Alexandra allowed some of the importunate individuals to guard certain of her fortresses.

Alexandra herself was evidently a good administrator, apart from the question of the Pharisees. She doubled the size of the Jewish military forces, in addition to keeping a large mercenary contingent, and as a result was able to maintain peaceful relations with the surrounding rulers. The one thorn in Alexandra's side was her son Aristobulus. The elder son Hyrcanus had been appointed high priest on Alexander Jannaeus's death and would have been the natural heir to his mother.

Yet Aristobulus seems to have been the more dynamic of the two, and there were doubts about Hyrcanus's ability and even desire to rule. When Alexandra became ill, Aristobulus took his chance. He occupied twenty-two fortresses in which a number of his supporters had been made guards, hired a mercenary army, and proclaimed himself king. He apparently used the pretext that if he did not, the Pharisees would seize power on his mother's death. Alexandra quickly responded to this by imprisoning Aristobulus's wife and children, but her illness prevented her from taking further action. As Aristobulus was amassing a large army, she died at the age of seventy-three after a reign of nine years.

After the death of Alexandra, the Hasmonaean dynasty descended into sordid conflict between her two sons. Their rivalry was to lead to the end of Hasmonaean rule, which we shall discuss in the next chapter.

Conclusions

This chapter has covered a significant century and a half of Jewish history. Things began with the Seleucid retaking of Coele-Syria (Syria Palestine). The Jews seem to have prospered under Seleucid rule for twenty-five years or so, until Antiochus IV came to the throne. At this time, Jason the brother of the high priest had ambitions not only to take the office but also to make Jerusalem into a Hellenistic city. He succeeded by bribing Antiochus with a promised increase in tribute and managed to implement his plans for Jerusalem. Most of the Jews seem to have welcomed his reforms, especially the inhabitants of Jerusalem itself.

But another individual, also a priest, named Menelaus pulled the same trick on him by promising Antiochus even more money. Menelaus had now displaced Jason as high priest, though there is no indication that Menelaus was interested in the Hellenistic reform of Jerusalem. At this point Jewish affairs become entangled with the Sixth Syrian War, in which Antiochus responded to Egyptian aggression by marching to Egypt and reordering the administration. When this was reversed by the Egyptian rulers, he marched into Egypt again but was forced to withdraw by the Romans. Judaea was thought to be in revolt, and the Seleucid army took Jerusalem. But for reasons that are still unclear, one measure taken was to suppress Jewish worship at the temple. Religious suppression was unprecedented in history up to this point.

The result was a Jewish revolt to restore the temple and Jewish worship. The family of the Maccabees (also known as Hasmonaeans) probably did not initiate this revolt, but they soon gained the leadership of it under Judas Maccabee. Although Judas's military conduct was not "miraculous" (as some have described it), he was able to succeed on the battlefield and to retake Jerusalem. He restored temple worship apparently in December 165 BCE, though Judas was himself killed in fighting only a few years later. At this point, most of the inhabitants of Judah seemed to be content to go back to the status quo of Seleucid rule. But Hasmonaeans continued to fight, now seeking independence for Judaea from Seleucid control. Under subsequent leadership by the Maccabaean brothers Jonathan and then Simon, they continued the struggle; however, it was the development of a rival for the Seleucid throne that allowed the Hasmonaeans to negotiate concessions and gain privileges, including the high priesthood itself.

Independence came only slowly, with important setbacks. It was declared under Simon about 143/142 BCE but was perhaps more symbolic than actual. But by the time of Simon's son John Hyrcanus, the Hasmonaeans—now a dynasty of priest-kings—ruled over an independent kingdom. This lasted until the middle of the first century BCE, when the sons of Queen Alexandra Salome fought for the throne after her death. This struggle and its major consequences will be discussed in the next chapter.

12

The Roman Takeover and the Reign of Herod the Great

We left the last chapter in mid-battle, as it were. Queen Alexandra Salome had two sons, the eldest of whom (Hyrcanus II) had become high priest. But the younger (Aristobulus II) led a revolt against her and Hyrcanus that continued until her death. The present chapter describes the continuation of that conflict, the intervention of the Romans who made Judah a component in the developing Roman Empire, and the establishment of rule by Herod the Great. We must always keep in mind the backdrop to this part of Jewish history: the dying decades of the Roman Republic and the establishment of the Roman Empire. Herod ruled with the permission of the Romans, and Judaea now came firmly under Roman control as long as the Roman Empire lasted.

The Last of the Hasmonaeans: Aristobulus II and Hyrcanus II (67–63 BCE)

Hyrcanus II took the high priesthood and, formally, the Hasmonaean throne in 70 to 69 BCE, two or three years before Alexandra died. In spite of this, Aristobulus II was not ready to accept Hyrcanus as king and declared war on his brother as soon as their mother was in her grave. They met in battle near Jericho, and Aristobulus quickly defeated Hyrcanus. Using Aristobulus's family (whom he had as prisoners) as a bargaining chip, Hyrcanus arranged a deal in which he was permitted to live unharmed as a private citizen while the rulership went to his brother.

At this juncture, a character by the name of Antipater is introduced. It is said that he was an Idumaean, whose father, Antipas, had been appointed governor of Idumaea by Alexander Jannaeus. Antipater stirred up the leading Jews against Aristobulus. After a time, he also persuaded Hyrcanus that he had made a mistake in giving up the kingship and indeed was in danger of being executed by Aristobulus. Receiving a guarantee of safety from the Nabataean ruler Aretas III, Hyrcanus fled to Petra. He managed to obtain the aid of an army under Aretas, and attacked Aristobulus, defeated him, and besieged him in Jerusalem to which he had fled. The outcome of the siege was still in the balance when the Romans intervened.

The Roman general, Pompey, had been campaigning in the East, fighting against the Armenians. The Armenian king surrendered in 66 BCE. Pompey then sent his lieutenant, Scaurus, to Syria. Delegates from both the sons of Alexandra met him with bribes, but Scaurus sided with Aristobulus (who supposedly gave the larger bribe) and forced Aretas to raise the siege of Jerusalem. Scaurus returned to Damascus, but shortly afterward Aristobulus defeated Hyrcanus in battle. This was the way things stood until Pompey himself arrived in Syria where he was entreated by both sides.

Also appearing before Pompey was a delegation from "the Jewish nation" (consisting of more than two hundred of the leading men), asking that Judaea be allowed to continue as a theocracy without the high priest also acting almost like a king.[1] It was clear that many of the national leaders were fed up with Hasmonaean rule, though it appears that their entreaties were ignored. After hearing the different sides, Pompey delayed a decision, saying he first needed to deal with the Nabataeans. This was too much for Aristobulus (who had presented a large bribe to Pompey), and he set off for Judaea.

Pompey marched after him immediately, before he had time for much preparation. Aristobulus realized the folly of resistance and met Pompey on the last leg of his march, between Jericho and Jerusalem, promising money as well as entry into Jerusalem. Aristobulus's followers had a different idea, however, and shut the city against the Romans. The people of the city were divided between the supporters of Aristobulus and those of Hyrcanus. The former withdrew into the temple, cutting the bridge to the upper city, while the latter opened the gates to Pompey. The siege of the temple lasted three months, apparently until about mid-summer. The Romans were assisted by Hyrcanus and his followers. The Roman army also took advantage of the Sabbath to advance their siege works since the Jews would not fight on the Sabbath if not directly attacked.

During this time and even in the final assault when many were being killed, the priests continued their sacrificial duties. When the Romans finally broke through, many of the defenders were slaughtered by their fellow Jews who were adherents of Hyrcanus. Pompey and others of the Romans entered the temple area and even went inside the Holy of Holies. This may have been partly out of curiosity but also to demonstrate that the Romans were now in charge; however, the temple itself was respected: neither the vessels nor the temple treasure was touched, and the temple was cleansed, and the cult resumed the next day at Pompey's command.

Thus, Judaea as an independent kingdom came to an end. Although it was to be a "friendly kingdom" (essentially a vassal kingdom) of Rome for many years under Herod the Great and his grandson Agrippa I, it was not again to be a sovereign nation for another two millennia. The territory gained by successive Hasmonaean rulers was taken away to leave only the area that roughly made up the province of Judah under the Babylonians and Persians. Although Hyrcanus was restored to the high priesthood, he did not have the title of king, and a heavy tribute was imposed on the country.

Roman Administration in Judaea

With his reorganization of the kingdoms in the region Pompey felt his work here was done. He turned the whole domain over to Scaurus and made his way back to Rome, taking Aristobulus and his sons with him as captives (though one son Alexander escaped on the way). Now, Scaurus continued with the military operations that Pompey had not managed to complete. The main one of these was to get control of the Nabataeans. When he marched against Petra, however, his men lacked sufficient food. Antipater and Hyrcanus stepped in and provided grain and other provisions from Judaea. Scaurus then sent Antipater to negotiate with King Aretas, persuading him to pay 300 talents as tribute so that the Romans would leave him alone.

In the meantime, Aristobulus's son Alexander had raised a small army and was threatening Hyrcanus by making raids on Judaea, but Scaurus's term of office came to an end. Gabinius, a former consul, was appointed governor of the region in 57 to 54 BCE. In contrast with Antipater's perspicuity, the shortsightedness of the Hasmonaeans was soon demonstrated in several attempts by Aristobulus and his son Alexander (and later Alexander's brother Antigonus) to lead revolts and reestablish their rule. Gabinius defeated them, not only with Roman troops (partly led by Mark Antony) but also a Jewish force including Antipater's picked troops. Hyrcanus could now take up his place as high priest in the temple.

Pompey's initial settlement may have seemed very unfortunate from the Jewish point of view, but it was mild compared to the drastic further reorganization that came about under Gabinius. It has usually been interpreted as a way of bringing the potentially rebellious province to heel by a process of divide and conquer. The continual rebellions led by Aristobulus and his sons clearly had a good deal of popular support. Instead of quietly shouldering the yoke of Roman rule, Judaea looked to be a continuing problem. Gabinius's solution was to divide the country into five administrative councils. Gabinius left his arrangements in effect for only a few years, perhaps because they were not succeeding. After a further revolt in 55 BCE, he more or less turned the administration over to Antipater.

About the year 56 BCE, Aristobulus II himself, along with his son Antigonus, escaped from Rome and led a new rebellion. As a former priest-king, he had no trouble gaining a large following, collected in a short time. Unfortunately, the outcome was completely predictable, and Aristobulus and Antigonus were taken prisoner and returned to Rome. The two sons (Alexander and Antigonus) were released by the Senate to return to Judaea, however, because Gabinius had promised this to their mother when negotiating to have the fortresses surrendered. This soon proved to be a mistake because Alexander revolted a second time. Antipater managed to persuade many Jews to abandon their following of Alexander; nevertheless, the latter was still left with a large army with which he met the Romans near Mount Tabor, but again it was to no avail.

The Roman civil war began in 49 BCE, with Julius Caesar's crossing of the Rubicon and Caesar's and Pompey's opposing each other. Caesar released Aristobulus from prison with the intention of putting him at the head of two legions; the plan was thwarted, however, when adherents of Pompey poisoned him before he even left Rome. Likewise, his son Alexander was executed in Antioch by the proconsul of Syria at Pompey's orders, but Antigonus and his two sisters were taken under the protection of Ptolemy, king of Calchis. The decisive battle between Caesar and Pompey was at Pharsalus in 48 BCE. Pompey was defeated but escaped to Egypt with a small company; however, he was killed by the men of Ptolemy XII as soon as he landed. (His death is referred to in the *Psalms of Solomon* 2:15-31.) Caesar followed and spent the winter in Alexandria where Cleopatra VII, the sister of Ptolemy and joint ruler, became his mistress.

After Pompey's death in 48, Antipater quite decisively took the side of Caesar and distinguished himself in aiding Mithridates of Pergamum, the leader of the Roman forces, to capture Egypt. This was done by diplomacy in securing Arab and Syrian aid, and in persuading the Jews in the district of Onias to support Caesar and allow his army through, as well as by military prowess in which Antipater showed both outstanding personal bravery and strategic ability in battle. Apparently at this time, or probably earlier, Antipater was appointed governor of the Jews.[2]

Caesar rewarded Antipater and Hyrcanus for their usefulness. Hyrcanus was confirmed in the priesthood and Antipater given Roman citizenship and exemption from taxation. These honors were increased when Antigonus, Aristobulus's son, foolishly accused Antipater and Hyrcanus before Caesar: Antipater was made "procurator" of Judaea. Hyrcanus was apparently also raised to ethnarch of Judah by Caesar.[3] Permission was also given to rebuild the walls of Jerusalem, which had been in ruins since Pompey's siege.

After the assassination of Julius Caesar, the last days of the Roman Republic played out. The two main players were Mark Antony and Caesar's grand-nephew Octavian. After the defeat and death of the main conspirators, the Empire was now essentially divided between Octavian and Antony. But there was friction between the two major leaders from the beginning. Antony went to the East to raise funds and organize the region, but when he returned to Italy in 40 BCE, he was refused admission, for which he blamed Octavian. Whatever the reason for the misunderstanding, what seemed like imminent war was averted with some difficulty. Instead, in October 40, Octavian and Antony agreed to the Treaty of Brundisium, which gave Italy and the West to Octavian, with Antony having the East, and another triumvir Lepidus got Africa.

Early Career of Herod

It is commonplace to state that Herod was only partially Jewish, or even that he was a foreigner ruling over Judaea.[4] Several points should be made about this:

- While some traditions make Herod Idumaean, other traditions give a different ancestry. For example, Nicolaus of Damascus, who was Herod's secretary and wrote the account drawn on by Josephus, said that his family came from among the leading Jewish families who migrated to Judaea from Babylon.[5] Josephus's argument that Nicolaus said this only out of a desire to flatter Herod is a two-edged sword, since his own version could arise from a desire to *slander* the Herodaean family. Also, it is difficult to see why Herod would be pleased to be linked with Babylonian Jews if this were not true. Most important, why should Herod feel ashamed of Idumaean ancestry?
- The Idumaeans had converted and remained within the Jewish community at least well into the first century CE. It may have been that Herod's family were Jews who simply lived in the Idumaean area. But even if they were originally of completely Idumaean ancestry, the indication is that they were Jewish converts.

- Herod appears to have lived as a Jew. Any conclusion about his ethnicity cannot ignore this point. If he was not originally of Jewish descent, his family had adopted Judaism.
- *Testament of Moses* 6.2-6, a passage normally interpreted as referring to Herod, accuses him among other things of being a non-priest. On the other hand, nothing is said about his being a foreigner or non-Jew.

What is clear is that even if he was Idumaean, Herod lived as a Jew. If his family had been originally Jewish, they were still possibly converts. Whatever else his identity might have included, it was certainly Jewish.

Antipater was in charge of organizing the province of Judaea. This led him to appoint Herod governor of Galilee while his older brother, Phasael, was placed over Jerusalem (c. 47 BCE). Herod was quite young (probably about twenty-five). His energy and leadership ability were quickly demonstrated by one of his first acts, which was to catch and execute Ezekias (Hezekiah) a bandit leader. This earned him the favor of the Syrians in this area, because Ezekias had been a serious threat to them, and brought him to the attention of the Syrian governor Sextus Caesar. In attempting to emulate his younger brother by sound rule, Phasael gained the good will of the people of Jerusalem. Because of his own actions and those of his sons, Antipater himself was respected by the nation and allowed to exercise the authority which in name belonged to the high priest Hyrcanus.

Not surprisingly, opposition soon developed to the growing power of Antipater's family. Herod was singled out as a special target for attack. Although Hyrcanus's exact attitude at first was unclear, the constant criticism and lobbying by some of the leading Jews eventually goaded him into calling Herod to account before the Sanhedrin. The pretext was his execution of Ezekias without benefit of a trial first before the Sanhedrin. Herod's response was a model of sagacity: he complied but came with a bodyguard large enough to show that he was not intimidated but not so large as to imply a threat to Hyrcanus. The precise course of the trial is unclear, but what does seem plain is that Sextus Caesar sided with Herod, sending instructions to Hyrcanus for the charges to be dropped. One reason for Sextus's intervention is probably that as a Roman citizen Herod did not have to stand trial before a local court. In any case, Sextus gave greater authority to Herod, making him governor of Coele-Syria and Samaria as well.

After Julius Caesar's assassination in 44 BCE, Cassius came to take over the Roman forces in the area. He imposed tribute on the whole of Syria to raise funds for the coming war, including 700 talents of silver from Judaea, with responsibility for collecting from the different regions apportioned to various individuals. Herod was the first to produce his quota from Galilee (100 talents), winning Cassius's favor by this and other acts of friendship. Another Jewish leader, Malichus, gained his disfavor, however, and would have been executed had not Antipater intervened with a large gift to Cassius.

In 43 BCE Cassius and Murcus raised an army in Syria to support Cassius and Brutus against Octavian and Antony. They saw Herod as a valuable tool in their enterprise and, according to some sources, they made him governor of Syria. Herod's exact position is somewhat vague, and he might not have been at the top of the hierarchy over the province. In any case, they apparently promised him that he would be king of Judaea after the war. Herod was clearly seen as the rising star.

Malichus rewarded Antipater by plotting against him. Whatever the cause of Malichus's opposition to Antipater, one of his multiple plots eventually bore fruit, and he succeeded in poisoning him. Herod was persuaded by his brother Phasael's argument that they should bide their time about taking revenge, lest a direct attack with soldiers be seen as starting a revolt. On the other hand, when Herod had to intervene in Samaria, to put down a sedition and civic quarrels, he returned with his troops at the time of a festival. But when Malichus tried to keep him and his troops out of Jerusalem, Herod simply ignored the message that came through Hyrcanus. He then wrote to Cassius for permission to get rid of Malichus, which Cassius was happy to give. Herod got his revenge when Malichus was in Tyre and had him executed for plotting to return to Jerusalem and raise a revolt against the Romans while Cassius was preoccupied with his war against Anthony.

There were others with plans, as well. The international situation was such that several revolts broke out together. As soon as Cassius left Syria in 42 BCE, a Jewish general, Helix, attacked Phasael who defeated him. Also, Antigonus, the son of Aristobulus II, had been allowed to return to the area. Herod led the campaign against him with considerable success. It was after this military victory that Herod was publicly betrothed to Hyrcanus's granddaughter Mariamme. She would become his second wife, he having already married a Jewish woman named Dora.

Herod and Hyrcanus do not seem to have been particularly affected by their support of Cassius in the fight against Antony and Octavian. After Cassius's defeat and death, Antony came to take over rulership of the East (42 BCE). An embassy of leading Jews met him and accused Herod and Phasael of governing the country with Hyrcanus as a mere puppet. Antony ruled in favor of the two brothers, not only because of his personal regard for Herod but also allegedly because of a large bribe. The opposition did not cease, however, and two more delegations came before Antony with accusations. When the second of three made their charges, Antony asked Hyrcanus who were the better rulers of the nation, and the latter indicated Herod and Phasael.

The result was that Antony made Herod and his brother tetrarchs while imprisoning a handful of their opponents. The last delegation was much larger, a thousand men, but now Antony was losing patience. Herod and Hyrcanus met the delegation and urged them to back down, for the sake of national peace and also their own safety, but they refused. Antony had had enough and sent troops who killed a large number of them. It must be recognized, however, that the size of the group and its attitude indicated the beginnings of a revolt.

How Herod Became "King of the Jews"

In the spring of 40 BCE, the Parthians invaded Syria and Palestine. They were aided by the Roman turncoat Quintus Labienus Parthicus, who had been a supporter of Pompey. This invasion was the opportunity for the opponents of Herod. Antigonus, son of Aristobulus II, once more planned to take over Judah, this time with Parthian aid. He apparently promised 1,000 talents and five hundred women to the Parthians to depose Hyrcanus and make him king, as well as to get rid of Herod and his entourage. A Parthian general came to Jerusalem claiming to help settle the fight that was taking place between factions. Phasael received him cordially and even agreed that he and Hyrcanus should go to discuss matters with the Parthian satrap near Tyre, against the advice of Herod who remained in Jerusalem.

Herod's suspicions proved right, for Phasael and Hyrcanus were taken prisoner by the Parthians. The plan was to capture Herod as well, but already wary he received advance news of what had happened to Phasael and avoided the trap. Instead, he collected his family and followers and fled Jerusalem in the middle of the night to Idumaea. He left his immediate family with a guard in the desert fortress of Masada and scattered the rest around the country, because of the number of refugees with him (supposedly about nine thousand). He made his way to Petra with the thought of raising ransom money for his brother from King Malchus, but Malchus refused and ordered him out of his territory. Herod then pushed toward Egypt. It was on the way there that he received word of what had happened: the Parthians had given the throne to Aristobulus who had mutilated Hyrcanus's ears so he could no longer be high priest (cf. the priestly requirements in Lev. 21:16-23). Phasael had bravely committed suicide.

Herod hurried on to Alexandria and took a ship for Rome even though it was now the winter sailing season and thus a dangerous time to be on the seas. At Rome he was well received by Antony and Octavian, who were currently cooperating because of the recent treaty of Brundisium. They determined that the best way to oppose Antigonus and the Parthians was to make Herod king. Herod was not expecting to be given the kingship but was planning to propose it for a grandson of Hyrcanus. So, it was apparently in late 40 that Octavian and Antony presented Herod to the Senate, and he was declared king of Judaea.

After being declared king by the Senate, Herod had immediately returned to the East (about December 40 or January 39 BCE) and gathered an army to fight against Antigonus. In the meantime, his brother Joseph had been able to hold Masada against the enemy. Ventidius the Roman general in the area was supposed to be giving aid to Joseph but did nothing because of alleged bribery by Antigonus; instead, he left his subordinate Pupedius Silo with a body of troops encamped near Jerusalem, while he went off to chase the Parthians. Antigonus was able to suborn Silo as he had Ventidius.

By now it was well into 39 BCE. Galilee, as a whole, went over to Herod. Ostensibly, Ventidius and Silo had been ordered to aid him, but Ventidius was occupied with local revolts caused by the Parthian invasion, and Silo had to be rescued by Herod from attacks by Jews. Herod relieved Masada, secured Idumaea, sent his relatives to Samaria, then finally came against Jerusalem. Herod offered an amnesty to the defenders, but Antigonus rejected it. An attempt was made to thwart the siege by Silo who claimed that his men did not have enough food, but Herod quickly remedied the situation and, to ensure secure supplies in the future, took Jericho and garrisoned it.

Galilee, Idumaea, and Samaria were now firmly in Herod's hands, and he was able to winter his troops in these districts. Although it is difficult to assess Antigonus's strength, he evidently had areas of support in Palestine as well as a line of influence still to Silo. Herod did not rest even in the winter: he sent his brother Joseph with troops to occupy Idumaea. Herod himself took Sepphoris, which had been in Antigonus's hands, and then used the opportunity to go against certain "brigands" living in caves in the area near Arbela. Some of them may have been ordinary bandits, but others were probably opposition groups to Roman and Herodian rule.[6]

Herod now had Galilee under control and could pay his men and send them to their winter quarters. At this point, Silo's underhand dealings with Antigonus came back to haunt him. Silo had allowed Antigonus to winter some of his troops near Lydda, in exchange for the latter's provisioning Silo's own soldiers. Antigonus did supply them for a month but then suddenly stopped, instructing the local inhabitants to gather up all available provisions and take refuge in the hills, leaving the Roman soldiers to starve. Silo had no choice but to come cap in hand to Herod. The latter tasked his younger brother, Pheroras, with provisioning Silo's troops, which he did in abundance.

About this time (autumn 39 BCE) Antony went to Athens, where he made his home for a couple of years. He defeated the Parthians in the summer of 38 BCE. Herod met Antony on the Euphrates and provided assistance to him, leaving his brother Joseph in charge. With the siege won, Antony dispatched Gaius Sosius, his governor of Syria, with several legions to Herod's aid. As he was on his way back, however, Herod learned that his brother Joseph had foolishly taken to the field against some of Antigonus's forces, and his inexperienced troops had been massacred and Joseph himself killed. Immediately following this, Galilee and apparently Idumaea had revolted.

Herod had his revenge. He made a forced march through Mount Lebanon to Jericho. Antigonus send his own general against Herod. In the battle Herod was himself wounded by a javelin, but his forces were victorious. Herod now besieged Jerusalem where Antigonus had holed up. After setting up the siege, Herod showed his contempt of Antigonus's military prowess by going off to Samaria to marry Mariamme. There were in effect two generals: Herod at the head of his own army and Sosius who had been sent by Antony in command of the Roman force.

With the size of the besieging army, the outcome was quite predictable; nevertheless, the defenders fought ferociously. Yet when the Lower City and the outer portions of the temple had fallen to the Romans and Herod, the defenders asked for sacrificial animals to be brought to them, and Herod agreed, thinking it might make them more likely to surrender. But since they fought even more strongly, he pressed the attack. When the attackers finally broke through, none of the defenders were spared; indeed, the Jews of Herod's army were as determined to leave no living opponents as the Romans. Antigonus surrendered to Sosius, however, and was taken prisoner. Herod had two concerns: one was to keep his non-Jewish troops from violating the temple; the other was to prevent wholesale looting of the city and slaughter of the population. He managed the latter only by promising generous gifts to all the officers and men from his own purse, a promise that he was quick to fulfill.

The exact length of the siege of Jerusalem and the time of its fall is uncertain. The siege had probably begun sometime in the spring of 37 BCE: this fits nicely with the defeat of the Parthians and Herod's return with Sosius's troops. The city fell most likely sometime in the summer of 37 BCE.[7] Antigonus was executed by Antony in Antioch by beheading,[8] thus bringing the Hasmonaean kingly rule to an end. That Antigonus can be considered the last of the Hasmonaean kings is indicated by his many coins, which give his title in Hebrew as "Mattathias the high priest and the *hever* [community] of the Jews" but in Greek as "king Anti(gonus)."

Antony, Cleopatra, and Herod

To retrace our steps a bit: once the differences between Antony and Octavian were temporarily sorted out by the treaty of Brundisium (about September 40 BCE), Antony's major task was to deal with the Parthians who had overrun Syria in 40 BCE. In 39 BCE, Antony pushed the Parthians back beyond the Euphrates. By this time, he had become involved with Cleopatra, who had done away with her brother Ptolemy XIV to reign as sole ruler. In 37 he sent his wife Octavia (Octavian's sister) back to Italy, though not divorcing her, and openly acknowledged his children by Cleopatra. With Cleopatra's financial support, he invaded Parthia in 36 BCE in a disastrous campaign that cost him a third of his force. His successful invasion and capture of Armenia in 34 BCE hardly made up for this.

Herod had numerous troubles caused by Cleopatra who not only wanted to take over control of Palestine but also seemed to have disliked Herod personally. Fortunately, Antony was well disposed toward Herod despite his infatuation with Cleopatra; this, along with skillful diplomacy on Herod's part, managed to keep his throne and kingdom for himself even though certain territories were taken away. Cleopatra's designs were allegedly not just on Judaea but on Arabia and other territories as well. She was given an area in Coele-Syria by Antony when she first pressed him. Later, he added certain territories in Arabia; he also included Jericho, which Herod leased back from her, along with a large section of the coast of Palestine and Phoenicia. Cleopatra apparently even visited Jerusalem (or at least Judaea) on one occasion.[9]

After Antigonus mutilated Hyrcanus, the Parthians had allowed him to settle among the Jews in Babylon where he was greatly honored. He wanted to return to Palestine, however, and Herod invited him to come home, sending an envoy with gifts to the Parthian king asking for his return. The Parthians let him go, and Herod received him with a splendid homecoming. Hyrcanus could no longer be high priest, and Herod appointed Ananel (Hananel) from a priestly family in Babylon. This angered Hyrcanus's daughter Alexandra who thought that her own son Jonathan Aristobulus should have been given the office. She appealed to Cleopatra to use her influence on Antony.

Antony's friend (and lover?) Quintus Delius visited Herod and was impressed with Aristobulus's charm and beauty. He suggested to Antony to send for the boy (as a possible paramour?). But by this time, Herod had decided the best course of action was to make an excuse as to why the boy could not leave Judaea and appointed him (who was only seventeen) as high priest. When the lad presided at the altar during the Feast of Tabernacles (c. 35 BCE), he was acclaimed enthusiastically by the people there, which was a danger sign that there might be threats to Herod's kingship. Thus, when a year later Aristobulus was drowned while swimming at the palace in Jericho, Alexandra blamed Herod and wrote to Cleopatra with an accusation of murder against him. Cleopatra persuaded Antony to summon Herod to answer the charges, but Herod was cleared by Antony.

This did not stop the allegations that Herod was responsible for his death. But did Herod have the youth assassinated as Josephus alleged? Most modern writers on Herod have accepted the verdict of Josephus—and Alexandra—as reliable, in spite of the evident bias of both individuals. This scenario is less than credible, however, because Aristobulus's death created great problems for Herod.[10] First, to assassinate him in his own palace was bound to bring questions and accusations down on his head. Second, he was already under scrutiny from Cleopatra, who had Antony's ear. If she decided to accuse him to Antony (as she did), the outcome was unpredictable: Herod could well have lost his throne. Finally, he needed to get the people on his side, and getting rid of a popular, young, handsome high priest was the last thing he needed to do. Herod was a shrewd calculator throughout his career, as we have already seen demonstrated, and if he had contemplated removing Aristobulus, he would have realized this was a poor way to go about it. Aristobulus's death at this time and in this manner brought him nothing but grief.

Although Antony was under Cleopatra's thumb, he was clearly reluctant to condemn one whom he had made king not that many years before. There was also Herod's charm, rhetorical ability in defending himself, and the fact that he was very useful to Antony. The result was that he even accompanied Antony part of the way on his Parthian venture in 36 BCE. Nevertheless, there were repercussions for Herod's household. Herod had left his brother-in-law Joseph in charge, with instructions to put Mariamme to death if anything happened to him when he went with Antony.[11] Unfortunately, Joseph told Mariamme about these orders. She accused Herod of wanting her dead, but this convinced him that Mariamme would have learned of this from Joseph only if he was intimate with her. Herod had Joseph executed.

Antony's involvement with Cleopatra was becoming a propaganda weapon for Octavian who was also strengthening his position by espousing traditional Italian values and customs. When Antony proclaimed Cleopatra's son Caesarion as Caesar's legitimate son and King of Kings, ruling jointly over Egypt with Cleopatra as Queen of Kings, it was an additional factor to make the powers in Rome question Antony's judgment. When the official triumviral powers (made in 40 BCE) lapsed in 33 BCE, Octavian laid aside his title, although Antony did not. In the developing crisis, Octavian largely had the support of Italy and the western provinces. A proclamation was issued removing Antony's powers and declaring war on Cleopatra.

The decisive battle was at Actium in September 31 BCE. Although Antony would supposedly have had a strong fleet, the battle was quickly given up. Antony and Cleopatra sailed back to Alexandria with a few ships while most of the fleet came into Octavian's hands. It was another year before Octavian pursued Antony to Egypt since he had to deal with his veterans. At that time Antony, deserted by his troops, committed suicide. Cleopatra was taken prisoner but also committed suicide in captivity. After a century of continual civil war, Rome was finally at peace again.

Herod, Friend of Augustus Caesar

At the battle of Actium in 31 BCE, Herod was ready to aid Antony in any way possible but, fortunately for Herod, Antony did not feel he needed him. Instead, he sent him to fight the Nabataeans who were refusing to pay the tribute owed. There is reason to be skeptical of this explanation, however, since it seems very unlikely that Antony would have refused help if it had come. The fight with the Arabs was rather convenient when we look at subsequent events: it made sure that Herod was otherwise engaged when the time came for the battle between Antony/Cleopatra and Octavian. A politician as astute as Herod could no doubt see what was coming, with the odds very much against Antony's succeeding. He also knew that if Antony was successful, Cleopatra's full fury might well have been unleashed on him. There are signs that already a year or two before Actium, he was preparing to take any steps needed to survive in the new order.

Antony's defeat at Actium in September 31 BCE left Herod on the losing side. He also had enemies or potential enemies in his own court. The high priest Hyrcanus appealed to the Nabataean king for refuge, but the correspondence was betrayed to Herod. Herod went to the Sanhedrin with these letters and had Hyrcanus condemned to death. After Hyrcanus's execution, Herod imprisoned his mother, sister, and children. Herod was now ready to make his move in the changed circumstances in which the Actium defeat had left him. The question was what action he should take. Typically, he made a bold stroke.

Sometime in the spring of 30 BCE he sailed to meet Octavian at Rhodes. He appeared before the Roman victor without his crown and dressed as a commoner but otherwise with regal demeanor. He candidly stated that he had supported Antony as a faithful ally and would have been at Actium if Antony had not given orders to the contrary. He had been a fast friend and adviser of Antony, even after the latter's defeat. Now, he placed his crown before Caesar but would serve him just as staunchly as he had Antony if allowed to.

The result was that Octavian urged him to be his friend now, as he had been to Antony, and restored his diadem. There were probably a number of reasons why Octavian was happy to restore Herod's crown and confirm his rule, not least his past record and his administrative ability. Also, it was Octavian's policy to leave Antony's client rulers in power once they had acknowledged his sovereignty. Nevertheless, one suspects Octavian admired in Herod's actions the same courage and sheer guts that he himself possessed. *Whatever one might think of Herod in other respects, he had what it took to be leader in a crisis.*

The genius of Octavian's reign was that he acted as a constitutional monarch while maintaining the outward trappings of the Republic. Further, the machinery of government was so well designed that it was not only passed on in a smooth transition at his death but continued to work and keep the peace at home—for the most part—for another two centuries. The first desire of the people was for peace, and the veterans wanted their rewards of discharge and land. So after taking Egypt in 30 BCE, he returned to Rome and began the task of building a stable government in a welcome respite from fighting. His military career was by no means at an end, but his greatest achievements were civil, governmental, and domestic, with most of the fighting on the frontiers being conducted by subordinates.

Things were sufficiently in progress that he was able to make a bold but calculated move in early 27 BCE to renounce all his powers and offices before the Senate. The result was that the Senators would not hear of it. Thus, his carefully planned move was such that he could keep the forms of the Republic while maintaining his actual power of supreme ruler. An additional bonus was that he was voted the title Augustus, declared *princeps* or first citizen, and the sixth month of the Roman calendar (which at that time began in the spring) was named August in his honor. This is referred to as the First Settlement.

The so-called Second Settlement conferred civil, provincial, and military authority practically without limit, which continued to be the basis of the rule of the emperors who succeeded him. Throughout most of his reign, Herod kept in close touch with Augustus and was able to maintain a good relationship with the emperor himself as well as other members of the family.

The Rest of Herod's Reign (30–4 BCE)

Octavian's friendship was immediately evident after confirming Herod in his kingship. The emperor came through Palestine some months later while on his way to retaking Egypt (30 BCE). Herod not only lavishly entertained him and his troops but also made available ample provisions for the march across the desert; he was similarly unsparing in expense on Augustus's return from Egypt. His personal accommodation for Octavian was not only most splendid but was accompanied by a gift of 800 talents. The effect was for the Roman emperor to conclude that he was being generous beyond the means of his small kingdom and to reward him with additional territories. Throughout most of his reign, Herod enjoyed the close friendship and confidence of Augustus and was honored with titles and other accoutrements of status as well as further grants of territory.

These gifts do not just represent Roman greatness of heart toward Herod. Judaea was a frontier kingdom, and it was known that Herod would take great care for its security, thus also keeping a vital link in the Roman boundary safe from barbaric encroachment. For example, the territories of Trachonitis, Batanaea, and Auranitis (roughly equivalent to the areas of Bashan and Gilead often mentioned in the Hebrew Bible) had a problem with brigands who hung out in the mountainous and wilderness areas. A local ruler was in league with some of the robber bands who especially preyed on the people of Damascus. Since the region had come under Roman rule, the local people appealed to Governor Varro who reported the matter to Caesar. This was one of the reasons Augustus assigned the territories to Herod, because he expected him to take care of the problem—which he did. The local ruler went to Rome to complain against Herod but without success.

Herod ruled as a "client king" (or "friendly king") of Rome. There were a number of these during the late Republic and early Empire, especially as long as the boundaries of the Empire continued to be expanded. Client kingship was useful to the Romans because the client kingdom served as a buffer to the areas not under Roman control and could be called upon to render military aid when needed. On the other hand, Rome did not have to expend valuable resources in administration and the posting of legions on a permanent basis, for the client king took care of his own administration and defense of his borders under normal circumstances. Thus, by the end of his reign Herod controlled a state reaching from southern Lebanon to the Negev and from the Mediterranean to the Transjordan. It was an area basically as large as that under Alexander Jannaeus and probably as large as—perhaps larger than—anything under the Israelite monarchy.

One of the major achievements of Herod's rule was his building program, which was spectacular even by Roman standards. There were two aspects to the internal program, the civic/personal and the military/defenive, though some works had elements of both connected with them. These included a theater and a large amphitheater in Jerusalem; also a hippodrome, though this was perhaps identical with the amphitheatre.[12] Of particular interest is the story that the decoration of the theater caused a disturbance among certain Jews. Herod had a number of "trophies" scattered around the theater that commemorated his success in war. But some were convinced that these had human images at their heart. When Herod learned of this, he called some of the prominent leaders of the group to view them. When he had the ornaments that decorated the outside of the trophy removed, they could see for themselves that no image lay at the core. Most only laughed and accepted that they had been mistaken; unfortunately, a few refused to change their opinion that Herod was introducing unlawful ways.

The fortifications of the realm were naturally very important. In Jerusalem this included the Antonia and other protective fortified towers. South of Jerusalem he created the fortress of Herodium. Probably about 27 to 25 BCE he rebuilt Samaria, renaming it Sebaste, the Greek equivalent of "Augustus." Only a day's journey from Jerusalem, it could also serve as a fortress to control the entire country if necessary. Because it was dedicated to the emperor, it had a magnificent temple at its center. About six thousand of Herod's veteran allies were settled in and around it and were offered equitable laws. On the coast, the old city of Straton's Tower was rebuilt with a magnificent man-made harbor and called Caesarea, again after Augustus. It was later to be the seat of the Roman government of Palestine.

The crowning achievement of his building projects, and one that would have done most to endear him to the Jewish people, was the restoration and rebuilding of the temple at Jerusalem, probably beginning about 19 BCE.[13] The care with which this was carried out and the enormous cost involved (apparently paid for by Herod himself) suggests that its alleged fame throughout the Roman Empire was not exaggerated.[14] He doubled its area. The work of building could be done only by priests and had to be carried out in such a way as to maintain the dignity of the house and not disrupt the regular cultic services. He assured the people that he would tear none of it down until the building materials for the reconstruction were all assembled. The main work was completed in a year and a half, though work continued for more than eighty years until not long before it was destroyed by the Romans.[15]

Herod also made a name for himself for his generosity in funding building projects in the Greek and Roman worlds (*War* 1.21.11-12 §§422–8; *Ant.* 15.9.5 §§326–30). This included gymnasia, marketplaces, theaters, aqueducts, and even temples for cities in Phoenicia and Syria, but also Asia Minor, Rhodes, and even Greece itself. He endowed the Olympian games (which seemed to be declining) and was made president of the celebrations. He was careful, however, not to erect temples, statues, or other pagan religious buildings in Judaean territory. One area where he also tried to make a difference was in the realm of laws and justice.

About 25 BCE, the country was hit by a major drought for at least two years. Herod's treasury was low because of his building projects, and in any case neighboring regions were also suffering drought and famine and not able to sell food to Judaea. As was typical for him, he took bold action: he stripped his palace of gold and silver, including artistic ornaments, and turned it into money. He then applied to his friend who was prefect of Egypt to buy grain from there. Egypt was the breadbasket of

FIGURE 12.1 *Reconstruction of Herod's temple.*

Rome, and its grain was normally restricted to official Roman use. The prefect made an exception in Herod's case, however, and supplied him with much of what was needed. Herod also gave aid to cities in the region and helped out as far away as Syria. He even took care to supply clothing, since many flocks had had to be used as food, which caused a shortage of wool. When the drought turned, he resourced fifty thousand men to bring in the harvest. His solicitude and generosity toward his people and the region went a long way to changing attitudes toward his rule.

Marcus Agrippa, Caesar's son-in-law, trusted friend, and general, came to the East the first time about 23/22 BCE. While he wintered on the island of Lesbos at Mitylene, Herod, who was a close friend, visited him. Despite famine in Rome, which he dealt with without accepting a dictatorship, Augustus himself visited the East for three years (22–19 BCE). It was about 20 BCE (Herod's seventeenth year) that Augustus came to visit Syria. It was on this occasion that Augustus gave territory lying between Trachonitis and Galilee to Herod. Caesar also instructed the procurators of Syria to gain Herod's consent for matters affecting his kingdom. Herod asked Augustus for his brother Pheroras to have a tetrarchy. Apparently, Peraea (Transjordan) was assigned to him. After Augustus left the area, Herod built a magnificent temple to the emperor near Paneas, which later became Caesarea-Philippi.

Shortly afterward, Herod reduced the taxes for the people of his kingdom by a third. It is alleged that citizens were not allowed to assemble, were spied on, and were sometimes secretly detained, imprisoned, and even killed by Herod. This is probably correct, but this seems to have been normal in empires and monarchies of the time. He required an oath of loyalty from all his subjects, punishing those who objected. Yet he also exempted Pollion the Pharisee and Samaias and their disciples, as well as the Essenes. In both cases it was because of their support or alleged predictions of his success at crucial points in his career.

Marcus Agrippa was again sent to Asia Minor in 14 BCE to place a king friendly to the Romans on the throne of Cappadocia. Herod went to meet him and invited him to Judaea. There he gave Agrippa a magnificent welcome in the autumn of that year, showing him the new cities of Sebaste and Caesarea. He ended the tour in Jerusalem where people welcomed him with great acclaim. Agrippa had to sail before winter, but the next spring Herod engaged in a protracted sea voyage to catch up with him in Pontus. Agrippa was delighted to see him, and they returned overland. Herod demonstrated his generosity to many of the peoples and cities en route. He also supported petitions or made recommendations on behalf of some diaspora Jews who approached Agrippa with requests for favors.

It was on this occasion that the Jews of Ionia petitioned Agrippa because they were being mistreated, especially in not being able to observe their own laws (e.g., they were being required to appear in court on Jewish holy days, undertake military and civic duties from which they had been exempted, and not being allowed to send the temple tax to Jerusalem). The result was that Agrippa granted their petition and confirmed their traditional religious rights. After Agrippa sailed away, Herod remitted a quarter of the taxes in his realm for one year in honor of his friendship with him and the accomplishments of the visit. Unfortunately, Agrippa himself died only a year later in 12 BCE.

A conflict with the Arabs occurred in 10/9 BCE. A group of men from the Trachonitis had traditionally supplemented their living by brigandage. When Herod took over rule, he put a stop to this so that they had to earn their living only by farming. This caused problems because the soil was poor and probably also because it went against their traditional way of life. While Herod was in Rome, a revolt developed which was quickly put down, but about forty of the leaders fled to Arabia. Although the Arab king was Obodas II, the real power behind the throne was a high noble named Syllaeus who gave refuge to the brigands and allowed them to raid Judaea and Coele-Syria from a secure base in Arabian territory.[16] Herod killed many of their relatives in Trachonitis, but they continued to attack his territory. To add insult to injury, Syllaeus reneged on repayment of a loan from Herod. Part of the problem may have been personal since Syllaeus had once been betrothed to Herod's sister, Salome, but the marriage had been prevented by Herod's insistence that Syllaeus adopt Jewish practices (including circumcision).

Herod was unable to stop the raiders by normal methods and finally lost patience. He consulted with the Roman governors of Syria, Saturninus, and Volumnius. They produced an agreement that each party—Herod and Syllaeus—would return the other's subjects who had taken refuge in his territory; also Syllaeus would repay the debt to Herod in thirty days. The result was that many of the brigands were found to be in Arab territory (in spite of Syllaeus's denials). But then Syllaeus went away to Rome without meeting his responsibilities according to the agreement.

The local Roman officials gave Herod permission to take unilateral action. They supported him by agreeing that he would be justified in taking his army into Arabia. Herod was wholly successful, destroying the brigand stronghold and capturing the defenders; however, he was then attacked by an Arab force and killed its commander in defending himself. To prevent future recurrences of brigand activity, Herod settled a military colony of three thousand Idumaeans in Trachonitis. He reported what he had done to the Roman authorities in Phoenicia, and they judged that he had acted reasonably.

Yet Herod was on thin ice here. A friendly king of Rome, such as he was, had pretty much a free hand in his own kingdom and could do more or less what he wanted. But it was a quite different matter when it came to external matters, such as acting against a fellow client king, and in spite of getting local Roman approval Herod had overstepped his authority—an exceptional misjudgment on his part. Furthermore, on the diplomatic front he was outwitted by Syllaeus who was in Rome during Herod's military actions. Putting his case before Augustus, Syllaeus was able to convince him against Herod to the extent that the emperor wrote him a harsh letter and would not even receive a delegation to give his side of the event. This was serious for Herod who had enjoyed Augustus's support and friendship up to this point.

Syllaeus wrote back to Arabia and told them not to hand over the brigands, so they continued their plundering of Herod's territory. They even attacked the military colony of Idumaeans that he had settled in the area. Herod could do nothing but endure the raids and the general humiliation for a period of time. Then, Obodas died and Aretas IV took the throne. This action irritated Augustus whose permission should normally have been sought; on the other hand, it meant that the Arabian camp was now divided. Aretas sent a golden crown and many gifts to Caesar, but he also wrote a letter with a number of accusations against Syllaeus; however, Augustus ignored the accusations and returned the gifts. Now, however, Herod tried once more to present his case to Caesar by sending his assistant Nicolaus of Damascus. This time Augustus heard Herod's case and was persuaded by Nicolaus who not only was an effective orator but also had the support of Aretas's faction in his charges against Syllaeus (e.g., some incriminating letters).

Augustus was sorry for the breach that had been created with Herod and became reconciled with him. Syllaeus, on the other hand, he condemned to death. Augustus was apparently even of a mind to add Arabia to Herod's domain but decided against it because of Herod's age and family troubles. So he confirmed Aretas on the Arabian throne, though rebuking him for his boldness in taking the kingship without first receiving Roman confirmation.

In spite of Augustus's death sentence on Syllaeus, he seems to have had freedom of movement. He had returned home to the kingdom of Aretas and had apparently been involved in the assassination of several prominent Nabataeans but had not paid his debt to Herod as directed by Augustus. He returned to Rome at the same time as Herod's son Antipater was there (c. 6 BCE). Antipater brought charges against him, including a plot to have Herod killed by an Arab servant. Herod arrested the servant and two other Arabs in his household who confirmed the plot. Saturninus, the governor of Syria, sent them to Rome for trial. Also, Syllaeus was apparently responsible for the failure of a Roman expedition against south Arabia, as well as other offenses. As a result, he was beheaded in Rome.

Family Quarrels and the Death of Herod

Most of the rest of the narrative about Herod is taken up with the rather unedifying spectacle of family jealousies, hates, intrigues, and executions. The problem for the historian is how to evaluate this information. It is not the stuff of history but of soap opera. This does not mean that many of the events described did not take place, or even did not occur much as recounted, but woven into the narrative is continual moral evaluation, assigning of motives, descriptions of states of mind, and general pseudo-psychoanalysis. To take this at face value—as many writers unfortunately have done—is to treat the stuff of romance as if it were straightforward history. Most of the data can be summarized briefly and lose nothing by conciseness.

The first episode in this business has already been recounted: the execution of Herod's wife Mariamme (the granddaughter of Hyrcanus) and his brother-in-law Joseph (see p. 252). Yet if we trust Josephus's rather overheated narratives, Herod seems to have been very much in love with Mariamme—or at least obsessed with her. If she had been more astute, she undoubtedly could have manipulated him and got him to do whatever she wanted. Instead, she played on her "royal" Hasmonaean connections and openly showed her contempt for and hatred of her husband. He would get angry but would then cool off and seek reconciliation, but she apparently refused to bend.

Perhaps more fatefully her contempt also extended to the females in Herod's family, his mother, Cypros, and his sister, Salome. Mariamme's attitude toward them was eventually a significant cause of her downfall, because his mother and sister worked on Herod to make him jealous and suspicious until he finally acted against Mariamme despite his feelings for her. But once she had been executed, Herod seems to have had a mental breakdown. At times he seemed to think she was still alive; he went off by himself in the wilderness under the pretext of hunting. This evident mental distress after a time led to his contracting a serious illness and seeming to be on his deathbed. Mariamme's mother Alexandra, not for the first time scheming against Herod, tried to get control of two key fortresses. But those in charge of the fortresses were loyal friends of Herod and informed the convalescing king of her scheme and he had her put to death.

Intrigues among Herod's relatives also eventually led to the execution of Alexander and Aristobulus, Mariamme's two sons by Herod.[17] They seem to have been very resentful over the treatment of their mother, though Josephus also claims they had a "desire to get control/have power." The accounts in Josephus generally take the view that they were just rather bitter young men who spoke up when it would have been wiser to keep their mouths shut, rather than guilty of actual plots against Herod's life. A further complication was the question of their half-brother, Antipater, son of Herod's first wife, Doris. Rivalry was inevitable between the potential heirs, especially since Antipater was the firstborn even though not considered heir after Herod married Mariamme. He seems to have been the main instigator of charges, rumors, and lies against the sons of Mariamme. He was now declared Herod's successor, both publicly and in Herod's will.

Events first came to a head about 12 BCE when Herod finally took Alexander to be accused before Augustus in Rome. The outcome of this was a reconciliation of Herod and his son(s) through the good offices of Augustus. The accused sons and Antipater returned with him to Jerusalem, where all three were declared joint heirs. The reports of plottings against Herod did not cease, however. Josephus ascribes much of this to Antipater who was allegedly skillful in manipulating matters to implicate Alexander and Aristobulus.

At one point, three of Herod's personal servants who were eunuchs admitted to relations with Alexander. Only under torture did they reveal supposed intimate talk which suggested that he would be ruling instead of Herod before long. After further inquiries, Herod had Alexander imprisoned. Eventually, a letter of Alexander's was found (though he claimed it was a forgery) in which he planned to assassinate Herod and flee to the fortress Alexandrium. Herod imprisoned Alexander and Aristobulus and wrote to Augustus for his permission to punish them.

Augustus gave Herod permission to deal with his sons according to the nature of their crimes but advised him to examine them before a council. Herod assembled such a council of Roman governors and officials, and appropriate family members—150 in all. Although several argued for a more lenient punishment, the council as a whole voted for the death penalty. It was now about 6 BCE. Herod had his sons put to death by strangling at Sebaste and then buried in Alexandrium. Yet he was concerned to take care of the widows and orphans. He sent Glaphyra back to her father but also gave her back her dowry. He then arranged marriages for Aristobulus's widow Bernice and for a number of the children of Alexander and Aristobulus.

Antipater is alleged to be not only the chief plotter against the two sons of Mariamme but also against Herod himself. Herod seems to have turned management of his court over to Antipater because of confidence in him. Herod's brother Pheroras found it useful to pay homage to Antipater, but he was undone by his devotion to his wife. She, with her mother and some other women, were alleged to have formed a cabal against Herod. They insulted two of Herod's daughters and aroused the animosity of Herod's sister, Salome.

One of the incidents that aroused suspicions about Pheroras's wife concerned the Pharisees. Herod required an oath of loyalty to Caesar and also to himself. The six thousand Pharisees refused to swear this oath, and Herod punished them with a fine. Pheroras's wife paid the fine on their behalf, however, after which some of them predicted that the throne would be taken from Herod and come to her and her husband. This by itself was bad enough, but Herod found that Pharisees had made inroads into his court and corrupted certain individuals. Apparently promises of offspring and rulership were made to a certain eunuch (cf. Isaiah 56:3-5). Herod put him and some other courtiers to death but also some of the Pharisees.

Finally, Herod convened an assembly of friends and accused Pheroras's wife before them. Pheroras was called on to divorce her but refused. Eventually, Herod banished both Pheroras and his wife. Pheroras went back to his tetrarchy in Transjordan where he became ill and died. But some of his men claimed that he had been poisoned by his wife. Inquiry confirmed this to Herod who confronted her. She tried to commit suicide, failed, and revealed all under the promise of immunity. She admitted the poisoning but her testimony and that of various servants also implicated Antipater and his mother Doris.

The question was what to do about Antipater who had now been accused from a variety of quarters. In spite of his previous confidence in Antipater, Herod now believed the various charges against him. Antipater had traveled to Rome a while before to meet Augustus and also to take Herod's will, which designated him as Herod's successor. He had made himself useful in prosecuting Syllaeus at this time but had also been instrumental in getting letters sent to Herod that accused some of Herod's other sons (Archelaus and Philip, who were later to be tetrarchs after Herod's death) of plotting against him. Antipater did not suspect anything, having heard nothing of the accusations against him, but returned home after seven months in Rome. Herod assembled a council of friends and relatives. Although Antipater defended himself, Herod had him bound and imprisoned, and both he and the Roman legate of Syria wrote to Caesar. Shortly afterward, letters as if from Salome were found to have been forged by a servant of Empress Livia, at Antipater's instigation, a further charge against him. Herod altered his will making Herod Antipas his heir (and passing over both Archelaus and Philip).

Josephus goes on at great length about the accusations and Herod's morbid fears that put him in a state of mental torture. He then has Herod on a campaign of suspicion and torture against all, even his long-term and intimate friends. How much of this we can believe is a question. One of the main reasons for being cautious is that Herod's other actions and decisions during this time seem rational and reasonable.

By this time, it was late 5 or early 4 BCE. Herod became seriously ill and steadily got worse. The description of it is horrendous but part or even much of this could be a literary concoction; certainly, one should be careful in taking the description at face value to the point of some modern medics trying to determine the precise affliction as has sometimes been done. Herod's attempts to find a cure or even relief from the pain were unsuccessful.

On one occasion, rumor had it that Herod was dead. There were two religious teachers by the name of Matthias, son of Sepphoraeus, and Judas, son of Margalus or Margalothus. These two men are called "sophists" or "teachers" and are said to have a reputation of being experts in the ancestral laws and their interpretation. They are often identified as Pharisees, but knowledge of and expertise in the laws was hardly limited to Pharisees, and Josephus has no hesitation in identifying people as Pharisees. *The fact that he does not do so here is a good indication that they were not Pharisees.* No images had been allowed in the refurbished temple; however, over the main gate of the temple Herod had had a golden eagle erected as a votive offering (but perhaps also in homage to Augustus specifically or the Romans generally).

Matthias and Judas instigated their disciples to tear it down. An officer of the king (and of the temple?) brought a large force and arrested about forty of those who did not flee, fearing that more extensive riot or even revolt was in the making. When brought before the king, they defended themselves with the statement that they were serving God and death would be only a passage to a greater reward. Herod had them taken to the amphitheater in Jericho and charged them with sacrilege. He had the teachers and chief culprits burned alive and the rest executed. Josephus claims an eclipse of the moon took place on the day of the executions, which was probably seen as a divine sign by some (perhaps even Josephus himself).

Herod's health continued to deteriorate. He went to the warm baths at Callirrhoe near Jericho, but this did not help. Josephus claims he gathered notable Jews from all over his kingdom into the hippodrome. He is then alleged to have instructed Salome and her husband Alexas to have them shot down by the soldiers when he died, so that the nation would mourn at his death—even if not for him! This is another damning anecdote whose credibility is often taken at face value in spite of serious doubts about its truth. First, no such slaughter in fact took place, which immediately casts doubt on Herod's supposed intent. Second, it has been plausibly argued that as a precaution against a revolt against his successor, he assembled the elite among the Judaeans in Jericho as hostages, though no harm came to them nor was meant to. After his death an anti-Herodian but false tradition then developed that he was planning to kill them.

More credible is the statement that letters arrived from Caesar, giving Herod the authority to banish or execute Antipater. The sentence was not carried out immediately. Then Herod tried to kill himself with a paring knife but was prevented; however, a rumor went around the palace that he was dead. Antipater heard this and tried to bribe his jailor to release him. When this was reported to the king, he had Antipater summarily executed and buried in the fortress Hyrcania. Herod then changed his will one last time, giving kingship of Judaea to Archelaus (son of his wife Malthace), a tetrarchy of Galilee and Peraea to Antipas (also son of Malthace), and a tetrarchy of Trachonitis, Batanaea, and Paneas to Philip (son of his wife Cleopatra). Five days after Antipater's execution, Herod died. This was shortly before Passover, in late March or early April 4 BCE. He had reigned thirty-seven years since he was made king in 40 BCE, and thirty-four years since the execution of Antigonus in 37 BCE.

Assessment of Herod's Reign

Herod has been such a notorious and controversial figure that any evaluation of him is very difficult. In assessing his reign, one must ask: Against what standard? Other Graeco-Roman despots? The Hasmonaean rulers? Some golden ideal of kingship? Ancient views of Herod were generally negative and have gone a long way toward shaping the modern ones. Perhaps one of the views that has had most influence in later Christian history is the labeling of Herod as "slaughterer of the innocents." *But it is clear that no "slaughter of the innocents," in fact, took place.*

According to Matthew 2:16-18, Herod asked the Magi to tell him where the baby born king of the Jews was located. When they disregarded this, he is alleged to have slain all males who were two years old and under in Bethlehem. Some histories and commentaries still take this at face value, but it is clearly a piece of legend, probably Christian, though whether it was meant consciously to be anti-Herodian or only to demonstrate opposition to the Christ child seems uncertain. The legendary nature of the story is indicated by (a) the whole context of men from the east following a star; (b) the idea that Herod would have taken such a mission to find a newborn "king of the Jews" seriously; (c) the fact that Josephus, who has many distinctly anti-Herodian passages and even outright slander, says nothing about such a thing; for example, the criticisms of Herod by a Jewish delegation before Augustus do not use such an illustration even though it would have been an unparalleled example of cruelty and despotic rule;[18] (d) the fact that no other writer mentions what would surely be a point of interest to any Roman reader about this Jewish king; (e) the common motifs found in a variety of accounts of the birth of important religious figures.

Modern scholarship has presented a mixed picture of Herod. To its credit there are those who have attempted to provide a positive side of the man, but probably the majority of accounts that one reads tend to take much of Josephus's assessment at face value. The autocratic and even tyrannical aspect of Herod's rule can be taken for granted, but such is the nature of one-ruler states throughout history. *It was just as true of the Hasmonaeans as of Herod*. The question is to what extent his rule should be characterized by the negative aspects and to what extent these are countered by other, more positive features. Several recent studies have attempted a revision of the negative view. The studies would hardly be classified as a whitewash, but they do go a long way toward pointing out the positive features of Herod's rule, which not only helped the Jews in many ways during his lifetime but paved the way for his descendants (such as Agrippa I and Agrippa II) to act as advocates for the Jewish people on a number of occasions.

Herod's problems within his own family occasioned the anecdote which ascribed to Augustus the observation, "I would rather be Herod's pig (Greek *hus*) than his son (Greek *huios*)" (Macrobius, *Saturnalia* 2.4.11). The ascription does not have to be correct to illustrate the tradition about Herod preserved in the non-Jewish world. But even if Augustus said such a thing, it could hardly have escaped his notice that he experienced similar troubles within his own family during his long reign. Thus, Herod was not the only capable ruler whose competence changed remarkably as he passed from the throne room into the living quarters.

The point must be made that Herod considered himself a Jew, by all indications. It is common to label him a "foreigner" because some of his enemies are alleged to have identified him as "a half-Jew."[19] But apart from the question of descent, which is not an easy one (see pp. 246–7), he regarded himself—and was regarded by the Romans—as a Jew. Notice the following considerations:

- His respect for Jewish customs. There are no examples of blatant disregard for them. Even in the midst of a tirade about the introduction of "foreign" and "unlawful" customs by Herod, Josephus has then to admit that this did not really involve breach of Jewish law, as Herod himself demonstrated to his critics.[20]
- His coins with no human portraits on them.
- His requirement that a Nabataean convert to Jewish practices before he would marry his sister Salome to him.[21]
- The amount of money and interest he put into the Jerusalem temple.
- His fortress at Herodium, considered by many to have had a synagogue in it. Even his most private quarters at Masada used no offensive motifs in the skillful decorations.
- His speech about building the temple refers to the ancient Israelites as "*our* fathers."[22]

Unfortunately, the tendency is to judge Herod by an artificial standard because of prejudice against him. For example, no one seems to question the Jewish identity of Agrippa I, yet all his coins outside Judaea have human portraits on them, whereas his grandfather Herod did not use human images on any of his coins. Why should the one be ignored for his benefit, while the positive side of the other is dismissed as mere politics? It has sometimes been alleged that Herod would not have been considered Jewish because his mother was not Jewish; however, this appears to be anachronistic since the matrilineal descent of Jewishness is a later development (in Herod's own time Jews seem to have regarded the ethnicity of the father the important factor).

On the economic side, it is often stated that he burdened his subjects with taxes. All rulers taxed their subjects, and this would always weigh more heavily on the poor and politically impotent, but there is no indication that Herod's taxes were greater than those of previous or later rulers. On the contrary, his rule probably relieved some of the burden since the indication is that the taxes placed by the Romans were crushing in the period between 63 and 40 BCE when Herod took over, partly because of war expenses and partly because a good deal of territory was taken away from Jewish control. Under Herod most of this was regained; in addition, he opened new land to cultivation in certain desolate regions. Also, it now seems clear that Herod did not pay regular tribute to the Romans (despite the assertion in many standard works that he did). Friendly kings were considered independent, and the Romans did not try to collect taxes in their realm.

Further on the financial side, he was able to diffuse criticism at various times by acts of generosity to his own people: He prevented the soldiers from looting Jerusalem when it fell in 37 BCE by rewarding them from his own pocket (p. 250). He relieved a famine at considerable expense to himself, which silenced his critics and established general good will even among many who were formerly hostile (p. 256). In honor of his meeting with the Roman noble Agrippa, he rescinded a quarter of the taxes for the year 12 BCE, which is said to have won over his immediate audience of a large assembly consisting of the people of Jerusalem and many from the country (p. 257). The enormous expenses of the temple building supposedly came from his own coffers (p. 255). Much of the cost of his other building projects may have come from the traditional half-shekel offering required of all Jews, including those in the diaspora.

Yet one would hardly call him a benevolent monarch: at least, he was no better than other rulers of the time—though also no worse. He governed as absolute ruler and could be completely ruthless in suppressing opposition.[23] At the beginning of his rule he made the Sanhedrin completely impotent—as far as any check on his activities is concerned—by executing a number of its members and cowing the rest.[24] Although it was subordinate to the Hasmonaean rulers, it does seem to have functioned as a form of restraint on them, whereas it ceased to have any political function under Herod, as far as can be determined. But was he worse than other monarchs of the time—whether local potentates, monarchs of sizable kingdoms, or even the Roman emperor himself? Indeed, was he really any different from the Hasmonaean rulers before him? Remember the concerted opposition especially to Alexander Jannaeus—but also to John Hyrcanus and others.

It is very difficult to judge public opinion in the days before scientific polls. There were certainly those who detested him and his rule, but to extrapolate beyond that to say that he was unpopular with the Jews—as is so often done—is simply to go beyond our knowledge. We do not know that he was any more unpopular than, for example, Alexander Jannaeus. Some who were critical changed their minds, at least temporarily, according to statements in Josephus. Certain groups and individuals evidently benefited from his rule, not least the temple priests and personnel. Much of his contribution to building projects elsewhere in the Hellenistic world could have been primarily egocentric but would still help the reputation of the Jews who were often being criticized for their unusual customs at this time. And he was able to intercede on behalf of certain Jewish communities with the Roman authorities on occasion.[25] In fact, he seems to have had a special concern for Jews in the diaspora. Any judgment on Herod must consider the positive as well as the negative.

There lies the final question: Whatever his faults, was Herod's rule not preferable to that of direct Roman rule? Some thought not at the time of his death, but what about in the decades after 6 CE when Judaea was once again a Roman province? *The Jewish delegation that asked Augustus for direct Roman rule may have rued their words when Judaea did actually revert to being a Roman province once again!*

13
The First Century CE: Roman and Herodian Rule to the Fall of Jerusalem

The death of Herod the Great left a large gap in leadership and a period of great uncertainty for Judaea. As will be clear to readers of this chapter, the next century was a traumatic time for the Jews as a whole, especially those living in Judaea itself. It was also a momentous century with a number of beginnings and other major events. It saw of course the origins of Christianity but also a seminal time for what became the rabbinic movement. It also brought the permanent destruction of the Jerusalem temple and a war that affected all Jews, not just those in Judaea itself.

The problematic reign of Archelaus was followed by a period of Judaea as once more a Roman province was governed by Roman prefects. A brief period as once again a kingdom under Agrippa I was then followed by a renewed rule by Roman procurators, ending with a Jewish revolt and the Roman siege of Jerusalem. The events packed into the seventy-five years from the death of Herod to the fall of Masada were astounding.

Governed by Tetrarchs

After the death of Herod, Archelaus saw himself as the likely successor to his father's rule. He headed for Rome, leaving in charge Sabinus, Caesar's procurator in Syria. Others also went to Rome, including Salome and Herod Antipas; only Philip evidently remained at home to look after the country. Augustus convened a council of leading Romans and listened to the case of each side. He then made no decision but decided to think the matter over.

But while they were waiting, a letter arrived, reporting a revolt in Judaea. The Roman official Sabinus who remained in Jerusalem ended up stirring up the populous by planning to take over the various fortresses under his control and seek for Herod's treasures (evidently for the purpose of personal gain!). When Pentecost came, many from Galilee, Idumaea, and Transjordan joined Judaeans with the intent of confronting Sabinus. He sent soldiers to attack the Jews, and the fight encompassed portions of the temple, allowing the Romans to loot the temple treasury; Sabinus is said to have taken 400 talents for himself.

A serious revolt was now gaining momentum. The rebels were besieging Sabinus. Most of the Jewish royal troops had joined the rebels, but an elite group of three thousand from Samaria remained loyal. In Idumaea, about two thousand of Herod's veterans also rebelled, and rebel leaders arose in several different places. In a number of cases these leaders were evidently messianic pretenders, claiming royalty and a divine mission. Judas, the son of the Brigand Chief Ezechias (executed by Herod), organized a group in Galilee and aimed for royalty. A king's slave, Simon, took the crown and made raids in the countryside in Peraea, though his group was stopped by the Sebastenians, and he was killed. A shepherd named Athrogaeus also took on the persona of a king, and with his four brothers led effective raids against not only Romans and those loyal to the king but apparently all fellow Jews as well.

The Roman governor in Syria at the time was Varus. When he received word about the revolt, he set out with two legions and collected additional auxiliaries on the way. By the time Varus reached Jerusalem, the besieging rebels had fled, while the remaining Jews in the city asserted to him that they were innocent bystanders, caught up in the fighting. Sabinus, meanwhile, had slipped off to the coast, apparently not wanting to be confronted by Varus about his thoroughly botched military operation. The Romans went through the countryside, hunting out rebels. Varus was willing to pardon most of the rebels but sent the leaders to Rome, where Augustus in turn pardoned many of them but not those of Herod's relatives who had joined the rebels. Varus left a legion in Jerusalem and returned to Antioch.

Philip was now also in Rome, sent there on the advice of Varus. Also arriving to present a case before Augustus was a delegation of fifty Jews. Supported by a large number of local Jews from Rome itself, they were allowed to petition against Herod's rule and Archelaus as his successor, asking for Judaea to be joined to Syria and no longer have a king—in other words, to revert to being part of a Roman province. August deliberated for several days, then essentially followed Herod's final will:

Archelaus to have half the territory (including Judaea, Samaria, and Idumaea);

Antipas, the tetrarchy of Galilee and Peraea; and

Philip, the tetrarchy of Trachonitis, Batanaea, and Auranitis.

Caesar also rejected the 1,500 talents left to him by Herod and had it distributed among the king's offspring, keeping only a few inexpensive ornaments as mementos of the king.

At this point, it should be noted that *the name "Herod" is often mistakenly added to the names of Herod the Great's successors*. Antipas had the name Herod, as apparently did Archelaus; however, Philip did not, nor did Agrippa I and Agrippa II. Thus, it is *erroneous to talk of "Herod Agrippa" or to refer to the tetrarch as "Herod Philip"* (there was a Herod Philip but he was a different person from the tetrarch).

Archelaus was ethnarch, not king, though the possibility of the title in future was dangled before him by the emperor. Of the Archelaus's reign, we know little. Archelaus divorced his wife Mariamme and married Glaphyra, the daughter of the king of Cappadocia and widow of his brother Alexander (who had been executed by his father Herod). He was her third husband. Josephus recounts two dreams.

His wife had a dream in which her former husband Alexander stood beside her and accused her of taking her brother as a husband, contrary to Jewish law, and said he was reclaiming her. She supposedly died two days later.

Another dream Archelaus had himself, in which he saw nine (or ten) ears of grain being eaten by oxen. He requested interpretations, and various meanings were suggested to him. But an Essene by the name of Simon interpreted it "correctly": the nine ears of grain were years and the oxen a revolution. So he would reign nine years and die after changes to his affairs. Indeed, in either his ninth or tenth year—the year 6 CE—Augustus deposed him and exiled him to Vienna in Gaul. The precise reason for this removal from office is not given; however, he is said to have treated both Jews and Samaritans "brutally": both Jews and Samaritans complained of his "brutality" or "cruelty and tyranny." This was allegedly because he did not forget "old feuds," but the precise circumstances are not given; however, the Roman historian Dio (55.27.6) says his brothers accused him. Continuing as tetrarchs were Herod Antipas, over Galilee, and Philip over parts further north (mostly non-Jews) for several more decades (see below, pp. 275–6).

Judaea a Roman Province (6–41 CE)

After the deposition of Archelaus, Judaea was turned into a Roman "province." The Roman governors of Judaea are variously referred to as "governor," "prefect," and "procurator." Because of these titles in the sources, it was long assumed that the governors of Judaea held the title of procurator, until an inscription with the name of Pilate was discovered that labeled him "prefect." It now appears that the governor of Judaea held both the offices of "prefect" and "procurator," at least in the period after 44 CE, which would in part explain the confusion of terminology. Yet it is also clear that the governor of Judaea was subordinate to the imperial legate of Syria in Damascus, who could intervene at any point in the actions of the Judaean governor. We know this happened on a number of occasions. Therefore, it was administratively a part of Syria but nevertheless had its own identity and autonomy—up to a point.

The imperial provinces, under direct rule of the emperor, included some of the more turbulent regions and required troops to be stationed in the vicinity. Judaea was one of these regions, with a governor of the equestrian order, who could be closely monitored by the higher-ranking legate of the main province (in this case, Syria). Now that Judaea was a province rather than a "client kingdom," it was now necessary to set up the Roman administrative system in place of the Herodian one. This meant that taxation had to be done directly by the Romans rather than being in the hands of the "friendly king" or ethnarch (under Herod the Judaeans had paid no direct tax to the Romans).

Coponius, a Roman knight, was delegated as governor of Judaea. His boss was the proconsul Quirinius (having served as consul in Rome in 12 BCE) who had been sent as imperial legate to govern Syria. The first task of Quirinius and Coponius was to conduct a registration or census of persons and property. It is important to be aware that Luke 2:1-5 makes several mistakes about this process. He says—

wrongly—first, that it happened under Herod the Great; second, that the census covered the whole Roman Empire (there was never any census of the whole Roman Empire); and third, that one had to go to one's birthplace to be registered—when registration was logically made at the place where one lived and owned property. This change of administration and the census of Judaea took place in the thirty-seventh year after Actium or 6 CE.[1]

Some have tried to salvage Luke's account by claiming an earlier census during Herod's reign. That this census was an unprecedented action, though, is quite clear because of the Jewish reaction. Many were very upset by it, though most acceded to the arguments of the high priest that there was nothing to do but submit; however, Judas the Galilean, from Gamala, and Saddok the Pharisee led some sort of rebellion. Their view was that only God was their master, and to accept the assessment of the census was to submit to slavery. They called on Judaeans to try for independence. The reference made to Judas in Acts 5:37 suggests a brief revolt, but this information may not be reliable since the movement survived him, contrary to the statement put into the mouth of Gamaliel.

In any case, this was the origin of what Josephus calls "the Fourth Philosophy," alongside the sects of Pharisees, Sadducees, and Essenes. In a highly rhetorical passage, Josephus talks of "great hordes of brigands" and "men of the highest standing assassinated," with the seeds of future troubles planted.[2] This sounds grossly exaggerated, until one sees that he was probably referring to the subsequent period of sixty years during which various members of the Fourth Philosophy and others carried out assassinations and otherwise fomented trouble. He suggests that the main result was to inspire zeal in the young men through the actions of Judas and Saddok.

The next twenty years are almost completely a blank. We do know who the governors were, however, with some indication of events in Judaea during their office:

Coponius (6–c. 9 CE): Josephus claims that some Samaritans polluted the temple during the Passover festival by scattering human bones in it.

Marcus Ambivulus (c. 9–12 CE): during his governorship, Herod's sister Salome died.

Annius Rufus (c. 12–15 CE): in 14 CE Augustus died at age seventy-seven, after a reign of fifty-seven years.

Valerius Gratus (c. 15–26 CE): he had a long term of office, eleven years, and made several changes of high priest.

Pontius Pilate (26–36 CE).

Marcellus (36–41 CE).

The only other significant event recorded by Josephus in this period was not about the Jews in Palestine but in Rome: the expulsion of the non-citizen Jewish residents in 19 CE, probably for complex reasons. These can be recounted briefly. Josephus (*Ant.* 18.3.5 §§81–4) is our most detailed source, but the incident is also mentioned by Roman writers.[3] The background to this was a scandal in connection with the Isis temple in Rome.[4] A young Roman knight wished to seduce a noble married lady named Paulina and offered her a large cash inducement, which she refused. Since she was a devotee of Isis, however, the priests of the temple were bribed to tell her that the god Anubis wished to spend the night with her. She acceded to the invitation, though it was the rather earthly Roman knight rather than the god who took advantage of the situation. When it was later revealed to her that she had been tricked, her husband complained to Tiberius who had the priests crucified, the temple destroyed, and the equestrian exiled.

About the same time, another Roman matron named Fulvia had converted to Judaism. She followed a Judaean confidential trickster who had fled prosecution in Palestine but was pretending to be an interpreter of the Mosaic law, in association with three other miscreants. They cheated her out of purple cloth and gold that she thought were going to the temple in Jerusalem. When she found out that she was being tricked, her husband went to Tiberius, and the emperor expelled the entire Jewish community from Rome. The consuls of the time also sent four thousand of the young Jewish men to Sardinia for military duties (a large number refused, for reasons of religious observance, and were punished). Josephus (*Ant.* 18.3.5 §§84) concludes that the whole community suffered because of the actions of these four rogue Jews.

Yet the incident was probably much more complicated than that. It must first be recognized that Josephus's account of the Roman matron Fulvia looks suspiciously like a romantic folktale and needs to be treated cautiously. Yet in a fragment often dated to 19 CE, the Roman historian Cassius Dio (57.18.5a) refers to a considerable number of converts to Judaism among the Roman upper class, with active proselytizing by some Jews in Rome.

Further, in spite of his distaste for foreign cults, Tiberius's actions regarding Jews is generally anything but hostile. For example, after the death of Sejanus (who is said to have been anti-Jewish [p. 273]), Tiberius issued instructions to provincial governors to reassure the Jews in their provinces (Philo, *Gaius* 159–61).

We should note that 19 CE saw the expulsion of Egyptians (including Isis worshipers) as well as Jews, and the illness and death of the well-liked Roman noble Germanicus, nephew of Tiberius, all in the same year. The popular rumor was that Germanicus's death had been due to poison and various magical arts. It seems that the Romans generally felt they were under the shadow of divine wrath that needed appeasing. A public show of commitment to the ancestral divinities by expelling practitioners of "alien rites" would seem most appropriate.[5]

Contrary to the impression made by Josephus's rhetoric, only police measures were taken against noncitizens with the military conscription of about four thousand young men. But Jews who were Roman citizens were in no way affected. Yes, the Jewish community in Rome, along with other groups, were made scapegoats, but it seems to have suffered no major continuing effects, only some temporary inconvenience. As so often in the past, Jews gradually returned to the city over time, without incident. The community continued to grow and flourish.

We now come to the governorship of Pontius Pilate (26–36 CE). His was a long term in office, probably because it was the custom of Tiberius to leave provincial governors in their posts rather than replace them frequently as had been the former custom. According to the accounts of both Josephus and Philo (Tacitus is the only Roman author to mention Pilate [*Ann.* 15.44.3]), Pilate's governorship was not a particularly successful one. Three specific incidents have come down to us in the sources.

The first was probably at the beginning of his governorship when he moved the army from Caesarea (the Roman capital of Judaea) to winter quarters in Jerusalem.[6] Although previous Roman governors and military commanders had respected the Jewish objection to the imperial images, Pilate sent his men in with standards that had medallions bearing the image of Caesar attached to them. It was done at night and was thus a *fait accompli* by the time the Jews realized what had happened. Their entreaties and protests did no good, even though they journeyed to Caesarea to make them. Finally, Pilate had a large group of soldiers suddenly surround the importuning Jews and threatened them with death if they did not give up their demonstration. Their response was to lie down and expose their necks to the swords. This so astonished Pilate that he relented and removed the standards back to Caesarea.

Then, Philo (*Gaium* 299–305), ostensibly quoting a letter of Agrippa I, refers to an episode in which some shields dedicated on behalf of Tiberius were introduced into Herod's palace in Jerusalem by Pilate. Even though there was only a dedication inscription and no images on the shields, the Jews were affronted and complained bitterly, with four Herodians (probably Herod Antipas, Philip, and two other sons of Herod the Great) representing their case to the provincial administration. Pilate backed down and allowed them to petition Tiberius, who ordered Pilate to remove the standards to a temple dedicated to the emperor outside Jewish territory. The problem is why the aniconic shields should have caused such offense to the Jews. The most likely explanation is this: Pilate was no doubt trying to honor the emperor, as would any provincial governor of the time. He assumed that the lack of images on the shields would make them acceptable to the Jews. What he did not know, though, was that Jews would be aware of the *dedication* of the shields as a part of the emperor cult and raised objections because of this.

The third incident involved a protest that was not so peacefully settled. Pilate took money from the temple treasury (money donated for sacrifices, labeled *Korban*) to build an aqueduct to bring water to Jerusalem.[7] This was probably a further addition to the existing aqueduct system dating from the Hellenistic period. The aqueduct construction may well have been finished when the incident occurred. The large crowd that assembled, while Pilate was in Jerusalem presiding over the governor's tribunal, raised an angry protest. This time Pilate directed his soldiers, carrying cudgels instead of swords, to mix with the crowd disguised in Jewish garments. At a signal from Pilate, they attacked the unarmed crowd so that many Jews were allegedly killed by being trampled in the panic, as well as injured.

On the surface, this sounds like another provocation by an insensitive governor, and many modern commentators have assumed the fault lay with Pilate. But a closer look shows it to be more complicated than it first appears. First, the project had no particular benefit for Pilate but would have been an important contribution to the infrastructure of the city and thus the province. There seems no personal reason for Pilate to carry out this except as a service to the population of Jerusalem. Second, it would have needed the cooperation, and indeed the approval, of the city and/or temple authorities. Thus, those who protested were actually protesting against the Jewish leadership of the city and province and were doing so long after they knew about the construction. Finally, the Roman central government would have contributed funds toward the project.

Whether temple funds could have been used is not so clear, but according to later rabbinic sources, excess funds could be so used (*M. Šeqal.* 4.2).[8] It is also important to note that Josephus (*Ant.* 18.3.2 §62) refers to the protest as a "revolt," which would have been seen as a serious matter to be dealt with ruthlessly from the Roman point of view. Thus, it is possible that the aqueduct was only a pretext for some to stir up the masses and instigate an uprising. This might also explain why the Jews did not take their complaint to Pilate's superiors in the Roman hierarchy, such as the imperial legate in Syria.

Part of the problem might lie with Tiberius's protégé and confident Sejanus, who is alleged to have pursued an anti-Jewish policy.[9] From this it has often been concluded that Pilate's actions in Palestine reflected the same anti-Jewish attitude since, it is also argued, he was a protégé of Sejanus. But this argument has been opposed, for several reasons. There is no evidence of a direct connection between Pilate and Sejanus. Since Tiberius's policy was to keep the provinces quiet, it is unlikely that Pilate would have deliberately stirred up trouble, however powerful a patron he might have had. In any case, Tiberius came to believe the allegations secretly made against Sejanus. The emperor sent a message to the Senate toward the end of 31 BCE, which denounced the unsuspecting Sejanus who was actually present when it was read out publicly. Any supposed influence of Sejanus on Pilate would have abruptly ended at that point!

Pilate went too far, apparently, in quelling a disturbance among the Samaritans. A man promised to show the Samaritans the sacred vessels of the tabernacle which according to Samaritan tradition had been buried in a hidden site on Mount Gerizim. A large group gathered in a nearby village with the intention of climbing Mount Gerizim for the demonstration at a particular time. Whether it was anything more than a peaceful gathering is not indicated, but Pilate evidently interpreted it as the prelude to a revolt. Before they could make the ascent of the mountain, they were intercepted by Roman troops who killed and captured many and scattered the rest.

The main leaders and most prominent individuals among those captured were executed at Pilate's orders. This was too much for the Samaritan council who protested to Vitellius the governor of Syria. Exactly why he accepted their accusations is not clear, but he did so, sending Marcellus to take over in Judaea and ordering Pilate to return to Rome and appear for trial before Tiberius. This Pilate did, but Tiberius had died (March 37 CE) by the time he reached Rome. At this point our information ceases and we know nothing further about Pilate's fate or subsequent activities.

"The Jesus Movement": Another Jewish Sect

Pilate is of course important for the history of early Christianity, since the New Testament gospels give Pilate a prominent role in the trial and execution of Jesus. In recent years, scholars have come to recognize that the "Jesus movement" began as just another sect or movement within Judaism, with followers accepting the basic tenets of Judaism and its teachings but acknowledging the teachings of Jesus. There seem to have been different views about Jesus's messiahship and his relationship to the Father, with some apparently seeing him as an enlightened and inspired teacher but nothing beyond this, while others viewed him as no less than the "son of God" and in some way divine. We need to keep in mind that the New Testament gives only a particular perspective on Jesus, while there were groups who evidently believed somewhat differently.

The earliest source to mention Jesus is Josephus, writing about 90 CE.[10] He refers to the trial and execution of James the brother of Jesus by the Sanhedrin.[11] There is also the so-called *Testamonium Flavianum*.[12] This is also a passage in Josephus that mentions Jesus, but its authenticity is highly disputed since it states that "this was the Christ," a very unlikely statement for Josephus. Also, some versions do not have this or give a different wording. Keep in mind that Josephus's writings were preserved in Christian circles, not Jewish. Although the Christians seem to have preserved his writings intact, there may be one or two passages that have been altered in transmission. The explanation that Josephus referred to Jesus but that pious scribes Christianized the passage, as it were, is widely accepted. That is, most modern scholars think that Josephus did indeed mention Jesus but that Christian scribes added words and phrases to give a more favorable opinion.

Although some passages of the New Testament suggest that Christianity was separate from Judaism from the beginning, this does not appear to be the case. We must keep in mind that the New Testament was written over most of the first century and parts of it even into the second century CE, with a good many writings late in this period. The question then becomes one that is very current in contemporary debate: "the parting of the ways." Most now recognize that this was not a single event but a process, and that various streams of Judaism and Christianity parted in different ways and times. Also, whereas we all accept that Judaism and Christianity share a great deal, there is also no question that Christianity became a separate religion. There was definitely a "parting of the ways," at least by the time that Christianity became the religion of the Roman Empire under Constantine the Great. Each religion came to have its own identity, however much they may have shared.

The question of identity was an important one from the Roman government's point of view, however, because Christianity was often proscribed and persecuted. On the other hand, however much some Romans despised Judaism, Jewish religion was never made illegal or suffered official persecution. Individual Jews or Jewish groups may have been pursued by the Roman authorities if they were seen as breaking the law, especially if they were thought to be rebelling, but like most religions, Judaism was tolerated under Roman law. Christianity, on the contrary, was often outlawed until the time of Constantine.

Judaea Becomes Once More a Kingdom

The legate of Syria Vitellius had installed Marcellus as governor of Judaea in place of Pilate in 36 CE. Marcellus seems to have been the last Roman governor of the province during this period of direct Roman rule. As far as we know, Marcellus continued as governor until Judaea became a kingdom again under Agrippa I's rule, in 41 CE. The entanglement of Jewish events with Roman history becomes very apparent at this point. To set the background, the reigns of Herod Antipas and Philip must be described and the rise of Caligula to emperor delineated. The two tetrarchs over portions of Herod the Great's old kingdom are important for Jewish history. Both were builders of noted cities, both made their way into the pages of the New Testament as well as into Josephus, and both were succeeded by Agrippa I as king.

Philip (4 BC–34 CE) the tetrarch ruled over territories to the north and east of Galilee: Trachonitis, Auranitis, Gaulanitis, Batanaea, and Paneas. Only a few Jews lived in his realm. He rebuilt the ancient city of Paneas at the sources of the Jordan, which had been named for its shrine to the god Pan. Founded about 3/2 BCE, he named it after Augustus, but it became known as Caesarea-Philippi to distinguish it from the city built by his father. His mode of government was said to be "moderate" and "trouble-free." Certainly, no unrest is recorded during his rule, which seems to have been a peaceful one. We also know that he was married to Salome, daughter of Herodias, though this was possibly after the incident relating to John the Baptist (see below). Philip died in the twentieth year of Tiberius (i.e., probably the winter of 33/34 BCE); he had reigned thirty-seven years. Tiberius put his territory under the administration of the Syrian legate, but the income was kept in trust. A few years later in 37 CE, it was given to Agrippa I.

Herod Antipas (4 BCE–39 CE) was appointed tetrarch over Galilee and Peraea in Herod's will and subsequently confirmed by Augustus. The jewel in the crown of his building projects was Tiberias, which he built as a new foundation on the western shores of the Sea of Galilee. Josephus (*Ant.* 18.2.3 §37) states that the inhabitants were a "rabble," including many poor people and some who were compelled to settle there by force. The reason for settling many undesirables there was allegedly that the city was built on a site of tombs, which many Jews would have avoided. Tiberias was capital of Galilee much of the time, creating a rivalry between it and the city of Sepphoris.

Antipas's marriage to Herodias is supposed to have led to one of the most notorious episodes of his life. He arrested John the Baptist and had him executed. According to Mark 6:14-28 (//Matt. 14:1-12//Luke 9:7-9, followed by countless stories, sermons, passion plays, dramas, operas, movies, etc.), the arrest was because of John's criticism for taking his brother's wife, and the execution was at the instigation of Herodias and her daughter Salome, as usually interpreted. Josephus (*Ant.* 18.5.2 §§116–19), however, knows nothing of this story of the dancing girl. Instead, he ascribes the arrest and execution to Antipas's fear that John's popularity with the crowds might lead to sedition.

When we compare the two accounts, the version in Mark is suspect. For one thing, it states that Herodias had been the wife of Philip, whereas it was her daughter Salome who was the wife of Philip (the Tetrarch). For another, the account of the plot by Herodias and Salome to have John beheaded looks very much like a folktale without historical foundation (Antipas's promise to her of half his kingdom is an absurdity). Finally, according to Josephus, John was imprisoned and executed in Machaerus in Transjordan, whereas the banquet scene of Mark 6 seems to be set in Galilee (cf. Mark 6:21).

Enormous amounts of New Testament scholarship have been expended on Antipas's alleged part in the trial of Jesus. This is found only in Luke 23:6-12, which has Pilate send Jesus to Antipas for trial, when he hears that Jesus is a Galilean. It might be asked why Pilate would allow someone else to try an accused person when he had clear jurisdiction. It is indeed unlikely that he felt the need for guidance by Antipas, as has sometimes been suggested, especially since neither Pilate nor his assistants were present at the appearance before Antipas.[13] But Pilate might have done it as a courtesy, or it might even have seemed to him a good way to rid himself of a troubling situation. In any event, Antipas is said to have returned Jesus to Pilate. This account is not intrinsically improbable since Antipas frequently came to Jerusalem for the festivals, and Pilate's action is easily explained.

We now come to the important Jewish noble Agrippa I. Agrippa's full name was evidently Marcus Julius Agrippa, judging from the name of his son Agrippa II; thus, the common reference to him as "Herod Agrippa" (based on Acts 12:1) is incorrect. No early sources refer to him as Herod, and it is not clear that Luke knew he was writing about Agrippa I in Acts 12:1. He possibly confused Agrippa I with his brother, Herod of Chalcis. Whatever the reason for the confusion, the name "Herod Agrippa" for Agrippa I should be deleted from scholarly usage forthwith.

The son of the executed Aristobulus and grandson of Herod the Great, he was heir of both the Hasmonaeans and the Herodians. He was educated in Rome and lived there many years. He married Cypros, granddaughter of Herod's brother Phasael. After the death of his mother, however, he proceeded to go through a king's ransom in personal living and especially in expensive gifts for his Roman friends. His poverty became such that he felt it necessary to go away from Rome, even then leaving behind large debts. For a time, he lived in Malatha in Idumaea and was even said to be contemplating suicide. Agrippa's sister Herodias was married to Herod Antipas. At the request of Agrippa's wife to Herodias, Antipas allowed him to live for a time in Tiberias, holding the office of market commissioner, but the two brothers-in-law soon fell out.

Next, he sponged off the proconsul Flaccus, the governor of Syria, until they broke up their friendship (over a bribe paid to Agrippa to influence Flaccus's judgment in a boundary dispute between Damascus and Sidon). Agrippa's brother Aristobulus, who was also on poor terms with him, was partly the cause of this breakup. But it left Agrippa destitute, and he decided to return to Italy, managing to borrow money from his mother's freedman (a freed slave who continued to work for his mistress). However, Herenius Capito the procurator of Jamnia heard about Agrippa's presence and sent soldiers to gain payment for the large amount he owed the Roman treasury (50 talents or 300,000 drachmas). Fortunately, he managed to slip away to Alexandria, where he tried to borrow more money from Alexander the alabarch (the brother of the Jewish theologian and philosopher Philo—p. 278). The latter refused to lend money to Agrippa but agreed to do so to his wife (200,000 drachmas). Agrippa sailed on to Italy, and she returned to Judaea with their children.

Arriving back in Italy, Agrippa was well received by Tiberius and stayed with him and his family on the island of Capri. Things went fairly smoothly for a time, though Agrippa's failure to pay his large debt to the imperial treasury caused a problem until he managed to borrow a further sum from Antonia (sister-in-law of

Tiberius and mother of Germanicus and Claudia) to pay it off. Agrippa kept in with Antonia by borrowing 1 million drachmas (nearly 167 talents) from a Samaritan freedman of Tiberius and repaying her. He developed a close association with Antonia's grandson (and Tiberius's grandnephew) Caligula at this time, which was to stand him in good stead later. However, it first cost him his freedom and may have endangered his life: he made a careless remark to Caligula that he hoped he would soon be ruling in place of Tiberius, which was overheard by a freedman. Later, when this freedman was accused of theft by Agrippa, he told all to the emperor. Agrippa was put in prison where he remained for six months until Tiberius's death.

In the end Agrippa owed a good deal to Caligula. Gaius Caligula (37–41 CE) is probably one of the hardest of the emperors to evaluate dispassionately, perhaps rivaled only by Nero. Son of the popular Germanicus and grandnephew of Tiberius, he spent much of his youth living in army camps, from which he got the nickname *caligula* ("little boots"). Caligula's accession was greeted with enthusiasm because of the idiosyncrasy of Tiberius's last years and the senatorial prejudice against him. The idyllic promise of the initial part of Caligula's reign (perhaps the first year or two) was overtaken by a drastic change, about the time the emperor was struck by an illness, which (according to Philo, *Gaius* 14–22) marked the beginning of strange behavior. Opposition developed, including a conspiracy among officers in the army of the Rhine that had to be suppressed. Like Tiberius, Caligula was accused of a reign of terror against all sorts of alleged conspirators but also as a means of gaining money by confiscating the estates of those executed. Finally, it all came to a head in January 41 when he was assassinated by some of his own Praetorian guard while on his way to lunch from the theater.

When Caligula was declared emperor, he released Agrippa as soon as Tiberius's funeral had taken place and then turned over the former tetrarchy of Philip and also another tetrarchy in the Lebanon to him, granting him the title of king (37 CE). With Caligula's permission, Agrippa left Rome for his kingdom in 38 CE, sailing through Alexandria. Agrippa's fortunes had now considerably changed and, rather than an importunate of his brother-in-law Herod Antipas, he was now his superior in having the title king whereas the other was only tetrarch.

Herod Antipas's downfall was primarily due to ambition, according to Josephus (*Ant.* 18.7.1-2 §§240–56) who mainly blames his wife. The irony is that the chief instigator was his brother-in-law Agrippa I whom he had earlier helped. Antipas seems not to have been overly put out by this change of fortunes with regard to his brother-in-law. But supposedly Herodias resented this and egged on Antipas to seek the title king from Caligula. Antipas is supposed to have resisted her urgings for a time but eventually sailed with her to Rome to appear before the emperor. Agrippa learned of what Antipas intended and wrote letters of accusation to Caligula that arrived about the time that Antipas did. One charge was that Antipas was stockpiling arms, with the intention of revolt in league with the Parthians. This accusation of planning a revolt is very unlikely, but when Antipas admitted to possessing the arms, Caligula took it as evidence of the conspiracy and removed him from office. Herodias, as the sister of Agrippa, was to be spared, but she refused to abandon her husband: the result was that she was also exiled with Antipas, and their possessions all went to Agrippa. Agrippa now ruled over a considerable kingdom but not the core province of Judaea.

Philo's Mission from the Alexandrian Jews to Caligula

It was at this time that matters relating to the Jews of Alexandria came to a head. The Jewish community in Alexandria had a long history. We have no indication of any major difficulties between the Jewish community and the Greek inhabitants of the city until Roman times when a sea change in attitude seems to have taken place. The Greek citizens of Alexandria had an enormous pride in their ancestry and tradition, and the Roman takeover was a great blow to their prestige and self-esteem. Further, the leaders of Judaea (Hyrcanus II and Antipater) had contributed a good deal to the conquest of Egypt and had gained the Roman good will as a result. These facts seem to have been the foundation of anti-Judaism in Egypt which increased as time went by.

Two treatises of the Jewish theologian and philosopher Philo (c. 20 BCE to c. 50 CE) describe some important events relating to the Jewish community in Alexandria (*In Flaccum* and *Legatio ad Gaium*). Around the year 38 CE, the Greeks of the city were stirred up against the Jews, at least in part over the question of citizenship. The main instigators were the gymnasiarchs Isidorus and Lampo, the two leaders of the gymnasium that formed the center of Greek cultural life in the city. These put great pressure on the Roman governor Flaccus to remove the special privileges of the Jews. Most of the Jews were not citizens of the city, but they nevertheless enjoyed special privileges that citizens also had, such as exemption from the *laographia* or poll tax.

The visit of Agrippa I on his way to take up his kingship over the old domain of Philip apparently exacerbated the situation. Behind Agrippa's visit may lie some hidden but important dealings.[14] Caligula had a difficult political problem that he wanted Agrippa to help resolve. This was why Agrippa had been granted praetorian honors (those of a magistrate)—conferred by the Senate but no doubt at Caligula's request—the first foreigner to receive them. Normally, a governor of a province received a *mandata*, an official confirmation of and instructions in the office, but Flaccus had been in Egypt when his term under Tiberius had expired at Tiberius's death, and he had not come back to Rome to receive reappointment by Caligula. Agrippa was on his way to Judaea but journeyed via Alexandria, therefore, in an official capacity, to deliver the emperor's *mandata* to Flaccus. He also outranked Flaccus, as was necessary to carry out this task.

Agrippa was welcomed in Alexandria, particularly by the Jewish community. But during his visit he was publicly mocked by some of the local people. After Agrippa left, anti-Jewish measures were put in force, which led to riots against the Jewish community. As governor, Flaccus was responsible for keeping order, and he had been put in a bad situation by the riots. His concern was to gain back control and establish peace before his Roman masters took sterner measures against the city and against him personally. Yet Flaccus was evidently not even-handed in his necessary actions. His measures seem to have been heavily weighted toward a crackdown on the Jewish community: synagogues were closed (and in some cases destroyed), and all Jews were ghetto-ized by being forced to live in the *Delta* area (one of the five districts) of the city. Order was restored only when Flaccus was sent to stand trial before Caligula and replaced by Pollio in October 38 CE.

The peace established was a very uneasy one. Permission was granted for the Jewish community to send an embassy to Caligula, as well as for the Greek community to do likewise. Philo headed the delegation which left in the winter of 38/39 CE (or 39/40). Caligula only heard the mission while inspecting a building project and—according to Philo—was not very attentive to their concerns. Instead, he abruptly asked them why Jews did not eat pork.[15] Even though Philo claims the delegation was in danger of their lives, his highly partisan account shows that Caligula actually dismissed the Jews with the simple statement, "They seem to me to be not wicked but unfortunate people, lacking understanding in not believing that I was allotted the nature of a god" (*Gaius* 367), hardly the actions of a mad tyrant and rabid hater of the Jews. In any event, the mission was overtaken by Caligula's plans to place his statue in the temple (see next section).

But the story continues into the reign of the emperor Claudius. On Caligula's death, the Jews seem to have been the ones who rioted in Alexandria this time.[16] A report was sent to Claudius by the prefect. Finally, the delegations led by Philo and his Alexandrian opponents were heard by Claudius who maintained the traditional Roman policy of religious and ethnic tolerance. His decree reaffirmed Jews' rights to practice their religion without hindrance, but he did not give permission for them to live outside the *Delta* quarter, as some of them had done before 38 CE. He also warned them about agitating for citizenship or other special privileges. Peace was restored but much of the bitterness no doubt remained and was passed on to future generations until it culminated in the revolts under Trajan (chapter 14, pp. 327–8).

The somewhat legendary *Acta Alexandrinorum* suggest that two of the Alexandrian delegates, the gymnasiarchs Isidorus and Lampo, were tried before Claudius and perhaps even executed by him.[17] Agrippa (probably Agrippa I but possibly Agrippa II) was also brought in as an accuser in the trial by the *Acta Isidori* (part of the *Acta Alexandrinorum*). The *Acts* had Agrippa debate with the Alexandrian gymnasiarch Isidorus before Claudius, but it is doubtful that Agrippa appeared at Isidorus's trial. What offense the Alexandrians had committed and when the trial took place are not clear. Isidorus seems to have had a part in various hearings before the emperor.

Caligula's Attempt to Place His Statue in the Temple

We now come to one of the most important threats to the Jewish religion in ancient history—exceeded only by the anti-Judaism of Antiochus IV Epiphanes (discussed in chapter 11). This was the intent of Emperor Caligula to set up his statue in the temple at Jerusalem. Agrippa evidently played a key role in the episode. Without doubt this was a monumental occurrence in the religious history of Judah. The consequences might have been as violent as the Maccabaean revolt, though it is unlikely that the Jews would have won this time. Luckily, Agrippa was instrumental in getting Caligula's plans canceled. There is more than one version of the story,[18] but the events that seem the most historically trustworthy are the following:

An incident occurred in Jamnia (Yavneh), which had a mixed population of Jews and others. The Roman policy was one of religious tolerance to Judaism, but they expected this tolerance to be reciprocated. When local Jews tore down an altar dedicated to the emperor, they committed a serious breach not only against the local freedom of worship but against Roman authority. Their actions could be taken as an act of open rebellion. In retaliation for this, Caligula proposed setting up his own statue in the Jerusalem temple.[19] That Caligula responded with punishment is only to be expected. The Jews (including Philo and Josephus) found it convenient to interpret this as a sign of personal animosity against themselves, but this was only propaganda. The one thing still unexplained is why Caligula chose the idea of a statue in the Jerusalem temple as punishment for the Jewish political act in Jamnia, but one plausible reason is this: Judaism was tolerated on condition that it had no political implications. If the Judaeans thought otherwise, then the Temple would have to be destroyed or Romanized; this is the likely rationale of Gaius' decision.[20]

Petronius, the Syrian legate, was sent from Antioch with the task of carrying out the order. He was met at Ptolemais by a large crowd of Jews who begged him to desist. He went to Tiberias and held an audience with the people and the leading figures of the nation, attempting to show them the senselessness of defiance since they could not win against Rome. But the people proved intractable, and Petronius saw that they were not sowing the fields even though it was time to do so. Apparently, Agrippa I's brother Aristobulus, with others of the family and leaders of the Jewish community, petitioned Petronius to write to Caligula, which he did despite the personal risk.

Although Caligula was furious at this, he is alleged to have given a respectful reply which nevertheless urged Petronius to go on with the project. This would have been in 40 CE. According to one version of the story, Agrippa is depicted as giving a banquet for Caligula, which pleased the latter greatly by its sumptuousness. He offered to grant Agrippa anything he wanted, and Agrippa asked that the placing of the statue be canceled. Another version says that when Agrippa heard of the plan, he simply wrote a long rhetorical letter, at risk to his own life, which Caligula reluctantly heeded. In any case, because of his regard for Agrippa, Caligula wrote to Petronius canceling his plans. Both Philo and Josephus make Petronius a hero of the situation, who did all he could to avoid carrying out Caligula's order.

The Rest of Agrippa I's Reign

After Caligula's assassination, we know of the appointment of Claudius as emperor, unlikely as it would have seemed to many at the time. The various sources agree that Agrippa was involved in the negotiations by which Claudius became recognized as emperor. The problem is his precise role since the two fullest accounts (in Josephus) give somewhat different pictures. Regardless of the precise details, Agrippa was the mediator between Claudius and the Senate. Evidently, he showed his skill at manipulation in helping to bring the senators around to accepting Claudius despite their claimed great reluctance.

Claudius promoted Agrippa to consul in rank, and his brother Herod to that of a praetor. Both were allowed to attend the Senate and thank Claudius in Greek. Claudius not only confirmed the territories given to Agrippa by Caligula but added to them Judaea and Samaria. Thus, Agrippa's kingdom was even more extensive than that of his grandfather Herod the Great. To Agrippa's brother Herod was given the kingdom of Chalcis, located in the Lebanon valley.

With such honors, Agrippa returned to Jerusalem. Even in his brief reign over Judah, Agrippa was able to accomplish some important projects. He began his reign over Judaea by the first of many acts of piety toward the temple, which included the dedication of his golden chain (given to him by Caligula and modeled on the iron chain that held him when imprisoned by Tiberius), placing it over the temple treasury. Soon after his return to Palestine, Agrippa showed himself useful to the Jews once again when a statue of the emperor was placed in the synagogue of Dora by a certain young hothead. Agrippa took the matter up with Petronius, who was still the Syrian governor at that time. Petronius wrote a letter to the leaders of Dora, denouncing the incident, calling for the instigators to be brought to trial, and reminding them of Claudius's edicts about the rights of Jews to practice their religion.

On another occasion, however, he did not show the greatest of sagacity. After presiding over games in Berytus (Beirut), he entertained his brother and four other client-kings in Tiberias. From the evidence given, the intent was only social and completely innocuous. By this time Petronius had been replaced by Vibius Marsus as Syrian governor. Marsus arrived during the celebrations and received a cordial reception from Agrippa and the others, but he was suspicious and ordered the individual rulers back to their kingdoms. This caused a breach between him and Agrippa; on the other hand, it was the task of a Roman governor to anticipate trouble, and it was not particularly surprising that he viewed the situation with a critical eye.

It was evidently Agrippa's aim to demonstrate that, despite his past and continuing somewhat spend-thrift ways, he could leave behind a rather happier memory than that of his grandfather. Agrippa strengthened the walls of Jerusalem at its most vulnerable point, the north side, in the Bezetha district. Marsus the governor of Syria reported the building to Claudius who stopped it as potentially revolutionary.[21] To conciliate the inhabitants of Jerusalem, Agrippa remitted the house tax, which was apparently collected to pay for maintaining the city walls. Like his grandfather, he also supported building projects in the broader Hellenistic world, such as a theater and amphitheater in Berytus.

Most of the other information about Agrippa is anecdotal, though it does tend to confirm the positive picture and evaluation of Josephus. One story is that he was accused by a religious leader of entering the temple area while in a state of ritual impurity. Agrippa's diplomatic response was sufficient not only to show the baselessness of the charge but also to win the man over. This is used to illustrate not only Agrippa's lack of arrogance about his position but also his devotion to the Jewish religion, for he was said to be scrupulous in offering sacrifice and otherwise adhering to traditional practice. Interestingly, this does not seem to have prevented his using his image on his coins outside the Jewish areas of his kingdom and even setting up statues of his daughters.[22] However, unlike his grandfather, Herod the Great, Agrippa has had more of a popular image in ancient and modern literature—which seems rather unfair to Herod the Great.

His relationship to the Pharisees is not a simple one. It is often alleged that he favored them and attempted to cultivate good relations with them. But others have opposed this and instead argued that it was the Sadducees who flourished under Agrippa, though this was in spite of rather than because of the king's policies.[23] The difficulty with both hypotheses is that they depend heavily on rabbinic traditions and certain questionable assumptions about the Pharisees and Sadducees.[24] Rabbinic traditions are indeed positive about Agrippa I, but he was generally popular with his Jewish subjects as a whole: this may imply nothing about the Pharisees in particular. On the other hand, there is some evidence of growing priestly power after the death of Agrippa, which might bear on the Sadducee hypothesis.

Agrippa's reign has been made notorious in Christian tradition in the Acts of the Apostles: Acts 12:1-19 makes him a persecutor of the Christians who killed James the brother of John and arrested Peter, though the latter was supposedly rescued from harm in a completely miraculous way. The question of the persecution of Christians cannot be confirmed, though several recent studies accept it as having a basis in fact.[25] There may be a genuine memory here even if it also suits the theological motives of Luke. However, any arrests are likely to have been limited to a few individuals (only Peter and the sons of Zebedee are named), and to have been for reasons of "affairs of state." A general persecution of the church is not indicated and improbable at this time.

We have two accounts of the death of Agrippa, both of which have a number of points in common. According to Josephus (*Ant.* 19.8.2 §§343–50), he appeared in a special garment at games in Caesarea, was proclaimed by the crowds as more than human, and became immediately seized with an illness from which he died in a few days. Acts 12:20-23 gives a similar account, similar enough to suggest a common origin, though a number of the details differ. It states that Agrippa was acclaimed as a god by the people of Tyre and Sidon and was smitten by God for allowing it, being eaten by worms and dying a painful death. One immediately recognizes both literary and theological stereotypes in this account. Like so many accounts of death in literary sources, one should be cautious about seeing something akin to a medical diagnosis. Whatever the cause and whether or not worms had a hand in it, Agrippa was only fifty-four at his death. He had reigned seven years, four of them over the territories of Philip and Antipas under Caligula and three over the rest of Herod the Great's kingdom under Claudius. In many ways, this was probably a high point for Judaeans as a nation in the first century, not to be repeated for many centuries.

The Emperor Claudius and the Jews

Claudius (41–54 CE) was a most unlikely candidate for emperor. The uncle of Caligula, he had been pointedly kept out of public office and affairs by both Augustus and Tiberius, for reasons that are still somewhat obscure (though he is said to have had certain mannerisms which made him the object of ridicule). Nevertheless, he possessed a mind of unusual ability and had a reign which was positive on the whole, despite the contemporary Roman tradition which was often hostile. To distance himself from Caligula he made every attempt to reconcile the Senate with his rule and show it respect in the manner of Augustus.

Where Claudius was both strongest and most controversial was in his development of the administrative structure. His wife Agrippina seems to have had a positive effect on Claudius's development of the administrative system, changing it from a repressive dictatorship to a relatively benign partnership between ruler and ruled. His motive seems chiefly to have been concerned with efficiency, but the result was a considerable step toward centralization as well as the embryonic stage of a later bureaucracy. He put trusted freedmen in charge of several departments, which became the basis of a sort of civil service. Both the removal of the traditional senatorial privilege and the use of freedmen were an affront to the upper classes and aroused their opposition. From a historical perspective, it led to putting further power into the hands of the emperor and upsetting the balance that Augustus's settlements had tried to achieve.

The pro-senatorial tradition paints Claudius as the puppet of his wives and freedmen. While perhaps to some extent true for the last few years of his reign, it has still been exaggerated, but he proved unlucky in his choice of wives. His first wife, Messalina, has become infamous as a model of promiscuousness, and Claudius finally had to order her execution. His second wife was his niece Agrippina, the mother of Nero. She is alleged to have been a woman of such cruelty and malice as to destroy anyone whom she disliked. When Claudius died suddenly in 54, the story had it that she had given him a dish of poisonous mushrooms, a common charge in the case of unexplained deaths.

One important event under Claudius was an expulsion of Jews from Rome.[26] The reasons for it remain controversial among specialists. This has points in common with earlier expulsions, especially that under Tiberius (pp. 270–1 above). Some have referred to Dio 57.18.5a (often dated to 19 CE), which refers to proselytizing activity on the part of Jews. There are problems with this interpretation, however. It seems unlikely that there would have been major attempts at conversion in Rome at this time, and the Senate's response looks like having been against a rather more serious situation.

One possible cause was problems with the grain supply to inhabitants of Rome, which had supposedly occasioned riots at times during the years 18 to 23 CE (cf. Tacitus, *Ann.* 2.87; 4.6).[27] The Jews, many being poverty stricken, had been part of the unrest: the Jews were viewed as a group that posed a potential threat of staging a revolt, which drew attention because of their numbers. This led to the Senate taking drastic measures. Yet such supposed unrest on the part of the Jews is not cited in the accounts of the expulsions by Tacitus, Cassius Dio, or Suetonius.

A few years later, Claudius had gone out of his way to promote traditional Roman religion and had banned astrologers and magicians. Since he had defended Jewish rights in Alexandria, the Jews were not singled out. Yet they were part of a larger grouping that included foreign cults in general, but, like an earlier expulsion in 139 BCE, it was a routine "crackdown" to appease public opinion and had few long-term consequences.[28]

To summarize one argument (which affects the expulsions under both Tiberius and Claudius), the cause was an interplay between Roman values, especially those relating to Roman religion, and "foreign" (in Roman eyes) cults.[29] Foreign cults were often associated with magic, especially as used to curse or destroy opponents, and divination. Concerns about magical practice were expressed under Claudius. Nevertheless, Romans did not seem to be apprehensive of Jewish numbers or power, and the Jewish communities remained mainly undisturbed.

With regard to the expulsion under Claudius, however, the question remains as to whether there were two or only one, and when one or both occurred.[30] An alleged expulsion in 41 CE seems to be based on a misunderstanding. Cassius Dio (60.6.6) does not refer to an expulsion but to an edict in 41 CE that deprived the Jews of the right of assembly because of their large numbers; he makes the specific point that they were not expelled. Suetonius (*Claud.* 25.4) refers to an undated expulsion caused by riots over "Chrestus." This is usually taken to be a reference to Christians, but that would of necessity suggest a late date for the event since a conflict between Jews and Christians was not likely to have occurred as early as 41. There are problems with taking this "Chrestus" (a common name at the time) as meaning Christians, and Suetonius's precise meaning is still debated.

Acts 18:2 suggests that sometime around 50 CE Aquila and Priscilla had only recently been forced to leave Rome with other Jews. The patristic writer Orosius (7.6.15-16) quotes Josephus to the effect that an expulsion took place in 49 CE. Orosius is not always reliable, however, and it seems unlikely that he had access to a passage of Josephus lost to us, since no such statement is found in our extant text of Josephus. A date toward the end of Claudius's reign seems more reasonable in the light of Suetonius's comment (though we are not bound by the date 49). An argument that seems most convincing to me concludes that in 41 CE Claudius forbade the Jews to hold assemblies because of disturbances; later at an indeterminate date (49 CE?), when the disturbances continued, some (by no means all) Jews were expelled from Rome, among whom were Aquila and Priscilla.[31] The most secure data thus point to a single expulsion toward the end of Claudius's reign, though more than one expulsion is by no means out of the question.

Agrippa II (44–94? CE)

The aftermath of Agrippa I's death was unpleasant for the Judaeans in that Judah came once more under Roman administration. But it was made doubly unpleasant by the reaction of some of the non-Jewish population in the areas ruled by Agrippa. Some in Caesarea and Sebaste, instead of mourning, held celebrations and toasted Agrippa's death, offering sacrifices to the underworld deity Charon. Some of the local soldiers also took the statues of the king's daughters and exhibited them in brothels in pornographic displays. Claudius dispatched Fadus to govern Judaea.

Agrippa's son, named Marcus Julius Agrippa (apparently like his father), was only seventeen at his father's death. Since Agrippa II had been educated in Rome, he was well known to Claudius who might have given him his father's kingdom. Supposedly, Claudius was minded to do this but was dissuaded by his freedmen advisors, and Judaea instead came once more under a Roman governor.[32] The reason for this recommendation from Claudius's advisors was allegedly the boy's young age; however, this explanation sounds like one given for public consumption since a regency could easily have been established until Agrippa II was older. There may have been more grave reasons for the decision. The most likely explanation is that this fits with the emperor's general policy of integrating vassal kingdoms into the Empire as provinces at that time.

Although not ruling over Judaea itself, Agrippa was able to serve the Judaeans and other Jews on a number of occasions. For example, a dispute arose with the Roman governor Fadus over control of the high priestly garments. The special robes worn at the three major festivals plus the Day of Atonement had traditionally been kept in a special building by the temple. Under Herod the Great, this building was turned into the Antonia, and he took control of the vestments as a means of potential control of his Jewish subjects. After the exile of Archelaus, control of the vestments was assumed by the Romans. However, when Vitellius was well received by the people of Jerusalem at one point, he consented to place the sacred garments under their own authority as a reciprocal gesture and even requested Tiberius's approval for this.[33] Fadus now ordered the garments to be turned over to Roman custody again, but the Jews petitioned Claudius who granted their request that they remain under Judaean control, at Agrippa's instigation.

Agrippa came to rule over several territories. When in 48 or 49 CE Herod of Chalcis died, Claudius presented the kingdom to him. He also inherited some new privileges previously held by Herod of Chalcis. The right to appoint the high priest had been taken by the Romans in 6 BCE but was restored to Agrippa I when he became king in 37 CE. After Agrippa I's death, it was given to Herod of Calchis. Now Agrippa II received the right of appointing the high priests as well as authority over the temple, even though Agrippa did not rule over any actual Judaean territory.[34] In 53 CE, Claudius assigned a new kingdom to the Jewish king, the tetrarchy of his Great-Uncle Philip (Trachonitis, Batanaea, Gaulanitis) plus Abila, the former kingdom of Lysanias, and the former tetrarchy of Varus; however, rulership of Chalcis was taken away. When Nero came to office, he gave Agrippa the Galilean cities of Tiberias and Tarichaea as well as Julias in the Peraea.

Close to Agrippa for much of his life was his sister Berenice. She had originally married Marcus Julius Alexander, the son of the Alexandrian alabarch named Alexander, in about 43/44. When he died, she was given by her father to Herod of Chalcis who himself died in 48. She now lived for a lengthy period with her brother, but a rumor began to circulate that she was having an incestuous affair with him. As a result of this she married Polemo, king of Cilicia, who agreed to be circumcised. This marriage lasted only a short time before she left him. She bore the title of queen, as is known not only from Josephus but also from an inscription from Athens that actually uses the title "great queen."[35] (On her relationship with the future emperor Titus, see p. 318 below.)

Both Agrippa and Berenice are mentioned together in Acts 24:24–26:32 in conjunction with Festus the governor of Judaea. Although this may constitute original source material, there are reasons to be cautious.[36] The actual number of data that can be checked are few, and the narrative significantly omits Berenice's title of queen. The omission of any address to her or the use of her title in the direct address of Acts 25:24 would have been an inexcusable breech of protocol. Whether Luke had any information at this point beyond a few commonplaces about the two is very questionable.

One episode (before the 66–70 war) involved a wall of the temple.[37] When in Jerusalem, Agrippa liked to watch the proceedings within the temple court from a part of his palace which overlooked the area while dining. Certain "eminent men" of Jerusalem were incensed by this and erected a wall that blocked Agrippa's view. Since it also blocked the view of the Roman sentries posted to watch the crowds during the festivals, both Agrippa and the Roman procurator Festus objected; however, the latter allowed the high priest Ishmael to lead a delegation to Nero over the matter. Nero's mistress Poppaea, although probably not a Jewish convert as sometimes alleged, interceded on behalf of the Jews, and Nero allowed the wall to remain in place.

Yet Agrippa was not without influence and even authority in Jerusalem. This is illustrated by a petition to Agrippa from the Levites who were temple singers.[38] They requested permission to wear linen robes like the priests. The king obtained the support of the Sanhedrin and allowed the singers to wear linen robes; also, to learn the hymns by heart (no explanation is given, though presumably they had previously been sung from written sheets of some sort). In another incident, work on the temple was completed about this time, leaving an alleged eighteen thousand builders out of work.[39] They appealed to the king to be allowed to raise the height of the east portico. Agrippa concluded that this was impractical, but he approved employing the temple workmen to pave the city with white stone. The king also enlarged Caesarea Philippi and renamed it Neronias in honor of the emperor. He spent money on the Phoenician city of Berytus (Beirut), building a theater and providing for sculptures to adorn the city. Josephus claims that he was hated by his subjects because of spending money on a "foreign" city.

When the 66–70 war with Rome began, Agrippa attempted to dissuade the Jews from carrying through with their folly, but both he and Berenice were forced to withdraw from the city by the people. His part in the Judaean revolt and his later life is described below (pp. 294–308, 316).

The Emperor Nero (54–68 CE)

Nero has been so vilified in the tradition that it is difficult to give a sober assessment of his rule. In this sense he is very much like Caligula, though ruling longer and less bizarrely. Undoubtedly, many of the criticisms of him are well justified as even recent epigraphic finds indicate, but it is still difficult to penetrate the rumor, slander, and anecdote to the historical Nero. His reign began well and was very positive for about the first five years. Although his tutor the philosopher Seneca should perhaps receive credit for much of this, it is by no means certain that Nero's own thinking was not an important part of the success. However, even these years were clouded by his relationship with his mother, "Agrippina the younger." She had worked hard to secure the throne for him, then attempted to dominate him even to the point of co-rulership; eventually he ordered her execution—supposedly in secret, but of course it got out—and Nero forever entered history as a matricide (cf. *SibOr* 4.121).

Nero had divorced his wife Octavia in 62 and married his long-time mistress Poppaea Sabina (30–65 CE). She has been of considerable interest because of her peripheral place in Jewish history, but the idea that she was a Jewish convert is unlikely. It was about the time of his marriage to Poppaea that Nero began to reign badly. He was also blamed for the great fire of Rome in the summer of 64, though this is probably slander caused by his evident enthusiasm for rebuilding the city according to his own plans.

The final few years were turbulent ones, in which Nero devoted more and more time to his "artistic" pursuits. These years were also marked by the outbreak of a number of real or imagined conspiracies in which some prominent individuals were forced to end their lives by suicide (e.g., the philosopher Seneca, and Nero's own arbiter of taste, the writer Petronius, author of the *Satyricon*). In 68 CE, his Gallic Governor Vindex revolted. Although Vindex was defeated, Galba the governor in Spain declared himself a legate of "the Senate and people of Rome"—that is, emperor—rather than of Nero. Instead of taking firm action, Nero dithered until finally one of the Praetorian prefects fled and the other bribed the Praetorian Guard to declare for Galba. Nero was proclaimed an enemy by the Senate and took his own life in June 68 at the age of thirty.

Judaea Once Again a Roman Province (44–66 CE)

The history of Judaea between the death of Agrippa I and the Great War with Rome was taken up with Judaea once more a Roman province with Roman governors. Some were capable, but many were not and had periods of office that only exacerbated an unhappy experience of the Jews under Roman rule. There is the question of whether making Judaea once more a province would create problems for Roman rule of the area. The silence in Josephus's account suggests the change from kingdom to province was a smooth and unproblematic one. The Roman administrative apparatus from 41 CE may still have remained by and large in place even when Agrippa I became king.

Thus, the kingdom was divided up, as had happened in 6 CE, with the core area becoming once more the Roman province of Judaea but under the ultimate control of the Syrian governor. The two decades following Agrippa I's death is the story of Judaea's gradual slide into war. The phrase "spiral of violence" has sometimes been used for the situation during this period, but there is a certain aptness about its succinct summary of the situation. The equestrian governors of Judaea varied in their actions and competence, but the overall effect was detrimental to Judaean–Roman relations.

Cuspius Fadus (44–46? CE)

The first procurator Cuspius Fadus arrived to find a major problem of brigandage that was especially affecting Idumaea and the Nabataeans, but he captured Tholomaeus one of the chief leaders and executed him. His actions are supposed to have purged the province of brigands. It was also during his office that Theudas arose as a prophet and claimed to be able to divide the Jordan River as had happened in the time of Joshua, attracting a significant following. He was killed and his followers scattered by a contingent of cavalry before he had a chance to attempt the deed. This is probably the same individual mentioned in Acts 5:36; if so, he has been misdated by the author of Acts to a much earlier time than he actually lived. Another incident, concerning the high priest's vestments, has already been discussed (p. 285 above). Finally, Josephus mentions Fadus's success in keeping the peace by respecting local customs, though he mentions that both Fadus and Tiberius Alexander did this.[40]

Tiberius Julius Alexander (46?–48 CE)

Tiberius Julius Alexander was the son of the Alexandrian alabarch Alexander and nephew of the philosopher Philo of Alexandria, whose tracate *De animalibus* consists of a dialogue between uncle and nephew; he had a brother, Marcus Julius Alexander. His father was reputed to be one of the wealthiest men in the world at the time.[41] According to Josephus, Tiberius Alexander "did not remain in the ancestral laws," though exactly how that statement is to be interpreted is difficult since no details are given. Had he simply abandoned the religion of his people, or is it just that his father Alexander was more pious? Devotion to religion was a relative matter: perhaps Tiberius Alexander was simply not so devout.

Evidently, Tiberius Alexander went through the normal offices of an upper-class Roman. His term as governor of Judaea was basically peaceful because he understood the Jewish way of life, though there is no indication that he was less than firm in his administration: he had James and Simon, the sons of Judas the Galilean, tried and crucified; the charge is not specified but was presumably that of revolution (Acts 6:36-37 is confused over the order of Theudas and Judas and also seems mistaken in suggesting that Judas was executed). Also during Tiberius Alexander's governorship a famine arose over a large area of the eastern Mediterranean.[42] Helena, the queen mother of Adiabene and a convert to Judaism, was in Jerusalem at the time and spent a considerable sum in importing grain from Egypt and figs from Cyprus to distribute to the needy. In addition, her son Izates, king of Adiabene and a convert as well, sent money to the leaders of Jerusalem to help with the famine.

To complete the story of Tiberus Alexander, the next time he appears is as a member of the staff of the Roman General Domitius Corbulo in his engagement with the Parthians in 63 CE.[43] Then, he became the equestrian governor of Egypt where he was appointed by Nero, evidently in 66 CE just before the Jewish revolt.[44] An edict of his has come down to us from 68 CE, outlining his administration policy and forms one of the most interesting of the surviving edicts from the prefects of Egypt. A few months after the Jewish rebellion in Palestine had begun, riots broke out in Alexandria between the Greek citizens and the Jews, with the Jews seizing the initiative. At first Alexander tried to calm them without the use of force, but when that was unsuccessful, he turned his two legions loose on the Jewish quarter.[45] His part in the war of the Jews with Rome is recorded below (p. 305). Tiberius Alexander apparently ended his career as one of the two prefects of the Praetorian Guard, the elite protection for the emperor in Rome.

Ventidius Cumanus (48–52 CE)

Under Ventidius Cumanus, a succession of incidents disturbed the order that had prevailed under Tiberius Alexander. The first incident involved the temple. It was normal practice, as a precautionary measure, for the Roman administration to post soldiers on top of the temple portico during religious festivals to guard against any disturbances that might break out. During Passover time one year (c. 50 CE) a soldier defiantly exposed himself and made a rude gesture as an insult to the celebrating Jews, and a riot soon followed, with some Jews throwing stones at the soldiers. Cumanus sent additional troops to the area to quell the disturbance. As they approached, the Jews attempted to flee through narrow exits, which resulted in many being crushed to death.

Another incident happened shortly after this. One of Caesar's servants, who may have been carrying official post, was attacked and robbed outside Jerusalem, near Beth-Horon. The Roman way of dealing with this was to punish the neighboring villages for not having intervened to help the Roman representative, also probably suspecting that some of the band were inhabitants of these same villages. However, during the attack on the villages, one of the soldiers defiled and destroyed a copy of "the laws of Moses" (a Torah scroll?). Such a protest arose over this action, with a large delegation coming to Caesarea, that Cumanus hastily had the soldier brought out and publicly executed to appease the Jewish anger. The action apparently prevented what looked like developing into an uprising.

A final episode was quite detrimental to Cumanus himself as well as the Jews. At Ginaea (modern Jenin), some Samaritans attacked a group of Galileans on their way to Jerusalem for a festival and killed some. While a mob of Galileans was gathering to take the law into their own hands, leading Jews went to Cumanus and asked him to come to Galilee and punish the Samaritan attackers before the Jews took action. Despite this appeal to Cumanus, he did nothing, allegedly because he had been bribed by the Samaritans.

Word had now reached Jerusalem, and apparently a mob made up of Jews from both Jerusalem and Galilee, led by the brigands Eleazar son of Deinaeus and a certain Alexander, attacked some Samaritan villages. Josephus indicates the beginnings of a mass revolt since the Galileans urged them to assert their "freedom." At this point, Cumanus finally intervened with troops while the Jewish leaders attempted to persuade the rebels to return home; the two forms of persuasion eventually worked, though some of the mob seem to have continued to rob and pillage. The Samaritans felt it important to appeal to the Syrian governor, Quadratus, but the Jews were quick to answer the charges. After a preliminary investigation, Quadratus proceeded to the Palestinian area to see things at first hand. After a further hearing, he had some of the chief participants in the fighting executed, both Jews and Samaritans. Concerned about a revolt, he proceeded to Jerusalem but found the people quietly celebrating Passover.

Before returning to Antioch Quadratus sent the Governor Cumanus, the military tribune Celer, some of the Samaritan notables, and the high priests Jonathan and Ananias and other Jewish leaders to Rome for a trial before Claudius. Since a number of Claudius's freedmen and other prominent Romans supported Cumanus, Agrippa II appealed to Agrippina (Claudius's wife) and petitioned Claudius on behalf of the Jews. Claudius found in favor of the Jews, executing some of the Samaritan delegation and exiling Cumanus. The tribune Celer was taken back to Jerusalem and there publicly executed.

Antonius Felix (52–59? CE)

In a play on his name, Antonius Felix was not one of the happiest choices as governor (*felix* meaning "happy" in Latin). This was despite the Christian tradition that he even showed an interest in the teachings of the apostle Paul (Acts 24:22-27). Paul is supposed to have been brought before him because of Jewish threats to his life (Acts 24:12-34), but after examining him, Felix left Paul in prison during the rest of his governorship. According to the Roman historian Tacitus (*Hist.* 5.9), Felix "practised every kind of cruelty and lust, wielding the power of king with all the instincts of a slave." He was the brother of Pallas, the influential freedman of Claudius, and was noted for having married "three queens," one of these being Drusilla, a sister of Agrippa II.[46]

A number of events happened during Felix's term of office. Agrippa gave his sister Drusilla in marriage to the king of Emesa, Azizus, who had agreed to be circumcised. This was after a proposal of her marriage to Antiochus's son Epiphanes had fallen through, because he backed out of converting to Judaism. After he became procurator of Judaea, Felix fell for Drusilla. She was apparently unhappy in her marriage and left Azizus for Felix. They had a son, but both Drusilla and her son disappeared at the time of the eruption of Mount Vesuvius (79 CE). About this time Agrippa's other sister, Berenice, now a widow, married Polemo, the king of Cilicia, who agreed to convert to Judaism; however, the marriage soon broke up.

Josephus tells us that under Felix, things were going from bad to worse, with Judaea experiencing widespread brigandry and "imposters."[47] Felix took stern measures with some success, capturing and executing many of those causing trouble. For example, he captured and sent to Rome the bandit chief Eleazar who was said to be one of the leaders in the strife between the Jews and Samaritans under Cumanus. But during his procuratorship arose another menace which was much harder to deal with: the terrorists known as the Sicarii. Their method was to conceal a curved dagger (called a *sika*) under their clothes, and in a crowd, especially during a festival, it was no problem to get close to their victim, quickly dispatch him with the dagger, and then escape back into the crowd. Their targets were not primarily the Romans but those of the Jews who cooperated with them, meaning primarily the leading priests, the wealthy, and those with an office in the administration of the country. One of their means of financial support was to be hired to get rid of personal enemies. Josephus alleges that Felix, whose job it was to contain such assassins, hired them to assassinate the former high priest Jonathan because the latter had criticized Felix's administration of Judaea.

Named among the "imposters" were various prophets who arose and drew followings after themselves. Many of these were revolutionary movements and not just religious cults. Some apparently led their followers into the desert, with promises of deliverance. Josephus gives only one example to back up his blanket statement that there were many such groups: an unnamed Egyptian Jew who led a group to the Mount of Olives where he was going to cause the walls of Jerusalem to fall so that they could enter the city. Apparently, they needed this to happen to overcome the Roman garrison. One account states that this was a prelude to the prophet's setting himself up as dictator of Jerusalem.[48] Felix quickly intervened to kill and scatter his followers, though the prophet himself apparently escaped (cf. also Acts 21:38). But this seems to be Felix's general way of dealing with these movements.

Josephus summarizes the escalation of revolt and disorder under Felix in extravagant terms, concluding that "this war was surging day by day."[49] Even allowing for a good deal of rhetorical exaggeration, this statement suggests a steady increase of popular sentiment against Roman rule being translated into action. Ideological support came from nostalgia for better times in the past, feelings of nationalism, and religious teachings and prophecies of various sorts, but there also seem to have been important socioeconomic factors. At the core of these movements was the desire for freedom, which put them not only against the Romans but also against Jews who were seen to be cooperating with Roman rule.

One event toward the end of Felix's term of office was a forerunner of what was to happen at the beginning of the war with Rome. The Jews of Caesarea began to agitate for citizenship of the city (at that time, just living in a city was not sufficient to make you a citizen), arguing that they should have this by right since a Jew (Herod the Great) had founded the city. They were opposed by the Syro-Greek population, who pointed out that if the city had been meant for Jewish residence the various statues and temples to the family of Caesar would not have been erected by Herod. It seems that over the years the noncitizen Jewish population, formerly in the minority, increased to the point that it outnumbered the Syrians who were citizens. Despite attempts by the city magistrates to keep order by punishing any who started quarrels, they could not prevent the escalation of provocative language that ended in physical clashes. The Jews seem to have prevailed.

The situation was disturbing to Felix who saw this as a war and intervened, killing and capturing a number of the rioting Jews when they defied him in person. Since the issue was obviously not settled, Felix took representatives from both sides and sent them to Rome to present their case to Caesar. Shortly after this Felix was replaced as governor, and the Jews of Caesarea accused him of misdeeds in their presentation before Nero. The charge did not stick, allegedly because of his brother Pallas's influence with Nero; Josephus also alleges that the Syrian delegation bribed Nero's secretary. Be that as it may, Nero sided with the Syro-Greek population of Caesarea against the Jews and issued a rescript with his ruling against their being citizens. Evidently, the Jews did not accept this and continued their agitation with the Syrians until it finally came to a head again a few years later.

This civil strife also affected Jerusalem and even the temple itself. Hostility developed between the high priests (the high priestly families, including those who had been high priests before) and the other priests and the leaders of Jerusalem.[50] The former high priest Ananias is said to have increased his position with the people by means of bribes. But he also sent his servants directly to the threshing floors to demand the priestly tithe, even to take it by force if necessary. This bypassed the ordinary priests, many of whom "starved to death," no doubt an exaggeration but it illustrates a serious problem: the lower ranks of the priesthood had more and more trouble receiving their traditional source of income from the tithes. Apparently, uncontrolled revolutionary individuals attached themselves to both priestly factions, which only increased the internal strife and even violence.

Porcius Festus (59?–62 CE)

Porcius Festus succeeded Felix. From Acts 25:1-12, you would think his most urgent concern as soon as he arrived in Palestine was to hear the case of the apostle Paul! Not only is this rather unlikely, but although Festus sent Paul to Rome for trial, whether he (and allegedly Agrippa) thought Paul innocent after interviewing him is not a question we can answer (since Acts cannot be considered reliable for many aspects of Jewish history).[51] Festus's first concern was no doubt the major threat to Roman order—the numerous brigand groups and the Sicarii. He proceeded against them, capturing and killing many, though to what extent he was able to achieve success in clearing the country of the menace is difficult to say. He also killed a certain "deceiver" and scattered his following; this individual had promised salvation to those who followed him into the desert. Festus was concerned with the building of a wall on the temple (see pp. 285–6 above). He died in office.

Lucceius Albinus (62–64 CE)

After Festus died Lucceius Albinus was appointed governor, but before he had arrived, the high priest Ananus, son of Ananus (a Sadducee), convened the Sanhedrin and had James the brother of Jesus brought before them for trial. They condemned him for breaking the law and had him stoned to death. Many moderate Jews were offended by this and secretly called on Agrippa II to act. They also met Albinus when he arrived and charged Ananus with convening the Sanhedrin without consent of the governor. The result was that Agrippa deposed Ananus as high priest and replaced him with Jesus, son of Damnaeus.

He attempted to clear the land of the Sicarii who were the major problem. One of the bad moves by Albinus was to release those imprisoned for robbery because of the ransom paid by their relatives, but his efforts were in part thwarted by a new tactic well known from modern terrorists: the kidnapping of prominent persons who were then held hostage against the release of some of their own number from prison. This of course only encouraged repeated kidnappings until many of the Sicarii captured by Albinus were again free to carry on their activities. As a final gesture before vacating his office, perhaps to leave some good will behind, Albinus is said to have cleared the prisons by executing those who deserved it but releasing those committing lesser offenses. "The revolutionary party in Jerusalem" became more audacious, since they could do what they wanted if they bribed Albinus. Exactly who this revolutionary party was and what it did is left rather vague by the Jewish historian, but he goes on to say that various individuals from the common people set themselves up as leaders and gathered a band of followers, using robbery to gain funds for their activities.[52]

Gessius Florus (64–67 CE)

Gessius Florus was appointed as procurator of Judaea because of the influence of Nero's wife Poppaea who was a friend of his wife Cleopatra.[53] He is alleged to have permitted any crime as long as he got his cut, and his wife Cleopatra was as bad as him. Even allowing for gross rhetorical exaggeration on Josephus's part, Florus seems—like many Roman provincial governors—to have enriched himself during his term of office. The result was that a large crowd gathered around the Syrian legate Cestius Gellius when he visited Jerusalem during the Passover season (probably in 65 CE) and complained about Florus. Cestius promised to alleviate the harsher aspects of Florus's rule but returned to Antioch apparently without having done very much.

In the meantime, an event happened in Caesarea to which Josephus gives special significance. This was about May 66 CE. When the Jews attempted to buy a piece of land adjoining their synagogue, the owners refused and instead decided to build on the property in such a way as to restrict access to the synagogue. Jewish hotheads attempted to disrupt the building by physical violence, which Florus suppressed. When Florus vacated the city to deal with a matter in Samaria, a Syrian insulted the Jews by sacrificing birds on an upturned pot in front of the synagogue as they came for worship, perhaps suggesting that they were lepers (cf. Lev. 14:4-5). Violence broke out which the Roman cavalry commander was not able to contain, so the Jewish community took their copy of the Torah and withdrew to a place called Narbata outside the city. A Jewish delegation of twelve leading men tried once more to gain Florus's help but was simply imprisoned by him, with the charge that they had taken the Torah out of Caesarea without authorization!

Already agitated by this set of events, the people of Jerusalem converged on the temple after being provoked when Florus took 17 talents from the temple treasury (probably because Jerusalem and its adjacent countryside alone were 40 talents in arrears on tribute). The people called on Caesar to deliver them from Florus. The governor marched into Jerusalem with troops, refusing the greetings of the people, and set up a tribunal to punish certain individuals who had publicly insulted his administration (by pretending to beg copper coins for him after he took the money from the treasury). When the Jewish leaders asserted that it was impossible to identify the culprits, Florus sent his men to the agora in the upper city, with permission to sack it.

Agrippa was away in Egypt, but his sister was in Jerusalem, fulfilling a Nazarite vow. Queen Berenice's attempts to make Florus halt the slaughter were ignored. Florus then inflamed the situation further by calling the chief priest and leaders and instructing them to greet two Roman cohorts being marched into Jerusalem; however, he had secretly commanded the soldiers not to return the greetings. When this happened, some of the Jews began to protest and thus gave an excuse for further action against them by the soldiers. In the fighting that followed, Florus himself tried to take possession of the Antonia fortress next to the temple, the alleged reason being that he wanted to seize the temple treasury, but the reason was more likely to be military than just to confiscate the temple money.

Florus left a cohort of soldiers to keep order but sent a report to the Syrian Governor Cestius Gallus, accusing the Jews of various crimes and especially of revolt. On the Jewish side, too, the Jerusalem magistrates and Berenice wrote letters with their side of the story. Cestius sent the tribune Neapolitanus to investigate; about the same time Agrippa returned from his visit to Alexandria and met up with the tribune in Jamnia. Although feelings were running high, the two apparently found Jerusalem basically calm. Neapolitanus was assured that the inhabitants were submissive to the Roman administration, except for Florus because of his treatment of them. He commended their loyalty and called on them to keep the peace; he then honored the sanctuary (in the Court of Gentiles) and reported back to Cestius.

The War with Rome (66–70 CE)

Beginning Stage of the War

It was not yet apparent that Judaea was at war with Rome. In retrospect, however, the first steps had already been taken. But the people requested the chief priests and the king to send a delegation to Nero to accuse Florus. This created a dilemma for Agrippa, since choosing a suitably diplomatic embassy to accuse Florus would be difficult, but he dared not ignore the growing resentment among the people. He elected to address the populace from a prominent site with a public speech about the impossibility of fighting Rome and of the dangerous path on which they had already embarked. It is commonly recognized that the speech found in the *War* (2.16.4 §§345–401) is Josephus's own composition. But reading the speech two millennium later shows it to be a *tour de force*: if something like it was delivered it must have had an impact on many of the hearers.

In this purported speech, Agrippa accepts the excesses of the procurators over Judaea but argues this is not because of orders from Caesar. As for those who called for liberty, it is too late: the time to have resisted Rome was when Pompey first appeared. The Jewish leadership was much better placed to oppose Roman rule at that time, but it failed. This is not surprising because from Greece to Asia Minor to Gaul, Spain, Germany, and Britain—whose resources were much greater than Judaea's—they were all conquered by the Romans. Yes, even the Parthians, Carthaginians, and peoples of Africa. All the peoples and regions subdued by Rome are enumerated. No ally can be expected, not even those from across the Euphrates. The Jewish people are also wrong to expect divine aid, since fighting will make them break the law (e.g., the Sabbath), or it will be used to the advantage of the Romans. They will not spare the people nor the holy city nor the sanctuary, and those Jews living in various diaspora cities will be slaughtered.

It is likely that the substance of this speech was in some form or other conveyed to his audience. According to Josephus, the initial response to his words was favorable, and the collection of outstanding taxes in the Jerusalem region and the repair of damage done to the temple porticos in the fighting against Florus were carried out. But suddenly the mood changed, and Agrippa and Berenice were formally expelled from Jerusalem. All Agrippa could do was to send leading citizens to Florus in Caesarea to arrange for arrears of tribute to be collected from the whole province.

Up to this point wholesale war could still probably have been avoided; however, things now moved rapidly. The Sicarii captured the fortress of Masada and killed its Roman garrison. Eleazar, son of the high priest Ananias and the captain of the temple, halted all sacrifices by foreigners, which meant that the daily offerings for Caesar were stopped. Although the chief priests and leading citizens were against this, the bulk of the ordinary priests supported Eleazar, and the decision was not reversed. This was a crucial escalation of hostilities: the Romans allowed this daily sacrifice to be evidence of loyalty, whereas most people subject to Roman rule had to participate in the emperor cult. Stopping these sacrifices was a blatant act of rebellion and probably an irretrievable step in the path to all-out war with Rome.

When the priests refused to budge, the foremost citizens—which included the chief priests and the most notable of the Pharisees—met and called the people in front of the Bronze Gate of the temple. They argued vehemently that sacrifices by non-Jews had always been accepted. They even called priestly experts in the ancestral laws to show that their ancestors had always accepted such sacrifices, but to no avail.[54] Seeing that they were not listened to and that they had no means of quelling the revolt, for their own self-protection they sent messages to both Florus (who did nothing) and Agrippa (who sent two thousand cavalry to their aid). With these the "peace party" occupied the upper city but the lower city and temple were in the hands of the "war party" led by Eleazar.[55] Efforts to oust each other from their respective domains were unsuccessful, despite many casualties on both sides.

By this time, it was August 66 CE. At the festival of wood-gathering a number of Sicarii slipped into the city and joined the rebels who were now strong enough to expel Agrippa's troops from the upper city. The insurgents first burned the house of Ananias the high priest and the palaces of Agrippa and Berenice. Next, they burned the record office where debts were recorded, which they hoped would endear them in the eyes of the poor whose debts were recorded here. The troops and leaders (including Ananius the former high priest and his brother Ezechias) fled to the old palace of Herod the Great where they were besieged. The rebels next attacked the fortress of Antonia by the temple and put the garrison to death and then set it on fire.

The siege was being directed by the Sicarius leader Menahem (who was the son [grandson?] of Judas the Galilaean who had rebelled back in 6 CE when Judaea was first returned to being a Roman province). As just noted, he had taken a group to Masada, broken into Herod's armory, and was able to provide arms for many of his followers among the rebel group. But they had no siege engines, and those holed up in the palace could hold out only until their provisions were consumed. Eventually, the Jews and the troops of Agrippa requested to withdraw and were allowed to leave. This amnesty was refused to the Roman soldiers, however, who moved into the fortress towers of Hippicus, Phasael, and Mariamme where they remained under siege.

Shortly afterward, Ananias and his brother were found hiding and were slain by the insurgents. At this point, however, the fault lines in the rebel movement began to show up. Menahem had taken on the role of a tyrant. When Menahem went up to the temple, dressed in the robes of royalty and escorted by an entourage, Eleazar led his own followers to attack him. Menahem and his supporters fled, but Menahem was found hiding and executed. Some of his followers, however, including a relative Eleazar son of Jairus, managed to escape to Masada where they waited out the revolt until finally besieged by the Romans in 73 CE (see chapter 14, pp. 314–16). Some apparently hoped that this falling out among the insurgents would bring an end to the war, but far from it. When the Roman captain of the besieged soldiers offered to surrender their arms if allowed to leave unmolested, Eleazar agreed. But as soon as the Romans laid down their weapons, his followers slaughtered them. Only their captain was spared because, ironically, he promised to be circumcised and become a Jew; even more ironically this massacre of the Romans occurred on the Sabbath!

Whatever the potential consequences of previous actions up to this point, the rebels had now crossed a line. This massacre of Roman soldiers was an act that Rome was bound to avenge. Inevitable and inexorable revenge for acts of hostility was the one characteristic that had made Rome what it was. There was now nothing that the Judaeans could do to avoid paying the price. Even if they had laid down their arms at this point and returned to their homes, the Romans would have had to make them pay a terrible price for this grave insult to Rome's honor.

Even before the Romans started to respond to the events, the acts of the insurgents in Jerusalem had horrifying consequences for many Jewish communities elsewhere in the eastern Mediterranean, many of which were massacred by their Gentile neighbors. One of the first was in Caesarea, where the troubles had started: apparently the entire Jewish population was wiped out (or perhaps driven out), alleged to be twenty thousand deaths. In retaliation, gangs of Judaeans attacked a number of towns and cities in which the population was mainly non-Jewish. In the wake of such violence on the Jewish side, it is hardly surprising that in many cities, non-Jewish citizens turned on their Jewish residents. Some of them no doubt saw it as a preventative measure to deter Jewish violence from breaking out in their area. "Judaizers" are also said to have been treated with suspicion, by which seems to be meant converts to Judaism, perhaps non-circumcised "Godfearers."[56]

In Alexandria, where calm had been established some decades earlier, further rioting broke out. Certain Jews attended a public gathering (called to send an embassy to Nero) and three were killed by a mob; when the Jews attempted to retaliate, however, war threatened to break out in the city. The governor Tiberius Alexander first tried to calm them by entreaties, sending leading citizens among them. When this did not work, however, he finally turned two Roman legions and another two thousand auxiliaries on them. Now the community sued for peace, and Tiberius Alexander withdrew the troops and restrained the Greek citizens of the city.

Why this attack on Jewish populations who were evidently not part of the revolt? There are probably a variety of reasons, one of the main ones being the panic that the uncontrolled Jewish gangs generated and the fear that revolution would spread to Jews in their own area. There were also more selfish reasons: greed for property, the chance to settle old scores, and general anti-Judaism. But the fact that Jewish bands were attacking and pillaging villages over a large area up and down Syria cannot be underestimated as an important factor. Yet some cities refused to punish their own Jewish populations for the sins of their brethren.

It was September 66, only some weeks after the events that triggered the catastrophe in Jerusalem, when the Syrian Governor C. Cestius Gallus finally began military operations against the revolt. As he marched out of Antioch, he had the Twelfth Legion and the equivalent of another legion plus other infantry, cavalry, and auxiliaries. Also, Agrippa brought an equivalent in foot soldiers and cavalry and accompanied him. The first encounter was in Galilee, where the whole district was attacked, pillaged, and villages destroyed.

The Roman forces approached the city of Jerusalem during the Feast of Tabernacles, probably early October 66. The Jews were able to mobilize a large body of fighters from the festival pilgrims and temporarily halt the Roman advance. The figure of Simon, son of Gioras, appears for the first time, though he later becomes an important figure in the revolt. Cestius took the opportunity to attack the Jews, who were now in disorder, and pushed on to Jerusalem where he laid siege in October 66 CE. The city was only partially prepared to defend itself, and the defenders abandoned the suburbs and outer city along with the unfinished third wall, taking refuge in the temple and inner city.

According to Josephus, who may well be relying on Roman historians here, the city would have fallen and the war ended then and there if Cestius had pressed his advantage.[57] Indeed, some of the citizens (instigated by Ananus, son of the former high priest Jonathan) secretly negotiated to open the city gates to the Romans without success until they were discovered by the war party and driven into their houses. The Romans were engaged in siege craft against the walls when Cestius suddenly decided to withdraw from the city.

All during their march back to Caesarea they were harassed by the Jews but especially in the pass at Beth-Horon; the withdrawal became more of a rout. Some of the leadership was killed, and they abandoned their siege engines and most of their baggage. The Jews pursued them as far as Antipatris before giving up and collecting their spoils. The Romans had lost more than five thousand foot soldiers—the equivalent of a legion—and almost a five-hundred-man cavalry. According to Suetonius they also lost their eagle, a further insult to honor that Rome had to avenge.[58]

Preparations to Resist an Inevitable Roman Campaign

The Jews now had the opportunity for war preparations which, in hindsight, probably only prolonged the suffering and increased the casualties. At the time it undoubtedly seemed a much-needed breathing space for those who thought the Roman military machine could be taken on. The precise attitudes to the war varied radically. For example, several individuals are named as fleeing the city to Agrippa, and some were dispatched on a mission to Nero. Josephus is probably correct in stating that the opposition to war was strongest among the upper classes of the priests and municipal leaders in Jerusalem. It is also probable that some of these felt strongly enough to flee the city, but many in this group clearly supported the war, as has so carefully been documented, even if some had private misgivings.[59] It is Josephus's account that gives us most of the detail about the war, but he has discretely played down the extent to which the priests and upper classes were active supporters of the rebels.

After the rout of Cestius, the rebels met in the temple to organize the conduct of the war. While it would have been difficult to remain neutral at this time for those still in Jerusalem, it indicates that even the "moderates" were integrated into the resistance by one means or another. The rebels also appointed military leaders and a governing apparatus to conduct the war. The overall leaders for Jerusalem were Joseph, son of Gorion, and the former high priest Ananus (apparently son of Ananus). Eleazar, son of Simon, despite his major part in the earlier events, was initially not trusted sufficiently to be given office; however, he had control of much of the public treasury so that later things were to change drastically. The rest of the country was divided up into six districts, each one entrusted to a commander who acted in both military and civil capacity:

1. Idumaea: Jesus, son of Sapphas (a chief priest), and Eleazar (son of Neus the high priest; unfortunately, no such high priest is known; should it be Eleazar, son of Ananias?);
2. Jericho: Joseph, son of Simon;
3. Peraea: Manasses;
4. Thamna, with Lydda, Joppa, and Emmaus: John the Essene;
5. Gophna and Acrabetta: John, son of Ananias;
6. Lower Galilee and Gamala: Josephus, son of Matthias (he also claims to have been given Upper Galilee, but this is doubtful).

The greatest suspicion falls on Josephus's own alleged intentions: even though he claims that he was against the war and even a fifth columnist in Galilee, this is both too convenient for his later position and contrary to his own conduct. The simplest interpretation of his actions is that whatever initial reservations he may have had, he embarked on his task in Galilee with considerable enthusiasm and a constant eye to self-advantage. If he were as much against the war as he states, it would have been a simple matter to defect to Agrippa.

Ananus the high priest was leading in Jerusalem at this time. Josephus claims that Ananus intended to subvert the drive toward war, but this is hardly compatible with his actions: directing the repair of the walls, the assembly of war engines, collecting weapons and armor, and training young men to fight.[60] It is no doubt correct that Ananus wanted to control the so-called Zealots (on these see below, p. 303), but this could well have been to bring all military activity under his full command. Simon, son of Gioras, also seems to have been active but with plundering and stealing from the population. Finally, Ananus sent a force against him, and he fled with his followers to Masada. Later, Simon was to play an important role in the affairs in Jerusalem during the siege.

We are given little information about five of the districts created by the governing council in Jerusalem, but the situation in Galilee is known from the detailed (if highly partisan and contradictory) narratives of its commander Josephus. Galilee serves to highlight one of the major problems which the Jews faced: internal divisions and rivalries that were probably as destructive as anything the Romans would do. A section of Galilee was not Jewish, and even some of the Jewish cities were basically pro-Roman or at least antiwar. For example, of three chief cities of Galilee, only Gabara seems to have been pro-revolt while Sepphoris was pro-Roman and Tiberias prevaricated.[61]

The actual number of those fighting under Josephus's command at any one time is never more than a few thousand and these seem to be mainly his mercenaries and bodyguard. A number of these mercenaries were "brigands" whom Josephus hired because he had little hope of controlling them directly. The major cities and defendable sites were also fortified. But most of Josephus's energy seems to have been taken up with his rivalry with John of Gischala (also called John, son of Levi).

Josephus's tirade against John probably masks a political power struggle between two officially appointed commanders. That is, contrary to his own statement, Josephus was probably appointed commander only of Lower Galilee and John was the commander of Upper Galilee. John was thus not straightforwardly the upstart or troublemaker which Josephus makes him out to be; on the contrary, there were many in Jerusalem (e.g., Simon son of Gamaliel) who viewed Josephus as the troublemaker who kept encroaching on John's command instead of sticking to his own.[62] He spends a good part of the *Life* (38-64 §§189–335) describing his attempt to outflank the embassy sent from Jerusalem to remove him from command (though, in the end, he managed to keep his position).

In the Meantime … the Situation in Rome

Matters were coming to a head not just in Judaea but also in Rome itself. A crisis had developed in 68 CE when Nero was still on the throne. With Nero's death and the end of the Julio-Claudian line of rulers, one would have been surprised if a period of turmoil did not erupt in which various individuals staked a claim to the throne. *Galba*, the governor of Hispania, had challenged Nero's rule, which led to the latter's suicide. Galba returned to Rome and was generally accepted by the Senate and military. He faced large problems, however, and was very much on trial as to how well and how quickly he faced them. He immediately addressed the financial crisis by attempting to raise taxes and effect some economies. In a short time, though, his maladministration had begun to alienate many. At the beginning of January 69, the armies of the Rhine refused to renew their oath to him. Galba recognized the peril and tried to appease his opponents by associating a young senator with him in office. This did nothing for the military and alienated Otho, a former close friend of Nero and governor of Lusitania, who would have considered himself an obvious choice as successor to Nero.

Otho made arrangements for the usual bribe to the Praetorian Guard and was declared emperor in the middle of January 69 CE. Although he immediately did away with Galba, the army of the Lower Rhine acclaimed their own commander, *Vitellius*, as emperor and began to march on Rome. Otho tried to come to an arrangement with Vitellius but failed. The stage was now set for another civil war. Superior tactics allowed the Vitellian army to make it safely over the Alps, even though it was still winter, and surprise the supporters of Otho. The initial campaign went against Otho who committed suicide rather than continue the fight.

It soon became clear, however, that the new emperor's fight for his office was not at an end, for in July 69 the governor of Egypt, Tiberius Alexander, and the eastern legions declared for *Vespasian*. This was soon followed by the legions of the Danube who had originally supported Otho. Antonius Primus their commander made a forced march on Italy where he caught the Vitellians off guard. After Primus had gained two decisive victories, it was clear to Vitellius that he had little hope and so negotiated terms of abdication with Vespasian's elder brother who was in Rome. But before the agreement could be implemented, the Praetorian Guard once again took matters into their own hands: they attacked and killed Vespasian's brother in the Capitol, setting the temple of Jupiter on fire in the process.

Primus now arrived in Rome and fought with the remaining Vitellian resistance. Vitellius was captured and killed, and Vespasian's son Domitian was made viceregent. Discipline was quickly breaking down and it looked as if the Danube troops were about to sack the city; however, Vespasian's legate, Mucianus, arrived and established control, sending the legions of the Danube back to the frontier. Vespasian himself arrived in Rome a few months later in the summer of 70, where he was formally crowned emperor.

The family of Vespasian (69–79 CE) was one newly arrived to the ranks of the *Equites*, or knights, social class, and he himself had never been a member of the Senate. He was above all a military man who had campaigned in Britain and Africa before being appointed commander about age fifty-seven for the Judaean campaign by Nero. His appointment as emperor marked an innovation in several ways. To lessen the effects of this he attempted to create the fiction of a relationship to the previous line of rulers, the Julio-Claudians. On the other hand, he came at a time when Rome was desperate for peace and calm, and he proved a good administrator and ruler, becoming perhaps the most popular emperor since Augustus.

Vespasian's handling of the economic crisis was a sign of his ability, for he managed to cut spending and raise new taxes without alienating his supporters or provoking major discontent in the provinces that bore the brunt of increased imposts. Although still making some use of freedmen, he avoided the problems created by Claudius and Nero by appointing most governmental officers from the equestrian ranks. Like Augustus he kept enough of the forms of republican government to satisfy the Senate while continuing to reduce its power.

It was not Vespasian's policy to expand the frontiers of the empire as such. On the other hand, it became clear that proper maintenance of the current frontiers required some further annexation of territory. He began the push west and north in Britain, which eventually ended in bringing northern England, southern Scotland, and much of Wales under Roman control by Domitian's time. He also began to bring further areas of Germany into the defense system, specifically the Black Forest.

Perhaps one of the greatest contributions made to peace by Vespasian was the establishment of the dynastic principle. He made it quite clear from the beginning that Titus was to be his successor and Domitian after that if Titus had no children. (The fact that Vespasian had two suitable sons was indeed one of the things which had led many to support him.) Therefore, when Vespasian died in 79, Titus was able to make the transition into the office without incident.

Vespasian's Campaign Against Galilee[63]

To return to the rebellion in Judaea, once the scale of the Jewish revolt and Cestius's defeat was reported to Nero in 66, he quickly recognized its seriousness and lost no time in appointing Vespasian to take charge. Vespasian sent his son Titus to Alexandria to bring the Fifteenth Legion while he made his way to Antioch, the regional capital. Here he was met by King Agrippa II. Vespasian now had at his disposal the Fifth, Tenth, and Fifteenth Legions, along with other cohorts and squadrons, as well as the soldiers of Agrippa, Antiochus IV of Commagene, and Soaemus of Emessa—about sixty thousand fighting men. It was now the spring of 67 CE, just a year since the initial troubles in Caesarea.

When Vespasian arrived in Ptolemais, the inhabitants of the Galilean town of Sepphoris showed their pro-Roman support and asked for a garrison. Vespasian recognized the strategic value of Sepphoris and complied as best he could. Galilee was only a region to be secured by the Romans so that they could concentrate on their real task that was Jerusalem. Josephus, the Jewish commander of Lower Galilee, was waiting not far from Sepphoris. Hardly had the Romans reached the neighborhood before the bulk of Josephus's men deserted him and fled. With his remaining troops Josephus holed up in Tiberias. Vespasian took Gabara on the first assault and killed all the grown males, probably both in revenge for the defeat of Cestius and as an example to the Jewish defenders of other cities. Neighboring villages were also destroyed and the inhabitants sold into slavery. Josephus wrote to the Jerusalem authorities, asking for permission to negotiate or to receive reinforcements sufficient to defend the region.

Not having heard from Jerusalem, Josephus left Tiberias and took up his place in Jotapata at the beginning of June 67 CE. Vespasian immediately prepared to besiege it as one of the major fortified cities in Galilee. Josephus managed to hold out about six weeks during June–July. It was clearly an important target for the Romans, because of both its size and its defenses. Josephus himself managed to survive the final assault and hide in a cave with some other soldiers; when discovered by the Romans, they agreed on a suicide pact. Although Josephus describes this all in great detail, his account is extremely suspect, especially since he appears to have drawn the lot to be last to kill himself. In any case, he was taken captive by the Romans and brought before Vespasian where he predicted that the Roman general would be emperor (he claims to have had regular prophetic dreams).[64]

His account at this point is believable in that something along these lines must have happened, not only to explain his subsequent treatment by Vespasian but also because the *War* was later read (or at least intended to be read) by Vespasian and Titus. We also have to remember that several Roman writers describe the circulation of predictions that Vespasian would become emperor.[65] As it happens Vespasian was slightly wounded in the battle for Jotapata, and Titus is said to have led the final assault.

During the siege of Jotapata, a large group of Samaritans assembled on Gerizim.[66] Josephus alleges they were thinking of revolt. In any case, the Romans interpreted this as a threat, and the commander of the Fifth Legion led troops against them. When the Samaritans refused to lay down their arms, they were all slain, the number said to be over eleven thousand. This was mid-July 67 CE. Although it was midsummer (late July), Vespasian took his troops to Caesarea, evidently with the intention of wintering there and undertaking the invasion of Judaea the next spring. Joppa had been resettled by Judaeans who had built a fleet of pirate ships to raid the coastal sea traffic. A Roman force was dispatched: the pirates took to their ships to escape but a storm destroyed most of the fleet; the survivors were massacred and Joppa razed.

Vespasian apparently believed that Galilee was now sufficiently cowed to be a threat no longer. He accepted an invitation of Agrippa to visit his kingdom and went off to Caesarea Philippi; however, word soon arrived that the cities of both Tiberias and Tarichaea were in revolt. Tiberias's actions seem to have been due only to a minority faction of its citizens, led now (if not before) by one of its magistrates named Jesus, son of Saphat. Although a small force of Roman cavalry sent to offer terms to the city was attacked and forced to flee, a delegation of citizens made haste to the Roman camp and, with Agrippa's support, offered the submission of the city to Vespasian. Jesus and his men withdrew to Tarichaea. Tiberias opened its gates to Vespasian and was spared any looting or major destruction.

Many rebels among the Jews had gathered in Tarichaea, not just those from Tiberias; it had also been fortified earlier by Josephus and was ready to offer considerable resistance to the Romans. Titus was sent against the city, reinforced by Trajan (the father of the future emperor). They defeated the Jewish force drawn up outside the city, which then fled inside the wall. Like Tiberias, however, Tarichaea had many native inhabitants (as opposed to refugees and fighters from elsewhere in Galilee) who were against resistance to the Romans. These inhabitants clashed with the fighters who fled back into the city.

When this became known to the Romans, they were able to take the city in a surprise attack, though many native inhabitants suffered as well as the rebels. Many of the defenders fled in boats onto the Sea of Galilee but were pursued and slain by the Roman soldiers on specially made war rafts. Vespasian then had to decide what to do with the captured rebels in Tarichaea. He separated them from the natives of the city and allowed them to make their way to Tiberias. There he executed the non-useful, sent a large number of young men to work on digging the Corinthian canal, and sold the rest into slavery. This all took place in September 67 CE.

At this point, all of Galilee had surrendered—all the fortresses and towns—except Gischala and Gamala, a city in Gaulanitis on the eastern side of the Sea of Tiberias, which continued to remain belligerent when most of the other cities had surrendered. The reason was that Gamala was set in rugged mountainous terrain and had been well fortified, which the defenders thought would allow them to repel any attack. Vespasian besieged it; Agrippa led his own troops alongside the Romans and was severely injured by a sling stone that hit him on the elbow as he tried to talk the occupants into surrendering. The siege was hard fought, with many casualties on the Roman side and Vespasian himself cut off and endangered at one point; it lasted from early October to early November 67. When the city finally fell, many of the defenders threw themselves over the cliffs but the rest, including women and children, were slaughtered by the attackers, though a few fighters escaped to Jerusalem.

Only Gischala was now left of those refusing to surrender. Gischala was the hometown of John, son of Levi (Josephus's bugbear who later allied with the Zealots). Titus was dispatched with a cavalry unit to take Gischala. He first offered terms. John agreed to think about them if left in peace over the Sabbath, but during the night he fled with many of his supporters (Vespasian would not have fallen for this trick!). Although many, especially the families, were killed or captured when the Romans caught up with them the next day, John made it safely to Jerusalem. Gischala opened its gates to Titus, and Galilee was now completely under Roman control.

Jerusalem Isolated and Surrounded

The Roman advance had now so unnerved the Jewish defenders that few were willing to take a stand in the various fortresses or cities. As a result, many of the rebels in the villages and countryside—along with a great number of simple refugees seeking asylum—now made their way to Jerusalem. The large number of refugees was to create significant problems during the siege of Jerusalem. The arrival of outsiders, such as John of Gischala, also changed the balance of power in Jerusalem and was soon to lead to a series of internal fights and factions that put Jew against Jew.

For the moment the upper-class leadership in Jerusalem remained intact. Although Josephus is probably slanting the story by making the chief priestly families ready to surrender to the Romans, it does appear that the upper-class priestly families were opposed to some of the other factions. One group took over the temple area. Apparently at this time a number of "brigand" chiefs and their men had allied themselves to form a group known as the *Zealots*.[67] Although the term "zealot" has often been used by modern scholars as a general term to characterize any revolutionary group of this period, it is clear that *Josephus confines his usage here to a specific group in Jerusalem which he first mentions only in 68 CE. This suggests an express grouping in this context, and the term "Zealot" should not be extended to include all revolutionary groups indiscriminately.*

The Zealots decided to appoint a new high priest by an earlier custom of drawing lots. They chose a man named Phanni, son of Samuel. Josephus (*War* 4.3.8 §155) claims he was ignorant and not of the high priestly family. Various of the priestly and upper-class leaders opposed this appointment and also the actions of these Zealots in general, including Gorion, son of Joseph and Simon, son of Gamaliel. They were supported by some from the high priestly families, such as Ananus, son of Ananus and Jesus, son of Gamalas. Ananus appears to have tried to instigate the Jerusalem population against those occupying the temple area, but the bloody conflict that followed left many dead and wounded without achieving anything except to drive them into the inner courts.

John of Gischala became involved, apparently pretending to serve the priestly group but also helping the Zealots by providing intelligence on what was being planned by the former. He advised summoning the Idumaeans as the allies of the Zealots. The Idumaeans, although living in the old area of Idumaea, generally identified themselves with Jews and practiced Jewish customs. They responded immediately, with an alleged number of twenty thousand. Ananus, enlisting the aid of the chief priest Jesus, tried to shut them out of Jerusalem. Taking advantage of a storm, some of the Zealots opened the city gates and let the Idumaeans in. A great slaughter ensued, with the Zealots and Idumaeans on one side and the guards and others on the other. The former group then hunted down Ananus and Jesus (and apparently others of the high priestly families) and butchered them.

When news of the internecine fighting in Jerusalem came to Vespasian, there were those who advised an immediate march on Jerusalem in hopes that they could take it quickly. However, it was decided that the factional strife would only weaken the defenders if left to themselves; therefore, the policy of systematic reduction of the country was continued. Vespasian left his winter camp to march south about March 68. His force came down from Caesarea on the western side of the country. Then, he turned east, marching toward Idumaea, which he reduced. He then retraced his steps back north, through Neapolis (Shechem) and turned back down to Jericho where he established a garrison. It was probably about this time that Qumran was destroyed, while many villages around the shores of the Dead Sea were also looted.

Jerusalem was now surrounded and isolated from the rest of the country. Vespasian returned to Caesarea and was preparing for the march on Jerusalem itself when word came of Nero's death. It would now have been July or August 68. Rather than continue the war Vespasian decided to wait to see developments; to what extent he already had ideas of becoming emperor is difficult to say, but his judicious wait at this point would have been in line with such thoughts. When news came of Galba's acclamation (summer of 68 CE), he sent Titus to salute the new emperor, with Agrippa II accompanying him, but also requesting instructions about proceeding with the Jewish war. However, while apparently still in the area of Greece, they received word of Galba's death and Otho's accession (probably January 69). Agrippa continued on to Rome, but Titus returned to his father in Caesarea.

In the meantime, the Roman Civil War advanced, but the waiting apparently continued, with Otho and Vitellius fighting each other in Italy. Finally in June 69 Vespasian began once again his push to Jerusalem, which he had postponed for almost a year. Certain areas north of Jerusalem were quickly reduced. He then took Hebron, slaying the inhabitants and burning it. The only fortresses now in rebel hands were Herodium, Masada, and Machaerus, while the Romans were at the walls of Jerusalem. Vespasian again returned to Caesarea and again word came from Italy, this time to say that Otho had committed suicide, and Vitellius had taken Rome earlier (in April 69 CE). Vespasian was in a dilemma: he was reluctant to acclaim Vitellius, but should he himself go for the supreme office? By now it was the summer of 69 CE, but things developed rapidly.

According to Josephus (*War* 4.10.2-4 §§588–604), Vespasian's own troops in Judaea were the first to declare him emperor. But more officially Tiberius Alexander, the governor of Egypt, acclaimed Vespasian as emperor (at Vespasian's request), followed shortly by other legions of the East and in Europe.[68] Also, local rulers supported him; indeed, Queen Berenice was a strong adherent.[69] She and others summoned Agrippa back from Rome (where he managed to slip away without Vitellius's knowing) to back Vespasian. Mucianus the legate of Syria, was dispatched with troops to Italy, though he decided to march overland since it was winter. As a side point, Vespasian released Josephus from his bonds at this time and gave him his freedom. (This was apparently because of his prediction that Vespasian would become emperor.) Vespasian and Titus moved on to Egypt to secure the grain supply. Here they learned that Vitellius had been defeated and executed (December 69 CE). As Vespasian prepared to embark for Rome, he sent Titus with the army to finish the task of taking Jerusalem.

Jewish Infighting in Jerusalem

Back in Jerusalem the Idumaeans now aided the Zealots in a reign of terror against those perceived as enemies. With time, however, the Idumaeans changed their minds, allegedly because of finding out the real crimes of the Zealots and learning that Ananus and other individuals who had been slaughtered were not traitors as claimed.[70] Although they were all said to have returned home, later passages mention them as still in Jerusalem, which suggests that only a part of them quitted Jerusalem.

Before leaving Jerusalem, they are said to have released two thousand citizens from prison who had been placed there by rebel groups. Many of these joined Simon, son of Gorias, and subsequently left Jerusalem. Leaving Jerusalem was becoming more difficult, however. The Zealots had guards on all the gates and refused to let anyone leave unless they paid a bribe; many of those who had no means of payment were killed.

The Sicarii had earlier taken Masada and were now using it as a base for raids on the countryside. They were joined at this time by Simon, son of Gioras. He then marched back up to Jerusalem where the Zealots felt threatened by him. He set up camp outside the walls, with the people of Jerusalem being oppressed by the Zealots within and Simon without. In the meantime, John of Gischala had apparently thrown his lot in with the Zealots, at least temporarily, but now he created his own faction as a rival to them.[71] The Idumaeans in his army are now said to have attacked him and the Zealots.

John and the surviving Zealots fled into a local palace but were driven from there into the temple where other Zealots from across the city joined them to prepare to attack the people and the Idumaeans. The Idumaeans met with the chief priests, and together they decided to let in Simon to help them fight against the group in the temple. Once inside, Simon quickly became master of the city (about April or May 69 CE). A rebel leader named Eleazar grew tired of John's tyranny and broke away with part of the Zealots.[72] Eleazar was a priest and one of the original Zealot leaders. A three-way split was now in evidence, as Josephus (*War* 5.1.1-3 §§1–20) summarizes the situation:

- Eleazar and his group occupied the inner court of the temple;
- John and his group were in the outer court; and
- Simon and his group held the Upper City and much of the Lower City.

All three were fighting each other with considerable bloodshed on all sides. Surprisingly, Tacitus (*Hist.* 5.12) mentions these three factions and the names of their leaders, as well (even though he appears not to know Josephus).

Final Siege of Jerusalem

This was the state of things in Jerusalem as Titus marched on the city with four legions in the spring of 70. Vespasian had requested Tiberius Alexander to come from Egypt and be Titus's chief of staff.[73] This is quite understandable since Titus as a young and rather impetuous individual could use the steadying influence and experience of the much older Tiberius Alexander who served him throughout the Judaean campaign.

Titus set up camp on Mount Scopus and Mount Olivet and proceeded to attack the north side of the city as had been traditional for invaders for centuries. The only experienced fighters on the Jewish side were the rebel militias. For the most part, the Jerusalem leadership had no military training or experience. This lack plus the selfish focus on only what was good for their individual group meant that no strategic plan was devised and no coordinated attempt to defend against the Romans took place. The rebel groups were intent only in furthering their own ends, which primarily meant fighting against other rebel groups who were seen as rivals. This lack of strategic planning resulted in important military opportunities against the Romans being lost.

Yet when the Jewish groups did finally engage the Roman forces, they were formidable fighters. This was because their guerrilla tactics were suited to the situation. The terrain was often more amenable to the rebels who had little or no armor, often charged suddenly from secret locations, and frequently fought with little thought of safety for their own lives. The Jewish defenders generally outfought the Romans in hand-to-hand combat. Also, although there may have been some skilled slingers on the Jewish side, stones thrown by hand could be deadly, and a ready supply was all round them.

The legionaries, on the other hand, found that their armor often hampered them because of the broken ground on which they were attacked, and disciplined maneuvers to which they were accustomed were not possible. The rebel weapons were mainly swords and knives, though catapults and other siege engines had been captured from Cestius and were used, first against other rebel groups, but then against the Romans. Time and again it was the Roman cavalry that swayed the balance in favor of the Romans.

Yet the sheer number of Roman soldiers, the resources available, and superior fighting technology (such as the use of cavalry and archers) meant that the outcome was inevitable. According to the Roman historian Dio (65.5.4), there were deserters to the rebel side, not only from the ranks of Agrippa's troops and other allies of the Romans but even from among the Roman troops themselves. But once the siege was instigated, it was only a matter of time before the city fell.

The rebel groups evidently called a temporary truce among themselves when the Romans set up the siege of the city; nevertheless, the three basic internal divisions continued until Passover time of 70 CE. Then when Eleazar was allowing worshipers into the inner court of the temple, John was able to slip some of his men in secretly. They attacked Eleazar's faction and eventually won, uniting the two groups once more into one. John was in charge, but Eleazar also retained a position of command. The united group numbered about 8,500 (since about 2,400 Zealots had joined them) and maintained control of the temple and the Kedron valley. Simon's group of 15,000 (10,000 plus 5,000 Idumaeans) continued to oppose them, having possession of the Upper City and part of the Lower. This all despite the progress of the Roman siege.

During the inter-rivalry between the various Jewish groups, much of the food stockpiles were apparently destroyed. The result was a famine within the walls, beginning even before Titus invested the city. The rebels were able to control sufficient food for their own fighters initially, but even they eventually suffered from lack of provisions.[74] Many people also escaped the city to the Romans, or at least tried to.

Josephus paints a picture in which the majority of those in Jerusalem wanted to escape or for the city to surrender to the Romans; also, that the aristocracy was under constant threat of execution by the rebels. Yet Josephus needs correction from his own data, which often contradict the dismal picture that he describes. The fact is that most of the upper class survived until the end of the war, many of whom were fully committed to opposing the Romans. Granted, some prominent individuals were killed, but these were the ones seen as the most direct threat to the rebel leadership. The fact that Josephus's father apparently lived through the siege without harm indicates that the insurgents were perhaps not the out-and-out monsters as he portrays them to be—at least, not very efficient monsters.[75]

The details of the siege are given at length by Josephus and would be tedious to relate here. There were countless heroic deeds by ordinary soldiers on both sides, as well as atrocities against innocent victims. According to the Roman historian Tacitus (*Hist.* 5.13.3), Jewish women even engaged in the fighting. But Josephus's long rhetorical passages, with their stereotyped descriptions, soon become repetitive and tedious. Josephus was himself sent to talk from a distance to the defenders with the hope that some would desert or even that they could be parlayed into surrendering. At one point, he was knocked unconscious by a stone hurled by one of the defenders but survived without major harm.

Titus began his operations against Jerusalem apparently in early May of 70 CE. After fifteen days the Romans took the First Wall (also called the Third or Agrippa's Wall). Another five days was sufficient to capture the Second Wall, at the end of May. Titus made preparations to take the Third Wall and built earthworks over the next two or three weeks (to the middle of June). But Jewish countermeasures frustrated the Roman efforts and destroyed much of the siege equipment. Finally, he decided to build a siege wall around the city to isolate it from the rest of the country. This siege wall also had the effect of preventing food supplies from being brought into the city, exacerbating the famine that was already underway. This took only a few days, after which Titus resumed building earthworks to take the final wall. Despite the best efforts of the defenders, these new earthworks were completed by the middle of July, and the battering rams began their work of demolishing the final defenses of the city, with a focus on the Antonia tower.

Once through this wall, the attackers found that the rebels had built a second wall behind it, a common practice of defenders in such cases. A night assault let the Romans temporarily take this wall, but they were eventually driven back. It was early August (Panemus 17 or Tammuz 17, according to both Josephus and Jewish tradition) that the *tamid* or daily sacrifice ceased in the temple, probably because of lack of lambs. Titus supposedly had Josephus shout to John of Gischala a message in Aramaic (or Hebrew) that he would allow the sacrifices if John would agree, apparently suggesting that he would allow sacrificial victims to be taken into the temple from outside the walls. John's reply was that (as quoted by Josephus) "he did not fear capture of the city, for it was God's property."[76] This might indicate a belief on the part of the defenders that God would ultimately not allow his city to be captured—the so-called inviolability of Zion tradition—a belief parallel to the one allegedly held by some Jews in the last days of the kingdom of Judah in the time of Jeremiah.

Another night attack failed to make a breakthrough, but about this time a number from the families of the chief priests plus a number of the aristocracy took this opportunity to escape to the Romans and were allowed to settle in Gophna. This demonstrates that not all the upper class of priests and laymen had been killed, contrary to what Josephus alleges, nor that escape was impossible at this time. The Romans had demolished the foundations of the Antonia and were now ready to assault the temple.

Destruction of the Temple and End of the War

A new, very risky phase of operations took place at this time (the middle of August). Both the rebels and the Romans began to burn various parts of the temple porticos. In one instance, the Jews enticed some Roman soldiers onto the roof of the west portico, then set it on fire. But the Romans also used fire as a mode of attack. Now Titus ordered the temple gates to be set on fire. This was at the end of August. Two prominent leaders of the rebels deserted about this time: although Titus was inclined to execute them, in the end he allowed them to live.

Titus ordered the burning gates to be extinguished, in preparation for a final assault. He then called a council of his leading generals (including the procurator of Judaea, Marcus Antonius Julianus) to discuss the fate of the temple. Josephus claims that Titus gave orders not to burn the temple. When a Roman soldier supposedly tossed in a torch contrary to orders, Josephus gives us a picture of the Roman commander trying to stop the fire which was destroying the temple. But in spite of his orders, the soldiers were in such a frenzy that they continued the destruction and lighting of fires to the point that Titus gave up.

This picture that Josephus gives us about Titus's intent and actions is of course absurd. For other sources—and strategic sense—indicate that Titus saw the temple as a continuing instigation of rebellion and determined that it should be reduced to ruins.[77] He probably did feel some of the pity for the people and perhaps even for such a notable edifice as the temple, but he was also a soldier with a task to do. The council that Josephus allegedly reported clearly decided on the destruction of the temple, not the supposed clemency of Titus that he imagines.

With the leveling of Antonia's foundations, the Romans were ready for their final assault. Making use of cavalry, they shut the defenders in the inner court of the temple. Then right at the end of August (the 10th of the Hebrew month of Av) they attacked the inner court of the temple. During the process the chambers surrounding the temple were set on fire. Titus took the opportunity to view the inner parts of the temple, including apparently the Holy of Holies. The fire was not extinguished, and the temple burned.

Josephus tells us of various signs and portents that presaged the destruction of the temple, reports also found in some Roman writers.[78] Such a catalogue of portents was often standard in accounts of ancient disasters. More interesting are Josephus's reports of oracles that were being circulated among the Jews. One was cited by Josephus himself, to the effect that the city would fall when someone would begin to kill his fellow countrymen.[79] Another prophecy was that the temple and city would be captured when the temple became "four-square," which supposedly happened after the destruction of the Antonia tower.[80] A final oracle was that one from their country would become ruler over the world.[81] Josephus states this was misinterpreted as a reference to a ruler from Judaea when actually it referred to Vespasian who was declared emperor while in Judaea.[82]

That some people—perhaps many—stayed in Jerusalem because they expected divine deliverance from the Romans is indicated by another incident.[83] About six thousand people, including women and children, assembled at a portico of the outer temple court, because a prophet had proclaimed that God commanded them to go there for deliverance. In fact, most were killed by the Romans. Josephus claims that the leaders of the rebels had bribed false prophets to deceive the people by proclaiming divine deliverance. In actual fact, such prophets may have arisen spontaneously and voiced a message that they themselves believed in. Also, although Josephus quotes only so-called prophets who prophesied the destruction of the temple and city, it is just as likely that there were others predicting divine salvation for both—though Josephus would not have told us of these!

The temple was destroyed sometime toward the end of August in 70 CE, though the traditional date of the 9th of Av is a stereotype and at variance with Josephus's date of 10th of Av. Many of the defenders had fled into underground passages. A group of priests surrendered to Titus but were executed. A group of followers of Simon and John asked to negotiate with Titus; however, they then refused to accept an offer of life from him, if they laid down their arms, but instead asked to take their families and go out into the wilderness unmolested. Titus refused, saying time for clemency was past and they must fight or die. He now gave the soldiers permission to sack and burn the city.

The sons and brothers of Izates, king of Adiabene (who converted to Judaism), came to Titus, asking for clemency. He kept them in custody for the moment but later took them to Rome in chains to serve as hostages for the good behavior of their country. Some Idumaeans attempted to negotiate with Titus but were discovered by Simon and the leaders put to death. Jesus, son of Thebuthi, one of the priests, delivered up the temple treasury to Titus, and Phineas the temple treasurer revealed where many of the priestly garments, the spices for sacrifices, and other ornaments were kept. Further effort was needed to reduce the city, but the spirit of the rebels was broken and their resistance to further siege activity low. The city was finally taken completely toward the end of September.

Many of the survivors in the city were now allowed to live (at least, the able-bodied) but sold as slaves, though Titus is said to have spared and released forty thousand citizens of Jerusalem. But he (rather contradicting Josephus' description of his tenderness toward the besieged) kept a large number of captives to throw to the beasts or for gladiatorial fights in shows at Caesarea Philippi and Berytus (Beirut). Some were also taken back to Rome to be exhibited in his triumphal procession. Among them was Simon, son of Gioras, and John of Gischala. Both had fled into underground passages but later surrendered when they ran out of food. Simon had come out where the former temple had stood, clad in white tunics and a purple robe. What the significance of this is can be surmised. Josephus says he was trying to startle the Romans, but they seem not to have been much taken in. The purple robe sounds like a claim to royalty, though it did not seem to impress his captors. After being dragged through the streets of Rome in chains in the triumph for the Flavians, Simon was then sent to be executed. Surprisingly, John of Gischala was allowed to live, though sentenced to life imprisonment.

Why Did They Hold Out?

A question many have wondered about is why the defenders of Jerusalem continued to fight to the bitter end, when defeat seemed inevitable. It is a question often asked in such cases: compare for example the continued resistance of the German military in the final months of World War II when it was clear that the Allies' advance was unstoppable. Several reasons suggest themselves:

- Many of the defenders of Jerusalem, especially in the early days of the war, evidently believed that the city was too strong to be taken.
- Some probably thought they could escape if things got too bad. Some of these may have been individuals who remained in Jerusalem primarily to protect their property or other interests. Desertions took place throughout the siege, in spite of attempts by rebel groups to prevent people escaping to the Romans. In several instances, upper-class Jews who had been heavily involved in the revolt then went over to the Romans and were allowed to live and settle elsewhere.
- There is an instinct among some soldiers to fight to the end, whatever the odds, especially when the alternatives are considered: no doubt many felt that if they lost, there was nothing left for them except death or slavery, not only for themselves but also for their families.
- There was a hope against hope of miraculous deliverance on the part of some. In World War II there were some convinced that Hitler had secret weapons that would be launched in the nick of time to force the Allies to come to terms. In Jerusalem some clearly believed in divine intervention to save God's city and temple. How widespread this belief was is difficult to quantify, but several hints have already been noted above.

Conclusions

This chapter has covered about seventy-five years of important events in Jewish history. After the death of Herod in 4 BCE, his territory was divided among three of his sons. Archelaus, the ruler over Judaea proper, lasted only a decade before being deposed by Augustus. But Herod Antipas (over Galilee) and Philip (parts further north, mostly settled by non-Jews) exercised their rule for more than three decades. Judaea itself became a Roman province in 6 CE and remained so until 41 CE, controlled by Roman governors. Agrippa I had become a friend of Gaius Caligula, and was given the territory of, first, Philip (who had died) and then Herod Antipas (who was deposed) beginning in 37 CE. Finally, Claudius gave him also Judaea in 41 CE because of his help in convincing the Senate to accept Claudius as emperor.

Agrippa died in 44 CE, and Judaea became once more a Roman province. His son Agrippa II was given territory to govern but not Judaea. Later, however, he was given authority over the temple and allowed to appoint the high priest. Judaea had Roman governors until 66 CE, but friction between the Jews and the Roman administration grew during this time, sometimes exacerbated by the Roman procurators. Finally, a revolt broke out in which many even of priests and upper-class Jews participated. Yet rather than prepare properly for defense of the city for the inevitable Roman siege, the rebels spent much of their energy fighting each other. The 66–70 war with Rome was further complicated by internal fighting in Rome over the throne. Vespasian who was sent to put down the revolt paused the siege of Jerusalem in 68 CE, after pacifying the Galilee. But he was declared emperor in 69 CE, and it fell to his son Titus to conduct the final assault on Jerusalem and the destruction of the temple in 70 CE.

14
Last Gasps: The Final Jewish Revolts under Trajan and Hadrian

Much of Jerusalem, including its unparalleled temple, was destroyed in 70 CE. Yet this did not end the desire on the part of some Jews to gain independence from Roman control. Indeed, the 66–70 war continued in certain peripheral areas and did not come to an end until 73 (or possibly 74) CE. But in the six decades or so that followed, it became clear that the Jews under the Roman yoke had not fully accepted their overlords. Two further major rebellions broke out before the Jews finally acquiesced and submitted, with Jerusalem even off limits to Jews for a considerable period of time. This chapter covers these "last gasps" of Jewish resistance before the following dark centuries in which Jews were generally second-class citizens and often persecuted for their religion and ethnicity.

Continued Resistance after the Fall of Jerusalem

The fall of Jerusalem brought the Jewish war to a close as far as the main Roman and Jewish forces were concerned; unfortunately, it did not end all Jewish resistance. The Tenth Legion was left to guard the ruins of Jerusalem, but three fortresses still lay in the hands of Jewish factions: Herodium, Machaerus, and Masada. The pressure for a quick victory was now removed from the Roman leadership, and these remaining pockets of resistance could be dealt with at greater leisure. Nevertheless, they had to be dealt with. Lucilius Bassus was named as the legate for Judaea. To him fell the task of taking these final holdouts. Bassus managed to get Herodium to surrender, though no details are given.

Machaerus, east of the Dead Sea, was a formidable stronghold, first built by Alexander Jannaeus but greatly fortified by Herod the Great. It had a mixed population of Jews and non-Jews. The Jews had taken over the fort, forcing the non-Jews to live in the nearby town. Bassus besieged the fort, and the skirmishes on both sides left many casualties without a decisive outcome. But then a daring youth named Eleazar, a formidable fighter, was captured by the Romans who proceeded to threaten to crucify him in sight of the fortress. The defenders at this point negotiated with the Romans to be allowed to surrender the fort and leave, taking Eleazar with

FIGURE 14.1 *The Jewish fortress Masada.*

them. Bassus agreed to this. In the meantime, the inhabitants of the town planned to flee in secret but were betrayed. Of those who did not manage to escape, the men were massacred and the women and children enslaved. The irony is that the townspeople suffered this, while those who fought in the fortress were allowed to leave unharmed.

This now left all of Judaea in Roman hands except for Masada. Bassus died soon after this and was replaced by Flavius Silva whose task it was to reduce the remaining fortress. As noted earlier (chapter 13, p. 294) Masada had been captured at an early stage in the war by the Sicarii (*not* "the Zealots," as sometimes claimed). Their leader Menahem was assassinated by other Jewish groups, and they were driven out of the city and took refuge in Masada already in 66 CE.[1] The Sicarii in Masada were led by Eleazar son of Jairus who was a descendent of the Judas who opposed the Roman enrollment by Quirinius in 6 CE. These Sicarii had basically avoided getting involved in fighting the Romans but lived by raids on fellow Jews.

Masada has become a modern legend, in no small part because of the discoveries of the Dead Sea Scrolls and excavations of the fortress by Y. Yadin. The new information has been so interpreted as to expand the legend rather than demythologize it.[2] Whether the defenders of Masada should be labeled "martyrs" or only "assassins" is a matter of opinion: their fellow Jews upon whom they preyed would no doubt use the latter term. Josephus also castigates them, yet his account still makes heroes of them.

The siege was actually brief, lasting a few months at most.[3] Silva quickly dominated the region around Masada, establishing garrisons as needed. He then rapidly surrounded the fortress with a siege wall so that no one could escape. Supplies, including water, had to be brought in, but (local?) Jews were commandeered to do this work. Silva had his troops throw up a ramp of earthworks on the west side of Masada until near the top, after which layers of stone were laid to give stability and to make a base for a siege tower and a battering ram. Once the siege ramp had reached the top and they were able to deploy the battering ram, the climax came quite quickly.

Josephus says nothing about attacks on the Romans by the defenders. As the Romans were besieging the site and constructing a ramp to get to the top, they fired arrows and other missiles from the siege tower at the defenders to keep them at bay. In Josephus's account, all the defenders did was to try to defend against the siege measures, the main such defense being the building of a second wall when the first was breached. No doubt some defenders would have been killed by the Roman siege engines and archers, but nothing is said of their fighting back against the Romans as such. The second wall, made partly of earth, was effective in slowing down the work of the battering ram, but then the Romans set the wooden part of this wall on fire, and it was clear that they would break through shortly. Josephus says that instead of attacking immediately, as one would expect, the Romans drew back with plans to attack the next day.

According to Josephus's account, Eleazar made a long speech. It was, of course, common for Greek and Roman historians to invent speeches and put them into the mouths of historical characters. The speech supposedly given by Eleazar was an invention of Josephus though, interestingly, it is very religious: God as the only king, God's having abandoned the Jews, and the immortal soul trapped temporarily in the mortal body. It makes great copy for modern readers of the story, but we have no idea whether Eleazar made a speech or, if he did, what its contents were. The effect for the defenders was evidently to choose suicide for themselves and their families. They are said to have drawn lots, with ten chosen to dispatch the others, then each other. The last man then had to kill himself. Almost a thousand people are said to have died, but there were survivors: two women (one with five children) hid themselves and then surrendered to the Romans.

We have long been dependent on Josephus's account, but in recent years archaeological expeditions have worked on Masada. We can now compare the remains of the Roman siege operations with the literary narrative. Remains of a siege ramp on the west side of Masada, a circumvallation wall with watch towers, and evidence of eight Roman camps all fit with Josephus's description. Of course, there are aspects of Josephus's account that the material remains have not confirmed, such as Eleazar's speech (commented on above) and the mass suicide of the defenders.

On the other hand, various aspects of Josephus's account are plausible and seem correct. For example, he could easily have presented a scenario of a heroic defense against the Roman troops by the Sicarii, and it would have fitted his general approach in the *War* of emphasizing Jews as heroic combatants. The fact that he did not suggests that no such defense took place. The mass suicide was said to have taken place on the 15th of the Jewish month Nisan (March/April)—that is, Passover time or the beginning of April. However, the year is not specified, and the question has been much debated, generally with the choice between 73 and 74 CE. At the moment, either date—73 or 74—still seems a possibility.

As a postscript to the Great War, Masada was not the last hurrah of the Sicarii. With the fall of Masada, all Palestine was now in Roman hands, but some of the Sicarii had managed to flee to Egypt.[4] Did some Sicarii find a way to escape from the siege at Masada? We are not told. In any case, these Sicarii began to try to stir up the Jewish community in Egypt; however, the leading Jews feared that they might suffer the fate of their brothers in Judaea and captured as many Sicarii as they could, turning them over to the Romans. When news of the Sicarii disturbances was conveyed to Vespasian, he sent orders for the Egyptian governor Lupus to close the temple of Onias at Leontopolis as another potential focus for revolt (on this temple, see chapter 11, p. 214).

The Years after the Great War with Rome

One of the major problems with writing a history of the Jews after 70 CE is that Josephus's narrative—an invaluable survival from antiquity despite all its problems—ceases and the history has to be pieced together from scattered bits and pieces. Most of what we know of specific events revolves around two periods of revolt, yet despite recent important discoveries, even today only a few facts are known regarding the extremely important rebellions under Trajan and Hadrian.

The years following the 66–70 revolt were bad ones for many Jews in Palestine. Not only had thousands been killed and sold into slavery but portions of Judaea, especially around Jerusalem, had suffered the ravages of war. Some interpret the data to mean that the economic situation was desperate, assuming that large tracts of land had been taken over by the emperor and redistributed to Roman supporters.

Recently, others have argued that that picture needs revision. Rather than taking over much of Judaea into his personal possession, Vespasian confiscated only the property of rebels and founded just the one colony of soldiers in Judaea itself. Also, much of the country had suffered little direct damage from the war since most of the fighting had been in Judaea proper, primarily around Jerusalem, and only to a lesser extent in Galilee and elsewhere. On the other hand, the annual donations for the temple from the diaspora were now lost by being converted to a Jewish tax, *fiscus Judaicus*; further, the basis for the significant industry that catered for the thousands of pilgrims who came for the annual festivals in Jerusalem was gone forever. Judaea was evidently reduced to an agrarian and basically subsistence economy.

Agrippa II kept his territory, however, which would have meant parts of Galilee, Gaulanitis, and Batanaea, Trachonitis, and so on. Some sources indicate that Agrippa's realm was enlarged by Vespasian. It seems clear, however, that he had lost his position as intermediary between the Jews and Rome, because his engagement on the Roman side in the revolt meant that he had lost the confidence of the Jewish people. Josephus (*Life* 65 §§362–7) corresponded with him about his work and allegedly received his confirmation of their accuracy. The date of his death has been disputed. Recent study suggests either 93/94 or 96/97.

The status of Judaea changed. Whereas before 66 CE, Judaea was formally a part of the province of Syria, now Judaea was an independent province, and a new type of governor was created by Vespasian: governorship by a senator of praetorian rank who was also commander of the Legion X Fretensis that was permanently stationed there. Then later Judaea became a consular province when a second legion was deployed. Otherwise, the government of the province seems to have carried on much as it had before 66, as was customary under Roman rule, but details are lacking.

Yet the legal position of Jews seems not to have changed. A number of scholars have postulated an anti-Jewish policy on the part of the Romans, either by Hadrian or even going back to the Flavians. There is no question that those responsible for the 66–70 revolt were punished by death or enslavement when captured during the war or by seizure of land from survivors afterward. Part of Flavian propaganda was their suppression of the Jewish revolt, to establish their right to rule. There was also the *fiscus Judaicus* imposed by Vespasian and continued by later emperors. Yet there are counterarguments to this scenario, some quite strong. One can argue that the Flavian propaganda was predictable: a *cause célèbre* was needed to strengthen the claims of the family to the office of emperor, and the Judaean war was the main event to use for this purpose.

Otherwise, from the Roman point of view the Flavian measures were not particularly high handed. Even the *fiscus* could be said to cause no harm, since the Jews could no longer pay to the temple—why not divert the money to something useful to the Romans? Also, although the *fiscus* affected the Jews, different forms of taxation were heavily enforced on all subjects of the Roman empire; the Alexandrians, for example, were not exempted from burdensome taxation. The main argument for seeing no particular anti-Judaism on the part of the Romans is that toleration of Jewish religious practices continued, and there is no evidence that Jews were disadvantaged as such under Flavian rule.

Yet there was a major crisis from a religious perspective. The Jerusalem temple— until now the center of Judaism—was in ruins. Not only were those whose hope was in the temple affected but also those whose power base lay there, primarily the priests but also probably such groups as the Sadducees. This does not mean that the identity of the priestly families was forgotten, for many Jews even today maintain a tradition that they are "Aaron" or "Levi," but this identification is and was of little use when no temple existed. Most privileges formerly possessed were now removed, and their worth could be established only when they found a part in the new order (which some of them did, of course).

The Roman Emperors: Titus to Nerva

We must not forget that the Jews were still part of the Roman world, and the Romans were very much in charge. The Roman emperors at this time often took actions that had effects on the Jews, whether in Palestine or elsewhere in the Empire. The reign of Vespasian was surveyed in the previous chapter (chapter 13, p. 300). We now need to consider some of those emperors who followed him.

Titus (79–81 CE)

The reign of Titus might be characterized as "short and sweet." He was still less than thirty when he took up a command post under Vespasian during the Jewish war. Already he had experience as a military tribune in Germany; now he showed himself a skilled diplomat when acting on his father's behalf during the war and especially in the events relating to Vespasian's being declared emperor, notable in a young man still in his twenties. One of our main sources for his activities during the war is Josephus who lost no opportunity to praise Titus's abilities as a soldier, general, and man. Josephus's picture is clearly exaggerated. No doubt Titus had ability and was certainly an individual of courage and action, but he was also impetuous to the point of being foolhardy in battle and no great strategist. He also had the steadying hand of Tiberius Alexander (chapter 13, p. 305).

Titus's behavior after victory led to misunderstanding and rumor and gave the impression that he was trying to become a rival to his father. When this became known, Titus immediately sailed for Rome and reported to Vespasian, dispelling the rumors of seeking to take over. Vespasian for his part gladly shared many of his offices and responsibilities to ensure that Titus would succeed him. Indeed, Titus became the first Roman emperor to receive the throne from his father. Between 70 and 79, he obtained a variety of high offices, including consulship, censorship, priesthood, and tribuneship, which he occupied jointly with Vespasian to the point that he was practically co-ruler with his father.

Of special interest is his relationship with Berenice the sister of Agrippa II. He first met her when he came to Syria with his father to put down the Jewish revolt.[5] Their affair was carried on fairly openly until he returned to Rome in 71. Because of regard for public opinion, and probably on the advice of his father, he did not invite her to Rome until 75 and then along with her brother Agrippa. Agrippa was given the rank of praetor, while Berenice took up residence in Titus's palace, where they resumed their affair.[6] Apparently, they were expected to marry, but two Cynic philosophers denounced them publicly. The Cynics were punished (one with death), but Titus realized that the people of Rome would not approve, since it no doubt evoked shades of Cleopatra and Antony among other objections. He sent her away, whether in 79 when he became emperor or earlier is not clear. She returned to the Middle East, but later when she came again to Rome during his term of office, they did not meet.[7]

His brief reign included the completion of the famous Colosseum, which Vespasian had begun, as well as the Baths built in his honor. He is reported to have been generous to the point of extravagance in giving gifts to the Roman public and to many individuals. After the destruction of Pompeii in 79 and a fire and plague in Rome itself in 80, he gave considerable aid to the survivors. The historian Dio (66.19.3a) nevertheless states that he governed frugally, making precise judgment difficult. It is also difficult to judge his rule, as a whole, because it was so short. Dio (66.18.4-5) thought that things would have gone downhill if he had ruled longer.

Domitian (81–96 CE)

Although the third Flavian and the second son of Vespasian to rule, Domitian has unfortunately gone down in both Christian and Roman history as a bad ruler. This is due mainly to the strict measures he took to maintain his hold on the throne, especially the revival of treason trials. In actual fact, though, Domitian was an efficient administrator of the empire and essentially continued the policies of Vespasian with similar consequences. The opposition came because of traits of personality in large part because of his position as the younger son who had been overshadowed by Titus all his life. Although he had even functioned briefly as vice-regent in late 69 after the Vitellians were defeated, he had also blotted his copybook at the time. Consequently, he was not given any office or honor of substance, whereas Titus was groomed for government by a succession of appointments with real responsibility.

Therefore, when he had the chance to govern, he took the reins firmly in hand and did not bother to keep up the appearances of respecting the Senate as his father had done. Continuing the policies of Vespasian to entrust the administration to professionals of equestrian rank, Domitian began the tendency (though possibly it had already started under Vespasian) to divide the work of governing large provinces between a civilian official (*iuridicus*) and a military governor. He completed the reorganization of the frontier defenses in several areas, including Britain and Germany.

After a rebellion on the Rhine in 88, Domitian began to fear conspiracies and revived prosecutions for treason. It was last under Nero that the senatorial class had had to suffer condemnation of many of its own number. From a historical perspective, this does not negate the positive nature of much of Domitian's administration, but it is hardly surprising that it colored his entire reign for those upper-class writers who suffered through the period. His own wife, Domitia, instigated his assassination in 96, and his memory was condemned by the Senate. It has been speculated that he was planning an attack on the Jews, which only his death prevented, but this hypothesis does not seem well founded. However, he did extend the Jewish tax (*fiscus Judaicus*) in certain ways, a subject still debated. One interpretation said that he extended it to all those circumcised, even those who had abandoned the Jewish religion.

Nerva (96–98 CE)

The plot against Domitian seems to have been a limited one without a specific candidate in mind to replace him. Thus, the choice fell to the Senate who appointed Nerva because of his seniority rather than distinction of personal qualities (he was already over sixty-five), but he was popular with the Senate as one of their own. He took an oath not to execute any senator except after a free trial by the Senate itself, one later repeated by both Trajan and Hadrian.

Nevertheless, Nerva clearly led a caretaker government. He had no military prowess to claim the loyalty of the army, and he quickly had trouble with the Praetorian Guard who was angry about the murder of Domitian. Nerva was forced to accede to their demands, but this only showed how vulnerable he was to the whims of the military and invoked images of "the year of the four emperors" (a name sometimes applied to the year 69 CE). However, Nerva had the sense to resolve the problem by gaining the support of Trajan who was commander in northern Germany. Nerva adopted him and made him co-ruler, thus ensuring stability for the few months left in his reign. One interesting decree by Nerva was a change in the Jewish tax, which he commemorated by an inscription on some of his coins. It was now placed on all who practiced Judaism, whether born Jewish or not.

Movements That Flourished after 70 CE

Since the destruction of the holy place had happened once before and yet the temple had been rebuilt, no doubt many hoped that it was only a matter of time before a new edifice was erected on Zion. Nevertheless, as long as Jerusalem and the temple remained in ruins, this was still an important theological problem for many Jews. We find that there were several different approaches taken to attempt to resolve this problem.

The groups which survived and flourished were those with built-in mechanisms allowing them to provide substitutes for the temple and its cultus, primarily the Pharisees and the Christians. The indications are that Christians by this time had begun to substitute Christ for the temple and its sacrificial system. Although Luke (whether rightly or wrongly) pictures the Jewish members of the early church as continuing to observe temple and ritual practice (Acts 2:1; 21:17-26), he also preserves a tradition that rejects the temple completely in the speech of Stephen (Acts 7:44-50). The Epistle to the Hebrews includes a long exposition on how the temple cult was a detailed symbol of the sacrifice of Christ. There is little indication that the destruction of the temple was in any way a theological problem for the emerging Christian church.

Apart from the Christians, two further Jewish groups took different approaches, one of which allowed survival and one of which did not. We shall now consider these two groups in more detail: the apocalyptic approach and the approach of rabbinic Judaism.

The Apocalyptic Approach: The Apocalypses of Ezra, Baruch, Abraham, and John

It appears that a significant number of Jews sought to resolve the current difficulties of their existence through the medium of apocalyptic expectations: the hope in divine intervention to destroy Rome and exalt the faithful Jews in the near future. It is hard to say how widespread this view was, but we do find strong apocalyptic expectations in some circles. This was laid out not only by such Jewish apocalypses as 4 Ezra, *2 Baruch*, and probably the *Apocalypse of Abraham*, but also the Christian Apocalypse of John.

These suggest why the rebellions in 115 to 117 CE and the Bar Kokhva revolt a few years later came about: the apocalyptic expectations known from earlier times had not ceased to have their force. Contrary to the developing rabbinic tradition, coming to terms with the new situation was not to the taste of all Jews, as events in the early second century CE demonstrate. They wanted to revive the supposed glorious past by violent revolution, though there was a major expectation that God would also take a hand.

The *Apocalypse of Ezra*, the *Apocalypse of Baruch*, the *Apocalypse of Abraham*, and the New Testament book of Revelation all seem to arise from approximately the same time: about 100 CE. Although Revelation is very much Christian in its present form, a good deal of Jewish material seems to be drawn on, and it represents the same spirit as the Jewish apocalypses of the same time. All four have much in common in spite of different (fictional) settings and a different patriarchal figure as the main actor (though 4 Ezra and 2 Baruch are probably related organically in some way). Most commentators agree that the Revelation of John—like 4 Ezra and 2 Baruch—is predicting the impending destruction of Rome and the deliverance of the faithful by the return of Jesus Christ.

The *Apocalypse of Ezra* or 4 Ezra (also sometimes referred to as 3 Ezra or 2 Esdras) is preserved in Latin and Syriac translations, the original (probably Hebrew) being entirely lost. It forms chs 3 through 14 in the work called 2 Esdras in the Apocrypha (chs 1–2 are usually referred to as 5 Ezra, and chs 15–16 as 6 Ezra). The *Apocalypse of Baruch* or 2 Baruch is preserved only in a Syriac translation from a lost original (presumably Hebrew). From the number of passages closely parallel to 4 Ezra, scholars have tended to see it as dependent on 4 Ezra, though some argue that the converse is true.

Both works seem to represent the situation some years after the Roman destruction of Jerusalem and the Second Temple. In both books the fact of the destruction is a major theological problem, and both address the question of theodicy (i.e., Why would God allow such a disaster to happen to his people?). Although they deal with a variety of issues, the primary answer is that God will shortly intervene to rectify matters. The victorious conqueror—the Roman Empire (the "eagle" of 4 Ezra 11–12)—has not much longer to enjoy its evil gains, for God will take a hand to destroy it. The Eagle Vision appears to outline the history of the Roman emperors to about the time of Domitian, suggesting the intervention of the messiah in the near future. This will commence the end time process which will include the temporary Messianic Age and finally the creation of a new heaven and new earth.

The *Apocalypse of Abraham* is known only in a Slavonic version (though the original language was probably Hebrew). The first part of the book (*Apoc. Abr.* 1–8) is how Abraham destroyed his fathers' idols; the second half (*Apoc. Abr.* 9–32), a description of a heavenly journey and the things Abraham saw there, including the original Adam and Eve in Eden. The author has priestly interests and may have been a priest. The demon Azazel has a prominent part to play as the tempter and opponent of God (*Apoc. Abr.* 13; 14:5; 22:5–23:13; 29:5-7; 31:2-7), while the angel Iaoel is equally important (*Apoc Abr.* 10:3). The temple has been destroyed (*Apoc. Abr.* 25; 27:1-5) but will be rebuilt (*Apoc. Abr.* 29:17-18).

Although there are many differences in content and approach between the four books, they have much in common, even given that Revelation is a Christian work with an outlook not found in any of the Jewish apocalypses (especially the return of Christ). The following points about Judaism arise from these books:

- A preoccupation with Roman rule and an expectation of the imminent end of the Roman empire. The Eagle Vision of 4 Ezra 11–12, the beast from the sea (Rev. 13:1-8) as well as the beast ridden by the scarlet women of Revelation (Rev. 17), and the fourth kingdom of 2 Baruch (39–40) are all symbols of Rome's expected destruction. In each case the Roman empire as it existed about 100 CE is pictured, but heavenly intervention (by Christ in Rev. 18, though announced by an angel; by a messianic figure in 4 Ezra 12:31-34) will bring about the destruction of Rome. The *Apocalypse of*

Abraham (32:1) speaks more generally of punishment of the heathen, but it predicts the restoration of the temple and cult.

- The rise or coming of a messianic figure. In Revelation this is naturally the heavenly Christ who returns for judgment of the wicked, but the messiah of *2 Baruch* (29–30; 39:7–40:3; 70:9; 72–74) is also apparently a heavenly figure, though hardly divine. 4 Ezra 7:26-32 posits a Messianic Age: an earthly messiah who will rule for four hundred years, after which he and all mankind will die, but then the resurrection and judgment will follow after seven days and finally new heavens and a new earth. In 4 Ezra 13, however, the "man from the sea" appears to be a heavenly messianic figure. The *Apocalypse of Abraham* (31:1) speaks more generally of the coming of a "chosen one" who will gather God's chosen people.

- The "messianic woes" (the various problems, plagues, and unnatural events preceding the end time) have a prominent place in all the apocalypses (4 Ezra 5:1-13; 6:18-28; *2 Bar.* 70; *Apoc. Abr.* 29:15; 30:2-8; Rev. 6, 8–9, 15–16). The "four horsemen" of Revelation 6:1-8 are based on a traditional list of plagues of war, famine, pestilence (e.g., Ezek. 6:11).

The Rabbinic Approach: Nascent Rabbinic Judaism at Yavneh (70–130 CE)

It is generally agreed that rabbinic Judaism arose in some way from the Pharisaic movement of the pre-70 period. The first-century Pharisees were, among other things, evidently in many ways a table-fellowship sect in which the home represented the temple; the hearth, the altar; and the Pharisee, himself, the priest. A Pharisaic layman in his home was able to reenact the temple cult in symbol. Although Pharisees would have—and clearly did—participate in the official temple worship as did other Jews, their religious system was fully capable of operation without a physical temple. They had also been a political movement, seeking power and authority in Jewish society; therefore, it is hardly surprising that they were a significant factor in the post-70 religious reconstruction.

Yet Rabbinic Judaism was a post-70 phenomenon. Although it retained the old core of Pharisaism, its new center was an element not characteristic of pre-70 Pharisees: from all we can determine it developed *study of the Torah as a substitute for the temple and its service*. The Pharisees had their religious traditions which included certain interpretations of written scripture; however, study of biblical writings was evidently not seen as their main concern. With rabbinic Judaism, on the contrary, study was the main focus of their devotion and worship—both the written Torah and the interpretive Pharisaic traditions that became known in rabbinic Judaism as "the oral law."

Coincidentally, the post-70 situation was also favorable to the Pharisees in that it had removed many rivals from the scene. The Essenes seem to have been wiped out; Qumran—whatever its relationship with the Essenes—was overrun and destroyed. Some no doubt escaped from that destruction and perhaps other threats (such as the fall of Jerusalem), but we have the impression that few Essenes were any longer around in Jewish society. The destruction of the temple made the Sadducees and the priests more or less irrelevant. Some Pharisees were priests, but priests no longer had a formal place in religion.

But rabbinic Judaism was a new form of Judaism. It contained many elements known from pre-70 groups, but it was a new synthesis. Yes, Pharisaic tradition was brought in as a major content of its teaching. Yet the tradition of study of the written word may have been imported from the priesthood and scribes. Even the Essenes may have made their contribution. The driving force of this innovation was the academy which the Romans allowed to be established in the *town of Yavneh* (often given in the Latin form "Jamnia"). It can be said with certainty that what happened at Yavneh had great consequences for the development of Judaism after 70. The preserved tradition seems to be unanimous that the reconstruction of the rabbinic version of Judaism after the fall of Jerusalem was due to the Jewish teacher *Yohanan ben Zakkai*, an intriguing figure about whom much is still a puzzle.[8]

According to legend, Yohanan was given permission to establish an academy in the city of Yavneh by Emperor Vespasian himself.[9] Although that is scarcely credible, local Roman authorities must have been involved. The grant made to Yohanan represented an important concession to Judaism by the Romans: it means that the reconstruction which began under Yohanan had, if not Roman sanction, at least Roman tolerance. We in fact know very little of the details of what happened at Yavneh. The precise interactions at Yavneh have been obscured by the later editing and interpretation of the period in rabbinic literature. The intervention of the Bar Kokhba revolt, the executions or deaths of some important rabbinic leaders, and the reevaluation of some of the Yavnean leaders by a later generation, all led to the heavy censorship and recontextualization of the Yavnean traditions.

Almost all our knowledge of what happened is contained in rabbinic literature which has little or no interest in historiographic matters. Yet, whatever the origins of the academy, it goes down as an extremely important episode in Jewish history because the rabbinic version of Judaism gradually grew stronger until it came to dominate the practice of Judaism in later centuries and is the basis of Orthodox Judaism today. It is important to put out of our minds the often *misinterpretation* of what happened at Yavneh, especially the depiction found in some Christian works which refer to it as the "synod of Jamnia," as if it were like a church council. It was not a council and was not a decision-making body, at least for the whole of Judaism. What was happening here may even have gone largely unnoticed by most Jews at the time.

It is usually thought that Yohanan ben Zakkai was a Pharisee, but his characteristics according to the earliest traditions do not fit well what we know of pre-70 Pharisaism.[10] He looks more like a scribal figure whose religion centered on scripture, and since this is an important feature of rabbinic Judaism, it was probably Yohanan who pushed matters in this direction in the religious reorientation. Perhaps more important was his apparent ability to work with a variety of groups. According to one statement (*M. Avot* 2:8), a number of groups were represented at Yavneh; if so, a variety of viewpoints may have fed into what became a Yavnean synthesis. As mentioned above, Yavneh is often misrepresented as a "synod," as if it were something analogous to a church council; on the contrary, it was more like an academy, and the number of participants seems to have been quite small at first, nor were the members necessarily recognized as representatives of Jews of the country. The group behind the Mishnah came to be influential for Jewish society, but this took a long time, perhaps centuries.

Whatever Yohanan's sectarian affiliation, there is evidence that the dominant influence in the Yavnean discussions was Pharisaic. That is, much of the content of debates appears to be based on tradition or interests that have been identified with the pre-70 Pharisees. Two "schools" had become dominant in the late pre-70 period of Pharisaism: the schools of Hillel and Shammai. But there were other important Pharisaic figures. One of these was the family of Gamaliel (apparently the person mentioned in Acts 5:34; 22:3). His grandson Gamaliel II was an important person at Yavneh.[11] Later tradition makes the Gamaliel faction a part of the Hillel family, but this is not the case in the earliest layer of traditions: the Gamaliel "school" was probably separate from that of Hillel. We seem to have a jockeying for power in which the school of Hillel eventually wins, though the family of Gamaliel maintained a significant influence, with the school of Shammai losing out.

The major concern of pre-70 Pharisaism, at least in the first century, seems to have been with religious law. Therefore, most of the pre-70 tradition centered on legal discussions and disputes. Each school had its own rulings, some or many of which may have differed from those of other schools. These traditions also represented the interests and sphere of authority of the Pharisees, namely, their own homes and inter-sectarian concerns. At Yavneh the differences had to be threshed out between the various schools and whatever non-Pharisaic parties were represented there. The exact maneuverings that went on can only be guessed at, but at some point agreement was reached that the opinions of both the school of Hillel and the school of Shammai would be preserved. As already noted, the school of Hillel eventually became the dominant one, though this seems to have taken time since the school of Shammai was apparently more influential in pre-70 Pharisaism.

Although neither biography nor narrative history is possible because of the nature of the traditions, there is still material of value to the historian in the rabbinic literature.[12] Most importantly, source analysis shows the development of religious ideas in the major periods of the growth of the Mishnah, which extends back to the Yavnean period and even before.[13] Prior to 70, the areas of most interest were those of purity, agriculture, festivals, and women—that is, the areas of importance for a sect who had control of its own membership and internal affairs but not of society as a whole. That this was the Pharisees is a very reasonable inference.

The Yavnean layer shows an interesting transitional phase toward the eventual outlook of the Mishnah (on this, see below) in its final form. There is little development in the order dealing with civil law (*Neziqin*), indicating the group is not administering society at large. The considerable discussion about the cult does not seem rooted in the experience of cultic personnel but in the biblical text alone; that is, the interest is in creating a new, idealized cult according to the sect's principles, not in extending or developing the old Second Temple practices, which were, of course, in the hands of the priests. Understanding the situation at Yavneh should bury a lot of myths, such as the notion that the Hebrew Bible was canonized there or that the leaders of the academy ran society, whether in the civil or religious sphere. Rather, Yavneh presents only a transitional period on the way toward the dominance of Jewish life by the rabbis (though this took a long time, probably centuries).

Apart from Yohanan ben Zakkai perhaps the most intriguing figure at Yahweh was Rabbi Aqiva. Unfortunately, older and traditional studies are uncritical and simply conflate the various early and later traditions. The aspect that is most fascinating is Aqiva's relationship to Bar Kokhva. Did Aqiva declare Bar Kokhva the messiah? There is some evidence that Aqiva held a nationalistic-messianic view,[14] which would put him at odds with the general outlook of the Mishnah which has a completely different world view from the apocalyptic-messianic.[15] On Aqiva and Bar-Kokhva, and on the messianic view of Bar Kokhva, see further below (pp. 333–4).

After the Bar Kokhva revolt the center of rabbinic Judaism shifted to a town in Galilee called Usha where debate about rabbinic tradition and rabbinic law continued. This eventually led to the first major document or book of rabbinic Judaism. Although there is a vast number of rabbinic writings, extending into the medieval period and later, some of the most influential can be briefly outlined here. But first some terms that are often found in discussions: two important terms are *halakhah*, basically legal material, and *haggadah*, generally applied to all non-halakhic material, meaning stories and recitation of nonlegal material. The literature falls into two chronological periods: *the Tannaitic period*, that is, the time of the Tannaim or earlier rabbinic figures, up to about 300 CE; and *the Amoraic period*, that is, the time of the Amoraim, the rabbinic figures after the period of the Mishnah and other Tannaitic writings.

The earliest document of the Tannaitic period is the *Mishnah*. The editing of it is attributed to Rabbi Judah the Prince about 200 CE. It is mainly a book of legal rulings, divided into six orders: "Seeds" (mainly agricultural regulations); "Festivals" (the Sabbath and the annual holy days); "Women" (rulings relating to women); "Damages" (the regulations closest to civil law); "Holy Things" (matters relating to the temple); and "Purities" (regulations on clean and unclean objects and states). Although some of this material arose from the time before 70 CE, it has all been edited and developed, first in the period of Yavneh (up to about 120 CE), then in the decades following the Bar Kokhva revolt (the period of Usha). The other main Tannaitic document is the *Tosephta*, dating to perhaps 250 to 300 CE. It consists mainly of material that supplements the Mishnah. Divided into the same six orders, it is more detailed where the Mishnah is brief, and vice versa. There are also Tannaitic commentaries on parts of Exodus, Leviticus, Numbers, and Deuteronomy, known as the *Tannaitic Midrashim*.

The main Amoraic writings are the two Talmuds, which are basically commentaries on the Mishnah. The main one is the *Babylonian Talmud*, compiled in the Babylonian Jewish community, probably after 500 CE but based on oral traditions of rabbis mainly in the period 200 to 500 CE, though sometimes earlier. There is no comment on the orders of "Seeds" or "Purities." When "the Talmud" is referred to without any other designation, the Babylonian Talmud is usually in mind. The other is the *Palestinian Talmud* (also called the *Jerusalem Talmud*). It is about a third of the size of the Babylonian Talmud, but the text has been less well preserved, and it has been less studied by scholars. Some tractates of the Mishnah are not commented on, though "Seeds" and "Purities" do have comment. There is also the *Midrash Rabba*, later commentaries on the five books of Moses, and the *Megillot* or festival books (Song of Songs, Ruth, Lamentations, Ecclesiastes, Esther). Some of the commentaries are from the fourth century or so CE, but others (e.g., Numbers) are medieval.

To summarize briefly, developing rabbinic Judaism at Yavneh appears to owe a great deal to the pre-70 Pharisaic tradition, yet it is also a synthesis of a variety of elements. The important factor toward the religious development was the injection of a perspective from another source. This was the concept of Torah-centeredness and the religious efficacy of study. Things of interest to some Jews—especially apocalyptic ideas like the messiah and the end of the world—seem not to have been given up, but they were relegated to an indefinite future. If any of the early rabbis were expecting the end of the world, their views seem to have been edited out of the tradition. But the Judaism that evolved at Yavneh and then Usha was not the religion of most Jews initially. It was only in subsequent centuries that it spread and gained influence to become the dominant form of Judaism.

The Roman Emperor Trajan (98–117 CE)

We now come to the time of new Jewish rebellions, those under Trajan and Hadrian. First, the reign of Trajan: he had many of the qualities of Vespasian. The army considered him one of themselves, and he maintained the outward forms of the republic sufficient to keep the Senate happy. To the personal contrast with Domitian was added the administrative ability of the latter to inaugurate a period of relative order and peace which lasted through a good portion of the second century CE. (This did not include the frontiers that were always a potential source of trouble.) Indeed, Trajan began his reign by having to deal with the Dacians. This was the start of Trajan's policy of expansion, pushing the boundaries of the Roman Empire to their widest limits.

After the Dacians, it was the turn of the East. In 106 he annexed Arabia (Nabataea) to form a new province, but this was only a prelude to the campaigns that came toward the end of his reign, his wars in the East. Although the precise reason for them has been debated, they were undoubtedly undertaken primarily out of strategic motives, whatever secondary aims there may have been. The immediate cause was the threat to the Armenian throne. Trajan left Rome in October 113 for Antioch where he spent several months preparing for war. He probably had the equivalent of eleven legions (plus auxiliaries) when he set out in the spring of 114 for Armenia. The crown was removed from the pretender to throne and Armenia—or at least the western part of it—made into a Roman province. In the area of the Caucasus, Trajan established a number of client-kings to help hold the frontier in this area.

In the autumn of 114, Trajan turned south into Mesopotamia. The precise course of events for the next year is uncertain, but he obtained the submission of various peoples and territories, including Nisibus, Edessa, Singra, and even areas beyond the Tigris. He did not return until late in 115; however, he was in Antioch when the earthquake of December 13, 115 occurred. Trajan had now established a new province of Mesopotamia, but he was not finished. In the spring of 116 he set out for the conquest of Assyria and Babylonia. He took Adiabene, Seleucia, and Ctesiphon by the summer, establishing the new province of Assyria, then sailed down the river to the Persian Gulf to add further client-kings, and returned to the site of ancient Babylon to spend the winter.

A counterattack by the Parthians, combined with revolts in Mesopotamia itself, threatened to undo everything, but these were effectively suppressed and most of the conquered areas remained under Roman control. Lusius Quietus received much of the credit for this. However, it was 117 and something had to be done about the serious situation with the Jewish revolts in Cyprus, Cyrene, and Egypt (see next section), including sending back to the west military units originally removed from there for the Parthian invasion. It was time to stop advancing and consolidate. Trajan left this task to Hadrian and began to make his way back to Rome. He died on the way in August 117.

The Revolts under Trajan

During the period 115–17, Jewish revolts broke out in Cyrenaica, Egypt, Cyprus, and Mesopotamia (according to some, even in Palestine, though this is doubtful). The brief statements we have by Eusebius (*Hist. Eccl.* 4.2.1-5) and the Roman historian Cassius Dio (68.32) give very few data. This can be filled out to some extent by papyri in Egypt and by archaeology. For Mesopotamia almost nothing is known.

The Mesopotamian revolts seem to have begun in the wake of Trajan's Eastern conquests. When he sailed down the Tigris to the Persian Gulf in the middle of 116, a general revolt took place in the newly created provinces of Mesopotamia and Assyria during his absence. Although Trajan and his generals put down the revolt, he died soon afterward. Jewish participation seems only part of a broader backlash against the Roman conquest, which included the Parthians and other native inhabitants of Mesopotamia. Other than the brief knowledge that Jews were among those trying to throw off the recently acquired Roman yoke, we know nothing about it.

The revolt that began in the West in 115 was primarily a Jewish affair. Although the revolt may not have begun in Cyrene, it reached a critical mass first there and spilled over into Egypt. Cyrene was devastated in the fighting. Although excavation has concentrated on sacred and public buildings, sufficient has been found to suggest that the entire city of Cyrene was completely destroyed, and there was damage or destruction at other sites. Multiple inscriptions tell of buildings and temples which were rebuilt to replace those torn down by the Jews. Not surprisingly, the Jews seem to have concentrated their efforts on pagan temples and statues wherever they were found. According to literary authors, the fight was led by a "king" named Lukuas (Eusebius) or Andreas (Dio). This is important because the proclamation of a king shows not only a desire for national independence but even suggests messianic impulses.

The revolt in Egypt eventually covered the entire country, judging from the spread of places mentioned. A riot or something larger took place in Alexandria which was put down straight away sometime before October 115. The Greeks then used this opportunity to attack the pacified Jews, who now required the Romans to intervene on their behalf. However, such periodic friction was not unusual and does not seem at first to have led to a general revolt. Taxes continued to be paid until the summer of 116, by which time the main revolt seems well underway. The revolt lasted approximately a year and was not put down until Roman reinforcements arrived. Even then it was not easy because in anticipation of the legions' arrival the Jews seem to have concentrated their forces around Memphis to prevent the Romans from crossing the river and even succeeded in defeating one legion. It was not until a second joined the first that they were able to defeat the Jews about January 117.

The ferocity of the fighting is indicated by records of new recruits into the Roman centuries in the months after the battle, which seem to average about one-third of total strength and thus suggest a high rate of casualties. Areas of Egypt were so devastated by the fighting that they were still unfruitful many decades later. But the Jews suffered more. They are said to have been "exterminated," undoubtedly true for many areas since references to Jews practically cease after this.[16] Because the revolt was quickly stifled in Alexandria, there were survivors. Many of these were resettled in an area adjacent to the city, but the magnificent great synagogue in the city had been destroyed and the Jewish court seems to have been suspended.

The rebellion in Cyprus was also led by a "king" named Artemion, again having overtones of a messianic movement. The number of 240,000 slain by the Jews according to Dio is incredible, like his figures for Cyrene, but it certainly suggests widespread killing and destruction in both places. A few building inscriptions could be interpreted as representing rebuilding after the fighting, but nothing is specifically said to show this. Potentially more telling is a statue, possibly of a Flavian emperor, which has been heavily damaged, especially the divine images on the cuirass. According to Dio, when the Jews were finally defeated, an edict was issued forbidding Jews to settle on the island, while any accidentally shipwrecked there would be executed.

The revolts were probably due to a variety of factors. To take Egypt first, there had been continual friction between the Jews and the Greek population going back at least a century. Also, the strength of the Roman military forces in Egypt had always been low, because of lack of significant unrest through much of Roman rule and was now further reduced by Trajan's call for various units to aid in his Parthian war. The revolts in Cyprus and Cyrene had a definite catalyst in the "kings" who took the lead in rebelling against Roman rule, evidently messianic figures of some sort. This might suggest that the cause in Egypt was similarly messianic/eschatological, since the Jews could not rationally have hoped to win by ordinary military means. This suggestion has *prima facie* merit, especially if the Cyrene uprising was the cause of that in the Egyptian countryside. We cannot be sure about a messianic cause of the revolt, but it could still be an important element since eschatological speculation was significant at this time.

Did the Jews of Palestine also revolt at this time? Some have suggested that they did, but this cannot go much beyond speculation. The arguments are all indirect. Some of them are extremely weak and depend on data that have been overinterpreted and even emended. Against them one must oppose the silence of the early historians: none of the surviving accounts—Dio, Eusebius, Orosius—mentions Palestine, which still seems strange despite their general brevity. In the light of arguments advanced so far, it seems best to allow for the possibility of some unrest but recognize that the evidence is very uncertain. It is possible that there were attempts at an uprising there but, if so, they seem to have been quickly put down by the governor Quietus.

The Roman Emperor Hadrian (117–138 CE)

As a protege of Trajan, Hadrian had been well trained for his role as emperor. He had campaigned with Trajan and oversaw the army in the East at Trajan's death. He was already in his early forties and had apparently been designated as Trajan's heir. It was under Hadrian that the push of the borders of the empire further east was halted; he quickly abandoned the recent conquests in Mesopotamia as too difficult to defend and came to terms with the Parthians. This meant that most of his reign was a time of peace, which allowed him to exercise his considerable skills in overhauling the administration and establishing formal procedures for regular military training. It also let him take a number of tours of the empire, which occupied the bulk of his twenty-one-year reign.

After three years in Rome working on the administration of the empire, Hadrian began his first tour of the empire in 120 or 121.[17] His second tour most likely began in early 128. It was probably in the spring of 130 that he visited Jerusalem and gave the order for it to be rebuilt as Aelia Capitolina. The occasion was marked by the issue of a series of coins with the inscription, "for the arrival of Augustus [Hadrian] in Judaea (*ADVENTVI AVG[VSTI] IVDAEAE*)."[18] In late summer 131, he returned to Syria, apparently spending some time there. He wintered in Athens in 131/132, after which the revolt in Judaea began. The next firm date is his presence in Rome in 134: precisely what he did in the intervening time is uncertain. However, it seems probable that he personally inspected the theater of war in Judaea sometime in 133/134. It may have been the exertions of his tours that brought on an illness in 136 which only worsened through the final years of his reign. He died in July 138 CE.

The Bar-Kokhva Revolt (132–136 CE)

We know a bit more about the Palestinian revolt of 132 to 136 than about the earlier revolts in Egypt, Cyrene, and Cyprus—thanks in large part to recent discoveries of manuscripts and coins—but not much more. Again, there is not enough information to give a history of the war or even a rough sequence of events. The only account of consequence preserved is that of Dio Cassius (69.12-14), though Eusebius has some additional information (*Hist. Eccl.* 4.6.1-4). The points of relevance in their accounts can be summarized as follows:

- Hadrian founded the city of Aelia Capitolina and built a new temple to Jupiter on the site of the Jewish temple, which caused a significant war (Dio 69.12.1-2). Eusebius (*Hist. Eccl.* 4.6.4) suggests that the city of Aelia was built after the revolt and settled by non-Jewish inhabitants.

- As long as Hadrian was close by, the Jews were at peace but revolted when he moved on. But when they manufactured weapons for the Romans, they made (some?) of poor quality so that they would be rejected and could be used by the Jews (Dio 69.12.2).

- The Jews did not dare to meet the Roman army in open combat but made use of underground hiding places (69.12.3).

- The Romans were not too concerned at first, but as the hostility advanced among the Jewish population, others (not specified) joined them (69.13.1-2).
- Hadrian sent his best generals against the Jews, first Julius Severus, governor of Britain (though Dio does not mention any other generals) (69.13.2). Eusebius (*Hist. Eccl.* 4.6.2) names only Rufus, governor of Judaea.
- The Jewish leader was named *Barchochebas* (Βαρχωχεβας), which seems to represent the Aramaic phrase "son of the star." He was a murderer and bandit but claimed to be a "light-bringer," come down from heaven to cast marvellous light on the miserable (Eusebius, *Hist. Eccl.* 4.6.2). Dio does not mention a specific Jewish leader.
- Because of their numbers and fanaticism, Severus did not attack the Jewish fighters in the open but proceeded by destroying small groups and shutting them up and cutting off their food supplies (Dio 69.13.3).
- The pinnacle of the war was reached in Hadrian's eighteenth year (August 135 to August 136 CE) at Βηθθηρα (Betar), which fell only after a long siege (Eusebius, *Hist. Eccl.* 4.6.3).
- Eusebius (4.6.2) says thousands of Jews—men, women, and children— perished, while Dio (69.13.3-14.2) says most of Judaea was made desolate, with 580,000 men killed in fighting and famine and disease killing many more; fifty forts and 985 villages were destroyed.
- So many Romans also died (Dio 69.14.3) that Hadrian refrained from using the common opening in his report to the Senate, "I and the legions are in health."
- Hadrian forbade Jews from entering Jerusalem or even the surrounding district (Eusebius, *Hist. Eccl.* 4.6.3).
- Even before the war there had been portents of the destruction, with the tomb of Solomon collapsing into pieces and wolves and hyenas running howling into cities (Dio 69.14.2).

Whereas the First Revolt produced a number of leaders but no single outstanding one, the Second Revolt is dominated by the name of its leader. In rabbinic literature he is referred to as Shim'on ben Koziba, which has usually been considered a denigrating wordplay (*koziba* means "lie" in Aramaic). The explanation that this is a title, based on the messianic interpretation of Num. 24:17, is probably correct, especially now that recent documents contain his actual name. In various Hebrew letters he is called "Simon son of Kosiva." But other than his father's name and his personal name, we know extremely little about this unusual individual, even with the discoveries of his own personal letters.

The governor of Judaea, Tineius Rufus, apparently first attempted to crush the revolt but was singularly unsuccessful. The reasons are not known, but there have long been arguments that the *legio XXII Deiotariana*, which is known to have disappeared about this time, was wiped out in the initial stages of the revolt. Normally, a more junior pro-consul would have been chosen for the job of sorting out the revolt, but the situation was clearly grave. This is why Sextus Iulius Severus, a senior official with the major responsibility of governing Britain was brought in. And many reinforcements of soldiers were also transferred to the new command.

Dio states that Hadrian's best "generals"—plural—were sent. These were probably Publicius Marcellus, the governor of Syria, and Haterius Nepos, the governor of Arabia, both of whom seem to have been honored at this time by Hadrian.

Bar Kokhva's military strategy is revealed by two factors: (1) the location of his "kingdom" or territory in the area to the south of Jerusalem and west of the Dead Sea bordering on the Judaean desert, and (2) the discovery of a number of man-made hideouts tunneled into the rock in the Shephelah and elsewhere.

It seems that Bar Kokhva's men waged war primarily in guerrilla fashion rather than in pitched battles with the Romans. The den-like dwellings dug into the rock formed bases of operation that allowed the Jewish fighters to hide undetected, emerge when the opportunity presented itself for a swift blow at the enemy, and then disappear once more as if into thin air. Even if a hideout was discovered, it was so constructed as to make it very difficult to attack those within. But Dio's statement that the Romans also tried to engage only with small Jewish contingents could also relate to this mode of fighting on the part of the Jews. The hideouts were constructed surreptitiously over a period of time preceding the war and used to make a surprise attack on the Romans at the beginning of the uprising, with considerable success. But such hideouts were used in many periods, and the attempt to relate them all to the Bar Kokhva revolt is disputed. A second stage was the construction of more conventional fortifications above ground to meet the Roman counterattack.

The position of the territory also made invasion difficult except from certain predictable directions. Most of the named sites border on the Judaean desert. En-gedi, an important oasis on the Dead Sea, is prominent in some of the correspondence. This would not only make the territory held by Bar Kokhva less accessible to the Romans, but the wilderness would provide the Jews with a quick place of retreat, either after guerrilla raids or if a pitched battle went against them. Manuscript finds occur only along the west coast of the Dead Sea, but more important are the sites actually mentioned in the documents and those where coins have been found; these include Hebron, Latrun, Herodium, Tekoa, Ir Nahash, and En-gedi.[19] These all occur roughly in a rectangle bounded on the north by Jerusalem and Latrun; on the east by the Dead Sea; on the south by Nahal Hever, and on the west by a line running south from Latrun.

Surprisingly, there is no evidence that they held Masada, but this could be explained by the suggestion that they were also concerned not to defend fortresses from which there was no possible retreat. The wilderness was at their backs and a refuge of last resort. The oasis of En-gedi on the west side of the Dead Sea served as a point of provisioning and a communications center. Whether there was one main headquarters is a moot point, though it has been argued that Herodion served this purpose for at least part of the war. Several other place names occur in the documents, all from the area to the south of Jerusalem and west of the Dead Sea. Although it has often been asserted that the Jews took Jerusalem, there is little hard evidence for this beyond hints in minor literary sources. A strongly negative argument is the lack of any Bar Kokhva coin finds from the extensive archaeological excavations in Jerusalem.

Another important site was Betar (Bethar) about 10 kilometers (6–7 miles) southwest of Jerusalem, which eventually served as the place of Bar Kokhva's last stand against the Romans. It was a modest settlement, apparently with public buildings using ashlars in their construction. At the time of the Roman siege, a fortification wall was built on the summit of the hill, using material from the village's buildings and preexisting fortifications; it shows evidence of hasty and inadequate construction. The Romans set up camps to the south of the hill (remains still visible) and threw up a siege wall around it. A Latin inscription on a rock near the spring (southeast of the village) seems to name the besieging legions as *legio V Macedonica* and *legio XI Claudia*. Many sling stones were found from the time, indicating how the besieged defended themselves. We have little reliable information on the battle itself. Eusebius claims that the siege lasted a long time, and the defenders were defeated by hunger and thirst (*Hist. Eccl.* 4.6.3).

The letters and other documents of Bar Kokhva show neither a messianic figure nor a fighter in action. Instead, they mirror a mundane world in which land is leased (Mur 24), the Sabbath observed (Mur 44), the festivals scrupulously celebrated (*P. Yadin* 57), and the ownership of a cow disputed (Mur 42). A couple of letters assert Bar Kokhva's authority because he had apparently not been obeyed (Mur 43; *P. Yadin* 49), and another mentions that something was not done because the "Gentiles" (Romans) were nearby (Mur 42). This appears to be the closest to military activity found in these contemporary records. None of this is incompatible with Bar Kokhva as a messianic figure, but we hardly find the heroic military leader that being the messiah often implies, and certainly not a heavenly figure (on the question of his messiahship, see pp. 333–4 below). An intriguing statement by Dio (69.13.2) is that non-Jews also participated in the fight against the Romans.

According to Dio (69.14.1), half a million Jews died in the fighting alone, not counting those who perished from famine and disease or who were enslaved. This seems an exaggerated figure but at least indicates the serious cost of the Second Revolt in Jewish lives. According to the patristic writer Jerome (*In Zach.*, on Zech. 11:4-5; *In Hier.* 6.18, on Jer. 31:15), after the defeat the glut of slaves was so great that the price dropped drastically in the eastern markets for a time, a striking image, though the reliability of this tradition remains uncertain. But judging from the comments of Dio (69.14.3), the Roman casualties were also very high, to the extent that Hadrian in his report to the Senate dropped the customary formula, "I and the legions are well." Aelia Capitolina now became a reality, and Jews were long excluded even from entry into the city. Only in the fourth century do we learn that Jews were again allowed access to the temple site, though only once a year on Av 9, the traditional date of its destruction.

There was, no doubt, a variety of causes for the revolt. Briefly, we can note here that many of the factors that led to the 66–70 rebellion were still in existence. There is evidence of periodic unrest in Judaea since the fall of Jerusalem in 70. All that was needed was the right catalyst. Whether that catalyst was a single action of Hadrian or the rise of Bar Kokhva as a leader or something else again, the Jews were not yet ready to remain under the Roman yoke without one more try for independence. The war was evidently preceded by a certain amount of unrest in Palestine, which would explain why it was felt necessary to bring a second legion into the area sometime before 120.

One older suggestion should no longer be seriously entertained. This was the idea that Hadrian at first gave permission for the Jews to rebuild the temple but then withdrew that permission. Debate in recent scholarship has tended to center around two causes. The first one is the assumption that Hadrian issued a decree against castration, which was interpreted to include circumcision, thus constituting a serious attack on Jewish religious practice.

There is no doubt that a decree prohibiting circumcision would have been a significant reason for the revolt, but the question is whether it conforms with Hadrian's general character and policies and whether the sources for this allegation should be believed. The main problem is that Roman law at no time forbade circumcision by ethnic groups. It was Antonius Pius who introduced regulations about circumcision, but these were only for the purpose of protecting slaves: Jews were still allowed to circumcise their own sons, as the law explicitly states. Also, circumcision was not generally regarded as "mutilating the genitals," which one questionable source states.[20] In fact, Hadrian's decree regarding castration was not a new one but only the renewal of a decree already issued by Domitian and renewed by Trajan.

Hadrian's visit to the region in 130 CE seems to have relevance for the revolt, though it is difficult to be sure about what he did that brought it on. But it may be related to another possible cause, which is that Hadrian attempted to rebuild Jerusalem as the Roman city Aelia Capitolina. This depends primarily on the statement of Dio Cassius (69.12.1) that Hadrian constructed a city on the site of (ruined) Jerusalem, called Aelia Capitolina (after Hadrian himself), including on the Jewish temple site a temple to Zeus; as a result, a long, great war took place. One difficulty with this explanation is that it seems to be contradicted by Eusebius (*Hist. Eccl.* 4.6.4) who states that Aelia Capitolina was founded *after* the Jewish defeat, making it a consequence rather than a cause of the revolt. However, modern scholars have generally seen these two statements as complementary rather than contradictory; that is, Hadrian's plans to found Aelia sparked the revolt so that the actual execution of the project was postponed until the revolt was put down. Coins more recently discovered indicate that Aelia Capitolina was definitely planned before the revolt. Thus, it seems likely that the refounding of Jerusalem was planned—and perhaps even begun—as Aelia Capitolina *before* the revolt. However, one group of coins seems to have been minted after the revolt, suggesting that the real process of building did indeed come afterward.[21]

Thus, the founding of Aelia Capitolina has been supported by several discussions as the major cause of the revolt. Yet it seems likely that there were a variety of causes and Hadrian's plans for Aelia served only as the catalyst to bring things to a head. Many of the factors that led to the 66–70 revolt were still in existence in the early second century, including strong feelings of nationalism and resentment against Roman rule. One further major cause has already been discussed in a previous section (pp. 320–2 above): messianic expectations and apocalyptic prophecies in certain circles seem to have helped fuel the revolt. The *Apocalypses of Ezra and Baruch* were probably completed not long before the Bar Kokhva revolt and show that speculations about the supernatural destruction of Roman rule were still much in evidence. These and the New Testament book of Revelation (and the *Apocalypse of Abraham*, if it was this early) allow us to surmise the existence of other such apocalypses that have not survived.

This brings us to the question of whether Simon saw himself as a messianic figure. There is no indication in the documents as such to show that he claimed to be the messiah. The symbols on his coins have been interpreted messianically,[22] however, and rabbinic and Christian tradition shows that his role was regarded as messianic by some. Hence, the Aramaic title Bar Kokhva ("son of the star"), which became attached to him at some point. Also, it has become a part of modern scholarly tradition that the famous Rabbi Aqiva at Yavneh declared Bar Kokhba the messiah and was active in preparations for the revolt. It is argued that Aqiva's alleged travels had the purpose of raising money and gaining arms for the war. The most recent study concludes that there is no evidence to suggest that Aqiva undertook journeys to prepare for the war. On the other hand, it is very possible that Aqiva was "a calculator of the end of days," looked on Bar Kokhva as messiah, and was thus involved in the revolt.[23]

Yet, did Simon himself and his followers see him as a messianic figure? We have one important contemporary indication: the title of "prince" (*nāśî'*) found on coins and in some documents. The title of "king" had lost its cache by the second century CE, but *nāśî'* had taken its place as its equivalent. Usage in Ezekiel and Qumran indicates that the term had messianic overtones, with the *nāśî'* becoming an eschatological figure.[24]

The term "son of the star" was probably not a self-designation by Simon but applied by others. We must keep in mind that at this time the concept of the messiah varied considerably, all the way from a full-blown heavenly figure to little more than a human hero. If the letters and documents from the Judaean desert indicate a rather mundane figure for Simon, this is probably because he interpreted the messiah as a human figure, a priest or military leader, not a heavenly figure.

Examples of "Ordinary" Lives: The Stories of Two Jewish Women

Much of our discussion has of necessity centered on leaders, upper-class individuals, and activists of various sorts. Yet one of the aims of recent history writing has been to include ordinary men and women in its purview. This is often easier said than done because literary sources tend to focus on the upper classes and the wealthy, or present fictional, idealized models, and we know little of ordinary people, whether men or women.

Yet we are very fortunate to have—in defiance of the norms of historical evidence—archaeological finds that have helped to redress the balance, with insight into the lives of two "ordinary" Jewish women. This information is unique in early Jewish history at present. These two women are Babatha and Salome Komaïse. We possess direct, private information, because they took personal and family documents with them when they sought to escape the Roman soldiers by going into hiding places during the Bar Kokhva revolt. As far as we know, they perished when the Romans found their places of refuge in the Judaean Desert, but their documents remained hidden until found more than half a century ago. The marriage, court, and real estate documents allow us to piece together some of the major events in the lives of these two women.

Both women were from Maḥoza in Arabia, a village on the shore of the Dead Sea, probably near the southern end, in the district of Petra. How they ended up in

En-gedi and became caught up in the Bar Kokhva revolt is an intriguing puzzle. In any case, the two women apparently knew each other, since they had contiguous property and the names of some of the same witnesses are found in their documents.

Babatha

Most is known about Babatha, whose thirty-five documents cover the period 94 to 132 CE.[25] The first document (*P. Yadin* 1) is a note of indebtedness by a husband, guaranteeing that his wife's dowry would be repaid in the event of death or divorce. He was borrowing from her dowry to pay rent on a property. The guarantor is the husband's partner, the Nabataean 'Abad-'Amanu/'Amiyu. Then come two sales contracts (*P. Yadin* 2–3), both ostensibly for the same piece of property (a plantation of date palms at Maoza) but dated only a month apart. According to the second contract, the property came into the possession of Babatha's father, Shim'on ben Menahem, but why there should be two sales contracts within a month is a puzzle. The first purchaser was a high-up Nabataean official named Archelaus, who seems to be the son of 'Abad-'Amanu/'Amiyu. It has been suggested that Archelaus had bought the property but then rescinded the purchase in favor of Shim'on, for the reason that his father had died, and he had to pay off the loan contracted by his father and his partner.

Babatha was apparently widowed, with an orphan son, by 124 CE, when the city council appointed two guardians for her son (*P. Yadin* 12). Since he was still a minor, requiring guardians some eight years later (*P. Yadin* 27), this would make him very young in 124 CE. This would probably make Babatha only fifteen to twenty years of age in 124, putting her birth about 105 CE, and her marriage around 120 CE. Her first husband was named Jesus ("Yashua"), as was her son. It was only shortly after the appointment of guardians for her son that she was complaining to the governor that the guardians were neglecting their responsibilities to provide adequate maintenance (*P. Yadin* 13). It is hardly surprising, then, that shortly afterward she seems to have remarried, about 125 CE, to Yehudah, son of El'azar (*P. Yadin* 10). Yehudah appears as her guardian the next year in continuing action against the guardians of her son (*P. Yadin* 14; *P. Yadin* 15).

P. Yadin 4 has been identified as a guarantor's agreement—that is, a third party guarantees that he will refund the purchaser's price if it happens that there was a prior lien against the property. In other words, it guarantees that the seller owns the property and is in a position to sell it, under the law. Because of the fragmentary state of the papyrus, the names of the various parties have not been preserved. It may be that the document is, rather, an additional grant of property to Shim'on (Babatha's father), to justify the higher purchase price for the property originally bought by Archelaus.[26]

We know that Shim'on did acquire various pieces of agricultural land, which he passed on to his wife Miryam in 120 CE by deed of gift, though the grant was to take effect only after his death (*P. Yadin* 7). The date-palm orchard that he purchased in 99 CE is not included, however, indicating he had already given it to Babatha, perhaps on the occasion of her first marriage. *P. Yadin* 16 indicates Babatha owned the date-palm property in 127 CE because she declared it at the time of the Roman census.

We have two loan documents with regard to Babatha's second husband, Yehudah. The first (*P. Yadin* 11) is a loan from a Roman centurion in 124 CE, at a time when he was about to marry Babatha or had already married her. In the second (*P. Yadin* 17), Yehudah borrowed a large sum from Babatha in 128 CE. This may have been occasioned by the anticipated marriage of his daughter Shelamzion to Judah Qimber, which took place a few months later (*P. Yadin* 18). As a wedding gift her father gave Shelamzion property in En-gedi, half to come to her immediately and the other half on his death (*P. Yadin* 19).

The documents *P. Yadin* 20–26 tell a poignant story. Sometime between his daughter's marriage in April 128 and June 130 (the date of *P. Yadin* 20), Babatha's husband, Yehudah, died. Since he had not repaid the loan made to him by his wife, Babatha took possession of several properties as compensation. We know she sold one crop of dates in September 130 (*P. Yadin* 21–22). Yehudah had had a brother Yeshua, however, who had also died before June 130, leaving some orphaned children. The guardians of these orphans launched a lawsuit against both Babatha and Yehudah's daughter Shelamzion. They gave up the suit against Shelamzion in June 130 (*P. Yadin* 20), conceding ownership of a courtyard given to her by her father in *P. Yadin* 19. But they continued their lawsuit against Babatha (*P. Yadin* 23–26), though she has countered their charges in some of the documentation. Since Babatha preserved the documents in her archive, she must have come out on top in the legal proceedings.

What happened after that is not found in the documentation. At some point she moved from Arabia to the En-gedi area, and toward the end of the Bar Kokhva revolt she hid her possessions in a cave before being taken by the Romans. What happened to her after that is unknown, though she did not retrieve her possessions.

Salome Komaïse

Salome's story is represented by a series of documents.[27] Salome was the daughter of Levi and Salome Grapta (sometimes Gropta). We know of her story from January 125 CE to August 131, which is the time period covered by the documents. The earliest document (dated to January 125 CE) is a receipt (XHev/Se 60), apparently for taxes paid by Menahem son of Iohannes, who owned property abutting Salome's half courtyard (see below). As far as we know, this Menahem was not related to Salome, but the taxes had been remitted via Sammouos son of Simon (Shim'on) who was apparently Salome's first husband.

The next document (XHev/Se 61) is a declaration of land arising out of the Roman census in Arabia in April 127 CE. The name of the one making the declaration is lost in a lacuna, except for the ending *-los* or *-las*, but he is "son of Levi" and appears to be Salome's brother. A second land declaration of December 127 (XHev/Se 62) is by Sammouos, son of Simon, Salome's husband. The next document (XHev/Se 63) is a renunciation of claims to certain property by Salome toward her mother Salome Grapta. This seems to be property left by Grapta's deceased husband and her deceased son, *-los* son of Levi.

Thus, it appears that Salome's father was dead by this date (sometime between April and December 127) and that her brother had also died after April in the same year when he had declared certain property for the census. Evidently, there had been a dispute between Salome and her mother about ownership of the property, but that dispute had now been resolved. Salome's husband at the time appears as her "guardian," though all except the end of his name (-*os* or -*as*) is lost in a hole in the document; but he is son of Simon and appears to be the same Sammouos mentioned earlier.

The reconciliation between Salome and her mother Salome Grapta might have occasioned the next document (XHev/Se 64), but a second marriage was probably also a factor. For Salome Grapta had remarried, her new husband being Joseph, son of Simon, who appears in the document as her guardian. She made over several properties to her daughter. Salome's husband is not mentioned in the document, so we do not know if he was still alive. Later, we know (from the marriage certificate: Hev/Se 65 = *P. Yadin* 37) that in August 131 CE she married a second husband, Jeshua, son of Menahem. At some point in the next few years, she moved to En-gedi and ended up in nearby caves where she was evidently taken by the Romans, either for death or slavery.

Looking at the stories of both these women, we see that legally and in other ways they lived in what some have labeled a patriarchal society; however, one researcher has argued that this term is inappropriate.[28] She makes the point, "In short, male dominance was real; but it was fragmentary, not hegemonic."[29] But within that framework, the situation of a female person was often more complex, with more freedoms and autonomy, than sometimes admitted. The situation also varied from community to community, with the diaspora communities sometimes showing women as being more equal or independent than those in Palestine itself.

The remarkable stories of these two women show us in a small way how so many ordinary Jews lived. Yes, their religion was important, but the trials and events of ordinary life was similar to those of many in other cultures and places at the time. Yet like so many Jews, their lives were overtaken by traumatic events in the wider panorama of history. It is only because of their tragic fate that we possess documents outlining their lives at certain points during their existence.

Conclusions

What has been termed "Second Temple Jewish history" did not really end with the destruction of the temple in 70 CE. It really came to an end with the Roman victory over Bar Kokhva. The fall of Jerusalem in 70 had not quenched the Jewish desire for liberty, but two further revolts—under Trajan and then Hadrian—had finally shown most Jews that eschatological expectations for the end of Rome were doomed to disappointment. How this affected even ordinary Jews was illustrated by the sad fates of two women at the time of Bar Kokhva, Babatha and Salome Komaïse.

It was clear that the Jewish people were fated to remain in a subservient position for many centuries. Not only this but to suffer religious persecution as the former Jewish sect, now the Christian religion, took control of the Roman Empire. The many Jews who came under Arab rule in the seventh century and later did not generally undergo religious persecution, though they often had to pay a special tax to practice their religion. But from the small beginnings in Yavneah in 70 CE, a new form of Judaism evolved and developed—rabbinic Judaism. This eventually spread and displaced other versions of Judaism to become dominant in most Jewish communities. Other modes of Judaism also flourished at times (Karaite Judaism, for example) but rabbinic Judaism generally prevailed, even to the present day. And, finally, after almost two millennia, beginning in 1948 Jews once again have a free, independent state.

15
Summary: History of the Jewish People over Two Thousand Years

The Early Period

The first reference to a group called "Israel" dates from about 1200 BCE. Yet we know that the ancestors of Israel were likely to be various Semitic peoples known from Egyptian sources going back to 2000 BCE and possibly even earlier. These may have been the Shasu or the Hyksos or other peoples known to be from Canaan—or a combination of several of them. Unfortunately, these are not discussed in such detail in our sources as to give us their identity in most cases. Nothing resembling Israel is known from the Amarna Letters from the mid-fourteenth century BCE, but an "Israel" may have been part of the unnamed population of one or more of the city-states in Canaan at the time.

Israel is first attested in the last part of the Late Bronze Age. A stela of Pharaoh Merenptah dated to about 1208 BCE is the first mention of Israel by name in history. What can we say about this Israel? Very little, beyond its existence. The hieroglyphic determinative used with the name suggests that "Israel" is a people. The name is used alongside several topographical names (e.g., the cities Ashkelon and Gezer in southern Canaan, and the city Yenoam perhaps near Beth-Shean). This suggests that Israel was somewhere in Canaan, though Transjordan cannot be ruled out.

Much speculation has been expended about the makeup of this Israel. A number of different groups are known from texts in the Late Bronze Age. These include the Apiru and the Shasu. The "Apiru" seem to be a social group, made up of those on the margins of society who have left their people to make their living as outcasts or migrants or even outlaws. The term "Shasu" looks primarily like a reference to a particular lifestyle, pastoralism. Yet here and there are texts that talk about tribes and settlements and seem to suggest an ethnic group. It may of course be that the Egyptians were lumping more than one group together under the name.

Because Apiru is almost certainly a cognate of the word "Hebrew," it was once thought that the two could be equated, and the Apiru of the Amarna texts were the "Hebrews" or "Israelites." Further study now suggests that the term "Hebrew" as an ethnic term for Israelites was a development from the original social usage.

This would suggest a connection between Apiru and Israel, but an indirect one, so that while some of Israel's ancestors might have been Apiru, one should not equate the term with all Israelites. Perhaps more relevant are the group known as the Shasu. They are often associated with Edom and the area around the southern end of the Dead Sea. We also have one reference to "the Shasu of Yahwa'" (*Yhw3 S3sw*), which has been seen as the origin of the divine name *Yahweh*, the primary Israelite deity.

What seems clear is that a variety of peoples made contributions to Israel. "Canaanites" was used in ancient Near Eastern texts to refer to people who lived in Canaan (Palestine) regardless of their ethniciy. Israelites were certainly Canaanites, but that does not exclude some or even many of them from being Shasu, some of whom may have settled in the central highlands. It has been demonstrated that some of those settling in the hill country were former pastoralists, but others may have been farmers moving to less settled areas, migrants from outside Canaan, and people in general seeking land and a new life. This was because the highlands had been largely uninhabited in the Late Bronze Age (c. 1600–1200 BCE) and provided land for the taking to those willing to put in the effort to make it productive.

For our knowledge about the earliest history of Israel, we are primarily dependent on ancient Near Eastern texts and archaeology. But you may ask, the Bible claims to tell us about this time—why not just follow the biblical text, beginning with Genesis? We explained the reason for this in the first couple of chapters of this book. These discussed how we got the Bible—how it was written. The Bible is a book of theology—a book with strong religious messages. But what I have written in the present volume is not primarily about theology but about history. While some parts of the Bible do contain some historical information, it is not primarily a history book, and many of its stories contain little or no history. For example, the early chapters of Genesis borrowed from various stories about creation and early human history that circulated not only in Israel but elsewhere in the ancient Near East. These were important stories that told us many things about theology, religion, and people, but they were not history as such.

The very first chapter of Genesis was about creation. It is a beautiful, almost poetic tale, but it does not tell us about the real origin of the earth and the universe. It says nothing about the Big Bang, or the early stars known as Blue Giants or the development of galaxies or the long process of configuration of the earth from dust, gas, and debris left over from the formation of the sun. The Bible does not tell us what we know from science, that the life of plants and animals evolved over millions of years from single-celled creatures until humans finally developed from primate ancestors some hundreds of thousands of years ago. The Bible tells us of Adam and Eve, but the finds and careful palaeontological study of fossil remains shows no such origins for humans. The first generations of humans came to an end with a worldwide flood according to Genesis, but not even geologists with a strong religious faith have found any evidence for such a catastrophic event. Again, these are stories with great theological messages, but they are not history.

The Pentateuch and Joshua talk of the doings of patriarchal figures, an exodus from Egypt, a wandering in the wilderness for forty years, and a conquest and settlement of the land of Canaan in a matter of half a decade. Once again, we found little actual history here. The stories about the patriarchs were often contradicted by what we know of the history of the Levant in the second millennium BCE. There was no place in Egyptian history for the devastation of the ten plagues nor of a population of several million leaving. No archaeological evidence has been found for a large population that lived for many decades in the wilderness of southern Palestine. While Israel certainly settled in Canaan, there was nothing in the material culture to show a violent conquest and destruction of the cities and native population at that time.

Of course, a small core of history might be found in some of these events as described in the early books of the Bible. While no exodus as described in the Pentateuch occurred, several possible scenarios might well have given rise to the greatly expanded and developed exodus narrative of the Bible. One possibility, long argued, is that a small group of slaves escaped from Egypt, perhaps pursued by a unit of soldiers who were unaccountably thwarted or even destroyed in their pursuit, an event that then became blown up into the story found in the book of Exodus. Other proposals are possible, but the story was in any case developed at a much later time when there were many Jews living in Egypt.

Nevertheless, among the sources—and questions—considered in each chapter has been the biblical text: to what extent is the Bible reliable—to what extent can we use it in writing our history? Most scholars do not pitch their tents at the extreme ends of the spectrum, either accepting or dismissing the text without question. For those who do not immediately embrace or reject the text, no easy answer arises from our pages: we cannot say that the biblical text is reliable or unreliable, because it all depends on which episode or text one has in mind. A general trend, however, is that the later one moves in history, the more reliable the biblical account.

The Period of the Monarchies

What happened between the first mention of "Israel" about 1200 BCE and the second mention some 350 years later? We have no information from primary written sources, only archaeology, plus we have the secondary source of the Bible. Archaeology is very important for writing a history of Israel in this period. Also, although archaeology helps us bridge the gap between 1200 and 850 BCE, there is still much debate over how to interpret it and, therefore, much debate over how much of the text we can accept. But fortunately, recent archaeological finds have added vastly to our knowledge of early Israel. In addition, there is more and more agreement among the majority of archaeologists about what the excavations tell us about Israel's history.

The first major event in Israel's history is the settlement. Far from a quick conquest by outsiders, as the Pentateuch and Joshua picture it, archaeology shows it to have been a slow process. Rather than being outsiders, the new settlers in the Central Highlands were mainly natives, moving from other parts of Canaan into relatively unsettled land in the highlands (though there may have been a few outsiders). As the population grew, they gradually formed tribes and then eventually gained a common identity as a people. Somewhere among their number was most likely the "Israel" mentioned by the Merenptah Stela. Eventually, for whatever reason, the entire population of highland settlers adopted this name for themselves.

In Early Iron Age I (c. 1200 BCE and following), settlements in the Canaan highlands suddenly blossomed. About the same time, the coastal plain was settled by a group whose material culture seems strongly influenced by Aegean and Cypriot forms. Egyptian texts refer to them as the Sea Peoples who settled along the Palestinian coast. One of the main groups or tribes went by the name of "Philistines." The much later biblical text also refers to a variety of groups who inhabited the interior of Palestine, as well as the Israelites who are associated with the highlands in some passages. Although the biblical references are sometimes garbled or improbable, a number of the names coincide with peoples from Syria and Asia Minor (the Amorites, Hittites, Hurrians [Horites], Hivites, Girgashites), as well as the (indigenous?) Canaanites.

How did the highlanders coalesce into the "Kingdom of Israel"? Some have blamed pressure from the Philistines; others have argued for other factors, but all agree that Israel eventually came together into a state. The relationship of the Israelites with the Philistine cities was evidently a complicated one. The archaeology suggests that the inhabitants of the coastal plain were likely to be stronger in population and resources than those in the hill country. There is also the question of whether they would have felt the need to expand into the highlands at this stage.

Therefore, far from the Philistines attempting to spread their settlement into the hill country, they seem to have been happy with their lives in the lowlands (their prosperous agrarian land had not by any means reached "carrying capacity" and put pressure on them to expand). It seems more likely that the highland people—the Israelites—periodically raided the lowland areas for plunder and especially to steal livestock and grain supplies; they also seem to have wanted to control the trade routes across their territories.

The first stage of Israel as an integrated people seems to have been the kingdom led by Saul. But Saul's rise to leadership was most probably based on military skills and potential. Yet his choice might well have been confirmed and legitimated by the ritual actions of a senior priestly/prophetic figure such as Samuel. The narrator could have told David's story without Saul, but he seems to have been stuck with an entangled narrative in which David was not the first king and whose dynasty was legitimated only because another dynasty was cut off. Hence, the story of Saul as the first king of Israel is entirely plausible.

David himself also rose to prominence as a warrior. Although the David-and-Goliath story is incredible and seems to have originally been a story about another Israelite hero, David's prowess as a fighter looks genuine. But he was also an inventive and ruthless politician who first gained rulership over the tribe of Judah and then kingship over a united Israel and Judah. This suggests a "united monarchy" but one on a much-reduced scale compared to the biblical one, with David perhaps more like a chieftain. David's rule was not achieved without bloodshed: it included deals with those on the other side, such as Abner, a member of the Saulide family. Once David occupied the throne, he also seems to have made a deal with the Philistines and neutralized that threat. But not everyone was reconciled with David's rule, which is why several rebellions took place in the latter part of his reign. He apparently went on to expand his territory, probably being the one to take Jerusalem into his domain, but this is unlikely to have included the Aramaeans who were far north of his kingdom.

The exaggerated legend of Solomon does not fit well with David. The archaeology in Jerusalem so far does not corroborate a massive capital city with much monumental architecture. There is some monumental architecture, but it seems limited to the Stepped Stone Structure: it looks unlikely that anything like the city envisaged in the Bible remains to be found. Although David controlled a certain amount of territory, gained in part through his personal military ability and leadership, Solomon suddenly—though he fights no battles nor leads an army—controls land from Egypt to Anatolia, monopolizes trade in the region, sends his ships to far-off lands, and brings in vast sums of gold that match or exceed those of later great empires such as Persia.

Solomon's wealth and wisdom are so great that the Queen of Sheba must travel to Israel to meet him. When she does, she finds that they were even greater than the legend had claimed! Yet the one account we have of his wisdom is a banal story about two prostitutes, nothing like the great Oriental tales of cleverness and wisdom about such figures as Ahiqar or Alexander. Solomon probably existed, but he was evidently a minor local ruler whose domain covered only a portion of Palestine, which he had inherited from David. The extensive conquests of David and the empire of Solomon from the "river of Egypt" to the Euphrates are not supported by the archaeology, the international context, or the resources available. The visit of the "Queen of Sheba" simply has no support in the sources.

Solomon appears to have managed to hold together the kingdom he had inherited. But after his death, it reverted to the natural division that had been there from the beginning: it split back into a Kingdom of Israel and a Kingdom of Judah, once again rivals with one another as they apparently had been in the past. When "Israel" next occurs in original sources outside the Bible—in this case, the Assyrian inscriptions—it is now a kingdom in the northern part of Palestine, allied with the Aramaean king of Damascus and others against the expanding Assyrian Empire. Assyrian inscriptions make clear that alongside Israel was another kingdom to the south, that of Judah.

But from early in the "divided monarchy," we suddenly find aspects of the text supported fairly consistently by external sources: Assyrian records and other sources confirm the names of Israelite and (later) Judahite kings, their relative time and order of reign, and some of their deeds. In other words, it is during the reigns of Rehoboam and Jeroboam I that we first start to find evidence that the narrator has used a contemporary source. This was probably a *court chronicle*. This chronicle was brief, giving the name of the king and recounting a few military exploits and building projects. It was a "Chronicle of the Kings of Judah" but also included information about the Kingdom of Israel. This appears to have been the backbone of the story of the kings of Judah and Israel. In some cases, in 1 and 2 Kings, much of the king's reign seems to be drawn from such a chronicle, but in other cases much found in the narrative is legend or religious invention. In some cases, much of the narrative is actually about prophetic figures (as with the reign of Ahab).

The first kingdom for which we have solid evidence apart from the Bible is the state founded by Omri. This fits what we would expect from the broad picture of ancient Near Eastern history. Already by the time of Omri Israel was caught between the great empires to the north and south. Hardly has Omri passed from the scene and his son Ahab begun reigning before the Assyrians were threatening. This continued until the Assyrians besieged and conquered Samaria about 720 BCE, bringing the

Kingdom of Israel to an end. But the Kingdom of Judah, too, came under the Assyrian thumb even before Samaria fell. The story of Israel and then Judah from about 850 BCE is domination by the Mesopotamian or Egyptian Empires.

We also find the religion developing and changing. Even in the earlier period when Israelites were clearly polytheistic, Yahweh was still their main deity. He seems to have had a consort until fairly late, but she disappears by or during the seventh century. It is also shortly after this time that some of the biblical writers present a solidly monotheistic picture of the deity—even if some Jews and Israelites still looked to more than one god. The Bible talks of a reform under Hezekiah, but this seems doubtful. Certainly, the high places do not disappear; they seem to have continued in use until or almost until the fall of Jerusalem. Better attested is reform under Josiah, though it probably did not reach further north than Bethel. Exactly how much of the story of finding a book of the law in the temple should be believed is a question, but it does appear that the book of Deuteronomy originated or becomes known in the period after 700 BCE.

From the Persian period on, the Jews as a whole worship one God, without images. The Jews also focus their worship on a single temple in Jerusalem. There were other temples, including the one on Gerizim that the Samaritans claim as the correct one. We also know of one at Elephantine in Egypt, but it ceased to function after 400 BCE. The temple at Leontopolis that Onias IV founded was an aberration caused by the suppression of Jewish worship under Antiochus IV. But having no local temple became a problem for the many Jews in the diaspora, which led to the concentration of religion on the book of the law and the rise of synagogues.

As for our knowledge of Judah after the fall of Samaria, the biblical text shows the same type of records preserved that helped us with the Northern Kingdom: the same mixture of chronicle data, oral tales, legends and other material that marks the descriptions of the reigns of kings until the fall of Jerusalem. In some cases, material has clearly been inserted for theological reasons, such as the accusations against Manasseh designed to blacken his name, and the claims that Josiah reformed the cult even as far as Samaria. Yet there is a gradual increase in reliability the later the narrative progresses. In the last years of the kings of Judah, when there are times that we know what was happening year by year, the biblical text can be remarkably accurate, and in the last few years (after 594 BCE) when our external sources cease, we can still have reasonable confidence that the basic narrative is correct. Yet plenty of inaccurate biblical text can also be found, such as the book of Daniel, which means that it must always be subject to critical analysis.

Judaism in Transition

It is important to characterize the Jewish religion after the end of the monarchy, for there were many changes and developments. When the Second Temple period is viewed as a whole, two points relating to religion stand out:

- First, many of the trends in Judaism, as well as its characteristics, have their origins in the Persian period, which is one of the reasons the Persian period should begin the Second Temple period (not the coming of Alexander, as some well-known histories do). These characteristics include the centrality of the Jerusalem temple for most Jews, the high priest as the leader (or co-leader, with the officially appointed governor) of the state, the rise of the Sanhedrin as the high priest's advisory council, apocalyptic, monotheism, angelology and demonology, and sacred authoritative writings.

- Second, a number of trends that became important owe their origin or important developments to Jews living in the diaspora. These include synagogues, the centrality of scriptural study, non-sacrificial worship, and prayer. They managed to observe the Passover without a lamb, while the translation of the biblical books into Greek—the Septuagint—made the scriptures available to the many diaspora Jews who did not know Hebrew.

Yet the core of Jewish worship throughout the Second Temple period was the Jerusalem temple. Even many Jews in the diaspora attempted to make a pilgrimage to the temple at some point in their lives. Israelite religion—as far back as one can trace it—had centered on the sacrificial cult. At the heart of the cult was blood sacrifice. The sacrifice was also a social and communal act, for in most cases the animal sacrificed served as the basis of a cultic meal in which only certain parts were burned on the altar, some other parts went to the priests, and the rest was for the worshiper and family to consume in a state of ritual purity. But there were other elements in temple worship (such as music and singing) and other means to worship, such as prayer.

It must be recognized that the mundane and physical acts of the daily temple cult were invested with deep symbolic meaning. This meaning is not usually discussed in ritual texts which focus on the correct performance of the ritual, however, and we are often left to guess at the meaning which the worshiper saw in the acts. We gain some idea of the cosmic, mythical significance of the temple and its worship from various hints in early biblical texts and rather more detail in later texts. But no doubt both priests and worshipers would have stood aghast at the thought that the sacrifice itself could be jettisoned once one appreciated its spiritual meaning. Many Jews regarded the cessation of the daily (*tamid*) sacrifice through the actions of Antiochus Epiphanes as shaking the cosmos to its foundations and heralding the eschaton itself, according to a contemporary witness (Daniel 7–12).

For most Jews, this was *the* primary form of worship: participation in the temple cult was the *sine qua non* of service to God. This was how your sins were forgiven and how you renewed your relationship with God. This is what it meant to be a temple-centered religion. Worship in the Land of Israel was dominated by the annual festival calendar and the pilgrimage to Jerusalem to the temple. It was probably the custom for many or most of those in Judaea and also in such neighboring areas as Galilee to make a regular journey to the temple at one of the festivals, even if not several times a year. But for those who lived at a distance from the city, it was simply impractical, and especially so for those living in the diaspora.

Personal and communal devotion apart from the temple began to develop, especially toward the end of the Second Temple period and especially in the diaspora. In the diaspora, the synagogue originated and evolved, with time, as a major communal place of instruction and worship, probably first in the early Greek period. The institute eventually spread to the homeland itself. However, even though synagogues are sparsely attested in Judaea before 70 CE, they seem to be a late introduction there, well after the Maccabaean revolt from all archaeological and literary evidence. The temple was still the religious center of the land of Israel up until its destruction in 70 CE. The essential place of the temple is demonstrated by the extreme reaction to its pollution in the time of the Maccabees. To repeat, the religious life of the people in Palestine revolved around the temple and its regular cultic activities.

Yet, as with all Jewish practices, not everyone thought or acted in the same way. The Jerusalem cult was not universally revered to the exclusion of any other by every Jew. Apart from the existence of some other temples (noted above), certain groups clearly regarded the Jerusalem holy place and the current priesthood as polluted, for example, the Essenes, yet even the Essenes would apparently have accepted a "purified" temple. Contrariwise, it seems that in a few circles, the idea of a "temple made with hands" at all was already being questioned or even rejected. The *Fourth Sibylline Oracle* is one of the few examples—if not the sole one—of a total rejection of the temple in a Jewish source. More problematic is Stephen's speech in Acts 7 which castigates a physical, earthly temple. This is of course found in a post-70 Christian source and thus suspect; on the other hand, it has parallels with the *Fourth Sibylline Oracle* and may represent the ideas of an early Jewish or related group.

There were also certain other traditional observances that were probably adhered to by most Jews, such as some purity laws, especially those clearly laid down in the Pentateuch, and the agricultural priestly dues. Important in the late first century BCE and the first century CE were the use of *miqva'ot* (ritual baths) and stone vessels (that did not contract ritual impurity), which were indication of popular concerns for ritual purity. Ossuaries and other burial customs may show some views about the afterlife. But the average Jew certainly did not attempt to make his home into a model of the temple as possibly the Pharisee did. How people were educated in their religion is not completely clear. According to the Hebrew Bible, the primary duty lay with the family, especially the father. There was undoubtedly some instruction in the temple during the festivals since the cult would otherwise be meaningless. This may have been through scribes as primary official communicants regarding religious law, but such scribes were probably connected to the temple, perhaps being Levites or even priests.

There were many Jewish religious systems (some use the term "Judaisms") extant in Judaea and the surrounding area before 70. Some of these were associated with particular religious sects. For a proper understanding, we ought to examine each one individually on its own terms. Lamentably, we do not have sufficient information for a coherent description of most of them. Instead, we find only partial information or even no more than hints in the extant literary and material remains. Many discussions of the past have lumped the sources together to describe *the* Jewish belief or practice regarding eschatology, messianism, worship, and so on. While in some cases this was carefully done, the tendency has been to present a monolithic portrait (often with assumptions about "orthodoxy" underlying the reconstruction) so that the description of one system or form of Judaism—or even no actual system but only an artificial construct—masquerades as a portrait of all Judaism.

There is still a tendency to see the religion of this period in terms of sects, with special emphasis on the Pharisees, but there is no reason to see such minority movements as anything more than just a part of the picture. According to our sources, such groups formed only small numbers (whatever influence they had beyond their actual adherents). The sects varied greatly, not only in their history but also in their aims. The three main sects—the Sadducees, Pharisees, and Essenes—had already originated in the Hasmonaean period (or possibly earlier), but they were also prominent during Roman rule. What we especially see during the Roman period is the rise of various revolutionary movements. Some of these may have been primarily religious movements, whereas others were possibly more political and nationalistic in origin. Drawing lines between these two categories would not be easy, however, even if we had a great deal of information: many movements combined physical activism and violence with religious justification and ideology.

Even though most people were not members of a religious sect, a religious outlook is frequently influenced by teachers and groups who may not have had a large number of actual followers. There are indications that mysticism was important to some Jews, for example, though by nature this was kept secret by devotees. Magic, astrology, and other forms of divination were clearly practiced, but as they were esoteric arts not much information has been left about them. People who were ill or "had a demon" would seek out those whom they thought could help, whether it was the priest in the temple, the local "Jerusalem Lourdes" (e.g., John 5:2-7, cf. variant reading), or the traveling healer-cum-exorcist. Astrologers probably did not starve in Judaea any more than they did elsewhere in the Graeco-Roman world.

The peripatetic preacher—whether Pharisee, Essene, ascetic, mystic, Gnostic, or whatnot—could always draw a crowd. If nothing else, it was a diversion and one of the few forms of entertainment available (as Monty Python's *Life of Brian* so brilliantly illustrates). Of course, there were always a few persons in these crowds attracted by curiosity who experienced personal enlightenment. These might continue to follow the preacher when he moved on, perhaps abandoning their home and livelihood. Such periods of discipleship were probably brief for all but the hard core, but almost always a few individuals in any village would become engaged in such discipleship even if it did not last.

Life for most people was not easy, being mainly a struggle for enough to eat and to provide a reasonable amount of clothing and shelter. Religion was important, as was religious and ethnic identity, but we have little indication that this personal piety was very extreme. As so often, local people adapt their religion to their needs and eschew those aspects requiring major inconvenience. This is why Pharisaic practices, with the minute emphasis on ritual purity in daily life, would not have been adopted by most people, however much some of them may have looked up to Pharisees as models of piety. The same would apply to an even greater degree to exclusivistic groups like the Essenes who were apparently seen as examples of piety and special favor from God. Most people did not join sects; they did not have the luxury of leisure and money. Some destitute people may have been attracted to sects because they provided food for all members, but this is unlikely to have been a major factor in recruitment, since the group ultimately had to find the resources to support themselves.

The average Jew was probably what the later rabbis would refer to as an *am ha-aretz*—"a person of the land." That is, they were men and women pious in their own way but whose main attention was taken up with making a living. They could not afford the luxury of devoting a great portion of their time and energy to the picayune details of religious observance, which some sectarians may have regarded as essential. We have some small inkling about the lives of ordinary Jewish men and even women (e.g., marriage contracts; bills of sale; burial customs; the Babatha and Salome Komaïse archives). They marry, they have children, they buy and sell property, they divorce, they die and are buried. The catacombs of Rome and the papyri of Egypt have been valuable sources on the communities living outside Palestine during this period.

Poverty was no barrier to intense devotion, so that even those living on the edge of subsistence might well turn to religion for solace and hope. Judging from the preserved literature, many had a keen expectation that God would bring in a better future. Few could have been fully content with the status quo throughout most of the Second Temple period (with perhaps the exception of the early Hasmonaean period). For much of that time Judah was a subject nation, yet according to tradition she had once been a proud, independent country and even a great empire by the grace of God. Some Jews could think on this subject only with extreme bitterness at the current state of their nation. With the correct action this might be put right, either by God alone or by human agents with God's help, was their thought. Some espoused revolution as the appropriate means of rectifying the situation. There were plenty of precedents in the Hebrew Bible, and in the post-Hasmonaean period the Maccabees served as exemplars. "By God and my right hand" might be their motto (as well as that of a modern royal family).

Others felt just as passionately but saw the human role as being a more passive one: prayer, obedience, even the shedding of one's own blood in martyrdom—but primarily patient waiting for God to fulfill his divine plan. God would do what needed to be done—it was not up to humans to take matters into their own hands. They had a part, but their part was waiting on the Lord. Of course, they could also calculate and speculate, and these calculations and speculations fill many extant, and presumably even lost, apocalypses. While the exact moment of God's wrath might be uncertain, there was never any doubt that he would descend in fury—when the time was right—to punish the wicked, reward the righteous, and bring about new heavens and a new earth.

It would be a mistake to think every Jew had an apocalyptic view of the future; yet a number of apocalyptic and related writings were produced during this period, showing the beliefs and concerns of some segments of the population. To some extent we can probably draw a distinction between Judaea (and the other Jewish areas of Palestine) and the diaspora. A number of diaspora writings of this period show no evidence of apocalyptic expectations, even after some major incidents with the Romans such as Caligula's attempt to place his statue in the Jerusalem temple. For example, Philo's view of eschatology is personal rather than national or cosmic, as is the Wisdom of Solomon's. Nevertheless, major revolts in a variety of areas in 115 to 117 CE indicate that eschatology was important to some Jews in the diaspora, and some apocalypses apparently circulated there, even if they did not originate in the diaspora.

How many Jews were caught up in this apocalyptic world view at various times, especially at the turn of the era? Some scholars have assumed that the vast majority were, but we really do not know. There are plenty of known apocalyptic and revolutionary writings, but how widespread were they? In Palestine itself many Jews had enough on their plates with the daily struggle to make a living so that any involvement with apocalyptic matters was not their first concern though, as already noted, it may have served as a diversion from a life of misery for certain individuals. It is impossible to quantify the number of people who took the different approaches, but the literature and other indications are sufficient to recognize a variety of paths followed.

The Hellenistic period was characterized by religions of personal salvation. Contrary to certain older religions of the Graeco-Roman period, Judaism still retained many of its ancient Near Eastern characteristics as a national religion. That is, it continued to be primarily an ethnic religion, even in the diaspora, whereas certain other national religions developed much more universalistic tendencies during the Hellenistic period. Isis worship, to take just one example, had transformed from a national cult of Egypt to a religion of salvation that actively sought converts and penetrated many parts of society in the Roman Empire.

Similarly, in certain respects Judaism in the Graeco-Roman world fitted the category of a salvation religion. It seems evident that Judaism was viewed by many educated Greeks and Romans as another imported Hellenistic mystery cult, which would explain some of the attitudes by Greek and Romans to the Jewish religion. Although the extent of Jewish influence might be debated, there seems no question that many Romans and others were attracted by the religion, and we find sporadic examples of outright conversion to Judaism, though Jewish sympathizers seem to have been more common.

Temple worship did not require written scripture since the priests could instruct the people on the proper cultic procedures and decorum, and the religious meaning of the cult. Many traditional societies need no "book" to tell people how to worship. Away from the temple, though, the written word was a vital link and pillar of worship, along with public and private prayer. This is why the translation of the Pentateuch into Greek (probably in the third century BCE) was such a significant event in the history of Judaism: now the many Greek-speaking Jews who knew little or no Hebrew had access to their Holy Scriptures. The exact form of worship undertaken in the diaspora is uncertain, though the Greek writer Agatharchides mentions the Jewish "temples" (= synagogues?) where the worshipers pray with outstretched hands until evening on the seventh day (Josephus, *Ag. Apion* 1.22 §§208–9).

The text of various holy books was still developing, and no standard collection or text seems to have become established until the first century CE, but the Pentateuch, the Prophets, and some of the Writings of the later Hebrew canon seem to have been widely accepted long before Pompey threatened Jerusalem. Even groups in the region of Palestine are attested as basing themselves on the written word by this time, notably Qumran. Temple worship was being simultaneously enriched, supplemented, and diluted by other forms of worship coming from the diaspora. Biblical interpretation in its widest sense had become well developed by the Roman period and took its place alongside cultic worship (though many of the interpreters evidently had priestly associations of some sort). If the temple had not been destroyed, it would have been interesting to see how temple worship evolved in the light of these new practices.

The Persian Period

We can now return to our historical survey and look in some detail at how the Jews lived and worshiped in the Second Temple period—the Persian, Greek, and Roman periods (c. 540 BCE to 70 CE). Judah began the Second Temple period (the time from about 540 BCE to 70 CE) with the loss of the monarchy. The Babylonians had removed the king from reigning over Judah. When the Persians established their rule, the monarchy was not restored; instead, Judah became a province in the Persian Empire. Thus, if there is one word to characterize the nation of Judah throughout the Second Temple period, it would be *theocracy*. By this is meant a political entity or country ruled by priests, primarily the high priest, during most of this time. That was both its strength and its weakness. The priestly oversight allowed for a union of the civil and religious at a time when Judah was under foreign rule and a native king might not have been acceptable to the overlords.

After Jerusalem fell in 587/586 BCE, Judah was not an "empty land" as was once proposed, but the settlement varied greatly. The population overall had been considerably reduced by fighting and disease and was now concentrated to the north of Jerusalem in Benjamin. Mizpah (Tell el-Nasbeh) seems to have been designated as the administrative center of the province by the Babylonians and then by the Persians. Jerusalem appears to have been largely uninhabited during the four decades or so from the fall of Jerusalem until Persian rule. Its revival during the Persian period was evidently slow, and the rebuilding of the destroyed temple probably took some decades.

The impression of some of the Jewish literature that the Persian king favored the Jews and provided great resources for the Jerusalem temple is pure propaganda. There is no evidence that the Persians dealt with the Jews any differently from other peoples in their empire, and the Jerusalem temple was not singled out for special treatment. Yet the Jews generally thrived under Persian rule, from the information available. The documents from Elephantine show how a Jewish community lived their lives and how they interacted with the Persian administration.

The first concern after the return of exiles from Babylonian captivity (beyond making a living) was the rebuilding of the temple. Because of the nature of the sources, it is difficult to be precise about the course of events, but the building seems to have begun in earnest early in Darius's reign, about 520 BCE. When it was finished is unknown (very likely is the sixth year of Darius [Ezra 6:15] or 516 BCE), as is much of the history of Judah for the next seventy-five years. Then sometime around the middle of the fifth century BCE, a new force was unleashed on the province, one aimed at isolating the people from the surrounding nations and cultures. This was Governor Nehemiah.

In one sense, this was not new since the idea that mixing with Gentiles was bad for religious purity had been around a long time in certain circles. But the zealot Nehemiah came not only with a single-minded view of what Judaism should be but also with powers as governor backed by Persian authority. In this he may have been preceded or—more likely—followed by Ezra (though assessment of the Ezra tradition is much more difficult and controversial; in any event, most of the measures ascribed to Ezra look very similar to those of Nehemiah).

Who constituted a part of the Jewish community was given a very narrow definition. The boundaries were drawn and non-Jews excluded as far as possible; indeed, there seems to have been an attempt also to exclude those Jews who were descended from inhabitants of the land who had not been deported by the Babylonians. They are called "peoples of the land," as if they were separate from the Jews, even classified as foreigners. Nehemiah could enforce his rulings as law and evidently did, to the consternation of not a few of his fellow Jews. The community became exclusivistic and inward looking, with barriers put up to keep the outside world as far away as possible.

How long such an approach lasted after the passing of Nehemiah (and Ezra?) is uncertain, though there is evidence that at least some—perhaps many—of the community did not share Nehemiah's vision. The indication is that his measures did not last. Some of those whom he opposed, such as the Tobiads, seem to have maintained their position in Judaean society (see below). But one of the literary products was a version of the Pentateuch, though this appears to have been promulgated late in the Persian period, after 400 BCE.

Nehemiah's opposition to the governor of Samaria, Sanballat, was the beginning of a long-term rivalry between the Judaeans and the Samaritans. The relationship was not a simple one, and despite frequent theological and even physical clashes the two communities still evidently traded ideas and even sacred books (since the Samaritan Pentateuch probably originally came from Judaea, though the text was changed and developed over time by the Samaritan community). A final breach between the two communities does not appear to have taken place for several centuries.

The Coming of the Greeks

The transition from Persian to Greek rule (c. 330 BCE) apparently took place without major trauma or significant change for the Jews. The legend that Alexander the Great himself visited Jerusalem is incredible, and Judah does not seem to have been affected by Alexander's army, though it would have submitted formally to the Greeks like all the peoples of the region (Samaria, on the other hand, apparently rebelled and became a Macedonian colony). Perhaps more unhappy was the period of the Diadochi when armies marched back and forth over the whole Near East for almost forty years. We do not know the details, but Jerusalem seems to have been taken at least once, as well as experiencing a transfer of population to Egypt on one or more occasions.

Palestine, however, came permanently under Ptolemaic rule by about 300 BCE, and Judaea was more or less at peace for the next century. Egypt had taken Coele-Syria (Syria Palestine), but the Seleucids had a legal claim on it. There were five "Syrian wars" over those one hundred years: during the first four Syrian wars, the Seleucids failed to take what they argued was rightfully theirs but succeeded in the "Fifth Syrian War" about 200 BCE. As far as we know, little if any of this struggle affected the small province of Yehud, isolated as it was from the main invasion routes and the most fertile areas of the region, until Jerusalem was taken by the Seleucids in the Fifth Syrian War.

We have some insights into this period of the third century BCE. Especially important is the archive of Zenon, the agent of the Ptolemaic finance minister, who took a tour through Palestine in 259 BCE. We also have the legend of the Tobiad family in Josephus. There are many incredible elements in the story, but the existence of the individuals named is largely confirmed from the Zenon papyri, some references in the books of Maccabees, and the archaeology of the Transjordanian site of Iraq al-Amir. We also have references to Jews in some of the Egyptian papyri. Some Jews are attested as having served in the Ptolemaic army, including being members of a military colony such as that of the Tobiads or even mercenaries. And of course we have one of the most significant religious events: the translation of the Pentateuch into Greek in Alexandria.

Otherwise, we hear little about the Jews. Underneath the calm surface, however, changes were taking place—slowly, quietly, but inexorably the developing Hellenistic culture was making its impact felt, even in the remote and mainly rural province of Judaea. The assumption that the Greeks brought something completely new and radically challenging to Judaism, however, simply follows the prejudice of some Jewish sources and especially of their modern interpreters. We know that Greek influence had already begun long before Alexander, primarily through two media: coastal trading (the Phoenician cities were especially affected) and Greek mercenary troops. We should not exaggerate the pre-Alexander inroads of Greek culture into Palestine, but the point is that things Greek were not new. A second false assumption is that what the Greeks did was replace the native culture or customs, either by cultural superiority or by force, with the Jews being the sole exception to this tide of Hellenization.

In fact, the Greeks only brought a new element to the venerable and deeply entrenched cultures of the ancient Near East, nor did they seem to have much interest in having their ways of doing things adopted by the native peoples. On the contrary, their belief in Greek culture as superior made them want to keep it as a privilege for themselves alone. It was the natives who wanted to share in this new entity in their midst because they saw it as a stepping stone to achieving success, as a symbol of status, and as desirable for a better and happier life. The upper classes quickly acted to gain for themselves and/or their children a Greek education, and a few did give up their traditional lifestyle for one modeled completely on the Greek. Most did not go so far, however, but adopted those aspects of Greek culture that seemed useful while not abandoning their own.

How you gonna keep 'em down on the farm when they've seen Antioch, Ptolemais, or gay Laodicea? A century or so of quiet development and influence—and attitudes changed—new interests were kindled: Hellenization had its impact. Of course, for the rest of the people, the non-aristocrats, the peasants who made up the vast bulk of the population, their lives changed little. They had new rulers and paid taxes to a different regime. The language of the higher levels of bureaucracy was now in Greek, but much of the work of administration, especially that which came in contact with most people, was carried out in the local language; for Palestine and much of the Seleucid Empire this was Aramaic.

The local agents for the Greek government were often natives, anyway. People were aware of the many new Greek cities, either new foundations or old Oriental cities with a new charter, and many natives lived in them. Thus, most people became aware of new cultural elements in their midst, but these Greek ways did not usually affect the average person all that much. This new Hellenistic world was, therefore, something new: a synthesis of the Greek and the native, nor was there a blending or melting (*Verschmelzung*) of the two in most cases. As time went on, the mixture changed and eventually some blending of styles developed, but this took centuries.

The only urban area of Judaea was that of Jerusalem, but there was an upper class; there were cosmopolitan individuals; and there was regular contact with the outside world—perhaps not least because of the large Jewish diaspora that now existed, especially in Egypt but also elsewhere. These Jews of the diaspora still looked to Jerusalem and the temple, with a not insignificant number of pilgrims coming at each of the major festival periods. The small upper class would have watched developing events with some interest. For a few, the potential commercial advantages of Greek culture would have excited attention. The political question of whether the region might come under Seleucid control was a concern for many. These were practical matters, but also no doubt various members of the priestly and lay aristocracy found themselves intrigued by the novelties of Hellenistic culture—an attraction perhaps enhanced by communication with relatives who lived in some of the Greek cities. For such people, the narrow and exclusivistic vision of Nehemiah must have seemed decidedly blinkered.

The Seleucids Take Over

Coele-Syria changed hands: about 200 BCE, Antiochus III was finally able to take as the southern part of his empire what his ancestors had been trying to gain for almost a century. Judaea was now under Seleucid rule, but the old Jewish constitution was affirmed by official decree of Antiochus himself (apparently because of help the local Jews had given him in taking Jerusalem from Seleucid troops), and nothing seems to have changed immediately. After the stormy period under Antiochus III, Seleucus IV reigned for a quiet few years, to be succeeded in 175 BCE by his vigorous brother Antiochus IV. What did he do about the Jews?

According to 2 Maccabees, Antiochus did nothing! The time had come for sudden action—or so some thought—but these were Jews who thought this, not Antiochus. What had been building up for decades burst forth in the so-called Hellenistic reform. This was not something imposed from above by the Seleucid king; on the contrary, it seems to have blossomed naturally from below out of seeds long nurtured in an environment stimulated by the proximity of Greek institutions. When Antiochus became king, there is no indication that the province of Judaea was any special concern of his.

According to 2 Maccabees, it was Jason the brother of the high priest Onias III who went to Antiochus IV and asked for the high priesthood in exchange for a raised annual tribute. He also asked for Jerusalem to become a *polis* or Greek-style city (for a further payment). To Antiochus it looked like a good deal, and he accepted it. Surprisingly, there is no record of any adverse reaction. Many if not most Jews (at least, of those in Jerusalem) apparently took it in their stride: even the most potentially scandalous act of having the king depose the serving high priest in favor of another seems to have been accepted without overt protest.

Yet it would be difficult to overestimate the importance of the "Hellenistic reform" for the subsequent history of Judaea. It brought the full impact of a more sophisticated culture and its economic benefits onto an economically and culturally backward nation. Judaea could no longer exist quietly and let the rest of the world pass them by. Not only did the full light of a new way of living fall on the Jews of the city, but its glare also exposed them to the rest of the world. The long relative isolation had come to an end. It is important to note, however, that Jason did not disturb the official cult or break Jewish law. Apart from the illegitimate act of usurping the office of high priest, his actions regarding the temple were all those of a traditional high priest. *Jason's innovations were political and cultural, not religious.*

If this new situation had been allowed to take its course in a steady, peaceful manner, it is hard to predict how things may have evolved. However, a crisis soon developed. After only a few years, a member of another priestly family named Menelaus, did the same trick as Jason, offering even more tribute to have the office of high priest. Antiochus saw only a positive gain for himself from this and accepted. This brought Jason's enterprise to an end, but there was no need for a major crisis. Yet one developed. The first problem was that Menelaus had offered an impossible sum to Antiochus and was unable to pay it. He is alleged to have sold temple vessels to gain money for payment. Whether this accusation was true or not, it was believed and the people of Jerusalem rioted against Menelaus's brother who was in charge while Menelaus was himself away in Antioch. After the mob killed the brother, the *gerousia* (temple council) sent some of their own members to Antiochus to accuse Menelaus, but he turned the tables on his accusers (by bribery, according to the sources). Menelaus was safe for the moment.

About this time Antiochus became engaged in a war with Egypt. This was in 170 or early 169 BCE, and he was very successful. In the spring of 168, he invaded again, but the Romans were unhappy with things and ordered him to call off his military expedition. As he did so, Jason took the opportunity to assault Jerusalem to try to take back the high priesthood. Antiochus interpreted this as a revolt (with some justification) and sent his army to stop it. They took Jerusalem with no difficulty, and Jason fled; Menelaus was restored to his position. But then something inexplicable happened. In December 168 BCE Antiochus stopped the daily sacrifice in the temple and all practice of Jewish worship. *For three years Judaism was officially prohibited.*

Although religious tolerance has often been seen as a product of modern enlightenment, in fact this is only because of long centuries of monotheistic persecution. The polytheism common in the ancient world was tolerant by its nature. Other gods and worship were accepted and permitted. The Persian, Greek, and Roman governments did not restrict the practice of Judaism as a religion, whatever the personal feelings of individuals. Thus, Judaism was sometimes ridiculed, and rebel Jews were attacked under Roman rule, but this did not affect the official tolerance. *Now, under Antiochus, the one exception in history up to this time to this general policy of tolerance took place—a religion was proscribed and persecuted.*

The event is still mysterious, despite important and ingenious suggestions. That Antiochus should have taken such a drastic step was out of keeping with his normally shrewd administration. Whatever else Antiochus was, he was no fool; indeed, he seems to have been one of the most able of the Seleucid rulers. It may be that he was wrongly advised by Menelaus. In any case, his assault on the Jewish religion was a serious miscalculation and plunged him into an unnecessary war which took valuable resources at a time when finances were a problem.

The Maccabaean Revolt and the Hasmonaean Kingdom

What form the Antiochean persecution took is debated. Some have denied that it was conducted against individual Jews, in spite of stories of torture and execution. Yet there is no question that the temple was polluted, and its service interdicted, which is persecution by any definition. There were Jews who were not prepared to stand by and let this state of things exist without opposition; hence, violent resistance developed. Whether the family of the Maccabees were the initiators in this is a question, but in a short period of time they evidently became the revolt leaders.

Reports that the father Mattathias initiated things by slaying a Seleucid individual may or may not be true. But what is clear is that the son Judas became the acknowledged leader. What began as guerrilla tactics against both the Seleucids and Jews that they saw as traitors developed into more formal battlefield confrontations. There were some surprising Maccabaean victories, though these were not miraculous as the legends have it: they used local knowledge as an advantage, they brought forces the equivalent in size to or even larger than the opposing Seleucid army, and they sometimes lost battles that were still reported as victories!

Yet they succeeded in their primary goal, which was to retake and cleanse the temple and re-commence its service, most likely in December 165 BCE, almost exactly three years after its pollution. Antiochus IV died at the end of 164 BCE, and the new Seleucid ruler Antiochus V apparently wanted to conclude the fighting and made some concessions to Judas Maccabee. He also executed the would-be high priest Menelaus, which was no doubt a relief to many. But Alcimus, who succeeded Menelaus as high priest, was accepted by most Jews, though not by the Maccabees. Alcimus died of natural causes a few years later.

Yet the Maccabees continued the struggle which soon led to the death of their leader, Judas Maccabee. Why they persevered in fighting is debated, but it shows that their goal (perhaps developed later in the campaign) was not just restoration of religious rights but ultimately independence from Seleucid rule. Judas's brother Jonathan became the new leader of the Maccabaean rebels, but few of his fellow countrymen were now willing to continue fighting, and Jonathan and his small number of followers were basically on the run from the Seleucid forces for many years. Most Jews were apparently happy with the restoration of the temple and saw no need to engage in further conflict now that the status quo had been restored.

But then a new situation developed that was to be the salvation of the Maccabaean cause: a rival Seleucid dynasty arose. Jonathan was quick to play off one side against the other, allying himself first with one rival ruler, then another. The result was that about 153 BCE he was officially granted the office of high priest by one Seleucid pretender, Alexander Balas, and became his Friend (a high position close to the Seleucid king). This also seems to have consolidated Jonathan's leadership authority among his fellow Judaeans. Jonathan also sent an embassy to Rome to effect a treaty of friendship and alliance. It must be kept in mind, however, that the Romans made such treaties without any expectation of providing military or other assistance to their treaty partners: the benefit to the Maccabees was not actual intervention by the Romans but prestige in the eyes of their own people that they had such a prominent "partner" by formal acknowledgment.

Jonathan's ballet with the Seleucid rivals eventually came to grief: he was captured by Tryphon through a ruse. Although his brother Simon Maccabee negotiated for their release, Tryphon eventually executed Jonathan and his sons. The result (some argue that it was intentional) was that Simon and his descendants became the sole leaders of the nation. In his first year Simon declared the independence of Judah (about 143–142 BCE), and in his third year "the priests and people" acclaimed Simon with a stela that confirmed his priesthood and leadership. One should be careful not to take these declarations at face value: Judah was still under the Seleucid thumb for another decade or more, and the acclamation of the priests and people had been negotiated and was granted only conditionally and—notably—says nothing about Simon's sons and descendants. Nevertheless, these measures had important symbolic significance, both for Simon and for the status of Judah in the Seleucid realm.

Simon's reign was short, and, like his brothers, he died violently about 135 BCE. He was succeeded by his eldest son, John Hyrcanus (Hyrcanus I). Under John's oversight, Judah finally achieved independence from the Seleucids. He also began a program of expansion. One of his main actions was the conversion of the Idumaeans to Judaism. Most Idumaeans subsequently seem to have remained loyal to Judaism and apparently considered themselves part of the Jewish people. He also destroyed Samaria and Shechem/Mt Gerizim, which did not help Jewish-Samaritan relations.

The Jewish historian Josephus first makes some of the main sects active during Hyrancus's reign, though whether they originated at that time or earlier is uncertain. Josephus tells a story concerning John Hyrcanus that involved the Sadducees and Pharisees. Whether there is truth to the story, it at least connects Hyrcanus with these two groups. It is only much later (during the reign of Alexandra Salome) that the Pharisees are said to have particular legal traditions and to be seeking political power to enforce them on the populace. It is in the New Testament and the Mishnah that we may get an inkling of the Pharisees' main concerns (Josephus's account of them tells us only about their beliefs that would be of interest to his Graeco-Roman readers). But in neither case, nor in the case of the Essenes, does Josephus suggest how or when they originated.

After a long reign Hyrcanus I was succeeded by Aristobulus I about 104 BCE. Since he reigned only a year, we know little about him, but he is alleged to have taken the title of "king" (though some think it was his successor who first used it); his coins do not use the title. He also supposedly converted the Ituraeans (an Arab or possibly Aramaean group in southern Syria, north of Galilee) to Judaism by force, though there is little evidence of this in the archaeology, and any adoption of Judaism was soon given up by them.

The next Hasmonaean ruler was Alexander Jannaeus. The title "king" is found on his coins, and he expanded the Hasmonaean state to its widest extent. He seems to have married his brother's widow; in any case, his wife Alexandra Salome was a remarkable woman who was to succeed him. Internal opposition developed to Jannaeus to the extent that some of the rebels brought the Seleucid pretender Demetrius III against him; however, after the crucial battle, in which Jannaeus was defeated, the Jews fighting for Demetrius supposedly changed sides. In any event, Demetrius withdrew, and Jannaeus wreaked vengeance by crucifying eight hundred of his opponents and killing their families while he feasted with his concubines (an event apparently mentioned in the Qumran document 4QNahum Pesher). Some have assumed that these opponents were Pharisees, but this assumption is not supported by evidence: Josephus at no point suggests they were Pharisees (though there might have been Pharisees among them). The *Antiquities* claims that Jannaeus, on his death bed, advised his wife to make peace with the Pharisees. The problem is that the *War* makes no mention of the Pharisees at any point in his reign, and the *Antiquities* says nothing about them except in this one anecdote.

Yet what we know about the nine-year reign of Alexandra is that it was nevertheless dominated by the Pharisees. They were able to get rid of a number of their enemies to the point that Alexandra sent some of the Pharisees' opponents to guard some of her fortresses to spare their lives. She was a good administrator on the whole, but the last part of her reign was plagued by the opposition between her sons, Hyrcanus II and Aristobulus II: the elder son Hyrcanus became high priest and assumed leadership of Judaea, but Aristobulus raised an army and proclaimed himself king. The matter had not been resolved when Alexandra died. Outmaneuvered, Hyrcanus agreed to give up the high priesthood and live as a private citizen. But then a new figure entered the picture, Antipater. According to Josephus, he was an Idumaean, though by all accounts he lived as a Jew and some sources make him Jewish (possibly he was only the Jewish governor of Idumaea). He convinced Hyrcanus not to give up his claim to the throne and helped him escape to the Nabataean king Aretas III. With this support Hyrcanus defeated Aristobulus and besieged Jerusalem.

The Roman general Pompey was on the scene, having come to fight the Armenians. Both Hyrcanus and Aristobulus appealed to him. When he delayed his response, Aristobulus impatiently broke away and marched toward Jerusalem. Pompey now came after him, and he surrendered, but his followers shut the gates of Jerusalem against the Romans. They besieged the city for three months until it fell, apparently in the summer of 63 BCE. Judah had lost its independence, and the Judaeans were now once again under foreign rule.

The Jews under Roman Control

The first few decades of imposed Roman rule were difficult ones for the nation. The renewed servitude chafed. The unstable situation created by the Roman civil war, which came on a few years later in 49 BCE, encouraged nationalistic movements and revolts. One part of the nation—or its leadership, at least—accepted compromise with the Romans as unavoidable; another part tried to restore Hasmonaean rule, first under Aristobulus II, and then under his sons, Alexander and Antigonus, but without success. Hyrcanus ostensibly ruled (under Roman supervision), but Antipater was the power behind the throne; he also brought his sons Phasael and Herod into the administration.

Then, in 40 BCE the Parthians invaded the region and took over Palestine; they made Antigonus a puppet king. Phasael was captured and committed suicide, but Herod escaped and traveled to Rome. There he was championed by both Mark Antony and Octavian, presented to the Senate, and declared king of Judaea. With the aid of a Roman army, he besieged Antigonus in Jerusalem, which fell in the summer of 37 BCE, though Herod bribed the soldiers not to plunder the city. Herod now ruled as "client king" or "friendly king" of the Romans. This was important because it allowed Herod—and Judaea—a great deal of independence, and it brought him into close contact with the Roman leaders. As a client king, the Romans kept hands off his finances. He gave gifts to the Romans, which often amounted to a considerable amount of wealth, but his kingdom was not taxed by the Romans.

Mark Antony was in control of the East, and Herod worked with him, though he was put under considerable pressure by his Egyptian consort Cleopatra who was antagonistic to Herod. These arrangements all came to an end in 31 BCE when Octavian defeated Mark Antony and Cleopatra at Actium. Herod had been fighting the Nabataeans and was not at Actium, but he was still on the wrong side. He went boldly to Octavian but without his crown, admitted that he had been a friend of Mark Antony, but promised that he would be equally a friend of the new emperor. Octavian accepted his offer of loyalty and restored his kingdom. The two were to remain fast friends for most of the rest of Herod's life.

Several times it had appeared possible that Aristobulus II or his sons could shake off the Roman yoke and renew the Hasmonaean kingdom. Hope continued even after the declaration of Herod as king in 40 BCE, and Herod had to put down some periodic uprisings; however, once Octavian had prevailed at the battle of Actium the fate of the nation was sealed: life was possible only by recognizing the overlordship of Rome. Whether as a client kingdom or as a province, Judaea was a subject people of the Romans until the Arab conquest.

The Herodian Kingdom

Despite centuries of a concerted bad press, Herod was—on balance—good for Judaea. Given the inevitability of Roman rule, he was able to champion many Jewish causes. A ruthless response to any challenge to his power could be taken for granted even without some striking examples (e.g., his decimation of the Sanhedrin), but those who suffered directly from his measures to maintain power were few, primarily a few families of the priesthood and aristocracy. The idea of a reign of terror against the people, as a whole, is unsubstantiated and unlikely. The picture of the gospel of Matthew that he was "slaughterer of the innocents" is patently false—all other sources, even hostile ones, are completely silent about such an atrocity. The claim that he bled the nation financially is often repeated but is also to be rejected. Like all rulers, Herod collected taxes, but there is no evidence that he was more exploitative than the Hasmonaeans and certainly no more so than the Romans when they ruled directly.

His friendship with Augustus, his good works for the Greek world, his magnificent building program in Judaea, and especially his rebuilding of the temple to make it one of the most famous edifices of the time could only have enhanced the prestige of the Jewish nation and people. Also, work on the temple kept a large work force employed until the 60s CE. He responded to periods of famine with aid and reduced taxes. He was also concerned with the Jewish diaspora. seeing to it that Jewish religious privileges were restored in Asia Minor where they had been eroded by local opposition. He established peace and unified the country into one large kingdom, as large as that alleged for Solomon. It is true that direct opposition would not have been allowed: Herod's security system seems to have been quite efficient. But it meant that most Jews under his rule lived in a condition of relative peace and public order. Herod not only respected Jewish sensibilities but also clearly lived as a Jew himself. In the absence of modern polling, it is hard to estimate how popular he was, but the legacy of his rule was positive.

Demotion to a Roman Province

As soon as Herod died, his surviving offspring headed for Rome to lobby Augustus for leadership of the country. In the end, Augustus followed Herod's will and divided his kingdom between Archelaus, who was given Judaea (and the title ethnarch), Herod Antipas who received Galilee and Peraea, and Philip who acquired Batanaea, Trachonitis, and Paneas. The last two had the title of tetrarch. *Note: although Antipas had "Herod" as a part of his name, and probably also Archelaus (judging from his coins), most of the Herodian rulers did not: terms such as "Herod Philip" and "Herod Agrippa" are incorrect and should disappear from usage.*

Archelaus had apparently been told that he might be given the title "king" if he ruled well, but within a decade he had been ousted from his territory and exiled at Augustus's prerogative. One reason were complaints about his rule from both Judaeans and Samarians. We are given little in the way of specifics, though one suggestion is that he was also insufficiently active in promoting honor of the Roman emperor (unlike Herod the Great who had been enthusiastic in this area). Judaea now became a Roman province attached to the province of Syria (6–41 CE), with Roman governors.

Those Jews who wanted to get rid of Herodian rule now got their wish—and it is likely that many lived to regret it, for trying to accommodate rule by Roman governors turned out to be a thorny and difficult task. This was the case even when the governor was probably trying his best to be considerate of Jewish sensibilities, which was not always true. Most of the governors simply did not understand their Jewish subjects. For example, this seems to have been the situation in a couple of incidents under Pontius Pilate, though a third example (relating to the funding of an aqueduct project) probably represents an excuse by some Judaeans to protest.

Yet members of the Herodian family still had a good deal of power, and for the most part they were helpful in representing Jewish concerns to the Roman administration. Philip the tetrarch had a peaceful time, dying about 34 CE. Herod Antipas, however, ran into conflict with his brother-in-law Agrippa I (whom he had tried to help at one time) and was eventually removed from office by the Roman emperor Caligula and his territory given to Agrippa about 39 CE. The New Testament of course emphasizes Antipas's actions regarding John the Baptist and Jesus; Josephus also mentions the Baptist episode, with different—and more accurate—details, but has nothing about the trial of Jesus.

Agrippa I and Agrippa II

In his brief reign, Agrippa I (37–44 CE) accomplished a good deal for the Jews. One of the most important menaces to Jewish worship was Caligula's threat to place a statue in the Jerusalem temple about 40 CE. This was an enormous religious crisis, potentially comparable to Antiochus Epiphanes's pollution of the temple; however, Agrippa's intervention seems to have been an extremely important reason that Caligula withdrew his orders, because Agrippa had been a close friend of Caligula before the latter became emperor. Then, after Caligula was assassinated, Agrippa appears to have acted as an intermediary in getting the Senate to approve Claudius's elevation to the imperial throne. Claudius rewarded him by making Judaea and Samaria a part of his kingdom (he was already ruling the former tetrarchies of Philip and Herod Antipas).

Agrippa I is an example of a Herodian ruler who was popular, at least with his Jewish subjects. This is ironic because he did a number of the same things done by Herod the Great—at times, even going further—yet not receiving the opprobrium that came Herod's way. For example, his realm produced approximately the same income that Herod's had, yet there is no statement preserved that he impoverished the country, similarly with his projects of aid to cities and areas outside Palestine. He also put the images of the emperor and his family on his coins (something Herod never did) without being castigated as acting contrary to Jewish law. Later rabbinic literature remembers him with affection, something not accorded other Herodian rulers. The one exception to this general good will was with some of his non-Jewish subjects, who insulted his memory after his death by disgraceful exploitation of his daughters' statues.

At his early death, Agrippa's son was still a minor, and Claudius finally decided not to pass the kingdom on to him. Eventually, he gave him Chalcis, the realm of his uncle about 48 or 49 CE. Later he exchanged that for the tetrarchy of his Great-Uncle Philip (Trachonitis, Batanaea, Gaulanitis and some further territories around Galilee). Although Agrippa II was not king over Judaea, Claudius granted him authority over the temple and the power to appoint the high priest. Agrippa spent a good deal of time in Jerusalem and evidently had considerable influence there. For example, he used temple funds to pay workers (laid off because work on the temple had finally been completed) to pave Jerusalem in white stone. The limits of Herodian power were demonstrated, however, at the beginning of the war with Rome. Agrippa is presented as attempting to address the people and convince them that the path of war they had embarked on was mistaken. His audience—the people of Jerusalem—rejected his message and forced him to leave the city. He was to aid the Romans in putting down the revolt.

Demoted to a Province a Second Time and the Path to War

After Agrippa I's death, Claudius decided to make Judaea once more a Roman province. Apart from Agrippa II's youthfulness, it became general Roman policy not to make use of client kings in the way they had done in the past. As with previous governors, the Roman procurators over Judaea seem to have varied in competence and conduct, from Tiberius Alexander who was from a Jewish family to Felix whom even the Roman historian Tacitus (*Hist.* 5.9) condemns. A number of seemingly random acts led to the revolt. One of these was the cessation of sacrifices in the temple on behalf of the emperor and his family. This might seem trivial, but this was the main way that the Jews showed their loyalty to the Roman emperor, since they did not participate in the emperor cult. This chain of events led to driving out Governor Cestius Gallus from Jerusalem, the massacre of the Roman garrison, and the taking of a Roman eagle. There was now no going back: Rome was bound to avenge these defiant acts.

One cannot help feeling that a war between the Judaeans and the Romans was bound to happen because of the continued buildup of tensions under Roman rule. An interesting aspect of the revolt was the extent to which the initial leadership was in the hands of men from the leading priestly families and the Jerusalem aristocracy, including some younger members of the Herodian family. Although Josephus strives to give the impression that a few low-born gangsters caused it all, a careful study of his own data shows the true leadership. As a member of the aristocracy Josephus himself was one of these very people and—once again, despite his efforts to divert the issue—seemed to be an enthusiastic supporter of the war until captured by the Romans.

The war itself still presents many puzzles, not least why so many intelligent people thought it would be possible to defeat the Romans, especially without better preparation and coordination of efforts. The various groups who fought one another in Jerusalem through much of this time would be characters in a farce if it were not so tragic. Josephus does not explain this. One has an inkling that apocalyptic speculations fuelled the hopes of some, if not all, of the fighters; if so, Josephus wanted to downplay that aspect of the situation.

"The Seventy Years' War"

Once the Judaeans revolted in 66 CE, the violent struggle with Rome continued, off and on, for another seventy years. At least, this is one way of looking at it, because in spite of successive defeats the spirit of revolution took seven decades to die. The Roman war in Galilee and Golan in 67 CE does not seem to have caused widespread destruction, since many of the cities surrendered immediately to the Roman forces. Only a few held out and were taken by force, such as Jotapata and Gamala. The destruction in and around Jerusalem was a different matter. After surrounding the city Vespasian held off attacking because of the Roman civil war. This gave the various Jewish factions the opportunity to make war on one another. This meant the death of many citizens by starvation and violence even before the Romans renewed their active siege in 70 CE under Titus. The result was the wholesale destruction of the city and temple, and the death or enslavement of many of the inhabitants and refugees in the city. A large area around the city had also been pillaged for resources for the Roman army and to build siege equipment.

After the 66–70 revolt, there was a mopping up operation against the fortresses of Herodium, Machaerus, and Masada. With the fall of Masada about 73/74, things seem to have been quiet for a long time. The destruction of population and property was minimal except for Jerusalem itself and its immediate surroundings. Yet Judaea could not go back to being a temple state, because the Romans had taken certain measures that made this difficult, not least the destruction of the temple. It is true that many of the pre-70 high priestly families survived and continued to have a good deal of power for some decades. The Herodian family was weakened after 70, but Herodians continued to have some influence, as well. Agrippa II lived until the early 90s CE. It was probably in the 90s, however, that the old power structures had become so weakened that they were ousted by new forces. We know little of the politics or even the details of the general situation in Palestine at the time. But new power structures and a new form of Judaism began to take shape shortly after the destruction.

We have some evidence that the Jews of Palestine recovered economically and socially over the decades after 70. Efforts began by a small group at the city of Yavneh to produce a synthesis of various forms, factions, and sects of pre-70 Judaism. How significant it was seen at the time and how widely it was even known about are questions we cannot answer at the present. But this nascent "Rabbinic Judaism"—based largely on Pharisaism but also other traditions—eventually came to dominate Judaism (though it took several centuries). Although descriptions of Second Temple Judaism have been characterized by discussions of the various sects, this is a wrong emphasis. Most Judaism of the time falls within certain parameters, giving a broad common ground held by almost all Jews. But the cult-centeredness and other characteristics of Judaism then meant there was no "orthodoxy" as such, beyond a few broad concepts: belief in one God, God's covenant with Israel, a general ethnic identity, male circumcision, common acceptance of Sabbath and holy day observance, and certain laws of ritual purity. The picture that emerges is a complex one.

But we know that a longing—indeed, an expectation on the part of some—for throwing off the Roman yoke, even the destruction of the Roman Empire continued to exist among the people (witness the various apocalyptic writings). The result was that less than half a century after the fall of Jerusalem, in 115–117 CE, major Jewish revolts took place in Cyrenaica, Cyprus, Egypt, and Mesopotamia. We know little in detail about them, but the indication is that there was huge loss of life among both the Jewish and the non-Jewish populations. They were put down, but the apocalyptic fervor continued in many Jewish circles.

The final decisive fight was 132–135/136 CE in the Palestinian region under the Jewish leader Bar Kokhva. We are fortunate in having letters and other documents and coins from that period, though many questions remain unanswered. It appears that Bar Kokhva was indeed seen as a messianic figure, at least by some, especially in the title "prince, messiah" (*nāśî'*) that Bar Kokhva himself appears to have used. The progress of the war is unknown, but it seems to have been fought mainly by guerrilla tactics, with the Jews making use of underground hiding places, though the Romans also fought by attempting to isolate and attack small groups of Jewish fighters. The fighting appears to have been confined mainly to the region south of Jerusalem and between the Dead Sea and the Mediterranean (but there may have been unrest in Arabia and even elsewhere). The final battle was the siege of Bethar, which ended in the death of Bar Kokhva. A large portion of the Jewish population is said to have been killed or enslaved, but the Roman army also suffered heavy losses. Jerusalem was rebuilt as the Roman colony of Aelia Capitolina, and Jews were forbidden to enter the city.

The Jewish documents found in the Judaean desert do give us a brief glimpse into the lives of ordinary Jews during this period, such as through the archives of two ordinary Jewish women, Babatha and Salome Komaïse, but this is not enough to answer many of our major questions. What does emerge is the amount of religious change and redirection going on, the results of which become apparent in the post-135 period. Priests existed but they had nowhere to exercise their priesthood, and any continuation of the temple tradition had to take on new forms. It was the nascent rabbinic movement (as well as the breakaway sect of Christianity) that had the dynamics to fit the new situation.

As already noted, many of the strands of pre-70 religion continued into post-70 Palestine, including messianism and the imminent expectation of the eschaton, which were an ominous pointer to the revolts to come. But new entities also began to form. The influence of diaspora innovations had started to have an effect before 70, and some of these proved quite productive in the new situation (e.g., synagogues and the place of scripture). At the beginning of the period, there was probably still a widespread hope that the temple might be rebuilt in time; by the end of the Bar Kokhva revolt that hope had been decisively dashed. It is difficult to find apocalypses and other Jewish works with a strong apocalyptic-messianic worldview after 135 CE.

From all we can tell, apocalyptic expectations ceased in their old form, having disappointed once and for all. The earliest rabbinic document Mishnah (from about 250 CE) eschews eschatology and messianic expectations. One way of understanding this is that the conceptual world of the Mishnah simply excludes eschatology; the lessons of the failed messianic and resistant movements of the pre-70 period had been learned, and a new worldview was developed in which eternity consisted of a focus on the timeless observance of the Torah. There seems no question that this is the outlook of the Mishnah as it stands, while the messianic views that developed subsequently have a different character. This may be a post-Yavneh development, however, since Aqiva and, perhaps, some other rabbis seem to have supported Bar Kokhva, though the matter is complicated.

The death of Bar Kokhva brought Jewish hopes of an independent state to an end. The Jews remained under Roman rule until the Arab conquest in the seventh century. They were also prohibited from entering Jerusalem until perhaps the fourth century. Judaism took on an inward focus and a concern for *halakhic* (legal) traditions that were often centered on the temple that had now long been in ruins. Yet the Judaeans were not exiled from their land (despite assertions to the contrary on the part of some today), and their ability to practice their traditional religious customs was not generally abridged under Roman and then Arab rule (though Arab rulers usually imposed a religious tax). It was primarily in the Christian realm that they were persecuted and sometimes even forbidden to practice Judaism. It was nearly two millennia later, in 1947, before an independent Jewish state came into existence once again—after centuries of oppression, persecution, and attempts to suppress Jewish worship.

REFERENCES AND NOTES

Chapter 1

General information on the principles of writing history are outlined in my *Ancient Israel: What Do We Know and How Do We Know It?* (2nd edn; London/New York: T&T Clark, 2017), 4–38.

For a discussion on how the Bible was written and developed, see, for example, John Barton, *A History of the Bible: The Book and Its Faiths* (London: Penguin, 2019).

For a discussion of principles of a modern critical study of the Bible, see, for example, John Barton, *The Nature of Biblical Criticisms* (Louisville/London: Westminster John Knox, 2007).

Chapter 2

Much of the content of this chapter is given in more detail in my book *Faith and Fossils: The Bible, Creation, and Evolution* (Grand Rapids, MI: Eerdmans, 2018).

Notes

1. *ANET* 93–95.
2. Quoted by Syncellus 28.
3. Wolgemuth, Ken, Bennett, Gregory S., and Davidson, Gregg, "Theologians Need to Hear from Christian Geologists About Noah's Flood," Lecture given to the Evangelical Theological Society, November 18, 2009, https://www.asa3.org/ASA/topics/Physical%20Science/Geologists_Noahs_Flood_Paper_at_ETS_by_Wolgemuth_Bennett_Davidson.pdf (accessed October 10, 2024).

Chapter 3

Much of the material in this chapter is covered in more detail in my *The Dawn of Israel: A History of Canaan in the Second Millennium BCE* (London: T&T Clark, 2023); and in *Ancient Israel: What Do We Know and How Do We Know It?* (2nd edn; London/New York: T&T Clark, 2017), especially chapters 2 and 3.

Notes

1. *ANET* 230.
2. Josephus, *Against Apion* 1.14 §§73–92.
3. *ANET* 378.
4. Sapir-Hen, Lidar, and Ben-Yosef, Erez, "The Introduction of Domestic Camels to the Southern Levant: Evidence from the Aravah Valley," *TA* 40 (2013): 277–85.
5. A more detailed examination is available in Grabbe, *The Dawn of Israel*, 153–62.
6. Hoch, James E., *Semitic Words in Egyptian Texts of the New Kingdom, and Third Intermediate Period* (Princeton, NJ: Princeton University Press, 1994) is a study on Semitic words in Egyptian texts of the New Kingdom and Third Intermediate Period. This study found that in the five hundred words gleaned from a wide range of Egyptian texts (mainly from the Eighteenth to Twenty-Fourth Dynasty), Egyptian *s* (*ś*) was used to transcribe Semitic [ṯ], [š], and [šš] (= Hebrew ש), while ס (*samek*) was used to represent Egyptian ṯ. If the Egyptian name Ramesses (*Rʿ-ms-sw*) had been written in Hebrew of the fifteenth to twelfth centuries BCE, it would have had *shin* ש, whereas the name in the biblical text has *samek*.

Chapter 4

Much of the information in this chapter is covered in more detail in my *The Dawn of Israel: A History of Canaan in the Second Millennium BCE* (London: T&T Clark, 2023), especially chapters 7 and 8; and in *Ancient Israel: What Do We Know and How Do We Know It?* (2nd edn; London/New York: T&T Clark, 2017), especially chapter 3.

Notes

1. A number of studies have investigated this event: Cline, Eric H., *1177 BC: The Year Civilization Collapsed* (Turning Points in Ancient History; Princeton, NJ, and Oxford: Princeton University Press, 2014); Drews, Robert, *The End of the Bronze Age: Changes in Warfare and the Catastrophe ca. 1200 BC* (Princeton, NJ: Princeton University, 1993); Millek, Jesse Michael, *Destruction and Its Impact on Ancient Societies at the End of the Bronze Age* (Columbus, GA: Lockwood Press, 2023); Ward, William A., and Joukowsky, Martha Sharp (eds), *The Crisis Years: The Twelfth Century BC from Beyond the Danube to the Tigris* (Dubuque, IL: Kendall/Hunt Publishing, 1992).
2. Hesse, Brian, and Wapnish, Paul, "Can Pig Remains Be Used for Ethnic Diagnosis in the Ancient Near East?" in Neil A. Silberman and David B. Small (eds), *The Archaeology of Israel: Constructing the Past, Interpreting the Present* (JSOTSup 239; Sheffield, UK: Sheffield Academic Press, 1997), 238–70, quote from 261.

Chapter 5

Much of the information in this chapter is covered in more detail in my *The Dawn of Israel: A History of Canaan in the Second Millennium BCE* (London: T&T Clark, 2023), especially chapters 7 and 8; and in *Ancient Israel: What Do We Know and How Do We Know It?* (2nd edn; London/New York: T&T Clark, 2017), especially chapters 2 and 3.

Individual studies important for this chapter include:
Paul S. Ash, *David, Solomon and Egypt: A Reassessment* (JSOTSup 297; Sheffield, UK: Sheffield Academic Press, 1999).

Notes

1. Maeir, Aren M. (ed.), *Tell es-Safi/Gath I: The 1996–2005 Seasons: Part 1: Text* (Ägypten und Altes Testament 69; Wiesbaden: Harrassowitz Verlag, 2012), 18.
2. Galling, Kurt, "Goliath und seine Rüstung," in *Volume du Congrès Genève 1965* (VTSup 15; Leiden: Brill, 1966), 150–69; also Finkelstein, Israel, "The Philistines in the Bible: A Late-Monarchic Perspective," *Journal for the Study of the Old Testament* 27, no. 2 (2002): 131–67; Maran, Joseph, "Goliath's Peers: Interconnected Polyethnic Warrior Elites in the Eastern Mediterranean of the Thirteenth and Twelfth Centuries BCE," in Itzhaq Shai et al. (eds), *Tell It in Gath: Studies in the History and Archaeology of Israel: Essays in Honor of Aren M. Maeir on the Occasion of His Sixtieth Birthday* (Ägypten und Altes Testament 90; Münster: Ugarit-Verlag, 2018), 223–41.
3. For a comparison of David and El Ci, see Grabbe, Lester L., "King David and *El Cid*: Two *'Apiru* in Myth and History," in Rannfrid I. Thelle, Terje Stordalen, and Mervyn E. J. Richardson (eds), *New Perspectives on Old Testament Prophecy and History: Essays in Honour of Hans M. Barstad* (VTSup 168; Leiden: Brill, 2015), 230–45.
4. Na'aman, Nadav, "In Search of Reality Behind the Account of David's Wars with Israel's Neighbours," *IEJ* 52 (2002): 200–24.
5. Killebrew, Ann E., "Biblical Jerusalem: An Archaeological Assessment," in Andrew G. Vaughn and Ann E. Killebrew (eds), *Jerusalem in Bible and Archaeology: The First Temple Period* (SBLSymS 18; Atlanta, GA: Society of Biblical Literature, 2003), 334.
6. Steiner, Margreet L., "Jerusalem in the Tenth and Seventh Centuries BCE: From Administrative Town to Commercial City," in Amihai Mazar (ed.), *Studies in the Archaeology of the Iron Age in Israel and Jordan* (JSOTSup 331; Sheffield, UK: Sheffield Academic Press, 2001), 280–88; Steiner, Margreet L., "Expanding Borders: The Development of Jerusalem in the Iron Age," in Thomas L. Thompson, with the collaboration of Salma Khadra Jayyusi (ed.), *Jerusalem in Ancient History and Tradition* (JSOTSup 381; CIS 13; London/New York: T&T Clark International, 2003), 68–79; Steiner, Margreet L., "The Evidence from Kenyon's Excavations in Jerusalem: A Response Essay," in Andrew G. Vaughn and Ann E. Killebrew (eds), *Jerusalem in Bible and Archaeology: The First Temple Period* (SBLSymS 18; Atlanta, GA: Society of Biblical Literature, 2003), 351–61.
7. See especially, Lehmann, Gunnar, "The United Monarchy in the Countryside: Jerusalem, Judah, and the Shephelah During the Tenth Century BCE," in Andrew G. Vaughn and Ann E. Killebrew (eds), *Jerusalem in Bible and Archaeology: The First Temple Period* (SBLSymS 18; Atlanta, GA: Society of Biblical Literature, 2003), 134–6; Steiner, Margreet L., "Re-Dating the Terraces of Jerusalem," *IEJ* 44 (1998): 13–20; "The Archaeology of Ancient Jerusalem," *CRBS* 6 (1994): 143–68.
8. Mazar, Eilat, "Did I Find King David's Palace?" *BARev* 32, no. 1 (2006): 16–27, 70; Mazar, Eilat, *The Palace of King David: Excavations at the Summit of the City of David: Preliminary Report of Seasons 2005–2007* (Jerusalem: Shoham Academic Research and Publication, 2009).
9. Finkelstein, Israel, Herzog, Ze'ev, Singer-Avitz, Lily, and Ussishkin, David, "Has King David's Palace in Jerusalem Been Found?," *TA* 34 (2007): 142–64.

10 Garfinkel, Yosef, "The Davidic Kingdom in Light of the Finds at Khirbet Qeiyafa," *City of David Studies of Ancient Jerusalem* 6 (2011): 14*–35*; Garfinkel, Yosef, Ganor, Saar and Hasel, Michael G., "The Iron Age City of Khirbet Qeiyafa After Four Seasons of Excavations," in Gershon Galil, Ayelet Gilboa, Aren M. Maeir, and Dan'el Kahn (eds), *The Ancient Near East in the Twelfth–Tenth Centuries BCE: Culture and History* (AOAT 392; Münster: Ugarit-Verlag, 2012), 149–74; Garfinkel, Yossi, Ganor, Sa'ar, and Hasel, Michael, "Khirbat Qeiyafa 2010–2011," *Hadashot Arkheologiyot* 124 (April 19, 2012): 1–12; Garfinkel, Yosef, Streit, Katharina, Ganor, Saar, and Hasel, Michael G., "State Formation in Judah: Biblical Tradition, Modern Historical: Theories, and Radiometric Dates at Khirbet Qeiyafa," *Radiocarbon* 54 (2012): 359–69.

11 El-Amarna tablet 4; cf. Ash, *David, Solomon and Egypt*, 112–19.

12 Schipper, Bernd Ulrich, *Israel und Ägypten in der Königszeit: Die kulturellen Kontakte von Salomo bis zum Fall Jerusalems* (OBO 170: Freiburg: Universitätsverlag; Göttingen: Vandenhoeck & Ruprecht, 1999), 84–90.

13 Ash, *David, Solomon and Egypt*, 119.

14 Josephus, *Against Apion* 1.17–18 §106–27.

15 Liverani, Mario, *Israel's History and the History of Israel*, translated by Chiara Peri and Philip R. Davies (London: Equinox, 2005), 315.

16 Mazar, Amihai, "The Spade and the Text: The Interaction between Archaeology and Israelite History Relating to the Tenth-Ninth Centuries BCE," in Hugh G. M. Williamson (ed.), *Understanding the History of Ancient Israel* (Proceedings of the British Academy 143; Oxford: Oxford University Press for the British Academy, 2007), 164–5.

Chapter 6

For more detailed information on the contents of this chapter, see my
Ancient Israel: What Do We Know and How Do We Know It? (2nd edn; London/New York: T&T Clark, 2017), especially chapters 4 and 5; and *1 and 2 Kings: History and Story in Ancient Israel: An Introduction and Study Guide* (T&T Clark Study Guides to the Old Testament; London/New York: T&T Clark, 2017).

Individual studies important for this chapter include:

Becking, Bob, *The Fall of Samaria: An Historical and Archaeological Study* (SHANE 2; Leiden: Brill, 1992);

Becking, Bob, "West Semites at Tell Šēḫ Ḥamad: Evidence for the Israelite Exile?" in Ulrich Hübner and Ernest Axel Knauf (eds), *Kein Land für sich allein: Studien zum Kulturkontakt in Kanaan, Israel/Palästina und Ebirnâri für Manfred Weippert zum 65. Geburtstag* (OBO 186: Freiburg [Schweiz]: Universitätsverlag; Göttingen: Vandenhoeck & Ruprecht, 2002), 153–66;

Grabbe, Lester L., "Omri and Son, Incorporated: The Business of History," in Martti Nissinen (ed.), *Congress Volume Helsinki 2010* (VTSup 148; Leiden: Brill, 2012), 61–83;

Grayson, A. K., *Assyrian and Babylonian Chronicles* (Texts from Cuneiform Sources 5; Locust Valley, NY: J. J. Augustin, 1975);

Grayson, Albert Kirk, *Assyrian Rulers of the Early First Millennium BC II (858–745 BC)* (Royal Inscriptions of Mesopotamia: Assyrian Periods 3; Toronto: Canada: University of Toronto Press, 1996);

Greer, Jonathan S., *Dinner at Dan: Biblical and Archaeological Evidence for Sacred Feasts at Iron Age II Tel Dan and their Significance* (CHANE 66; Leiden: Brill, 2013);

Kuan, Jeffrey Kah-jin, *Neo-Assyrian Historical Inscriptions and Syria-Palestine: Israelite/ Judean-Tyrian-Damascene Political and Commercial Relations in the Ninth-Eighth Centuries BCE* (Jian Dao Dissertation Series 1 = Bible and Literature 1; Hong Kong: Alliance Bible Seminary, 1995);

Schipper, Bernd Ulrich, *Israel und Ägypten in der Königszeit: Die kulturellen Kontakte von Salomo bis zum Fall Jerusalems* (OBO 170: Freiburg [Schweiz]: Universitätsverlag; Göttingen: Vandenhoeck & Ruprecht, 1999).

Tadmor, Hayim, *The Inscriptions of Tiglath-Pileser III King of Assyria: Critical Edition, with Introductions, Translations and Commentary* (Jerusalem: Israel Academy of Sciences and Humanities, 1994);

Wilson, Kevin A., *The Campaign of Pharaoh Shoshenq I into Palestine* (FAT 2/9; Tübingen: Mohr Siebeck, 2005).

Notes

1   Glassner, Jean-Jacques, *Mesopotamian Chronicles*. Ed. Benjamin R. Foster (SBL Writings from the Ancient World 19; Atlanta: Society of Biblical Literature, 2004), 193–203; Chronicle 1 in Grayson, A. K., *Assyrian and Babylonian Chronicles* (Texts from Cuneiform Sources 5; Locust Valley, NY: J. J. Augustin, 1975).
2   Schipper, Bernd Ulrich, *Israel und Ägypten in der Königszeit: Die kulturellen Kontakte von Salomo bis zum Fall Jerusalems* (OBO 170: Freiburg [Schweiz]: Universitätsverlag; Göttingen: Vandenhoeck & Ruprecht, 1999), 189–91.
3   Campbell, Edward, and Magen, Itzhak, "Shechem," in Stern, Ephraim (ed.), *New Encyclopedia of Archaeological Excavations in the Holy Land* (Jerusalem: Israel Exploration Society; New York: Simon & Schuster, 1993), vol. 4: 1352–3.
4   Greer, Jonathan S., *Dinner at Dan: Biblical and Archaeological Evidence for Sacred Feasts at Iron Age II Tel Dan and their Significance* (CHANE 66; Leiden: Brill, 2013), 97–100; and Davis, Andrew R., *Tel Dan in its Northern Cultic Context* (SBL Archaeology and Biblical Studies 20; Atlanta, GA: Society of Biblical Literature, 2013), 31–2.
5   Finkelstein, Israel, *The Forgotten Kingdom: The Archaeology and History of Northern Israel* (Society of Biblical Literature Ancient Near East Monographs 5; Atlanta, GA: Society of Biblical Literature, 2013), 75–81.
6   Greer, *Dinner at Dan*, 119–20.
7   Wilson, Kevin A., *The Campaign of Pharaoh Shoshenq I into Palestine* (FAT 2/9; Tübingen: Mohr Siebeck, 2005).
8   For details of the sites, see Wilson, *The Campaign of Pharoah Shoshenq I into Palestine*, 102–18; Schipper, *Israel und Ägypten in der Königszeit*, 125–8; Kitchen, K. A., *The Third Intermediate Period in Egypt (1100–650 BC)* (2nd edn, Warminster, Wiltshire: Aris & Philips, 1986), 432–9; Weippert, Manfred, *Historisches Textbuch zum Alten Testament* (Grundrisse zum Alten Testament 10; Göttingen: Vandenhoeck & Ruprecht, 2010), 233–8.
9   See the discussion and references in Finkelstein, Israel, "The Campaign of Shoshenq I to Palestine: A Guide to the Tenth Century BCE Polity," *ZDPV* 118 (2002): 110; Niemann, Hermann Michael, "The Socio-Political Shadow Cast by the Biblical Solomon," in L. K. Handy (ed.), *The Age of Solomon: Scholarship at the Turn of the Millennium* (Studies in the History and Culture of the Ancient Near East 11; Leiden: Brill, 1997), 197–9.

10 See especially the discussions in Sergi, Omer, *The Two Houses of Israel: State Formation and the Origins of Pan-Israelite Identity* (Archaeology and Biblical Studies 33; Atlanta, GA: SBL Press, 2023).
11 Schipper, Bernd Ulrich, *Israel und Ägypten in der Königszeit: Die kulturellen Kontakte von Salomo bis zum Fall Jerusalems* (OBO 170: Freiburg [Schweiz]: Universitätsverlag; Göttingen: Vandenhoeck & Ruprecht, 1999), 133–9, quote translated from 139.
12 For a detailed presentation of sources and a reconstruction of Omri's reign, see Grabbe, Lester L., "Omri and Son, Incorporated: The Business of History," in Martti Nissinen (ed.), *Congress Volume Helsinki 2010* (VTSup 148; Leiden: Brill, 2012), 61–83.
13 For a detailed presentation of sources and a reconstruction of Ahab's reign, see Grabbe, "Omri and Son, Incorporated."
14 Miller, J. Maxwell, "The Elisha Cycle and the Accounts of the Omride Wars," *JBL* 85 (1966): 441–54; Miller, J. Maxwell, "The Fall of the House of Ahab," *VT* 17 (1967): 307–24; Miller, J. Maxwell, "The Rest of the Acts of Jehoahaz (I KINGS 20 221-38)," *ZAW* 80 (1968): 337–72; Pitard, Wayne T., *Ancient Damascus: A Historical Study of the Syrian City-State from Earliest Times until its Fall to the Assyrians in 732 BCE* (Winona Lake, IN: Eisenbrauns, 1987), 114–25; Kuan Jeffrey Kah-jin, *Neo-Assyrian Historical Inscriptions and Syria-Palestine: Israelite/Judean-Tyrian-Damascene Political and Commercial Relations in the Ninth-Eighth Centuries BCE* (Jian Dao Dissertation Series 1 = Bible and Literature 1; Hong Kong: Alliance Bible Seminary, 1995), 36–9.
15 Rofé, Alexander, *The Prophetical Stories: The Narratives about the Prophets in the Hebrew Bible: Their Literary Types and History* (Jerusalem: Magnes, 1988).
16 Biran, Avraham, and Naveh, Joseph, "An Aramaic Stele Fragment from Tel Dan," *IEJ* 43 (1993): 81–98; Biran and Naveh, "The Tel Dan Inscription: A New Fragment," *IEJ* 45 (1995): 1–18.
17 Cf. Smith, Morton, *Palestinian Parties and Politics That Shaped the Old Testament* (New York: Columbia, 1971).
18 *ANET* 280.
19 Grayson, Albert Kirk, *Assyrian Rulers of the Early First Millennium BC II (858–745 BC)* (Royal Inscriptions of Mesopotamia: Assyrian Periods 3; Toronto: Canada: University of Toronto Press, 1996), 17–18 (A.0.102.2: 15, 24, 27); also the discussion in Tadmor, Hayim, *The Inscriptions of Tiglath-Pileser III King of Assyria: Critical Edition, with Introductions, Translations and Commentary* (Jerusalem: Israel Academy of Sciences and Humanities, 1994), 149; Kuan, *Neo-Assyrian Historical Inscriptions and Syria-Palestine*, 52–53n167.
20 Cf. Grayson, *Assyrian Rulers of the Early First Millennium BC II*, 211 [A.0.104.7: 4–8]; *ANET*, 281–2.
21 Tadmor, *The Inscriptions of Tiglath-Pileser III King of Assyria*, 69–71.
22 This invasion of Aram and death of Rezin is described in Tigath-pileser's Summary Inscription 4; see Tadmor, *The Inscriptions of Tiglath-Pileser III King of Assyria*, 138–41.
23 Ibid., 138 (*Summary Inscription 4*, 7'–8'), 186 (*Summary Inscription 9*, reverse 3–4).
24 Ibid., 140 (*Summary Inscription 4*, 15'–19'), 188 (*Summary Inscription 9*, 9–11).
25 Tiglath-pileser had Pekah removed for disloyalty and replaced by Hoshea (Tadmor, *The Inscriptions of Tiglath-Pileser III King of Assyria*, 140 [*Summary Inscription 4*, 15*–19*], 188 [*Summary Inscription 9*, 9–11]). Shamaneser III conquered Samaria (Grayson, *Assyrian and Babylonian Chronicles*, 73 [*Babylonian Chronicle* 1.i.27-28]).
26 Schipper, *Israel und Ägypten in der Königszeit*, 149–58; "Wer war "Sōʾ, König von Ägypten" (2 Kön 17,4)?" *BN* 92 (1998): 71–84.

27 Schipper, *Israel und Ägypten in der Königszeit*, 151–8.
28 Becking, Bob, *The Fall of Samaria: An Historical and Archaeological Study* (SHANE 2; Leiden: Brill, 1992); Becking, Bob, "West Semites at Tell Šēḫ Ḥamad: Evidence for the Israelite Exile?" in Ulrich Hübner and Ernest Axel Knauf (eds), *Kein Land für sich allein: Studien zum Kulturkontakt in Kanaan, Israel/Palästina und Ebirnâri für Manfred Weippert zum 65. Geburtstag* (OBO 186; Freiburg [Schweiz]: Universitätsverlag; Göttingen: Vandenhoeck & Ruprecht, 2002), 153–66.
29 Zertal, Adam, "The Wedge-Shaped Decorated Bowl and the Origin of the Samaritans," *BASOR* 276 (1989): 77–84.
30 Becking, *The Fall of Samaria*, 61–104; 2002; Na'aman, Nadav, and Zadok, Ran, "Assyrian Deportations to the Province of Samerina in the Light of Two Cuneiform Tablets from Tell Hadid," *TA* 27 (2000): 159–88; Oded, Bustanay, *Mass Deportations and Deportees in the Neo-Assyrian Empire* (Wiesbaden: Reichert, 1979), 69–71; Oded, Bustanay, "The Settlements of the Israelite and Judean Exiles in Mesopotamia in the Eighth–Sixth Centuries BCE," in G. Galil and Moshe Weinfeld (eds), *Studies in Historical Geography and Biblical Historiography Presented to Zecharia Kallai* (VTSup 81; Leiden: Brill, 2000), 91–99; Cogan, Mordechai, and Tadmor, Hayim, *II Kings: A New Translation with Introduction and Commentary* (AB 11; Garden City, NY: Doubleday, 1988), 197, 209–10.

Chapter 7

More material and detailed references on this religion is found in my
Ancient Israel: What Do We Know and How Do We Know It? (2nd edn; London and New York: T&T Clark, 2017), chapter 4; also *Leviticus* (Society for Old Testament Study, Old Testament Guides; Sheffield, UK: Sheffield Academic Press, 1993).
Individual studies of importance to the subjects of this chapter include:
Albertz, Rainer, *A History of Israelite Religion in the Old Testament Period*, vol. 1, *From the Beginnings to the End of the Monarchy*, vol. 2, *From the Exile to the Maccabees* (London: SCM, 1994);
Becking, Bob, Dijkstra, Meindert, Korpel, Marjo C. A., and Vriezen, Karel J. H., *Only One God? Monotheism in Ancient Israel and the Veneration of the Goddess Asherah* (Biblical Seminar 77; Sheffield, UK: Sheffield Academic Press, 2001);
Davies, Graham I., *Ancient Hebrew Inscriptions: Corpus and Concordance* (Cambridge, UK: Cambridge University Press, 1991);
Day, John, *Yahweh and the Gods and Goddesses of Canaan* (JSOTSup 265; Sheffield, UK: Sheffield Academic Press, 2000);
Dever, William G., *Did God Have a Wife? Archaeology and Folk Religion in Ancient Israel* (Grand Rapids, MI: Eerdmans, 2005);
Dietrich, Walter, and Klopfenstein, Martin A. (eds), *Ein Gott allein? JHWH-Verehrung und biblischer Monotheismus im Kontext der israelitischen und altorientalischen Religionsgeschichte* (OBO 139; Freiburg [Schweiz]: Universitätsverlag; Göttingen: Vandenhoeck & Ruprect, 1994);
Edelman, Diana V. (ed.), *The Triumph of Elohim: From Yahwisms to Judaisms* (Contributions to Biblical Exegesis and Theology 13; Kampen: Kok Pharos; Grand Rapids, MI: Eerdmans, 1995);
Gnuse, Robert Karl, *No Other Gods: Emergent Monotheism in Israel* (JSOTSup 241; Sheffield, UK: Sheffield Academic Press, 1997);

Gogel, Sandra Landis, *A Grammar of Epigraphic Hebrew* (Society of Biblical Literature Resources for Biblical Study 23; Atlanta, GA: Scholars Press, 1998);

Grabbe, Lester L., *Priests, Prophets, Diviners, Sages: A Socio-historical Study of Religious Specialists in Ancient Israel* (Valley Forge, PA: Trinity Press International, 1995);

Keel, Othmar, and Uehlinger, Christoph, *Gods, Goddesses, and Images of God in Ancient Israel*. Translated by Thomas H. Trapp (Minneapolis, MN, and Edinburgh, UK: T&T Clark, 1998);

Lemaire, André, *Nouvelles inscriptions araméennes d'Idumée, Tome II Collections Moussaïeff, Jeselsohn, Welch et divers* (Supplément no. 9 à *Transeuphratène*; Paris: Gabalda, 2002).

Nakhai, Beth Alpert, *Archaeology and the Religions of Canaan and Israel* (ASOR Books 7; Boston, MA: American Schools of Oriental Research, 2001);

Smith, Mark S., *The Origins of Biblical Monotheism: Israel's Polytheistic Background and the Ugaritic Texts* (Oxford, UK: Oxford University Press, 2001);

Smith, Mark S., *The Early History of God: Yahweh and the Other Deities in Ancient Israel* (2nd edn, San Francisco, CA: Harper, 2002);

Toorn, Karel van der, Becking, Bob, and van der Horst, Pieter W. (eds), *Dictionary of Deities and Demons in the Bible* (2nd edn, Leiden: Brill, and Grand Rapids, MI: Eerdmans, 1999).

Notes

1. Some of the studies that will be important in this chapter include Albertz, Rainer, *A History of Israelite Religion in the Old Testament Period*, vol. 1, *From the Beginnings to the End of the Monarchy*, vol. 2, *From the Exile to the Maccabees* (London: SCM, 1994); Smith, Mark S., *The Origins of Biblical Monotheism: Israel's Polytheistic Background and the Ugaritic Texts* (Oxford, UK: Oxford University Press, 2001); Smith, Mark S., *The Early History of God: Yahweh and the Other Deities in Ancient Israel* (2nd edn, San Francisco, CA: Harper, 2002); Keel, Othmar, and Uehlinger, Christoph, *Gods, Goddesses, and Images of God in Ancient Israel*, trans. Thomas H. Trapp (Minneapolis, MN, and Edinburgh, UK: T&T Clark, 1998); Becking, Bob, Dijkstra, Meindert, Korpel, Marjo C. A., and Vriezen, Karel J. H., *Only One God? Monotheism in Ancient Israel and the Veneration of the Goddess Asherah* (Biblical Seminar 77; Sheffield, UK: Sheffield Academic Press, 2001); Day, John, *Yahweh and the Gods and Goddesses of Canaan* (JSOTSup 265; Sheffield, UK: Sheffield Academic Press, 2000); Edelman, Diana V. (ed.), *The Triumph of Elohim: From Yahwisms to Judaisms* (Contributions to Biblical Exegesis and Theology 13; Kampen: Kok Pharos; Grand Rapids, MI: Eerdmans, 1995); Dietrich, Walter, and Klopfenstein, Martin A. (eds), *Ein Gott allein? JHWH-Verehrung und biblischer Monotheismus im Kontext der israelitischen und altorientalischen Religionsgeschichte* (OBO 139; Freiburg [Schweiz]: Universitätsverlag; Göttingen: Vandenhoeck & Ruprect, 1994); Nakhai, Beth Alpert, *Archaeology and the Religions of Canaan and Israel* (ASOR Books 7; Boston, MA: American Schools of Oriental Research, 2001); Dever, William G., *Did God Have a Wife? Archaeology and Folk Religion in Ancient Israel* (Grand Rapids, MI: Eerdmans, 2005); Gnuse, Robert Karl, *No Other Gods: Emergent Monotheism in Israel* (JSOTSup 241; Sheffield, UK: Sheffield Academic Press, 1997); *DDD*.
2. Diodorus Siculus 1.94.2; Varro, apud Lydus, *De Mensibus* 4, no. 53: 110–11.
3. *KTU* 1.16.3.6, 8.
4. Cf. Morton Smith, *Palestinian Parties and Politics That Shaped the Old Testament* (New York: Columbia, 1971).

5   *TAD* B7.3:3 = AP #44:3; C3.15:127–8 = AP #22:124–5.
6   Nakhai, *Archaeology and the Religions of Canaan and Israel*; Dever, *Did God Have a Wife?* 110–75; Vriezen, Karel J. H., "Archaeological Traces of Cult in Ancient Israel," in Becking et al., *Only One God?* 45–80.
7   Gogel, Sandra Landis, *A Grammar of Epigraphic Hebrew* (Society of Biblical Literature Resources for Biblical Study 23; Atlanta, GA: Scholars Press, 1998), #6.1.11; Davies, Graham I., *Ancient Hebrew Inscriptions: Corpus and Concordance* (Cambridge, UK: Cambridge University Press, 1991), #15.005.
8   Aharoni, Yohanan. 1981. *Arad Inscriptions*, in cooperation with Joseph Naveh; Jerusalem: *Israel Exploration Society* 16, no. 3; 18, no. 2; 21, no. 2, 4; 40, no. 3.
9   Gogel, *A Grammar of Epigraphic Hebrew*, #6.1.15; *TSSI* #12: Lachish 2.1-2, 5; 3.2-3, 9; 4.1; 5.1, 7; 6.1, 12.
10 For further information, see the discussion in Grabbe, Lester L. 2010. "'Many Nations Will Be Joined to Yhwh in That Day': The Question of Yhwh outside Judah," in Francesca Stavrakopoulou and John Barton (eds), *Religious Diversity in Ancient Israel and Judah* (London/New York: T&T Clark International, 2010), 175–87.
11 Gogel, *A Grammar of Epigraphic Hebrew*, #6.1.14; Davies, *Ancient Hebrew Inscriptions*, #8.017 and #8.021.
12 Gogel, *A Grammar of Epigraphic Hebrew*, #6.1.12; Davies, *Ancient Hebrew Inscriptions*, #25.003; see also Zevit, Ziony, *The Religions of Ancient Israel: A Synthesis of Parallactic Approaches* (New York and London: Continuum, 2001), 359–70.
13 For example, Albertz, Rainer, *A History of Israelite Religion in the Old Testament Period: Volume 1: From the Beginnings to the End of the Monarchy; Volume 2: From the Exile to the Maccabees* (London: SCM, 1994), 417–18; Smith, *The Origins of Biblical Monotheism*, 179–94; Smith, *The Early History of God*, 191–9; Becking et al., *Only One God?* 191–2.
14 Diodorus of Sicily 40.3.4.
15 I give a brief summary of the more detailed discussion in my study guide Grabbe, *Leviticus* 1993.
16 Lisbeth E. Fried, "The High Places (BĀMÔT) and the Reforms of Hezekiah and Josiah: An Archaeological Investigation," *JAOS* 122 (2002): 437–65.
17 Lemaire, André, *Nouvelles inscriptions araméennes d'Idumée, Tome II Collections Moussaïeff, Jeselsohn, Welch et divers* (Supplément no. 9 à *Transeuphratène*; Paris: Gabalda, 2002), 149–56.
18 Further information on the king as the leading cultic figures is found in Grabbe *Priests, Prophets, Diviners, Sages*, chapter 2, 20–40.
19 Gunneweg, A. H. J., *Leviten und Priester: Hauptlinien der Traditionsbildung und Geschichte des israelitisch-jüdischen Kultpersonals* (FRLANT 89; Göttingen: Vandenhoeck & Ruprecht, 1965); Cody, Aelfred, *A History of Old Testament Priesthood* (AnBib 35; Rome: Pontifical Biblical Institute, 1969); Albertz, *A History of Israelite Religion in the Old Testament Period*, 219–22, 427–36; Gunneweg, A. H. J., *Leviten und Priester: Hauptlinien der Traditionsbildung und Geschichte des israelitisch-jüdischen Kultpersonals* (FRLANT 89; Göttingen: Vandenhoeck & Ruprecht, 1965); Cody, *A History of Old Testament Priesthood*; Nurmela, Risto, *The Levites: Their Emergence as a Second-Class Priesthood* (SFSHJ 193; Atlanta, GA: Scholars Press, 1998); Schaper, Joachim, *Priester und Leviten im achämenidischen Juda: Studien zur Kult- und Sozialgeschichte Israels in persischer Zeit* (FAT 31; Tübingen: Mohr Siebeck, 2000).
20 Grabbe, Lester L., *"The Spirit of the Lord Came upon Me": Prophets in Ancient Israel from a Cross-Cultural Perspective* (London and New York: T&T Clark, 2024). See also the chapter on prophets in Grabbe, *Priests, Prophets, Diviners, Sages*.

21 Grabbe, Lester L., "Maccabean Chronology: 167–164 or 168–165 BCE?" *Journal of Biblical Literature* 110 (1991): 59–74.
22 See, especially, Greengus, Samuel, "Law in the OT," *IDBSup* (1976): 532–7.
23 Grabbe, *Priests, Prophets, Diviners, Sages*, 119–51.
24 Grabbe, Lester L., *Judaic Religion in the Second Temple Period: Belief and Practice from the Exile to Yavneh* (London/New York: Routledge, 2000), 317–18.
25 Grabbe, Lester L., Review of M. Douglas, *Leviticus as Literature*, *Journal of Ritual Studies* 18 (2004): 157–61.
26 Toorn, Karel van der, "The Nature of the Biblical Teraphim in the Light of the Cuneiform Evidence," *CBQ* 52 (1990): 203–22.
27 *KTU* 1.5.5.17-22.
28 Kramer, Samuel Noah, *The Sacred Marriage Rite: Aspects of Faith, Myth, and Ritual in Ancient Sumer* (Bloomington: University of Indiana, 1969); Lapinkivi, Pirjo, *The Sumerian Sacred Marriage in the Light of Comparative Evidence* (SAAS 15; Helsinki: The Neo-Assyrian Text Corpus Project, 2004).
29 Barstad, Hans M., *The Religious Polemics of Amos: Studies in the Preaching of Am 2, 7B-8; 4,1-13; 5,1-27; 6,4-7; 8,14* (VTSup 34; Leiden: Brill, 1984), 21–33; Goodfriend, Elaine Adler, and Karel van der Toorn. "Prostitution," *ABD* (1992): 5.505-13.
30 For example, see the various arguments in Schwartz, Jeffrey H., Houghton, Frank, Macchiarelli, Roberto, and Bondioli, Luca, "Skeletal Remains from Punic Carthage Do Not Support Systematic Sacrifice of Infants," *PLoS ONE* 5, no. 2 (2010); Schwartz, Jeffrey H., Houghton, Frank D., Bondioli, Luca, and Macchiarelli, Roberto, "Two Tales of One City: Data, Inference and Carthaginian Infant Sacrifice," *Antiquity* 91 (2017): 442–54; Smith, Patricia, Avishai, Gal, Greene, Joseph A., and Stager, Lawrence E., "Aging Cremated Infants: The Problem of Sacrifice at the Tophet of Carthage," *Antiquity* 85 (2011): 859–75; Smith, Patricia, Stager, Lawrence E., Greene, Joseph A., and Avishai, Gal, "Age Estimations Attest to Infant Sacrifice at the Carthage Tophet," *Antiquity* 87 (2013): 1191–9; Xella, Paulo, Quinn, Josephine, Melchiorri, Valentina, and van Dommelen, Peter, "Phoenician Bones of Contention," *Antiquity* 87 (2013): 1199–207.

Chapter 8

Further information and references for the material in this chapter can found in my *Ancient Israel: What Do We Know and How Do We Know It?* (2nd edn; London/New York: T&T Clark, 2017); chapter 5 also in my edited volume: *Good Kings and Bad Kings: The Kingdom of Judah in the Seventh Century BCE* (Journal for the Study of the Old Testament Supplement 393 = European Seminar in Historical Methodology 5; London/New York: T&T Clark International, 2005).

Individual studies of importance to this chapter include:

Albertz, Rainer, *A History of Israelite Religion in the Old Testament Period*, vol. 1, *From the Beginnings to the End of the Monarchy*, vol. 2, *From the Exile to the Maccabees* (London: SCM, 1994);

Knauf, E. Axel, "Hezekiah or Manasseh? A Reconsideration of the Siloam Tunnel and Inscription," *TA* 28 (2001): 281–7;

Knauf, E. Axel, "The Glorious Days of Manasseh," in Lester L. Grabbe (ed.), *Good Kings and Bad Kings: The Kingdom of Judah in the Seventh Century BCE* (JSOTSup 393 = ESHM 5: London/New York: T&T Clark International, 2005), 164–88;
  Na'aman, Nadav, "The Kingdom of Judah under Josiah," *TA* 18 (1991): 3–71;
  Na'aman, Nadav, "The Kingdom of Judah under Josiah," in Lester L. Grabbe (ed.), *Good Kings and Bad Kings: The Kingdom of Judah in the Seventh Century BCE* (JSOTSup 393 = ESHM 5: London/New York: T&T Clark International, 2005), 210–17;
  Uehlinger, Christoph, "Was There a Cult Reform under King Josiah? The Case for a Well-Grounded Minimum," in Lester L. Grabbe (ed.), *Good Kings and Bad Kings: The Kingdom of Judah in the Seventh Century BCE* (LHBOTS 393 = ESHM 5; London and New York: T&T Clark International, 2005), 279–316.

Notes

1 For a more technical and detailed account of this period of history, see Grabbe (ed.), *"Like a Bird in a Cage": The Invasion of Sennacherib in 701 BCE* (JSOTSup 363 = European Seminar in Historical Methodology 4; Sheffield, UK: Sheffield Academic Press, 2003).
2 See Grabbe, *Ancient Israel*, 238–44 for further information and references; see also the essays in Grabbe (ed.) 2003.
3 For example, Albertz, *A History of Israelite Religion in the Old Testament Period*, vol. 1, 180–6; Na'aman, Nadav, "The Debated Historicity of Hezekiah's Reform in the Light of Historical and Archaeological Research," *ZAW* 107 (1995): 179–95.
4 Knauf, "Hezekiah or Manasseh? A Reconsideration of the Siloam Tunnel and Inscription"; Ussishkin, David, "The Date of the Judaean Shrine at Arad," *IEJ* 38 (1988): 142–57.
5 Fried, Lisbeth E., "The High Places (*BĀMÔT*) and the Reforms of Hezekiah and Josiah: An Archaeological Investigation," *JAOS* 122 (2002): 437–65.
6 It was then argued that 2 Kgs 18:13, 17 to 19:9a was parallel to 19:9b-37 (duplicated in Isa. 36–7). This gives the following analysis (Childs, Brevard S., *Isaiah and the Assyrian Crisis* [Studies in Biblical Theology, Second Series 3; London: SCM, 1967]):
  Account A: 2 Kings 18:13-16.
  Account B_1: 2 Kings 18:17-19:9a, 36-37//Isaiah 36:1–37:9a
  Account B_2: 2 Kings 19:9b-35//Isaiah 37:9b-36
  Neither of these narratives B_1 or B_2 could be considered trustworthy historical sources but were both "legendary," even if here and there they contained a correct historical datum, as we shall see.
7 See, for example, Shea, William H., "Sennacherib's Second Palestinian Campaign," *JBL* 104 (1985): 410–18.
8 Yurco, Frank J., "The Shabaka-Shebitku Coregency and the Supposed Second Campaign of Sennacherib against Judah: A Critical Assessment," *JBL* 110 (1991): 35–45.
9 See Grabbe (ed.) 2003. For an overview and sources, see Grabbe, *Ancient Israel*, 239–40.
10 Grabbe, Lester L., "The Kingdom of Judah from Sennacherib's Invasion to the Fall of Jerusalem: If We Had Only the Bible," in Lester L. Grabbe (ed.), *Good Kings and Bad Kings: The Kingdom of Judah in the Seventh Century BCE* (JSOTSup 393 = ESHM 5; London/New York: T&T Clark International, 2005), 78–122.
11 Na'aman, Nadav, "Hezekiah's Years of Reign in Light of the Epigraphic Evidence," in Robert Deutsch and André Lemaire (eds), *Gabriel, Tell this Man the Meaning of His*

Vision (Daniel 8:16): Studies in Archaeology, Epigraphy, Iconography and the Biblical World in Honor of Gabriel Barkay on the Occasion of His 80th Birthday (22 June 2024) (Tel-Aviv: Archaeological Center Publications, 2024), 216–30.
12 Parpola, Simo, "The Murderer of Sennacherib," in B. Alster (ed.), *Death in Mesopotamia: Papers Read at the XXVIe Rencontre assyriologique international* (MESOPOTAMIA: Copenhagen Studies in Assyriology 8; Copenhagen: Akademisk Forlag, 1980), 161–70.
13 Finkelstein, Israel, "The Archaeology of the Days of Manasseh," in Michael D. Coogan, Cheryl J. Exum, and Lawrence E. Stager (eds), *Scripture and Other Artifacts: Essays on the Bible and Archaeology in Honor of Philip J. King* (Louisville, KY: Westminster John Knox, 1994), 169–87; Finkelstein, Israel, and Neil Asher Silberman, *The Bible Unearthed: Archaeology's New Vision of Ancient Israel and the Origin of its Sacred Texts* (New York: Free Press, 2001), 264–74.
14 Tatum, Lynn, "Jerusalem in Conflict: The Evidence for the Seventh-Century B.C.E. Religious Struggle over Jerusalem," in Andrew G. Vaughn and Ann E. Killebrew (eds), *Jerusalem in Bible and Archaeology: The First Temple Period* (SBLSymS 18; Atlanta, GA: Society of Biblical Literature, 2003), 300.
15 Knauf, "Hezekiah or Manasseh?"; Grabbe, *Good Kings and Bad Kings*, 170.
16 Claburn, W. E., "The Fiscal Basis of Josiah's Reforms," *JBL* 92 (1973): 11–22.
17 Na'aman, "The Kingdom of Judah under Josiah," 33–41.
18 Knauf, "The Glorious Days of Manasseh"; Albertz, *A History of Israelite Religion in the Old Testament Period*, vol. 1, 198–201; "Why a Reform Like Josiah's Must Have Happened," in Lester L. Grabbe (ed.), *Good Kings and Bad Kings: The Kingdom of Judah in the Seventh Century BCE* (JSOTSup 393 = ESHM 5; London/New York: T&T Clark International, 2005) 27–46; Lohfink, Norbert, "Gab es eine deuteronomistische Bewegung?" in Walter Gross (ed.), *Jeremia und die "deuteronomistische Bewegung"* (BBB 98; Beltz: Athenäum, 1995), 313–82; Davies, Philip R., "Josiah and the Law Book," in Lester L. Grabbe (ed.), *Good Kings and Bad Kings: The Kingdom of Judah in the Seventh Century BCE* (JSOTSup 393 = ESHM 5; London/New York: T&T Clark International, 2005), 65–77.
19 See, for example, the opposing arguments of Uehlinger, "Was There a Cult Reform under King Josiah?"; Niehr, Herbert, "'Die Reform des Joschija: Methodische, historische und religionsgeschichtliche Aspekte," in Walter Gross (ed.), *Jeremia und die "deuteronomistische Bewegung"* (BBB 98; Beltz: Athenäum, 1995), 33–55.
20 Uehlinger, "Was There a Cult Reform under King Josiah?"; Hardmeier, Christof, "King Josiah in the Climax of DtrH (2 Kgs 22–3) and the Pre-Dtr Document of a Cult Reform at the Place of Residence (23.4-15): Criticism of Sources, Reconstruction of Earlier Texts and the History of Theology of 2 Kgs 22–23," in Lester L. Grabbe (ed.), *Good Kings and Bad Kings: The Kingdom of Judah in the Seventh Century BCE* (LHBOTS 393 = ESHM 5; London/New York: T&T Clark International, 2005), 123–63.
21 Na'aman, "The Kingdom of Judah under Josiah," 51–5, with earlier literature.
22 Grabbe, Lester L., "Fundamentalism and Scholarship: The Case of Daniel," in B. P. Thompson (ed.), *Scripture: Method and Meaning: Essays Presented to Anthony Tyrrell Hanson for his Seventieth Birthday* (Hull: Hull University Press, 1987), 138–40.
23 Grabbe, *The Dawn of Israel*, 232–3.
24 Ibid., 233–4.
25 Our knowledge of Pharaoh Apries from native Egyptian sources is deficient; however, we have some information from Greek sources that has generally been accepted by Egyptologists (Herodotus 2.161-9; Diodorus Siculus 1.68.1-6).
26 Becking, Bob, "Inscribed Seals as Evidence for Biblical Israel? Jeremiah 40:7–41:15 Par Example," in Lester L. Grabbe (ed.), *Can a "History of Israel" Be Written?* (JSOTSup 245 = ESHM 1; Sheffield, UK: Sheffield Academic Press, 1997), 75–80.

Chapter 9

A much more detailed study, with extensive references, is my *A History of the Jews and Judaism in the Second Temple Period 1: Yehud: A History of the Persian Province of Judah* (LSTS 47; London and New York: T&T Clark International, 2004) and *Ezra and Nehemiah* (London: Routledge, 1998).

A number of individual studies important for this period include:

Briant, Pierre, *From Cyrus to Alexander: A History of the Persian Empire*, translated by Peter T. Daniels (Winona Lake, IN: Eisenbrauns, 2002);

Grabbe, Lester L., "Another Look at the *Gestalt* of 'Darius the Mede,'" *Catholic Biblical Quarterly* 50 (1988): 198–213;

Lipschits, Oded, "Demographic Changes in Judah between the Seventh and the Fifth Centuries BCE," in Oded Lipschits and Joseph Blenkinsopp (eds), *Judah and the Judeans in the Neo-Babylonian Period* (Winona Lake, IN: Eisenbrauns, 2003), 323–76;

Lipschits, Oded, *The Fall and Rise of Jerusalem: Judah under Babylonian Rule* (Winona Lake, IN: Eisenbrauns, 2005);

Pearce, Laurie E., "'Judean': A Special Status in Neo-Babylonian and Achemenid Babylonia?" in Oded Lipschits, Gary N. Knoppers, and Manfred Oeming (eds), *Judah and the Judeans in the Achaemenid Period: Negotiating Identity in an International Context* (Winona Lake, IN: Eisenbrauns, 2011), 267–77;

Porten, Bezalel, and Yardeni, Ada, *Textbook of Aramaic Documents from Ancient Egypt: 1–4*, Hebrew University, Department of the History of the Jewish People, Texts and Studies for Students (Jerusalem: Hebrew University, 1986–1999);

Reinmuth, Titus, *Der Bericht Nehemias: Zur literarischen Eigenart, traditionsgeschichtlichen Prägung und innerbiblischen Rezeption des Ich-Berichts Nehemias* (OBO, 183; Fribourg: University Press; Göttingen: Vandenhoeck & Ruprecht, 2002).

Notes

1 Weidner, Ernst F., "Jojachin, König von Juda, in babylonischen Keilschrifttexten," in *Mélanges Syriens offerts a Monsieur Rene Dussaud par ses amis et ses élèves* (Paris: Geuthner, 1939), II, 923–35; *DOTT*, 84–6.

2 Joannès, F., and Lemaire, André, "Trois tablettes cunéiforme à onomastique ouest-sémitique (collection Sh. Moussaïeff)," *Transeuphratène* 17 (1999): 17–34; Pearce, Laurie E., "New Evidence for Judeans in Babylonia," in Oded Lipschits and Manfred Oeming (eds), *Judah and the Judeans in the Persian Period* (Winona Lake, IN: Eisenbrauns, 2006), 399–411; Pearce, Laurie E., "'Judean': A Special Status in Neo-Babylonian and Achemenid Babylonia?" in Oded Lipschits, Gary N. Knoppers, and Manfred Oeming (eds), *Judah and the Judeans in the Achaemenid Period: Negotiating Identity in an International Context* (Winona Lake, IN: Eisenbrauns, 2011).

3 Pearce, "'Judean,'" 269–70.

4 On this story see Grabbe, Lester L., "Another Look at the *Gestalt* of 'Darius the Mede,'" *Catholic Biblical Quarterly* 50 (1988): 198–213.

5 Beaulieu, Paul-Alain, *The Reign of Nabonidus, King of Babylon 556–539 BC* (Yale Near Eastern Researches 10; New Haven, CT: Yale University Press, 1989).

6 Grabbe, "Another Look at the *Gestalt* of 'Darius the Mede.'"

7 Stolper, Matthew W., *Entrepreneurs and Empire: The Murašû Archive, the Murašû Firm, and Persian Rule in Babylonia* (Uitgaven van het Nederlands Historisch-Archaeologisch Instituut te Istanbul 54; Leiden: Nederlands Historisch-Archaeologisch Instituut te Istanbul, 1985).

8 Lipschits, Oded, "Demographic Changes in Judah between the Seventh and the Fifth Centuries B.C.E.," in Oded Lipschits and Joseph Blenkinsopp (eds), *Judah and the Judeans in the Neo-Babylonian Period* (Winona Lake, IN: Eisenbrauns, 2003), 365.
9 Ibid., 329.
10 Olmstead, A. T., "Tattenai, Governor of 'Across the River,'" *JNES* 3 (1944): 46.
11 There will always be questions about the precise texts to include in NM. For the sake of convenience, the present chapter will use the following delineation unless otherwise noted: Neh. 1:1-4, 11; 2:1-20; (the list in 3:1-32 has been incorporated into the narrative by Nehemiah himself); 3:33–4:17; 5:1-19; 6:1-19; 7:1-5; 12:31-32, 37-40; 13:4-17, 19-25, 27-31. On this, see Reinmuth, Titus, *Der Bericht Nehemias: Zur literarischen Eigenart, traditionsgeschichtlichen Prägung und innerbiblischen Rezeption des Ich-Berichts Nehemias* (OBO, 183; Fribourg: University Press; Göttingen: Vandenhoeck & Ruprecht, 2002); also for the definitive discussion of the NM up to the present.
12 Smith, Morton, *Palestinian Parties and Politics That Shaped the Old Testament* (London: SCM, 1987; corrected reprint of New York: Columbia, 1971); Blenkinsopp, Joseph, "Temple and Society in Achemenid Judah," in Philip R. Davies (ed.), *Studies in the Second Temple: 1. The Persian Period* (JSOTSup 117; Sheffield: JSOT, 1991), 29; Kippenberg, Hans G., *Religion und Klassenbildung im antiken Judäa* (2nd edn, SUNT 14; Göttingen: Vandenhoeck & Ruprecht, 1982/1982), 55–62; Yamauchi, Edwin M., "Two Reformers Compared: Solon of Athens and Nehemiah of Jerusalem," in Gary Rendsburg et al. (eds), *The Bible World: Essays in Honor of Cyrus H. Gordon* (New York: Ktav, 1980), 269–92.
13 Grabbe, "What Was Nehemiah Up To? Looking for Models for Nehemiah's Polity," in Isaac Kalimi (ed.), *New Perspectives on Ezra-Nehemiah: History and Historiography, Text, Literature, and Interpretation* (Winona Lake, IN: Eisenbrauns, 2012), 27–36.
14 A useful overview can be found in Andrewes, A., "The Growth of the Athenian State," in CAH 3, no. 3 (1982): 36–91, especially 375–91; see also Buckley, Terry, *Aspects of Greek History 750–323 BC: A Source-Based Approach* (London and New York: Routledge, 1996). On trying to reconstruct Solon's own writings, see Ruschenbusch, Eberhard, *ΣΟΛΩΝΟΣ ΝΟΜΟΙ: Die Fragmente des solonischen Gesetzeswerkes mit einer Text- und Überlieferungsgeschichte* (Historia-Einzelschriften 9; Wiesbaden: Franz Steiner Verlag, 1966).
15 Blenkinsopp, "Temple and Society in Achemenid Judah," 29; Smith, *Palestinian Parties and Politics That Shaped the Old Testament*, 108. On Pericles's reforms, see Rhodes, P. J., "The Athenian Revolution," in CAH 5.62-95 (1992), especially 77–87; Buckley, *Aspects of Greek History 750–323 BC*, 241–51.
16 This is one explanation but is probably also a simplistic one. One factor seems to be the number of individuals coming from abroad and settling in Athens at this time. If they married an Athenian, as many did, their children would be citizens. It is clear that there was a feeling against allowing the ranks of citizens to expand in such a way at this time, though precisely what arguments were used is not clear from the extant sources.
17 Brunneau, P., "'Les Israélites de Délos' et la juiverie délienne," *BCH* 106 (1982): 465–504; Kraabel, A. T., "New Evidence of the Samaritan Diaspora Has Been Found on Delos," *BA* 47 (1984): 44–47.
18 WDSP 7:17; also perhaps in WDSP 9:14.
19 WDSP 11r:13; cf. WD 23.
20 TAD A4.7:29//A4.8:27-28 = AP 30:29//31:27-28.
21 TAD A4.9:1-2 = AP 32:1-2.
22 WD 22.

23 WDSP 8:12; 5:14.
24 Josephus, *Ant.* 11.7.2–11.8.6 §§302–45.
25 Meshorer, Ya'akov, and Qedar, Shrahga, *Samarian Coinage* (Numismatic Studies and Researches 9; Jerusalem: Israel Numismatic Society, 1999), 27, 93.
26 Eshel, Hanan (Hebrew), "The Rulers of Samaria During the Fifth and Fourth Centuries BCE," *EI* 26 (1999): 10.
27 The most complete collection of documents from Elephantine is *TAD*: Porten, Bezalel, and Yardeni, Ada, *Textbook of Aramaic Documents from Ancient Egypt*, vols 1–4 (Hebrew University, Department of the History of the Jewish People, Texts and Studies for Students. Jerusalem: Hebrew University, 1986–1999).
28 Karel van der Toorn, "Previously, at Elephantine," *Journal of the American Oriental Society* 138 (2018): 255–70.
29 *TAD* A4.1.
30 Rowley, H. H., "The Chronological Order of Ezra and Nehemiah," *The Servant of the Lord and Other Essays* (Oxford: Blackwell, 1965), 135–68; Widengren, Geo, "The Persian Period," in John Hayes and J. Maxwell Miller (eds), *Israelite and Judaean History* (Philadelphia, PA: Fortress, 1977), 489–538; Emerton, J. A., "Did Ezra Go to Jerusalem in 428 BC?" *JTS* 17 (1966): 1–19; Ackroyd, P. R., *Israel under Babylon and Persia* (New Clarendon Bible, OT 4; London: Oxford, 1970), 191–6.
31 See especially Grabbe, Lester L., "The 'Persian Documents' in the Book of Ezra: Are They Authentic?" in Oded Lipschits and Manfred Oeming (eds), *Judah and the Judeans in the Persian Period* (Winona Lake, IN: Eisenbrauns, 2006), 531–70.
32 A standard rate of gold to silver in the Persian Empire seems to have been about 13 to 1 (Herodotus 3.95).
33 See further Grabbe, "Penetrating the Legend: in Quest of the Historical Ezra," in Marjo C. A. Korpel and Lester L. Grabbe (eds), *Open-Mindedness in the Bible and Beyond: A Volume of Studies in Honour of Bob Becking* (LHBOTS 616; London and New York: T&T Clark, 2015), 97–110.
34 *Tôrāh* in Nehemiah occurs primarily in chs 8–10, which concern the public reading of the law. Nehemiah 8 is about Ezra's reading of the law, but 9 and 10 do not feature Ezra. Although Nehemiah is listed as a signatory in Nehemiah 10:2, he has nothing to do with events in 9 and 10. Yet it would be totally unlike Nehemiah to be a passive observer, which suggests that if this was based on an archival document (which is not certain, of course), his name has been added by the editor. In any event, there is no mention of the book of *tôrāh* in the Nehemiah Memorial, which would be congruous with promulgation of the book of the law after his time (for a recent analysis of the Nehemiah Memorial or Memoir, see Reinmuth, *Der Bericht Nehemias*).
35 Cf. Grabbe, Lester L., *A History of the Jews and Judaism in the Second Temple Period 2: The Coming of the Greeks: The Early Hellenistic Period (335–175 BCE)* (Library of Second Temple Studies 68; London/New York: T&T Clark International, 2008), 341. On the authenticity of the Hecataeus passage, see ibid., 113–19.
36 For a further discussion, see chapter 10, pp. 200–3 of this volume.
37 See further Grabbe, *A History of the Jews and Judaism in the Second Temple Period 1*, 331–43; Grabbe, Lester L., "Elephantine and the Torah," in Alejandro F. Botta (ed.), *In the Shadow of Bezalel: Aramaic, Biblical, and Ancient Near Eastern Studies in Honor of Bezalel Porten* (Culture and History of the Ancient Near East 60; Leiden/Boston: Brill, 2013), 125–35.
38 See further Grabbe, *A History of the Jews and Judaism in the Second Temple Period 1*, 209–16.

39 Contrary to a number of scholars, I have argued that the governor of Judah Bogoses and the high priest Joannes are the same as the individuals named in Aramaic papyri from Elephantine dated to 407 BCE.
40 Briant, *From Cyrus to Alexander*, 674.
41 Ibid., 683–5.
42 Ibid., 685.
43 Ibid., 589–90.

Chapter 10

For a more detailed study and references for material in this chapter, see my
A History of the Jews and Judaism in the Second Temple Period 2: The Coming of the Greeks: The Early Hellenistic Period (335–175 BCE) (Library of Second Temple Studies 68; London/New York: T&T Clark International, 2008).

Here are some individual studies important for aspects of this chapter:

Cowey, James M. S., and Klaus Maresch (eds), *Urkunden des Politeuma der Juden von Herakleopolis (144/3-133/2 v. Chr.) (P. Polit. Iud.)* (Abhandlungen der Nordrhein-Westfälischen Akademie der Wissenschaften, Papyrologica Coloniensia 19; Wiesbaden: Westdeutscher Verlag, 2001);

Kuhrt, A., and S. Sherwin-White (ed.), *Hellenism in the East* (London: Duckworth, 1987);

Sherwin-White, Susan, and Amélie Kuhrt, *From Samarkhand to Sardis: A New Approach to the Seleucid Empire* (London: Duckworth, 1993).

Notes

1 Smith, Morton, "Palestinian Judaism in the First Century," in Moshe Davis (ed.), *Israel: Its Role in Civilization* (New York: Harper, 1956), 67–81.
2 See especially Kuhrt and Sherwin-White, *Hellenism in the East*; Sherwin-White and Kuhrt, *From Samarkhand to Sardis*.
3 For example, it is widely accepted among biblical scholars that the book of Deuteronomy has been heavily influenced by the form of the Assyrian vassal treaty. Cf. McCarthy, Dennis J., *Treaty and Covenant* (2nd edn; Rome: Pontifical Biblical Institute, 1978), 157–205.
4 Eusebius, *Chronicle* on Olympiad CXII (205F).
5 *Raphia Decree* 15–17, trans. Austen, M. M., *The Hellenistic World from Alexander to the Roman Conquest: A Selection of Ancient Sources in Translation* (Cambridge, UK: Cambridge University, 1981), 482–3.
6 See especially *CPJ 1* and Horbury, William, and Noy, David, *Jewish Inscriptions of Graeco-Roman Egypt* (Cambridge, UK: Cambridge University Press, 1992).
7 Cowey and Maresch, *Urkunden des Politeuma der Juden von Herakleopolis*.
8 See *P. Polit. Iud.* (Cowey and Maresch, *Urkunden des Politeuma der Juden von Herakleopolis*), 1.1; 2.1; 3.1; 6.1.
9 Modrzejewski, J. M., *The Jews of Egypt: From Rameses II to Emperor Hadrian*, trans. Robert Cornman (Philadelphia, PA: Jewish Publication Society, Edinburgh: T&T Clark, 1995), 111–12; LeFebvre, Michael, *Collections, Codes, and Torah: The Re-characterization of Israel's Written Law* (LHBOTS 451; New York/London: T&T Clark International, 2006), 171–3.

10 P. *Polit. Iud.* 4 (Cowey and Maresch, *Urkunden des Politeuma der Juden von Herakleopolis*, 23–9); see also the discussion in Honigman, Sylvie, "The Jewish Politeuma at Heracleopolis," *SCI* 21 (2002): 259–66; Honigman, Sylvie, "*Politeumata* and Ethnicity in Ptolemaic and Roman Egypt," *AncSoc* 33 (2003): 95–102.
11 Manning, J. G., *Land and Power in Ptolemaic Egypt: The Structure of Land Tenure* (Cambridge, UK: Cambridge University Press, 2003), 221.
12 Hughes, George R., and Jasnow, Richard (with a contribution by James G. Keenan), *Oriental Institute Hawara Papyri: Demotic and Greek Texts from an Egyptian Family Archive in the Fayum (Fourth to Third Century BC)* (Oriental Institute Publication 113; Chicago: Oriental Institute of the University of Chicago, 1997), #9, square brackets part of the original.
13 On the whole subject of prophecy and apocalyptic, see my *"The Spirit of the Lord Came upon Me": Prophets in Ancient Israel from a Cross-Cultural Perspective* (LHBOTS 738; London: T&T Clark, 2024).
14 Cf. Grabbe, *A History of the Jews and Judaism in the Second Temple Period 2*, 341. On the authenticity of the Hecataeus passage, see Grabbe, *A History of the Jews and Judaism in the Second Temple Period 2*, 113–19.
15 See further, Grabbe, Lester L., *A History of the Jews and Judaism in the Second Temple Period 1: Yehud: A History of the Persian Province of Judah* (LSTS 47; London/New York: T&T Clark International, 2004), 331–43.

Chapter 11

For much more information and references for this chapter, see my study *A History of the Jews and Judaism in the Second Temple Period 3: The Maccabaean Revolt, Hasmonaean Rule, and Herod the Great (175–174 BCE)* (Library of Second Temple Studies 95; London/New York: T&T Clark, 2020).

Notes

1 Mittag, Peter Franz, *Antiochos IV. Epiphanes: Eine politische Biographie* (Klio Beiheft, N.F. Band 11; Berlin: Akademie Verlag, 2006); Mørkholm, O., *Antiochus IV of Syria* (Classica et Mediaevalia, Dissertationes 8; Copenhagen: I Kommission Hos, 1966).
2 Celsus 7.25.1.
3 E.g., Russell, D. S., *Between the Testaments* (London: SCM, 1960), 27; Russell, D. S., *The Jews from Alexander to Herod* (The New Clarendon Bible, Old Testament 5; Oxford: Oxford University Press, 1967), 37.
4 Bernhardt, Johannes Christian, *Die jüdische Revolution: Untersuchungen zu Ursachen, Verlauf und Folgen der hasmonäischen Erhebung* (Klio Beihefte, Neue Folge 22; Berlin/Boston: De Gruyter, 2017), 222, 540; Bringmann, Klaus, *Hellenistische Reform und Religionsverfolgung in Judäa: Eine Untersuchung zur jüdisch-hellenistischen Geschichte (175–163 v. Chr.)* (Abhandlungen der Akademie der Wissenschaften in Göttingen, Phil.-hist. Klasse, 3. Folge, Nr. 132; Göttingen: Vandenhoeck & Ruprecht, 1983), 15–28; Grabbe, Lester L., "Maccabean Chronology: 167–164 or 168–165 BCE?" *JBL* 110 (1991): 59–74.
5 1 Macc. 10.1-14; Polybius 33.15.1-2; 33.18.6-14; Justin 35.1.6–2.4.
6 Cf. *Ant.* 13.2.4 §58–61; Justin 35.1.9.

7 1 Macc. 10.67-89; Justin 35.2.1–4; Diodorus 32.9c-d; 33.3-4; Appian 11.67; Livy, *Periochae*, 52.
8 1 Macc. 11.13-19; Justin 35.2.1-4.
9 1 Macc. 11.38-53; cf. *Ant.* 13.4.9 §129–30; Diodorus 33.4.1-4.
10 1 Macc. 11.54-59; Diodorus 33.3-4a; Appian, *Syr.* 68.
11 Cf. Josephus, cf. *Ant.* 13.5.4 §146.
12 1 Macc. 11.60-74; Josephus, *Ant.* 13.5.5-7 §§148–62.
13 Josephus, *Ant.* 13.7.2 §223; Appian, *Syr.* 11.68; Strabo 14.5.2; Syncellus 351.13.
14 For a detailed discussion, see Grabbe, *A History of the Jews and Judaism in the Second Temple Period 3*, 143–65.

Chapter 12

For much more information and references for this chapter, see my study
A History of the Jews and Judaism in the Second Temple Period 3: The Maccabaean Revolt, Hasmonaean Rule, and Herod the Great (175–174 BCE) (Library of Second Temple Studies 95; London/New York: T&T Clark, 2020).

Notes

1 Diodorus 40.2.
2 Josephus, *Ant.* 14.8.1 §127.
3 Josephus, *Ant.* 14.10.2 §190, but he seems to have been called "king" by the Jews themselves: *War* 1.10.4 §§202–3; 1.10.9 §214; *Ant.* 14.8.5 §§148, 151; 14.9.1 §157; 14.9.3 §165; 14.9.4 §§168, 172.
4 Cf. Josephus, *Ant.* 14.15.2 §403.
5 Ibid., 14.1.3 §9.
6 Ibid., 14.15.6 §§432–3.
7 Ibid., 14.16.2 §473.
8 So also Strabo, as quoted in *Ant.* 15.1.2 §§8–10; Plutarch, *Antony* 36; Dio 49.22 says he was crucified and flogged, though then beheaded.
9 Josephus, *War* 1.18.5 §§361–62; *Ant.* 15.4.2 §§96–103.
10 Baltrusch, Ernst, *Herodes: König im Heiligen Land—Eine Biographie* (Munich: C. H. Beck, 2012), 186–8.
11 Josephus, *Ant.* 15.3.5-9 §§65–87.
12 Ibid., 15.8.1-2 §§267–79; *War* 1.21.8 §415; *Ant.* 17.10.2 §255.
13 Josephus, *War* 1.21.1 §401; *Ant.* 15.9.1-7 §§380–425.
14 Ibid., 15.11.1 §380.
15 Josephus, *Ant.* 20.9.7 §§219–20; cf. John 2:20.
16 Josephus, *Ant.* 16.7.6 §§220–5; 17.1.1. §10.
17 Josephus, *War.* 1.23.1-27.6 §§445–551; *Ant.* 16.1.2 §§6–11.
18 Josephus, *War.* 2.6.2 §§84–6; *Ant.* 17.11.2 §§304–10.
19 Josephus, *Ant.* 14.15.2 §403.
20 Ibid., 15.8.1-2 §§267–79.
21 Ibid., 16.7.6 §§221–5.
22 Ibid., 15.11.1 §385.
23 Ibid., 15.10.4 §§365–72.
24 Ibid., 14.9.4 §175.
25 E.g., Josephus, *Ant.* 16.2.3-5 §§27–65.

Chapter 13

For much more information and references for this chapter, see my study *A History of the Jews and Judaism in the Second Temple Period 4: The Jews under the Roman Shadow (4 BCE–150 CE)* (Library of Second Temple Studies 99; London/New York: T&T Clark, 2021).

Individual studies shedding light on aspects of this chapter include:

Grabbe, Lester L., "What Did Author of Acts Know about Pre-70 Judaism?" in J. Harold Ellens, Isaac W. Oliver, Jason von Ehrenkrook, James Waddell, and Jason M. Zurawski (eds), *Wisdom Poured Out Like Water: Studies on Jewish and Christian Antiquity in Honor of Gabriele Boccaccini* (Deuterocanonical and Cognate Literature Studies 38; Berlin/New York: De Gruyter, 2018), 458–9;

Gruen, Erich S., *Diaspora: Jews amidst Greeks and Romans* (Cambridge, MA: Harvard University Press, 2002);

Price, Jonathan J., *Jerusalem under Siege: The Collapse of the Jewish State 66–70 CE* (Brill's Series in Jewish Studies 3; Leiden: Brill, 1992);

Rogers, Guy MacLean, *For the Freedom of Zion: The Great Revolt of Jews Against Romans, 66–74 CE* (New Haven, CT: Yale University Press, 2022);

Schwartz, Daniel R., *Agrippa I: The Last King of Judaea* (TSAJ 23; Tübingen: Mohr Siebeck, 1990).

Notes

1 Josephus, *Ant.* 18.2.1 §26; Cassius Dio 55.25.1: consuls M. Aemilius Lepidus and Lucius Arruntius.
2 Josephus, *Ant.* 18.1.1 §§7–10.
3 Cf. Tacitus, *Ann.* 2.85.4; Suetonius, *Tib.* 36; Cassius Dio 57.18.5.
4 Josephus, *Ant.* 18.3.4 §§65–80; cf. Moehring, Horst R., "The Persecution of the Jews and the Adherents of the Isis Cult at Rome A.D. 19," *NovT* 3 (1959): 293–304.
5 Gruen, *Diaspora*, 34.
6 Josephus, *War* 2.9.2-3 §§169–74; *Ant.* 18.3.1 §§55–9.
7 Josephus, *War* 2.9.4 §175; *Ant.* 18.3.2 §§60–2.
8 Cf. also Agrippa II's later use of temple funds for a paving project to provide employment, as described by Josephus (*Ant.* 20.9.7 §§219–22).
9 Philo, *Gaius*, 159–60; *Flaccus* 1; cf. Eusebius, *Hist. Eccl.* 2.5.7.
10 For a survey and discussion of sources outside the Bible, see my article, "'Jesus Who Is Called Christ': References to Jesus Outside Christian Sources," in Thomas L. Thompson and Thomas S. Verenna (eds), *"Is This Not the Carpenter?" The Question of the Historicity of the Figure of Jesus* (Copenhagen International Seminar; Sheffield: Equinox, 2012), 57–69.
11 Josephus, *Ant.* 20.9.1 §§199–200.
12 Ibid., 18.3.3 §§63–4.
13 Cf. Wilker, Julia, *Für Rom und Jerusalem: Die herodianische Dynastie im 1. Jahrhundert n.Chr.* (Studien zur Alten Geschichte 5; Frankfurt am Main: Verlag Antike, 2007), 123–7.
14 Gambetti, Sandra, *The Alexandrian Riots of 38 CE and the Persecution of the Jews: A Historical Reconstruction* (JSJSup 135; Leiden: Brill, 2009), 151–65.
15 Philo, *Gaius*, 361.
16 Josephus, *Ant.* 19.5.2 §§278–9.

17 Musurillo, H. A. (ed.), *The Acts of the Pagan Martyrs: Acta Alexandrinorum* (Oxford: Clarendon, 1954); *CPJ* 2:55–107, texts 154–9.
18 Philo's treatise, *Legatio ad Gaium*, mainly in 184–338; Josephus, *War* 2.10.1-5 §§184–203; *Antiquities* 18.8.2-9 §§261–309.
19 Philo, *Gaius*, 334.
20 Schwartz, *Agrippa I*, 82.
21 So Josephus, *Ant.* 19.7.2 §§326–7; *War* 2.11.6 §§218–19 is less likely correct in stating only that Agrippa's death stopped the project, as is *War* 5.4.2 §§151–5, which makes him stop the project voluntarily.
22 Josephus, *Ant.* 19.9.1 §357.
23 Schwartz, *Agrippa I*, 16–30.
24 On the Pharisees and Sadducees, see chapter 11, **pp. 234–6** on their beliefs. As noted there, the idea that the Pharisees dominated Jewish religious life at this time is mistaken.
25 Lüdemann, Gerd, *Early Christianity according to the Traditions in Acts: A Commentary* (London: SCM, 1989), 139–46; Schwartz, *Agrippa I*, 119–24.
26 Suetonius, *Claud.* 25.4; Orosius 7.6.15; cf. Dio 60.6.6.
27 Williams, Margaret H., "The Expulsion of the Jews from Rome in AD 19," *Latomus* 48 (1989): 765–84.
28 Cf. Grabbe, Lester L. *A History of the Jews and Judaism in the Second Temple Period 3: The Maccabaean Revolt, Hasmonaean Rule, and Herod the Great (175–4 BCE)* (Library of Second Temple Studies 95; London/New York: T&T Clark, 2020), 241-2.
29 Gruen, *Diaspora*, 29–41.
30 Smallwood, E. Mary, *The Jews under Roman Rule* (SJLA 20; Leiden: Brill, corrected reprint, 1981), 27–38.
31 Josephus, *War* 2.22.1 §§650–1.
32 Josephus, *Life* 22 §§104–11; 25 §§123–4.
33 Josephus, *War* 2.21.7 §§626–8; *Life* 38–9 §§189–98.
34 The rest of the present account is only a summary of Josephus's detailed account in the *War* (2.22.1 §647–7.11.5 §455), though with critical observations. For a discussion of more of the detail, one should consult Price, *Jerusalem under Siege*; Rogers, *For the Freedom of Zion*; Cohen, Shaye J. D., *Josephus in Galilee and Rome: His Vita and Development as a Historian* (CSCT 8; Leiden: Brill, 1979); and Mason, Steve, *A History of the Jewish War AD 66–74* (Cambridge, UK: Cambridge University Press, 2016).
35 Josephus, *War* 3.8.3 §§351–3; 3.8.9 §§405–7.
36 Tacitus (*Hist.* 5.13), Suetonius (*Vesp.* 4–5), and Cassius Dio (Epitome 66.1).
37 Josephus, *War* 3.7.32 §§307–15.
38 Ibid., 4.3.4-9 §§138–61.
39 Cf. Tacitus *Hist.* 2.74-86; Suetonius, *Vesp.* 6.3.
40 Tacitus, *Hist.* 2.81.
41 Josephus, *War* 4.5.5 §§345–52.
42 Ibid., 4.7.1 §§389–96.
43 Ibid., 5.1.1-4 §§1–26.
44 Ibid., *War* 5.1.6 §§45–6; 6.4.3 §237.
45 Ibid., 5.9.3 §370; 6.2.8 §157.
46 Ibid., 5.13.1 §533.
47 Ibid., 6.2.1 §98.
48 As the later Christian writer Sulpicius Severus reports (*GLAJJ* 2:64-7 [#282]; cf. also Price, *Jerusalem under Siege*, 170–1; Alon, G., "The Burning of the Temple," in *Jews, Judaism and the Classical World: Studies in Jewish History in the Times of the Second Temple and Talmud* (Jerusalem: Magnes, 1977), 252–68; Weikert, Christopher,

Von Jerusalem zu Aelia Capitolina: Die römische Politik gegenüber den Juden von Vespasian bis Hadrian (Hypomnemata 200; Göttingen: Vandenhoeck & Ruprecht, 2016), 83–90. According to Severus, Titus summoned a council of his senior officers and consulted them about whether the temple should be destroyed. Some were against it, but others—including Titus himself—thought the temple should be destroyed so that the religions of the Jews and Christians could be exterminated more easily.

49 Josephus, *War* 6.5.3 §§288–309; Tacitus, *Hist.* 5.13.
50 Josephus, *War* 6.2.1 §109.
51 Ibid., 6.5.4 §311.
52 Ibid., 6.5.4 §312–13.
53 Interestingly, several Roman historians also refer to this oracle: Tacitus, *Hist.* 5.13; Suetonius, *Vesp.* 5; Cassius Dio, Epitome 66.1.
54 Josephus, *War* 6.5.2 §§283–7.
55 Ibid., 2.17.5 §422.
56 Ibid., 2.18.2 §463.
57 Ibid., 2.19.4 §531.
58 Suetonius, *Vesp.* 4.5.
59 Price, *Jerusalem under Siege*, 27–38.
60 Josephus, *War* 2.22.1 §§650–1.
61 Josephus, *Life* 22 §§104–11; 25 §§123–4.
62 Josephus, *War* 2.21.7 §§626–8; *Life* 38–9 §§189–98.
63 The rest of the present account is only a summary of Josephus's detailed account of the *War* (2.22.1 §647—7.11.5 §455), though with critical observations. For a more detailed discussion, one should consult Cohen, *Josephus in Galilee and Rome*; Price, *Jerusalem under Siege*; and Mason Steve, *A History of the Jewish War AD 66–74*.
64 Josephus, *War* 3.8.3 §§351–3; 3.8.9 §§405–7.
65 Tacitus (*Hist.* 5.13), Suetonius (*Vesp.* 4.5), and Cassius Dio (Epitome 66.1).
66 Josephus, *War* 3.7.32 §§307–15.
67 Ibid., 4.3.4–9 §§138–61.
68 Cf. Tacitus, *Hist.* 2.74–86; Suetonius, *Vesp.* 6.3.
69 Tacitus, *Hist.* 2.81.
70 Josephus, *War* 4.5.5 §§345–52.
71 Ibid., §§389–96.
72 Ibid., 5.1.1–4 §§1–26.
73 Ibid., 5.1.6 §§45–6; 6.4.3 §237.
74 Ibid., 5.9.3 §370; 6.2.8 §157.
75 Ibid., 5.13.1 §533.
76 Ibid., 6.2.1 §98.
77 As the later Christian writer Sulpicius Severus reports (*GLAJJ* 2:64–7 [#282]; cf. also Alon, "The Burning of the Temple"; Price *Jerusalem under Siege*, 170–1; Weikert *Von Jerusalem zu Aelia Capitolina*, 83–90). According to Severus, Titus summoned a council of his senior officers and consulted them about whether the temple should be destroyed. Some were against it, but others—including Titus himself—thought the temple should be destroyed so that the religions of the Jews and Christians could more easily be exterminated.
78 Josephus, *War* 6.5.3—§§288–309; Tacitus, *Hist.* 5.13.
79 Josephus, *War* 6.2.1 §109.
80 Ibid., 6.5.4 §311.
81 Ibid., 6.5.4 §312–13.
82 Interestingly, several Roman historians also refer to this oracle: Tacitus, *Hist.* 5.13; Suetonius, *Vesp.* 5; Cassius Dio, Epitome 66.1.
83 Josephus, *War* 6.5.2 §§283–7.

Chapter 14

For much more information and references for this chapter, see my study *A History of the Jews and Judaism in the Second Temple Period 4: The Jews under the Roman Shadow (4 BCE–150 CE)* (Library of Second Temple Studies 99; London/New York: T&T Clark, 2021).

Individual studies shedding light on aspects of this chapter include:

Cotton, Hannah, and Ada Yardeni (eds), *Discoveries in the Judaean Desert XXVII: Aramaic, Hebrew and Greek Documentary Texts from Naḥal Ḥever and Other Sites, with an Appendix Containing Alleged Qumran Texts (The Seiyâl Collection II)* (Oxford, UK: Clarendon Press, 1997);

Lewis, Naphtali (ed.), *The Documents From the Bar Kokhba Period in the Cave of Letters: Greek Papyri*, with Y. Yadin and J. C. Greenfield (eds), *Aramaic and Nabatean Signatures and Subscriptions* (Judean Desert Studies 2; Jerusalem: Israel Exploration Society, 1989);

Meshorer, Ya'akov, *Ancient Jewish Coinage*, vol. 1, *Persian Period through Hasmonaeans; Volume II: Herod the Great through Bar Kokhba*, 2 vols. (New York: Amphora, 1982);

Mildenberg, Leo, "Bar Kokhba Coins and Documents," *HSCP* 84 (1980): 311–35;

Mildenberg, Leo, *The Coinage of the Bar Kokhba War* (Typos 6; Aarau/Frankfurt/Salzburg: Sauerlander, 1984);

Neusner, Jacob, *Development of a Legend: Studies on the Traditions Concerning Yohanan ben Zakkai* (SPB 16; Leiden: Brill, 1970);

Neusner, Jacob, "The Formation of Rabbinic Judaism: Yavneh (Jamnia) from AD 70 to 100," *ANRW II* 19, no. 2 (1970): 3–42;

Neusner, Jacob, *The Rabbinic Traditions About the Pharisees before 70*, 3 vols (Leiden: Brill, 1971);

Neusner, Jacob, *Judaism: The Evidence of the Mishnah* (Chicago, IL: Chicago University Press, 1981);

Neusner, Jacob, *Messiah in Context: Israel's History and Destiny in Formative Judaism* (Philadelphia, PA: Fortress, 1984);

Schäfer, Peter, "Aqiva and Bar Kokhba," in William Scott Green (ed.), *Approaches to Ancient Judaism*, vol. 2 (BJS 9; Atlanta, GA: Scholars Press, 1980), 113–30;

Schäfer, Peter, *Der Bar Kokhba-Aufstand: Studien zum zweiten jüdischen Krieg gegen Rom* (TSAJ 1; Tübingen: Mohr Siebeck, 1981);

Schäfer, Peter, "Bar Kokhba and the Rabbis," in Peter Schäfer (ed.), *The Bar Kokhba War Reconsidered: New Perspectives on the Second Jewish Revolt against Rome* (TSAJ 100; Tübingen: Mohr Siebeck, 2003), 1–22;

Yadin, Yigael, Greenfield, Jonas C., Yardeni, Ada, and Baruch A. Levine (eds), *The Documents from the Bar Kokhba Period in the Cave of Letters: Hebrew, Aramaic and Nabatean-Aramaic Papyri* (Judean Desert Studies 3; Jerusalem: Israel Exploration Society, 2002).

Notes

1 Josephus, *War* 2.17.8-9 §433–48; 4.7.2 §§398–405.
2 On the modern "Masada complex," see Ben-Yehuda, Nachman, *The Masada Myth: Collective Memory and Mythmaking in Israel* (Madison: University of Wisconsin Press, 1995); Ben-Yehuda, Nachman, *Sacrificing Truth: Archaeology and the Myth of Masada* (Amherst, NY: Humanity Books, 2002); Zerubavel, Yael, *Recovered Roots: Collective Memory and the Making of Israeli National Tradition* (Chicago: University of Chicago Press, 1995).

3   Josephus, *War* 7.8.2-9.2 §§275–406.
4   Ibid., 7.10.1–11.4 §§407–53.
5   Cf. Tacitus, *Hist.* 2.2.
6   Dio 66.15.3-5; Suetonius, *Titus* 7.1-2.
7   Cf. Dio 66.18.1.
8   Neusner, *Development of a Legend*.
9   *Avot de Rabbi Natan*, 4.
10 Cf. Neusner, "The Formation of Rabbinic Judaism," 30–2, 36–7.
11 Kanter, S., *Rabban Gamaliel II* (BJS 8; Atlanta, GA: Scholars, 1979).
12 Neusner, Jacob, "The Present State of Rabbinic Biography," in G. Nahon and C. Touati (eds), *Hommage à Georges Vajda: Etudes d'histoire et de pensée juive* (Leuven: Peeters, 1980), 85–91; Neusner, Jacob, "Evaluating the Attributions of Sayings to Named Sages in the Rabbinic Literature," *JSJ* 26 (1995): 93–111; Green, William Scott, "What's in a Name?—The Problematic of Rabbinic 'Biography,'" in William Scott Green (ed.), *Approaches to Ancient Judaism: Theory and Practice* (BJS 1; Atlanta, GA: Scholars, 1978), 77–96; Green, William Scott, "Context and Meaning in Rabbinic 'Biography,'" in William Scott Green (ed.), *Approaches to Ancient Judaism*, vol. 2 (BJS 9; Atlanta, GA: Scholars, 1980), 97–111; Goodblatt, David, "Towards the Rehabilitation of Talmudic History," in Baruch Bokser (ed.), *History of Judaism: The Next Ten Years* (BJS 21; Atlanta, GA: Scholars, 1980), 31–44.
13 Neusner, *Judaism*.
14 Schäfer, "Aqiva and Bar Kokhba," 124–5.
15 Cf. Neusner, *Messiah in Context*.
16 Appian, *Bel. Civ.* 2.90.380.
17 Cf. Opper, Thorsten, *Hadrian: Empire and Conflict* (London: British Museum, 2008); Birley, Anthony R., *Hadrian: The Restless Emperor* (London: Routledge, 1997).
18 Mildenberg, *The Coinage of the Bar Kokhba War*, 97–99; Hendin, David, *Guide to Biblical Coins* (New York: Amphora, 2010), 460.
19 Mildenberg, "Bar Kokhba Coins and Documents," 320–3; Mildenberg, *The Coinage of the Bar Kokhba War*, 84–94.
20 *Scriptores Historiae Augustae*, *Hadr.* 14.2: "At that time the Jews also waged war because they had been forbidden to mutilate their genitals."
21 Mildenberg, *The Coinage of the Bar Kokhba War*, 100–1.
22 Cf. Meshorer, *Ancient Jewish Coinage*, vol. 2, 138–50.
23 Schäfer, "Aqiva and Bar Kokhba"; Aleksandrov, G. S., "The Role of Aqiba in the Bar Kokhba Rebellion," in Jacob Neusner, *Eliezar ben Hyrcanus*, vol. 2 (SJLA 4; Leiden: Brill, 1973), 427.
24 Schäfer, *Der Bar Kokhba-Aufstand*, 67–73; Schäfer, "Bar Kokhba and the Rabbis," 15–20.
25 Lewis (ed.), *The Documents from the Bar Kokhba Period in the Cave of Letters*; Yadin, *The Documents from the Bar Kokhba Period in the Cave of Letters*.
26 Esler, Philip F., *Babatha's Orchard: The Yadin Papyri and an Ancient Jewish Family Tale Retold* (Oxford, UK: Oxford University Press, 2017), 176–220.
27 XHev/Se 60–65 in Greek (including *P. Yadin* 73 = XHev/Se 65: Cotton and Yardeni [eds], *Discoveries in the Judaean Desert XXVII*, 133–79), plus perhaps Aramaic XHev/Se 12 (Cotton and Yardeni [eds], *Discoveries in the Judaean Desert XXVII*, 60–4). See especially Cotton, Hannah M., "The Archive of Salome Komaïse Daughter of Levi: Another Archive from the "Cave of Letters,'" *ZPE* 105 (1995): 171–208.
28 Meyers, Carol L., "Was Ancient Israel a Patriarchal Society?" *JBL* 133 (2014): 8–27.
29 Ibid., 27.

INDEX

Aaron 82, 165–166, 167, 202, 317
Aaronites 124, 130
'Abad-'Amanu/'Amiyu 335
Abdi-Heba 38–39, 59
Abiathar 124
Abijam 89–90, 92, 95
Abila 285
Abimelech 60
Abiram 202
Abishalom 89
Abner 72, 73, 76, 78, 342
Abraham 320–322
Abrahamic 17
Abram/Abraham 5, 14, 27–28, 41–42, 44–46, 49–50
   Apocalypse/Apocalyptic texts and approaches 320–322
   Bar-Kokhva 333
   beginnings of religious "scripture" 201
Absalom 78, 79, 224
Achaemenid 153, 167, 180
Achish 67, 79
Acrabetta 298
Actium 252–253, 270, 358
   Antony, Cleopatra, and Herod 252
Adad-'idri *see* Hadaezer
Adad-narari II 98
Adad-narari III 99
Adam 14, 23–28, 32, 42, 49, 340
   Apocalypse/Apocalyptic texts and approaches 321
   beginnings of religious "scripture" 201
   early Israelite deities and worship 117
Adrammelech 133
Adiabene 288, 309, 326
Aelia Capitolina 329, 332–333, 363
Africa 246, 294, 300
Agrippa I 267–268, 272–282, 287, 310, 359–361
   after the Great War with Rome 316
   and Agrippa II 284–285
   assessment of Herod's reign 263

   last of the Hasmonaeans 244
   see also Aristobulus
Agrippa II 276, 279, 284–286, 304, 310, 360–362
   and Antonius Felix 290
   assessment of Herod's reign 263
   and Lucceius Albinus 292
   and Porcius Festus 292
   tetrarchs 268
   and Titus 318
   and Ventidius Cumanus 289
   Vespasian's campaign against Galilee 300–301
Agrippa, Marcus 256–257
Agrippina 282–283, 286, 289
Ahab 97, 98, 100–104, 105–109, 114, 118, 134, 343–344
   and Jehoshaphat 104
Ahaz 112
Ahaziah 101, 107, 108–109
Ahaziah of Israel 105–106, 118
Ahaziah of Judah 105–106
Ahijah 92, 107
Ahimelech 124
Ahiqar 83, 343
Ahitub 124
Ahmose 37, 38
Akhenaten 38
Akkadian 29, 31, 38, 46, 103, 108
Akko 52, 208
Akra/Acra 216–218, 220, 225–226, 229–230, 232
Albinus, Lucceius 292
Alcimus 226–229, 234, 355
Aleppo 42–43
Alexander Balas 209, 228–230, 355–356
Alexander the Great 177, 178, 183–187
Alexandra 239–243, 356–357
Alexandria 204, 276–279, 327–328, 352
   Alexander the Great and his conquests 183–184
   Antiochus and the sixth Syrian war 217

Antony, Cleopatra, and Herod 252
beginning stages of the war with Rome 296
Claudius and the Jews 283
Ezra as lawgiver 172
and Gessius Florus 293–294, 296
Herod, "King of the Jews" 249
the Jews and Hellenization 182–183
the Jews and their communities in Egypt 195
and Philo's mission 278–279
"province" of Judaea under the Ptolemies 188–189
revolts under Trajan 327–328
Roman administration in Judaea 245
the Tobiads 192–193
Vespasian's campaign against Galilee 300–301
Alexandrian (citizen of Alexandria) 185, 278–279, 285, 288, 317
Alexandrium 208, 260
altar 80, 101, 112, 119, 130, 345
Antony, Cleopatra, and Herod 251
beginnings of Jewish religious "scripture" 202–203
Caligula and his statue 279–280
conflict and religious suppression, Judaea 219–220
historical problems in the Ezra story 168
Holy Days and festivals 125–126
Jason's "Hellenistic Reform" 212
Pharisees and Sadducees 234
priests, prophets, sages, and others 124
rabbinic approach 322
sacred/profane, pure/impure concepts 126
and Seleucid rule 207, 212
temple religion versus "popular"/"folk"/"family" religion 128
views different from Nehemiah's 161
worship in ancient Israel 122
Amarna 37, 38–39, 42, 49, 56, 59, 81, 85, 339
"The Amarna Age" 38–39
Amaziah 105, 110
Ambivulus, Marcus 270
Amel-Marduk 141
Amenemhet I 36
Amenhotep I 38
Amenhotep II 38

Amenophis IV *see* Akhenaten
Ammon 79, 101–102, 105, 171, 184–185
Ammonite 60, 110, 154–155, 160
Amon 135
Amorites 342
amphitheater 254–255, 261, 281
Amu 35, 37
Ananel (Hananel) 251
Ananiah 162, 165
Ananias 239, 289, 291, 294–295, 298
Ananus 292, 297–298, 303, 304
Anatolia 57, 66, 343
Angel 203
Annius Rufus 270
Antigonus 233, 238, 245–246, 262, 357–358
  Antony, Cleopatra, and Herod 251
  Herod, early career 248
  Herod, "King of the Jews" 248–250
Antiochus 216–217
Antiochus Epiphanes 345, 360
Antiochus I Soter 209
Antiochus II Theos 177, 209
Antiochus III (Antiochus the Great) 177, 193–194, 207, 209, 353–355
Antiochus IV Epiphanes 182, 207, 241–242, 344, 355
Antiochus V Eupator 209, 355
Antiochus VI Epiphanes Dionysus 209
Antiochus VII Euergetes Sedetes 209
Antiochus VIII Gryphus Epiphanes Philometor Kallinikos 209, 239
Antiochus IX Cyzicenus Philopator 209, 239
Antiochus X Eusebes Philopator 209
Antiochus XI Epiphanes Philadelphus 209
Antiochus XII Dionysus Epiphanes 209
Antiochus XIII Philadelphus Asiaticus 209
Antipas *see* Herod Antipas
Antipater 243, 258–262, 278, 357
  early career of Herod 247–248
  the Jews under Roman control 357–358
  Roman administration in Judaea 244–246
Antonia (fortress) 255, 285, 293, 295, 307–308
Antonius *see* Felix, Antonius
Antony (Mark Antony) 245–253, 318, 358
Apamea 209, 232

Aphek 103
Apiru 39, 56–58, 60, 77, 81, 339–340
Apocalypse/Apocalyptic texts and
    approaches 200, 344–345,
    348–349, 361–363
  Bar-Kokhva 333
  Ezra, Baruch, Abraham, and John
    320–322
  rabbinic approach 325–326
Apollonius 190, 218, 222, 229
Apries 138
Aqiva 325, 334, 363
aqueduct 255, 272, 273, 359
Arab/Arabia 334–338, 356, 358, 362–364
  and Ahab 101–102
  and Alexander Jannaeus 239–240
  Amaziah and Azariah (Uzziah) of Judah
    110
  Antony, Cleopatra, and Herod 251
  Bar-Kokhva revolt 331
  Herod, and Augustus Caesar 252–253
  Herod's reign (30–4 BCE) 257–258
  Jewish communities in Babylonia
    144–145
  Near Eastern culture and Hellenization
    181
  opposition to Nehemiah 152–154
  question of "the patriarchs" 44
  reign of Manasseh 134
  Roman administration in Judaea 246
  and Solomon 84
  sources for history 4
  and Trajan 326
Arad 53–54, 55, 93–94, 119–120, 121, 131
Aramaean 57, 67, 74, 79, 342–343, 356
  and Ahab 101–102
  Ahaziah and Jehoram of Israel and
    Joram and Ahaziah of Judah 105
  Athaliah and Joash of Judah 109
  Jehoahaz and Jehoash of Israel 109
  Jehoshaphat 104
  and Jehoshaphat 104
  and Jehu 108
  Jeroboam (II) of Israel 111
  Jotham and Ahaz of Judah 112
  Last Kings of Israel and the Fall of
    Samaria 112
  and Omri 98
  reign of Asa of Judah 95–96
Aramaic (language) 9, 16, 141, 307,
    333–334, 352
  Bar-Kokhva 330

Elephantine Jewish community 165–166
Ezra as lawgiver 171
historical problems in the Ezra story
    167–168
Jehoahaz and Jehoash of Israel 109
the Jews and Hellenization 183
near Eastern culture and Hellenization
    180
reign of Manasseh 134–135
"repopulation" of Judah 146
Araunah 80
Archelaus 260–262, 267, 310, 335, 359
  Agrippa II 285
  Judaea 269
  tetrarchs 267–269
Aristobulus (brother of Agrippa I) 280
Aristobulus I 233, 238–239, 241, 356
  and Alexander Jannaeus 239
Aristobulus II 243–246, 248, 357
  Herod, "King of the Jews" 248–249
  the Jews under Roman control 357–358
Aristobulus, Jonathan 251–252
Aristobulus (son of Herod) 259–260, 276
Armenia/Armenian 31, 244, 251, 326, 357
Arrian 7–8, 184, 185, 186
Artaxerxes 142, 151–152, 166–168,
    173–174
Asa 89, 95–98, 100–101, 104
  Jehoshaphat 104
  Omri 97–98
Ashdod 52, 67, 160, 171, 208, 229
Asher 61
Ashur-dan II 98
Ashur-dan III 99
Ashurbanipal 134
Asiatic 35–37, 66
Assyria/Assyrians 29, 72, 77, 139, 143–144,
    343–344
  beginnings of religious "scripture" 203
  early Israelite deities and worship 119
  and Hezekiah 131–134
  and Jehoahaz 137
  Jewish communities in Babylonia
    143–144
  the Jews and Hellenization 182
  and Josiah 136–137
  and Manasseh 134–135
  Near Eastern culture and Hellenization
    179–181
  "repopulation" of Judah 146, 148
  rise of the Omrides/Israeli statehood
    87–89, 97–113

and Solomon 84
and Trajan 326
revolts under Trajan 327
views different from Nehemiah's 161
Athaliah 105, 108–109
Athens 209–210, 250, 285, 329
Atonement, Day of 165, 285
Augustus 300, 310, 329, 359
   assessment of Herod's reign 262–263, 265
   Claudius and the Jews 282–283
   death of Herod 259–261
   friend to Herod 252–254
   Herodian Kingdom 359
   Herod's reign (30–4 BCE) 254–256, 258
   and Judaea as a Roman "province" 270
   Judaea's reunification as a kingdom 275
   tetrarchs 267–269
Av (Hebrew month) 308–309, 332
Azariah 92, 110, 165, 226

Baal 21, 60, 73, 164–165
   "abominations" of the Canaanite religion 129
   and Ahab 100–101, 104
   Ahaziah and Jehoram of Israel and Joram and Ahaziah of Judah 105
   Athaliah and Joash of Judah 109
   development of monotheism 121
   divine names in the biblical text 116
   early Israelite deities and worship 117–119
   Elijah and Elisha and the prophetic narrative cycle 107
   and Jehu 107–108
   Jeroboam (II) of Israel 111
   Yahweh and Israel 121
Baasha 95, 96–97
   Omri 97
Babatha 334, 335–336, 337, 347–348, 363
Babel 32, 42, 49
Babylon/Babylonia 11, 131, 133–140, 350–351
   "abominations" of the Canaanite religion 129
   Alexander and his conquests 184–185
   Antony, Cleopatra, and Herod 251
   Aristobulus II and Hyrcanus II 244
   and Ashurbanipal 100
   Court/Royal Chronicle 88
   creation account 22–23
   the "Diadochi" 187

   early career of Herod 246
   early Israelite deities and worship 117
   the Jews and Hellenization 182
   Judah and the Jews in 141–176
   Near Eastern culture and Hellenization 179–180
   Neo-Babylonian period 44–46, 119, 141, 143–145, 180, 211
   priests, prophets, sages, and others 125
   "province" of Judaea under the Ptolemies 188
   rabbinic approach 325
   and Sargon II 99
   story of The Flood of Genesis 29, 30
   and Trajan 326
Babylonian Empire 141–145
Bacchides 223, 227, 228
Bagohi 164–165
Balas *see* Alexander Balas
bamah/bamot 119, 131
Baptist *see* John the Baptist
Bar-Hadad 95–96, 101, 103–104, 108–110, 111
Bar-Kokhva 325, 329–334
Baruch 320–322
Bashan 107, 254
Bassus, Lucilius 313–314
Batanaea 254, 262, 268, 275, 285, 316, 359–360
Bathsheba 84
Beersheba 44, 131, 134
Beirut 281, 286, 309
Belshazzar 144
Ben Sira 125, 167, 172, 201–203
Ben-Hadad *see* Bar-Hadad
Benjamin/Benjaminite 53, 62, 85, 145–148, 350
   "The Amarna Age" 39
   and Asa of Judah 95–96
   and Eshbaal 73
   Israel and Judah compared 72
   Israel's origins 57
   Jason's displacement by Menelaus 214
   and Judges 59
   and King David 74, 77–80, 90
   and Saul 70–71
   Saul and David traditions 76
   "Song of Deborah" 61
Berenice 285–286, 290, 293–295, 304, 318
Berenice IV 210
Berossus 30–31
Berytus *see* Beirut

Betar/Bethar 331–332
Bethel 53, 62, 70, 72, 344
　early Israelite Deities and worship 119
　and Josiah 136
　and King David 81
　Rehoboam and Jeroboam 92–93
　Saul and David traditions 76
　temples and sacred spaces 123
Bethlehem 76, 262
Beth-Shean 52, 62, 71, 230, 233, 339
Boaz 161
Boethusians 234–235
Booths, Festival of *see* Tabernacles
Borsippa 88, 144
brigands 270, 298
　and Cuspius Fadus 287
　Herod, "King of the Jews" 249–250
　Herod's reign (30–4 BCE) 254, 257–258
　Israel's origins 56–57
　and Ventidius Cumanus 289
Britain 5–7, 181, 294, 300, 319, 330
Brundisium 246, 249, 251

Caesar
　Antony, Cleopatra, and Herod 252
　death of Herod 260–262
　fall of Jerusalem 267–268, 272, 289, 291, 293–295
　Herod's reign (30–4 BCE) 256, 258
　see also Augustus; Julius
Caesarea 255–257, 293–297, 300–304, 309
　and Agrippa I and II 282, 284, 286
　and Antonius Felix 291
　and Gessius Florus 293
　Herod's reign (30–4 BCE) 255–257
　and Judaea as a Roman "province" 272
　Judaea's reunification as a kingdom 275
　and Ventidius Cumanus 289
Caesarion 252
Caleb 202
Caligula 275, 277–282, 310, 348, 359–360
　Agrippa I and II 360
　Claudius and the Jews 282
　and Nero 286
Cambyses 142, 163
Canaan 35, 37–41, 49, 339, 340–342
　Israelite settlement 51, 52, 56–59, 61–62, 63
　Israel's becoming a kingdom 65, 67, 69, 71
Canaanite 36, 38–39, 48–49, 340, 342
　"abominations" of 115, 129–130

　and Asa of Judah 96
　Israelite settlement 53–56, 58–60, 62–63
　"repopulation" of Judah 147
　and Saul 71
Canon (biblical) 1, 5–6
　and the Book of Genesis 17–33
　　Adam and Eve 23–28
　　another Israelite creation account 20–22
　　compared with the Babylonian creation account 22–23
　　Flood story 28–32
　　main creation account 18–20
　divine names 115–119
　and its writing 8–9
　origins 9–15
Capitolina *see* Aelia
Cappadocia 257, 268
Carthage/Carthaginian 129–130, 294
Cassius 247–248, 271, 283, 284, 327, 329–330, 333
castration 332–333
census 148–149, 269–270, 335, 336–337
Cestius 292–294, 296–297, 300–301, 306, 361
Chalcis *see* Herod of Chalcis
Chelkias 239
Chemosh 119–120
Chronicles 12, 49, 65, 73, 139–140, 343–344
　Apocalypse/Apocalyptic texts and approaches 200
　beginnings of Jewish religious "scripture" 203
　divine names in biblical text 116
　and Eshbaal 73
　Israelite statehood 87–91, 95–101, 105, 108–111, 113–114
　and Jehoiachin 138
　and Jehoiakim 137–138
　and Josiah 135–137
　and Manasseh 134–135
　priests, prophets, sages, and others 124–125
　"repopulation" of Judah 147
　and Zedekiah 138
Cilicia/Cilician 184, 285, 290
circumcision 219–220, 290, 295–296, 362
　and Agrippa II 285
　and Antonius Felix 290
　Bar-Kokhva 332–333
　and Domitian 319

INDEX

Herod's reign (30–4 BCE) 257
Jason, and Seleucid rule 213
and Judah Aristobulus I 239
Claudius 279–282, 289–290, 300, 310, 360–361
   Agrippa II 284–285
   and the Jews 282–284
Clearchus of Soli 183
Cleopatra 181, 251–252, 262, 292–293, 318, 358
   and Herod 252–253
Cleopatra II 210, 217
Cleopatra III Berenice 239
Cleopatra VII 210, 245
cleruchy 190, 197, 205
coins 4, 281, 356–357, 359
   Agrippa I and II 360
   assessment of Herod's reign 263
   Bar-Kokhva 329, 331, 333–334
   and Gessius Florus 293
   and Hadrian 329
   Herod, "King of the Jews" 250
   John Hyrcanus I 233
   Judah Aristobulus I 239
   and Nerva 319
   Sanballat and the Samaritan community 162, 163
   "The Seventy Years' War" 362–363
   Simon (143–135 BCE) 231
Colosseum 318
Coponius 269–270
corvée labor 90, 92
crucify 240, 271, 288, 313–314, 357
cult (temple worship) 130, 225, 344–346, 349, 354, 361–362
   "abominations" of the Canaanite religion 129
   Ahaziah and Jehoram of Israel/Joram and Ahaziah of Judah 105
   and animal sacrifice 123
   Antonius Felix 290
   Apocalypse/Apocalyptic texts and approaches 320–322
   Aristobulus II and Hyrcanus II 244
   Asa of Judah 95–96
   Book of Joshua/Israelite "conquest" 54
   Claudius and the Jews 283
   conflict and religious suppression, Judaea 217–221
   Court/Royal Chronicle 89
   and David 82
   early Israelite Deities and worship 118, 119
   Elephantine Jewish community 163
   Elijah and Elisha and the prophetic narrative cycle 107
   Herod's reign (30–4 BCE) 255
   and Hezekiah 131
   Holy Days and festivals 125–126
   how the Bible was written 8
   Jason and Menelaus 215–216
   and Jehu 108
   Jewish revolt against the Seleucids 212–214
   the Jews and Hellenization 181–182, 183
   the Jews and their communities in Egypt 195–196
   Judaea (6–41 CE) 271, 272
   Judaea under the Ptolemies 189
   law and ethics 128
   and Manasseh 134–135
   nascent rabbinic Judaism at Yavneh 322, 324
   Near Eastern culture and Hellenization 179
   and Nehemiah's governorship 157
   Persian period and Judaism 175
   priests, prophets, sages, and others 3, 123–125
   rabbinic approach 322, 324
   Rehoboam and Jeroboam 92–93
   "repopulation" of Judah 146
   "resettlement" of the "province" of Judah 148
   sacred/profane, pure/impure concepts 126–127
   temple religion versus "popular"/"folk"/"family" religion 128–129
   versus "popular"/"folk"/"family" religion 128–129
   war with Rome (66–70 CE) 294–295
   worship in ancient Israel 122–123
   Yahweh and Israel 121
   see also Baal
Cumanus, Ventidius 288–289, 290
cuneiform 3–4, 29–31, 45, 56, 144, 149
Cyprus 22, 94, 239, 288, 327, 362
   Bar-Kokhva 329
   revolts under Trajan 327–328

Cyrenaica/Cyrene 327, 362
  Bar-Kokhva 329
  revolts under Trajan 327–328
Cyrus 141–146, 148
  Persian period and Judaism 175
  "repopulation" of Judah 146
  "resettlement" of the "province" of Judah 148–150

Dacians 326
Dagon 229, 232
Daliyeh (Wadi) 161–162, 186
Damascus 79, 92, 98–99, 106, 108, 110–112
  and Alexander Jannaeus 239–240
  Aristobulus II and Hyrcanus II 244
  assessment of Herod's reign 254
  and Judaea as a Roman "province" 269
  Judaea's reunification as a kingdom 276
Dan 55, 61, 92–93
Daniel 9, 11, 12, 16, 219, 344
  Apocalypse/Apocalyptic texts and approaches 200
  beginnings of Jewish religious "scripture" 201, 203
  and Jehoiakim 138
  Jewish communities in Babylonia 144–145
  the Jews and Hellenization 182–183
  Pharisees and Sadducees 234
Darius I 142, 148–150, 162, 350
Darius II Ochus 142, 165, 175
Darius III Codommanus 142, 184
Dathan 202
David 11, 65, 70–91, 114, 129, 342–343
  Amaziah and Azariah (Uzziah) of Judah 110
  and Asa of Judah 96
  beginnings of Jewish religious "scripture" 202
  crowning 77–78
  cultic personnel and religious specialists 124
  Israelite statehood 90–91
  Jerusalem 79–81
  and Josiah 136
  origins/early life 76–77
  relationship with Saul traditions 75–76
  Sea Peoples and Philistines 67
  Tel Dan inscription 74
  temple religion versus "popular"/"folk"/"family" religion 129

views different from Nehemiah's 161
  wars 78–79
Debir 55
Deborah 12, 60–61
deities in Ancient Israel 115, 116–119
  see also worship in Ancient Israel
Delaiah 162, 164
Delta/Delta region 35–38, 40, 47, 66, 113, 278, 279
Demetrius I Soter 209–210, 226–227, 228–229
Demetrius II 209, 229–233
Demetrius III Eucaerus Theos Philopator 209, 239–240, 357
Deuteronomy 28, 136, 325, 344
Diadochi 177, 186–187, 204, 351
diaspora 344–346, 348–349, 353, 359, 363
  Alexander the Great and Ptolemaic rule 174–177, 177, 189, 195, 204, 206
  final Jewish revolts under Trajan and Hadrian 316, 337
  Judah and the Jews, Babylonian and Persian Empires 143
  Roman rule and the fall of Jerusalem 294
  Roman takeover and reign of Herod the Great 257, 264–265
Dio *see* Cassius
Diodorus Siculus 173–174
divine names in the biblical text 115–119
Domitian 300, 318–319, 333
  Apocalypse/Apocalyptic texts and approaches 321
  and Nerva 319
  and Trajan 326
Doris 259, 260
drachmas 199, 213, 276–277
Drusilla 290

Eagle/eagle (Roman) 261, 297, 321, 361
Ebir-nari 145, 149, 152, 161, 168–170
Ebla 42–43
Edom/Edomite 48, 56, 105, 340
  Ahaziah and Jehoram of Israel and Joram and Ahaziah of Judah 105
  Amaziah and Azariah (Uzziah) of Judah 110
  cultic personnel and religious specialists 125
  Israel's origins 56
  Jotham and Ahaz of Judah 112

and the wars of King David 79
Yahweh and Israel 120
Egypt 35–37, 93–95, 197–199
   Egyptian New Kingdom 37–38
   see also Alexandria; *individual Egyptian rulers...*; Pharaoh/pharaoh(s)
Ekron 67, 78–79, 134, 229
Elam/Elamite 4, 88, 99–100
Elath 112
Eleazar 202, 289–290, 294–298, 305–306, 313–315
Elephantine 119, 130, 162–167, 344, 350
   early Israelite Deities and worship 119
   Ezra as lawgiver 172
   temple religion versus "popular"/"folk"/"family" religion 128
   temples/sacred space 123
Elephantine Jewish community 163–166
Elhanan 77
Eliashib 167
Elijah 106–107
Elisha 103–107, 109, 114, 116, 125, 203
Elkanah 76
Elohim 116
el-Rimah 109–110
Emesa 290
Emmaus 222–223, 298
Enki 29–31
Enoch/Enoch 14, 186, 200–201
Enosh 14, 201
Enuma Elish 22–23, 117
ephebate 211
Ephraim/Ephraimite
   context of Israelite settlement 53
   fall of Samaria/Jerusalem 112
   and King David 76, 78, 82
   and Saul 70
   "Song of Deborah" 61–62
Epiphanes *see* Antiochus IV
Esarhaddon 99, 134
eschatology 346, 348, 363
Eshbaal 70, 73, 77–78, 85, 116
   and David 73
Essenes 233–238, 256, 270, 322–323, 346–347, 356
Esther 12, 125, 138, 145, 174–175, 325
   Persian period and Judaism 175
ethics 127–128
   see also law and ethics
ethnarch 246, 268–269, 359

Euphrates 42–43, 82–83, 294, 343
   beginnings of the Maccabean revolt 222
   beginnings of religious "scripture" 201
   historical problems in the Ezra story 168–169
   "King of the Jews" 250–251
   question of "the patriarchs" 42–43
   and Solomon 82–83
Eusebius 30–31, 327–333
Eve 23–28, 32, 42, 49, 321, 340
evolution (Darwin) 17, 25–28, 32
exile 350, 359, 363–364
   history and the Bible 5
   Judah and the Jews, Babylonian and Persian Empires 147, 148, 175
   rise of the Omrides, and statehood 91, 99, 112
   Roman rule and the fall of Jerusalem 269, 271, 277, 285, 289
"exilic period" 139, 143, 146
exodus 5, 22, 39–41, 46–50, 62–63, 325, 340–341
Ezekias 131–135, 139, 187, 203, 247, 344
Ezekiel 125, 138, 143, 203, 334
Ezra 9, 16, 124–125, 146–151, 350–351
   Apocalypse/Apocalyptic texts and approaches 320–322
   Bar-Kokhva 333
   beginnings of Jewish religious "scripture" 200–203
   first twenty-five years of Seleucid rule 207–208
   historical problems with the Ezra story 167–170
   importance of the Persian period for Judaism 175
   as lawgiver 171–173
   marriage with "foreign" wives 170–171
   views different from Nehemiah's 160–161
   when did Ezra work 166–167
Ezra-Nehemiah 147–148, 151, 160–161, 165–167, 171–173
   Nehemiah's vision for Judaea 160

Fadus, Cuspius 284–285, 287–288
feasts/festivals, Jewish 125–126, 219, 285–290, 345–346, 353
   and Agrippa II 285–286
   and Alexander Jannaeus 239–240
   and Antonius Felix 290

Bar-Kokhva 332
beginning stages of the war with Rome 295–297
beginnings of religious "scripture" 202
early career of Herod 248
Firstfruits of Oil 125–126
Firstfruits of Wine 125–126
fourth and fifth Syrian wars 194
Hanukkah 125–126, 225
Jason, and Seleucid rule 212–213
and Judaea as a Roman "province" 270
Judaea's reunification as a kingdom 176
of Lights 225
rabbinic approach at Yavneh 324–325
Tabernacles 172–173, 229, 233, 239, 251, 296–297
and Ventidius Cumanus 288–289
of Weeks 165, 235
Woodgathering 125–126, 295
worship in ancient Israel 122
years after the Great War with Rome 316
see also Passover
Felix, Antonius 290–291, 361
Festus, Porcius 285–286, 292
fiscus Judaicus 316, 317, 319
Flaccus 276, 278
Flood story *see* Noah
Florus, Gessius 292–295
"foreign" wives 170–171

Gabara 298, 301
Gabinius 245
Gabriel 143
Galba 287, 299, 304
Galilee 87, 345, 356, 359–362
  Book of Joshua and the Israelite "conquest" 54
  death of Herod 262
  early career of Herod 247
  final deeds of Judas 225–226
  Herod, "King of the Jews" 249–250
  Herod's reign (30–4 BCE) 256
  and Jehu 107
  and Josiah 136
  rabbinic approach 325
  Roman rule and the fall of Jerusalem 267–269, 275–276, 289, 296, 298–302, 310–311
  and Saul 70–71
  and the wars of King David 79
  years after the Great War with Rome 316
Gamala 208, 270, 298, 302, 361
Gamaliel 270, 299, 303, 324
Gath 38, 39, 53, 67–68, 78–79, 106, 109
Gaulanitis 275, 285, 302, 316, 360
  see also Gilead
Gaza 67, 99, 113, 134, 162, 184–187, 208
Gedaliah 139, 147
gender
  Jewish women in legal documents 199–200
  see also marriage
Genesis 1, 14–15, 49–50, 57, 340
  divine names in biblical text 116
  early Israelite Deities and worship 117
  history and the Book of 17–33
  Israel's origins 57
  question of "the patriarchs" 41–46
Gerizim 130, 344, 356
  first twenty-five years of Seleucid rule 208
  and John Hyrcanus I 233
  and Judaea as a Roman "province" 273
  Sanballat and the Samaritan community 162–163
  temple religion versus "popular"/"folk"/"family" religion 128
  temples/sacred space 123
  Vespasian's campaign against Galilee 301
Germanicus 271, 276–277
Geron 218–219
gerousia 189, 215, 354
  see also Sanhedrin
Geshem 47, 152–153, 154
Gezer 38, 40, 222, 339
Gibeon/Gibeon 53, 55, 71, 94
Gideon 60
Gilead 60, 61, 70, 103, 106, 107, 239, 254
  see also Gaulanitis
Girgashites 57, 342
Gischala 302
Golan 226, 361
Goliath 71, 76–77, 81, 342
Gophna 222, 298, 307
Gorgias 222–223, 226
Gratus, Valerius 270
Greek Empire 177–206, 351–353
  Alexander the Great 177, 178, 183–186

the Jews and Hellenization 181–183
Near Eastern culture and Hellenization 179–181
Ptolemaic rule 177, 187–205
   Apocalypse/Apocalyptic texts and approaches 200
   beginnings of Jewish religious "scripture" 200–203
   fourth and fifth Syrian wars 193–194
   the Jews and legal practice in Egypt 197–199
   the Jews and their communities in Egypt 195–197
   Judaea in the Zenon papyri 190–191
   Pentateuch into Greek 204
   the Tobiads 191–193
   women in legal documents 199–200
gymnasiarch 278, 279
gymnasium 180, 211, 213, 255, 278

Haberu see Apiru
Hadadezer 98–99, 101–102, 104, 108
Hadrian 313, 316–317, 319, 326–327, 329–338
Hagar 27–28
Haggai 148–150, 200
Hamath 92, 101–102, 108, 109–110, 113, 120
Hammurabi 127
Hanan 161–162
Hananiah 155, 162, 163, 165
Hanukkah 125–126, 225
Hasidim 182, 221, 234, 235
Hasmonaean 347–348
   and Alexander Jannaeus 239, 241
   and Alexandra Salome 242
   Aristobulus II and Hyrcanus II 243–244
   assessment of Herod's reign 262–264
   death of Herod 259
   Herod, "King of the Jews" 250
   Herodian Kingdom 358
   the Jews under Roman control 357
   and Jonathan Maccabee 228–229
   Judaea's reunification as a kingdom 276
   Roman administration in Judaea 245
Hasmonaean Kingdom 207, 231–241, 355–357
   fall of 243–244
   rise of, and the Maccabean revolt 207–231, 355–357

Antiochus and the sixth Syrian war 216–217
beginnings of the revolt 221–223
concessions by the Seleucids to the Jews 223–224
conflict and religious suppression in Judaea 217–221
final deeds of Judas 225–227
first twenty-five years of Seleucid rule 207–210
Jason's displacement by Menelaus 214–216
Jason's "Hellenistic Reform" 210–214
leadership of Jonathan Maccabee 228–251
retaking of the Temple 225
Hazael 9, 53, 67, 73–74, 98
   Ahaziah and Jehoram of Israel and Joram and Ahaziah of Judah 105–106
   Athaliah and Joash of Judah 109
   Hazael, and Jehu 107, 108
   Jehoahaz and Jehoash of Israel 109–110
   and Jehu 103
Hazor 38, 52, 54, 55
Hebron 45, 55, 57, 145–146, 331
   and Eshbaal 73
   Israel and Judah compared 72
   and King David 74, 77–78
   Roman rule and the fall of Jerusalem 304
   Yahweh and Israel 120
Hecataeus 121, 172, 187–188, 200–201
Helena 288
Heliodorus 209, 210–211
Hellenization 177, 179–183, 212, 215–216, 234, 352
Hellenization/Hellenistic 179–183
   Apocalypse/Apocalyptic texts and approaches 200
   Jason, and Seleucid rule 210–214
Heracleopolis 195
Herod the Great/Herodian Kingdom 243–311, 313, 357–360
   Antony/Cleopatra 251–252
   assessment of his reign 262–265
   and Augustus Caesar 252–254
   death 258–262
   early career 246–248
   "King of the Jews" 248–250

reign (30–4 BCE) 254–258
  see also Romans
Herodias 275–277
Herodium 304, 313, 331, 362
  assessment of Herod's reign 263
  first twenty-five years of Seleucid rule 208
  Herod's reign (30–4 BCE) 255
Herodotus 83, 129, 133, 169
Heshbon 53–54, 55
Hezekiah 131–135, 139, 187, 203, 247, 344
Hillel 324
Hiram 84
history 1–16
  and the Book of Genesis 17–33
  entering of Israel 35–50
    "The Amarna Age" 38–39
    exodus 46–49
    Palestine and Egyptian New Kingdom 37–38
    question of "the patriarchs" 41–46
    Ramesside pharaohs and first mentions of Israel 39–41
    Semitic peoples in Egypt 35–37
  historians 6–8
  sources 1–5
Hittite 4, 342
  Court/Royal Chronicle 89
  Israel's origins 57
  King David and Jerusalem 80
  Ramesside pharaohs and first mentions of Israel 39–40
  Sea Peoples and Philistines 66
Hivite 57, 342
Holy Days 125–126
  see also feasts/festivals, Jewish
Homer 29, 211
Horeb 202
Hosea 99
Hoshea 112–113, 133
Hurrians 4, 38, 80, 342
Hyksos 37–38, 49, 339
Hyrcanus I (John Hyrcanus) 232–235, 238, 242, 264, 356
  and Alexander Jannaeus 239, 241
  and Judah Aristobulus I 238–239
Hyrcanus II 243–249, 251, 253, 278, 357–358

Iaō 115–116
Iao 187

Idumaea/Idumaeans 123, 134, 145, 356–357
  and Alexander Jannaeus 240
  Aristobulus II and Hyrcanus II 243
  and Cuspius Fadus 287
  early career of Herod 246–247
  final deeds of Judas 225–226
  Herod, "King of the Jews" 249–250
  Herod's reign (30–4 BCE) 257–258
  and John Hyrcanus I 233
  Judaea's reunification as a kingdom 276
  and Judah Aristobulus I 239
  tetrarchs 267–268
  war against the Romans 298, 303–306, 309
incense 110, 126, 164
India 83, 181, 183, 185
Ipsus 187, 188
'Iraq al-Amir 128, 192, 208, 352
Isaac 14, 28, 45, 201
Isaiah 20–21, 23, 112, 121, 125
  Apocalypse/Apocalyptic texts and approaches 200
  beginnings of Jewish religious "scripture" 203
  death of Herod 260
  and Hezekiah 132–133
  Sanballat and the Samaritan community 162
  views different from Nehemiah's 160–161
Ishbosheth see Eshbaal
Ishmael 28, 139, 285–286
Isidorus 278, 279
Isis 270–271, 349
Israelite settlement 51–63
  archaeology 51–52
  and becoming a kingdom 65–68
  Book of Joshua and the Israelite "conquest" 53–56
  context of Israelite settlement 52–53
  origins 56–58
  "Song of Deborah" 60–61
  summary 61–63
  times of Judges 58–60
Israelite statehood 87–114
Issachar 61
Italy 246, 251, 252, 276–277, 299, 304
Ituraeans 239, 356
Izates 288, 309

Jaddua 162–163
Jael 175
James (brother of Jesus) 274, 292
Jamnia *see* Yavneh
Jannaeus, Alexander 238–241, 243, 254, 264, 313, 356–357
Jason 207, 210–218, 221, 234, 241–242, 353–354
Jeb 163, 164–165
Jebusite 57, 79–80, 82, 83–84, 124
Jedaniah 164–165
Jeddous 190–191
Jehoahaz 109–110, 137
Jehoash 83, 109–110
Jehoiachin 137–138, 144, 147
Jehoiada 108–109
Jehoiakim 137–138
Jehoram 101, 102–103, 105–106, 108–109, 118
Jehoram of Israel 105–106
Jehoshaphat 104–105, 108
Jehu 100, 102, 103, 105–109
Jephthah 60
Jeremiah 12, 125, 307
  beginnings of Jewish religious "scripture" 203
  and Jehoiachin 138
  and Jehoiakim 137–138
  Jewish communities in Babylonia 143
  and Josiah 136–137
  "repopulation" of Judah 146–147
Jericho 298, 303
  Alexander the Great and Ptolemaic Rule 186
  Israelite settlement 54–55
  Judah and the Jews, Babylonian and Persian Empires 174
  Maccabean revolt, and the Hasmonaean Kingdom 208, 232
  Roman rule and the fall of Jerusalem 298, 303
  Roman takeover and Herod the Great 243–244, 249–251, 261–262
Jeroboam I 89–97, 100–101, 107, 114, 202, 343
  and Jehu 107
Jeroboam II 84, 91–92, 96, 111
Jerubbaal 60
Jeshua 203, 337
Jesse 76

Jesus 320–321, 335, 359–360
  history and the Bible 15, 27–28
  Israel's entry into history 47
  Maccabean revolt, and the Hasmonaean Kingdom 236
  Roman rule and the fall of Jerusalem 273–276, 292, 298, 301–303, 309
"The Jesus Movement" 273–274
Jezebel 100–101, 103–104, 105–108, 118, 134
Jezreel 53, 60–61, 62, 70–71, 79, 87, 94, 105
Joab 78
Joash 92, 106, 108–110, 111
Job 12, 21, 23, 116, 125, 203
Johanan 164–165, 167
John *see* Hyrcanus I
John (author of Revelation) 320–322
John the Baptist 275–276, 359–360
John of Gischala (son of Levi) 298–299, 302–303, 305, 307, 309
Joiada 158, 162–163
Jonah 92, 160–161
Jonathan Aristobulus 251
Jonathan (high priest) 238, 289, 290, 297
Jonathan Maccabee 228–231, 242
Jonathan (son of Saul) 71, 75, 116, 226, 231, 355–356
Joppa 298, 301
Joram 105–106
Joram of Judah 105–106
Jordan
  Alexander and the Jews 186
  Judaea's reunification as a kingdom 275
  and Saul 70–71
  and the Tobiads 192–193
  see also Transjordan/Transjordanian
Jordan River 51, 53, 57, 186, 287–288
Jordan valley 70–71, 145–146
Joseph (brother of Herod) 249–250
Joseph (brother-in-law of Herod) 252, 259
Joseph (son of Gorion) 297–298, 303
Joseph (son of Jacob) 50
Joseph (son of Simon) 298, 337
Joseph son of Zecharias 226
Joseph Tobiad 191–193, 205
Josephus 1, 2, 37, 84, 359–361
  and Agrippa I 280–282
  and Agrippa II 285, 286
  and Alexander Jannaeus 239–241
  Alexander and the Jews 185

Antony, Cleopatra, and Herod 251–252
assessment of Herod's reign 262–265
beginnings of the Maccabean revolt
    221–222
and Caligula 280
Claudius and the Jews 284
coming of the Greeks 352
death of Herod 259, 261–262
early career of Herod 246
final century of Persian rule 173
and Hellenization 183
Holy Days and festivals 125–126
"Jesus Movement" 274
the Jews and their communities in Egypt
    205
and John Hyrcanus I 233
and Judaea as a Roman "province"
    270–273, 287
    Antonius Felix 290–291
    Cuspius Fadus 287–288
    Gessius Florus 292–293
    Tiberius Julius Alexander 288
    Ventidius Cumanus 289
Judaea in the Zenon papyri 190
Judaea's reunification as a kingdom
    275–277
Maccabaean Revolt and Hasmonaean
    Kingdom 356–357
Pharisees and Sadducees 235–236
and Ptolemy I 187
Qumran and the Essenes 236–238
Sanballat and the Samaritan community
    162–163
tetrarchs 268–269
and the Tobiads 191–192
war with Rome 294, 297
    continued resistance after the war
        314–316
    end of war 308–309
    final siege of Jerusalem 306–307
    Jewish infighting in Jerusalem 305
    opposition to war 297–299
    surrounding of Jerusalem 303, 304
    and Titus 318
    Vespasian's campaign against Galilee
        301–302
    years following 316
Joshua 12, 51, 62–63, 65, 287–288,
    340–341
    beginnings of Jewish religious
        "scripture" 201–203

Book of, and the Israelite "conquest"
    53–56
Ezra as lawgiver 173
historical problems in the Ezra story 167
importance of Persian period for
    Judaism 175
Israel's origins 56
rebuilding/completion of the Temple 150
"repopulation" of Judah 147
"resettlement" of the "province" of
    Judah 148–149
Sanballat and the Samaritan community
    161–163
times of Judges 58–59
Josiah 107, 135–137, 139–140, 344
and Amon 135
beginnings of Jewish religious
    "scripture" 203
development of monotheism 121
Elijah and Elisha and the prophetic
    narrative cycle 107
and Hezekiah 131
and Jehoahaz 137
and Jehoiachin 138
Jotapata 301, 361–362
Jotham 110, 112
Judaea
    conflict/religious suppression, Jason and
        Menelaus 217–221
    Roman Empire 259–260, 269–277,
        287–294, 359–360, 361
    under the Ptolemies 188–189
    in the Zenon papyri 190–191
Judah
    Abijam 95
    appointment of Nehemiah 151–161
    Asa 95–96
    Athaliah and Joash 108–109
    Book of Esther 174–175
    compared to Israel 72
    Elephantine Jewish community
        163–166
    Ezra the scribe 166–173
    fall of Samaria/Jerusalem 131–140
    final century of Persian rule 173–174
    importance of Persian period for
        Judaism 175–176
    and the Jews in the Babylonian and
        Persian Empires 141–176
    Joram and Ahaziah 105–106
    Jotham and Ahaz 112

rebuilding/completion of the Temple
  150–151
 "repopulation" 146–148
 "resettlement" 148–150
 Sanballat and Samaritan communities
  161–163
Judas the Galilean 270, 288, 295
Judas Maccabaeus 225–226, 227, 228, 234,
  242, 355
Judges 58–61
Julius *see* Agrippa I; Agrippa II; Tiberius
  Alexander
Julius Caesar 245–247

Karaite *see* Qaraite
Kedron 80, 306
Kenan 14
Khirbet Beit Lei 119
Khirbet el-Qom 120
Khirbet Qeiyafa 80–81
Khirbet Rabud 55
Khnum 163–165
Kislev 221, 225
Kokhba, Kokhva *see* Bar-Kokhva
Komaïse *see* Salome
Kuntillet Ajrud 120

Lab'ayu/Labayu 39, 85
Lachish 38, 52, 54–55, 110, 119–121, 132
Lamech 14
Latin 4, 15, 115–116, 332
 and Antonius Felix 290
 Apocalypse/Apocalyptic texts and
  approaches 321
 the "Diadochi" 186–187
 Rabbinic approach 323
 sacred/profane, pure/impure concepts
  126
law and ethics 127–128, 171–173, 197–200
Lebanon 150, 239, 254, 277, 280–281
Lebo-Hamath 92
legate
 death of Herod 260–261
 resistance after the war with Rome 269,
  273, 274–275, 313
 Roman rule and the fall of Jerusalem
  280, 287, 293, 300, 304
legion, legion(s) 299–301, 304–306
 Bar-Kokhva 330, 332
 beginning stages of the war with Rome
  296–297

Herod's reign (30–4 BCE) 254
 "King of the Jews" 250
 resistance after the war with Rome 313
 Roman administration in Judaea 245
 tetrarchs 268
 and Tiberius Julius Alexander 288
 and Trajan 326
 revolts under Trajan 327–328
 years after the Great War with Rome
  317
Leontopolis 123, 128, 130, 214, 316, 344
leprosy 110
Levant 36, 44, 87, 340–341
 and Ahab 100, 102
 Alexander and his conquests 184
Levi 60–61, 298, 302, 317, 336
Leviathan 20–23, 118
Levites 82, 110, 130, 155, 157–158, 346
 and Agrippa II 286
 Elephantine Jewish community 165–166
 historical problems in the Ezra story
  168–169
 priests, prophets, sages, and others
  124–125
 sacred/profane, pure/impure concepts 126
Leviticus 122–123, 125–129, 165–166, 325
Libya/Libyan 40
Lusius Quietus 327
Lydda 250, 298
Lysimachus 187, 214–216

Maacah 89
 Abijam of Judah 95
 Asa of Judah 95
Maccabaean 207, 216–232, 234, 242, 279,
  345–346, 355–357
Maccabean revolt 207, 210–231, 355–357
Maccabees 345–346, 348, 352–356
 Antiochus and the sixth Syrian war
  216–217
 beginnings of the Maccabean revolt
  221–223
 concessions by the Seleucids to the Jews
  223–224
 conflict and religious suppression in
  Judaea 217–221
 final deeds of Judas 226–227
 fourth and fifth Syrian wars 194
 Holy Days and festivals 125–126
 Jason's displacement by Menelaus
  214–216

Jason's Hellenistic reform 210–214
Jewish communities in Babylonia 144
the Jews and Hellenization 182
the Jews and legal practice in Egypt 198
Jonathan Maccabee 228–231, 242
Judas Maccabaeus 225–226, 227, 228, 234, 242, 355
   Pharisees and Sadducees 234
   retaking of the Temple 225
   and Simon 231
   worship in ancient Israel 123
Macedonia/Macedonian 183–185, 186, 187, 209, 217, 351
Machaerus 208, 275–276, 304, 313, 362
Machir 60–61
magic/magicians 128, 271, 283, 347
Mahalalel 14
main creation account 18–20
Malichus 247–248
Manasseh 53, 60–61, 131–135, 139, 162–163, 344
Manetho 37
Marcellus 270, 273, 274–275, 330–331
Marduk 21, 22–23, 117, 144
Marduk-baladan 99
Mari 98–99
Mariamme 248, 250, 252, 259–260, 268, 295
marriage 260, 275, 285, 290, 348
   Ahab 103–104
   Alexander's conquests and Ptolemaic rule 192, 198, 199, 205
   Israel's origins 58
   Jews in Babylonian and Persian Empires 158–162, 166–167, 170–171, 174–175
   Maccabean revolt, and the Hasmonaean Kingdom 236–238
   "sacred marriage" rites in Mesopotamia 129
   sacred/profane, pure/impure concepts 127
   Solomon 82–83
Marsus, Vibius 281
Masada 208, 249, 263, 267, 362
   Bar-Kokhva 331
   beginning stages of the war with Rome 294–295
   infighting in Jerusalem during Roman rule 304–305
   preparation against Roman invasion 298
   resistance after the war with Rome 313–316
Masoretic 12–15
Mattathias 221, 250, 355
Matthias 261, 298
Medes 143
Mediterranean 185, 254, 288, 296, 363
   history and the Bible 9, 22
   Israelite settlement 52, 61
   Israel's entry into history 36
   rise of the Omrides, and statehood 99, 100, 102, 109
   Saul, David, and Solomon 66
Megiddo 38, 52, 93–94, 137
Menahem 99, 111–112, 295, 314, 335–337
Menelaus 214–218, 221–226, 234, 241–242, 354–355
Mephibosheth 116
Merenptah 49–51, 63, 65, 339, 341
   Israel's origins 58
   question of "the patriarchs" 41–42
   Ramesside pharaohs and first mentions of Israel 40–41
Meribbaal 116
Merodach-baladan *see* Marduk-baladan
Mesha 97, 102–104, 119
Mesopotamia 3–4, 28–31, 43–46, 343–344, 362
   "abominations" of the Canaanite religion 129
   and Ashurbanipal 100
   Court/Royal Chronicle 88
   the "Diadochi" 187
   and Hadrian 329
   Israel's origins 57
   Jewish communities in Babylonia 142–145
   the Jews and Hellenization 181–182
   last kings of Israel and the fall of Samaria 113
   law and ethics 127–128
   and Rehoboam and Jeroboam 91
   revolts under Trajan 327
   Sanballat and the Samaritan community 161
   and Solomon 82–83
   and Trajan 326–327
   and Zedekiah 138
messiah/messiahship 235, 273–274, 362–363

Apocalypse/Apocalyptic texts and
approaches 321–322
Bar-Kokhva 332–334
rabbinic approach 325–326
Methuselah 14
Michal 75
Miqne, Tel 134
miqva'ot 346
Mishnah 235, 323–325, 356, 363
Mizpah 60, 95, 96, 146, 222–223, 350
Moab/Moabite 79, 97, 102–105, 119–120, 171
and Alexander Jannaeus 239
marriage with "foreign" wives, Ezra 171
views different from Nehemiah's 160–161
Modein 222, 227, 230
monarchies, period of the 341–344
monotheism 84, 129–130, 175, 218–219, 344–345, 354
development of 121
divine names in biblical text 115–116
early Israelite deities and worship 116–119
Yahweh and Israel 119–121
Mordechai 175
Moses 46–47, 50, 121, 124, 136, 139, 143
beginnings of Jewish religious "scripture" 201
conflict and religious suppression in Judaea 220
early career of Herod 247
Elephantine Jewish community 165–166
Ezra as lawgiver 171–173
Ptolemy I and the Jews 187–188
rabbinic approach 325
translation of the Pentateuch into Greek 204
and Ventidius Cumanus 289
Mucianus 300, 304
Murashu 144–145

Nabataea/Nabataeans 243–245, 252–253, 357, 358
assessment of Herod's reign 263
and Babatha 335
Cuspius Fadus 287
Herod's reign (30–4 BCE) 258
and Trajan 326
Nabonassur 88
Nabonidus 141, 144

Nadab 91, 92, 96–97
Nahor 14, 45
Nahum 240, 357
Naphtali 61
nascent rabbinic Judaism 322–326
nāśî 334, 362–363
Nazirite 13–14
Near Eastern culture and Hellenization 179–181
Nebuchadnezzar 137–138, 140, 141, 144, 147–148, 171
and Jehoiachin 138
and Zedekiah 138
Nehemiah 143, 147–149, 151–163, 350–351, 353
beginnings of Jewish religious "scripture" 203
building the Wall 155
and Ezra 166–167
historical problems in the Ezra story 167, 170
as lawgiver 171–173
marriage with "foreign" wives 170–171
final century of Persian rule 173
fiscal crisis 156–157
importance of Persian period for Judaism 175
opposition to 152–155
as a reformer 158–160
remainder of his governorship 157–158
and the Tobiads 191
views different from Nehemiah's 160–161
vision for Judaea 160
Neo-Babylonian period 44–46, 119, 141, 143–145, 180, 211
Nero 277, 283–288, 291–301, 304, 319
Nerva 317, 319
Nicanor 223, 226–227
Nicolaus 246, 258
Nikaso 162–163
Nile 35, 66, 163
Nimshi/Nimshides 107, 109
Nippur 144–145
Noah 14, 28–32, 201
Nubians 66, 133
Nuzi 45

Obadiah 101, 118
Octavia (sister of Octavian) 251, 286

Octavian 246–249, 251–254, 358
Omri 61, 84, 96–104, 108, 114, 343–344
　Athaliah and Joash of Judah 108–109
　Jeroboam (II) of Israel 111
Omrides 87–114
oracle 184, 308, 346
Orosius 284, 328
ostracon/ostraca 111, 118–121, 123, 163, 165
Otho 299, 304

Palestine 37–38, 99–100, 208
Paneas 208, 256, 259, 262, 275
Parthia/Parthians 248–252, 277, 288, 294, 327, 358
　and Hadrian 329
　Jewish communities in Babylonia 143
　and John Hyrcanus I 233
　revolts under Trajan 327–328
　and Simon 232
Passover 5, 47, 50, 163–165, 270, 345
　death of Herod 262
　Elephantine Jewish community 163–165
　first siege of Jerusalem by the Romans 306
　and Gessius Florus 293
　resistance after the war with Rome 315–316
　and Ventidius Cumanus 289
patriarchs 15, 41–46, 49–50, 66–67, 320–321, 337, 340–341
Paul 27–28, 290, 292
Pekah 99, 112
Pekahiah 112
Peleg 14, 45
Peleset *see* Philistines
Pentateuch 13–15, 49, 206, 340–341, 346, 349–352
　beginnings of Jewish religious "scripture" 200–201, 203
　Elephantine Jewish community 165–166
　Ezra as lawgiver 171–173
　final century of Persian rule 173
　importance of the Persian period for Judaism 176
　and Josiah 136
　law and ethics 127
　Palestine and the Egyptian New Kingdom 37
　translation into Greek 204
Pentecost 234–235, 267–268

Penuel 92, 94
Peraea 268, 275, 285, 298
Pergamum 84, 246
Pericles 158–159
Persian Empire 99, 141–142, 145–176, 350–351
Petra 243, 245, 249, 334–335
Petronius 280, 281, 287
Pharaoh/pharaoh(s) 133, 137–140, 339
　Israeli statehood 91–96
　Israelite settlement 61
　Israel's becoming a kingdom 61, 65–66, 83
　Israel's entry into history 35–41, 46–47, 49
　Near Eastern culture and Hellenization 181
pharaohs 39–41
Pharisees 233–236, 270, 320, 346–347, 356–357
　and Agrippa I 281–282
　and Alexander Jannaeus 240–241
　beginning stages of Israel's war with Rome 295
　death of Herod 260–261
　nascent rabbinic Judaism at Yavneh (70–130 CE) 322–324
Phasael 247–249, 276, 295, 357–358
Pheroras 250, 256, 260
Philadelphia 45, 190, 208, 232–233
Philip 183–184, 209, 218, 310, 359–360
　and Agrippa I and II 282, 285
　beginnings of the Maccabean revolt 222–223
　death of Herod 260–262
　final deeds of Judas 226
　Roman rule and the fall of Jerusalem 267–269, 272, 274–278
Philip II 183–184
Philip III 186
Philip V 209
Philippi 256, 275, 286, 301–302, 309
Philistia/Philistines 136, 202, 229, 342
　Israelite settlement 53–54, 57, 61–62
　Israel's entry into history 44
　rise of the Omrides, and statehood 96–98, 106, 110
　Saul, David, and Solomon 65–71, 77–81, 85
Philo 27–28, 182–183, 236–238, 348
　Caligula and his statue 280

and Judaea as a Roman "province" 271–272
Judaea's reunification as a kingdom 276–277
mission From the Alexandrian Jews 278–279
and Tiberius Julius Alexander 288
Phineas 309
Phoenicia/Phoenicians 4, 46, 66, 84, 130, 352
  "abominations" of the Canaanite religion 129–130
  and Agrippa II 286
  and Ahab 101
  Alexander the Great 184, 185
  and Alexander Jannaeus 240
  Antiochus and the sixth Syrian war 216
  Antony, Cleopatra, and Herod 251
  early Israelite deities and worship 118
  and Esarhaddon 99
  final century of Persian rule 173–174
  Herod's reign (30–4 BCE) 255, 257–258
  and Nehemiah 152, 160
  Ramesside pharaohs and first mentions of Israel 39–40
  and Zedekiah 138
Pilate, Pontius 269–276, 359
Pithom 47
Pliny 236–238
Polemo 285, 290
politeuma 195–196
Pollio 278
Pollion 256
Polybius 193–194
polytheism 115
Pompey 244–246, 248–249, 294, 349, 357
Popilius Laenas 217
Poppaea 285–287, 292–293
Potiphar 46
praetor 280–281, 318
Praetorian Guard 277–278, 287–288, 299, 317, 319
prefect 161–162, 255–256, 267, 269, 279, 287–288
priests 3, 123–125, 238, 289–290, 297
prince/princess 40, 42, 83, 91–92, 362–363
  and Ashurbanipal 100
  Bar-Kokhva 334
  beginnings of Jewish religious "scripture" 202
  historical problems in the Ezra story 170

and Jehu 107–108
rabbinic approach 325
proconsul 245, 269–270, 276
procurator
  Roman rule and the fall of Jerusalem 267, 285–294, 310–311, 361
  beginning stages of the war 269
  destruction of the Temple, end of the war 308
  Judaea's reunification as a kingdom 276
  tetrarchs 267
  Roman takeover and Herod the Great 246, 256
prophecy/prophet 8, 130, 143, 146–150, 342–343, 349
  Ahab 100, 118
  and Antonius Felix 290–291
  Apocalypse/Apocalyptic texts and approaches 200
  appointment of Nehemiah 154
  Bar-Kokhva 333
  beginnings of Jewish religious "scripture" 201–203
  as cultic personnel 123–125
  and Cuspius Fadus 287
  destruction of the Temple/end of the war with Rome 308–309
  Elijah 106–107, 114
  Elisha 105–107, 109, 114
  and Jehu 108
  Jewish communities in Babylonia 143
  law and ethics 127
  narrative cycle 106–107
  Rehoboam and Jeroboam 92
  Samuel 69–70
  Saul 71
  Saul and Davidic traditions 75, 81
  Vespasian's campaign against Galilee 301
  Yahweh and Israel 121
prophets 123–125
Proverbs 125, 202
Psalms 11, 23
Psammetichus I 46
Psammetichus II 138
Ptolemies/Ptolemaic rule 177, 187–205, 208, 280, 301, 352
Ptolemy I Soter 177, 186–188, 195, 198–200, 204, 205
  and Judaea as a Roman "province" 188
Ptolemy II Philadelphus 177, 190

Ptolemy III Euergetes I 177, 205
Ptolemy IV Philopter 177, 193–194, 205, 210
Ptolemy (son of Abubus) 232
   and John Hyrcanus I 232–233
Ptolemy V Theos Epiphanes 177, 194
Ptolemy VI Philometor 210, 216–217, 230
Ptolemy VII Neos Philopator 210
Ptolemy VIII Euergetes II Physcon 210, 217
Ptolemy IX Soter II Lathyrus 210, 239
Ptolemy X Alexander 210
Ptolemy XI Alexander II 210
Ptolemy XII Neo Dionysus Auletes 210, 245
Ptolemy XIII 210
Ptolemy XIV 210, 251
Ptolemy XV 210
pure/impure concepts 126–127
Purim 125, 175, 226

Qadesh-barnea 50, 134
Qohelet (Ecclesiastes) 11, 16, 125
Quadratus 289
queen 118, 129, 174, 175, 252, 285
"Queen of Heaven" 121
Queen of Kings 252
queen mother 95–96, 107, 288
Queen of Sheba 84, 343
Quintus Curtius 185, 186
Quintus Delius 251
Quintus Labienus Parthicus 248
Quintus Memmius 224
Quirinius 269–270, 314
Qumran 303, 322–323, 334, 349, 357
   history and the Bible 12–14
      Maccabean revolt, and the Hasmonaean Kingdom 208, 233–234, 236–238, 240
polytheism/monotheism 117, 125–126

rabbi/rabbinic 267, 273, 320, 337–338, 347–348, 362–363
   and Agrippa I and II 281–282, 360
   Apocalypse/Apocalyptic texts and approaches 320
   Bar-Kokhva 330, 333–334
   nascent rabbinic Judaism at Yavneh (70–130 CE) 322–326
   Pharisees and Sadducees 235
Rahab 21–23, 118
Ramah 95, 97

Ramesses 39–40, 47–48, 65–66
Ramoth 103, 106
Raphia 193–194, 205
Rehoboam 89–95, 114, 202, 343
resurrection 28, 322
Reuben 61
Revelation 200, 320–322, 333
Rezin 112
Rhine 277, 299, 319
Rhodes 253, 255
rite 122, 129, 271
Romans 243–311, 317–319, 357–358
   administration in Judaea 244–246
   Agrippa I and II 280–282, 284–286, 360
   Antony, Cleopatra, and Herod 251–252
   Caligula 278–280
   Claudius and the Jews 282–284
   Domitian 318–319
   fall of Hasmonaean Kingdom 243–244
   Hadrian 313, 329–338
   Herod the Great 243
      Antony/Cleopatra 251–252
      assessment of his reign 262–265
      and Augustus Caesar 252–254
      death 258–262
      early career 246–248
      "King of the Jews" 248–250
      reign (30–4 BCE) 254–258
   "The Jesus Movement" 273–274
   Judaea, 6–41 CE 269–273
   and Judaea as a Roman "province" 259–260, 269–273, 287–294, 359–361
   Judaea's reunification as a kingdom 274–277, 287–294
   Nero 286–287
   Nerva 317, 319
   Philo's mission/Caligula 278–279
   tetrarchs 267–269
   Titus 317, 318
   Trajan 326–328
   triumph 216–217, 309
   see also individual rulers of Rome...
Rome 294–310, 316–317, 361
   see also Romans
Roxane 186
Rufus 330

Sabbath 125–126, 158–161, 165, 175, 187, 362
   Aristobulus II and Hyrcanus II 244

Bar-Kokhva 332
beginning stages of the war with Rome 294–296
beginnings of the Maccabean revolt 221
the Jews and Hellenization 182
the Jews and legal practice in Egypt 199
nascent rabbinic Judaism at Yavneh (70–130 CE) 325
Pharisees and Sadducees 235
Ptolemy I and the Jews 187
Qumran and the Essenes 237
Vespasian's campaign against Galilee 302
Sabinus 267–268
sacred/profane concepts 126–127
sacrifice 307, 309, 320, 345, 354, 361
"abominations" of the Canaanite religion 129–130
and Agrippa I and II 281, 284
and Alexander Jannaeus 239
Amaziah and Azariah (Uzziah) of Judah 110
Aristobulus II and Hyrcanus II 244
beginning stages of the war with Rome 294–295
conflict and religious suppression, Judaea 220
Elephantine Jewish community 163–166
first twenty-five years of Seleucid rule 207
fourth and fifth Syrian wars 194
Herod, "King of the Jews" 250
Jason's "Hellenistic Reform" 212–213
and Judaea as a Roman "province" 272
priests, prophets, sages, and others 124
Ptolemy I and the Jews 187–188
Rehoboam and Jeroboam 92
sacred/profane, pure/impure concepts 126
story of The Flood of Genesis 30
temple religion versus "popular"/"folk"/"family" religion 128–129
temples/sacred space 123
worship in ancient Israel 122–123
Saddok 270
Sadducees 233–236, 270, 281–282, 292, 317, 322–323, 347, 356
sages 123–125
Saite 45–46, 48–50
Salome *see* Alexandra
Salome (daughter of Herodias) 275–276
Salome Grapta 336–337
Salome Komaïse 334, 336–337, 348, 363
Salome (sister of Herod) 257, 259, 260–261, 263, 267, 270
Samaias 256
Samaria/Samarian 343–344, 351, 356, 359, 360
and Agrippa I 280–281
Alexander the Great 184, 186
"Amarna Age" 39
beginnings of the Maccabean revolt 222
conflict and religious suppression in Judaea 218
context of Israelite settlement 53
early career of Herod 247–248
early Israelite deities and worship 119–120
fall of 131, 133, 134
final century of Persian rule 174
first twenty-five years of Seleucid rule 208
and Gessius Florus 293
Herod, "King of the Jews" 249–250
Herod's reign (30–4 BCE) 255
and Hezekiah 133
Israelite statehood 87, 94, 97–101, 107–114
the Jews and their communities in Egypt 196
and John Hyrcanus I 233
and King David 78
and Manasseh 134
Nehemiah, opposition to 153
as part of the Persian Empire 161–164
Ptolemy I and the Jews 187
tetrarchs 268
and the Tobiads 192
Samaritans 14–15, 161–163, 344, 351, 356
beginnings of Jewish religious "scripture" 203
the Jews and their communities in Egypt 195
and John Hyrcanus I 233
and Judaea as a Roman "province" 170, 173
Judaea's reunification as a kingdom 276–277
tetrarchs 169
and Ventidius Cumanus 289–290
Vespasian's campaign against Galilee 301

Samson 59
Samuel 13–14, 303, 342
    beginnings of Jewish religious "scripture" 202
    cultic personnel and religious specialists 124–125
    divine names in the biblical text 116
    Israel's becoming a kingdom 61, 65, 68–71, 78–79, 81
    "Song of Deborah" 61
Sanballat 152–155, 158–164, 171, 351
Sanhedrin 235–236, 247, 344–345, 358
    and Agrippa II 286
    assessment of Herod's reign 264
    first twenty-five years of Seleucid rule 208
    Herod and Caesar 253
    Jason's displacement by Menelaus 215
    "The Jesus Movement" 274
    and Judaea as a Roman "province" 189
    and Lucceius Albinus 292
    see also gerousia
Sarah 27–28, 45, 143
Sargon II 99, 113, 119
Satrap 173–174
Saturninus 257–258
Saul 65, 69–82, 85, 342
    divine names in biblical text 116
    and Israeli statehood 87, 90
    temple religion versus "popular"/"folk"/"family" religion 129
scapegoat 122, 271
Scaurus 244
    Roman administration in Judaea 244–245
"school" 1–2, 42, 51–52, 136, 324
scribe 87–88, 346
    and Ahab 102–103
    Ben Sira and "wisdom books" 125
    Ezra 9, 16, 124–125, 146–151, 166–173, 350–351
    history and the Bible 3, 4, 10, 12, 16, 31
    Israelite settlement 63
    "The Jesus Movement" 274
    Jewish women in legal documents 200
    the Jews and their communities in Egypt 196
    and the wars of King David 79
    rabbinic approach 323

Scythopolis 208, 233
Sea Peoples 65–68
    see also Philistines
Sebaste/Sebastenian 208, 255, 257, 268, 284
sect/sectarian 207, 337, 346–348, 356, 362–363
    and Alexandra Salome 241
    "The Jesus Movement" 273–274
    and John Hyrcanus I 233–234
    and Judaea as a Roman "province" 270
    Qumran and the Essenes 237–239
    rabbinic approach 322, 324
Seder see Passover
Seir 56, 105
Sejanus 271, 273
Seleucids 351–357
    Alexander the Great and Ptolemaic Rule 177, 180–181, 187–188, 192–196, 201, 205
    Maccabean revolt, and the Hasmonaean Kingdom 207–232, 239–242
Seleucus I Nicator 177, 187–188, 209–211
Seleucus II Callinicus 177, 209
Seleucus III Ceraunus 177, 209
Seleucus IV Philopator 209, 228, 353
Seleucus VI Epiphanes Nicator 209
Semitic peoples in Egypt 35–37
Senate/senate 319, 326, 330, 332, 358, 360
    Antiochus and the sixth Syrian war 217
    final deeds of Judas 226–227
    Herod and Caesar 253
    Herod, "King of the Jews" 249
    and John Hyrcanus I 233
    leadership of Jonathan Maccabee 228–229
    Nerva 319
    "province" of Judaea under the Ptolemies 189
    Roman administration in Judaea 245
    Roman rule and the fall of Jerusalem 270, 273, 278, 280–283, 287, 299–300
    and Simon 232
Seneca 286–287
Sennacherib 99, 131–134, 139, 203
Sepphoris 208, 249–250, 275, 298, 301
Septuagint 9, 11–16, 116–117, 345
Seron 222
Serug 14, 45
Seth 14, 201

"The Seventy Years' War" 361–364
Severus, Julius 330
Sextus 247, 330
Shaddai 116
Shallum 111–112
Shalmaneser III 98, 101–103, 108
Shalmaneser IV 99
Shalmaneser V 99, 113
Shamgar 59–60
Shammai 324
Shasu 56–58, 62, 120, 339–340
Sheba 78, 84, 343
Shechem 35, 38–39, 303, 356
    and Alexander the Great 186
    and Alexander Jannaeus 239–240
    first twenty-five years of Seleucid rule 208
    Israel's origins 57
    and John Hyrcanus I 233
    and Rehoboam and Jeroboam 92
    times of Judges 60
Shelamzion 336
Shelemiah 164
Shem 14, 201
Shephelah 134, 145–146, 331
    Book of Joshua and the Israelite "conquest" 55–56
    context of Israelite settlement 53
    Israel's becoming a kingdom 68, 79, 81
Sheshbazzar 148–151
Shim'on 335, 336
Shim'on ben Koziba 330
Shim'on ben Menahem 335
Shishak *see* Shoshenq
Shoshenq 93–95
Shoshenq I 61, 91–92, 93–95
Sicarii 290, 294–295, 305, 314–316
    Lucceius Albinus 290
    Porcius Festus 290
Sicily 187–188
Sidon/Sidonian 99–104, 108, 138, 174, 276, 282
Silo, Pupedius 249–250
Siloam 131–132, 134
Silva, Flavius 314–315
Simon 214, 221, 226, 229–233, 238, 242
Sinai 27–28, 48, 202
Sisera 69, 72
So 113
Soaemus 300–301
Sodom 43

Solomon 78–87, 90–97, 114, 343, 348, 359
    Amaziah and Azariah (Uzziah) of Judah 110
    Bar-Kokhva 330
    beginnings of Jewish religious "scripture" 202
    cultic personnel and religious specialists 124–125
    and Jehoshaphat 105
    Roman administration in Judaea 245
Solomonic 76
Solon 158–159
"Song of Deborah" 60–61
Sosius, Gaius 250
Spain 77, 287, 294
statehood 87–114
    and Abijam of Judah 95
    and Ahab 100–104
    Ahaziah and Jehoram of Israel and Joram and Ahaziah of Judah 105–106
    Amaziah and Azariah (Uzziah) of Judah 110
    and Asa of Judah 95–96
    Athaliah and Joash of Judah 108–109
    Court/Royal Chronicle 87–90
    David's kingdom 90–91
    Elijah and Elisha and the prophetic narrative cycle 106–107
    invasion of Pharaoh Shoshenq 93–95
    Jehoahaz and Jehoash of Israel 109–110
    and Jehoshaphat 104–105
    and Jehu 107–108
    Jeroboam (II) of Israel 111
    Jotham and Ahaz of Judah 112
    last kings of Israel and the fall of Samaria 112–113
    and Omri 97–100
    Rehoboam and Jeroboam 91–92
    rulers of Israel to Omri 96–97
    Zechariah, Shallum, and Menahem of Israel 111–112
Stela 41, 97, 102, 119, 341
Suetonius 283–284, 297
Sumer/Sumerians 29, 31, 108
Susa 100, 174
Syllaeus 257–258, 260
synagogues 123, 328, 344–346, 349, 363
    and Agrippa I 281
    assessment of Herod's reign 263
    and Gessius Florus 293

the Jews and legal practice in Egypt 198–199
Pharisees and Sadducees 236
Philo's mission/Caligula 278
"province" of Judaea under the Ptolemies 189
Syrian wars 193–194, 216–217

Taanach 55, 119
Tabernacles, festival of 172–173, 229, 233, 239, 251, 296–297
Tabor, Mt. 245
Tacitus 220, 271–272, 283, 290, 305, 307, 361
Taharqa 99–100, 133
Talmud 325
tamid (offering) 123, 212, 219–221, 307, 345
Tannaim/Tannaitic 325
Tannin/Tanninim 20–21, 22, 118
Tarichaea 285, 301–302
Tattenai 149
Taurus Mountains 42–43, 184
Tekoa/Tekoaite 331
Tel Dan inscription 74
Tell el-Nasbeh 146, 350
Tema 144
temple religion versus "popular"/"folk"/"family" religion 128–129
Temple, temple 150–151, 225, 279–280, 308–309
Tennes rebellion 173–174
Terah 14, 45
teraphim 129
Testamonium Flavianum 274
tetrarch/tetrarchy 248, 256, 359–360
  Agrippa I and II 285, 360
  death of Herod 260–262
  Judaea's reunification as a kingdom 274–275, 277
theatre 329
  see also amphitheatre
Thebes 38, 195
theocracy 244, 350
Theophoric/Theophorous 101, 115–116, 118, 199
Theudas 287, 288
Thucydides 213
Thutmose/Thutmoses 38, 48
Tiamat 22–23, 117

Tiberias 275–276, 280–281, 285, 298, 301–302
Tiberius 271–278, 281, 283, 285
Tiberius Julius Alexander 288–289, 296, 299, 304–305, 318, 361
Tibni 97
  and Omri 97–98
Tiglath-pileser 44, 88, 98, 99, 111–113
Tigris 326–327
Timothy 223, 226
Tinneius Rufus, Quintus 330
Tirzah 55, 92, 94, 97
  and Omri 97–98
tithes 126, 157, 189, 291
Titus 300–311, 317, 318, 319, 361–362
Tobiads 191–193, 205, 351–352
  fourth and fifth Syrian wars 193
  Judaea in the Zenon papyri 190
  see also Joseph Tobiad
Tobiah 152–160, 191, 192
Tobias 143, 181, 190–191, 197, 205
  and the Tobiads 191–192
Tobit 143
Tophet 129–130
torah (law) 127, 165–166, 171–173
  see also law and ethics
Torah/*Torah* 105, 128–129, 167, 322, 326, 363
  beginnings of Jewish religious "scripture" 200–201, 203
  and Gessius Florus 293
  Jason's "Hellenistic Reform" 214
  and Ventidius Cumanus 289
Tosephta 235, 325
Trachonitis 275, 285, 316, 359–360
  death of Herod 262
  Herod's reign (30–4 BCE) 254, 256–258
  tetrarchs 268
Trajan 302, 313, 316, 326–328, 337
  Bar-Kokhva 333
  and Hadrian 329
  and Nerva 319
  revolts under 279, 327–328
Transjordan/Transjordanian 275–276, 339, 352
  and Alexander Jannaeus 240
  conflict and religious suppression in Judaea 217
  death of Herod 260
  final deeds of Judas 225–226
  fourth and fifth Syrian wars 194

Herod's reign (30–4 BCE) 254, 256
invasion of Pharaoh Shoshenq 94
Israelite settlement 51, 53–58
Israel's entry into history 44, 48, 50
Judaea in the Zenon papyri 190–191
opposition to Nehemiah 153
temple religion versus
  "popular"/"folk"/"family"
  religion 128
tetrarchs 267–268
and the wars of King David 79
translations 204
treasury 168, 210–211, 217, 255, 272,
  276–277, 281, 293, 297–298, 309
tetrarchs 267–268
tribune 289, 293–294, 318
tribute 205, 241, 293–294, 353–354
  and Ahab 103
  Amaziah and Azariah (Uzziah) of Judah
    110
  Antiochus and the sixth Syrian war 217
  Aristobulus II and Hyrcanus II 244
  assessment of Herod's reign 264
  early career of Herod 247
  first twenty-five years of Seleucid rule
    208
  Herod and Caesar 252–253
  and Hezekiah 132–133
  historical problems in the Ezra story
    169–170
  invasion of Pharaoh Shoshenq 94–95
  Jason's displacement by Menelaus 214
  Jehoahaz and Jehoash of Israel 109–110
  and Jehu 108
  John Hyrcanus I 233
  Jotham and Ahaz of Judah 112
  last kings of Israel and the fall of
    Samaria 113
  and Manasseh 134
  and Omri 98–99
  "province" of Judaea under the
    Ptolemies 189
  Roman administration in Judaea
    244–245
  and Simon 232
  and Solomon 83
  and the Tobiads 192–193
  Zechariah, Shallum, and Menahem of
    Israel 111–112
triumph (Egyptian) 93–95
triumph (Roman) 216–217, 309

Tryphon, Diodotus 209, 230–232, 356
Tyre/Tyrian 82, 84, 99–100, 103–104, 108,
  138, 144, 162, 184–186, 208, 213,
  215, 230, 248–249, 282

Ugarit/Ugaritic 4, 21–22, 66, 116–118,
  129–130
underworld 128, 284
Uriah 89
Usha 325–326
Utnapishtim 29–30
Uzziah 110, 112

Varro 254
Varus 268, 285
Vashti 174
Ventidius, Publius 249
Verschmelzung 180, 352–353
Vespasian 299–305, 308, 310–311,
  361–362
  campaign against Galilee 300–302
  and Domitian 318–319
  rabbinic approach 323
  resistance after the war with Rome
    315–316
  and Titus 317, 318
  and Trajan 326
  years after the Great War with Rome
    316–317
Vitellius 273, 274–275, 285, 299–300, 304
votive (offering/object) 95, 123, 261

Wall of Judah 155
"wisdom books", literature 125, 127,
  168–169, 200, 201, 202
wisdom and the city-state system 52–53
wisdom, Enki 29
wisdom and Hellenization 181–182
Wisdom of Solomon 82, 83–85, 343, 348
wisdom tradition 8
Woodgathering, Festival of 125–126, 295
worship in Ancient Israel 115, 116–119,
  122–123
  temples/sacred space 123

Xerxes 142, 144, 174

Yahweh/Yaho/Yahu 130, 201, 325, 340,
  344
  and Ahab 100–101, 104
  appointment of Nehemiah 161

and Asa of Judah 95–96
Court/Royal Chronicle 89
development of monotheism 121
divine names in the biblical text 115–116
early Israelite deities and worship 116–119
Elijah and Elisha and the prophetic narrative cycle 107
historical problems in the Ezra story 168
history and the Bible 13, 21–22
importance of the Persian period for Judaism 175
Israelite settlement 59–60
and Jehu 107–108
and Jeroboam (II) of Israel 111
Jewish communities in Babylonia 144
and King David 76
Rehoboam and Jeroboam 92
"repopulation" of Judah 146–147
Sanballat and the Samaritan community 161
and Saul 70
and Solomon 83–84
temple versus "popular"/"folk"/"family" religion 128
uniqueness to Israel 119–121

Yanoam 40
Yavneh 279–280, 322–326, 334, 362
Yehud 141, 145–146, 167, 175, 351
  appointment of Nehemiah 151, 155, 157, 160
  Elephantine Jewish community 163
  Ezra the Scribe 167, 171–173
  final century of Persian rule 173
Yehudah 335–336
Yohanan ben Zakkai 323–324

Zadok 82, 124, 234
Zakkur 98, 109–110
Zealots (Jewish sect) 298, 302, 303–306, 314
Zechariah 92, 111–112, 125, 148–149, 150, 200, 226
Zedekiah 138–139
Zenon 190–193, 197, 205, 352
Zenon papyri 190–191
Zerubbabel 147, 150, 167, 175, 203
  "resettlement" of the "province" of Judah 148–150
Zeus 219, 220, 333
Zimri 97
  and Omri 97–98
Zion 22, 307, 320
Ziusudra 29, 31

ABOUT THE AUTHOR

Lester L. Grabbe is Professor Emeritus of Hebrew Bible and Early Judaism at the University of Hull. He is founder and convenor of the European Seminar in Historical Methodology. He has written and edited numerous books on the history of the ancient Jewish people.